"The publication of this new translation of John Paul II's extraordinary catechesis on *Man and Woman He Created Them: A Theology of the Body* is almost as important an event as its appearance in English for the first time in 1981. Not only is it an accurate, consistent translation from the official Italian text, but it reintroduces the author's own original emphases. It clears up the confusion caused by indiscriminate use of words such as 'lust' for '*desiderio*' and '*concupiscenza*,' mistranslations that have gravely obscured key aspects of the redemption of the body. Above all, through research in the papal archives and recourse to John Paul II himself, Waldstein has supplied the original headings from the Polish edition, which enable the reader to grasp the work's structure as a whole and the integration of its parts. Waldstein's introduction is, in its own right, a significant contribution to the thought of John Paul II. Scholar and lay reader alike have reason to be profoundly grateful."

— MARY SHIVANANDAN, S.T.D.
Professor of Theology, John Paul II Institute for Studies on Marriage and Family at the Catholic University of America, Washington, DC

"Professor Michael Waldstein's new translation of the audiences given by Pope John Paul II on the theology of the body is absolutely superb. I have worked with the text over the past two and a half decades and compared the existing English translation with the Italian. I discovered many inconsistencies in the existing translation. Waldstein has given us a text faithful to the original and extremely helpful."

— WILLIAM E. MAY
Michael J. McGivney Professor of Moral Theology, Professor of Theology, John Paul II Institute for Studies on Marriage and Family at the Catholic University of America, Washington, DC

"[Michael Waldstein's introduction] is nothing less than stunning in its completeness, insight, and integrating power. I have rarely read a text with such pleasure! It modestly puts itself in the service of an introduction to the papal text, but could stand by itself as an interpretive monograph of the scope and depth of John Paul II's thought—not only in regard to the express topic, but more generally. Indeed, it articulates a quite general critique of the 'depersonalized' character of much of modern thought while at the same time formulating a positive understanding of the human person, and precisely regarding the role of the human body."

— KENNETH SCHMITZ
Professor of Philosophy Emeritus and Fellow
of Trinity College, University of Toronto

Man and Woman
He Created Them

JOHN PAUL II

Man and Woman He Created Them

A Theology of the Body

Translation, Introduction, and Index
by Michael Waldstein

Pauline
BOOKS & MEDIA
Boston

Nihil Obstat: William E. May, Ph.D.
Imprimatur: His Eminence Seán Cardinal O'Malley, OFM, Cap.
Archbishop of Boston
August 10, 2006

Library of Congress information on file.

ISBN 0-8198-7421-3

Cover design by Rosana Usselmann

Cover art: Michelangelo Buonarroti (1475–1564). The Sistine Chapel; ceiling frescoes after restoration. *The Creation of Adam*. Sistine Chapel, Vatican Palace, Vatican State. Photo Credit: Erich Lessing / Art Resource, NY.

NOTE ON THE COVER ART:

In the Sistine Chapel's *The Creation of Adam* by Michelangelo, we see that as God looks down at the passage of energy from his right arm through his index finger into Adam's left hand, he affectionately holds Eve under his other arm, her left hand resting gently above his wrist with her index finger slightly raised. Though she is still only an idea in God's mind, her eyes are intensely fixed on the eyes of Adam, who turns toward God's face and returns her look.

Reproduction of John Paul II's handwritten instructions for the theology of the body provided through the courtesy of Fr. Jan Głowczyk, director of the John Paul II Archives, Dom Polski, Rome.

Quotations from the works of St. John of the Cross excerpted from *The Collected Works of St. John of the Cross*, translated by Kieran Kavanaugh and Otilio Rodriguez, copyright © 1991 by Washington Province of Discalced Carmelites. ICS Publications, 2131 Lincoln Road, N.E. Washington, D.C. 20002-1199 U.S.A. www.icspublications.org.

Published by Pauline Books & Media, 50 Saint Paul's Avenue, Boston, MA 02130-3491. www.pauline.org.

Printed in the U.S.A.

Pauline Books & Media is the publishing house of the Daughters of St. Paul, an international congregation of women religious serving the Church with the communications media.

1 2 3 4 5 6 7 8 9   11 10 09 08 07 06

Contents

PART ONE

THE WORDS OF CHRIST

CHAPTER ONE

Christ Appeals to the "Beginning" 131

CONTENTS

From the Archives:
The Beginning of John Paul II's
Instructions for the Theology of the Body

General Instructions and TOB 1

(See Introduction, pp. 7–9)

a[d] m[aiorem] d[ei] g[loriam]   *1*   *totus tuus*
to the greater glory of God   all yours

1. The text "Theology of the Body" (Part One, Christ Appeals to the Beginning) divided into *22* discourses (reflections) for the Wednesday audiences.[1]

2. The small additions[2] do not in any way extend (nor do they change) the original structure of the text.[3] They are rather "interludes" that make it easier at the same time to keep the continuity of the topic. I have limited myself in them to the minimum necessary. It may be that some new circumstances will make it necessary in the future to extend these additions, but for the present there is no need.

3. The notes [are] to be published together with the corresponding sections.

I ask Sr. Emilia [Ehrlich, OSU] that we once again revise them.

4. The beginning of the cycle is intended for September 5, unless some substantive reason makes it necessary to postpone this date.

---

1. "The text" to which John Paul II refers is a book manuscript (entitled *Man and Woman He Created Them*) completed before his election in 1978. "Theology of the Body" is an alternate title given by John Paul II to the series of catecheses developed on the basis of "the text" of this book.

2. For these "additions," see the footnote on p. xviii.

3. According to this statement, the structure of Wojtyła's book as articulated in the manuscript by headings in four to five levels remained intact when John Paul II adapted the work for his Wednesday catecheses (see Introduction, p. 9).

arndz

1. Tekst „Teologia czata" (część I: Chrystus obiektywny do powstania) został podzielony na **22** przemówienia (rozważania) na audiencje środowe

2. Dodane fragmenty nie rozszerzają w niczym (ani nie zmieniają) pierwotnej struktury tekstu. Są to owe „przypisy", które właściwie równocześnie zachowują całość tematu. Ograniczyłem się w nich do niezbędnego minimum. Być może, że jakieś okoliczności nakażą w przyszłości rozszerzyć te dodatki — ale na razie nie widać potrzeby.

3. Przypisy prosimy by były publikowane razem z właściwymi fragmentami.
   Proszę o Eminencjo, abyśmy mogli je jeszcze przejrzeć.

4. Początek cyklu jest przewidziany na wrzesień (5. IX.), o ile jakiś wzgląd nieoczekiwany nie nakaże opóźnić tego terminu

<u>Gen[eral] Aud[ience] September 5[1]</u>   (I)

1. For some time now, preparations have been under way for the next ordinary assembly of the Synod of Bishops, which will take place in Rome in the fall of next year. The topic of the synod, "*De muneribus familiae christianae* (The Duties of the Christian Family)" will focus our attention on this community of human and Christian life, which has been fundamental *from the beginning*. The Lord Jesus used precisely this phrase "*from the beginning*" in the dialogue about marriage reported in the Gospels of Matthew and Mark. ~~It is precisely because of this phrase that~~ We want to ask ourselves ourselves what this word "beginning" means. In addition, we want to clarify ~~for ourselves~~ why Christ appeals to the "beginning" in this particular circumstance, and for this reason we look more precisely at the relevant text of ~~the Go[spel]~~ Sacred Scripture.

2. Twice ...

(as in the text)

3.

4. ... Christ's interlocutors today.

5. During the following Wednesday reflections at the general audiences, we will try, as Christ's interlocutors today, *to dwell at greater length on these words from Mt 19:?*. To follow the indication Christ put into them, we will try to penetrate into the

---

1. The two pages of John Paul II's instructions for TOB 1 show how he worked in adapting the book manuscript. In the book manuscript one finds Roman numerals added in John Paul II's own hand in the left margin that divide the text into pieces of appropriate length for the catecheses (22 catecheses in Chapter 1). There are also Arabic numerals that number the paragraphs within each piece of text. Arabic number 2 quotes the first word of paragraph 2 in the book; Arabic number 4 the last three words of paragraph 4, to signify that paragrapsh 2–4 of the book should be inserted here. Paragraph 5 is new. John Paul II seems to have followed the same system throughout.

Aud. gen. 5. IX (I)

1. Trwają już od pewnego czasu przygotowania do kolejnego zebrania wynajmego Synodu Biskupów, które ma odbyć w tej Rzymie jesienią roku przyszłego. Temat Synodu "de muneribus familiae christianae" (o zadaniach rodziny chrześcijańskiej) skupia naszą uwagę na tej wspólnocie życia ludzkiego i chrześcijańskiego, która jest od początku najbardziej podstawowa. Właśnie takim ewokiem "ad początku" postarzyż [...] Pan Jezus w rozmowie na temat małżeństwa, która została zapisana w Ewangelii wedle Mateusza a także wedle Marka. Chcemy postawić pytanie: co oznacza się "początek". Dlaczego równości wyjaśni[...], Dlaczego Chrystus w danym wypadku odwołuje w właśnie do "początku". I dlatego pragniemy wnikliwiej przyjrzeć się tej odniesieniu tekstów. Pismo rozumne i w tym odniesieniu tekstowi.

   dziełkowicie ... (jak w lekcie)

2.
3.
4.   wspisanych rozmowca Chrystusa.

5. W ciągu kolejnych rozważań stawiamy ze rozmaitych z audiencji generalnej, jako wypowiedzi w rozmówcy Chrystusa (postaramy się) nieco dłużej zatrzymać przy słowach Jezusa. Aby odpowiedzieć wskazanie, jakie w nich zawarł Chrystus, postaramy się iść w stronę owego ...

"beginning," to which he appealed in such a significant way; and in this way, ~~we will try~~ *to follow* ~~*so to speak*~~ *from afar the great work* [italics first added, then deleted] on this topic that the participants in the next ~~Ordinary Assembly~~ Synod of Bishops are undertaking right now. Together with the bishops, many groups of pastors and lay people are ~~undertaking it~~ participating in it who feel a particular responsibility for the tasks that Christ gives to marriage and to the Christian family; the tasks he has always given and gives also in our epoch, in the contemporary world.

The cycle of reflections we are beginning today, with the intention of continuing it during the following Wednesday meetings, has, among others, the goal *of accompanying,* ~~*so to speak*~~ *so to speak, from afar the work* in preparation for the synod, not, however, by directly touching its topic, but by turning attention to the deep roots from which this topic springs.

„początku", do którego ↝ wrócił w sposób tak bardzo znamienny. ~~Postaramy~~ ↝ tu sposób będziemy ~~widzieli~~ z daleka towarzyszyć tej wielkiej pracy, jaką w tym właśnie czasie i ~~zwiazku~~ z tematem najbliższego ~~spowadzenia wyrazi~~ ~~sego~~ ludu Biskupów pełniący ~~ty~~ ~~swisteriu i dzi~~ uczestnicy. Wraz z nimi ~~podejmuja te~~ pracy liczne ~~rzesze~~ duszpasterzy i świeckich, którzy czują ↝ w sposób niezbędny ~~sposiewialni~~ wobec tych zadań, jakie stawia ~~się~~ ~~rat~~ uczestnictwu i ~~naśladowaniu~~ chrześcijańskim Chrystus. ~~Marzeń zaczne~~ i stawia również w naszej epoce, w świecie współczesnym.

Cykl rozważań, który w dniu dzisiejszym rozpoczynamy, zamierza prawdziwie ~~popem~~ ~~swoja~~ ~~osoba~~ ~~szelkeś~~ ~~Natkych~~ ma także że i to na celu, aiby — ~~razem~~ widzieć z daleka towarzysząc ~~pracom~~ przystosować ~~się~~ do ludzie, nie ~~dosięgając~~ bezpośrednio ↝ tematu, ale ~~zawierając~~ ~~uwagi~~ ~~na~~ ~~najgłębsze~~ ~~konemic~~, z których ~~temat~~ ~~tu wyrasta~~.

Foreword

THE HERITAGE OF JOHN PAUL II is amazing in its richness and variety. Nevertheless, it has a clear center: the theology of marriage and the family and the pastoral commitment shaped by this theology. "As a young priest I learned to love human love.... If one loves human love, there naturally arises the need to commit oneself completely to the service of 'fair love,' because love is fair, it is beautiful" (John Paul II, *Crossing the Threshold of Hope*, 123).

Man and Woman He Created Them: A Theology of the Body is the main expression of this commitment to the beauty of love in John Paul II's teaching. Cardinal Wojtyła wrote the text before his election as Bishop of Rome and originally gave it the title *Male and Female He Created Them* (Gen 1:27). Reflection about creation stands at the very heart of his argument, as this title suggests. An alternate title given to the work by its author is *Human Love in the Divine Plan*. God's designs for the person, the designs of divine love for human love—this is the reality the theology of the body attempts to unfold on the basis of the teaching of Jesus.

As a philosopher, Wojtyła was clearly aware of the objections brought against the doctrine of creation in the modern era ever since Descartes and his scientific rationalism. In *Love and Responsibility* (1960), Wojtyła points out the habit widespread among intellectuals of confusing the order of nature with the biological order. The term "biological order," he argues, "does indeed mean the same as the order of nature, but only insofar as this is accessible to the methods of empirical and descriptive natural science, and not as a specific order of existence with an obvious relationship to the First Cause, to God the

Creator" (56–57). Biology "has man for its immediate author" since man abstracts certain elements from a larger and richer reality. The order of nature, by contrast, includes all these richer relationships among real beings. If one replaces the order of nature with the biological order, the consequences are devastating. "My soul had for a long time now been used to seeing in nature nothing but a *dead desert* covered by a veil of beauty, worn by nature like a mask that deceives" (Sergei Bulgakov). John Paul II's mature 1994 statement of the problem of this split between person and nature puts the matter in a nutshell.

> The philosopher who formulated the principle of "cogito, ergo sum"—I think, therefore I am—also gave the modern concept of man its distinctive dualistic character. It is typical of rationalism to make a radical contrast in man between spirit and body, between body and spirit. But man is a person in the unity of his body and his spirit. The body can never be reduced to mere matter.... The human family is facing the challenge of a new Manichaeism, in which body and spirit are put in radical opposition; the body does not receive life from the spirit, and the spirit does not give life to the body. Man thus ceases to live as a person and a subject. Regardless of all intentions and declarations to the contrary, he becomes merely an object. This neo-Manichaean culture has led, for example, to human sexuality being regarded more as an area for manipulation and exploitation than as the basis of that primordial wonder which led Adam on the morning of creation to exclaim before Eve: "This at last is bone of my bones and flesh of my flesh" (Gen 2:23). This same wonder is echoed in the words of the Song of Solomon: "You have ravished my heart, my sister, my bride, you have ravished my heart with a glance of your eyes" (Song 4:9). (John Paul II, *Letter to Families*, 19)

It is one of the chief merits of Professor Waldstein's extensive Introduction that it presents John Paul II's critique of scientific rationalism and his affirmation of the goodness of the body in detail.

It may seem strange to some, but it is a fact that in his theology of the body the Bishop of Rome upholds the dignity and truth of the bridegroom's cry of joy against scientific rationalism. The beauty of the body, which is the cause of this cry of joy, is not a mere veil, a deceptive mask behind which one must see the prosaic scientific truth of a mere chance mechanism that has no intrinsic meaning. The beauty is real and reliable. Its light can be traced back to God's original guiding intention for man and woman. Human reason can apprehend this light and see the deep reasonableness of God's design. The Catholic tradition has always upheld human reason. In John Paul II's theology of the body it upholds human reason in the ordinary experience of spousal love between man and woman: "You have ravished my heart, my sister, my bride, you have ravished my heart with a glance of your eyes."

One of the main goals of the theology of the body is the defense of Paul VI's prophetic encyclical *Humanae Vitae*. The defense must be seen in the context of John Paul II's defense of the ordinary human experience of love and its reasonableness. The teaching of *Humanae Vitae*, as John Paul II understands it, is based on the spousal meaning of the human body, that is, on the God-given power of the body to be a sign of the radical gift of self between man and woman.

On the basis of his defense of ordinary human reason in the experience of love between man and woman, John Paul II unfolds a theological argument that is in many respects new in Catholic magisterial teaching. Allow me to mention three of his striking theses. The image of God is found in man and woman above all in the communion of love between them, which reflects the communion of love between the persons of the Trinity (TOB 9:3). In God's design, the spousal union of man and woman is the original effective sign through which holiness entered the world (TOB 19:5). This visible sign of marriage "in the beginning" is connected with the visible sign of Christ's spousal love for the Church and is thus the foundation of the whole sacramental order (TOB 95b:7). These and the many related theses contained in the theology of the body will occupy theologians for a long time and lead to a renewal of theology as a whole. As Professor Waldstein shows in his Introduction, John Paul II's teaching—even if it is in some respects new—is deeply rooted in the Catholic tradition, above all in St. John of the Cross.

This new edition of the theology of the body is the fruit of ten years of intensive work at the International Theological Institute for Studies on Marriage and the Family (ITI) in Austria, founded at the request of John Paul II, which I serve as Grand Chancellor. Professor

Waldstein, ITI's founding President and St. Francis of Assisi Professor of New Testament, brings this work to a first important conclusion in his new translation and introduction. May God's blessing accompany the further fruits of this work.

CHRISTOPH CARDINAL SCHÖNBORN
Archbishop of Vienna

Preface

THE PHRASE "THEOLOGY OF THE BODY" strikes many people as an oxymoron. How could our bodies—so carnal, so earthy, so mortal—be a "study of God"? "The fact that *theology also includes the body should not* astonish or surprise anyone who is conscious of the mystery and reality of the Incarnation," John Paul II insisted. "Through the fact that the Word of God became flesh, the body entered theology...through the main door."[1] God has revealed his mystery through the Word made flesh—theology *of the body*. This phrase is not only the title of the first major teaching project of "John Paul the Great." It represents the very "logic" of Christianity.

John Paul II's theology of the body is most often cast as an extended catechesis on marriage and sexual love. It certainly is that, but it is also much more. Through the mystery of the incarnate person and the biblical analogy of spousal love, John Paul II's catechesis illumines the entirety of God's plan for human life from origin to eschaton with a splendid supernatural light. It's not only a response to the sexual revolution, it's a response to the Enlightenment. It's a response to modern rationalism, Cartesian dualism, super-spiritualism, and all the disembodied anthropologies infecting the modern world. In short, the theology of the body is one of the Catholic Church's most critical efforts in modern times to help the world become more "conscious of the mystery and reality of the Incarnation"—and, through that, to become more conscious of the *humanum,* of the very purpose and meaning of human life.

---

1. *Man and Woman He Created Them*, 23:4.

"The truth is that only in the mystery of the incarnate Word does the mystery of man take on light.... Christ, the final Adam, by the revelation of the mystery of the Father and his love, fully reveals man to himself and makes his supreme calling clear."[2] This familiar teaching of the Second Vatican Council was John Paul II's anthem. And his theology of the body is nothing but an extended commentary on this fundamental truth: Christ fully reveals man to himself through the revelation—*in his body*—of the mystery of divine love.

In the Word made flesh, the human body demonstrates its full, God-given capability "of making visible what is invisible: the spiritual and divine." Synthesizing the entire catechesis, John Paul observed that the human body "has been created to transfer into the visible reality of the world the mystery hidden from eternity in God, and thus to be a sign of it."[3] This "mystery hidden in God" is none other than the glory of trinitarian love and our "supreme calling" to participate in that love. "God himself is an eternal exchange of love, Father, Son, and Holy Spirit, and he has destined us to share in that exchange."[4]

How does the human body "transfer into the visible reality of the world" this divine mystery? It does so precisely through the gift of sexual difference and the call of the two to become "one flesh" (Gen 2:24). This is a "great mystery," as the author of Ephesians tells us. From the beginning, the male-female communion has been a kind of revelation—an "echo," so to speak, in the created order—of trinitarian communion and our destiny to share in that communion through Christ's spousal relationship with the Church (see Eph 5:31–32).

Thus, in a bold theological move, John Paul II concluded "that *man became the image of God not only through his own humanity, but also through the communion of persons, which man and woman form right from the beginning.*"[5] This will forever mark a critical development in Christian anthropology. To borrow a phrase from the Council, it "opens up vistas closed to human reason."[6] Man simply cannot pene-

---

2. *Gaudium et Spes*, no. 22.
3. *Man and Woman He Created Them*, 19:4.
4. *Catechism of the Catholic Church*, no. 221.
5. *Man and Woman He Created Them*, 9:3.
6. *Gaudium et Spes*, no. 24.

trate through reason alone the "great mystery" of the human body. Through reason, man can discover the workings of his own body as a biological organism, often with great precision and benefit to humanity. But the human body is not only *biological*. It is also, and even more so, *theological*. Only to the degree that we know what our bodies "say" theologically do we know who we really are and, therefore, how we are to live.

This, in a nutshell, is the gift of John Paul II's theology of the body. With profound insight and great originality, it helps us understand who we are according to God's original plan and how and why we fell from it. Most importantly, it shows us how the death and resurrection of Jesus Christ can effectively transform our understanding and experience of sexual embodiment, thus enabling us to reclaim our true identity. John Paul II's teaching remains more timely than ever. The world, which is now reaping a harvest of bitter suffering from the lies of the sexual revolution, is a mission field ready to soak up the good news of the "redemption of the body" that he proclaimed. But much work remains to be done, both at the academic and popular levels, if John Paul II's theology of the body is to become bread broken for all.

Michael Waldstein and the Daughters of St. Paul have made a tremendous contribution to that effort with this fine, new English translation. Its many improvements will delight scholars and lay enthusiasts alike. John Paul II's original structure and system of headings, never before translated from Polish, have been retrieved. The Pope's trademark use of italics, much of which had been lacking in the first translation or removed by subsequent editors, has been fully restored. Inconsistencies caused by different translators have been corrected. Sentences have been properly reconstructed. John Paul II's own numbering of paragraphs has been restored. And perhaps most excitingly of all, undelivered sections of Wojtyła's original manuscript have been unearthed and translated into English for the very first time. In short, nearly twenty-two years after John Paul II delivered the final address of the series, the English-speaking world is finally able to appreciate—inasmuch as any translation can offer—the original splendor of the Pope's project.

Furthermore, serious students of John Paul's teaching will benefit greatly from Waldstein's Introduction. As a popularizer of the Pope's theology, I can only tip my hat to the scholarship exhibited here. Waldstein not only provides a host of interesting archival discoveries about the original work as written by Karol Wojtyła and subsequently delivered by John Paul II. He also traces the development of Wojtyła's thought via a compact and insightful tour of modern philosophy. In the process we discover how the theology of the body offers a remarkably complete antidote to what ails the modern world.

It is my sincere hope that this brightly polished edition of John Paul II's revolutionary catechesis inspires a new generation of bishops, priests, theologians, religious educators, and lay enthusiasts to study, live, and proclaim the theology of the body to the world in the new evangelization. May Mary, in whom the redemption of the body has already been consummated, guide the efforts of all who participate in this important work.

CHRISTOPHER WEST, M.T.S., L.H.D.
Fellow, Theology of the Body Institute
April 19, 2006

Introduction by Michael Waldstein

————————— ∾ —————————

THE SEXUAL REVOLUTION was heralded by its advocates as a break-through for human development, for the freedom and happiness of the person. Wilhelm Reich, a student of Freud who saw himself at the forefront of the revolution, believed that the free availability of sexual pleasure beyond the limits imposed by the patriarchal Christian family would lead to health and happiness. It would even prevent insanity, mysticism, and war.

> Sexual energy is *the* constructive biological energy of the psychological apparatus that forms the structure of human feeling and thinking. "Sexuality" (physiological vagus function) is *the* productive vital energy, simply speaking. Its suppression leads not only to medical damage, but also quite generally to damage in the basic functions of life. The essential social expression of this damage is purposeless (irrational) action by human beings: their insanity, their mysticism, their readiness for war, etc.... The core of life's happiness is sexual happiness.[1]

A key element of the sexual revolution was the invention and general availability of effective contraceptives. Here too, hopes were high. Margaret Sanger, theoretician and founder of the Planned Parenthood Federation, urged women to revolt against sexual servitude. The first step in this revolt, she argued, is the use of contraceptives, because "no woman can call herself free who does not own and control her own body."[2] She elaborates thus: "What effect will the

---

1. Wilhelm Reich, *Die sexuelle Revolution* (first published in 1936), 15th ed. (Frankfurt: Fischer Verlag, 1999), 18–19; 22.

2. Margaret Sanger, *Women and the New Race* (first published in 1920; Elmsford, NY: Maxwell Reprint, 1969), 179–80; quoted according to Mary Shivanandan, *Crossing the Threshold of Love: A New Vision of Marriage in the Light of John Paul II's Anthropology* (Washington, DC: Catholic University of America Press, 1999), 187, no. 35.

practice of birth control have upon women's moral development?... It will break her bonds. It will free her to understand the cravings and soul needs of herself and other women. It will enable her to develop her love-nature separate from and independent of her maternal nature."[3] The more abundant love life made possible by eliminating the fear of pregnancy is the answer, Sanger adds, to women's search for deep meaning in their lives, including the religious and mystical dimensions of meaning. "I would even go so far as to state that there is no other source of true contentment or understanding of life values than that which comes from the realization of love in marriage.... In leading her successfully, nay triumphantly, through this mysterious initiation [of sex] he [that is, her husband] becomes for her a veritable god—worthy of her profoundest worship.... Through sex mankind may attain the great spiritual illumination which will transform the world, which will light up the only path to an earthly paradise."[4]

More than half a century after Reich and Sanger's utopian hopes, it is important to ask whether we have truly found "the only path to an earthly paradise" and "the core of life's happiness." In particular, has contraception enabled men to emerge in women's lives as "veritable gods...worthy of profoundest worship"? Or has it tended to transform them into episodic "users" and "consumers," who can dispense with their feminine objects of enjoyment once erotic excitement ebbs away?

In his *Man and Woman He Created Them: A Theology of the Body* (TOB), Pope John Paul II proposes a sexual politics of the radical gift of self of man and woman to each other, profoundly different from mere use and consumption.[5] From the very beginning of his ministry as a priest, he remarks in an important autobiographical passage, he had a special love for love. Deeply struck by the beauty of love between man and woman, he committed himself "to the service of 'fair love,' because love is fair, it is beautiful. After all, young people are always searching for the beauty in love."[6] Some of the most sensitive

---

3. Sanger, *Women and the New Race*, 179–80; see Shivanandan, *Threshold of Love*, 187.

4. Margaret Sanger, *Happiness in Marriage* (New York: Blue Ribbon Books, 1940), 121, 126, 271; see Shivanandan, *Threshold of Love*, 188, no. 43.

5. See Graham J. McAleer, *Ecstatic Morality and Sexual Politics: A Catholic and Antitotalitarian Theory of the Body* (New York: Fordham University, 2005).

6. John Paul II, *Crossing the Threshold of Hope* (New York: Alfred A. Knopf, 1994), 123.

and illuminating passages of world literature on erotic love can be found in TOB. John Paul II's argument has a compelling self-evidence because he allows love itself to show its beauty.

Yet, the full greatness of John Paul II's vision only emerges when one sees his concern for spousal love in the larger context of his concern about our age, above all for the question of scientific knowledge and power over nature, that is, the characteristically modern question of "progress." He argues that "the essence of the Church's teaching" about contraception lies in a more critical judgment about "the domination of the forces of nature" by human power (TOB 123:1). Like Reich and Sanger, John Paul II sees the question of contraception primarily as a question of "what *true progress* consists in, that is, the development *of the human person*" (TOB 133:3). He is concerned, no less than Sanger, with the quest for freedom, with "owning and controlling" one's own body, but he sees such individual autonomy (which is the only freedom Sanger speaks about, exactly like Descartes and Kant) as standing in the service of a still greater kind of freedom, "the freedom of the gift" (see Index at FREE).

The main purpose of the following Introduction is to present this larger context of John Paul II's vision as it emerged in his works before his election as Bishop of Rome. Wojtyła's theological and philosophical concerns have their roots in the spousal poetry and theology of St. John of the Cross (Section 2 of the Introduction). They took on a particular profile in an intense philosophical and theological dialogue with Immanuel Kant (Section 3) and Max Scheler (Section 4). The understanding of this dialogue allows one to grasp Wojtyła's concerns as a whole as documented in his seven major works published before his election (Section 5). In this light, one can approach the purpose of TOB (Section 6) as well as its structure and argument (Section 7).

Readers who do not wish to explore the larger context of TOB in so much detail may wish to jump from Section 1 immediately to Sections 6 and 7 of the Introduction, to take in the bird's eye view of the purpose, structure, and argument of TOB offered there.[7]

---

7. This Introduction is part of a larger argument presented in my forthcoming book: *John Paul II's Theology of the Body: Context and Argument.*

1. The Text

At the Wednesday General Audience on September 5, 1979, Pope John Paul II delivered the first of 129 catecheses on human love in the divine plan. Interrupted by the assassination attempt on May 13, 1981, and a long break for a Holy Year (from May 1983 to September 1984) as well as a number of catecheses on other topics, the cycle concluded a little more than five years later on November 28, 1984. The work as a whole is John Paul II's masterwork, in which the many strands of his philosophical and theological reflection come together in a rigorous and profound argument.[8]

Various titles have been given to this cycle of catecheses. The original title of the work is *Man and Woman He Created Them*. In the text itself, John Paul II describes the work as *reflections on the theology of the body*[9] and gives it the title *Human Love in the Divine Plan*, with the subtitle *The Redemption of the Body and the Sacramentality of Marriage*.[10] In the archival materials of the catecheses (see below), he uses the name *Teologia ciała, Theology of the Body*. This title has become customary in English.

Soon after being delivered, the catecheses were published one by one in *L'Osservatore Romano* (*OR*) and later in the complete series of the teachings of John Paul II published by the Holy See (*Insegnamenti*

---

8. As Carl Anderson points out, John Paul II set down seven major reference points for marriage and the family in the first five years of his pontificate. TOB is the first and most important of them. (1) Theology of the Body (1979–1984); (2) Synod on the Family (1980); (3) Pontifical Council for the Family (1981); (4) *Familiaris Consortio* (1981); (5) John Paul II Institute (1981); (6) Charter of the Rights of the Family (1983); (7) new ordering of marriage law in the 1983 Code of Canon Law.

9. "After a rather long pause, today we will resume the meditations that have been going on for some time, which we have defined as reflections on the theology of the body" (TOB 64:1; see also 11:2; 36:3; 63:7; 133:2). The reason why John Paul II uses the phrase "reflections on the theology of the body" rather than simply "theology of the body" may lie in their incompleteness. "These reflections do not include many problems that, with regard to their object, belong to the theology of the body (as, for example, the problem of suffering and death, so important in the biblical message)" (TOB 133:1).

10. "The whole of the catecheses that I began more than four years ago [in fact, more than five years ago] and that I conclude today can be grasped under the title, 'Human Love in the Divine Plan,' or with greater precision, 'The Redemption of the Body and the Sacramentality of Marriage'" (TOB 133:1).

di Giovanni Paolo II). In 1985, a one-volume edition appeared in Italian with the title *Uomo e donna lo creò: Catechesi sull'amore umano (Man and Woman He Created Him: Catechesis on Human Love)*, under the editorial direction of Carlo Caffarra, then president of the John Paul II Institute.[11] Since *Uomo e donna* (UD) is the most easily available Italian text and a common point of reference for those who study John Paul II, I will cite TOB by the number of the talk in UD, followed by the paragraph number (e.g., TOB 1:1).

UD contains five more catecheses than the *Insegnamenti*, a total of 134.[12] It has six instead of three meditations on the Song of Songs (TOB 108–13) and three instead of one on Tobit (TOB 114–16). In addition, the conclusion of the Ephesians cycle in UD (TOB 117) was not delivered and is not present in the *Insegnamenti*. The conclusion of the Ephesians cycle in the *Insegnamenti* (delivered on July 4, 1984) is omitted in UD, probably accidentally, because it begins with the same words as TOB 117.[13] Taking UD and the *Insegnamenti* together, the total number of distinct catecheses thus comes to 135.[14] More will be said below about this complicated textual situation and the policy of the present edition.

---

11. Giovanni Paolo II, *Uomo e donna lo creò: Catechesi sull'amore umano* (Rome: Città Nuova and Libreria Editrice Vaticana, 1985). Apart from the additions and omissions discussed below, the text of this edition differs from the *Insegnamenti* text only in minor details. For example, it brings consistency to the somewhat inconsistent use of capitals in the *Insegnamenti*.

12. UD counts only 133 because it presents the meditation of September 29, 1982, in an appendix (pp. 494–96). I have inserted it in its proper place according to date, between TOB 95 and 96, and numbered it as TOB 95b.

13. I have inserted the conclusion of the Ephesians cycle in the *Insegnamenti* immediately after TOB 117 and numbered it as TOB 117b. For details, see the overview on pp. 731–2.

14. The calculation is the following. If one begins with UD, the calculation is simple because UD omits two catecheses delivered by John Paul II and published in the *Insegnamenti*: 133 (the catecheses numbered sequentially in UD) plus one (for TOB 95b, which is printed as an appendix to UD) plus one (for 117b, which is the conclusion to the Ephesians section delivered but omitted in UD) equals 135. If one begins with the *Insegnamenti* text, the calculation is a little more complex: 129 (in the *Insegnamenti*) minus four (the four shorter catecheses on the Song of Songs and Tobit) equals 125, plus nine (the nine longer catecheses on the Song of Songs and Tobit as found in UD) plus one (the conclusion of the Ephesians section in UD that was not delivered and not published in the *Insegnamenti*) equals 135.

a. Textual Basis

In response to a letter sent on February 2, 2005, to Pope John Paul II, I received the following reply.

> Pope John Paul II has asked me to send you the following answer.
>
> As a textual basis for the new translation you should use the text of the catecheses as printed in the series edited by the Holy See, *Insegnamenti di Giovanni Paolo II* (II/2 p. 234 to VII/2 pp. 1316ff).
>
> In addition, the following points may be useful for your work.
>
> The original text of the catecheses is Italian.
>
> The titles you mention were added by the editorial offices of *L'Osservatore Romano* and are not part of the genuine Papal text.
>
> Emphasis by italics is original and should be preserved. This is a mark of the Holy Father's style.[15]

That the titles of individual catecheses are not part of the genuine papal text becomes further evident when one compares them in different language editions of *OR*.

TOB 1:
- *Italian:* In Dialogue with Jesus about the Foundations of the Family
- *English:* The Unity and Indissolubility of Marriage
- *German:* God Saw That Everything Was Good (1)
- *French:* Listening to Jesus on "The Origin" of the Family

TOB 2:
- *Italian:* In the First Account of Creation, the Objective Definition of Man
- *English:* Analysis of the Biblical Account of Creation
- *German:* God Saw That Everything Was Good (2)
- *French:* From the Beginning the Creator Made Them Male and Female

TOB 3:
- *Italian:* In the Second Account of Creation, the Subjective Definition of Man
- *English:* The Second Account of Creation: The Subjective Definition of Man

15. Letter from Archbishop Leonardo Sandri (Feb. 28, 2005).

German: Man Knows Good and Evil
French: "They Shall Be One Flesh"

These titles give readers some idea about a prominent topic in each catechesis, for the most part different topics in the different language editions. The *OR* editors did not have the complete work in front of them, and so they could not always pinpoint the focus of the argument, because focus depends in large part on context. The absence of context also explains why the titles do not supply what titles in modern books usually supply, namely, indications about the place of a particular section in the structure of the whole argument (Introduction, Chapter 1, Conclusion, etc.). I have omitted the *OR* headings and, instead, have inserted John Paul II's own chapter and section headings (see below).

John Paul II's statement, "The original text of the catecheses is Italian," should be understood in the sense that the Italian text is the authentic or authoritative text. The archives of the John Paul II Foundation at Dom Polski on the Via Cassia in Rome preserve the typescript of a book written in Polish by Cardinal Wojtyła before his election, entitled *Man and Woman He Created Them.*[16] The sister who typed the manuscript confirms that Pope John Paul II brought this text from Kraków to Rome after his election. The work seems to have been complete and ready for publication.

The archives also preserve materials that show how John Paul II used this manuscript as the basis of his Wednesday catecheses. A copy of the book typescript served as the basis. It contains Roman numerals in the margin that determine the beginning of the text to be used for each particular catechesis. It also contains Arabic numbers next to the paragraphs within each talk. Both sets of numbers seem to be in

---

16. Thanks are due to Fr. Wojtek Janusiewicz for accompanying me on a research trip to Dom Polski. Not only his knowledge of Polish, but also his sharp insights in the detective work of piecing together the evidence were essential to the success of the research. The director of the archive had been of the opinion that the Polish material was relevant only to the 1986 Polish edition, which he considered a translation from the original Italian into Polish. The paradigm shift from this hypothesis to the hypothesis that a pre-papal book manuscript in Polish served as the basis of the catecheses took place only gradually and with much uncertainty. It was fully confirmed only at the very end when we contacted the sister who actually typed the manuscript before John Paul II's election.

John Paul II's own handwriting. The main method of dividing the text into catecheses seems to have been the time needed to deliver a catechesis of regular length.

On separate sheets of paper, written in John Paul II's own hand, one finds introductory and concluding passages in Polish that were to be added to the Polish text of the book. The two sheets for TOB 1 have been reproduced above (see pp. xvii–xxi). The paragraph numbered 1 is new text to be added. At number 2 John Paul II writes the first word of the text from the book typescript with the marginal number 2, and at number 4 the last three words from the typescript with the marginal number 4. Between this beginning and end, he adds the remark, "as in the text," that is, the corresponding numbered paragraphs of the book manuscript were to be used unchanged, numbered according to the marginal numbers in the book.

Only the handwritten pages for the first chapter (TOB 1–23) are available in the archives at Dom Polski. Others are perhaps part of John Paul II's private papers, which are not publicly accessible. The continuation of the numbering system in the margins of the book manuscript at Dom Polski suggests that John Paul II continued working through the whole in the same way in which he had worked through Chapter 1.

The archives also contain the immediate product of these two elements, namely, clean typescripts of the catecheses in Polish that include both the text of the book (numbered according to John Paul II's instructions) and the passages added in the handwritten pages. Each Polish talk is followed by an Italian translation that served as the text read at the General Audience.

In substance, the catecheses follow the book typescript, but John Paul II added some large pieces of text (e.g., TOB 10, 23, and 133) and shortened others (e.g., the sections on the Song of Songs and Tobit). The 1986 Polish edition of TOB reproduces the original pre-papal book manuscript with some of the revisions introduced by John Paul II (e.g., the addition of TOB 10, 23, and 133). It does not contain any division into talks, nor does it contain the introductory and concluding paragraphs added by John Paul II in producing the catecheses. It also preserves the longer version of catecheses on the Song of Songs (six instead of three), and on Tobit (three instead of one). The archives contain an Italian version of these nine talks, but John Paul II shortened them before delivery, perhaps because of time considerations. The longer version is printed in the one-volume Italian edition (UD).

The 1986 Polish edition of TOB has an elaborate system of headings, four to five levels deep. The single most important result of examining the textual evidence at Dom Polski is the discovery that these headings were not added by the editors of the Polish edition, but are part of the original pre-papal work. They show how Wojtyła himself conceived the organic unity and order of his argument. There are altogether 219 headings with a total of about 1,600 words, a substantial amount of very precious text. Anyone who has attempted to understand the order of argument in TOB will realize how precious these headings really are. The headings are not reproduced in UD, nor in any translation (English, German, French, Spanish, Portuguese, etc.). Their use in the 1986 Polish edition, published with the approval of John Paul II by his closest collaborators, shows that they still expressed the author's intention in 1986, even though he had transformed his book into a series of catecheses.

The archives at Dom Polski also offer more direct evidence for the continuing importance of the headings. The set of instructions in John Paul II's own hand on the first leaf of his handwritten adaptations of the Polish text (reproduced above on pp. xvi–xvii) begins with the following two points:

1. The text, "Theology of the Body" (Part One, Christ Appeals to the Beginning) divided into *22* discourses (reflections) for the Wednesday audiences.

2. The small additions do not in any way extend (nor do they change) the original structure of the text. They are rather "interludes" that make it easier at the same time to keep the continuity of the topic. I have limited myself in them to the minimum necessary.

In the second point, John Paul II states explicitly that the structure of the original work as articulated by its headings remained the same when he used it for the Wednesday catecheses. In the first point, he explicitly mentions Part 1 and quotes the title of the first of the three chapters in Part 1, "Christ Appeals to the Beginning," which is the title found in the pre-papal book manuscript and the 1986 Polish edition.

One might argue that since the authoritative publication of the catecheses in the *Insegnamenti di Giovanni Paolo II* does not include these headings, they should not be considered part of the papal text. Yet, the absence of the headings in the *Insegnamenti* has a simple explanation. The *Insegnamenti* series reproduces the individual catecheses in the midst of other texts that happen to have been published on the same day. A system of headings five levels deep simply has no place in such a presentation of the text. As in many other cases, the *Insegnamenti* adopt the headings given by the editor of the Italian edition of *OR*. It is *these OR* headings that should be excluded as secondary and misleading. The relatively isolated life of the individual catecheses as well as the language barrier of the Polish original may be the reasons why the one-volume Italian edition does not include the original headings: it simply collects the isolated catecheses with their *OR* headings and divides them into cycles that do not entirely correspond to John Paul II's own organization of his work.[17]

To summarize, John Paul II used an apparently completed book manuscript as the basis for 129 catecheses. With two exceptions, he used the entire book.[18] He also added some sections not found in the original book manuscript (e.g., TOB 10 and 23).[19]

Given this complex situation, editors of one-volume editions of TOB have various choices. On one extreme stands the 1986 Polish

---

17. The concept of "cycle" has some support in the text of TOB (see Index at CYCLE). Its use as the main structuring device, however, goes back to the editor of UD, Carlo Caffarra. There is no evidence for this use in the archival materials. There are six cycles in UD and six chapters in John Paul II's own division. UD's Cycle 3 (The Resurrection of the Flesh) and 4 (Christian Virginity) are subsections of Chapter 3 of Part 1 in John Paul II's own division. John Paul II's Chapter 1 (The Dimension of Covenant and of Grace) and Chapter 2 (The Dimension of Sign) in Part 2 are both part of UD's Cycle 5 (Christian Marriage). For a more detailed discussion, see below pp. 112–14.

18. *The first exception*: Following the original book manuscript, John Paul II had prepared nine Italian catecheses on the Song of Songs and Tobit, but for actual delivery cut the text to less than half to fit into four audience talks. In the John Paul II archives, there is a copy of the longer version with markings in John Paul II's hand indicating which paragraphs were to be included in the shorter version and which were to be omitted. *The second exception*: John Paul II did not deliver one of the two talks that conclude the discussion of Ephesians (TOB 117), even though he had planned to (the talk had already been translated into Italian). The reasons for these exceptions may be scheduling pressures.

19. A complete comparison between the original Polish work and TOB will be prepared by Prof. Jaroslaw Merecki of the John Paul II Institute in Rome for a new Italian edition of TOB.

edition of TOB prepared by John Paul II's secretary, Stanislaw Dziwisz. This edition goes back to the original book manuscript, though it includes the newly written sections. It reproduces all the original headings but omits the division into catecheses as well as the introductions and conclusions that frame many individual catecheses. On the other extreme stands the 1997 English edition, which contains only the 129 catecheses as delivered, though it adds the division into cycles taken from UD and the headings added by *OR*. Somewhere between these two extremes stands the Italian edition (UD), which reproduces 134 discourses with their *OR* headings.

The present translation follows the standards of a critical edition. It is based on the conviction that readers should be supplied with all the data (and only the data) that come directly from John Paul II (thus his own headings, but no *OR* headings). A critical edition must allow readers to distinguish clearly between the various components of the text. In particular, I have marked the 129 catecheses actually delivered by a heading consisting of the date and citation in the *Insegnamenti*, and I have marked the catecheses not delivered by a heading consisting of "Not delivered" and the citation in UD. The shorter and the longer version of the Song of Songs and Tobit catecheses are presented parallel on facing pages, so that the reader can read both versions in their proper context and immediately see the differences.

b. Translation

Translations of papal documents in *OR* are excellent and have quasi-official status. In the case of TOB, however, the *OR* staff was faced with a task quite beyond the ordinary. In difficulty, TOB by far exceeds the traditional Wednesday catecheses by Paul VI and John Paul I. Even among the catecheses of John Paul II, TOB stands out as lonely Mount Everest among the hills.

The circumstances under which the first English translation had to be produced were difficult. Soon after its delivery at the Wednesday audience, each catechesis was sent to the English editorial office of *OR* to be translated. Since the translator(s) did not have the whole work before them, there are many examples of inconsistent translation. For example, the key concept, "*significato sponsale del corpo*" is translated in eight different ways: "nuptial meaning of the body" (in most catecheses up to TOB 101); "nuptial significance" (TOB 16, 39, and 69); "matrimonial significance" (TOB 40); "matrimonial meaning" (TOB 41); "conjugal meaning" (TOB 78); "conjugal significance" (TOB 96); and finally, in the last thirty catecheses, "spousal significance" as well as "spousal meaning" (TOB 102–32). A careful reader who works only from the English text would assume that John Paul II deliberately distinguishes between nuptial, matrimonial, conjugal, and spousal meanings as well as significances of the body and would wonder what the point of these subtle distinctions might be. Yet, the Italian is always "*significato sponsale del corpo,*" best translated as "spousal meaning of the body."[20] Similar inconsistencies can be seen in many other cases.

The English translator(s) at *OR* used the *Revised Standard Version* of the Bible and at times the *New American Bible,* both of which differ at many points from the version used by John Paul II, namely, the official translation published by the Conference of Italian Bishops (CEI).[21] For example, in the crucial verses about the reason for the creation of Eve (that is, Adam's solitude and the consequent need for a "help," Gen 2:18, 20), the CEI version follows the Vulgate and understands the Hebrew "kᵉneḡdô" as "*simile a lui,*" that is, "similar to him." Eve is created as "a help similar to him." In TOB 8:3, John Paul II uses this understanding of the Hebrew to argue that the likeness of nature between Adam and Eve is an important element for under-

---

20. The choice between "nuptial" and "spousal" is not an easy one. "Spousal meaning" is adopted in the official English translation of *Veritatis Splendor,* 15:2, and *Evangelium Vitae,* 97:2. "Nuptial" appears in the official English of *Pastores Dabo Vobis,* 29:1 and 44:2–3, as well as *Familiaris Consortio,* 37:5. The relatively rare word "nuptial," which is not part of the most widely shared vocabulary of English, has acquired a certain aura (aided by its lilting sound), partly through its connection with Hans Urs von Balthasar's concept of "*hochzeitlich* (nuptial)" and "*Hochzeitlichkeit* (nuptiality),*" a connection explored particularly by Angelo Scola, *The Nuptial Mystery* (Grand Rapids, MI: Eerdmans, 2005). Although "spousal" is not a perfect fit, it is closer to "*sponsale.*" TOB does contain several instances of "*nuziale* (nuptial)" (see Index at WEDDING). John Paul II could have written "*significato nuziale*" if this had been his intention. In instances of "*sponsale*" other than "meaning of the body," the *L'Osservatore* translation consistently uses "spousal." It would indeed be strange to translate "*amore sponsale*" as "nuptial love" rather than "spousal love" (see Index at SPOUSAL for other examples).

21. *Edizione Ufficiale della CEI (Conferenza Episcopale Italiana),* published in 1971 by the Conference of Italian Bishops.

standing the manner in which Eve is a "help." The *OR* translation has "a helper *fit for him*" (RSV), which is another acceptable way of understanding the Hebrew. Yet, it pulls the scriptural rug out from under John Paul II's argument. Why does "a helper fit for him" suggest a likeness of nature between Adam and Eve? Some textual argument would seem to be needed, but none is given.

In the *OR* translation, Jesus says, "Everyone who looks at a woman *lustfully* has already committed adultery with her in his heart" (Mt 5:28, RSV). The CEI translation, much closer here to the Greek original, has "*chiunque guarda una donna per desiderarla*: whoever looks at a woman *to desire her.*" The difference is important. Desire can be good or bad; lust is a vice. In the Italian text of TOB, the word "lust (*lussuria*)" occurs four times (see Index at LUST). To these four one can add six instances of lustful (*libidinoso*) and eleven of "*libido*" for a total of twenty-one defensible instances of "lust." In the *OR* translation, by contrast, "lust" recurs 343 times. The main reason for this massive multiplication of "lust" seems to lie in the RSV translation of Matthew 5:28 ("looks lustfully"). When John Paul II discusses Jesus' words in detail and repeatedly uses the word "desire" ("*desiderare*" or "*desiderio*") in agreement with the CEI translation ("looks to desire"), the *OR* translation attempts to preserve the connection with the term "lustfully" in the RSV and often translates "desire" as "lust." It multiplies "lust" further by frequently using it to translate "*concupiscenza.*" Yet, concupiscence is a wider concept than lust. Sexual concupiscence is only one of its species. The multiplication of "lust" introduces a note of pan-sexualism that is foreign to John Paul II. In order to avoid difficulties of this sort, the English Scripture quotes have been conformed to the CEI translation, always with an eye on the original Greek or Hebrew.[22]

The *OR* translations were compiled by Pauline Books and Media in four volumes: *Original Unity of Man and Woman* (1981); *Blessed Are the Pure of Heart* (1983); *The Theology of Marriage and Celibacy* (1986);

---

22. In some instances, I have maintained the CEI translation even against the original text. For example, the original Hebrew of Gen 2:23 reads, "This at last is bone of my bones and flesh of my flesh." The CEI translation for some reason inverts the order between bone and flesh. "This time she is flesh from my flesh and bone from my bones." In TOB 8:4 and 19:1, John Paul II follows the original order.

and *Reflections on Humanae Vitae* (1984). In 1997, Pauline published the whole text in one volume as *The Theology of the Body: Human Love in the Divine Plan.* The one-volume edition differs in a number of details from the earlier text. It omits the italicizing of phrases and sentences by which John Paul II regularly emphasizes particular points. It also omits many instances of quotation marks. John Paul II frequently uses quotation marks as a further means of emphasizing particular terms or signaling that they are the main topic of discussion. Finally, the 1997 edition recasts a number of difficult sentences to make them more readable.

The 1997 edition contains only the 129 catecheses translated by *OR.* The six additional catecheses contained in the Polish edition and UD are published here for the first time in English.

c. Literary Genre, Intended Audience, and Authority

"General Audience" is the genre by which the *Insegnamenti* series identifies the regular Wednesday discourses. Like Paul VI and John Paul I, John Paul II used the occasion of the Wednesday general audiences for catechesis. "Catechesis" is the more essential and interior category for defining TOB's literary genre. The particular group of pilgrims present on a particular Wednesday seems to represent the universal Church. TOB is a catechesis by the Bishop of Rome for the universal Church.

According to the Vatican II document on the pastoral office of bishops, "preaching and catechetical instruction...always hold the first place" in a bishop's teaching activity (*Christus Dominus,* 13). This is not to say that papal documents dedicated to particular issues, such as encyclicals and apostolic letters, are secondary and have less authority. It is to say, however, that the Wednesday catecheses have a certain primacy of place in the ordinary magisterium of the Bishop of Rome as pastor of the universal Church.

John Paul II explains his understanding of catechesis in *Catechesi Tradendae,* published on October 16, 1979, between the delivery of TOB 5 (October 10) and TOB 6 (October 24). One can assume that he had his catecheses on human love in mind when he wrote *Catechesi Tradendae* and, vice versa, that he had his account of catechesis in mind when he delivered TOB.

The primary and essential object of catechesis is, to use an expression dear to St. Paul and also to contemporary theology, "the mystery of Christ." Catechizing is in a way to lead a person to study this mystery in all its dimensions: "to make all human beings see what is the plan of the mystery...comprehend with all the saints what is the breadth and length and height and depth...know the love of Christ which surpasses knowledge...(and be filled) with all the fullness of God" (Eph 3:9, 18–19). It is therefore to reveal in the Person of Christ the whole of God's eternal design reaching fulfillment in that Person. It is to seek to understand the meaning of Christ's actions and words and of the signs worked by Him, for they simultaneously hide and reveal His mystery. Accordingly, the definitive aim of catechesis is to put people not only in touch but in communion, in intimacy, with Jesus Christ: only He can lead us to the love of the Father in the Spirit and make us share in the life of the Holy Trinity. (*Catechesi Tradendae*, 5)

This teaching is not a body of abstract truths. It is the communication of the living mystery of God. The Person teaching it in the Gospel is altogether superior in excellence to the "masters" in Israel, and the nature of His doctrine surpasses theirs in every way because of the unique link between what He says, what He does and what He is. (*Catechesi Tradendae*, 7)

To a remarkable degree, this account of catechesis resembles the actual method and content of TOB. Part 1 (TOB 1–86) focuses on three words of Christ that play a key role in his teaching about God's plan for the person and for human love. The focus lies on Christ as the Teacher. Part 2 (TOB 87–113) unfolds this teaching of Christ by turning to the Pauline teaching on "the mystery" of spousal love in Ephesians 5. The Final Part (TOB 114–33) applies the insights gained in Parts 1 and 2 to the concrete conjugal lives of men and women. No other catechetical cycle delivered by John Paul II after TOB has a similarly strict and close relationship with the very core and essence of catechesis as defined in *Catechesi Tradendae*. TOB seems to be John Paul II's catechesis par excellence.[23]

---

23. When one compares TOB with another major catechetical project realized in the pontificate of John Paul II, the *Catechism of the Catholic Church*, it quickly becomes apparent that the purpose of the two texts is quite different. The *Catechism* offers an overview of the Church's faith as a whole, while TOB focuses only on the essential core of catechesis, "the mystery" of Ephesians 5. TOB can thus serve as a John-Pauline lens for reading the *Catechism*, in particular for relating its many assertions to the one essential core of catechesis.

One must measure the authority of TOB in accord with these findings about office, genre, and content: the authority of a text is high if the Pope speaks (1) as pastor of the universal Church, (2) in a form of teaching central to his office of bishop, and (3) on a topic central to the faith. All three of these indicators are high in TOB.

Contrary to this evidence, some authors have dismissed the authority of TOB. In the traditionalist publication *Christian Order*, for example, G. C. Dilsaver argues that TOB should be considered a private theological work by Karol Wojtyła, not part of the papal magisterium of John Paul II.

> Pope John Paul II has used his Wednesday catechesis conference to read much of his private theological works. Among these is *The Theology of Marriage and Celibacy*. In this work, Karol Wojtyła (as a private theologian, since this work was completed prior to his ascending to the papacy) introduces the novel concept of "*mutual submission*" in his exegesis of Ephesians 5.[24]

All the signs that surround the Wednesday catecheses and that express John Paul II's intention make it quite clear that John Paul II intended the Wednesday catecheses to be precisely this: catecheses, not the recitation of private theological works. Dilsaver simply sidesteps the plain intention of John Paul II. The only argument he offers is that "this work was completed prior to his ascending to the papacy." This argument is irrelevant. The first publication of the text was its delivery by the Bishop of Rome as a cycle of catecheses. The original or authentic text of TOB is the Italian text as delivered by Pope John Paul II and published in the official *Insegnamenti* series.

A position similar to Dilsaver's is proposed by Charles Curran, who likewise ignores the genre "catechesis" and limits himself to the more external genre "General Audience" used by the *Insegnamenti* series.

> [*Man and Woman He Created Them* belongs to] a particular genre of teaching—the speeches given at the weekly audiences.... As such, talks to general audiences have little or no authoritative character. They are often just greetings to the various people in attendance and

---

24. G. C. Dilsaver, "Karol Wojtyła and the Patriarchal Hierarchy of the Family: His Exegetical Comment on Ephesians 5:21–33 and Genesis 3:16," *Christian Order*, June/July 2002.

exhortations.... These talks...have little or no importance from the point of view of authoritative teaching.[25]

Against both Dilsaver and Curran, one should insist that TOB is a catechesis proposed by the Bishop of Rome for the universal Church on the center of Christian faith, the "great mystery" of love (Eph 5).

John Paul II uses further concepts to describe the literary genre of TOB. He calls the catecheses "reflections" (146 times), which characterizes them in very general terms as a close and critically self-aware examination of their subject. He also calls them analyses (by far the most frequent term, 269 times) and meditations (twenty-one times). There is an apparent opposition between analysis and meditation: in a meditation, one assumes a receptive posture as one slowly ponders a whole in its meaning; in analysis, one takes a more active role to resolve the whole into its principles and elements. Yet the two movements of thought complement each other.

John Paul II also calls TOB a "study" (thirteen times), which seems to point to an academic setting. Wojtyła was trained as a philosopher and theologian and worked as a professor for a number of years. He kept contact with academic life even after his appointment as a bishop. TOB has many of the characteristics of an academic study, e.g., frequent technical expressions that recur in formulaic form (spousal meaning of the body, man of concupiscence, rereading the language of the body in the truth: many of these phrases are listed in the Index below), technical footnotes, etc.

Does this mean that TOB is an academic study presented as a catechesis? Would this not be an attempt to mix irreconcilable genres? The immediate audience assembled for the Wednesday audience consisted of people of all ages from all walks of life. Yet the text is at times so difficult that seasoned theologians and philosophers find themselves struggling with it. The scholarly footnotes, which are an integral part of the text (itself a curious fact in a catechesis), often quote sources in the original French, German, Latin, Greek, and Hebrew without any translation. There seems to be a disproportion between the text and its intended audience. "Quite frankly, the talks do not seem appropriate

---

25. Charles Curran, *The Moral Theology of Pope John Paul II* (Washington, DC: Georgetown University Press, 2004), 4–5.

for the occasion. They are somewhat theoretical and too detailed for a general audience.... I am sure that most of those in attendance at the audiences did not follow what the pope was saying."[26]

In answer to these queries, one can emphasize a point already made above: the group of pilgrims present at the Wednesday audiences stands for the universal Church. The true intended audience is the universal Church. In studying TOB, one has the impression that John Paul II is speaking with the full array of intellectual resources available to him, as if he were keeping a personal theological journal. At the same time, however, he is speaking consciously as the successor of Peter to the universal Church. To the objection that catechesis demands a lower level of intellectual sophistication, one can respond that catechesis is not only for the intellectually immature, but for all human beings of all degrees of sophistication, though academics may be less aware of their own need. In a similar way, the understanding of faith is unfolded in theology for the good of the whole Church with all intellectual resources available to theologians. Speaking to the whole Church on such a level can be fruitful, provided there are persons who help others to understand what is said. Besides, many passages in TOB are translucent in their simplicity and directness.

d. Reading of Scripture

John Paul II intends to present a theology of the body that is built on Scripture, above all on the words of Christ (see TOB 86:4). *What sort of reading of Scripture does he offer?* How is it related to historical-critical Scripture scholarship? John Paul II's view of historical-critical studies is quite positive.

> Catholic exegetes [must] remain in full harmony with the mystery of the Incarnation, a mystery of the union of the divine and the human in a determinate historical life. The earthly life of Jesus is not defined only by the places and dates at the beginning of the first century in Judea and Galilee, but also by his deep roots in the long history of a small nation of the ancient Near East, with its weaknesses and its greatness, with its men of God and its sinners, with its slow cultural evolution and its political misadventures, with its defeats and its victories, with its longing for peace and the kingdom of God. The

---

26. Curran, *Moral Theology of John Paul II*, 5.

Church of Christ takes the realism of the incarnation seriously, and this is why she attaches great importance to the "historical-critical" study of the Bible....

[Exegetes must strive] to understand the meaning of the texts with all the accuracy and precision possible and, thus, in their historical, cultural context. A false idea of God and the incarnation presses a certain number of Christians to take the opposite approach. They tend to believe that, since God is the absolute Being, each of his words has an absolute value, independent of all the conditions of human language. Thus, according to them, there is no room for studying these conditions in order to make distinctions that would relativize the significance of the words. However, that is where the illusion occurs and the mysteries of scriptural inspiration and the incarnation are really rejected, by clinging to a false notion of the Absolute. The God of the Bible is not an absolute Being who, crushing everything he touches, would suppress all differences and all nuances. On the contrary, he is God the Creator, who created the astonishing variety of beings "each according to its kind," as the Genesis account says repeatedly (Gen 1). Far from destroying differences, God respects them and makes use of them (cf. 1 Cor 12:18, 24, 28). Although he expresses himself in human language, he does not give each expression a uniform value, but uses its possible nuances with extreme flexibility and likewise accepts its limitations. That is what makes the task of exegetes so complex, so necessary, and so fascinating![27]

Although John Paul II has such a positive view of historical-critical scholarship, his temperament as a thinker does not tend toward assembling the many minute details by which such scholarship constructs its arguments. That he is capable of such arguments becomes apparent in his reconstruction of the cultural situation of Jesus' listeners in the Sermon on the Mount (see TOB 33–39). Still, he is more drawn to the question: What is the truth of things? His primary perspective, even as a reader of Scripture, is that of a philosopher and a systematic theologian.

At times, historical-critical scholars focus on the question of historical truth (What was intended by these words in this or that historical context?) in such an exclusive manner that they tend to lose

---

27. John Paul II, discourse on April 23, 1993, for the presentation of the document of the Pontifical Biblical Commission, "The Interpretation of the Bible in the Church," on the 100th anniversary of Leo XIII's encyclical *Providentissimus Deus* and the 50th anniversary of Pius XII's encyclical *Divino Afflante Spiritu*, 7–8.

sight of the question of the truth of things (What do these words show about God, about human life, etc.?). They tend to measure statements about the truth of things by the historical truth of the meaning of texts. John Paul II argues, for example, that we can "deduce" from the Yahwist creation narrative that "man became the image of God not only through his own humanity, but also through the communion of persons, which man and woman form from the very beginning" (TOB 9:3). One could object from a historical-critical point of view that the Yahwist narrative (Gen 2) does not contain the word "image" at all. "Image" is only found in the Priestly narrative (Gen 1). It is unlikely on historical grounds that the Priestly narrative understood man and woman in their distinction and communion as an image of God. Such a view is not attested elsewhere in Priestly texts. The image according to Genesis 1 lies more probably in dominion over the earth, which is explicitly mentioned.

Assuming for the sake of argument that this historical-critical observation is correct, the question of the truth of things remains open. Is the communion of persons *in actual fact* an image of God? Does what Genesis 2 says have any bearing on this question? The core of John Paul II's argument is very simple. According to Genesis 2, the creation of human beings reaches its perfection in the communion of persons between man and woman. According to Genesis 1, the image of God belongs to human beings precisely in their perfection. It is the point of arrival of the creation of the human being. It follows that the communion between man and woman is part of the divine image. It does not follow on historical-critical grounds, but on those of the truth of things.

A similar line of argument applies to John Paul II's reading of Ephesians 5:21 as implying the *mutual* submission of husband and wife (see TOB 89). It is easy to point out that the imperative "submit to one another" functions as a section heading in the letter and thus includes the one-sided subordination of children to their parents and of slaves to their masters (see Eph 6:1, 5). Hence Curran accuses John Paul II of being a liberal who goes against the patriarchal meaning of the text. "Here a liberal interpretation distorts the scriptural meaning."[28] Yet, it seems reasonable to assume that John Paul II considered

---

28. Curran, *Moral Theology of John Paul II*, 56.

this side of the matter (that is, a non-mutual kind of submission) but chose not to focus on it. He certainly does not contradict it. What he does focus on instead is a fascinating argument developed on the basis of "the fear of Christ" that gathers up the theological depth of Ephesians. One should consider John Paul II's account of the mutual submission of husband and wife on its own terms as revealing a profound truth of things.

The truth of things is, in the end, much more interesting than historical truths about texts, although historical truth must not be neglected. "Interpreters are thus not content with the question, What does what is said (as something merely said) mean in its historical place and in its historical context? Rather, they ask in the end, What things does the text speak of? To what realities does what is said lead?"[29]

John Paul II pays due attention not only to the human meaning (both in its original historical context "as something said" and as revealing the truth of things) but also to the divine meaning. The divine meaning constitutes the other side of the analogy between the Incarnation and Scripture. It is the meaning intended by God in the larger whole of his revelation.

> Studying the human circumstances of the word of God should be pursued with ever renewed interest.
>
> Nevertheless, this study is not enough. In order to respect the coherence of the Church's faith and of scriptural inspiration, Catholic exegesis must be careful not to limit itself to the human aspects of the biblical texts. First and foremost, it must help the Christian people more clearly perceive the word of God in these texts so that they can better accept them in order to live in full communion with God. To this end, it is obviously necessary that the exegete himself perceive the divine word in the texts. He can do this only if his intellectual work is sustained by a vigorous spiritual life.
>
> Without this support, exegetical research remains incomplete; it loses sight of its main purpose and is confined to secondary tasks. It can even become a sort of escape. Scientific study of the merely human aspects of the texts can make the exegete forget that the word of God invites each person to come out of himself to live in faith and love....

---

29. Rudolf Bultmann, "Das Problem einer theologischen Exegese des Neuen Testaments," *Zwischen den Zeiten* 3 (1925): 334–57, here 338.

Indeed, to arrive at a completely valid interpretation of words inspired by the Holy Spirit, one must first be guided by the Holy Spirit and it is necessary to pray for that, to pray much, to ask in prayer for the interior light of the Spirit and docilely accept that light, to ask for the love that alone enables one to understand the language of God, who "is love." (1 Jn 4:8, 16)[30]

The "language of God" that resounds in the whole of Scripture is, according to this text, closely connected with the truth that "God is love." TOB is at its core an attempt to read precisely this language in the spousal mystery (Eph 5).

"This mystery is great; I say this with reference to Christ and the Church" (Eph 5:32). In the overall context of Ephesians and further in the wider context of the words of Sacred Scripture, which reveal God's salvific plan "from the beginning," one can see that here the term *"mystērion" signifies the mystery* first hidden in God's mind and later revealed in man's history. Given its importance, the mystery is *"great" indeed*: as God's salvific plan for humanity, that mystery is in some sense the central theme of the whole of revelation, its central reality. It is what God as Creator and Father wishes above all to transmit to mankind in his Word. (TOB 93:2)

Of all the works of John Paul II, TOB is the most direct, profound, and extensive analysis of "what God...wishes above all to transmit to human beings in his Word." Just as TOB is *the* catechesis among John Paul II's catecheses, so it is *the* reading of the divine meaning of Scripture among all his readings. The encyclical *Dominum et Vivificantem* on the Holy Spirit comes perhaps closest to TOB since it contains an extensive meditation on the Gospel of John, particularly on the mystery that "God is love."

In his intimate life, God "is love," the essential love shared by the three divine Persons: personal love is the Holy Spirit as the Spirit of the Father and the Son. Therefore he "searches even the depths of God," as uncreated Love-Gift. It can be said that in the Holy Spirit the intimate life of the Triune God becomes totally gift, an exchange of mutual love between the divine Persons and that through the Holy Spirit, God exists in the mode of gift. It is the Holy Spirit who is the personal expression of this self-giving, of this being-love. He is Person-Love. He is Person-Gift. Here we have an inexhaustible treas-

---

30. John Paul II, discourse on April 23, 1993, no. 9.

ure of the reality and an inexpressible deepening of the concept of person in God, which only divine revelation makes known to us. (*Dominum et Vivificantem*, 10)

This trinitarian core of John Paul II's vision can be traced back to Karol Wojtyła's encounter as a young man with the poetry and theology of St. John of the Cross.

2. Wojtyła's Carmelite Personalism

a. *Gaudium et Spes*, 24:3, and the Sanjuanist Triangle

Pascal Ide has traced *Gaudium et Spes*, 24:3, through John Paul II's vast literary output and shown that it plays a key role in the comprehensive theology of gift developed by John Paul II, particularly in *Man and Woman He Created Them*.[31] This passage from *Gaudium et Spes* reads: "Indeed, the Lord Jesus, when he prays to the Father, 'that all may be one...as we are one' (Jn 17:21–22) and thus offers vistas closed to human reason, indicates a certain likeness between the union of the divine Persons and the union of God's sons in truth and love. This likeness shows that man, who is the only creature on earth which God willed for itself, cannot fully find himself except through a sincere gift of self; cf. Lk 17:33" (24:3). Two fundamental principles are contained in the last sentence of this text. First, God wills human beings for their own sake, for their good. Persons should thus not be used as mere means. Wojtyła calls this principle "the personalistic norm."[32] Second, persons can only find themselves in a sincere gift of self.

A triangle of theses connected with the second of these two principles runs like a deeply embedded watermark through the works of Wojtyła/John Paul II, from his doctoral dissertation, *Faith according to St. John of the Cross* (1948), to his last encyclical, *Ecclesia de Eucharistia* (2003).

---

31. See Pascal Ide, "Une théologie du don: Les occurrences de Gaudium et spes, n. 24, §3 chez Jean-Paul II," *Anthropotes* 17 (2001), 149–78; 313–44. See also Ide's unpublished commentary on TOB, Pascal Ide, "Le don du corps: Une lecture des catéchèses de Jean-Paul II sur le corps humain" (manuscript, 1992).

32. See Karol Wojtyła, *Love and Responsibility* (San Francisco: Ignatius Press, 1993), 40–44.

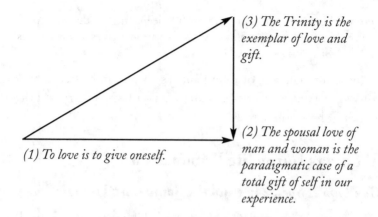

(3) The Trinity is the exemplar of love and gift.

(2) The spousal love of man and woman is the paradigmatic case of a total gift of self in our experience.

(1) To love is to give oneself.

The first point on this triangle is a general account of love as a gift of self. From this point, one line extends horizontally to the thesis that the gift of self is present with particular completeness in the spousal love between man and woman. Another line extends upward diagonally, to the analogous application of the same account of love to the Trinity. Love and Gift take place in complete fullness in the begetting of the Son and the procession of the Spirit (see *Dominum et Vivificantem*, 10, just quoted above). The descending line from point three to point two represents the thesis that communion between created persons, particularly the communion of spousal love between man and woman, flows as an image from God's own trinitarian communion.

Gaudium et Spes, 24:3, expanded in this way by a characteristic triangle, constitutes the very core of Wojtyła/John Paul II's philosophical and theological personalism. Wojtyła first encountered this personalism in the works of St. John of the Cross. The later encounter with the personalism of Kant and the very different personalism of Scheler enriched this Carmelite point of departure, but left its fundamental structure intact. The fundamental structure of Kant's personalism, and of Scheler's as well, is different. Wojtyła adopted neither the one nor the other (see below).

b. Wojtyła's Encounter with St. John of the Cross

In 1941, one year before he entered the underground seminary of Kraków, Karol Wojtyła, twenty-one years old, and a student of Polish literature, had a profound encounter with St. John of the Cross. The Gestapo played an instrumental and, in retrospect, historic role in bringing about this encounter. Hitler stripped Polish parishes of most of their priests in order to break the backbone of Polish religious and intellectual resistance. Consequently, Wojtyła came under the spiritual guidance of a layman, Jan Tyranowski, who introduced him to St. John of the Cross.[33] The young student was so struck by St. John of the Cross that he immediately learned Spanish to read the Mystical Doctor in the original. "Before entering the seminary, I met a layman named Jan Tyranowski, who was a true mystic. This man, whom I consider a saint, introduced me to the great Spanish mystics and in particular to St. John of the Cross. Even before entering the underground seminary, I read the works of that mystic, especially his poetry. In order to read it in the original, I studied Spanish. That was a very important stage in my life."[34]

Seven years after this first encounter with St. John of the Cross, now twenty-eight years old and a priest, Wojtyła defended his dissertation on the understanding of faith in St. John of the Cross, directed by Reginald Garrigou-Lagrange, then professor of spiritual theology at the *Angelicum*.[35] The dissertation, written in Latin, quotes the original text of St. John of the Cross in Spanish.[36] Looking back in 1982

---

33. He also introduced him to St. Louis de Montfort; see George Weigel, *Witness to Hope: The Biography of Pope John Paul II* (New York: Harper Collins, 1999), 58–62; George Huntston Williams, *The Mind of John Paul II: Origins of His Thought and Action* (New York: Seabury Press, 1981), 77–81.

34. John Paul II, *Crossing the Threshold of Hope*, 142. See also John Paul II, *Gift and Mystery: On the Fiftieth Anniversary of My Priestly Ordination* (New York: Doubleday, 1996), 23–25.

35. Karol Wojtyła, *La dottrina della fede in S. Giovanni della Croce* [*Doctrina de fide apud S. Joannem a Cruce*], ed. Massimo Bettetini, *Original Latin text with facing Italian translation* (Milan: Bompiani, 2003). English translation: Karol Wojtyła, *Faith according to St. John of the Cross* (San Francisco: Ignatius Press, 1981). See Jesús Castellano Cervera, "La rilettura della fede in Giovanni delle Croce (1948) e il magistero odierno di Giovanni Paolo II: Continuità e novità," in *Fede di studioso e obbedienza di pastore: Atti del Convegno sul 50o del dottorato di K. Wojtyła e del 20o del Pontificato di Giovanni Paolo II*, ed. Edward Kaczynski (Rome: Millennium Romae, 1999). Alvaro Huerga, "Karol Wojtyła, comentador de San Juan de la Cruz," *Angelicum* 56 (1979): 348–66; Raimondo Sorgia, "Approcio con l'«opera prima» di K. Wojtyła," *Angelicum* 57 (1980): 401–23; and Williams, *Mind of John Paul II*, 103–9.

36. According to Huerga, Wojtyła's understanding of the nuances of the Spanish original is excellent: Huerga, "Wojtyła, comentador de San Juan," 252.

at more than forty years of familiarity with St. John of the Cross, John Paul II says the following about his spiritual master in a homily delivered on November 4, 1982 (thus between TOB 99, October 27, 1982, and TOB 100, November 24, 1982). "To him I owe so much in my spiritual formation. I came to know him in my youth and I entered into an intimate dialogue with this master of faith, with his language and his thought, culminating in the writing of my doctoral dissertation on 'Faith in John of the Cross.' Ever since then I have found in him a friend and master who has shown me the light that shines in the darkness for walking always toward God."[37]

The main topic of Wojtyła's doctoral thesis is faith as a means of union between God and the human person. Faith as a means of union is also the point John Paul II emphasizes in his apostolic letter *Maestro en la fe* (1990) dedicated to St. John of the Cross.

> I myself have been especially attracted by the experience and teachings of the Saint of Fontiveros. From the first years of my priestly formation, I found in him a sure guide in the ways of faith. This aspect of his doctrine seemed to me to be of vital importance to every Christian, especially in a trail-blazing age like our own which is also filled with risks and temptations in the sphere of faith.... I wrote my doctoral thesis in theology on the subject of "Faith according to John of the Cross." In it, I devoted special attention to an analytical discussion of the central affirmation of the Mystical Doctor: Faith is the only proximate and proportionate means for communion with God. Even then I felt that John had not only marshaled solid theological doctrine, but that, above all, he had set forth Christian life in terms of such basic aspects as communion with God, the contemplative dimension of prayer, the strength that apostolic mission derives from life in God, and the creative tension of the Christian life lived in hope.[38]

Had Wojtyła chosen the topic of love rather than faith for his dissertation, the evidence of the strong impact of St. John of the Cross on his understanding of spousal love would be more direct and clear.

---

37. John Paul II, homily at Segovia (Nov. 4, 1982), *Insegnamenti* 5, no. 3 (1982): 1137–44, par. 2.

38. John Paul II, Apostolic Letter *"Maestro en la fe" to Felipe Sáinz de Baranda, Superior General of the Discalced Carmelites on the Occasion of the Fourth Centenary of the Death of John of the Cross* (Dec. 14, 1990), 2.

Still, in his dissertation he does quote and analyze a text that seems to be an important seed of much of his later thinking about love and personal subjectivity.

> O lamps of fire!
> in whose splendors
> the deep caverns of feeling,
> once obscure and blind,
> now give forth, so rarely, so exquisitely,
> both warmth and light to their Beloved.

The sense of personal subjectivity, which is so important to Wojtyła, is powerfully expressed in this stanza: caverns of feeling with fiery lamps that spread warmth and light across the whole distance to the beloved. In his commentary on the last two lines, St. John of the Cross writes:

> Since God *gives himself* with a free and gracious will, so too the soul (possessing a will more generous and free the more it is united with God) gives to God, God himself in God; and this is a true and complete gift of the soul to God.
>
> It is conscious there that God is indeed its own and that it possesses him by inheritance, with the right of ownership, as his adopted child through the grace of his *gift of himself*. Having him for its own, it can give him and communicate him to whomever it wishes. Thus it gives him to its Beloved, who is the very God who *gave himself* to it. By this donation it repays God for all it owes him, since it willingly gives as much as it receives from him.
>
> Because the soul in this gift to God offers him the Holy Spirit, with voluntary surrender, as something of its own (so that God loves himself in the Holy Spirit as he deserves), it enjoys inestimable delight and fruition, seeing that it gives God something of its own that is suited to him according to his infinite being. It is true that the soul cannot give God again to himself, since in himself he is ever himself. Nevertheless it does this truly and perfectly, giving all that was given it by him in order to *repay love, which is to give as much as is given.* And God, who could not be considered paid with anything less, is considered paid with that gift of the soul; and he accepts it gratefully as something it *gives him of its own.* In this very gift he loves it anew; and in this resurrender of God to the soul, the soul also loves as though again.
>
> A reciprocal love is thus actually formed between God and the soul, *like the marriage union and surrender,* in which the goods of both

(the divine essence that each possesses freely by reason of the voluntary surrender between them) are possessed by both together. *They say to each other what the Son of God spoke to the Father through John:* All that is mine is yours and yours is mine, and I am glorified in them [Jn 17:10].[39]

Wojtyła quotes key sections of this text and discusses them in some detail.[40] The most important passage highlights the trinitarian aspect of the transforming union between the soul and God.

This concept of the relationship between God and the soul, at once filial *and conjugal,* is based on two constant elements: [1] the adoptive communication of grace and [2] the power of love.

[Ad 1:] The soul becomes "God by participation" and therefore by participation it possesses divinity itself;

[Ad 2:] and the will gives to the Beloved through love nothing less than that which it had received from him: the gift of participated divinity. Hence the soul gives God to himself and through himself because the motion of the Holy Spirit is continuously transformed.[41]

Nevertheless, the one who gives is in fact the soul, which loves God in return to a supreme degree. Since its will is perfectly united with the divine will, it cannot carry out any other works than those that adhere to the divine will. Consequently, due to the perfection of the transforming union, the soul's will is entirely occupied in the same objectives of the divine will, namely, loving God and giving to him in love that which it has from him by participation—divinity itself, not only through the lover's will, but *as God loves, by the movement of the Holy Spirit.*

With this, we reach the *"Trinitarian"* mystical teaching that was already mentioned in the *Spiritual Canticle.*[42]

---

39. St. John of the Cross, *The Living Flame of Love,* commentary on st. B 3, par. 78–80, in *The Collected Works,* ed. Kieran Kavanaugh, rev. ed. (Washington, DC: ICS Publications, Institute of Carmelite Studies, 1991), 705–6; emphasis added.

40. See Wojtyła, *Apud Joannem a Cruce,* 421–30; Wojtyla, *St. John of the Cross,* 227–33, see also 89.

41. The Latin *"motio"* is in the nominative. Perhaps the ablative *"motione"* is to be read, in which case the text is to be translated, "because by the motion of the Holy Spirit, it [that is, the soul] is continually transformed.

42. Wojtyła, *St. John of the Cross,* 230; emphasis added, translation modified. Cf. Wojtyła, *Apud Joannem a Cruce,* 424 and 426.

c. The Sanjuanist Triangle in Detail

Three points of contact between the key text in *Living Flame of Love* (stanza 3, with commentary) and Wojtyła/John Paul II's vision are particularly clear and important. They correspond to the characteristic triangle of theses mentioned above: (1) Love implies a cycle of mutual giving, supremely the gift of self. (2) The paradigmatic instance of such self-gift in human experience is the spousal relation between man and woman. (3) The Trinity is the archetype of such love and gift from which the love between God and human persons as well as love between human beings derives as an imitation and participation. Let us look at each of these points in more detail.

(1) Love and the Gift of Self: St. John of the Cross describes the soul's relation to God as a cycle of mutual giving. The deep satisfaction and happiness of love is found in this cycle *as a cycle of giving*, not only of receiving (see TOB 68:2–3). In *Living Flame*, 3, what the bride gives is God, who has given himself to her. *Self*-gift is not explicit, but certainly implicit. In other texts, St. John of the Cross speaks more directly of the bride giving *herself*.

> There he gave me his breast;
> there he taught me a sweet and living knowledge;
> and I gave myself to him,
> keeping nothing back;
> there I promised to be his bride.[43]

In this stanza, the promise "to be his bride" seems to express in alternate words what immediately precedes it, "I gave myself to him, keeping nothing back." St. John of the Cross comments:

> In this stanza the bride tells of the *mutual surrender* made in this spiritual espousal between the soul and God, saying that in the interior wine cellar of love they were joined by the communication he made of himself to her....
>
> In that sweet drink of God, in which the soul is imbibed in him, she most willingly and with intense delight *surrenders herself wholly to him in the desire to be totally his and never to possess in herself anything other than him....*

---

43. St. John of the Cross, *Spiritual Canticle*, st. B 27.

Hence, not only in her will but also in her works she is *really and totally given to God without keeping anything back, just as God has freely given himself entirely to her.* This union is so effected that the two wills are mutually paid, surrendered, and satisfied (so that neither fails the other in anything) with the fidelity and stability of an espousal. She therefore adds: there I promised to be his bride.

Just as one who is espoused does not love, care, or work for any other than her bridegroom, so the soul in this state has no affections of the will or knowledge in the intellect or care or work or appetite that is not entirely inclined toward God. She is as it were divine and deified, in such a way that in regard to all she can understand she does not even suffer the first movements contrary to God's will.[44]

The characteristic feature of the spousal love between human beings and God, according to this text, is the totality of the gift of self, which is reflected in the totality of the orientation of affections toward the spouse. "I gave myself to him, keeping nothing back; there I promised to be his bride."

When there is union of love, the image of the Beloved is so sketched in the will, and drawn so intimately and vividly, that it is true to say that the Beloved lives in the lover and the lover in the Beloved. Love produces such likeness in this transformation of lovers that one can say each is the other and both are one. The reason is that in the union and transformation of love each gives possession of self to the other and each leaves and exchanges self for the other. Thus each one lives in the other and is the other, and both are one in the transformation of love.[45]

In this text, St. John of the Cross uses the concept of the gift of self to unfold the more traditional language of the "transformation" and "union" of love.

(2) The Paradigmatic Role of Love between Man and Woman: St. John of the Cross's comparison, "Just as one who is espoused," that is, one who is an earthly bride in relation to her human bridegroom, touches on the second important point of contact with Wojtyła. According to St. John of the Cross, the marriage analogy is appropriate across the whole breadth of Christian experience, even in its less perfect forms. It is most applicable, however, to what St. John of the

---

44. Ibid., commentary on st. B 27, par. 5–7.
45. Ibid., commentary on st. B 12, par. 7.

Cross calls "spiritual marriage," which follows "spiritual betrothal." In his commentary on stanza 22 (par. 3) of the *Spiritual Canticle*, he writes.

> This spiritual marriage is incomparably greater than the spiritual betrothal, for it is a total transformation in the Beloved, in which each surrenders the entire possession of self to the other with a certain consummation of the union of love. The soul thereby becomes divine, God through participation, insofar as is possible in this life.... Just as in the consummation of carnal marriage there are two in one flesh, as Sacred Scripture points out (Gen 2:24), so also when the spiritual marriage between God and the soul is consummated, there are two natures in one spirit and love, as St. Paul says in making this same comparison: Whoever is joined to the Lord becomes one spirit with him. (1 Cor 6:17)

The defining element of "spiritual marriage," according to this text, is the total surrendering of the self-possession of each to the other, analogous to the consummation of love by sexual union in marriage. St. John of the Cross uses this analogy to understand spiritual marriage by comparison with carnal marriage, but one can turn the comparison around to see what St. John of the Cross says about spousal love between man and woman. The conclusion one reaches in such an inversion is precisely Wojtyła's vision of spousal love: the gift of self is the defining mark of spousal love between man and woman in contrast with other forms of love. "Betrothed [=spousal] love differs from all the aspects or forms of love analyzed hitherto. Its decisive character is the giving of one's own person (to another). This is something different from and more than attraction, desire or even good will. These are all ways by which one person goes out toward another, but none of them can take him as far.... The fullest, the most uncompromising form of love consists precisely in self-giving, in making one's inalienable and non-transferable 'I' someone else's property."[46]

This important text from *Love and Responsibility* can be set next to some of St. John of the Cross's formulations and John Paul II's mature statement in *Familiaris Consortio*.

---

46. Wojtyła, *Love and Responsibility*, 96 and 97; emphasis added.

St. John of the Cross	Wojtyła	John Paul II
I gave myself to him, keeping nothing back; there I promised to be his bride.[47] ...[T]he bride tells of the mutual surrender made in this spiritual espousal between the soul and God....[48] [S]he most willingly and with intense delight surrenders herself wholly to him in the desire to be totally his....[49] Each surrenders the entire possession of self to the other with a certain consummation of the union of love.[50]	The essence of spousal love is self-giving, the surrender of one's "I".... The fullest, the most uncompromising form of love consists precisely in self-giving, in making one's inalienable and nontransferable "I" someone else's property.[51]	The total physical self-giving would be a lie if it were not the sign and fruit of a total personal self-giving, in which the whole person, including the temporal dimension, is present: if the person were to withhold something or reserve the possibility of deciding otherwise in the future, by this very fact he or she would not be giving totally.[52]

The striking similarity between these formulations suggests that Wojtyła's way of thinking about love was deeply formed by the language of "gift of self" found in St. John of the Cross.

(3) The Trinitarian Root of the Gift: The third decisive point of contact between Wojtyła/John Paul II and St. John of the Cross lies in the thesis that love as a gift of self is rooted in the relation between the Father and the Son in the unity of the Holy Spirit. Here is the key text again: "A reciprocal love is thus actually formed between God and the soul, *like the marriage union and surrender,* in which the goods of

---

47. St. John of the Cross, *Spiritual Canticle,* st. B 27.
48. Ibid., commentary on st. B 27, par. 3.
49. Ibid., commentary on st. B 27, par. 6.
50. Ibid., commentary on st. B 22, par. 3.
51. Wojtyła, *Love and Responsibility,* 96 and 97.
52. John Paul II, *Familiaris Consortio,* 11.

both (the divine essence that each possesses freely by reason of the voluntary surrender between them) are possessed by both together. *They say to each other what the Son of God spoke to the Father through John:* All that is mine is yours and yours is mine, and I am glorified in them [Jn 17:10]."[53] The Son of God is the first to say to the Father, "All that is mine is yours, and what is yours is mine." Both the soul's filial/spousal relation to God and the marriage union and surrender between man and woman are derived as images from this first cycle of giving within the Trinity. Neither St. John of the Cross nor Wojtyła/John Paul II apply spousal language directly to the Trinity. It is the father-son relation, not the bride-bridegroom relation, that is the normative image for the Trinity, in agreement with the teaching of Jesus. Yet, it is clear to both that the archetype and source of spousal love lies in the Trinity: "All that is mine is yours, and yours is mine."

In his writings and sermons, John Paul II returns frequently to St. John of the Cross.[54] The following two texts are good examples.

> Truly, the Father has sent his Son into the world that we, united to him and transformed by him, might be able to restore to God the same gift of love that he gave to us. "God so loved the world that he gave his only Son, so that everyone who believes in him might have eternal life" (Jn 3:16). Starting from this gift of love we can better understand and realize in us the eternal life of God, which consists in participating in the total and complete gift of the Son to the Father in the love of the Holy Spirit. A sublime reality, which St. John of the Cross expressed with the words, "Give to God, God himself in God" (*The Living Flame of Love*, stanza 3). I wanted to remind you of these Christian ideals in order to set before you in your mind and heart the final and grandiose goal of all evangelization.[55]

This text documents that the main passage expressing St. John of the Cross's trinitarian personalism, *Living Flame of Love*, 3, with commentary, was present to John Paul II in writing this sermon about a theme so dear to him, evangelization. In agreement with St. John of

---

53. St. John of the Cross, *Living Flame of Love*, B 80.

54. The *Insegnamenti* of John Paul II contain more than sixty documents mentioning St. John of the Cross.

55. John Paul II, homily at Buenos Aires (Mar. 10, 1987), *Insegnamenti* 10, no. 1 (1987): 1202–11, §2.

the Cross, he glosses the phrase "Give to God, God himself in God," by the language of the gift of self, "the total and complete gift of the Son to the Father in the love of the Holy Spirit." This is the eternal life of God in which human beings are called to participate. *Gaudium et Spes,* 24:3, is not far from these formulations: by showing us the union of the divine Persons, Jesus shows us that we can "find ourselves only through a sincere gift of self."

Another important text deals with human dignity, which is implicit in the first of the two principles in *Gaudium et Spes,* 24:3, (a creature "willed for itself"): "For St. John of the Cross, God is in all, and all is in God. All is presence and gift, all things carry us to God, and he offers us all as a gift to show how precious man is in his eyes as the crown of creation."[56] In this text, John Paul II sees human dignity in the framework of St. John of the Cross's theology of "presence and gift." Again *Gaudium et Spes,* 24:3, is not far away: God wills man for his own sake inasmuch as he creates man for a life of communion in receiving and giving the gift of self.

To conclude, it was in St. John of the Cross that Wojtyła first saw the triangle of theses that came to define the depth-structure of his vision of the person. The spiritual and intellectual roots of his personalism are Carmelite.

3. Wojtyła and Kant

In his penetrating study of Wojtyła, Kenneth Schmitz argues that the most significant challenge to which Wojtyła's personalism responds is a certain understanding of personal subjectivity and interiority that gained wide currency in the modern age.[57] A particular emphasis on subjectivity, Schmitz shows, emerged from the sixteenth century onward together with the rise of a mechanistic account of nature. Medieval accounts of nature had shared a sense of the interiority and depth of all natural beings. Natural beings were seen as constituted by their own interior principles and causes that involve a rela-

---

56. John Paul II, discourse to Congress on St. John of the Cross, Rome (Mar. 25, 1991), *Insegnamenti* 14, no. 1 (1991): 869–72, §2.

57. See Kenneth L. Schmitz, *At the Center of the Human Drama: The Philosophical Anthropology of Karol Wojtyła/Pope John Paul II* (Washington, DC: Catholic University of America Press, 1993), 121–45, esp. 131–37.

tion both to their creative origin and to their end and good. Nature comes from the wisdom of God and acts for an end. The good is the cause of causes. Human beings are not alone as beings of longing, as beings ordered to the good, but in their rational nature they experience a deep kinship with other natural beings and with their own sentient and bodily nature.

The mechanistic account of nature in the wake of Bacon and Descartes denied the interiority of material beings and consequently the kinship of the human person with the subrational natural cosmos. Alone in an inhospitable world that had been deprived of inner meaning, the freedom of the conscious subject becomes "absolute," detached from sources of meaning: "This, then, is the genesis of the modern sense of subject as subjectivity. We might say that subjectivity is the self-defense by which consciousness fends off a world either hostile to its inhabitation or at least without companionate room for it, even while consciousness subverts the integrity of that world by its imperious demands. The modern shift gave to the human subject an absolute status precisely in its character *qua* consciousness; for human consciousness not only sets its own terms but the terms for reality itself."[58]

Some have suggested that the particular context in which Wojtyła encountered this modern sense of subjectivity was the French personalist movement around Emmanuel Mounier and the journal *Esprit*.[59] There is indeed clear evidence that Wojtyła took part in the activities of a group of Polish personalists influenced by *Esprit* who founded the journal *Znak* or wrote regularly for it.[60] Nevertheless, it is German

---

58. Ibid., 135–36.

59. See John Hellman, "John Paul II and the Personalist Movement," *Cross Currents* 30 (1980–81): 415. See also Emmanuel Mounier, *Personalism* (Notre Dame, IN: University of Notre Dame Press, 1952). An account of the relation between Mounier and Maritain is offered by Joseph A. Amato, *Mounier & Maritain: A French Catholic Understanding of the Modern World* (Ypsilanti, MI: Sapientia, 2002). See also Kenneth L. Schmitz, "Jacques Maritain and Karol Wojtyła: Approaches to Modernity," in *The Bases of Ethics,* ed. William Sweet (Milwaukee: Marquette University Press, 2000).

60. This connection is documented in detail by Hellman, "Personalist Movement," 413–8. A detailed survey of French personalism, highlighting particularly its socialist and communist sympathies, is offered by John Hellman, *Emmanuel Mounier and the New Catholic Left 1930–1950* (Toronto: University of Toronto Press, 1981); see also Rufus William Rauch, *Politics and Belief in Contemporary France: Emmanuel Mounier and Christian Democracy, 1932–1950* (The Hague: Nijhoff, 1972).

personalism, particularly Max Scheler and, behind Scheler, the tower-ing figure of Immanuel Kant, that provides the true background.[61] Wojtyła writes about this background in *The Acting Person*:

> The author has given much thought to the work of M. Scheler, in particular his *Der Formalismus in der Ethik und die materiale Wertethik*....The critique of Kant contained in that work is of crucial significance for the present considerations and was for this author the occasion for reflection and the cause of a partial acceptance of some of Kantian Personalism. This refers specifically to the "ethical" Personalism expounded in *Grundlegung zur Metaphysik der Sitten*.... The discussion between Scheler (*Der Formalismus in der Ethik und die materiale Wertethik*) and Kant was in a way the "starting ground" for the reflection underlying the analyses of the "acting person" contained in this study.[62]

This statement is important as a guide for the study of Wojtyła. If indeed the discussion between Scheler and Kant is the "starting ground" of Wojtyła's main philosophical work, close attention to the relevant aspects of both Kant and Scheler will be helpful for under-standing it. Wojtyła's students testify that their teacher's most contin-uous and serious partner in philosophic dialogue, evident throughout his lectures and seminars, was indeed Kant.[63] "Kant, *Mein Gott!* Kant!"[64]

a. Bacon, Descartes, and a New Subjectivity

The ambition of power over nature played a pivotal role in the beginnings of modernity in Bacon and especially Descartes.[65] In his *Great Instauration* (1620), Francis Bacon (1561–1626) articulates the

---

61. The alternative between French or German personalism is, in the end, not absolute. Hellman shows that German personalism, particularly Scheler, stands at the origin of French personalism; see Hellman, "Personalist Movement," 410. Still, Wojtyła read the German personalists Kant and Scheler directly, not mediated by French personalists.

62. Karol Wojtyła, *The Acting Person* (Dordrecht, Boston, and London: D. Reidel, 1979), 22, no. 8 on 302.

63. According to the testimony of Stanislaw Grygiel, now occupant of the Wojtyła Chair at the Lateran University.

64. "Kant, *My God!* Kant!" Exclamation of John Paul II in the presence of guests when Kant was mentioned. Weigel, *Witness to Hope*, 128.

65. See Hans Urs von Balthasar, *Theodrama: IV: The Action* (San Francisco: Ignatius Press, 1994), 156–60.

fundamental philosophical principles that came to inform the overall shape of scientific reason. The title *Great Instauration* alludes, perhaps with some irony, to Ephesians, which speaks of God's action in the fullness of time "to gather everything under Christ as head, Vulgate: *instaurare omnia in Christo* (Eph 1:10)." Bacon states his purpose clearly in the preface: "The state of knowledge is not prosperous nor greatly advancing; and...a way must be opened for the human understanding entirely different from any hitherto known, and other helps provided, in order that the mind may exercise over the nature of things the authority which properly belongs to it."[66]

Authority over nature belonged to the human race before the fall, and it is to this primeval condition that Bacon intends to return, undoing the consequences of the fall as far as possible. The Scholastic "wisdom" of his own time, Bacon asserts, is immature: "For its value and utility it must be plainly avowed that that wisdom which we have derived principally from the Greeks is but like the boyhood of knowledge, and has the characteristic property of boys: it can talk, but it cannot generate, for it is fruitful of controversies but barren of works."[67] Human knowledge becomes mature and manly, able to beget children, only when it is directed to its true end, namely, power over nature in order to minister to the needs of life.[68]

The goal of power deeply determines what is, and what is not, a proper subject of knowledge and therefore what belongs, and what does not belong, into a true account of nature. Of the four causes investigated by the Aristotelian philosophy of nature, the two considered most important by Aristotle, namely, final and formal cause, should be dismissed. "The final cause rather corrupts than advances the sciences."[69] This is quite reasonable. Giving attention to the final cause hinders the concerns of power since power is concerned with subjecting something as material to a new superimposed purpose. A similar point applies for the same reason to the formal cause, understood as the nature of a thing: "Matter rather than forms should be

---

66. Francis Bacon, *The New Organon and Related Writings* (Indianapolis: Bobbs-Merrill, 1960), 3–4.
67. Ibid., 7–8.
68. Ibid., 267–68.
69. Ibid., 121.

the object of our attention, its configurations and changes of configuration, and simple action, and laws of action or motion, for forms are figments of the human mind, unless you call those laws of action forms."[70] The only remnant of form in Bacon's vision is mathematical law. "And inquiries into nature have the best result when they begin with physics and end in mathematics."[71] The strong orientation toward mathematics that came to dominate natural science may have other causes as well, e.g., Galileo's return against Aristotelian Scholasticism to a Pythagorean-Platonic vision, but the principal driving force seems to have been the goal of power.

Bacon's project of reconstructing the entire order of knowledge in light of the ambition of power over nature is connected with a premise developed earlier in the philosophical and theological current that stands behind the Reformation, namely, Nominalism: "Late medieval nominalism defended the sovereignty of God as incompatible with there being an order in nature which by itself defined good and bad. For that would be to tie God's hands, to infringe on his sovereign right of decision about what was good. This line of thought even contributed in the end to the rise of mechanism: the ideal universe from this point of view is a mechanical one."[72] Nominalism, however, did not yet formulate the goal of power as the measure of knowledge. Still, it eliminated from nature precisely those features that resist its subjection to power, namely, a strong teleology and formal causality. The universe most suited to the goal of power is a mechanical universe, grasped and made ready for use by the mathematical science of mechanics.

Bacon gives some thought to the question of the morality of the power he proposes. He is aware of the possible problem of an abuse of power, but dismisses it. "If the debasement of arts and sciences to purposes of wickedness, luxury and the like, be made a ground of objection, let no one be moved thereby. For the same may be said of all earthly goods: of wit, courage, strength, beauty, wealth, light and the rest. Only let the human race recover that right over nature which

---

70. Ibid., 53.

71. Ibid., 129.

72. Charles Taylor, *Sources of the Self: The Making of the Modern Identity* (Cambridge, MA: Harvard University Press, 1989), 82.

belongs to it by divine bequest, and let power be given it: the exercise thereof will be governed by sound reason and true religion."[73] It is chilling to read this statement about the automatically self-governing goodness of human power next to a statement about human ambition found only a few sentences earlier.

> It will not be amiss to distinguish the three kinds and, as it were, grades of ambition in mankind. The first is of those who desire to extend their own power in their native country, a vulgar and degenerate kind. The second is of those who labor to extend the power of their country and its dominion among men. This certainly has more dignity, though not less covetousness. But if a man endeavor to establish and extend the power and dominion of the human race itself over the universe, his ambition (if ambition it can be called) is without doubt both a more wholesome and a more noble thing than the other two. Now the empire of man over things depends wholly on the arts and sciences. For we cannot command nature except by obeying her.[74]

Bacon's leap in the third grade of ambition is extraordinary. The human heart is wayward in the first two grades of ambition for power. In the third grade, in "the empire of man over things," which simply consists in a greater universality of power by extension to the human race as a whole and to the whole "universe," the human heart is suddenly full of light and nobility.

At the height of its triumph in the twentieth century, as Hans Jonas argues, "the Baconian program" has revealed its insufficiency in the lack of control over itself. Both humanity and the earth now need protection because of the very magnitude of the power that has been achieved (e.g., nuclear weapons). Yet we do not seem able to offer such protection. Scientific and technological progress has its own dynamics in which power that *can* be used *will* be used. Bacon did not anticipate this deep paradox of the power derived from knowledge: that it leads indeed to some sort of domination over nature, but at the same time to a helpless subjugation under itself.[75]

Bacon's impact might have been small if the project of power had not been embraced by a mathematician and philosopher who can be

---

73. Bacon, *New Organon*, 119.

74. Ibid., 118.

75. See Hans Jonas, *The Imperative of Responsibility: In Search of an Ethics for the Technological Age* (Chicago: University of Chicago Press, 1984), 141.

considered the true father of the distinctively modern scientific-tech-nological project, Descartes. According to Descartes, "it is possible to reach knowledge that will be of much utility in this life; and...instead of the speculative philosophy which is now taught in the schools [that is, Scholastic philosophy] we can find a practical one, by which, know-ing the nature and behavior of fire, water, air, stars, the heavens, and all the other bodies which surround us...we can employ these entities for all the purposes for which they are suited, and so make ourselves masters and possessors of nature."[76] Descartes is very explicit. The speculative philosophy of the Scholastics must be replaced by a prac-tical, that is, technological philosophy. Doing and especially making must determine what is, and what is not, a relevant pursuit of philos-ophy and its eventual offshoot, natural science. Leon Kass points out the deep impact this view has on how nature is viewed: "The new sci-ence sought *first* power over nature, and *derivatively*, found a way to reconceive nature that yielded the empowering kind of knowledge: Seek power, and you will devise a way of knowing that gives it to you. The result can be simply put: knowledge permitting prediction and (some) control over biological events has been purchased at the cost of deep ignorance, not to say misunderstanding, of *living beings*, our-selves included."[77] The single most important exclusion from "objec-tive" being that Descartes insists upon is the exclusion of the final cause: "The entire class of causes which people customarily derive from a thing's 'end,' I judge to be utterly useless in Physics."[78] One can see immediately that a way of thinking formed in this Cartesian manner will have fundamental difficulties with an account of sex and marriage in terms of "ends."

It fits with Descartes' program of ordering knowledge in radical fashion to power over nature that he holds up free will as the greatest

---

76. René Descartes, *Discourse on Method*, 6, in *Discourse on Method and Meditations*, 3rd ed. (Indianapolis: Hackett, 1993), Adam and Tannery 61–62. Cf. also René Descartes, *Rules for the Direction of the Mind*, 13, in *Rules for the Direction of the Mind* (New York: Bobbs-Merrill, 1961), Adam and Tannery, 434.

77. Leon Kass, "The Permanent Limitations of Biology," in *The Ambiguous Legacy of the Enlightenment*, ed. William A. Rusher (Lanham, MD: University Press of America, 1995), 125.

78. Descartes, *Meditations*, 4, in *Discourse on Method and Meditations*, 83, Adam and Tannery, 55.

human good. "Now freewill is in itself the noblest thing we can have because it makes us in a certain manner equal to God and exempts us from being his subjects; and so its rightful use is the greatest of all the goods we possess, and further there is nothing that is more our own or that matters more to us. From all this it follows that nothing but freewill can produce our greatest contentments."[79] This apotheosis of the freedom of choice as the greatest human good seems to anticipate already the core of Kant's philosophy of freedom and autonomy. There seems to be a mutual harmonic reinforcement between this Cartesian view of freedom and the Baconian project. What distinguishes the master of nature above all is that he can decide freely what to do with nature. He is not bound by any preexisting purposes in nature, but sets his own purposes. Of course, the Christian tradition considers free choice a power of great dignity. Yet, it is a power subordinate to love. On this point Wojtyła maintains a view that is the direct opposite of Descartes' radical metaphysical liberalism: "Love consists of a commitment which limits one's freedom—it is a giving of the self, and to give oneself means just that: to limit one's freedom on behalf of another. Limitation of one's freedom might seem to be something negative and unpleasant, but love makes it a positive, joyful and creative thing. *Freedom exists for the sake of love....* Man longs for love more than for freedom—freedom is the means and love the end."[80]

The development of a mechanistic science of nature and the exaltation of the freedom of choice as an ultimate value in the wake of Descartes' choice of seeking "knowledge that will be of much utility in this life" had profound effects on the understanding of the place of the human person in the cosmos. Descartes took the path of a rigorous dualism. On the one side stands the mechanical cosmos of extended things (*res extensae*), whose only attributes are extension and movement, constituting an objective world of pure externality without any interiority. On the other side stands the human soul, the "thinking

---

79. Descartes, "Letter to Christina of Sweden," in Adam and Tannery, 5, 85; cf. *Meditations,* IV.8. Translation following Taylor, *Sources of the Self,* 147. One can perhaps temper the astonishing statement that freedom "exempts us from being his [that is, God's] subjects" by adding the word "seems." In fact, Descartes writes, "*semble* nous exempter de luy estre suiets..."; emphasis added.

80. Wojtyła, *Love and Responsibility,* 135–36.

thing" (*res cogitans*), whose only attribute is rational consciousness, that is, knowledge and free will, a world of pure interiority.[81]

Others followed more narrowly reductionist paths. For Bishop George Berkeley (1685–1753), a vigorous defender of the spiritual values of the Christian tradition, there is no independently existing material world, but every "material" thing is a mere perception of the soul (*esse est percipi*). All is personal consciousness.[82] According to Julien de La Mettrie (1709–1751), there is no thinking thing, but man is simply "machine man," a material mechanism.[83] In each case, the tension between the person and the material world of nature is the crucial issue, even in proposals that apparently abolish the person altogether in favor of mere mechanism. In de La Mettrie's "machine man," the fact remains that someone is thinking about the machine and freely harnessing it to his own ends.

John Paul II points out a close relation between the predominant scientific picture of the world and a particular form of ethics, namely utilitarianism: "The development of contemporary civilization is linked to a scientific and technological progress which is often achieved in a one-sided way and thus appears purely positivistic. Positivism, as we know results in agnosticism in theory and utilitarianism in practice and in ethics. In our own day, history is in a way repeating itself. Utilitarianism is a civilization of production and of

---

81. A more Christian reading of Descartes, relativizing the ambition for power and the primacy of free choice, is proposed by Gary Steiner, *Descartes as a Moral Thinker: Christianity, Technology, Nihilism* (Amherst, NY: Humanity Books, 2004), esp. chap. 4. At the very least, even if Descartes' own position is more complex, the *effect* of his writings in the growth of the modern project corresponds to the less Christian reading proposed above.

82. See George Berkeley, *A Treatise Concerning the Principles of Human Knowledge,* ed. Colin Murray Turbayne (Indianapolis: Bobbs-Merrill, 1970).

83. See Julien Offray de La Mettrie, *Machine Man and Other Writings,* ed. Ann Thomson (Cambridge; New York: Cambridge University Press, 1996). The second English edition of this work (1750) has an extended subtitle: "Man a Machine: Wherein the several systems of philosophers, in respect to the soul of man, are examined, the different states of the soul are shewn to be co-relative to those of the body, the diversity between men and other animals, is proved to arise from the different quantity and quality of brains, the law of nature is explained, as relative to the whole animal creation, the immateriality of an inward principle is by experiments and observations exploded, and a full detail is given of the several springs which move the human machine."

use, a civilization of things and not of persons, a civilization in which persons are used in the same way as things are used."[84]

The tension between nature and person runs as the central current through the various choices pursued by the seminal thinkers of modernity. What Jonas says about the existentialism of Bultmann and the early Heidegger applies in some way to the whole era. A change in the vision of nature, he argues, is at the bottom of the metaphysical situation that has given rise to existentialism and to its nihilistic implications. The essence of existentialism is a certain estrangement between man and the world, with the loss of the idea of a kindred cosmos—in short, an anthropological a-cosmism. Jonas compares this a-cosmism with the Gnostic religion, but finds it still more radical.

> There is no overlooking one cardinal difference between the gnostic and the existentialist dualism: Gnostic man is thrown into an antagonistic, anti-divine, and therefore anti-human nature, modern man into an indifferent one. Only the latter case represents the absolute vacuum, the really bottomless pit. In the gnostic conception the hostile, the demonic, is still anthropomorphic, familiar even in its foreignness, and the contrast itself gives direction to existence.... Not even this antagonistic quality is granted to the indifferent nature of modern science, and from that nature no direction at all can be elicited. This makes modern nihilism infinitely more radical and more desperate than gnostic nihilism could ever be for all its panic terror of the world.[85]

John Paul II develops a strikingly similar line of thought.

> The human family is facing the challenge of a new Manichaeism, in which body and spirit are put in radical opposition; the body does not receive life from the spirit, and the spirit does not give life to the body. Man thus ceases to live as a person and a subject. Regardless of all intentions and declarations to the contrary, he becomes merely an object. This neo-Manichaean culture has led, for example, to human sexuality being regarded more as an area for manipulation and exploitation than as the basis of that primordial wonder which led Adam on the morning of creation to exclaim before Eve: "This at last is bone of my bones and flesh of my flesh" (Gen 2:23). This same

---

84. John Paul II, *Letter to Families*, 13.

85. Hans Jonas, "Gnosticism, Existentialism and Nihilism," in *The Gnostic Religion: The Message of the Alien God and the Beginnings of Christianity* (Boston: Beacon, 1963), 338–39.

wonder is echoed in the words of the Song of Solomon: "You have ravished my heart, my sister, my bride, you have ravished my heart with a glance of your eyes" (Song 4:9).[86]

This text contains in miniature much of the program of TOB. John Paul II's main concern in TOB is to help overcome the body-spirit dualism that emerged from placing nature in the position of an "object" for human power. His argument in TOB is similar to that of the text just quoted, namely, reflection on the primal wonder of man and woman, whose bodies are not meaningless mechanisms, but means of expression in the language of love: you have ravished my heart with a glance of your eyes (Song 4:9).

b. Kant's Anti-Trinitarian Personalism

Kant built on Bacon and Descartes. He was convinced that, with Bacon, Descartes, and Newton, natural science had found the road of definitive progress that established mathematical-materialist determinism beyond any shadow of doubt as the valid way of understanding nature. The motto of Kant's *Critique of Pure Reason* is, in fact, a passage from the preface to Bacon's *Instauratio Magna* in which Bacon formulates the project for the new kind of knowledge. Kant defends the progress achieved in this direction against the sensualist irrationalism of Hume.[87]

Yet, the success of a mechanist natural science has disturbing consequences, in Kant's judgment, especially for morality and religion. If the universe is a self-contained material mechanism explained entirely by deterministic mathematical laws of nature, excluding recourse to a Divine Being, the three main pillars of morality and religion (as Kant sees them) are called into question: the freedom of the will, the immortality of the soul, and the existence of God.[88] While Kant is deeply committed to defending natural science, he is even more deeply committed to the preservation of morality and religion on these three pillars. He is particularly concerned about the defects of the ethical system that arose as the congenial counterpart of the Baconian and

---

86. John Paul II, *Letter to Families*, 19.

87. See Immanuel Kant, *Kritik der reinen Vernunft* [*Critique of Pure Reason*], *Gesammelte Schriften*, vols. 3–4 (Berlin: Königlich-Preußische Akademie der Wissenschaften, 1902–), B VII–XIV.

88. See ibid., B XXIX–XXXI.

Cartesian project, namely, utilitarianism, which considers all things as mere means to human happiness, that is, pleasure. Utilitarianism, he argues, abandons the holiness of the law in favor of mere calculation of an outcome that serves irrational inclinations, namely, the inclinations toward pleasure and the sum of pleasures, happiness.

Kant attempts to solve these tensions of modernity in two interrelated steps. The first step is to limit reason in its theoretical capacity, that is, in its statements about what *is or is not the case,* to the realm of appearances based upon received sense-data. The second is to limit freedom, the immortality of the soul, and the existence of God (all of which lie outside the scope of sense-data) to reason in its practical capacity, that is, in its precepts what *is or is not to be done.* One key step in this solution lies in the denial that theoretical reason has any competence regarding morality and religion. "I had to do away with *knowledge* to make room for *faith.*"[89]

Kant's way of doing away with knowledge to make room for faith is the "critical turn" in his account of knowledge spelled out in the *Critique of Pure Reason.* At its core, the turn consists in a reduction of "being" to "being an object for consciousness," that is, in its reduction to an appearance, a "phenomenon" in the strict sense of *a given for consciousness.*[90] "Things in themselves" are an exception, but Kant insists that we cannot know them.

Reason inescapably produces the ideas of the freedom of the will, the immortality of the soul, and the existence of God, but it goes wrong when it puts these ideas to theoretical use.[91] The problem with their theoretical use is not that the questions of freedom, immortality, and God are too difficult for theoretical reason. The problem is that the very asking of the question with the supposition that an answer is possible is an abuse of reason that necessarily ends in illusion.

Kant drives this point home most forcefully in his famous antinomies, each of which contains two proofs.[92] The first antinomy proves both that the world has a beginning in time and that it has no beginning in time. The second proves both that every composite substance in the world consists of simple substances and that no composite con-

---

89. Ibid., B XXX .
90. See the discussion of phenomena and noumena in ibid., B 294–315.
91. See ibid., B 394–95.
92. See ibid., B 454–89.

sists of simple substances. The third proves both that free will is one of the causes in this world and that there is no freedom, but all events in this world are determined. The fourth proves both that there must be a necessary Being that is the first cause of all events and that no necessary Being exists. Kant understands these four double-proofs as proofs in the strictest possible sense. He does not argue that one or the other side must be incorrect since they contradict each other. No, both sides are strictly demonstrated. Kant concludes that theoretical reason necessarily runs into illusion and self-contradictions when it attempts to expand knowledge beyond appearances based on received sense-data. Speculative or theoretical reason must not even *ask* the questions of the freedom of the will, the immortality of the soul, and the existence of God.[93]

In this light, it becomes clearer what Kant means by saying, "I had to do away with *knowledge* to make room for *faith*."[94] Kant does away with knowledge by excluding theoretical reason from any competence in the question of freedom, immortality, and God. Practical reason with its practical faith has room to settle in the protected vacuum. A mechanistic and deterministic natural science has complete sway in the world of external nature, but as a theoretical science, it is completely limited to the realm of appearances based on received sense-data. Practical reason can unfold in the sphere of pure thought, the sphere of the *person* as such.

It is difficult to conceive Kant's view in all its radicalism. That the will is free, that the soul is destined for a future life, and that a God exists and will reward those who do good—these three statements cannot be considered true or false on a theoretical level, that is, in the sense of corresponding (or of not corresponding) to what is actually the case. It is only "as if" God existed. "To believe in him [God] morally and practically means...acting in a manner *as if* such a rule of the world *were* real."[95] Likewise he maintains that the proof of the three practical postulates "is not a proof of the truth of these statements seen as theoretical statements, and thus not a proof of the

93. See ibid., B 490–504.

94. Ibid., B XXX

95. Immanuel Kant, *Von einem neuerdings erhobenen vornehmen Ton in der Philosophie* [*On a Recently Assumed Noble Tone in Philosophy*], *Gesammelte Schriften*, vol. 8, 396; emphasis added.

objective existence of the objects corresponding to them...but one that has only subjective and practical validity, one whose instruction is sufficient to produce the effect of our acting *as if* we knew that these objects *were* real."[96] Kant's faith only comes into play when morally good persons regulate their own conduct. Freedom, immortality, and God are matters of moral decency, not of being and of truth.

> I shall inevitably have faith in the existence of God and in a future life. And I am sure that nothing can shake this faith; for that would overturn my moral principles themselves, which I cannot renounce without being detestable in my own eyes.... The conviction is not a logical but a *moral* certainty; and because it rests on subjective bases (of the moral attitude), I must not even say, *It is* morally certain that there is a God, etc., but I must say, *I am* morally certain, etc. In other words, the faith in a God and in another world is so interwoven with my moral attitude that, as little as I am in danger of losing my moral attitude, so little am I worried that my faith could ever be torn from me.[97]

Kant's unshakable faith in God can preserve its certainty without fear, because it is perfectly insulated against any assault from theoretical reason. Kant's God is *a God without being*, a God who is an object of human consciousness alone, and of human consciousness only in its practical form. Schmitz's characterization of the form of personal subjectivity to which Wojtyła responds is fully and radically justified at this key point of Kant's system. "The modern shift gave to the human subject an absolute status precisely in its character *qua* consciousness; for human consciousness not only sets its own terms but the terms for reality itself."[98] It sets the terms for God.

Philosophy, Kant claims, aspires to being a doctrine of wisdom, but, contrary to Aristotle, who argues that wisdom is primarily theoretical,[99] Kant proposes an absolute priority of practical over theoret-

---

96. Immanuel Kant, *Welches sind die wirklichen Fortschritte, die die Metaphysik seit Leibnizens und Wolff's Zeiten in Deutschland gemacht hat?* [*What Are the Real Advances Made by Metaphysics in Germany since the Time of Leibniz and Wolff?*], *Gesammelte Schriften*, vol. 20, 298; emphasis added.

97. Kant, *Critique of Pure Reason*, B 856–87.

98. Schmitz, *Center of the Drama*, 136.

99. "It is right also that philosophy [that is, love of wisdom] should be called knowledge of the truth. For the end of theoretical knowledge is truth, while that of practical knowledge is action, for even if they consider how things are, practical men do not study what is eternal but what stands in some relation at some time." Aristotle, *Metaphysics*, 2.1 993b20; see also 1.2 982b11–28.

ical wisdom. It is in practical wisdom that the highest aspirations of the human mind are fulfilled.[100] The final purpose of the three problems of pure reason lies in the question of practical reason, "*What is to be done*, if the will is free, if there is a God, and if there is a future world?"[101]

Kant's starting point in his moral philosophy consists in the thesis, "Nothing can possibly be conceived in the world, or even out of it, which can be called good without qualification, except a good will."[102] What is a good will? A good will is a will that follows duty rather than the inclination toward pleasure or happiness. In fact, "inclination" and "happiness" are the main competitors of a good will. A morally good will is clearest and most certain when there is a clash between duty and inclination, when devotion to duty overcomes a contrary inclination to pleasure.[103] Inclination does not belong to the order of reason, but to that of sense-data. As such, however, sense-data are without order. They are radically individual and accidental. Kant's agreement with Hume's view of experience plays a key role in his argument.

A will is good when it springs from respect or reverence for duty. "I understand at least this much about it [that is, about reverence]: that it is an act of valuing the value that by far exceeds everything recommended by inclination; and that the necessity of my acts out of *pure* reverence for the practical law is what constitutes duty. Every other motive must give way to duty, because it is the condition of a will that is good *in itself*, the value of which surpasses everything."[104]

When the moral law confronts us in particular situations as the voice of duty, it has the form of a categorical imperative (from Greek *katēgoreō*, "speak directly, accuse"), "Do this!" rather than the form of a merely conditional imperative, "*If you wish to be happy*, do this!"[105] The moral law does not suggest or propose a good; it demands obedience.

---

100. See Immanuel Kant, *Kritik der praktischen Vernunft* [*Critique of Practical Reason*], *Gesammelte Schriften*, vol. 5, 108.

101. Kant, *Critique of Pure Reason*, B 828.

102. Immanuel Kant, *Grundlegung zur Metaphysik der Sitten* [*Groundwork for the Metaphysics of Morals*], *Gesammelte Schriften*, vol. 4, 393.

103. See Kant, *Critique of Practical Reason*, 87.

104. Kant, *Groundwork of Morals*, 403.

105. See ibid., 414.

How does the moral law arise? Why does it bind us? Kant sees the answer to these questions in the character of the human will. The human will, he holds,[106] has two essential features. It is, first, a power of *self-caused movement* without any external ground or cause, and it is, second, a *rational* power that works according to *universal* concepts. Both of these aspects are important for understanding what is required for a good will. First, since the will is an ultimately *self-moving* power, its goodness must lie in the absoluteness with which it moves *itself* apart from anything other than itself, and in particular, apart from any good and any end encountered in experience that might move it from the outside. Second, since the will is a *rational* power, its goodness must lie in the *universality* of the imperatives by which it directs itself. These two aspects are connected. It is by legislating to itself and all rational beings in the most universal form that the will achieves self-caused movement in the fullest sense: it itself posits for itself and all rational selves a universal law according to which it must act.

Kant accordingly arrives at what he calls "the categorical imperative" par excellence, which must inform any act if it is to be a morally good act: "Act only according to the maxim by which you can will at the same time that it becomes a universal law."[107] He also states it thus: "Act in such a way that at any time the maxim of your will can at the same time be valid as a principle of a universal legislation."[108]

This imperative fulfills the two requirements for the first principle of willing. It is an imperative of *self-determination* ("act!") according to the most *universal* form of any imperative, namely, universal law. It has no "material" content, that is, no motivation by any good such as the good expressed in the maxim, "Do good and avoid evil!" It prescribes only the *form* of willing. Good and evil, the *matter* of willing, belong to the unintelligible flux of Hume's world of sensation as opposed to reason. Only moral goodness belongs to the order of reason.

When it acts in accord with the categorical imperative, the human will does not subject itself to a law outside itself, but it legislates for

---

106. See Immanuel Kant, *Die Metaphysik der Sitten* [*The Metaphysics of Morals*], *Gesammelte Schriften*, vol. 6, 213.

107. Kant, *Groundwork of Morals*, 421.

108. Kant, *Critique of Practical Reason*, 30.

itself. "The will is not simply subject to the law, but subject in such a way that it must also be considered *as self-legislative* and for this reason, as the very first, subject to the law whose author it can consider itself to be."[109]

Kant's understanding of autonomy and heteronomy is rooted in this self-legislating character of the will. Autonomy can be defined *negatively* as the complete independence of the will from any motive of good or evil, that is, from any *matter* of desire. It can be defined *positively* as the absolute self-determination of the will according to the *form* of universal law. Heteronomy, by contrast, is the condition of the will when it is motivated by some good or evil encountered in experience.[110]

It is important to be clear on these definitions. They are so radical that one is tempted to dilute them by common sense, contrary to Kant's intentions. In classical Greek, a city is called heteronomous when it lives under the law (*nomos*) of *another* (*heteros*) *city*; it is autonomous when it is independent and can live under a law (*nomos*) that it makes for *itself* (*autos*). For Kant, the distinction between autonomy and heteronomy does not hinge on a distinction of persons or political bodies. It hinges, instead, on something more fundamental, on the two spheres found within each human person: the ultimately unintelligible sphere of sensory and emotional experience, which confronts us with various goods and evils, and the sphere of *pure reason* prior to all experience, prior to all good and evil. I am autonomous when I will what I will without being motivated by any good or evil, that is, when I move myself according to the categorical imperative. I fall into heteronomy when I will something *because* it is good. In heteronomy, I degrade my will and make it a servant of my irrational desires. I reach autonomy and freedom only when my will is completely independent from the whole sphere of appearances based on received sense-data, "for, independence of the determining causes of the world of sense (an independence which reason must always claim for itself) is freedom."[111]

---

109. Kant, *Groundwork of Morals*, 431.
110. See Theorem IV in Kant, *Critique of Practical Reason*, 33–34.
111. Kant, *Groundwork of Morals*, 452.

Kant's understanding of the dignity of human beings derives from his understanding of autonomy and freedom. He defends "the idea of the dignity of a rational being, which obeys no law except the law which it simultaneously gives to itself."[112] The goodness and value of a will that obeys the law does not derive from its obedience to a law that is wise and good, but from the power of the will as a true and universal legislator. To be an absolute causative beginning in the form of universal self-legislation—this is the heart of human dignity.

Inasmuch as persons have the dignity of autonomy, they are ends in themselves: "The only condition under which something can be an end in itself is when it has a value that is not merely relative, that is, a price, but an inner value, that is dignity."[113] Every good in the sphere of appearances based on received sense-data has a merely relative value, a price, because good and evil in the world of sense-data depend on what happens to be the inclination of the subject. There is no "true" good and evil. The one truly precious thing to which everything else must be ordered and which alone has the character of an end, is the autonomy of the person.

> Concerning man (and thus every rational being in the world) as a moral being one cannot ask further, For what end (*quem in finem*) does he exist? His existence has the highest purpose in itself. He can, as far as possible, subject the whole of nature to this purpose. At the least, he must not submit himself to any influence of nature contrary to this purpose.—Now if the beings of the world as beings that are contingent in their existence are in need of a highest cause that acts according to purpose, then man is the final purpose of creation. For, without man the chain of purposes subordinate to each other would not be explained in its entirety. It is only in man, and in man only as the subject of morality, that an unconditioned legislation concerning purposes can be found, which thus enables him alone to be a final purpose to which the whole of nature is teleologically subordinated.[114]

The cosmic grandeur of Kant's personalism in this text should not obscure a simple arithmetic fact. *Each and every person* is the final end

---

112. Ibid., 434.
113. Ibid., 435.
114. Kant, *Kritik der Urteilskraft* [*Critique of Judgment*], *Gesammelte Schriften*, vol. 5, 435–36.

of the whole of nature. There are as many final ends as there are persons.

Since each person is the final end of the universe, it is contrary to the dignity of persons if one uses them as mere means.

> While man is unholy enough, the *humanity* in his person must be holy to him. In all of creation, everything one might want and over which one has power can be used *as a mere means*. Only man himself and with him every rational creature is *end in itself*. For, in virtue of the autonomy of his freedom, he is the subject of the moral law, which is holy.[115]
>
> The practical imperative is thus the following. *Act in such a way that at all times you treat human nature in your own person as well as in the person of every other human being simultaneously as a purpose, never as a mere means.*[116]

The rule that we must not use human beings as mere means is closely related to the categorical imperative. In fact, it is simply another way of formulating the categorical imperative. The categorical imperative commands that I act as the universal lawgiver in absolutely self-impelled fashion. In acting according to this imperative, I grasp my own dignity as a person, that is, my dignity as the final end of the entire cosmos. I can only be consistent with myself in affirming my own dignity and autonomy if I grant the same dignity to other persons.

The contours of Kant's understanding of autonomy become clearer when one turns to his political philosophy. He insists emphatically that the purpose of government is not the happiness of its citizens, but only the protection of their rights.

> If a government is built on the principle of benevolence similar to that of a *father* towards his children, that is, a *paternal government* (*imperium paternale*), in which subjects are treated like children who have not yet come of age and who cannot distinguish what is truly beneficial from what is harmful for them, [a government] furthermore, in which subjects are forced to be passive, in order to await the judgment of the head of state, how they *should* be happy, and his sheer benevolence, whether he actually wills them to be so: this is the greatest *despotism* imaginable (that is, a constitution that annuls the entire freedom of

---

115. Kant, *Critique of Practical Reason*, 87, cf. 131. See also Kant, *Metaphysics of Morals*, 434.

116. Kant, *Groundwork of Morals*, 429.

subjects and leaves them without any rights.) Not a *paternal,* but a *patriotic* government (*imperium non paternale, sed patrioticum*) is the only government conceivable for human beings who are capable of rights.[117]

The superlative in this text is astounding: *the greatest* despotism *imaginable.* What is the greatest despotism imaginable? A slave state in which the head of state *does not intend* the good of citizens, but rules them *for his own* ends? No, a state under the benevolence of a father who *does* intend the good of the citizens—this is superlative despotism.

This astounding superlative can be understood in light of Kant's concept of autonomy. If the state were ordered to the happiness of its citizens, it would cast its citizens in a role of dependence, that is, of sonship, under a benevolent father. Dependence, however, is incompatible with human dignity as a dignity that resides in autonomy. Filial submission to a benevolent father destroys autonomy even more radically than slavish submission to a violent master, because it implies an interior and spiritual submission, not only an external conformity in actions. A slave's heart can be his own; a true son's heart belongs to his father. The direct clash between Kant's teaching on autonomy and the Lord's Prayer is remarkable. If the "Our Father" is indeed the paradigmatic prayer of Christians, then the destruction of human dignity, that is, the heteronomy of sonship, lies at the very heart of Christianity.

On this basis, one can grasp Kant's understanding of rational religion. A virtuous will, he argues, must be oriented not only toward duty, but also toward happiness. Moral virtue, that is, complete and utter autonomy of the will, is the "supreme" value to which everything else, including happiness, must be subordinated, but it is not by itself the "complete" human good, unless happiness is added. By being virtuous one becomes worthy of happiness.[118]

The pursuit of the complete good (virtue and happiness together) is (1) a free self-determination of the autonomous will that gives rise

---

117. Immanuel Kant, *Über den Gemeinspruch: Das mag in der Theorie richtig sein, taugt aber nichts für die Praxis* [*On the Common Saying: This May Be Right in Theory, but It Is No Good in Practice*], *Gesammelte Schriften,* vol. 8, 290–91.

118. See Kant, *Critique of Practical Reason,* 11.

to the postulates of (2) immortality and (3) the existence of God. The postulate of *immortality* derives from the first part of the complete good, namely, virtue. Since we cannot realize complete virtue in a finite life, we can only express our absolute commitment to virtue through faith in an eternal life of continuous moral progress.[119] The postulate of *the existence of God* derives from the second part of the complete good, namely, happiness. If we dutifully pursue the complete good, we necessarily postulate a cause of nature that distributes happiness to those who have made themselves worthy of it by their virtue.[120]

Kant strictly circumscribes the role of God in his rational religion: God gives happiness in proportion to deserving virtue. He is not free to issue any positive commands or enter into any relations, such as a covenant; nor is he free to offer his grace; nor is he the Supreme Good that moves human love as the final end. For, as a mere product of human practical reason, the idea of God does not have any theoretical bearing on the question whether there actually is a God.[121] In the same way, one cannot hold that there will actually be a real eternity of life in a real heaven in which a real God will give a real happiness. *The kingdom of God is wholly and exclusively moral and practical.*

Kant uses trinitarian language to express the central place of the human person in the religion he proposes.

> That which alone can make a world the object of divine decree and the end of creation is *Humanity* (rational being in general in the world) *in its full moral perfection,* from which happiness [that is, humanity's happiness] follows in the will of the Highest Being directly as from its supreme condition.—This man, who is alone pleasing to God ["This is my beloved Son in whom I am well pleased" (Mt 3:17)], "is in him from all eternity" ["The Word was with God" (Jn 1:1)]; the idea of man proceeds from God's being; man is not, therefore, a created thing but God's only-begotten Son [Jn 1:18; 3:16–18], "the Word (the Fiat!) through which all other things are, and without whom nothing that is made would exist" [Jn 1:1–3] (since for him, that is, for a rational being in the world, as it can be thought according to its moral determination, everything was made ["All things were

---

119. See ibid., 122–23.
120. See ibid., 124–32.
121. See ibid., 132–41.

created through him and for him" (Col 1:16)]).—"He is the reflection of his glory" [Heb 1:3].—"In him God loved the world" [Jn 3:16], and only in him and through the adoption of his dispositions can we hope "to become children of God" [Jn 1:12]; etc.[122]

Kant's remarkable dexterity in quoting Scripture should not obscure the central point of his rational faith: the human person is not a creature, but the absolute locus of all true meaning *a se, from itself.* The Son, that is, man, is equal to the Father, but not born from the Father.

It is with good justification that Wojtyła speaks of "Kantian Personalism."[123] Kant focuses all light in the person's moral dignity, that is, autonomy. He thus undercuts the relational character of trinitarian language (Father-Son, glory-reflection, etc.) in favor of an autonomous self, more precisely, in favor of each autonomous self, a series of juxtaposed and unrelated selves.

We can return with a fuller understanding to Schmitz's account of the dominant type of modern subjectivity to which Wojtyła's personalism responds. "This, then, is the genesis of the modern sense of subject as subjectivity. We might say that subjectivity is the self-defense by which consciousness fends off a world either hostile to its inhabitation or at least without companionate room for it, even while consciousness subverts the integrity of that world by its imperious demands. The modern shift gave to the human subject an absolute status precisely in its character *qua* consciousness; for human consciousness not only sets its own terms but the terms for reality itself."[124]

c. Kant and John Paul II on Sex and Marriage

Kant's anti-trinitarian personalism comes into clear focus in his account of sex and marriage. Wojtyła seems to have learned much from Kant in this area. Two points of contact are particularly striking.

The *first* principle of Kant's sexual ethics is what Wojtyła calls "the personalistic norm" according to which one must not "enjoy" a

122. Immanuel Kant, *Die Religion innerhalb der Grenzen der bloßen Vernunft* [*Religion within the Bounds of Reason Alone*], *Gesammelte Schriften*, vol. 6, 60–61.

123. Wojtyła, *Acting Person*, 22, no. 8 on 302.

124. Schmitz, *Center of the Drama*, 135–36.

person as a mere means for pleasure.[125] Mere enjoyment reduces a person to a thing or object, and this is contrary to the dignity of the person. The *second* principle of Kant's sexual ethics is that sexual union involves giving oneself to another person. These two principles are also the pillars of Wojtyła's sexual ethics.[126] They correspond to the two principles of the life of persons affirmed in *Gaudium et Spes*, 24:3.

Despite these points of close contact—or rather, precisely *in* these points of contact—Kant's view of sex and marriage could hardly be more opposed to Wojtyła's, not even if Kant were an advocate of promiscuous recreational sex, which he is definitely not. For Kant, sexual intercourse is a gift of self contrary to the dignity of the person. In all sexual relations, whether in marriage or outside it, both persons turn themselves into things by giving their sexual organs, and thus their own persons, to each other for the sake of being possessed and "enjoyed," that is, used for pleasure. This is contrary to the dignity and autonomy of the person, contrary to the right every person has to himself or herself.

The only remedy for this loss of autonomy in sex, according to Kant, is marriage. By marriage, I permanently acquire the user of my sexual organs as a thing. I thereby offset the loss of my self to her when she "enjoys" me in sexual intercourse. By a permanent contract, I own the one who episodically owns me. In this way, I regain myself and my autonomy. It seems to be like the case of a man who is afraid of losing a large sum of money in a casino, and so he buys the casino.

> *Sexual intercourse* (*commercium sexuale*) is the mutual use which one human being makes of the sexual organs and faculty of another (*usus membrorum et facultatum sexualium alterius*). It is either a *natural* use, by which a being of the same nature can be conceived, or an *unnatural* use either with a person of the same sex or with an animal that does not belong to the human species. These transgressions of the law, called unnatural vices (*crimina carnis contra naturam*) and unmentionable vices, must be rejected entirely, without any qualifications or exceptions, because they do injury to human nature in our own person.
>
> Now, the natural union of the sexes occurs either only according to animal *nature* (*vaga libido, venus volgivaga, fornicatio*) or according to *law*.—The latter is *marriage* (*matrimonium*), that is, the union of two

---

125. See Wojtyła, *Love and Responsibility*, 40–44.
126. See ibid., 28–44, 95–100.

persons for the lifelong mutual possession of their sexual characteristics.—The purpose of begetting and educating children may be a reason for which nature implanted a mutual inclination toward each other in the sexes, but for the legality of this bond it is not required that the one who marries *must* intend this goal for himself, for otherwise marriage would dissolve of itself when the begetting of children ends.

For, although it is based on pleasure for the mutual use of their sexual characteristics, the marriage contract is not accidental, but it is necessary in accord with legal principles of pure reason. That is, when man and woman want to enjoy (*genießen*) each other in their sexual characteristics, they *must* necessarily marry. This necessity follows from legal principles of pure reason.

For, the natural use that one sex makes of the sexual organs of the other is an *enjoyment* (*Genuß*) for which one partner gives himself (*sich hingiebt*) to the other. In this act, a human being makes himself into a thing, which is contrary to the right of human nature to one's own person. This is possible only under one single condition: when a person is acquired by another *in a manner equal to a thing*, correspondingly the former acquires the latter, for in this way the person gains itself back again and reconstitutes its personhood. Now, the acquisition of one bodily member of a human being is at the same time an acquisition of the whole person, because the person is an absolute unity. For this reason, the gift (*Hingebung*) and the acceptance of one sex for enjoyment by the other is not merely permissible *only* on the single condition of marriage, but it is *only* possible on this same condition. That this *personal right* is nevertheless at the same time also *a right in the manner of a right to a thing*, is clear, for when one part of the couple has run away or has given itself into the possession of another, the other spouse has the right at any time and without any condition to take it back into his or her power like a thing.

For the same reason, the relation of the married persons is a relation of *equality* of possession, equality both in their possession of each other (hence only in *monogamy*, for in polygamy the person who gives herself away gains back only part of the man whose possession she has become in her entirety and therefore reduces herself to a mere thing) and of external goods.[127]

Spousal love seems to be absent in Kant's account. John Paul II sees the sexual act as a "natural word" (*naturale verbum*)[128] connected

---

127. Kant, *Metaphysics of Morals*, 277–78.
128. John Paul II, *Familiaris Consortio*, 32, Latin text. The official English text has "innate language."

with "the spousal meaning of the body."[129] By its very nature as created by God, independently from any choice or determination made by human beings, the human body has the power to express love, to speak love in its own "natural word." In accord with this *nature,* sexual intercourse is not depersonalizing, but a deep fulfillment of the person through the gift of self. Wojtyła finds sharply anti-Kantian formulations in describing this gift of self: "The person no longer wishes to be its own exclusive property, but instead to become the property of that other. This means the renunciation of its autonomy and its inalienability. Love proceeds by way of this renunciation, guided by the profound conviction that it does not diminish and impoverish, but quite the contrary, enlarges and enriches the existence of the person."[130] One can see again the importance of the principle expressed some five years later in *Gaudium et Spes,* 24:3: "Man cannot fully find himself except through a sincere gift of self." Carmelite and Kantian personalism are most directly opposed to each other at this point.

One can also see why the issue of person and nature turns out to be so important in understanding human sexuality. The natural character of sexual language is one of its most important features, according to John Paul II. What we speak through the body in sexual union, whether we want it or not, is the gift of self in love. We cannot take away the spousal meaning of the body, though we can speak that meaning in a manner contrary to itself, that is, we can speak it in the form of a sexual lie.[131]

According to John Paul II, there *is indeed* a way of treating other persons in sexual intercourse that corresponds to Kant's way of understanding it: a "persistent mentality which considers the human being not as a person but as a thing, as an object of trade, at the service of selfish interest and mere pleasure: the first victims of this mentality are women."[132]

When Wojtyła describes this depersonalizing sexual use of one person by another, he chooses the term that is the key term of Kant's understanding of sex in general: to enjoy (*genießen*). In a course of

---

129. See Index at BODY 2.
130. Wojtyła, *Love and Responsibility,* 125–26.
131. See John Paul II, *Familiaris Consortio,* 11.
132. Ibid., 24.

action directed to mere enjoyment, the natural language of sex is distorted.

> Man, precisely because he has the power to reason, can, in his actions, not only clearly distinguish pleasure from its opposite, but can also isolate it, so to speak, and treat it as a distinct aim of his activity. His actions are then shaped only with a view to the pleasure he wishes to obtain, or the pain he wishes to avoid. If actions involving a person of the opposite sex are shaped exclusively or primarily with this in view, then that person will become only the means to an end—and "use" in its second meaning (=to enjoy) represents, as we see, a particular variant of "use" in its first meaning.[133]

The difference between Kant and John Paul II is particularly clear in their arguments against polygamy. According to Kant, polygamy is immoral because my second wife cannot retrieve the whole of her person, which she loses to me when I take depersonalizing sexual possession of her. The reason why she cannot retrieve the whole of her person is that I do not belong to her alone through a marriage contract, but also to my first wife. I divide myself by being permanently possessed by both my wives.

John Paul II's argument against polygamy is also a personalist argument. It is very close to Kant's, but at the same time quite the opposite. Polygamy is wrong because it is contrary to the logic of the communion that arises in the gift of love. "Such a communion is radically contradicted by polygamy: this, in fact, directly negates the plan of God which was revealed from the beginning, because it is contrary to the equal personal dignity of men and women who in matrimony give themselves with a love that is total and therefore unique and exclusive. As the Second Vatican Council writes: 'Firmly established by the Lord, the unity of marriage will radiate from the equal personal dignity of husband and wife, a dignity acknowledged by mutual and total love.'"[134]

To sum up, one fundamental reason for the divergence between Kant and John Paul II is the absence of truly personal conjugal love in Kant. Kant's personalism is at this point *not sufficiently personalistic*.

---

133. Wojtyła, *Love and Responsibility*, 33.
134. John Paul II, *Familiaris Consortio*, 19, citing *Gaudium et Spes*, 49.

Human sexuality, as he sees it, is not formed and penetrated by personal love, but is cut loose as a natural process foreign to the person.

Kant's sexual ethics may seem to be in many ways the opposite of the sexual revolution. Kant is no friend of sex. Nevertheless, he has a point of deep agreement with the sexual revolution: in both, sex is cut loose from the person. The difference is that the sexual revolution embraces this detached pleasure while Kant despises it. The dualism between person and nature, however, is similar and has the same roots.

This point leads to a second reason for the divergence between Kant and John Paul II, an equally fundamental reason. Kant's view of sex is an expression of his deeply disturbed relation to subrational nature. Subrational nature is a meaningless mechanism. The person is not at home in that nature, but stands outside it, carrying a rational order within itself a priori that it must impose on nature from the outside. The external natural world is ruled entirely by mechanistic laws grasped mathematically. Nature in its second aspect, namely, experience and inclinations, is subjective and irrational. Person and subrational nature are thus pitted against each other in a strict dualism. As mentioned above (see p. 43), Hans Jonas shows the reason why this dualism is even more desperate than the Gnostic dualism between spirit and matter. "Gnostic man is thrown into an antagonistic, anti-divine, and therefore anti-human nature, modern man into an indifferent one. Only the latter case represents the absolute vacuum, the really bottomless pit."[135]

Human sexuality is a point at which person and subrational nature intersect with particular intensity. Different ways of understanding and living the relation between person and nature show up particularly clearly in different ways of understanding and living sex. In John Paul II, there is a clear and strong sense of a kindred natural cosmos, gift of the Creator. The human body with the sexual language created by God has a deep kinship with the person. The sentient body is created *for the person* as an expression of personal love. In fact, the body is immediately and directly personal, because the person "is a body" (see Index at BODY 1).

---

135. Jonas, "Gnosticism, Existentialism and Nihilism," 338–39.

Kant's account of the role of children in marriage is helpful, because it shows his understanding of the relation between person and nature in the procreative meaning of sex: "The purpose of begetting and educating children may be a reason for which nature implanted in the sexes a mutual inclination toward each other, but for the legality of this bond it is not required that the one who marries *must* intend this goal for himself. Otherwise matrimony would end of itself when the begetting of children ends."[136]

Nature may have purposes of her own in linking sexual pleasure with procreation, but these purposes do not touch the order of the person, which derives a priori from reason, not from nature. Just as the person is violated in the sexual act, precisely inasmuch as that act involves a gift of self, so the person stands outside the procreative purpose of nature. One gets the sense that Kant would much rather do without sexual passion altogether. In fact, he explicitly says that he would much rather do without any inclinations at all: "Inclinations are so far from having an absolute value making them desirable in themselves that it must rather be the universal wish of every rational being to be completely free from them."[137]

What stands behind this negative view of inclinations in general and of sexual passion in particular is Kant's dualistic separation of the human person into animal nature, which, as he puts it, is worth less than money, and personhood, which is of a value beyond any commercial price.

> In the system of nature, man (*homo phaenomenon, animal rationale*) is a being of little importance and has a common value (*pretium vulgare*) together with other animals as products of the soil. Even the fact that he exceeds them by having reason and by being able to set goals for himself, even this gives him only an external value of usefulness (*pretium usus*). It gives one human being more [value] than another, that is, a price as a commodity in the commercial exchange of these animals as things, in which he has a lower value than money, the universal means of exchange. This is why the value of money is called eminent (*pretium eminens*). But man regarded as a person, that is, as the subject of moral-practical reason, is exalted above all price. For as such (*homo noumenon*) he is to be regarded as a purpose in himself,

---

136. Kant, *Metaphysics of Morals*, 277.
137. Kant, *Groundwork of Morals*, 428.

that is, he possesses dignity (an absolute inner value). By this dignity, he can compel all other rational beings to have respect for him, can measure himself against all other rational beings of the world and evaluate himself as standing on a footing of equality with every other being of this kind.[138]

Leon Kass, in agreement with Schmitz, points out that the image of the world created by natural science in the Baconian and Cartesian project conditions Kant's personalism at this point. "At the bottom of the trouble...is the hegemony of modern natural science, to whose view of nature even the partisans of personhood and subjectivity adhere, given that their attempt to locate human dignity in consciousness and mind presupposes that the subconscious living body, not to speak of nature in general, is utterly without meaning and dignity of its own."[139]

John Paul II is convinced, on the contrary, of the unity of nature and person. One can see this conviction in his account of procreation as the natural end of marriage. In *Familiaris Consortio*, 14, he repeats the traditional Catholic view in a formulation close to *Gaudium et Spes*, 50: "According to the plan of God, marriage is the foundation of the wider community of the family, since the very institution of marriage and conjugal love are ordained to the procreation and education of children, in whom they find their crowning."

Immediately after this traditional paragraph, one finds a truly remarkable paragraph in which John Paul II extends this understanding of nature in a personalist direction.

> In its most profound reality, love is essentially a gift; and conjugal love, while leading the spouses to the reciprocal "knowledge" which makes them "one flesh," does not end with the couple, because it makes them capable of the greatest possible gift, the gift by which they become cooperators with God for giving life to a new human person. Thus the couple, while giving themselves to one another, give not just themselves but also the reality of children, who are a living reflection of their love, a permanent sign of conjugal unity and a living and inseparable synthesis of their being a father and a mother.[140]

---

138. Kant, *Metaphysics of Morals*, 434–35.

139. Leon Kass, *Toward a More Natural Science: Biology of Human Affairs* (New York: The Free Press, 1985), 277.

140. John Paul II, *Familiaris Consortio*, 14.

John Paul II does not locate procreation outside the personal love between husband and wife, but most immediately and directly in it. The defense of nature's procreative purpose in marriage is at the same time a personalist defense of interpersonal love. John Paul II unfolds this line of thought in great detail in TOB.

To conclude, Kant's anti-trinitarian personalism, which considers sonship the worst slavery and autonomy the only human dignity, exalts the unrelated self. Sex occurs beneath the level of personhood and threatens personal autonomy. Marriage does the best it can to restore the right one has to oneself. John Paul II's trinitarian personalism exalts the related self that finds itself in the gift of self. Sex does not occur beneath the level of personhood, but is itself an event of personal love, even when it is distorted by being pursued for the sake of mere enjoyment. The natural purpose of sex, children, does not lie outside that love, but qualifies it essentially.

There is much that Wojtyła considers positive in Kant, particularly Kant's critique of utilitarianism and the consistent application of this critique to the understanding of sexuality. It is clear that Wojtyła let himself be guided by Kant's account of sex and marriage. In the end, however, he stands Kant on his head, based on his Carmelite personalism and his richer understanding of nature.

4. Wojtyła and Scheler

a. Scheler's Essentialist Personalism

In a text quoted above (see p. 36), Wojtyła explains that his main philosophical work, *The Acting Person*, grew out of his study of Scheler's major work, *Formalism in Ethics and a Material Ethics of Values: A New Attempt toward the Foundation of an Ethical Personalism*. He points in particular to Scheler's critique of Kant. "The critique of Kant contained in that work is of crucial significance for the present considerations and was for this author the occasion for reflection and the cause of a partial acceptance of some of Kantian Personalism."[141] Scheler's critique of Kant should thus be considered, at least briefly.

---

141. Wojtyła, *Acting Person*, 22, no. 8 on 302.

The very heart of Kant's system, according to Scheler, lies in the self-initiated activity or spontaneity of the subject, which imposes its own form both in the theoretical and practical sphere.[142] This spontaneity of the subject, Scheler argues, is purely "constructed." Kant has no evidence for it in anything truly apparent or given to him, that is, in any true "phenomena." He does not offer an account of the given, but imposes a construct.

The reasons that moved Kant to impose this construct, Scheler continues, are closely bound up with his uncritical acceptance of British empiricism, particularly Hume and Hobbes. Once the world is pulverized into a chaos of sensations and the human heart into an irrational flux of inclinations, there is need for a synthesizing power that produces the more unified world of experience as we know it.

"In short, *Hume's notion of nature required a Kantian understanding*, and *Hobbes's notion of man required a Kantian practical reason*, insofar as these theories were to be brought back to the facts of natural experience. But *without* this erroneous presupposition of a Humean nature and a Hobbesian man there is *no* need for such a hypothesis and *therefore* no need for an interpretation of the a priori as a 'law of functions' of such organizing activities."[143]

The roots of these views among the British empiricists, according to Scheler, lie in "an attitude of Puritan Protestantism,"[144] an attitude of distrust in principle for all that is "natural," all that has not passed through systematic-rational self-control, an attitude of distrust in principle for all relations between persons that have not been secured

---

142. In this context, "spontaneous" does not mean "impulsive, uncalculated, unplanned." The Latin "*spons*" can mean "free will" and the adjective "*spontaneus*" can mean "of one's own will." "Spontaneous" in this sense is the opposite of "receptive." It means that the subject is the *source or origin* of an action. See Max Scheler, *Formalism in Ethics and Non-Formal Ethics of Values: A New Attempt toward the Foundation of an Ethical Personalism*, 5th ed. (Evanston: Northwestern University Press, 1973), 65–68. German edition: *Der Formalismus in der Ethik und die materiale Wertethik: Neuer Versuch der Grundlegung eines ethischen Personalismus*, Gesammelte Werke, vol. 2 (7th ed.; Bonn: Bouvier Verlag, 2000), 84–86. The German edition will be cited immediately after the English, identified by "German."

143. Ibid., 66, German 85.

144. Ibid., 67, no. 23, German 86, no. 1. For Kant, of course, Lutheranism is more immediately formative than Puritanism. Puritanism, in turn, depends in many of its doctrines on Luther.

in contractual form. These historical roots, Scheler argues, grow into a fundamental "attitude" that is responsible for the overall form of Kant's system.

> This "attitude" I can only describe as a basic "hostility" toward or distrust of the given *as* such, a fear of the given as "chaos," an anxiety—an attitude that can be expressed as "that world there outside me, that nature there within me." "Nature" is what is to be formed, to be organized, to be "controlled"; it is the "hostile," the "chaos," etc. Hence this attitude is the opposite of *love* of the world, of trust in and loving *devotion* to the world. Strictly speaking, this attitude belongs only to modern times, which are permeated by *hatred for the world,* hostility toward the world, and a distrust of it, and by the *consequence* of this hatred: namely, the limitless need for activity to "organize" and "control" the world.... And all this has culminated in the mind of a philosophical genius.[145]

The opposition between Kant and Scheler goes to the very roots of philosophy. For Scheler the central animating principle of philosophy is the desire to dwell with love and devotion in a receptive, contemplative vision in order to grasp what is truly evident. Against the "constructions" of Kantian Idealism, he insists that philosophy must have a supple and obedient regard for what is given in experience. Philosophy must be an account (*logos*) of what is truly evident (*phainomenon*). In short, it must be phenomenology. In agreement with Scheler, John Paul II emphasizes love as the animating principle of phenomenology. "Phenomenology is primarily a style of thought, a relationship of the mind with reality, whose essential and constitutive features it aims to grasp, avoiding prejudice and schematisms. I mean that it is, as it were, an attitude of intellectual charity to the human being and the world, and for the believer, to God, the beginning and end of all things."[146] At the core of Scheler's critique of Kant, Wojtyła thus found a vigorous attack on the anthropological dualism of Kant and an attitude of love and devotion to the world, to what is truly given. This critique of Kant is Scheler's starting point for a more particular critique of Kant's ethical formalism and for his own argu-

---

145. Ibid., 67, German 86; translation modified.
146. John Paul II, address to a delegation of the World Institute of Phenomenology (Mar. 22, 2003).

ment that ethics must be based on what Kant calls the "matter" rather than the "form" of willing. It must be based on objective values.

Yet, Scheler's relation to Kant is more complex than his critique would suggest. He seems at times to be swept along by the genius of his favorite enemy, both in the form of exaggerated opposition and of uncritical acceptance. In particular, Scheler does not seem to escape from the loss of access to real being in Kant. One can see this loss of real being in Scheler's account of value and the person.

VALUE, according to Scheler, is manifest or given in a certain kind of feeling.[147] The German word Scheler uses for "feeling" is *Fühlen* rather than *Gefühl* or *Empfindung. Fühlen,* understood in the transitive sense of "to feel some object," refers to an intentional act, that is, an act that "tends" "into" something in the sense of being *about* something (see Index at INTENTIONAL). When I feel the roughness of a surface with my hand, the feeling I experience is *about* the roughness—it is intentionally related to the roughness. A toothache, by contrast, is not "about" some object. The feelings Scheler has in mind in his account of value are emotions, a specific kind of emotions, namely, those that have an "intentional" character in the sense that they are *about* a value.

Feelings—and here one can perhaps see an example of Scheler's exaggerated opposition to Kant—are the primary acts of the human person, more fundamental than willing and knowing. For Kant, all feelings (with the single exception of the reverence for duty) belong to the empirical and irrational realm of sense-desire, far from the rational core of the person. For Scheler, love as a feeling constitutes the innermost core of the person: the human person can be defined as *ens amans.*[148]

> He [Scheler] claims there is a primacy of the givenness of contents of values over any other acts of consciousness. Feeling values is basic to the mind's acts; emotive experiences are not internal chaos (Kant) but are suffused with an order of contents of values very different from the laws of logic pertaining to reasoning and thinking. Scheler's argument

---

147. See Scheler, *Formalism*, 35, German 56; 253-64, German 259-70.
148. Manfred Frings, *The Mind of Max Scheler: The First Comprehensive Guide Based on the Complete Works,* 2nd ed. (Marquette: Marquette University Press, 2001), 68.

is like this: just as colors can only be given to us "in" seeing them, so also values are given to us only "in" the feeling of them. Without "seeing" there are no colors. Without "feeling" there are no values.[149]

Scheler gives the example of different fruits that have different *kinds* of pleasant tastes to illustrate the interdependence between value and feeling. Each of these pleasant tastes as an object of enjoyment is a value, and each is *qualitatively* distinct from the others. What determines this qualitative difference is not a particular configuration of objective properties of the fruit's *being* that become apparent in sensation; nor is it simply a particular configuration of *states of feeling* in the one who eats the fruits. The objective value qualities that we feel in our delight are "authentic qualities of a value itself" *as distinct from being*.[150] In fact, we can experience values at times in their specific quality before we experience the being of their bearer, such as when we find a person repulsive without being able to name anything in the person's being that would account for this perception. In this case, we experience the value first and attach it secondarily to a being.[151]

Value qualities constitute a special essence-domain of objects with its own inherent intelligibility *distinct from being*. "Values are as a matter of principle given as indifferent with respect to being and nonbeing."[152] They do not themselves exist, but are given only as essences and only in acts of feeling. "As to the question: 'What is a value?' I submit the following answer: Insofar as in the question the word 'is' refers to existence (and not only to being as mere copula), a value 'is' not at all."[153]

Scheler does speak at times of the "being of values," but this being does not belong to them as values.[154] When we say, "This is good," existence does not properly belong to the value, but only, in a techni-

---

149. Ibid., 25. Frings' pithy summary is based on Scheler, *Formalism*, 9–23, German 32–45.

150. Scheler, *Formalism*, 13, German 35.

151. See ibid., 17, German 40.

152. Ibid., 206, German 214, translation modified.

153. Max Scheler, "Beiträge zur Feststellung der Beziehungen zwischen den logischen und ethischen Prinzipien [Doctoral Thesis]," in *Frühe Schriften: Gesammelte Werke 1* (Bern: Francke, 1971), 98. See Frings, *Scheler*, 23.

154. See Scheler, *Formalism*, 206–8, German 214–15.

cal term of phenomenology, to the "state of affairs" that carries the value, that is, to the fact that this is good. "The statement 'It is so' refers not to the value of the being in question, but only to the state of affairs that carries this value."[155] Value is an essence in consciousness distinct and independent from being.

One can observe a similar eclipse of being in Scheler's under-standing of the PERSON. Scheler denies that a person is a being in its own right, a substance. Instead, the person is a certain co-experienced unity of conscious life, an essence given in consciousness.

> The person must *never* be considered a *thing* or a *substance* with facul-ties and powers, among which the "faculty" or "power" of reason, etc., is one. The person is, rather, the immediately co-experienced *unity* of *experiencing*; the person is not a merely thought thing behind and out-side what is immediately experienced.[156]
>
> The person is not a "thing" or a "substance" which executes acts in the sense of a substance-causality. For such "things" could in fact be randomly obliterated or exchanged, if there is a multiplicity (one thinks of Kant's picture of electric spheres, which are dynamically uni-fied), with no change at all in immediate experience. In addition, everyone would carry the same "substance" with him, which—since *every* kind of manifold, e.g., time, space, number, plurality, would be missing—could not yield differences between one and the other.[157]

The second text shows one of the reasons why Scheler rejects the Aristotelian-Scholastic term "substance" as part of the definition of "person." He believes that this notion implies a naively spatial picture of an object *under* or *behind* attributes, as spheres of metal are located behind a surrounding magnetic field or a wall lies under a coat of paint.[158] His own position seems to be that the person's being is reducible to an experienced essence in consciousness.

---

155. Ibid., 208, German 215.

156. Ibid., 371, German 371.

157. Ibid., 384, German 384. Four years earlier, in his *Nature of Sympathy* (1912), Scheler seems to say the opposite. He speaks of "person-substances (*Personsubstanzen*) or act-substances (*Akt-substanzen*)." Max Scheler, *The Nature of Sympathy* (New Haven: Yale University Press, 1954), 123. Max Scheler, *Wesen und Formen der Sympathie: Gesammelte Werke 7* (Bern and München: Francke, 1973), 131. See Jonathan J. Sanford, "Scheler versus Scheler: The Case for a Better Ontology of the Person," *American Catholic Philosophical Quarterly* 79 (2005), 145–61.

158. Scheler, *Formalism,* 384–85, German 384–85.

b. Wojtyła's Critique of Scheler

At the beginning of his book on Scheler, Wojtyła explains why Scheler attracted the attention of Catholic thinkers. There were two main reasons. First, Catholic ethics had always focused on the *objects* of human acts, that is, the good or value. Scheler criticizes Kant for his failure to do justice to these objects of acts, and proposes an ethics based on such objects. This is what Scheler means when he calls his own ethics a "material ethics of values" in contrast to Kant's "formalism" in which moral goodness is a matter of the universal form of the categorical imperative (see above p. 49).

The second point of contact between Catholic ethics and Scheler is more specific. "There were also more particular theses that caused immediate associations with Christian ethics, especially with the ethical teaching of the Gospels. In his system Scheler underlines that love for the person and imitating an exemplary person have great importance and play a central role in ethical life as a whole."[159] Scheler and the Gospel's teaching on following and imitating Christ, Wojtyła says, meet in their "personalism."[160] "The personalist principle has a similar structure in Scheler and the Gospel: the principle of imitation is based on the expressly established ideal of the perfection of the person and it is supposed to help in reaching this ideal."[161] What Wojtyła calls "personalism" in these texts is a particular emphasis on the person in ethical life: the moral perfection of the person is proposed as a goal, love for the person and the imitation of Jesus are central.

The question Wojtyła attempts to answer in his book on Scheler is expressed in the title, *Evaluation of the Possibility of Constructing a Christian Ethics on the Assumptions of Max Scheler's System of Philosophy.* Wojtyła focuses the argument on the second and more specific reason that attracted him to Scheler, the imitation of Jesus.[162]

---

159. Karol Wojtyła, [*Evaluation of the Possibility of Constructing a Christian Ethics on the Assumptions of Max Scheler's System of Philosophy*] *Über die Möglichkeit eine christliche Ethik in Anlehnung an Max Scheler zu schaffen,* ed. Juliusz Stroynowski, *Primat des Geistes: Philosophische Schriften* (Stuttgart-Degerloch: Seewald, 1980), 38.

160. Ibid., 68.

161. Ibid., 75–76.

162. See Ibid., 70–74.

The Gospel's ideal of the moral perfection that is to be reached by following Jesus, Wojtyła argues, has three main characteristics.[163] (1) It is a *real* ideal, because it aims at a real perfection of the person in imitation of a real perfection already found in Jesus. (2) It is a *practical* ideal, because it is realized by acts of which the person is the responsible cause, acts by which the person therefore becomes really good or bad. (3) It is a *religious* ideal, both because the perfection to be imitated is that of the Father and the Son and because imitation establishes the right personal relation with God as the final end. These three points seem to be divided in accord with Aristotle's four causes minus matter: formal cause, efficient cause, and final cause. Wojtyła devotes a chapter to each.

(1) *The formal cause of the imitation of Jesus, moral goodness itself:* Scheler considers moral goodness only as an object of feeling. The disciples feel the individual ideal value-essence of Jesus and appropriate it as their own ethos. In his critique, Wojtyła argues that Jesus is not only a person to be imitated, but a true lawgiver who speaks about moral goodness as an objective and real property of certain acts. This aspect of Jesus' teaching places certain demands on a philosophy that claims to interpret the Gospel. In order to grasp ethical value in its real and objective position, one must pass beyond Scheler's phenomenology to metaphysics. "It is, therefore, due to its phenomenological principles that Scheler's system is unsuitable for the interpretation of Christian Ethics."[164]

> Despite its objectivist tendencies, Scheler's ethical system is not suitable for interpreting an ethics that has an objective character as Christian Ethics does. There is no doubt that Scheler's insufficient objectivism springs from his phenomenological principles. Because of these principles the ethical value always remains in an intentional and—despite everything—subjective position. In order to grasp ethical value in its real and objective position, one would have to proceed from different epistemological premises, namely, meta-phenomenological and even meta-physical premises.[165]

(2) *The efficient cause of the imitation of Jesus, the person as responsible origin:* Since Scheler considers moral goodness only as he considers all

---

163. See Ibid., 74–75.
164. Ibid., 97.
165. Ibid., 109.

value, namely, as an object of feeling, he does not focus on the person as the efficient cause responsible for moral goodness. In fact, just as value belongs to an order of essences quite independent from being, so also the person is not a being with a certain nature, from which acts of a certain nature can proceed as effects from inner principles. The person is "the immediately co-experienced *unity* of *experiencing.*"[166] "Due to its phenomenological principles, Scheler's system cannot directly grasp and express that the human person in its acts is the origin of moral good and evil. The whole difficulty is the result of the phenomenological premises of the system and we must assign the blame to these principles."[167]

Scheler rejects all duties and norms because they allegedly contain the negative spirit that dominates Kant's philosophy: hostility toward nature, distrust, fear of the given as chaos. Yet, Wojtyła responds, norms and duties are an integral part of human action in accord with the first principle of the practical order by which persons move themselves to act: *bonum est faciendum,* the good is *to be done.* Scheler's understanding of value does not allow him to grasp this principle.

> According to the premises of Scheler's system, value is by its nature indifferent with respect to existence. This means that it is a value regardless of whether it exists or not. ([Footnote:] It is quite different, for example, in the system of St. Thomas Aquinas, where the good is the true object of will, of striving (*appetitus*). When we will the good, when we strive for it, our concern is that it exists. The issue is the being of the good; cf. *Summa,* I.5....) This indifference in relation to existence is explained quite simply, because values are given as the proper objects of emotional perception. *Precisely because they are indifferent with respect to existence they do not give rise to an "ought."*[168]

In the commandment of love, Wojtyła argues, the experience of the good as good and of the commandment as norm work together and display the person as a truly responsible agent.

(3) *The final cause of the imitation of Jesus, blessedness:* Scheler's phenomenological essentialism has its most disastrous effect in his understanding of the final end, blessedness. Although Scheler says

---

166. Scheler, *Formalism,* 371, German 371.
167. Wojtyła, *Scheler,* 115.
168. Ibid., 139, with no. 29; emphasis added.

that personal life is "theomorphic," that is, intelligible only in a divine light, which is ultimately the divine *agape,* he understands this light as a detached essence quite apart from the living God. "In trying to intuit the *essence* of man, it is not the idea of God in the sense of an extant and positively determined reality that is presupposed; rather, it is only the *quality* of the divine, or the *quality* of the holy, that is given in an infinite fullness of being. On the other hand, whatever takes the place of this essence (in the historical time of earthly man and in the changing beliefs of positive religions) cannot be presupposed in any sense."[169] Wojtyła concludes from this and similar texts, "For the phenomenologist, man is a theomorphic being only and exclusively by virtue of experiencing the idea of God. Scheler is not concerned with the real relation to God as an existing, positive and defined reality. He is concerned with experiencing the idea of God."[170] It seems clear that human blessedness cannot lie in contemplating such a detached essence. Scheler finds blessedness, rather, in the depths of each person, a depth in which there is a quasi-identity between God and created persons. It is thus ultimately out of themselves that created persons draw their blessedness.

> Deepest happiness and complete bliss are dependent in their being on a consciousness of one's own moral goodness. *Only the good person is blissful.* This does *not* preclude the possibility that this very blissfulness is the *root* and *source* of all willing and acting. But happiness can *never* be a goal or even a "purpose" of willing and acting. *Only the happy person acts in a morally good way.* Happiness is therefore in no way a "reward for virtue,"[171] nor is virtue the *means* to reach bliss. Rather, happiness is the root and source of virtue, a fountainhead, although it is only a *consequence* of the inner *goodness* of the person.[172]
>
> In his existence and his acts the "good" person directly takes part in the nature of God, in the sense of *velle* in *deo* [to will in God] or *amare* in *deo* [to love in God], and he is blissful in this participation. A "reward" from God could only put a smaller and lower good in place of a higher one, and a superficial feeling in the place of a deeper pleasure.[173]

---

169. Scheler, *Formalism,* 292, German 296–97.

170. Wojtyła, *Scheler,* 161.

171. "[Happiness is]...the reward and end of virtue." Aristotle, *Nicomachean Ethics,* 1.9; 1099b.16–17.

172. Scheler, *Formalism,* 359, German 359–60.

173. Ibid., 368, German 368, translation modified.

Scheler's opposition to Kant is clear in these texts. According to Kant, happiness is the main competitor against duty in the moral life. The influence of the desire for happiness must be eliminated as far as possible. Duty must become the only motive. The poet Friedrich Schiller's ironic re-statement of Kant's ethics attacks this very point.

> Gladly would I serve my friends, but unfortunately I do it with inclination,
> and so I am much distressed that I am not virtuous.
> There is no other way: you must seek to despise them,
> and then do with disgust what duty commands.[174]

According to Scheler, happiness is the essential pre-condition of the moral life without which a morally good act is impossible. Happiness and moral goodness are inseparable.

Scheler draws the inevitable conclusion from this view. Essential happiness lies already in the human person prior to any divine reward. No reward given by God can constitute happiness. Such a reward would only add a lesser good to this essential happiness. Wojtyła comments:

> We see that in the teaching of revelation, all emphasis in the doctrine of eternal blessedness falls on the object of blessedness, namely, the divine nature, which is this object. In Scheler's phenomenological system, of course, this doctrine cannot be grasped and expressed.... No good that comes from outside the person can be a greater good than the good which the person finds in himself when he experiences himself as the source of a morally good act.... The greatest happiness and the greatest suffering—man draws these from within himself, he himself is its source for himself. This point of view seems to separate us completely from the Christian teaching. Given such a point of view, can we establish any point of contact with the revealed truth according to which the object of man's final blessedness is the divine nature?[175]

Wojtyła does look for a bridge between Scheler and Christianity. According to Scheler, he points out, there is a core of the person in which all social relations are left behind.[176] Yet, this "intimate person"

---

174. Friedrich Schiller and Johann Wolfgang von Goethe, *Xenien*, 387–88.
175. Wojtyła, *Scheler*, 183–84.
176. See Scheler, *Formalism*, 561–72, German 548–58.

and, more deeply, this "absolutely intimate person," is not utterly alone. It still allows for one relationship, the relationship with God. This relationship includes, in turn, a relationship with the community of the Church.

> However, solitude does *not* exclude one communal relation, namely, the relation to *God*, who by definition is neither an individual nor a comprehensive person, but one in whom both individual and comprehensive person are solidary. Thus it is in God alone that the intimate person may know himself to be condemned or saved. But he cannot do even this without his becoming indirectly aware of his solidarity (at least "in God") with the comprehensive person in *general* and, in the first place, with the Church. And without this certitude there would be no God, but merely a deceptive object of the highest nature, that is, an illusory God.[177]

Wojtyła remarks on this text that there is "a profound connection between these ideas of Scheler and the teaching of revelation."[178] The specter of the solitary human person drawing bliss out of himself alone in needless fullness of life seems to be definitively banished. "If in this most profound experience of oneself, which Scheler calls absolutely intimate person, the person does not cease to be in relation to God, then it experiences its happiness in the good and its despair in the evil of its own essence in relation to God. Does such a formulation help us to grasp and express eternal happiness in God and eternal rejection by God? Most certainly, Yes!"[179]

Yet, Wojtyła does not stop with this positive conclusion, but probes further. Scheler speaks about this relation to God only on the level of experience lived by the person in his or her subjectivity without any truly transcendent object. The really existing living God is bracketed in the phenomenological contemplation of essences. The person experiences a detached divine value-essence as an object of feeling. In the sources of revelation, he adds, the emphasis lies on the object of happiness. The real infinite goodness of God is the reason why he is the beatific end. When the person shares in the divine being, Scheler's phenomenological premises reduce this participation to an intentional feeling of the self-value of the person who experi-

---

177. Ibid., 563, German 550, translation modified.
178. Wojtyła, *Scheler*, 184.
179. Ibid., 185.

ences the value-essence of the holy, not the living God.[180] Wojtyła
concludes:

> A participation in God understood in this way *has nothing in common*
> with the real, essentially supernatural participation in God's nature
> and God's inner life. Only participation in God understood in this
> latter way constitutes the basis of final blessedness in God according
> to the teaching of revelation. The withdrawal of this participation is
> the basis of the definitive unhappiness of the human person as a con-
> sequence of its rejection by God. In Scheler's conception, by contrast,
> what the person feels as the real object of emotional bliss and
> despair—despite "participation in God"—is "good" or "evil" as self-
> values of the person that become perceptible at the source of the acts
> experienced by the person.[181]

At the end of his book on Scheler, Wojtyła raises once again the
question whether one can build Christian ethics on the foundations of
Scheler's phenomenology. He concludes that phenomenology can play
a secondary and assisting role, but a Christian thinker cannot be a
phenomenologist. The theologian, he writes,

> should not forego the great advantages which the phenomenological
> method offers his work. It impresses the stamp of experience on
> works of ethics and nourishes them with the life-knowledge of con-
> crete man by allowing an investigation of moral life from the side of
> its appearance. Yet, in all this, the phenomenological method plays
> only a secondary assisting role.... At the same time, these investiga-
> tions convince us that the Christian thinker, especially the theologian,
> who makes use of phenomenological experience in his work, cannot
> be a Phenomenologist.[182]

What Schmitz identifies as Wojtyła's overarching concern is clearly visible in this critique of Scheler. Despite his profound critique of
Kant, Scheler remains caught in the same subjectivist shift. "The
modern shift gave to the human subject an absolute status precisely in
its character *qua* consciousness; for human consciousness not only sets
its own terms but the terms for reality itself."[183] By giving such an
absolute status to human consciousness, Scheler's philosophy loses the

---

180. See ibid., 184–85.
181. Ibid., 185–86; emphasis added.
182. Ibid., 196.
183. Schmitz, *Center of the Drama*, 135–36.

personal subject; it loses real being; and it loses the final end of created persons.

> The philosophy of consciousness would have us believe that it first discovered the human subject. The philosophy of being is prepared to demonstrate that quite the opposite is true, that in fact an analysis of pure consciousness leads inevitably to an annihilation of the subject.[184]
>
> The analysis of the systems of Kant and Scheler shows the conclusion that a consistent teleology and perfectiorism has no room in the philosophy of consciousness. Of course, the end is something contained in consciousness, and the end is always some good or value, but as a [mere] content of consciousness, the end loses its perfective character. It possesses such a character only in connection with being, on the premises of a philosophy of the real. Only on this basis can one speak of a consistent teleology.[185]

Let us return from these key texts to the title of Wojtyła's habilitation thesis: *Evaluation of the Possibility of Constructing a Christian Ethics on the Assumptions of Max Scheler's System of Philosophy*. George Weigel writes in his biography of John Paul II (*Witness to Hope,* p. 128),

> That [Wojtyła] looked to Scheler as a possible guide, and that he put himself through the backbreaking work of translation so that he could analyze Scheler in his own language, suggests that Wojtyła had become convinced that the answers [to the question "Why ought I be good?"] were not to be found in the neo-scholasticism of Father Reginald Garrigou-Lagrange.

Weigel does not supply direct evidence that Wojtyła hoped to find a new foundation of ethics in Scheler. If one assumes that Wojtyła set out to study Scheler in this hope, one must conclude that he was disappointed. A Christian ethics cannot be built on Scheler. The reason

---

184. Karol Wojtyła, "The Person: Subject and Community," in *Person and Community: Selected Essays* (New York: P. Lang, 1993), 219–20. The paragraph containing this sentence was omitted in the first English publication of this essay in *Review of Metaphysics* 33 (1979/80): 273–308, perhaps because the judgment expressed in it is so categorically negative.

185. Karol Wojtyła, "Das Gute und der Wert [The Good and Value]," in *Lubliner Vorlesungen,* ed. Juliusz Stroynowski (Stuttgart-Degerloch: Seewald, 1981), 244. Wojtyła uses the concept "perfectiorism" derived from the Latin comparative *perfectior,* "more perfect"; an account based on a *greater* degree of perfection.

for the failure of Scheler's system is not due to particular errors here or there; it is systemic. As Wojtyła puts it (see above p. 71), "The whole difficulty is the result of the phenomenological premises of the system and we must assign the blame to these principles."

5. An Overview of Wojtyła's Concerns

a. Wojtyła's Seven Major Works

Before his election as Pope in 1978, Wojtyła wrote seven major works.[186] The following list arranges them in the chronological order of their composition or first publication.

1. 1948: *Faith according to St. John of the Cross.* Doctoral thesis in theology.

2. 1953: *Evaluation of the Possibility of Constructing a Christian Ethics on the Assumptions of Max Scheler's System of Philosophy.* Habilitation thesis in moral theology.

3. 1954–57: *Lublin Lectures.* Philosophical lectures on the foundations of ethics in dialogue with Plato, Aristotle, St. Augustine, St. Thomas, Kant, and Scheler.

4. 1957–59: *Love and Responsibility.* An integrated philosophical and theological account of love between man and woman, including a discussion of marriage and its ends.

5. 1969: *The Acting Person.* A philosophical account of the person.

6. 1972: *Sources of Renewal: The Implementation of the Second Vatican Council.*

---

186. Two further works come close to the category "major works": *Primer of Ethics* (1957), a collection of twenty popular articles on important topics in ethics, and *Man on the Field of Responsibility* (1972) intended as a sequel to *The Acting Person*, but left incomplete at seventy-four manuscript pages. TOB itself, though written before John Paul II's election, must be considered a papal document. In the fifties, Wojtyła wrote a two-volume work entitled *Catholic Social Ethics*, which was printed as a clandestine edition to escape government censure. It has not yet been republished in Polish and there seems to be no public access to it.

7. 1976:   *Sign of Contradiction*. Retreat preached to Paul
            VI and the papal household.

Four of these seven works are theological (1, 2, 6, and 7), two are mainly philosophical (3 and 5), and one (4) is philosophical with important theological aspects.

It is important to see the order in which the issues arise in Wojtyła's first two books, the book on St. John of the Cross and the book on Scheler. Wojtyła's point of departure as a philosopher and theologian is St. John of the Cross's personalism. It is a personalism shaped by the characteristic triangle of theses: love is a gift of self; spousal love between man and woman is the paradigmatic case of the gift of self; the origin and exemplar of the gift of self lies in the Trinity. It is also shaped by St. John of the Cross's keen attention to the lived experience of personal subjectivity. The book on Scheler shows that Wojtyła finds points of contact between this Carmelite personalism and Scheler in both of these characteristics of St. John of the Cross's teaching, the triangle of theses (especially the imitation of Christ, in which the trinitarian paradigm of personhood is realized; and self-giving *agape*) and its reflection in lived experience.

Yet he also finds an understanding of personal subjectivity that radically undermines the Christian understanding. As Wojtyła reads him, Scheler denies three core theses of the personalism implicit in the imitation of Christ. (1) Moral goodness is a real perfection of the person achieved in following Jesus. (2) The person is a really existing subject and the responsible causal origin of moral acts. (3) The goal of the imitation of Jesus is the infinite good, which consists in God's nature. Inasmuch as Scheler denies these three theses, his philosophy is *not personalistic enough*. Christian personalism is more deeply personalistic. Wojtyła's book on Scheler is thus an argument that affirms the deeper personalism of the theological tradition against the essentialist personalism of Scheler. Certainly, Wojtyła learned much from Scheler that is positive and one can trace many influences (they can be identified in part by following the references to Scheler in the indices of Wojtyła's works, in part by pointing out the many similarities), but his overall judgment is negative.

One can situate Wojtyła's main philosophical work, *The Acting Person* (1969), in relation to the three main points of his Scheler book.

The Acting Person focuses primarily on the second of the three points. It attempts to supply precisely what Scheler fails to supply, namely, an account of the person as a really existing subject and as the responsible origin of moral acts. It does so through a partial use of the phenomenological method and in light of many particular insights of Scheler. The main agenda of *The Acting Person*, however, is not dictated by Scheler, but by Wojtyła's roots in the spousal theology of St. John of the Cross, specifically by the key notion, "gift of self." In order to give oneself, one must be in responsible possession of oneself. *The Acting Person* supplies the account of the person that is presupposed by St. John of the Cross's spousal theology of self-gift.

Love and Responsibility (1957–59) attaches itself more immediately to the beginning of Wojtyła's formation, the spousal personalism of St. John of the Cross. St. John of the Cross does not thematically discuss love between man and woman. Yet, his frequent use of bride-bridegroom imagery contains a rich implicit theology of marriage inspired above all by the Song of Songs. In *Love and Responsibility*, Wojtyła makes this implicit theology of marriage explicit, enriching it by further insight. His pastoral experience with young couples enters into it, as does his study of Kant's account of sex and the Kantian critique of utilitarianism. The influence of Scheler can be seen particularly in the chapter on shame and in the disciplined attention to lived experience throughout.[187] Yet the core of Wojtyła's philosophical concern in *Love and Responsibility* is the understanding of the gift of self as the key element of spousal love. Kant touches on this theme, though in a sense opposite to Wojtyła. It is thus clear that the spousal theology of St. John of the Cross ultimately shapes the agenda of *Love and Responsibility*.

Like *Love and Responsibility*, Wojtyła's reading of Vatican II in *Sources of Renewal* (1972) and his retreat preached to the papal household (1976) stand in continuity with the book on St. John of the Cross, though the understanding of the person developed in *The Acting Person* plays an important role as well. A study of the theological background of TOB must be, in large measure, a study of *Sources of Renewal*. Let us therefore take a brief look at this book and its relationship with *Faith in St. John of the Cross*.

---

187. See Wojtyła, *Love and Responsibility*, 174–93.

b. Faith, Experience, and Personal Subjectivity

In *Sources of Renewal*, Wojtyła sets himself the task of outlining the implementation of Vatican II in a manner that corresponds to the actual intentions of the Council. The original guiding question of Vatican II, he argues, was *"Ecclesia, quid dicis de te ipsa?* Church, what do you say about yourself?"[188] "The People of God"—this is the Council's answer, Wojtyła claims.[189] The way both the question and the answer, "People of God," must be understood, he adds, is pastoral. How can the Church *grow in her awareness and life* as the People of God? Although the question is in the first place a question about the Church as a *social* organism, the growth of the Church's awareness must take place in the life of the individual *persons* that constitute it. It must take place in their lived experience of personal subjectivity. For this reason, the key question, "Church, what do you say about yourself?" is closely linked to the question, "What does it *mean* to be a believer, a Catholic, and a member of the Church?" in the context of today's world.[190]

Being a member of the Church means having faith, Wojtyła answers. For this reason, "the implementation of the Council consists first and foremost in enriching that faith," enrichment being understood as the reception and realization of faith in personal subjectivity, in conscious experience.[191] The overall goal of *Sources of Renewal* is to outline this enrichment of faith intended by the Council.

The emphasis on consciousness is a hallmark of the "philosophers of consciousness" from Descartes via Kant to Scheler. Wojtyła learned much from these philosophers, no doubt. Yet, St. John of the Cross seems to be the more important part of the picture. In some respects, the philosophers of consciousness resemble St. John of the Cross. As von Balthasar points out, St. John of the Cross's theology can be understood as a response to Luther, a specifically modern response in which personal subjectivity plays a pronounced role, yet without any

---

188. Karol Wojtyła, *Sources of Renewal: The Implementation of the Second Vatican Council* (San Francisco: Harper & Row, 1980), 420.

189. This thesis is unfolded in the lengthy chapter on "The Consciousness of the Church as the People of God," see ibid., 112–54.

190. Ibid., 17 and 420.

191. Ibid., 420.

polemical edge against the objective content of faith and its elaboration in monastic and scholastic theology. "What was challenging and scandalous in the Carmelite response to Luther was the manner in which it integrated the entire monastic tradition from the Greeks through the middle ages into the new Christian radicalism and gave to that tradition a hitherto unknown radicality by the modern turn toward the personal, the experiential and the psychological."[192]

Buttiglione makes a similar point when he says that Wojtyła "read in St. John of the Cross a kind of phenomenology of mystical experience."[193] Since Wojtyła's encounter with St. John of the Cross came before his encounter with phenomenology, the point is better put the other way around. Wojtyła read in phenomenology a Carmelite sensitivity to the lived experience of personal subjectivity. This chronological order holds not only for Wojtyła's biography, but also for the history of modernity. St. John of the Cross was born in 1544, Descartes half a century later, in 1596.

Wojtyła's dissertation strongly underlines the role of conscious experience in St. John of the Cross's account of faith as a means of union with God. "Speculative theology provided the principles, the spiritual authors gave the terminology and a vast area of comparative study, but the writings of St. John of the Cross are the fruit of experience. It was a vital experience of the supernatural reality that is communicated to the soul, a dynamic experience of participation in the intimate life of the Blessed Trinity, and, finally, an experience of the unifying power of that which serves as a 'means of union' with God."[194]

The experience of faith is, accordingly, the main thematic focus of Wojtyła's dissertation. What interests him, above all, is how faith, according to St. John of the Cross, becomes experience.

> We have already seen that the doctrine we shall study is a testimony of experience. It is expressed in scholastico-mystical language, using words and concepts well known in Scholastic theology, but its primary

---

192. Hans Urs von Balthasar, *The Glory of the Lord: A Theological Aesthetics: Vol. III: Lay Styles* (San Francisco: Ignatius Press, 1986), 106; trans. altered.

193. Rocco Buttiglione, *Karol Wojtyla: The Thought of the Man Who Became Pope John Paul II* (Grand Rapids, MI: Eerdmans, 1997), 45.

194. Wojtyła, *St. John of the Cross*, 22.

value and significance is as a witness of personal experience. It is there, in fact, that we can discover the living and dynamic reality of the virtue of faith, its activity in the human intellect, its corollaries and the effects on the movement of the soul toward union with God. For that reason, we take the experiential witness of St. John of the Cross as the material for our investigation. It will be our task to discover the concept of faith that can be gleaned from that witness and the theological precisions that are latent in it.[195]

Many theologians in modernity have given a prominent place to personal experience in their theology, often combined with an exaltation of feeling and a polemical edge against the objective content of faith. Schleiermacher is a particularly radical example of this tendency. Roman Catholic school catechesis in the post-Vatican II era has at times followed a similar direction. It is thus important to define Wojtyła/John Paul II's specific understanding of experience.

In his philosophical work (especially *The Acting Person* and its intended sequel, *Man on the Field of Responsibility*), Wojtyła focuses on the experience of *the person in action*, on the person in the ordinary and natural experience connected with living a human life both as an individual person and in community. A similar point holds for Wojtyła's theological work. Here, too, Wojtyła focuses on the experience of *the person in action*.

The starting point of Christian experience is faith. Faith is not replaced by experience, but it remains the comprehensive form of Christian experience. This is the first point to be made about Christian experience, as Wojtyła understands it: its origin and measure lies in faith, not the other way around. Faith must be "enriched," that is, it must become more mature and conscious, able to form the whole of experience. "Faith and the enrichment of faith is a supernatural gift of God and is not subject to human planning or causation; but man, and the Church as a human community, can and must cooperate with the grace of faith and contribute to its enrichment. The Council itself acted in this way, and its action, considering the level on which it took place, may be considered a plan of action for the whole Church."[196]

---

195. Ibid., 23.
196. Wojtyła, *Sources of Renewal*, 203–4.

The primacy of faith in Christian experience, even in the most exalted forms of experience characteristic of mysticism—this is the main point Wojtyła brings out in his dissertation when he situates St. John of the Cross historically.

> Against false interpretations of communion with God, the Mystical Doctor calmly taught that *faith* is the proper means of union—*faith in accord with all its implications: in complete nakedness, austerity, and obedience of the intellect*.... And now the issue becomes immediately clear. Against long-standing inclinations, the root of which is perhaps still present in the teaching of Averroes and in Arabian mysticism, inclinations that had recently been revived also by a false interpretation of Flemish authors and the Rhineland mystics, whose works were widely read in the Iberian peninsula, against these [inclinations] *the most interior manifestation* of the Spirit in the life of the Church proposed *faith, whose saving power and ability to unite the soul with God* is glorified in Sacred Scripture.[197]

The primacy in Christian experience belongs to faith "*in complete nakedness, austerity, and obedience of the intellect.*" Wojtyła sees St. John of the Cross as rejecting the opposite approach in which experience becomes the measure of faith.

> St. John of the Cross is consistent in his teaching: all these things [visions, locutions, and spiritual feelings] must be rejected in favor of the virtue of faith, which operates in the dark night and, by reason of its intimate proportion to divinity, surpasses any experience in which the natural faculties, however much purified, can find fruition and satisfaction. Faith, as we have seen, is the means of true and proper union with God, who by his essence incomparably transcends every created nature; for that reason faith surpasses even the most lofty mystical experience.[198]

The superiority of faith over all experience does not imply that the whole order of experience is irrelevant. On the contrary, it is relevant inasmuch as a living faith deeply transforms human experience by introducing the person to a path of union with God. "The virtue of faith is subordinated to union as means to the end."[199] St. John of the

---

197. Wojtyła, *St. John of the Cross*, 16–17, emphasis added, translation modified; Wojtyła, *Apud Joannem a Cruce*, 46.
198. Ibid., 123.
199. Ibid., 48.

Cross teaches *"the definitive power and essential characteristic of love—and therefore of the will—in* union.... The power and characteristic of love flows from its very nature insofar as it causes likeness and subjects the lover to the beloved. Hence if it is a question of union of likeness, love must necessarily be the unifying factor. This explains what the Mystical Doctor explains time and time again: union consists of the total conformation of the human will with the divine will."[200] St. John of the Cross, as Wojtyła understands him, sees faith as a means within human life as a whole. Human life as a whole is directed toward the end of a union of the human person with God through love. Human experience is not excluded from this process. On the contrary, it is to be formed by love. In this process, faith remains the proximate means of union that cannot be supplanted by feeling or some other surrogate.

In his apostolic letter on St. John of the Cross, John Paul II again emphasizes the fundamental and unsurpassable role of faith in the growth of a genuine Christian experience. He also identifies St. John of the Cross's understanding of Christian experience with the central concern of Vatican II.[201]

> In it [that is, the dissertation on St. John of the Cross], I devoted special attention to an analytical discussion of the central affirmation of the Mystical Doctor: Faith is *the only proximate and proportionate means* for communion with God.[202]
>
> The Mystical Doctor..., through his example and doctrine, helps Christians to make their faith strong with the very basic qualities of an adult faith which the Second Vatican Council asks of us. This faith is to be personal, free and convinced, embraced with one's entire being, an ecclesial faith, confessed and celebrated in communion with the Church, a praying and adoring faith, *matured through the experience of communion with God.*[203]
>
> The presence of God and of Christ, a renewing purification under the guidance of the Spirit, and the living of an informed and adult faith—is this not in reality the heart of the teaching of St. John of the Cross and his message for the Church and for men and women of today? ...Only faith enables us to *experience the salvific presence of God*

200. Ibid., 100.
201. See Angelo Scola, *L'esperienza elementare: La vena profonda del magistero di Giovanni Paolo II* (Genoa: Marietti, 2003), 47.
202. John Paul II, *Maestro en la fe,* 2; emphasis added.
203. Ibid., 7; emphasis added.

in Christ in the very center of life and of history. Faith alone reveals to us the meaning of the human condition and our supreme dignity as sons and daughters of God who are *called to communion with Him.*[204]

According to John Paul II's reading of St. John of the Cross, what is it that a living faith becomes increasingly conscious of? The decisive thing for the nature of an experience is its content or object. What is the object of Christian experience? The answer in the text just quoted is very clear: "the salvific presence of God in Christ in the very center of life and of history."

These words, in which John Paul II summarizes the doctrine of St. John of the Cross, resemble the opening words of his inaugural encyclical *Redemptor Hominis* (1979): "The Redeemer of Man, Jesus Christ, is the center of the universe and of history." Later in the same encyclical, John Paul II formulates the program of his pontificate in a similar way.

> While the ways on which the Council of this Century has set the Church going, ways indicated by the late Pope Paul VI in his first encyclical, will continue to be for a long time the ways that all of us must follow, we can at the same time rightly ask at this new stage: How, in what manner should we continue?... To this question, dear brothers, sons and daughters, a fundamental and essential response must be given. Our response must be: Our spirit is set in one direction, the only direction for our intellect, will and heart is—towards Christ our Redeemer, towards Christ, the Redeemer of man. We wish to look towards Him—because there is salvation in no one else but Him, the Son of God—repeating what Peter said: "Lord, to whom shall we go? You have the words of eternal life."[205]

In his dissertation, Wojtyła devotes an entire chapter to the personalist understanding of faith in St. John of the Cross. "Revealed truths are given to the intellect, but Christ himself is given as the life of Christians. In him is found the revelation of God to human beings, both in himself and as the exemplar that all should imitate and, through love, reproduce in themselves. In this way, and not in eager scrutiny of revealed truths, the manifestation of God is attained and shared by each one. For St. John of the Cross the revelation of God

---

204. Ibid., 3; emphasis added.
205. John Paul II, *Redemptor Hominis*, 7.

consists much more in personal witness than in the purely intellectual knowledge of revealed truths."[206] This summary of St. John of the Cross's teaching is akin to John Paul II's words of profound experience, "Our spirit is set in one direction, the only direction for our intellect, will and heart is—towards Christ our Redeemer." *Redemptor Hominis*, 10, unfolds what this "turning" involves.

> Man cannot live without love. He remains a being that is incomprehensible for himself, his life is senseless, if love is not *revealed to him*, if he does not *encounter* love, if he does not *experience* it and *make it his own*, if he does not *participate intimately* in it. This, as has already been said, is why Christ the Redeemer "fully reveals man to himself."... The man who wishes to understand himself thoroughly—and not just in accordance with immediate, partial, often superficial, and even illusory standards and measures of his being—he must with his unrest, uncertainty and even his weakness and sinfulness, with his life and death, *draw near* to Christ. He must, so to speak, *enter into Him with all his own self*; he must *"appropriate"* and *assimilate* the whole of the reality of the Incarnation and redemption in order to *find himself*.[207]

In this text, there is a remarkable density of words that express the assimilation of faith in the lived experience of personal subjectivity. Persons receive the revelation of God's love; they encounter it, experience it, make it their own, participate intimately in it, enter into it with all of their own self; they appropriate and assimilate it by bringing their unrest, uncertainty, weakness, and sinfulness to Christ in order to enter into Christ, and only in this way—find themselves. This emphasis on personal subjectivity coincides with what Wojtyła sees in the core teaching of St. John of the Cross. Wojtyła's understanding of St. John of the Cross, his understanding of Vatican II, and the program of his own pontificate as set forth in *Redemptor Hominis*—all three of these visions are expressions of one and the same vision, a Carmelite vision that was first formed in Wojtyła by St. John of the Cross.

In this reception of St. John of the Cross, Wojtyła resolutely takes the side of his thesis advisor Garrigou-Lagrange in the debate about

---

206. Wojtyła, *St. John of the Cross*, 174; see the whole chapter: 172–82.
207. John Paul II, *Redemptor Hominis*, 10; emphasis added.

the Mystical Doctor's relevance for the life of ordinary Christians. Against those who dismiss St. John of the Cross as preoccupied with extraordinary and miraculous mystical phenomena that are irrelevant for ordinary believers, Garrigou-Lagrange argues, in part by a careful comparison between St. John of the Cross and St. Thomas Aquinas, that St. John of the Cross's teachings concern the normal development of the supernatural life of faith and love.[208] Wojtyła may have come to the same conclusions on his own by his reading of St. John of the Cross, but it is likely that Garrigou-Lagrange helped significantly to shape the core of John Paul II's vision.[209]

To summarize, there is a strong continuity in Wojtyła's personalist vision that spans the period from his dissertation on St. John of the Cross (1948), through his interpretation of Vatican II (1972), to the pastoral program set forth in *Redemptor Hominis* (1979). Faith must penetrate and transform human experience. It must be received and enriched in the lived experience of personal subjectivity. Of course, the encounter with the philosophy of consciousness, particularly Kant and phenomenology, in the period of Wojtyła's habilitation thesis on Scheler (1953) as well as his own philosophical synthesis in *The Acting Person* (1969) were tributaries to this stream of tradition and sharpened Wojtyła's understanding of personal subjectivity.

c. The Trinitarian Nucleus of the Council

The nucleus of Wojtyła's theological personalism becomes clearer when one focuses on its trinitarian form as explained in *Sources of*

---

208. One focus of this debate was the gift of infused contemplation. See Reginald Garrigou-Lagrange, *Christian Perfection and Contemplation according to St. Thomas Aquinas and St. John of the Cross* (St. Louis: Herder, 1949), and *The Three Ages of the Interior Life: Prelude of Eternal Life*, 2 vols. (Rockford, IL: Tan, 1989).

209. Wojtyła is not the only one who was formed by Garrigou-Lagrange's understanding of the spiritual life. "If his [that is, Garrigou-Lagrange's] form of dogmatic theology failed to win the day at the Second Vatican Council, we will see that his most passionately held spiritual propositions were incorporated into official Catholic teaching by the Council Fathers." Richard Peddicord, O.P., *The Sacred Monster of Thomism: An Introduction to the Life and Legacy of Réginald Garrigou-Lagrange, O.P.* (South Bend, IN: St. Augustine, 2005), 179. See also the chapter on Garrigou-Lagrange and Wojtyła, pp. 214–20. Unfortunately, Peddicord focuses only on the philosophical points of contact between Wojtyła and Garrigou-Lagrange. A systematic comparison of their doctrines in spiritual theology must still be carried out.

Renewal. Sources of Renewal is divided into three parts. Part 1 explains the concept of "enrichment of faith" with the help of two further concepts, formation of the believer's *consciousness,* the cognitive aspect of a mature faith, and formation of the believer's *attitude,* the existential and ethical aspect of a life of faith, that is, the believer's active relationship with God.[210] "Attitude" is a concept close to Scheler's "ethos" that plays such a significant role in TOB. It is clear that Wojtyła learned much from Scheler in thinking through the concept of ethos. In Parts 2 and 3, *Sources of Renewal* takes up consciousness and attitude one by one: formation of the believer's *consciousness* in Part 2 and formation of the believer's *attitude* in Part 3.

PART TWO: Wojtyła unfolds the formation of the believer's *consciousness* in five steps. They correspond to the five chapters of Part 2:

1. the consciousness of creation;
2. the revelation of the Trinity and the consciousness of salvation;
3. Christ and the consciousness of redemption;
4. the consciousness of the Church as the People of God;
5. the historical and eschatological consciousness of the Church.

One can see a clear order of argument in these five chapters. Chapter 1 attends to the order of creation, of nature; the other chapters turn to the supernatural order of grace. Chapter 2, the first step in the order of grace, lays down the theological principle, namely, God's own trinitarian life made accessible to human beings. Chapter 3 discusses the manner in which God shares this life with us, namely, through Christ, the Redeemer. Chapters 4 and 5 draw the consequences for the Church's self-understanding, first in her essential nature (Chapter 4) and then in her life in history (Chapter 5). Chapter 2 is thus the crucial theological chapter in terms of which the others must be understood, including the more philosophical Chapter 1. Let us take a closer look at Chapters 2 and 4.

In Chapter 2, Wojtyła presents some of the most important Council texts on the Trinity and argues from them that the Trinity is the principal content of faith to which all other truths of faith must be related. He then asks a fundamental question: "Why are the missions

---

210. See Wojtyła, *Sources of Renewal,* 205.

of the divine persons addressed to him [man], and why do these in particular constitute the profoundest divine mystery of the Church?"[211] The question goes to the very heart, the nucleus, of the Council's teaching.

Wojtyła answers that the Church compares the revealed truth concerning God and the revealed truth concerning the human being and finds in this comparison her own mission and consciousness. The comparison brings to light a link between the exemplar in which the fullness of life is found and our imitation or participation in this exemplar. To unfold this answer, Wojtyła quotes *Gaudium et Spes*, 24:3: "Indeed, the Lord Jesus, when he prays to the Father, 'that all may be one...as we are one' (Jn 17:21–22) and thus offers vistas closed to human reason, indicates a certain likeness between the union of the divine Persons and the union of God's sons in truth and love. This likeness shows that man, who is the only creature on earth which God willed for itself, cannot fully find himself except through a sincere gift of self (cf. Lk 17:33)." Wojtyła comments:

> Man's resemblance to God finds its basis, as it were, in the mystery of the most holy Trinity. Man resembles God not only because of the spiritual nature of his immortal soul but also by reason of his social nature, if by this we understand the fact that he "cannot fully realize himself except in an act of pure self-giving" [*Gaudium et Spes*, 24:3]. In this way, "union in truth and charity" is the ultimate expression of the community of individuals. This union merits the name of communion (*communio*), which signifies more than community (*communitas*). The Latin word *communio* denotes a relationship between persons that is proper to them alone; and it indicates the good that they do to one another, giving and receiving within that mutual relationship.[212]

Many themes sounded in this text have a prominent place in TOB. The essential point to note is that Wojtyła sees the heart of the Council in the call to deeper personal awareness of love as self-gift rooted in the Trinity. In TOB he understands married life in the same terms. He had first seen this trinitarian vision of the life of the person in St. John of the Cross.

---

211. Ibid., 60.
212. Ibid., 61.

Wojtyła returns to the communion of persons in Chapter 4, when he discusses the Church's consciousness of herself in her essential nature as the "People of God." The concept of "*communio*," he argues, is the key defining concept in light of which one can understand what it means that the Church is the "People of God":

> If we want to follow the main thread of the Council's thought, all that it says concerning the hierarchy, the laity and the religious orders in the Church should be re-read in the light of the reality of *communio* for the community of the People of God. "For the members of the People of God are called upon to share their goods, and the words of the apostle apply also to each of the Churches, 'according to the gift that each has received, administer it to one another as good stewards of the manifold grace of God' (1 Pet 5:10)."
>
> Thus we have the *communio ecclesiarum* [communion of churches] and the *communio munerum* [the communion of gifts, tasks, or offices] and, through these, the *communio personarum* [communion of persons]. Such is the image of the Church presented by the Council. The type of union and unity that is proper to the community of the Church as People of God essentially determines the nature of that community. The Church as People of God, by reason of its most basic premises and its communal nature, is oriented towards the resemblance there ought to be between "the union of the sons of God in truth and love" [*Gaudium et Spes*, 24:3] and the essentially divine unity of the divine persons, in *communione Sanctissimae Trinitatis*.[213]

The point could not be clearer or more lapidary. *Ecclesia, quid dicis de te ipsa?* Church, what do you say about yourself? Increased awareness of the mystery of trinitarian communion—this is what allows a correct growth of the believer's *consciousness* of the nature of the Church as the People of God. "The Council devotes much attention to *making the faithful conscious of communio* as the link binding together the community of the People of God. Thus it appears that the internal development and renewal of the Church in the spirit of Vatican II depends to a very great extent on the authentic deepening of faith in the Church as a community whose essential bond is that of *communio*."[214]

This emphasis on the trinitarian understanding of Vatican II's teaching on the "People of God" is confirmed by *Sign of Contradiction*,

---

213. Ibid., 137–38. See Scola, *L'esperienza elementare*, 51 with footnotes.
214. Ibid., 144; emphasis added.

the retreat Cardinal Wojtyła preached for Paul VI in 1976, two years before his own election as Pope. At a highpoint of the retreat, the beginning of the seventh talk, he says,

> Let us turn our thoughts to God who is gift and the source of all giv-ing. The Fathers of the second Vatican Council were convinced that the complex reality of the Church cannot be adequately expressed in societal terms alone, even when the society constituted by the Church is called the "People of God." In order properly to describe this reali-ty and appreciate its underlying significance it is necessary to return to the dimension of mystery, that is to the dimension of the most Holy Trinity. That is why the Constitution *Lumen Gentium* starts with an introductory account of the divine economy of salvation, which ulti-mately is a Trinitarian economy (cf. *Lumen Gentium*, nn. 2–4).... Love, an uncreated gift, is part of the inner mystery of God and is the very nucleus of theology.[215]

Pascal Ide's argument that *Gaudium et Spes*, 24:3, plays a key role in John Paul II is confirmed by these passages.[216] *Gaudium et Spes*, 24:3, plays a key role already in Wojtyła's reading of Vatican II.

PART THREE: Wojtyła offers the following account of the believ-er's "attitude," which is the main subject of Part 3 of *Sources of Renewal*.

> The word ["attitude"] is usually applied analogically and denotes var-ious relationships which are endorsed as a whole by the individual consciousness. In simple terms we may say that an attitude is an active relationship but is not yet action. It follows upon cognition and increased awareness, but is something new and different from these. It involves "taking up a position" and being ready to act in accordance with it. In a sense it represents what Thomist psychology would call *habitus* and even *habitus operativus*, but the two are not identical.[217]

As mentioned above, Scheler's concept of "ethos" seems to stand behind this definition of "attitude," but St. John of the Cross's under-standing of a living faith that provides the source of Christian experi-ence is present as well.

---

215. Karol Wojtyła, *Sign of Contradiction* (New York: Seabury Press, 1979), 53 and 55.

216. See above p. 23.

217. Wojtyła, *Sources of Renewal*, 205. The remaining difference seems to be that Wojtyła's "attitude" emphasizes the aspect of *consciousness* while "*habitus*" does not.

Wojtyła's point of departure in Part 3 is *Dei Verbum*, 5. "To God who reveals himself one must give the obedience of faith by which man freely commits himself as a whole to God."[218] Wojtyła comments that faith "cannot consist merely of knowledge or the content of consciousness. Essential to faith is an attitude of self-commitment to God—a continual readiness to perform the fundamental 'action' which corresponds to the reality of revelation, and all other acts which spring from it and to which it gives their proper character. In speaking of the attitude of *self-gift*[219] *to God*, Vatican II touches on the most vital and vivifying point relating to the whole process of the enrichment of faith."[220]

It is not difficult to see in this reading of *Dei Verbum*, 5, Wojtyła's familiar emphasis on faith as a means of union with God and on love as a total gift of self, *totus tuus* (*Gaudium et Spes*, 24:3). Twenty-eight years later, in the year 2000, Pope John Paul II expressed the same understanding of the Council: "With the Council, *the Church first had an experience of faith*, as she abandoned herself to God without reserve, as one who trusts and is certain of being loved. It is precisely this act of abandonment to God which stands out from an objective examination of the Acts [of the Council]. Anyone who wished to approach the Council without considering this interpretive key *would be unable to penetrate its depths*. Only from the perspective of faith can we see the Council event as a gift whose still hidden wealth we must know how to mine."[221] What Wojtyła calls the fundamental "attitude" of the believer lies precisely in this self-gift to God. Part 3 unfolds this attitude in six chapters:

1. the attitude of mission and testimony;
2. the attitude of participation in the threefold saving power of Christ;

---

218. Vatican II, *Dei Verbum*, 5.

219. The German translation has "*Selbsthingabe*" (self-gift): see Karol Wojtyla, *Quellen der Erneuerung: Studie zur Verwirklichung des Zweiten Vatikanischen Konzils* (Freiburg: Herder, 1981), 180, cf. also 182. The English translation has "self-commitment" and in other contexts "self-abandonment."

220. Wojtyła, *Sources of Renewal*, 206.

221. John Paul II, address to the conference studying the implementation of Vatican II (Feb. 27, 2000).

3. the attitude of human identity and Christian responsibility;

4. the ecumenical attitude;

5. the attitude of the apostolate; and

6. the attitude required for building up the Church as *communio*.

Let us take a closer look at Chapter 1, in which Wojtyła lays down the theological foundation. The argument begins with the mission of the divine Persons. God reveals himself, saves the world, and constitutes his people by sending his Son and Spirit. "Thus in the Council's teaching, awareness of salvation is closely linked with the revelation of the Most Holy Trinity."[222] Since the missions of the Son and the Spirit are the origin of the Church as the People of God, they impart to that people a trinitarian form in the specific manner of mission. "The Church originated and continues to originate from that divine mission: this gives a 'missionary' character to its whole existence, and at the same time basically determines the attitude of every Christian."[223]

In reading Wojtyła's account of the believer's attitude we thus find ourselves right away in the depth of the trinitarian teaching on which Wojtyła reflected already in his doctoral dissertation on St. John of the Cross. By giving himself as a whole to the self-revealing God in the obedience of faith (*Dei Verbum*, 5), the believer grasps his own identity as a person who has come to share in the Person of the Son in relation to the Father by the gift of the Spirit. Mission is thus not in the first place an attitude of moral commitment in response to a moral duty, but a way of *being* that is rooted in the person of Jesus as the Son of God. "This [mission] does not initially imply a function or institution, but defines the nature of the Church and indicates its close link with the mystery of the divine Trinity through the mission of the Persons: the Son who comes to us from the Father in the Holy Spirit and the Spirit who proceeds from the Father and the Son. In this sense and on the basis of this reality, we can and should define the attitude of every human being in the Church."[224] To commit oneself

---

222. Wojtyła, *Sources of Renewal*, 206.
223. Ibid.
224. Ibid., 207.

to God's saving self-revelation thus means to follow and imitate Jesus. The imitation of Jesus was the point of departure of Wojtyła's Scheler book, in continuity with his book on St. John of the Cross. It appears once again at a key point of his book on Vatican II.

These samples from Wojtyła's book on Vatican II indicate the theological background of TOB. Not surprisingly, one finds *Gaudium et Spes*, 24:3, at the center of the argument, and at least two of the points on the Sanjuanist triangle, the first and the third: (1) love is a gift of self; (3) the primal reality of gift and pattern for all gift lies in the eternal love between the divine Persons.

6. The Purpose of the Theology of the Body

a. Why Theology "of the Body" in Particular?

The theology of the body gathers up the dominant concerns of Wojtyła's earlier philosophical and theological work. One can arrange these concerns schematically in three phases: the beginning, the challenge, and the response.

(1) *The Beginning:* The beginnings of Wojtyła's theological formation lie in the personalism of St. John of the Cross, a specifically modern personalism (as von Balthasar shows, see above p. 81). From this point onward, he focuses on the lived experience of personal subjectivity and develops the Sanjuanist triangle: love is a gift of self; spousal love is the paradigmatic gift of self; the Trinity is the archetype of such gift. These concerns are still the dominant concerns of TOB. There is a clear and strong continuity of concerns from Wojtyła's first book (1948) through his reading of Vatican II (1972) to TOB (originally written in the seventies, delivered 1979–84).

(2) *The Challenge:* Wojtyła's Carmelite point of departure was challenged by another modern sense of personal subjectivity, developed among others by Descartes, Kant, and Scheler. Schmitz's penetrating study of Wojtyła offers the key to understanding this challenge and Wojtyła's response to it (see above pp. 34–6).[225] The new sense of

---

225. See Schmitz, *Center of the Drama*, 135–36.

personal subjectivity is closely connected with the mechanization of the natural world. The ancient Gnostics found themselves in a demonic, anti-divine universe. Matter was evil. Yet, the truly bottomless pit is opened only by the Cartesian universe with its complete indifference to meaning. Matter is "mere matter," sheer externality. It is value-free. The reason for this indifference of matter to meaning lies in the rigorous reconstruction of knowledge under the guidance of the ambition for power over nature.

Desperately alone in an inhospitable world, orphaned by its own ambition for power, the Cartesian conscious subject is thrown back on itself; it must find all meaning in itself. The most powerful expression of this new kind of subjectivity is Kant's anti-trinitarian personalism. Kant set out to cure the modern subject of atheism and utilitarianism by setting religion and morality on a new foundation, namely, the dignity of the person. Kant's personalism glorifies the autonomy of the individual person as the only true value to which everything else must be subordinated. Man is equal to the Father, but not born from the Father. Fatherhood is the worst despotism imaginable, sonship the worst slavery. As Wojtyła reads him, Scheler offers a profound critique of Kant, but remains caught in a similar subjectivist shift in which human consciousness "sets the terms for reality itself" (Schmitz).

(3) *The Response:* Wojtyła's response is, at one and the same time, a defense of the goodness of nature and of the trinitarian paradigm of personhood. To be a person is to stand in a relation of gift. To be a human person is to live as a body that offers a rich natural expression for the gift of self in spousal love.

The defense of the body in this theological response to the Cartesian-Kantian-Schelerian form of subjectivity is pivotal. The scientific rationalism spearheaded by Descartes is above all an attack *on the body*. Its first principle is that the human body, together with all matter, shall be seen as an object of power. Form and final cause must therefore be eliminated from it.

The response to such a violent scientific-technological attack on the body must be a defense of the body in its natural intrinsic meaning. The spousal mystery is the primary place at which this defense must take place, because the highest meaning of the body is found there.

St. Paul's magnificent synthesis concerning "the great mystery" appears as the compendium or summa, in some sense, of the teaching about God and man which was brought to fulfillment by Christ. Unfortunately, Western thought, with the development of modern rationalism, has been gradually moving away from this teaching. The philosopher who formulated the principle of *"cogito, ergo sum"*—I think, therefore I am—also gave the modern concept of man its distinctive dualistic character. It is typical of rationalism to make a radical contrast in man between spirit and body, between body and spirit. But man is a person in the unity of his body and his spirit. The body can never be reduced to mere matter: It is a spiritualized body, just as man's spirit is so closely united to the body that he can be described as an embodied spirit. The richest source for knowledge of the body is the Word made flesh. Christ reveals man to himself. In a certain sense this statement of the Second Vatican Council [*Gaudium et Spes,* 22:1] is the reply, so long awaited, which the Church has given to modern rationalism.[226]

Put negatively, John Paul II's response to Descartes is, "The body can never be reduced to mere matter." Put positively, the response is, "The richest source of knowledge of the body is the Word made flesh." What then, precisely, does the Incarnation reveal about the body according to *Gaudium et Spes,* 22:1, that long-awaited reply to Cartesian rationalism? "Truly, it is only in the mystery of the incarnate Word that the mystery of man takes on light. For Adam, the first man, was a figure of the one to come, namely, Christ the Lord. Christ, the final Adam, in the very revelation of the mystery of the Father and his love, fully reveals man to man himself and makes his supreme calling clear" (GS 22:1). There is a close connection between *Gaudium et Spes,* 22:1 and 24:3. According to GS 22:1, Christ fully reveals man to himself through the revelation of the mystery of the Father and his love. According to GS 24:3, the trinitarian exemplar of union between the divine Persons shows that man can only find himself through a sincere gift of self. These two formulations seem to aim at one and the same thing: for man to be fully revealed to himself and to find himself are at least closely connected, if not identical, though "be revealed" may have a more cognitive character, "find" a more comprehensive existential one.

---

226. John Paul II, *Letter to Families,* 19.

This close connection suggests a similarly close connection between the conditions that lead to such revelation and finding, namely, on the one hand, the revelation of the mystery of the Father and his love, and, on the other, the sincere gift of self. From the Father's love and the Trinity of Persons, through the creation of the world, all the way to the body, there is a single logic of gift. The body must be seen in these terms, in what John Paul II calls a "hermeneutics of the gift" (TOB 13:2; 16:1). In the Incarnation, Christ's body is the place of the divine redeeming gift of self. *As "the great mystery" of spousal love (Eph 5), the Incarnation shows that the meaning of the body is spousal.* All things, and in particular the body, were created in Christ and for him: Christ's gift of self is thus the goal that most deeply explains God's original intention in creating the body.

Within this overarching hermeneutics of the gift, Wojtyła develops a complementary perspective that responds to Descartes' attack on the body in terms of the philosophy of nature. In 1953, Wojtyła assembled a group of physicists to discuss the question of nature. "[Jerzy] Janik recruited the scientists who began to meet regularly with Wojtyła. Their first project was to read St. Thomas Aquinas and discuss his concept of nature against the backdrop of what they were doing in their labs and classrooms every day."[227] It would be interesting to know what the results of this dialogue were. Cartesian principles are extremely difficult to eradicate, because for most practitioners of science they have taken on the unquestionable character of the self-evident.

In Wojtyła's sexual ethics, one can see the importance of the concern for nature. The main reason why it is difficult for people in the modern age, and particularly for modern intellectuals, to understand the Catholic vision of sex, he argues, is—biology. The restricted mechanist image of nature produced by natural science, and particularly by biology, obscures our vision for the order of living nature in all its richness and therefore prevents us from understanding and living sex in its full meaning. The nature of sex has become invisible through our Cartesian glasses.

---

227. Weigel, *Witness to Hope*, 100.

The expressions "the order of nature" and "the biological order" must not be confused or regarded as identical, the "biological order" does indeed mean the same as the order of nature but only in so far as this is accessible to the methods of empirical and descriptive natural science.... This habit of confusing the order of existence with the biological order, or rather of allowing the second to obscure the first, is part of that universal empiricism which seems to weigh so heavily on the mind of modern man, and particularly on modern intellectuals, and makes it particularly difficult for them to understand the principles on which Catholic sexual morality is based. According to those principles...the sexual urge owes its objective importance to its connection with the divine work of creation of which we have been speaking, and this importance vanishes almost completely if our way of thinking is inspired only by the biological order of nature. Seen in this perspective the sexual urge is only the sum of functions undoubtedly directed, from the biological point of view, towards a biological end, that of reproduction. Now, *if man is the master of nature*, should he not mould those functions—if necessary artificially, with the help of the appropriate techniques—in whatever way he considers expedient and agreeable? *The "biological order," as a product of the human intellect* which abstracts its elements from a larger reality, *has man for its immediate author.* The claim to autonomy in one's ethical views is a short jump from this. It is otherwise with the order of nature, which means the totality of the cosmic relationships that arise among really existing entities.[228]

In this penetrating passage, Wojtyła identifies a way of thinking and seeing that is deeply hammered into the minds of children in school and reinforced daily in adults by the cultural establishment—the way of thinking and seeing defined by a mechanist form of natural science, comfortably settled in the position of the self-evident.

The power of this mentality derives in part from *hiding its nature as a way of thinking and seeing that flows from a definite choice.* It understands the world of nature, which it sees so selectively, simply as "the objective order of nature." This is why Wojtyła's observation is extremely important: *"The 'biological order', as a product of the human intellect...has man for its immediate author."* Since we constructed this "biological order" based on our ambition for power over nature, it is

---

228. Wojtyła, *Love and Responsibility*, 56–57; emphasis added. For a similar text in TOB, see 59:3.

not in the least surprising that we think we can take our place in the biological order as masters of the machine without any questions, except perhaps environmental ones. To this way of thinking, contraception and its mirror image, in vitro fertilization, seem the most "natural" things in the world.

For Wojtyła, the two orders, the order of person and of nature, are strictly united. "In the order of love a man can remain true to the person only in so far as he is true to nature. If he does violence to 'nature' he also 'violates' the person by making it an object of enjoyment rather than of love."[229] Thirty-three years later, John Paul II writes, "The natural law thus understood does not allow for any division between freedom and nature. Indeed, these two realities are harmoniously bound together, and each is intimately linked to the other."[230]

The theological point (the spousal meaning of the body in the gift of self) and the philosophical point (person and nature are intimately united) were already highlighted above as the main points of difference in the comparison between the account of sex in Kant and in John Paul II (see above, pp. 55–63). (1) In Kant's anti-trinitarian personalism of the unrelated self, spousal love plays no role. Sex is always a depersonalizing use of the person for enjoyment. (2) In Kant's Cartesian view of nature, person and nature are alienated from each other. The procreative purpose is incidental to sex. According to Wojtyła/John Paul II, the body is not alien to the person in sex. The body is deeply meaningful with a twofold meaning: unitive and procreative. These two meanings bring us to the main thesis of *Humanae Vitae,* the inseparability of the unitive and procreative meaning of the conjugal act.

b. Why *Humanae Vitae* in Particular?

In the very last catechesis (TOB 133), John Paul II points to the encyclical *Humanae Vitae* as the true focus of TOB as a whole. Although he explicitly discusses *Humanae Vitae* only at the very end, in the last fifteen catecheses, *Humanae Vitae* sets the agenda from the beginning. "It follows that this final part [that is, the explicit discus-

---

229. Wojtyła, *Love and Responsibility,* 229–30.
230. John Paul II, *Veritatis Splendor,* 50.

sion of *Humanae Vitae*] is not artificially added to the whole, but is organically and homogeneously united with it. In some sense, that part, which in the overall disposition is located at the end, is at the same time found at the beginning of that whole. This is important from the point of view of structure and method" (TOB 133:4). John Paul II calls TOB as a whole a "rereading of *Humanae Vitae*" (TOB 119:5). Why does *Humanae Vitae* have such great importance for John Paul II that he dedicates his most carefully and profoundly elaborated work to it?

The "Majority Report" of Paul VI's birth control commission (intentionally leaked to the press in 1967) is unequivocal in its support for the Baconian program, unequivocal in identifying this program with the divine will. "The story of God and of man, therefore, should be seen as a shared work. And it should be seen that man's tremendous progress in control of matter by technical means and the universal and total 'intercommunication' that has been achieved, correspond entirely to the divine decrees."[231] It would be difficult to formulate a more unqualified allegiance with the Baconian program. Technical mastery over nature corresponds *"omnino," perfectly, entirely,* to the will of God. Compare this unqualified allegiance to John Paul II's prophetic warning in *Evangelium Vitae*: "Nature itself, from being 'mater' (mother), is now reduced to being 'matter,' and is subjected to every kind of manipulation. This is the direction in which a certain technical and scientific way of thinking, prevalent in present-day culture, appears to be leading when it rejects the very idea that there is a truth of creation which must be acknowledged, or a plan of God for life which must be respected."[232]

According to the "Majority Report," one of the reasons for the legitimacy of contraception is the legitimacy of power over nature (called a "duty"). "The reasons in favor of this affirmation [contracep-

---

231. Commission on Birth Control, "Majority Report," in *The Catholic Case for Contraception,* ed. Daniel Callahan (New York: Macmillan, 1969), 150. Commission on Birth Control, "Original Latin Text of the Majority Report: Documentum Syntheticum de Moralitate Regulationis Nativitatum," in *Contrôle des naissances et théologie: Le dossier de Rome: Traduction, présentation et notes de Jean-Marie Paupert,* ed. Jean-Marie Paupert (Paris: Seuil, 1967), 179.

232. John Paul II, *Evangelium Vitae,* 22.

tion is morally legitimate] are of several kinds: social changes in matrimony and the family, especially in the role of the woman; lowering of the infant mortality rate; new bodies of knowledge in biology, psychology, sexuality and demography; a changed estimation of the value and meaning of human sexuality and of conjugal relations; *but most of all,* a better grasp of the duty of man to humanize and to bring to greater perfection for the life of man what is given in nature."[233] The superlative *"but most of all"* deserves special attention. Among all the reasons for the moral legitimacy of contraception, the *foremost* reason, the reason that is *most of all* (*"maxime"*) a reason, is not the population explosion, not a personalist understanding of sexual intercourse, but the duty of humanizing nature. Humanizing is achieved, as the first text quoted above puts it, through "tremendous progress in the control of matter by technical means."

It appears that those aligned with the majority report saw the issue of contraception as a question of aggiornamento, as bringing the Church up-to-date by embracing a new loyalty to the Baconian project. The Church's openness to the modern age, her willingness to participate in the modern project, hinges in large measure on this new loyalty. In this light, one can perhaps understand one reason for the bitterness of the reaction of many Catholics against *Humanae Vitae.* The main problem of *Humanae Vitae* is not that it fails to grapple with social changes, infant mortality, the population explosion, and a personalist understanding of sexuality. The main problem is that it rejects loyalty to the Baconian program. It is an act of treason against the newly established alliance between Catholicism and modernity.

In *Humanae Vitae,* Paul VI accurately reports the important place of the Baconian program in the debate as exemplified by the "Majority Report." He mentions the argument from "control over matter by technical means" last in a list of reasons for reconsidering contraception and qualifies it with an adverb close to the superlative, namely, *praesertim,* above all. "Finally, one should take note *above all* that man has made such stupendous progress in the domination and

---

233. Commission on Birth Control, "Majority Report," 161, emphasis added; Latin 183.

rational organization of the forces of nature that he tends to extend this domination to his own total life: that is, to the body, to the powers of his soul, to social life and even to the laws which regulate the transmission of life."[234]

John Paul II highlights the issue of power over nature in a similar way as the very heart or essence of the Catholic understanding of the transmission of life.

> What is the essence of the teaching of the Church about the transmission of life in the conjugal community, the essence of the teaching recalled for us by the Council's pastoral constitution *Gaudium et Spes* and the encyclical *Humanae Vitae* by Pope Paul VI? The problem lies in maintaining *the adequate relationship* between that which is defined as *"domination...of the forces of nature"* (HV 2), and *"self-mastery"* (HV 21), which is indispensable for the human person. Contemporary man shows the tendency of transferring the methods proper to the first sphere to those of the second. (TOB 123:1)

> *The fundamental problem* the encyclical presents is the viewpoint of the *authentic development of the human person;* such development should be measured, as a matter of principle, by the measure of ethics and not only of "technology." (TOB 133:3)[235]

This agreement between the two sides, those who opt for contraception and those who reject it, is striking. There is agreement that the Baconian project of technological mastery over nature lies at the heart of the issue of contraception. The manner in which the Catholic advocates of contraception see the nature of sexuality seems to be formed precisely by the way of seeing nature that emerged from the scientific-technological project. What a moral theologian opposed to *Humanae Vitae* writes against *Veritatis Splendor* is an eloquent witness of this deeply Cartesian formation of the mind:

> It is not easy to avoid a sense of profound anticlimax, combined with a strong suspicion that what purported to be a critique of certain moral theories was after all only one more assault against critics who find no real plausibility in certain official Catholic teachings about sex

---

234. Paul VI, *Humanae Vitae*, 2.

235. For a moral judgment about contracepted sex, of course, the central issue is the object that proximately defines the moral essence of the act rather than the more general issue of power over nature. On "the essential evil" of contracepted sex, see TOB 123:7.

and, in particular, about contraception. It is certainly true that for a great many people who take morality very seriously the mere description of a bit of human behavior as, say, "sexual intercourse with the use of a condom" is morally significant; the statement, of itself, communicates nothing to elicit moral blame, moral praise, or even moral interest. To those people, of whom I am certainly one—and one who has read and pondered countless dreary pages on this subject—it is alternately funny and sad that an official doctrine of the Catholic church holds that anything identifiable as "contraceptive practices whereby the conjugal act is intentionally rendered infertile" can be denounced as "intrinsically evil" and "gravely disordered" behavior without knowing anything at all about the motives or results of these practices in individual cases.[236]

This text expresses the main issue particularly well in the dismissive formulation, "the mere description of a bit of human behavior as, say, 'sexual intercourse with the use of a condom'…communicates nothing to elicit moral blame, moral praise, or even moral interest." Sex appears in this statement, and particularly in its dismissive tone, as it does in Kant, namely, as a process that runs its course outside the realm of the person and of meaning. It is only when further motives of the person and results considered by the person enter that the biological process takes on moral interest.

The point of view of the author of this attack on John Paul II is hardly surprising. It is the default point of view of any person raised as a child and high school student in the twentieth century. No special effort is needed to breathe in the air of Cartesian anthropological dualism. It was a strange spectacle immediately after the publication of *Humanae Vitae* that theologians who meekly submitted to the dominant Cartesian mentality were celebrated in the secular press for their enlightened and courageous freedom from Church authority.

In contrast to the dominant mentality, John Paul II sustains *Humanae Vitae* to proclaim the good news—and it is indeed good news—that the human person "also *is* a body"—not merely "*has*" a

---

236. James Gaffney, "The Pope on Proportionalism," in *John Paul II and Moral Theology*, ed. Charles E. Curran and Richard A. McCormick (New York: Paulist, 1998), 59.

body, but "*is a body—è corpo*" (see Index at BODY 1). The meaning of the human body as experienced in sexual intercourse is deeply personal. The body, endowed with its own rich intrinsic meaning, speaks the language of self-gift and fruitfulness, whether the person intends it or not, because the person "is a body." The body is not outside the person. Self-gift and fruitfulness are rooted in the very nature of the body, and therefore in the very nature of the person, because the person "is a body."

John Paul II pinpoints this anthropological issue as the key issue in a passage of *Veritatis Splendor* that directly faces moral theories like the one just quoted.

> Faced with this theory, one has to consider carefully the correct relationship existing between freedom and human nature, and in particular *the place of the human body in questions of natural law.*
>
> A freedom which claims to be absolute ends up treating the human body as a raw datum, devoid of any meaning and moral values until freedom has shaped it in accordance with its design. Consequently, human nature and the body appear as *presuppositions or preambles,* materially *necessary* for freedom to make its choice, yet extrinsic to the person, the subject and the human act. Their functions would not be able to constitute reference points for moral decisions, because the finalities of these inclinations would be merely *physical* goods, called by some "pre-moral." To refer to them, in order to find in them rational indications with regard to the order of morality, would be to expose oneself to the accusation of physicalism or biologism.
>
> In this way of thinking, the tension between freedom and a nature conceived of in a reductive way is resolved by a division within man himself.
>
> This moral theory does not correspond to the truth about man and his freedom. It contradicts the *Church's teachings on the unity of the human person,* whose rational soul is *per se et essentialiter* [through itself and essentially] the form of his body. The spiritual and immortal soul is the principle of unity of the human being, whereby it exists as a whole—*corpore et anima unus*—as a person. These definitions not only point out that the body, which has been promised the resurrection, will also share in glory. They also remind us that reason and free will are linked with all the bodily and sense faculties. *The person, including the body, is completely entrusted to himself, and it is in the unity of body and soul that the person is the subject of his own moral acts.* The person, by the light of reason and the support of virtue, discovers in

the body the anticipatory signs, the expression and the promise of the gift of self.[237]

To conclude, the purpose of the theology of the body is to defend the body against its alienation from the person in Cartesian rationalism. Put positively, the purpose is to show the divine plan for human spousal love, to show the goodness and beauty of the whole sexual sphere against its cheapening in the "objective, scientific" way of looking at nature. God's plan and its renewal by Christ, the redeemer, is imprinted deeply within the bodily nature of the person as a pre-given language of self-giving and fruitfulness. For the person to live sexuality in an authentic manner is to speak spousal love in conformity with this truth of the language of the body. True human fulfillment in the sexual sphere can be found only by following this divine plan for human love. This is why the defense of *Humanae Vitae* is so important, important for the good of the human person. *"The fundamental problem the encyclical presents is the viewpoint of the authentic development of the human person;* such development should be measured, as a matter of principle, by the measure of ethics and not only of 'technology'" (TOB 133:3).

7. Structure and Argument

Many readers feel at sea in TOB with no clear sense of where they are and where they are going. The well disposed attribute this feeling to the "cyclical," or "mystical," or "Slavic," or "phenomenological" character of TOB; the less well disposed find TOB "mind-numbingly repetitious."[238] In fact, this impression is mistaken. It is in large measure due to the omission of John Paul II's own chapter and section headings in all editions of TOB except the Polish (see above pp. 9–10). TOB has a rigorous and clear order of thought throughout. When one follows John Paul II's divisions of the work with care, the structure and main argument become transparent. The following table gives an overview of the first three levels of the structure.

237. John Paul II, *Veritatis Splendor,* 48.

238. Luke Timothy Johnson, "A Disembodied 'Theology of the Body': John Paul II on Love, Sex & Pleasure," *Commonweal,* January 26, 2001.

Overview of the Structure

PART 1: THE WORDS OF CHRIST

CHAPTER 1: CHRIST APPEALS TO THE "BEGINNING" (TOB 1–23)
1. What Is Meant by "Beginning"?
2. The Meaning of Original Solitude
3. The Meaning of Original Unity
4. The Meaning of Original Nakedness
5. Man in the Dimension of Gift
6. "Knowledge" and Procreation (Gen 4:1)
7. [Conclusion: An Integral Vision]

CHAPTER 2: CHRIST APPEALS TO THE HUMAN HEART (TOB 24–63)
1. In the Light of the Sermon on the Mount
2. The Man of Concupiscence
3. Commandment and Ethos
4. The "Heart"—Accused or Called?
5. The Ethos of the Redemption of the Body
6. Purity as "Life according to the Spirit"
7. The Gospel of the Purity of Heart—Yesterday and Today
Appendix: The Ethos of the Body in Art and Media

CHAPTER 3: CHRIST APPEALS TO THE RESURRECTION (TOB 64–86)
1. The Resurrection of the Body as a Reality of the "Future World"
2. Continence for the Kingdom of Heaven

[Conclusion of Part 1: The Redemption of the Body]

PART 2: THE SACRAMENT

CHAPTER 1: THE DIMENSION OF COVENANT AND OF GRACE
(TOB 87–102)
1. Ephesians 5:21–33
2. Sacrament and Mystery
3. Sacrament and "Redemption of the Body"

CHAPTER 2: THE DIMENSION OF SIGN (TOB 103–17)
1. "Language of the Body" and the Reality of the Sign
2. The Song of Songs
3. When the "Language of the Body" Becomes Language of the
Liturgy (Reflections on Tobit)

CHAPTER 3: HE GAVE THEM THE LAW OF LIFE AS THEIR
INHERITANCE (TOB 118–33)
1. The Ethical Problem
2. Outline of Conjugal Spirituality

[CONCLUSION]

a. The Overall Structure

The structure of a text can be understood by asking two interrelated questions, again and again on each level of division. What is the purpose of the whole? What are the main parts that serve this purpose?

As argued above, the purpose of TOB as a whole is to defend the spousal meaning of the body against the alienation between person and body in the Cartesian vision of nature. All the fundamental questions of our age—questions about the meaning of the body, about the meaning of love, about nature, technology, and progress—come together in the issue of *Humanae Vitae* as in a tight knot. In order to understand these questions, one needs "an integral vision of man." "It is precisely by moving from 'an integral vision of man and of his vocation, not only his natural and earthly, but also his supernatural and eternal vocation' (*Humanae Vitae,* 7), that Paul VI affirmed that the teaching of the Church 'is founded upon the inseparable connection, willed by God and unable to be broken by man on his own initiative, between the two meanings of the conjugal act: the unitive meaning and the procreative meaning.'"[239]

Given that the overall goal of TOB is to present an integral vision of man, how do the main parts of TOB serve this goal? In the very last catechesis, John Paul II explains the first level of division as follows: "*The first part* is devoted to the *analysis of the words of Christ,* which prove to be suitable for opening the present topic.... *The second part* of the catechesis is devoted to the *analysis of the sacrament* based on Ephesians" (TOB 133:1). "The catecheses devoted to *Humanae Vitae* constitute only one part, the final part, of those that dealt with the redemption of the body and the sacramentality of marriage" (TOB 133:4). Although these texts mention three parts, the first two parts seem to belong together. They constitute John Paul II's theoretical account of human love in the divine plan, which he calls "an adequate anthropology" (see Index at ANTHROPOLOGY). The "final part" on *Humanae Vitae* turns to the concrete moral application of this anthropology in married life, above all in the question of contraception.

---

239. John Paul II, *Familiaris Consortio,* 32.

The reflections about human love in the divine plan carried out so far would remain in some way incomplete, if we did not try to see their concrete application in the area of conjugal and familial morality. We want to take this further step, which will bring us to the conclusion of our, by now, long journey, under the guidance of an important pronouncement of the recent magisterium, the encyclical *Humanae Vitae,* which Pope Paul VI published in July 1968. We will reread this significant document in the light of the conclusions we reached when we examined the original divine plan and Christ's words referring to it. (TOB 118:1)

In this text, one can see a clear distinction between a more theoretical discussion of "human love in the divine plan" and a more practical application of this discussion, particularly to the issue of contraception.

Ciccone draws attention to another feature that sets off the part on *Humanae Vitae* from the other two. In Parts 1 and 2, John Paul II focuses on Scripture: on the words of Jesus in Part 1, and the words of Paul in Part 2, while the Final Part turns to the text of *Humanae Vitae.* "This [final part on *Humanae Vitae*] does not stand in a series with the other two. This is clear already from the formal point of view, because it does not unfold on the basis of particular biblical texts. Very fittingly, therefore, is it called, not 'Third Part,' but 'Final Part,' as the point toward which the two preceding parts are oriented and on which they converge."[240]

Ciccone's last point should be highlighted. The Final Part is not a mere appendix to a work on biblical anthropology. It is the goal that shapes Parts 1 and 2. John Paul II himself explains the importance of the Final Part.

If I draw particular attention precisely to these final catecheses, I do so not only because the topic discussed by them is more closely connected with our present age, but first of all because *it is from this theme that the questions spring* that run in some way through the whole of our reflections. It follows that this final part is not artificially added to the whole, but is organically and homogeneously united with it. In some sense, that part, which in the overall disposition is located at the end, is at the same time found at the beginning of that whole. This is

---

240. Lino Ciccone, *Uomo—Donna: L'amore umano nel piano divino: La grande Catechesi del mercoledì di Giovanni Paolo II* (Leumann Turin: Elle Di Ci, 1986), 21.

important from the point of view of structure and method. (TOB 133:4)

One understands the structure of TOB correctly if one sees that the teaching of *Humanae Vitae* is present as the form-giving goal from the very beginning. It is first in intention, even if last in execution. The title of the final part is appropriate to its character as goal: "He Gave Them the Law of Life as Their Inheritance." John Paul II does not view the teaching of *Humanae Vitae* simply as a particular moral prohibition, but as a precious inheritance from the Creator that is closely connected with fostering life as a whole.

In his own division of the text, John Paul II attaches the final part as Chapter 3 to Part 2 rather than making it separate as Part 3. The actual arrangement of a book is dictated by a variety of considerations, including those of a literary sensibility that strives for symmetry and a certain evenness of length in major divisions. Division depends not only on the logic of the argument.

What is the relation between the two parts of the theological anthropology, "The Words of Christ" and "The Sacrament"? How do they serve the overall purpose in connection with each other? John Paul II characterizes them as follows: "*The first part* is devoted to the *analysis of the words of Christ,* which prove to be suitable for opening the present topic…. *The second part* of the catechesis is devoted to the *analysis of the sacrament* based on Ephesians (Eph 5:22–33), which goes back to the biblical 'beginning' of marriage expressed in the words of Genesis, 'a man will leave his father and his mother and unite with his wife, and the two will be one flesh' (Gen 2:24)."

On one level, the relation between these two parts is that between the words of Christ and the words of Paul: "The first part is dedicated to *the analysis of Christ's words*…. The second part…[is] based on Ephesians [5]." Yet, what John Paul II emphasizes in the italicized text is not the sequence from Jesus to Paul. There is a certain asymmetry. Part 1, he insists with italics, is dedicated "to *the analysis of Christ's words.*" Part 2, he insists again with italics, "was dedicated to the *analysis of the sacrament.*" It is only after this characterization of theological content or function that he adds "based on Ephesians."

If "analysis of the sacrament" is the theological function of Part 2, what is the theological function of Part 1? The titles John Paul II gives to the whole work provide a clue. "The whole of the catecheses that I began more than four years ago and that I conclude today can be grasped under the title, 'Human Love in the Divine Plan,' or with greater precision, 'The Redemption of the Body and the Sacramentality of Marriage'" (TOB 133:1). The overall title mentions a single subject, "Human Love in the Divine Plan," while the subtitle has two parts, "The Redemption of the Body" and "The Sacramentality of Marriage." Since John Paul II says in the text quoted above that Part 2 is about "the sacramentality of marriage," one is led to assume that Part 1 is about "the redemption of the body." The Conclusion of Part 1 (TOB 86) confirms this assumption. It focuses on "the redemption of the body." At the very end of that Conclusion, John Paul II writes, "Everything we have tried to do in the course of our meditations in order to understand the words of Christ has its definitive foundation in the mystery of the redemption of the body" (TOB 86:8).

The phrase "the redemption of the body" is taken from Romans: "Not only the creation, but we ourselves, who have the first fruits of the Spirit, groan inwardly while we wait for adoption, the redemption of our bodies" (Rom 8:23). In a theology of the body, the redemption of the body is the ultimate point of arrival, the end that determines all steps. In a letter written a few months after the conclusion of TOB, John Paul II seems to apply the concept "theology of the body" particularly to Part 1. "As you know, at my weekly General Audiences during the past several years, I presented a catechetical series of talks on the theology of the human body and the sacramentality of marriage, including within it a confirmation and further analysis and development of the teaching of Paul VI contained in *Humanae Vitae*."[241] The three parts distinguished in TOB 133 are clearly visible in this text. John Paul II appears to use the phrase "the theology of the human body" to refer specifically to Part 1, followed by Part 2 on "the sacramentality of marriage," and, set off from these two, the analysis of *Humanae Vitae*.

Part 1 is in some sense already the complete theology of the body. Since the "redemption of the body" is the final end considered by a

---

241. Letter to a meeting of bishops from North and Central America and the Caribbean in Dallas, Texas (Jan. 16, 1985).

theology of the body, reflection on it implies a complete theology of the body in all its essential articulations.

> To understand all that "the redemption of the body" implies according to Romans, an authentic theology of the body is necessary. We have attempted to build one, appealing first of all to the words of Christ. The constitutive elements of the theology of the body are contained in what Christ says when he appeals to the "beginning" concerning the question of the indissolubility of marriage (see Mt 19:8), in what he says about concupiscence when he appeals to the human heart in the Sermon on the Mount (see Mt 5:28), and also in what he says when he appeals to the resurrection (see Mt 22:30). Each one of these statements contains in itself a rich content of an anthropological as well as ethical nature. Christ speaks to man—and speaks about man, who is a "body" and is created as male and female in the image and likeness of God; he speaks about man, whose heart is subjected to concupiscence; and, finally, about man, before whom the eschatological perspective of the resurrection of the body opens up. (TOB 86:4)

This text is helpful for understanding the function of Part 1. When it analyzes the three words of Jesus from the point of view of "the redemption of the body," Part 1 presents all "the constitutive elements of the theology of the body." Ciccone rightly observes, "the two expressions [*redemption of the body* and *theology of the body*] are, in fact, equivalent to each other in the language of John Paul II."[242]

If Part 1 already presents the whole theology of the body in its constitutive elements, what is left for Part 2 to add? One aspect of the complementary roles of Parts 1 and 2 has already been mentioned, namely, the transition from the words of Jesus to the words of Paul (a technique used on three further occasions in TOB, twice in Chapter 3 of Part 1 and once in Chapter 1 of Part 2). As for theological content, Part 2 deepens and unfolds Part 1. The redemption of the body is closely connected with "the spousal meaning of the body." In fact, the definitive redemption of the body is nothing other than the final and glorious realization of the spousal meaning of the body in the resurrection and beatific vision (see TOB 67–68). From the very beginning, the spousal meaning of the body is "sacramental." It is a sign that manifests and communicates holiness (see TOB 19:3–6). It signifies the covenant between God and his people, between Christ and the

---

242. Ciccone, *Uomo—Donna,* 19.

Church, and ultimately the mystery of mysteries, namely, the communion between the divine Persons in the Trinity. For this reason, after a first comprehensive account of the redemption of the body in Part 1, John Paul II deepens and unfolds this account in Part 2 by focusing on the "*sacramentum magnum*," the great mystery of love revealed in Ephesians 5. In schematic form one can thus divide TOB as a whole as follows:

> PART 1:   The three words of Christ on the redemption
> of the body (TOB 1–86)
> PART 2:   The sacramentality of marriage according to
> Ephesians 5 (TOB 87–117)
> FINAL PART: *Humanae Vitae* (TOB 118–32)

b. Alternate Structures

The Italian one-volume edition (UD) divides *Man and Woman He Created Them* into six cycles that correspond to a large extent to the six chapters in Wojtyła's book.

1. The Beginning (TOB 1–23)
2. The Redemption of the Heart (TOB 24–63)
3. The Resurrection of the Flesh (TOB 64–72)
4. Christian Virginity (TOB 73–86)
5. Christian Marriage (TOB 87–117)
6. Love and Fruitfulness (TOB 118–133)

These six cycles differ from the six chapters in Wojtyła's book in two respects. The discussion of virginity in UD is a separate cycle rather than a subsection of Chapter 3; and the book's Chapters 4 and 5 come together to form UD's Cycle 5.

The first level of division in UD's headings and table of contents is the level of the six cycles. There is no division into two parts. Yet, as the titles given by the editor of UD already indicate, there is a close relation between Cycles 4 and 5: Christian virginity and Christian marriage belong together as the two concrete states of life in which the theology of the body is lived out. On this basis, one can readily see a two-part structure in UD. The first three cycles offer a general account of Christian anthropology while the last three cycles apply this anthropology to the concrete life of Christians in the two states of life, virginity and marriage. The boundary between the two parts suggested by UD is earlier than in Wojtyła's book. It comes before the discussion of virginity rather than after it.

On the basis of UD, West divides the work in a similar way as follows. [243]

PART 1: Who Are We? Establishing an Adequate Anthropology
Cycle 1: Original Man
Cycle 2: Historical Man
Cycle 3: Eschatological Man

PART 2: How Are We to Live? Applying an Adequate Anthropology
Cycle 4: Celibacy for the Kingdom
Cycle 5: The Sacramentality of Marriage
Cycle 6: Love & Fruitfulness

This way of dividing and reading the text seems in itself legitimate; it is also backed by the considerable authority of UD. It should not be rejected, but seen as an alternate and pedagogically effective way of organizing the argument.

When one compares the two divisions, the main difference is that, in John Paul II's own division of the text, virginity is seen predominately through the lens of the resurrection as an anticipatory sign of the resurrection. In UD and West, it is predominately seen as a state of life.

Another illuminating structural proposal is offered by Pascal Ide, who divides the first part of TOB according to the four historical states of the body. [244]

PART 1: The Theology of the Body
1. The body in the state of original innocence (TOB 1–23)
2. The body in the state of sinful nature (TOB 24–43)
3. The body in the state of redeemed nature (TOB 44–63)
4. The body in the state of glorified nature (TOB 64–72)
5. Application of the state of glorified nature to continence for the kingdom of heaven (TOB 73–86)

---

243. See Christopher West, *The Theology of the Body Explained: A Commentary on John Paul II's "Gospel of the Body"* (Boston: Pauline Books & Media, 2003), 51–53.

244. See Pascal Ide, «Don et théologie du corps dans les catéchèses sur l'amour dans le plan divin,» in *Jean-Paul II face a la question de l'homme: Actes du 6ème Colloque International de la Fondation Guilé,* edited by Yves Semen (Boncourt: Guilé Foundation Press, 2004), 159–212, here 207–9.

PART 2: The Theology of Marriage
    6. General Study of the Sacrament of Marriage (TOB 87–117b)
    7. Application to the Pastoral Care of Marriage and the Family (TOB 118–133)

The strength of Ide's structural proposal is that it highlights the sequence of the four historical states of man, a sequence objectively contained in John Paul II's argument. Reaching an overall number of seven cycles is, of course, a good thing as well. The fact remains, however, that John Paul II's primary division of Part 1 is tripartite, following the three words of Jesus that are the primary expressions of a Christian theology of the body; and his primary division of Part 2 is tripartite, two chapters on the two dimensions of any sacrament (grace and sign) and the final section on *Humanae Vitae*.

UD's, West's, and Ide's readings of the structure are theologically true and pedagogically helpful. Although authors must choose a single principle of division to avoid confusion in a book's headings and table of contents, they may well intend the text to allow several ways of reading. A certain "polyphony" of structures need not and should not be eliminated.

c. The Structure in Detail

PART 1: THE WORDS OF CHRIST: If the purpose of Part 1 is to present a theology of the body in its constitutive elements, what are its main parts and how do they serve this purpose? John Paul II divides it into three chapters, each of which analyzes a different word of Jesus about the redemption of the body:

> *The first part* is devoted to the *analysis of the words of Christ,* which prove to be suitable for opening the present topic. We analyzed these words at length in the wholeness of the Gospel text: and in the course of a reflection lasting several years, it seemed right to throw into relief the three texts analyzed in the first part of the catecheses.
>
> There is first of all the text in which Christ appeals "to the beginning" in the dialogue with the Pharisees about the unity and indissolubility of marriage (see Mt 19:8; Mk 10:6–9). Continuing on, there are the words Christ spoke in the Sermon on the Mount about "concupiscence" as "adultery committed in the heart" (see Mt 5:28). Finally, there are the words transmitted by all the Synoptics in which Christ appeals to the resurrection of the body in the "other world" (see Mt 22:30; Mk 12:25; Lk 20:35–36). (TOB 133:1)

John Paul II compares these three words of Jesus to a triptych, an altarpiece with three panels that form a meaningful whole with beginning, middle, and end.

> Next to the two other important dialogues, namely, the one in which Christ appeals to the "beginning" (see Mt 19:3–9; Mk 10:2–12) and the other in which he appeals to man's innermost [being] (to the "heart") while indicating the desire and concupiscence of the flesh as a source of sin (see Mt 5:27–32), the dialogue that we propose to analyze now is, I would say, *the third component of the triptych* of Christ's own statements, the triptych of words that are essential and constitutive for the theology of the body. In this dialogue, Jesus appeals to the resurrection, thereby revealing a completely new dimension of the mystery of man. (TOB 64:1)

The triptych of words forms a whole, beginning, middle, and end, inasmuch as the first word is concerned with the beginning, with God's original plan for human love; the second with the middle, that is, human history after the fall and before the resurrection, including the present time; and the third with the end, that is, the future resurrection and the definitive fulfillment of human life in the beatific vision. In these three words, Jesus speaks about one and the same thing: God's plan for human love. He speaks about it in the original intention of the Creator (Chapter 1: Christ Appeals to the "Beginning"), in its corruption by the fall and restoration by Christ (Chapter 2: Christ Appeals to the Human Heart), and in its definitive fulfillment after the resurrection (Chapter 3: Christ Appeals to the Resurrection). The perspective of the redemption of the body unites all three chapters.

CHAPTER 1: CHRIST APPEALS TO THE "BEGINNING": The opening chapter is particularly important, because it sets the content of the other two chapters. What is to be realized by Christ's redeeming power in human history (Chapter 2) and fully realized by that same redeeming power after the resurrection (Chapter 3) is nothing other than God's original plan for human love (Chapter 1). John Paul II's famous discussion of Genesis 1–2 is part of Chapter 1. It analyzes Genesis, not simply in itself as an account of the beginning, but as a component of *Christ's* teaching about the beginning.

If the overall purpose of Chapter 1 (TOB 1–23) is the presentation of God's original plan for human love, what are the main parts of that chapter, and how do they each serve this purpose? The teaching of *Humanae Vitae* hinges on "the two meanings of the conjugal act: the unitive meaning and the procreative meaning" (HV 12). These two meanings seem to be the main structuring principle of Chapter 1. After an introduction (Section 1), John Paul II first takes up the unitive meaning (Sections 2–5) and then develops the procreative meaning organically out of the unitive as essentially implied in the spousal meaning of the body (Section 6). "The procreative meaning...is rooted in the spousal meaning of the body and comes forth organically, as it were, from it" (TOB 39:5). The conclusion of the chapter is an important discussion of the "integral vision of man" based on this spousal meaning of the body in contrast to partial visions proposed by various sciences (Section 7).

In his discussion of the unitive meaning (Sections 2–5), John Paul II first analyzes three original experiences of man: original solitude, original unity, and original nakedness without shame (Sections 2–4). The fruit of this analysis is the concept "spousal meaning of the body," the central concept of TOB as a whole, first introduced in TOB 13:1. In Section 5, "Man in the Dimension of Gift," John Paul II then formulates a comprehensive theological program that he calls "hermeneutics of the gift" within which he analyzes the concept "spousal meaning of the body," first in itself (Section 5A) and then as manifested in original innocence (Section 5B).

1. What Is Meant by "Beginning"?
2. The Meaning of Original Solitude
3. The Meaning of Original Unity
4. The Meaning of Original Nakedness
5. Man in the Dimension of Gift
    A. The Spousal Meaning of the Body
    B. The Mystery of Original Innocence
6. "Knowledge" and Procreation (Gen 4:1)
7. [Conclusion: An Integral Vision]

CHAPTER 2: CHRIST APPEALS TO THE HUMAN HEART: "You have heard that it was said, 'You shall not commit adultery.' But I say to you: Whoever looks at a woman to desire her has already committed adultery with her in his heart" (Mt 5:27–28). After an introductory section on Christ's second word (Section 1), John Paul II turns to Genesis 3 to observe the origin of sexual concupiscence and the formation of "the man of concupiscence" (Section 2). He then analyzes the three main elements of Jesus' statement one by one: the commandment against adultery, the meaning of "looking at a woman to desire her," and the meaning of "has committed adultery in his heart" (Section 3). He then steps back from the details of Jesus' word to analyze the new "ethos of the body" expressed in it. He shows that Christ does not in the first place accuse the heart, but calls it (Section 4) to live according to the ethos of the redemption of the body (Section 5) according to the Spirit who creates purity of the heart (Section 6). He concludes with an overview of the Gospel of the purity of heart (Section 7).

1. In the Light of the Sermon on the Mount
2. The Man of Concupiscence
   A. The Meaning of Original Shame
   B. Insatiability of the Union
   C. The Corruption of the Spousal Meaning of the Body
3. Commandment and Ethos
   A. It Was Said, "Do Not Commit Adultery" (Mt 5:27)
   B. "Whoever Looks to Desire..."
   C. "Has Committed Adultery in the Heart..."
4. The "Heart"—Accused or Called?
   A. Condemnation of the Body?
   B. The "Heart" under Suspicion?
   C. Eros and Ethos
5. The Ethos of the Redemption of the Body
6. Purity as "Life according to the Spirit"
7. The Gospel of the Purity of Heart—Yesterday and Today
Appendix: The Ethos of the Body in Art and Media

CHAPTER 3: CHRIST APPEALS TO THE RESURRECTION: "In the resurrection they will not marry" (Mt 22:30). John Paul II takes up the question of the resurrection and the final fulfillment of the spousal meaning of the body in the vision of God, first in the teaching of Jesus (Section 1A) and then in the teaching of Paul (Section 1B). The immediately following discussion of continence for the kingdom of heaven considers virginity as an anticipatory sign of the resurrection, first in the teaching of Jesus (Section 2A) and then in that of Paul (Section 2B). An overview of "redemption of the body" concludes Part 1.

1. The Resurrection of the Body as a Reality of the "Future World"
   A. The Synoptics: "He Is Not God of the Dead but of the Living"
   B. Pauline Interpretation of the Resurrection in 1 Corinthians 15:42–49
2. Continence for the Kingdom of Heaven
   A. The Words of Christ in Matthew 19:11–12
   B. Paul's Understanding of the Relation between Virginity and Marriage (1 Cor 7)

PART 2: THE SACRAMENT: John Paul II's discussion of the "*sacramentum magnum*," the great mystery of spousal love in Ephesians, highlights the importance of his discussion of Genesis. Ephesians itself refers back to the beginning when it describes the mystery. "Therefore a man will leave his father and his mother and unite with his wife, and the two will form one flesh. This mystery is great; I say this with reference to Christ and the Church" (Eph 5:31–32). John Paul II accordingly reads Ephesians in light of Jesus' teaching about the beginning, including Genesis 1–2. Conversely, his reading of Ephesians sheds light on his reading of Genesis in Part 1.

The principle of division in Part 2 is the distinction between the *grace* of the sacrament and the sacramental *sign* that signifies and realizes this grace.

> Given that the sacrament is the sign by means of which the saving reality of grace and the covenant is expressed and realized, we must now consider it under the aspect of sign, while the preceding reflections were devoted to the reality of grace and the covenant. (TOB 103:3)

> The reflections about the sacrament of marriage were carried out in the consideration of the *two dimensions* essential to this *sacrament* (as to every other sacrament), namely, the dimension of covenant and grace and the dimension of the sign. Through these two dimensions,

we continually went back to the reflections on the theology of the body that were linked with the key words of Christ. (TOB 133:2)

CHAPTER 1: THE DIMENSION OF COVENANT AND OF GRACE: John Paul II offers a detailed reading of Ephesians 5:21–33 (Section 1). He then steps back from the details of the text to offer a more global view of the great mystery (Section 2). In the final section (3), he explores the connections between Ephesians and Christ's words as discussed in Part 1, first from the perspective of Christ's words (Section 3A) and then from the perspective of Paul's words (Section 3B).

1. Ephesians 5:21–33
    A. Introduction and Connection
    B. Detailed Analysis
2. Sacrament and Mystery
3. Sacrament and "Redemption of the Body"
    A. The Gospel
    B. Ephesians

CHAPTER 2: THE DIMENSION OF SIGN: In order to understand the sacramental sign, John Paul II develops the concept of "language of the body" (Section 1). The sacramental sign has one focal point in the words of conjugal consent and another focal point in sexual union, in which the bodies of man and woman speak "prophetically" in the name and with the authority of God. The Song of Songs presents this erotic language of the body in its full human integrity (Section 2). This section is clearly one of the most important in the whole work. At its beginning, John Paul II says, "It seems to me that what I want to set forth in the coming weeks is the crowning, as it were, of what I have explained" (*Insegnamenti* text of the catechesis on May 23, 1984, see p. 549). In Section 3, John Paul II uses Tobit as a springboard to develop an argument about the close relationship between the language of the body in sexual union and the language of the sacrament according to Ephesians and the Church's liturgy.

1. "Language of the Body" and the Reality of the Sign
2. The Song of Songs
3. When the "Language of the Body" Becomes Language of the Liturgy (Reflections on Tobit)

FINAL PART: HUMANAE VITAE (attached as Chapter 3 to Part 2; CHAPTER 3: HE GAVE THEM THE LAW OF LIFE AS THEIR INHERITANCE): John Paul II first presents the encyclical's teaching about contraception (Section 1) and then gives a panoramic view of conjugal spirituality according to *Humanae Vitae* (Section 2).

d. The Main Argument

There is a single main argument that runs through TOB. It is enriched by many subthemes, but is in itself clear and simple. What is at stake in the teaching of *Humanae Vitae* about the inseparability of the unitive and procreative meaning of the conjugal act is nothing else than "rereading the 'language of the body' in the truth" (TOB 118:6). John Paul II develops the concepts "language of the body" and "rereading [it] in the truth" in the section on the sacrament in the dimension of sign (TOB 103–16). The whole argument preceding TOB 103 can be understood as providing the foundation on which the concept of "rereading the 'language of the body' in the truth" can be understood. The key concept in this foundation is "the spousal meaning of the body." It is this meaning that is reread in the truth when man and woman engage in authentic sexual intercourse. Let us trace this argument in more detail by looking at some of the key passages that carry it forward.

PART 1, CHAPTER 1: CHRIST APPEALS TO THE "BEGINNING": The foundation of the argument is laid in Chapter 1, in which John Paul II interprets Jesus' teaching about God's original plan for human love. The highpoint of the argument is the extensive discussion of the spousal meaning of the body in the context of a hermeneutics of the gift (TOB 13–19). In the concluding passage, John Paul II writes:

> Man appears in the visible world as the highest expression of the divine gift, because he bears within himself the inner dimension of the gift. And with it he carries into the world his particular likeness to God, with which he transcends and also rules his "visibility" in the world, his bodiliness, his masculinity or femininity, his nakedness. A reflection of this likeness is also the primordial awareness of the spousal meaning of the body pervaded by the mystery of original innocence.
>
> Thus, in this dimension, a primordial *sacrament* is constituted, understood as a *sign that* efficaciously *transmits in the visible world the*

invisible mystery hidden in God from eternity. And this is the mystery of Truth and Love, the mystery of divine life, in which man really participates. In the history of man, it is original innocence that begins this participation and is also the source of original happiness. The sacrament, as a visible sign, is constituted with man, inasmuch as he is a "body," through his "visible" masculinity and femininity. The body, in fact, and only the body, is capable of making visible what is invisible: the spiritual and the divine. It has been created to transfer into the visible reality of the world the mystery hidden from eternity in God, and thus to be a sign of it.

...Original innocence, connected with the experience of the spousal meaning of the body, is holiness itself, which permits man to express himself deeply with his own body, precisely through the "sincere gift" of self [*Gaudium et Spes,* 24:3]. Consciousness of the gift conditions in this case "the sacrament of the body": in his body as man or woman, man senses himself as a subject of holiness. (TOB 19:3–5)

The key terms of John Paul II's whole argument are brought into play in this passage: the spousal meaning of the body linked with the gift of self, and the efficacious sacramental transmission of trinitarian life by the body in its spousal meaning.

PART 1, CHAPTER 2: CHRIST APPEALS TO THE HUMAN HEART: The spousal meaning of the body is also the criterion according to which one must judge man's historical state. In this state, a battle takes place between concupiscence and the spousal meaning of the body.

The image of the concupiscence of the body that emerges from the present analysis has a clear reference to the image of the person with which we connected our earlier analyses on the subject of the spousal meaning of the body. In fact, as a person, man is "the only creature on earth which God willed for itself" and at the same time the one who "cannot fully find himself except through a sincere gift of self" (*Gaudium et Spes,* 24:3). Concupiscence in general—and the concupiscence of the body in particular—attacks precisely this "sincere gift": *it deprives man, one could say, of the dignity of the gift, which is expressed by his body through femininity and masculinity,* and in some sense "depersonalizes" man, *making him an object "for the other."* Instead of being "together with the other"—a subject in unity, or better, in the sacramental "unity of the body"—man becomes an object for man, the female for the male and vice versa. (TOB 32:4)

The problem of concupiscence is thus not that it gives an excessive importance to sex, but that it fails to give it adequate importance.

It isolates sexual pleasure from its essential context in the life of persons.

PART 1, CHAPTER 3: CHRIST APPEALS TO THE RESURRECTION: John Paul II shows the final fulfillment of God's plan for human love in the beatific vision. This end, while being last in time, is first in intention. Being first in intention, it determines everything else, including God's original plan for human love. Again "the spousal meaning of the body" is the central concept.

> The reciprocal gift of oneself to God—a gift in which man will concentrate and express all the energies of his own personal and at the same time psychosomatic subjectivity—will be the response to God's gift of self to man. In this reciprocal gift of self by man, a gift that will become completely and definitively beatifying as the response worthy of a personal subject to God's gift of self, the "virginity" or rather the virginal state of the body will manifest itself completely as the eschatological fulfillment of the "spousal" meaning of the body, as the specific sign and authentic expression of personal subjectivity as a whole. (TOB 68:3)

Again, one should take note of the importance of the "spousal meaning of the body." The ultimate fulfillment of the human person, and thus the ultimate measure of all moral acts, lies in realizing the spousal meaning of the body.

PART 2, CHAPTER 1: THE DIMENSION OF COVENANT AND OF GRACE: Part 2 moves from the teaching of Jesus to its reflection in the "great sacrament" of Ephesians 5. In his account of the grace of the sacrament, John Paul II unfolds the content of the *"magnum mysterium"* of spousal love. This is "the truth" by which the spousal meaning of the body is measured.

> The analogy of the love of spouses (or spousal love) seems *to emphasize* above all *the aspect of* God's *gift of himself* to man who is chosen "from ages" in Christ (literally, his gift of self to "Israel," to the "Church"); a gift that is in its essential character, or as gift, total (or rather "radical") and irrevocable. This gift is certainly "radical" and therefore "total."...
>
> ...The analogy of marriage, as a human reality in which spousal love is incarnated, helps in some way to *understand the mystery of grace* as an eternal reality in God and as a "historical" fruit of the redemption of humanity in Christ. Yet, we said earlier that this biblical analogy not only "explains" the mystery but also, conversely, the mystery

defines and determines the adequate way of understanding the analogy and precisely that component of it in which the biblical authors see *"the image and likeness"* of the divine mystery. Thus, the comparison of marriage (due to spousal love) with the relationship between Yahweh and Israel in the Old covenant and between Christ and the Church in the New, is at the same time decisive *for the way of understanding marriage* itself and determines this way. (TOB 95b:4–5)

In this text, John Paul II describes spousal love in agreement with St. John of the Cross as a gift of self that is radical and thus total and irrevocable. God's covenant with human beings and the gift of his grace are essentially spousal. It is by this measure of God's gift of himself in Christ that spouses must measure the spousal meaning of their bodies. The *sacramentum magnum* in its dimension of covenant and grace is thus the measure of the sacrament in the dimension of sign.

PART 2, CHAPTER 2: THE DIMENSION OF SIGN: The concept of "reading" or "rereading" the "language of the body" appears first in the section on the sacramentality of marriage in the dimension of sign.

The words, "I take you as my wife/as my husband," bear within themselves precisely that perennial and ever unique and unrepeatable "language of the body," and they place it at the same time in the context of the communion of persons. "I promise to be faithful to you always, in joy and in sorrow, in sickness and in health, and to love you and honor you all the days of my life." In this way, the perennial and ever new "language of the body" *is not only the "substratum,"* but *in some sense also the constitutive content of the communion of persons.* The persons—the man and the woman—become a reciprocal gift for each other. They become this gift in their masculinity and femininity while they discover the spousal meaning of the body and refer it reciprocally to themselves in an irreversible way: in the dimension of life as a whole. (TOB 103:5)

What should be noted in this text is that John Paul II develops the concept of "the language of the body" out of "the spousal meaning of the body."

FINAL PART: *HUMANAE VITAE* (CHAPTER 3: HE GAVE THEM THE LAW OF LIFE AS THEIR INHERITANCE): The main teaching of *Humanae Vitae*, namely, the need to respect the inseparability of the unitive and the procreative meaning of the conjugal act, is equivalent, John Paul II argues, to the need to "reread the 'language of the body' in the truth." "Nothing else is at stake here than reading the 'language of the body' in the truth, as has been said several times in the earlier biblical analyses. The moral norm, constantly taught by the Church in this sphere, recalled and reconfirmed by Paul VI in his encyclical, springs from reading the 'language of the body' *in the truth*" (TOB 118:6). "The concept of a morally right regulation of fertility is nothing other than rereading the 'language of the body' in the truth" (TOB 125:1).

The main argument of TOB is thus very simple and clear. Its first step consists in unfolding the teaching of Jesus about the spousal meaning of the body (in its three dimensions: in God's original plan "from the beginning"; in the present struggle with concupiscence; and in the future fulfillment by the resurrection). Its second step consists in observing how this spousal meaning functions in the great sacrament of love, particularly in the language of the body that is the effective sign of this sacrament. Its third step consists in showing that *Humanae Vitae* simply asks men and women to reread this language of the body in the truth. The persuasive power of the argument lies in its ability to bring the teaching of Jesus to bear on the question of the genuine development and happiness of the human person. Jesus' teaching has an *inner* persuasive power, which lies in the beauty of God's plan for human love.

e. A Guiding Star for Reading TOB

With Pascal Ide, one can condense the whole argument of TOB in the statement, "Gift expresses the essential truth of the human body."[245] There is a deep continuity between Wojtyła's point of departure in St. John of the Cross's theology of the spousal gift of self, and this core of John Paul II's argument in *Man and Woman He Created Them*. "*Aimer c'est tout donner et se donner soi-même*. To love is to give everything and to give oneself," writes St. Thérèse of Lisieux, in full agreement with her teacher St. John of the Cross and her student John Paul II.[246] Her axiom can serve as a guiding star for the voyage through TOB.

---

245. Ide, "Don et théologie du corps," 161.

246. St. Thérèse of Lisieux, *Pourquoi je t'aime, ô Marie!, Why I Love you, Mary*, stanza 22.

Three important points should be kept in mind for a correct understanding of this guiding star. First, following John Paul II, one should avoid an excessive distinction between eros and agape, between sexual fulfillment and the disinterested gift of self in the love between man and woman.[247] It would not be agape, but a slap in the face of one's spouse to say, "I give myself to you only for your own good. I am not interested in any pleasure you might give me." Erotic tension and sexual enjoyment are essential parts of spousal agape. Through such tension and enjoyment, the human body speaks the spousal gift of self in sexual intercourse.

> As ministers of a sacrament...man and woman are called *to express* the mysterious *"language" of their bodies in all the truth properly belonging to it.* Through gestures and reactions, through the whole reciprocally conditioned dynamism of tension and enjoyment—whose direct source is the body in its masculinity and femininity, the body in its action and interaction—through all this *man*, the person, "speaks." (TOB 123:4)[248]

Second, in proposing his sexual politics of radical gift, John Paul II does not cast even a shadow of suspicion on sexual intercourse as

---

247. "Fundamentally, 'love' is a single reality, but with different dimensions; at different times, one or other dimension may emerge more clearly. Yet when the two dimensions are totally cut off from one another, the result is a caricature or at least an impoverished form of love" (Pope Benedict XVI, *Deus Caritas Est*, 8). *Agapē* is the word chosen by the Septuagint and the New Testament as the general word for love. It does not, as such, have the specific meaning of "purely self-giving love." *Erōs* is used only twice in the Septuagint (Prov 7:18; 30:16), never in the New Testament. One can see the breadth of "*agapē*" in 2 Samuel 13:15. After David's son Amnon raped his half-sister Tamar, "he was seized with a very great loathing for her; indeed, his loathing was even greater than the *agapē* with which he had agapically loved her, *hyper tēn agapēn hēn ēgapēsen autēn*." The *New Revised Standard Version* translates "*agapē*" in this context correctly as "lust." "His loathing was even greater than the lust he had felt for her" (2 Sam 13:15). The meaning "purely self-giving love" that has tended to attach itself to "*agapē*" seems to be mainly the result of the repeated use of "*agapē*" for love in the New Testament, particularly in the context of discussions of God's love for us.

248. It is difficult to see how a careful reader of TOB can accuse John Paul II of giving an incomplete picture of spousal love on this point. "A more complete picture should recognize that the gift of self also involves some human fulfillment and sexual enjoyment.... The papal teaching on marriage and sexuality fails to develop or even mention the role of sexual pleasure in marriage." Curran, *Moral Theology of John Paul II*, 170–72; 187. For the many passages overlooked by Curran, see Index at Pleasure, together with cross-references.

such, on sexual pleasure as such. In this respect, his vision of the ethos of the Sermon on the Mount differs profoundly from Manichaean contempt for sex.

> The adequate interpretation of Christ's words (Mt 5:27–28) as well as the "praxis" in which the authentic *ethos* of the Sermon on the Mount is realized step by step, must be absolutely free from Manichaean elements in thought and attitude. A Manichaean attitude would have to lead to the "annihilation of the body"—if not real, then at least intentional; to a negation of the value of human sex, that is, of the masculinity and femininity of the human person; or at least to their mere "toleration" within the limits of the "need" marked off by procreation. By contrast, on the basis of Christ's words in the Sermon on the Mount, the Christian *ethos* is characterized by *a transformation of the human person's consciousness and attitudes,* both the man's and the woman's, such as to express and realize, according to the Creator's original plan, *the value of the body and of sex,* placed as they are at the service of the "communion of persons," which is the deepest substratum of human ethics and culture. While for the Manichaean mentality, the body and sexuality constitute, so to speak, an "anti-value," for Christianity, on the contrary, they always remain "a value not sufficiently appreciated." (TOB 45:3)[249]

It is clear that John Paul II sees much need for change in this area. He sees an insufficient appreciation of the goodness of sexuality among Christians. In his view, Christians suffer from this defect not because they are Christians, but because they are affected by the Cartesian vision of nature characteristic of the Modern Age and the consequent banalization of sex characteristic of the sexual revolution. One might well summarize John Paul II's judgment about the sexual revolution in this way: the sexual revolution does not sufficiently appreciate the value and beauty of sex. It deprives sex of its depth by detaching it from the spousal meaning of the body. It favors the sexual lie, in which the language of radical gift is overlaid by the contrary language of individual autonomy and the use of persons for pleasure. John Paul II clearly and frequently affirms the goodness of sexual

---

249. Again, a careful reader could hardly write, "The impression given by *The Theology of the Body* is that passion and sexual pleasure are totally suspect and in need of control. The Pope does not seem to acknowledge a fundamental goodness about sexuality, despite the ever-present danger of lust and concupiscence." Curran, *Moral Theology of John Paul II,* 170.

pleasure (see Index at PLEASURE), but he sees sexual pleasure as belonging by its deepest and innermost nature to the dynamism of radical gift between man and woman.

Third, TOB is not primarily an admonition to follow the *law* of the body, but a persuasive proclamation of the *gospel* of the body. John Paul II does not see Jesus primarily as a moralist, as teaching a high ideal of self-giving love that leaves human beings in despair about the weakness of their flesh and the failure of their attempts to measure up to ideal love. On the contrary, Jesus speaks primarily as the redeemer, who overcomes sin and opens the way for a real transformation, for life in the Spirit. He is the redeemer of the body (see Index at REDEMPTION OF THE BODY), who has the power to inscribe the law of love on hearts of flesh. "I will remove the heart of stone from their flesh and give them a heart of flesh" (Ezek 11:19). "I will write my law on their hearts" (Jer 31:33). He can demand a radical gift of self, because he himself made such a gift of himself to the human race, and his gift is effective.

> Christ's words, which flow from the divine depth of the mystery of redemption, allow us to discover and strengthen the bond that exists between the dignity of the human being (of the man or the woman) and the spousal meaning of his body. On the basis of this meaning, they allow us to understand and bring about the mature freedom of the gift, which expresses itself in one way in indissoluble marriage and in another by abstaining from marriage for the kingdom of God. On these different ways, Christ "fully reveals man to man himself and makes his supreme calling clear" (*Gaudium et Spes*, 22:1). *This vocation is inscribed in man according to his whole psycho-physical compositum precisely through the mystery of the redemption of the body* [emphasis added].
>
> Everything we have tried to do in the course of our meditations in order to understand the words of Christ has its definitive foundation in the mystery of the redemption of the body. (TOB 86:8)

In *Veritatis Splendor,* John Paul II shows the implications of the centrality of redemption for the authentic form of Christian morality.

> Jesus shows that the commandments must not be understood as a minimum limit not to be gone beyond, but rather as a path involving a moral and spiritual journey towards perfection, at the heart of which is love (cf. Col 3:14). Thus the commandment "You shall not murder" becomes a call to an attentive love which protects and promotes the life of one's neighbor. The precept prohibiting adultery becomes an

invitation to a pure way of looking at others, capable of respecting the spousal meaning of the body.... *Jesus himself is the living "fulfillment" of the law* inasmuch as he fulfills its authentic meaning by the total gift of himself: *he himself becomes a living and personal law,* who invites people to follow him; through the Spirit, he gives the grace to share his own life and love and provides the strength to bear witness to that love in personal choices and actions (cf. Jn 13:34–35).[250]

In *Man and Woman He Created Them,* John Paul II left us the core of his great vision, deeply rooted in St. John of the Cross, a vision focused on the mystery of love that reaches from the Trinity through Christ's spousal relation with the Church to the concrete bodies of men and women. The voyage through TOB is long and at times very difficult, but it will richly reward you, the reader, for your time and effort.

---

250. John Paul II, *Veritatis Splendor,* 15.

Part One

THE WORDS OF CHRIST

CHAPTER ONE

Christ Appeals to the "Beginning"

―――――――⚬―――――――

1. What Is Meant by "Beginning"?

1 *General Audience of September 5, 1979*
(Insegnamenti, 2, no. 2 [1979]: 234–36)

1. FOR SOME TIME NOW, preparations have been under way for the next ordinary assembly of the Synod of Bishops, which will take place in Rome in the fall of next year. The topic of the synod, "*De muneribus familiae christianae* (The Duties [or Role, Gifts, Tasks] of the Christian Family)," will focus our attention on this community of human and Christian life, which has been fundamental *from the beginning.* The Lord Jesus used precisely this phrase *"from the beginning"* in the dialogue about marriage reported in the Gospels of Matthew and Mark. We want to ask ourselves what this word "beginning" means. In addition, we want to clarify why Christ appealed to the "beginning" in this particular circumstance, and for this reason we offer a more precise analysis of the relevant text of Sacred Scripture.

Approaching Genesis

2. Twice during the dialogue with the Pharisees who questioned him about the indissolubility of marriage, Jesus Christ appealed to the "beginning." The dialogue took place in the following way.

> Some Pharisees came to him to test him and asked him, "Is it lawful for a man to divorce his wife for any reason?" And he answered them,

"Have you not read that from the beginning *the Creator created them
male and female* and said, *'For this reason a man will leave his father and
his mother and unite with his wife, and the two will be one flesh'*? So it is
that they are no longer two, but one flesh. Therefore, what God has
joined let man not separate." They objected, "Why then did Moses
order to give her a certificate of divorce and send her away?" Jesus
answered, "Because of the hardness of your heart Moses allowed you
to divorce your wives, *but from the beginning it was not so.*" (Mt 19:3–8)

Christ does not accept the discussion on the level on which his
interlocutors try to introduce it; in a sense, he does not approve the
dimension they tried to give the problem. He avoids entangling himself in juridical or casuistic controversies; instead, he appeals twice to
the "beginning." By doing so, he clearly refers to the relevant words of
Genesis, which his interlocutors also know by heart. From these
words of the most ancient revelation, Christ draws the conclusion and
the dialogue ends.

3. *"Beginning" signifies therefore what Genesis speaks about.* It is
thus Genesis 1:27 that Christ quotes in summary form. "From the
beginning the Creator created them male and female," while the
complete original passage reads as follows: "God created man in his
image; in the image of God he created him; male and female he created them." A little later, the Teacher appeals to Genesis 2:24: "For
this reason a man will leave his father and his mother and unite with
his wife, and the two will be one flesh." Quoting these words almost
"in extenso," as a whole, Christ gives them an even more explicit normative meaning (given that in Genesis they sound like statements of
fact, "will...will unite...they will be one flesh"). The normative meaning is plausible, because Christ does not limit himself only to the
quote itself, but adds, "So it is that they are no longer two, but one
flesh. Therefore what God has joined let man not separate." That
phrase, "let man not separate," is decisive. In the light of this word of
Christ, Genesis 2:24 states the principle of the unity and indissolubility of marriage as the very content of the word of God expressed
in the most ancient revelation.

4. One could maintain at this point that the issue is settled, that
the words of Jesus Christ confirm the eternal law formulated and
instituted by God from the "beginning" as man's creation. It could

also seem that the Teacher, by confirming this primordial law of the Creator, does nothing else than establish its proper normative meaning, appealing to the very authority of the first Legislator. Yet, that significant expression, "from the beginning," repeated twice, clearly leads the interlocutors to reflect about the way in which, in the mystery of creation, man was formed precisely as "male and female," in order to understand correctly the normative meaning of the words of Genesis. And this is no less valid for interlocutors today than for those then. For this reason, in the present study, considering all this, we must put ourselves exactly in the position of Christ's interlocutors today.

5. During the following Wednesday reflections at the general audiences, we will try, as Christ's interlocutors today, to dwell at greater length on St. Matthew's words (Mt 19:3–8). To follow the indication Christ put into them, we will try to penetrate into the "beginning," to which he appealed in such a significant way; and in this way, we will follow from afar the great work on this topic that the participants in the next Synod of Bishops are undertaking right now. Together with the bishops, many groups of pastors and lay people are participating in it who feel a particular responsibility for the tasks that Christ gives to marriage and to the Christian family; the tasks he has always given and gives also in our epoch, in the contemporary world.

The cycle of reflections we are beginning today, with the intention of continuing it during the following Wednesday meetings, has, among others, the goal *of accompanying, so to speak, from afar the work* in preparation for the synod, not, however, by directly touching its topic, but by turning attention to the deep roots from which this topic springs.

2 General Audience of September 12, 1979
(*Insegnamenti*, 2, no. 2 [1979]: 286–90)

1. LAST WEDNESDAY, WE BEGAN the cycle of reflections on the response Christ the Lord gave to his interlocutors about the question of the unity and indissolubility of marriage. The Pharisee interlocutors, as we recall, appealed to the Law of Moses; Christ, by contrast, appealed to the "beginning," by quoting the words of Genesis.

The *"beginning," in this case, is what one of the first pages of Genesis speaks about.* If we wish to analyze this reality, we must doubtless turn first of all to the text. In fact, the words Christ spoke in the dialogue with the Pharisees, which Matthew 19 and Mark 10 report to us, constitute a passage that in turn fits into a well-defined context, without which they can neither be understood nor correctly interpreted. This context is given by the words, "Have you not read that from the beginning the Creator created them male and female...?" (Mt 19:4) and refers to the so-called first account of the creation of man inserted in the cycle of the seven days of the creation of the world (Gen 1:1–2:4). By contrast, the more immediate context of Christ's other words taken from Genesis 2:24 is the so-called second account of the creation of man (Gen 2:5–25), and indirectly also Genesis 3 as a whole. The second account of the creation of man forms a conceptual and stylistic unity with the description of original innocence, of man's happiness, and also of his first fall. Given the specificity of the content expressed by Christ's words taken from Genesis 2:24, one could also include in the context at least the first sentence of Genesis 4, which deals with the conception and birth of a human being from earthly parents. We intend to do so in the present analysis.

First Account of the Creation of Man

2. *From the point of view of biblical criticism,* one should immediately recall that *the first account of the creation of man is more recent than the second.* The origin of the latter lies much further back in time. One defines this more ancient text as "Yahwist," because it uses the term "Yahweh" to name God. It is difficult not to be impressed by the fact that the image of God presented there has some rather prominent anthropomorphic features (among other things we read there, "the Lord God formed man with dust of the ground and blew into his nostrils the breath of life," Gen 2:7). In comparison with this description, the first account, that is, the one considered chronologically more recent, is much more mature both with regard to the image of God and in the formulation of the essential truths about man. This account stems from the Priestly and "Elohist" tradition, from the term "Elohim," the term it uses to name God.

3. Given that in this narrative the *creation of man* as male and female, to which Jesus appeals in his answer according to Matthew 19, is placed in the rhythm of the seven days of the creation of the world, one could attribute to it above all a cosmological character: man is created on earth together with the visible world. At the same time, however, the Creator orders him to subdue and rule the earth (Gen 1:28): he is therefore placed above the world. Although man is so strictly tied to the visible world, nevertheless the biblical narrative does not speak of his likeness with the rest of creatures, but only with God ("God created man in his image; in the image of God he created him," Gen 1:27). In the cycle of the seven days of creation, a precise step-by-step progression is evident;[1] man, by contrast, is not created according to a natural succession, but the Creator seems to halt before calling him to existence, as if he entered back into himself to make a decision, "Let us make man in our image, in our likeness" (Gen 1:27).

4. *The level of this first account of* creation, even if *it is chronologically later, has above all a theological character.* An indication of this is above all the definition of man based on his relationship with God ("in the image of God he created him"), which includes at the same time an affirmation of the absolute impossibility of reducing man to the "world." Already in the light of the Bible's first sentences, man can neither be understood nor explained in his full depth with the categories taken from the "world," that is, from the visible totality of bodies. Nevertheless, man too is a body. Genesis 1:27 establishes that this essential truth about man refers to the male as much as to the

---

1. Speaking about matter not endowed with life, the biblical author uses different predicates, such as "separated," "called," "made," "put." Speaking about beings that have the gift of life, by contrast, he uses the terms "created" and "blessed." God orders them, "Be fruitful and multiply." This order applies to both animals and human beings, indicating that bodiliness is common to them (see Gen 1:22–28).

Still, in the biblical description, the creation of man is essentially distinguished from God's earlier works. Not only is it preceded by a solemn introduction, as if it were a case of God deliberating before this important act, but above all the exceptional dignity of the human person is highlighted by "likeness" with God, whose image he or she is.

When creating matter not endowed with life, God "separated"; he orders the animals to be fruitful and multiply, but the difference of sex is underlined only in the case of man: "male and female he created them," at the same time blessing their fruitfulness, that is, the bond of the persons (Gen 1:27–28).

female: "God created man in his image...; male and female he created them."[2] One must recognize that the first account is concise, free from any trace of subjectivism: it contains only the objective fact and defines the objective reality, both when it speaks about the creation of the human being, male and female, in the image of God, and when it adds a little later the words of the first blessing, "God blessed them and said to them, 'Be fruitful and multiply, fill the earth, subdue it, and rule'" (Gen 1:28).

5. The first account of the creation of man, which, as we have observed, has a theological character, contains hidden within itself a powerful metaphysical content. One should not forget that precisely this text of Genesis has become the source of the deepest inspirations for the thinkers who have sought to understand "being" and "existing" (perhaps only Exodus 3 can be compared with this text).[3] Despite some detailed and plastic expressions in this passage, man is defined in it primarily in the dimensions of being and existing ("*esse*"). He is defined in a more metaphysical than physical way. To the mystery of his creation ("in the image of God he created him") corresponds the perspective of procreation ("be fruitful and multiply"), of coming to be in the world and in time, of "*fieri*," which is necessarily tied to the metaphysical situation of creation: of contingent being ("*contingens*"). Precisely in this metaphysical context of the description of Genesis 1, one must understand the entity of the good, that is, the aspect of

---

2. The original text says, "God created man [hāʾāḏām, collective noun: "humanity"?] in his image, in the image of God he created him, man [zāḵār, male] and woman [nᵊqēḇāh, female] he created them." Gen 1:27; John Paul II's additions.

3. "*Haec sublimis veritas* [this sublime truth]," "I am he who am" (Ex 3:14), constitutes an object of reflection for many philosophers, beginning with St. Augustine, who held that Plato must have known this text, because it seemed to him so close to his conceptions. The Augustinian doctrine of the divine "*essentialitas* [essentiality]" exercised, through Anselm, a profound influence on the theology of Richard of St. Victor, Alexander of Hales, and St. Bonaventure. "To pass from this philosophical interpretation of Exodus to that proposed by St. Thomas, one necessarily had to bridge the gap that separated 'the being of essence' from 'the being of existence.' The Thomistic proofs of the existence of God bridged it."

Different from this is the position of Meister Eckhart, who on the basis of this text attributes to God the "*puritas essendi* [purity of being]": "*est aliquid altius ente* [he is something higher than being]." See E. Gilson, *Le Thomisme* (Paris: Vrin, 1944), 122–27; E. Gilson, *History of Christian Philosophy in the Middle Ages* (London: Sheed and Ward, 1955), 810.

value. In fact, this aspect returns in the rhythm of almost all the days of creation and reaches its high point after the creation of man, "God saw everything that he had made, and indeed, it was very good" (Gen 1:31). This is why one can say with certainty that the first chapter of Genesis has formed an incontrovertible point of reference and solid basis of a metaphysics and also for an anthropology and an ethics according to which "*ens et bonum convertuntur*" [being and good are convertible]. Of course, all this has its own significance for theology as well, and above all for the theology of the body.

6. At this point, we interrupt our considerations. In a week, we will occupy ourselves with the second creation account, that is, the one that, according to biblical scholars, is chronologically earlier. The expression "theology of the body" used just now deserves a more exact explanation, but we leave it for another meeting. We must first try to enter more deeply into the passage of Genesis to which Christ appealed.

Second Account of the Creation of Man

3 *General Audience of September 19, 1979*
(Insegnamenti, 2, no. 2 [1979]: 323–27)

1. IN REFERENCE TO CHRIST'S WORDS on the subject of marriage, in which he appeals to the "beginning," we turned our attention one week ago to the first account of the creation of man in Genesis 1. Today we will go on to the second account, often defined as "Yahwist" because in it God is often called "Yahweh."

The second account of the creation of man (linked with the presentation of original innocence, original happiness, and the first fall) has by its nature a different character. Although we do not want to anticipate the details of this narrative—because we will have to recall them in later analyses—we must observe that the whole text, *in formulating the truth about man, strikes us with its typical depth*, different from that of the first chapter of Genesis. One can say that this depth is above all subjective in nature and thus in some way psychological. Chapter 2 of Genesis constitutes in some way the oldest description and record of man's self-understanding and, together with chapter 3, it is the first witness of human consciousness. By means of deeper reflection on this text—through all the archaic form of the narrative, manifesting its early mythical[4] character—we find there "*in nucleo*" almost all the elements of the analysis of man to which modern, and above all contemporary, philosophical anthropology is sensitive. One could say that Genesis 2 presents the creation of man especially in the aspect of his

---

4. While in the language of rationalism of the nineteenth century, the term "myth" indicated what is not contained in reality, the product of the imagination (Wundt), or what is irrational (Lévy-Bruhl), the twentieth century has modified the conception of myth.

L. Walk sees in myth the natural, primitive, and nonreligious philosophy; R. Otto considers it an instrument of religious knowledge; for C. G. Jung, by contrast, myth is a manifestation of the archetypes, the expression of the "collective unconscious," symbol of the inner processes.

M. Eliade discovers in myth the structure of reality that is inaccessible to rational and empirical investigation: myth, in fact, transforms the event with respect to its category and makes one able to perceive the transcendent reality; it is not only a symbol of inner processes (as Jung affirms), but an autonomous and creative act of the human spirit, by means of which revelation occurs. See M. Eliade, *Traité d'histoire des religions* (Paris, 1949), 363; *Images et symboles* (Paris, 1952), 199–235.

According to P. Tillich myth is a symbol constituted by the elements of reality to present the absolute and the transcendence of being, to which the religious act tends.

H. Schlier underlines that myth does not know historical facts and has no need of them, inasmuch as it describes what is man's cosmic destiny and that [destiny] is always similar.

According to P. Ricoeur, "Myth is something else than an explanation of the world, of history and of destiny. Myth expresses in terms of the world—that is, of the other world or the second world—the understanding that man has of himself in relation to the foundation and the limit of his existence.... It expresses in an objective language the sense that man has of his dependence on that which stands at the limit and at the origin of this world." Paul Ricoeur, *The Conflict of Interpretations: Essays in Hermeneutics* (New York: Continuum, 1989), 386–87.

"The 'Adamic' myth is the anthropological myth *par excellence;* Adam means Man. But not every myth of 'the primordial man' is an 'Adamic' myth.... Only the Adamic myth is strictly anthropological. This means that it has three characteristics.

"In the first place, the etiological myth relates the origin of evil to an *ancestor* of the human race as it is now whose condition is homogeneous with ours....

"Second characteristic: the etiological myth of Adam is the most extreme attempt to *separate* the origin of evil from the origin of the good; its intention is to set up a *radical* origin of evil distinct from the more *primordial* origin of the goodness of things.... The distinction between radical and primordial is essential to the anthropological character of the Adamic myth; it is that which makes man a *beginning* of evil in the bosom of a creation which has already had its absolute *beginning* in the creative act of God....

subjectivity. When we compare the two accounts, we reach the conviction that this subjectivity corresponds to the objective reality of man created "in the image of God." And also, this fact is—in another way—important for the theology of the body, as we shall see in the following analyses.

2. It is significant that in his response to the Pharisees, in which he appeals to the "beginning," the Christ indicates in the first place the creation of man with reference to Genesis 1:27, "From the beginning, the Creator created them male and female"; it is only after this that he quotes the text of Genesis 2:24. The words that directly describe the unity and indissolubility of marriage are found *in the immediate context of the second creation account,* the characteristic feature of which is the separate creation of woman (see Gen 2:18–23), while the account of the creation of the first man (male) is found in Genesis 2:5–7. The Bible calls this first human being "man," (ʾāḏām), while from the moment of the creation of the first woman, it begins to call him "male," ʾîš, in relation to ʾiššāh ("woman," because she has been taken from the male = ʾîš).[5] And it is also significant that, when

---

"Finally—third characteristic—the Adamic myth subordinates to the central figure of the primordial man some other figures which tend to decentralize the story, but without suppressing the primacy of the Adamic figure." Paul Ricoeur, *The Symbolism of Evil* (San Francisco: Harper & Row, 1967): 232–34.

"The myth, in naming Adam, man, makes explicit the concrete universality of human evil; the spirit of repentance gives to itself, in the Adamic myth, the symbol of that universality. Thus we find again what we have called the universalizing function of myth. But at the same time we find the other two functions likewise evoked by the experience of repentance.... The proto-historical myth thus served not only to generalize the experience of Israel, applying it to all mankind, at all times and in all places, but also *to extend* to all mankind *the great tension between condemnation and mercy* that the teaching of the prophets had revealed in the particular destiny of Israel.

"Finally, there is the last function of the myth as it was motivated in the faith of Israel: the myth prepares the way for speculation by exploring the point of rupture between the ontological and the historical." Ibid., 241–42.

5. [Translator's note: ʾîš and ʾiššāh are pronounced eesh and eeshsha, with accent on the last syllable.] As far as the etymology is concerned, it is not excluded that the Hebrew ʾîš derives from a root that signifies "force" (ʾyš or ʾwš); ʾiššāh, by contrast, is tied to a series of Semitic terms whose meaning varies between "woman" and "wife."

The etymology proposed by the biblical text is popular in character and serves to underline the unity of the origin of man and woman; this seems confirmed by the assonance of the two words.

he appeals to Genesis 2:24, *Christ not only links the "beginning" with the mystery of creation, but also leads us to the boundary, so to speak, between man's primeval innocence and original sin.* The second description of the creation of man in Genesis is situated precisely in this context. There we read first of all, "With the rib that the Lord God had taken from the man he formed a woman and brought her to the man. Then the man said, 'This time she is flesh from my flesh and bone from my bones. She will be called woman because from man has she been taken'" (Gen 2:22–23). "For this reason a man will leave his father and his mother and unite with his wife, and the two will be one flesh" (Gen 2:24).

"Now both were naked, the man and his wife, but they did not feel shame" (Gen 2:25).

3. Then, immediately after these verses, Genesis 3 begins the account of the first fall of the man and the woman, linked with the mysterious tree that before this had already been called "the tree of the knowledge of good and evil" (Gen 2:17). A completely new situation thereby emerges, essentially different from the one before it. The tree of the knowledge of good and evil is a boundary line between the two original situations about which Genesis speaks. The first situation is that of original innocence in which man (male and female) finds himself, as it were, outside of the knowledge of good and evil, until the moment in which he transgresses the Creator's prohibition and eats the fruit of the tree of knowledge. The second situation, by contrast, is that in which man, after having transgressed the Creator's command at the suggestion of the evil spirit symbolized by the serpent, finds himself in some way within the knowledge of good and evil. This second situation determines the state of human sinfulness, contrasting with the state of primeval innocence.

Although the Yahwist text as a whole is very concise, it is sufficient for distinguishing and *contrasting these two original situations.* We are speaking of situations here, having before our eyes an account that is a description of events. Nevertheless, through this description and all its particulars, the essential difference *between the state of man's sinfulness and that of his original innocence* becomes clear.[6] In these two

---

6. "Religious language itself requires the transposition from 'images' or rather 'figurative modes' to 'conceptual modes' of expression.

antithetical situations, systematic theology was to see two different states of human nature, "*status naturae integrae*" (state of integral nature) and "*status naturae lapsae*" (state of fallen nature). All of this emerges from the Yahwist text of Genesis 2 and 3, which contains in itself the most ancient word of revelation and evidently has a fundamental significance for the theology of man and the theology of the body.

The Perspective of the "Redemption of the Body" (Rom 8:23)

4. When Christ, appealing to the "beginning," directs the attention of his interlocutors to the words written in Genesis 2:24, he orders them in some sense to pass beyond the boundary that runs, in the Yahwist text of Genesis, between man's first and second situation. He does not approve what Moses had allowed "because of hardness of...heart" and appeals to the words of the first divine order, expressly linked in this text with man's state of original innocence. This means that this order has not lost its force, although man has lost his primeval innocence. *Christ's answer* is decisive and clear. For this reason, *we must draw the normative conclusions from it,* which have an

---

"At first sight this transposition may seem to be merely an *extrinsic* change, I mean, one superimposed from the outside. Figurative language seems compelled to take the route of the concept for a reason which is peculiar to Western culture. In this culture, religious language has always been exposed to another language, that of philosophy, which is the conceptual language *par excellence.*... If it is true that a religious vocabulary is understood only within an interpreting community and according to a tradition of interpretation, it is also true that there exists no tradition of interpretation which is not 'mediated' by some philosophical conception.

"Thus the word 'God,' which in Biblical texts receives its meaning from the *convergence* of several modes of discourse (narratives and prophecies, legislative texts and wisdom literature, proverbs and hymns)—as both the intersection point and the horizon which escapes each and every form—had to be absorbed into the conceptual space, to be reinterpreted in terms of the philosophical Absolute, as prime mover, first cause, *Actus Essendi,* Perfect Being, etc. Hence our concept of God belongs to an ontotheology, within which it keeps organizing the entire constellation of the key-words of theological semantics, but within a framework of meanings prescribed by metaphysics." Paul Ricoeur, "Biblical Hermeneutics," *Semeia* 4 (1975): 29–145, here 129–30.

The question, whether the metaphysical reduction really expresses the content which the symbolic and metaphysical language conceals within itself, is another matter.

essential significance not only for ethics, but above all for the theology of man and the theology of the body, which, as a particular aspect of theological anthropology, is constituted on the foundation of the word of God who reveals himself. We will try to draw such conclusions in the next meeting.

4 General Audience of September 26, 1979
(*Insegnamenti*, 2, no. 2 [1979]: 378–82)

1. WHEN CHRIST RESPONDS TO THE QUESTION about the unity and indissolubility of marriage, he appeals to the words of Genesis about the subject of marriage. In our two foregoing reflections, we analyzed both the so-called Elohist text (Gen 1) and the Yahwist text (Gen 2). Today we want to draw some conclusions from these analyses.

When Christ appeals to the "beginning," he asks his interlocutors to go in some way beyond the boundary running in Genesis between the state of original innocence and the state of sinfulness that began with the original fall.

Symbolically, this boundary can be linked with the tree of the knowledge of good and evil, which delimits two diametrically opposed situations in the Yahwist text: the situation of original innocence and that of original sin. These situations have their own dimension in man, in his innermost [being], knowledge, consciousness, choice, and decision, and all of this in a relationship with God, the Creator, who, in the Yahwist text (Gen 2–3), is at the same time the God of the covenant, of the most ancient covenant of the Creator with his creature, that is, with man. The tree of the knowledge of good and evil, as an expression and symbol of the covenant with God broken in man's heart, marks out two diametrically opposed situations and sets them against each other: that of original innocence and that of original sin, together with man's hereditary sinfulness deriving from it. Yet, *Christ's words*, which appeal to the "beginning," *allow us to find an essential continuity in man and a link* between these two different states or dimensions of the human being. The state of sin is part of "historical man," of the human beings about whom we read in Matthew 19, that is, of Christ's interlocutors then, as well as of every other potential or actual interlocutor at all times of history and thus, of course, also of man today. Yet, in every man without exception, this state—the "historical" state—plunges its roots deeply into his theological "prehistory," which is the state of original innocence.

2. It is not a question of mere dialectic. The laws of knowing correspond to those of being. It is impossible to understand the state of "historical" sinfulness without referring or appealing to the state of original (in some sense "prehistoric") and fundamental innocence (and in fact Christ appeals to it). The emergence of sinfulness as a state, as a dimension of human existence, has thus from the beginning been linked with man's real innocence as an original and fundamental state, as a dimension of being created "in the image of God." And this point applies not only to the case of the first man, male and female, as "*dramatis personae*" and protagonists of the events described in the Yahwist text of Genesis 2 and 3, but also to the entire historical course of human existence. *Thus, historical man is rooted, so to speak, in his revealed theological prehistory;* and for this reason, every point of his historical sinfulness must be explained (both in the case of the soul and of the body) with reference to original innocence. One can say that this reference is a "co-inheritance" of sin, and precisely of original sin. While in every historical man this sin signifies a state of lost grace, it also carries with itself a reference to that grace, which was precisely the grace of original innocence.

3. When Christ, according to Matthew 19, appeals to the "beginning," he does not point only to the state of original innocence as a lost horizon of human existence in history. To the words that he speaks with his own lips, we have the right to attribute at the same time the whole eloquence of the mystery of redemption. In fact, already in the context of the same Yahwist text of Genesis 2 and 3, we witness the moment in which man, male and female, after having broken the original covenant with his Creator, receives the first promise of redemption in the words of the so-called Protoevangelium in Genesis 3:15[7] and begins to live *in the theological perspective of redemp-*

---

7. Already the Greek translation of the Old Testament, the Septuagint, which goes back to about the second century B.C., interprets Genesis 3:15 in the messianic sense, using the masculine pronoun *autos* in reference to the neuter Greek noun *sperma* [seed] (*semen* in the Vulgate). Jewish tradition continues this interpretation.

tion. Thus, "historical" man—both Christ's interlocutors then, about whom Matthew 19 speaks, and human beings today—participates in this perspective. He participates not only *in the history of human sinfulness,* as a hereditary, and at the same time personal and unrepeatable, subject of this history, but he also participates *in the history of salvation,* here too as its subject and co-creator. He is thus not merely shut out from original innocence due to his sinfulness, but also at the same time open to the mystery of the redemption realized in Christ and through Christ. Paul, the author of the Letter to the Romans, expresses this perspective of redemption, in which "historical" man lives, when he writes, "We ourselves, who have the first fruits of the Spirit, groan inwardly while we wait for...the redemption of our bodies" (Rom 8:23). We cannot forget this perspective as we follow the words of Christ, who, in his dialogue on the indissolubility of marriage, appeals to the "beginning." If that "beginning" indicated only the creation of man as "male and female," if—as we already mentioned—Christ only led his interlocutors across the boundary of man's state of sin to original innocence and did not open at the same time the perspective of a "redemption of the body," his answer would not at all be understood adequately. Precisely this *perspective of the redemption of the body guarantees the continuity and the unity* between man's hereditary state of sin and his original innocence, although within history this innocence has been irremediably lost by him. It is also evident that Christ, most of all, has the right to answer the ques-

---

Christian exegesis, beginning with St. Irenaeus (*Adv. Haer.* III, 23, 7), sees this text as the "Protoevangelium [first gospel]," which tells in advance the victory over Satan won by Jesus Christ. Although in the last centuries Scripture scholars interpreted this passage in different ways, and some have taken a stand against the messianic interpretation, nevertheless, in recent years there has been a return to that interpretation under a rather different aspect. In fact, the Yahwist author unites prehistory with the history of Israel, a history that reaches its high point in the messianic dynasty of David, which will bring the promises of Genesis 3:15 to fulfillment (see 2 Sam 7:12).

The New Testament illustrated the fulfillment of the promise in the same messianic perspective: Jesus is the Messiah descended from David (Rom 1:3; 2 Tim 2:8), born from woman (Gal 4:4), the new Adam-David (1 Cor:15) who must reign "until he has put all his enemies under his feet" (1 Cor 15:25). And finally, it presents the final fulfillment of the prophecy of Gen 3:15 (Rev 12:1–10), which, though it is not a clear and immediate foretelling of Jesus as the Messiah of Israel, nevertheless leads to him through the royal and messianic tradition that unites the Old and the New Testament.

tion presented to him by the teachers of the law and of the covenant (as we read in Matthew 19 and Mark 10) in the perspective of the redemption on which the covenant itself rests.

4. When, in the context of the theology of bodily man substantially delineated in this way, we reflect about the *method* of further analyses of the revelation of the "beginning," in which the appeal to the first chapters of Genesis is essential, we must immediately turn our attention to a factor that is particularly important for theological interpretation—important, because it consists in the relation between revelation and experience. In the interpretation of the revelation about man, and above all about the body, we must, for understandable reasons, appeal to experience, because bodily man is perceived by us above all in experience. In the light of the fundamental considerations just mentioned, we have every right to be convinced that this "historical" experience of ours must in some way stop at the threshold of man's original innocence, because it remains inadequate to it. Yet, in the light of the same introductory considerations, we must reach the conviction that in this case, *our human experience is in some way a legitimate means for theological interpretation* and that, in a certain sense, it is an indispensable point of reference to which we must appeal in the interpretation of the "beginning." A more detailed analysis of the text will allow us to have a clearer view of it.

5. It seems that the words of Romans 8:23 just quoted best express the direction of our research centered on the revelation of that "beginning" to which Christ appealed in his dialogue about the indissolubility of marriage (Mt 19; Mk 10). All our further analyses, also based on the first chapters of Genesis, will almost necessarily reflect the truth of the Pauline words, "We ourselves, who have the first fruits of the Spirit, groan inwardly while we wait for...the redemption of our bodies." If we place ourselves in this position—so profoundly in harmony with experience[8]—the "beginning" must speak to us with

---

8. When we speak here about the relationship between "experience" and "revelation," indeed about a surprising convergence between them, we only wish to observe that man, in his present state of existence in the body, experiences many limits, sufferings, passions, weaknesses, and finally death itself, which relates his existence at the same time to another and different state or dimension. When St. Paul speaks about

the great wealth of light that comes from revelation, to which, above all, theology desires to respond. The continuation of the analyses will explain for us why and in what sense this must be a theology of the body.

2. The Meaning of Original Solitude

5 *General Audience of October 10, 1979*
(Insegnamenti, 2, no. 2 [1979]: 712–16)

1. IN THE LAST REFLECTION of the present cycle, we drew a preliminary conclusion from Genesis about man's creation as male and female. The Lord Jesus appealed to these words, that is, to the "beginning," in his dialogue about the indissolubility of marriage (see Mt 19:3–9; Mk 10:1–12). However, the conclusion we drew does not yet put an end to the series of our analyses. In fact, we must reread the narratives of Genesis 1 and 2 in a wider context, which will allow us to establish a series of meanings of the ancient text to which Christ appealed. Today, accordingly, we will reflect *on the meaning of man's original solitude.*

A Twofold Context

2. The following words of Genesis directly give us the point of departure for such a reflection: "It is not good that the man" (male) "should be alone; I want to make him a help similar to himself" (Gen

---

the "redemption of the body," he speaks with the language of revelation; experience is not, in fact, able to grasp this content or rather reality. At the same time, within this content as a whole, the author of Romans 8:23 takes up everything that is offered to him, to him as much as in some way to every man (independent of his relationship with revelation), through the experience of human existence, which is an existence in the body.

We therefore have the right to speak about the relationship between experience and revelation; in fact, we have the right to raise the issue of their relation to each other, even if many think that a line of total antithesis and radical antinomy passes between them. This line, in their opinion, must certainly be drawn between faith and science, between theology and philosophy. In formulating this point of view, they consider quite abstract concepts rather than the human person as a living subject.

2:18). It is God-Yahweh who speaks these words. They are part of the second account of the creation of man and thus come from the Yahwist tradition. As we already recalled above, it is significant that in the Yahwist text the account of the creation of man (male) is a passage by itself (see Gen 2:7) that comes before the account of the creation of the first woman (see Gen 2:21–22). It is further significant that the first man (ʾādām), created from the "dust of the ground," is defined as "male" (ʾîš) only after the creation of the first woman. Thus, when God-Yahweh speaks the words about solitude, he refers with them to the solitude of "man" as such and not only to that of the male.[9]

It is difficult, however, merely based on this fact, to draw far-reaching conclusions. Nevertheless, the complete context of this solitude, about which Genesis 2:18 speaks, can convince us that here we are dealing with the solitude of "man" (male and female) and not only with the solitude of the man-male, caused by the absence of the woman. It seems, therefore, on the basis of the whole context, that this *solitude has two meanings: one deriving from man's very nature,* that is, from his humanity (and this is evident in the account of Genesis 2), and *the other deriving from the relationship between male and female,* and in some way, this is evident on the basis of the first meaning. A detailed analysis of the description seems to confirm it.

3. The problem of solitude shows itself only in the context of the second account of the creation of man. The first account does not mention this problem. There, man is created in a single act as "male and female," ("God created man in his image...male and female he created them," Gen 1:27). The second account—which, as we have already mentioned, speaks first about the creation of man and only afterward about the creation of woman from the "rib" of the male—concentrates our attention on the fact that "man is alone," and this

---

9. The Hebrew text constantly calls the first man hāʾādām, while the term ʾîš (male) is introduced only when the contrast with ʾiššāh (woman) emerges.

Man was thus solitary even without reference to sex.

In the translation in some European languages it is, however, difficult to express this concept of Genesis, because "human being" and "male" are usually named by the same word: "*homo,*" "*uomo,*" "*homme,*" "*hombre,*" "man."

turns out to be a fundamental anthropological issue that is in some way prior to the issue raised by the fact that man is male and female. This issue is prior, not only in the chronological sense, but rather in the existential sense: it is prior "by its very nature." This is how the issue of man's solitude will appear from the point of view of the theology of the body, if we are able to carry out a deeper analysis of the second creation account in Genesis 2.

Man in Search of His Essence

4. The statement of God-Yahweh "It is not good that the man should be alone" appears not only in the immediate context of the decision to create the woman ("I want to make him a help similar to himself"), but also in the wider context of motives and circumstances *that explain more deeply the meaning of man's original solitude.* The Yahwist texts links the creation of man above all with the need to "cultivate the ground" (Gen 2:5), and this would seem to correspond to the call to subdue and rule the earth found in the first account (see Gen 1:28). After this, the second creation account speaks about placing man in the "garden in Eden" and in this way introduces us to the state of his original happiness. Up to this moment, man is the object of the creative action of God-Yahweh, who at the same time, as Legislator, sets the conditions of the first covenant with man. Already this divine act underlines man's subjectivity. Subjectivity finds a further expression when the Lord God "formed every kind of animal of the field and all the birds of the air and brought them to the man" (male) "to see what he would call them" (Gen 2:19). Thus, the first meaning of man's original solitude is defined based on a specific "test" or on an examination that man undergoes before God (and in some way also before himself). Through this "test," man gains the consciousness of his own superiority, that is, that he cannot be put on a par with any other species of living beings on the earth.

In fact, as the text says, "whatever the man called every living creature, that was to be its name" (Gen 2:19). "In this way, the man gave names to all cattle, and to the birds of the air, and to every animal of the field; but the man" (male) "did not find a help similar to himself" (Gen 2:19–20).

5. This whole part of the text is undoubtedly a preparation for the account of the creation of woman. Nevertheless, it also has its own deep meaning independently of this creation. Thus, *the created man* finds himself from the first moment of his existence *before God* in search of his own being, as it were; one could say, in search of his own definition; today one would say, in search of his own "identity." The observation that man "is alone" in the midst of the visible world and, in particular, among living beings, has a negative meaning in this search, inasmuch as it expresses what man "is not." Nevertheless, the observation that he cannot identify himself essentially with the visible world of the other living beings (*animalia*) has, at the same time, a positive aspect for this primary search: even if this observation is not yet a complete definition, it nevertheless constitutes one of its elements. If we accept the Aristotelian tradition in logic and anthropology, one would have to define this element as the "proximate genus" ("*genus proximum*").[10]

6. The Yahwist text allows us, however, to discover also further elements of this admirable passage, in which man finds himself alone

---

10. "An *essential* (quidditive) definition is a statement that explains *the essence or nature* of things.

"It will be essential when we can define a thing by its *proximate genus* and *specific differentia*.

"The *proximate genus* includes within its comprehension all the essential elements of the genera above it and therefore includes all the beings that are cognate or similar in nature to the thing that is being defined; the *specific differentia*, on the other hand, brings in the distinctive element which separates this thing from all others of a similar nature, by showing in what manner it is different from all others, with which it might be erroneously identified.

"'Man' is defined as a 'rational animal'; 'animal' is his proximate genus, 'rational' is his specific differentia. The proximate genus 'animal' includes within its comprehension all the essential elements of the genera above it, because an animal is a 'sentient, living material substance.' ...The specific differentia 'rational' is the one distinctive essential element which distinguishes 'man' from every other 'animal.' It therefore makes him a species of his own and separates him from every other 'animal' and every other genus above animal, including plants, inanimate bodies, and substance.

"Furthermore, since the specific differentia is the distinctive element in the essence of man, it includes all the characteristic 'properties,' which lie in the nature of man *as man*, namely, power of speech, morality, government, religion, immortality, etc., realities which are absent in all other beings in this physical world." C. N. Bittle, *The Science of Correct Thinking, Logic*, 12th ed. (Milwaukee: Bruce, 1947), 73–74.

before God, above all to express, through a first self-definition, his own self-knowledge as the first and fundamental manifestation of humanity. Self-knowledge goes hand in hand with knowledge of the world, of all visible creatures, of all living beings to which man has given their names to affirm his own dissimilarity before them. Thus, consciousness reveals man as the one who *possesses the power of knowing* with respect to *the visible world*. With this knowledge, which makes him go in some way outside of his own being, *man* at the same time *reveals himself to himself in all the distinctiveness of his being*. He is not only essentially and subjectively alone. In fact, solitude also signifies man's subjectivity, which constitutes itself through self-knowledge. Man is alone because he is "different" from the visible world, from the world of living beings. When we analyze the text of Genesis, we are in some way witnesses of how man, with the first act of self-consciousness, "distinguishes himself" before God-Yahweh from the whole world of living beings (*animalia*), how he consequently reveals himself to himself and at the same time affirms himself in the visible world as a "person." That process of seeking a definition of himself, sketched so incisively in Genesis 2:19–20, leads not only—attaching ourselves again to the Aristotelian tradition—to indicating the "*genus proximum*," expressed in Genesis 2 with the words "gave the name" (to which corresponds the *specific "differentia*," which according to Aristotle's definition is *nous, zōon noētikon*). This process also leads to *the first delineation* of the human being *as* a human *person*, with the proper subjectivity that characterizes the person.

Here we interrupt the analysis of the meaning of man's original solitude. We will take it up again in a week.

Solitude and Subjectivity

6 *General Audience of October 24, 1979*
(Insegnamenti, 2, no. 2 [1979]: 841–44)

1. IN THE LAST CONVERSATION, WE BEGAN to analyze the meaning of man's original solitude. The starting point was given to us by the Yahwist text and in particular by the following words: "It is not good that the man should be alone; I want to make him a help similar to himself" (Gen 2:18). The analysis of the pertinent passages of Genesis

(see Gen 2) has brought us to surprising conclusions with regard to anthropology, that is, the fundamental science about man, contained in this book. In fact, in relatively few sentences, the ancient text sketches man as a *person with the subjectivity characterizing the person.*

When God-Yahweh gives to the first man, formed in this way, the commandment concerning all the trees that grow in the "garden in Eden," above all the tree of the knowledge of good and evil, this adds the aspect of choice and self-determination (that is, of free will) to the outline of man described above. In this way, man's image as a person endowed with his own subjectivity appears before us as finished in its first sketch.

The concept of original solitude includes both self-consciousness and self-determination. The fact that man is "alone" contains within itself this ontological structure, and at the same time, it indicates authentic understanding. Without this, we cannot correctly understand the next words, which constitute the prelude to the creation of the first woman, "I want to make a help." Above all, however, without that deep meaning of man's original solitude, one cannot understand and correctly interpret the whole situation of man, created in the image of God, which is the situation of the first, in fact primeval, covenant with God.

2. This man, about whom the account of the first chapter says that he has been created "in the image of God," is manifested in the second account *as a subject of the covenant,* that is, a subject constituted as a person, constituted according to the measure of *"partner of the Absolute,"* inasmuch as he must consciously discern and choose between good and evil, between life and death. The words of the first command of God-Yahweh (Gen 2:16–17), which speak directly about the submission and dependence of man-creature on his Creator, indirectly reveal precisely this level of humanity as subject of the covenant and "partner of the Absolute." *Man is "alone": this is to say that through his own humanity,* through what he is, he is at the same time set into a *unique, exclusive, and unrepeatable relationship with God himself.* The anthropological definition contained in the Yahwist text in its own way approaches the theological definition of man that we find in the first creation account ("Let us make man in our image and our likeness," Gen 1:26).

Solitude and the Meaning of the Body

3. Man, formed in this way, belongs to the visible world; he is a body among bodies. Taking up again and in some way reconstructing the meaning of original solitude, we apply it to man in his totality. The body, by which man shares in the visible created world, makes him at the same time aware of being "alone." Otherwise he would not have been able to arrive at this conviction, which in fact he reached (as we read in Gen 2:20), if his body had not helped him to understand it, making the matter evident to him. The awareness of solitude could have been shattered precisely because of the body itself. Basing himself on the experience of his own body, the man (ʾāḏām) could have reached the conclusion that he is substantially similar to the other living beings (*animalia*). By contrast, as we read, he did not arrive at this conclusion, but in fact reached the conviction that he was "alone." The Yahwist text never speaks directly about the body; even when it says, "the Lord God formed man with dust of the ground," it speaks about man and not the body. Nevertheless, the account taken as a whole offers us sufficient bases to perceive this man, created in the visible world, precisely as body among bodies.

The analysis of the Yahwist test will allow us, further, to *link man's original solitude with the awareness of the body*, through which man distinguishes himself from all the *animalia* and "separates himself" from them, and *through which* he is a *person*. One can affirm with certainty that man thus formed has at the same time the awareness and consciousness of the meaning of his own body. Moreover, [he has] this based on the experience of original solitude.

4. All of this can be considered an implication of the second account of the creation of man, and the analysis of the text allows us to develop it amply.

When at the beginning of the Yahwist text, even before it speaks about the creation of man from "dust of the ground," we read, "no one tilled the ground and made the water of the channels rise from the earth to irrigate the whole soil" (Gen 2:5), we rightly associate this passage with the one from the first account in which the divine commandment is expressed, "Fill the earth, subdue it, and rule" (Gen 1:28). The second account alludes in an explicit way *to the work man does* to cultivate the earth. One finds the first fundamental means for ruling the earth in man himself. Man can rule the earth, because only he—and none of the other living beings—is able to "cultivate" and transform it according to his own needs ("he made the water of the channels rise from the earth to irrigate the soil"). This first sketch of a specifically human activity seems to be part of man's definition as it emerges from the analysis of the Yahwist text. As a result, one can affirm that this sketch is intrinsic to the meaning of original solitude and belongs *to that dimension of solitude through which man has from the beginning been in the visible world as a body among bodies and discovers the meaning of his own bodiliness.*

We will return to this subject in the next meditation.

7 General Audience of October 31, 1979
(*Insegnamenti*, 2, no. 2 [1979]: 1007–10)

1. TODAY WE SHOULD RETURN ONCE MORE to the meaning of man's original solitude, which emerges above all from the analysis of the so-called Yahwist text of Genesis 2. The biblical text allows us, as we have already noted in earlier reflections, to throw into relief not only consciousness of the human body (man is created in the visible world as "a body among bodies"), but also that of the body's own meaning.

Taking into account the great conciseness of the biblical texts, admittedly one cannot extend this implication too far. It is certain, however, that here we touch the central problem of anthropology. Consciousness of the body seems to be identical in this case with the discovery of the complexity of one's own structure, which in the end, based on a philosophical anthropology, consists in the relation between soul and body. The Yahwist account expresses this complexity with its own language (that is, with its own terminology) by saying, "The Lord God formed man with dust of the ground and blew into his nostrils the breath of life and man became a living being" (Gen 2:7).[11] Moreover, precisely this man, a "living being," distinguishes himself continually from all other living beings of the visible world.

---

11. Biblical anthropology distinguishes in man not so much "body" and "soul," but rather "body" and "life."

Here the biblical author represents the conferral of the gift of life by the "breath," which does not cease to be the property of God: when God takes it back, man returns to the dust from which he was taken (see Job 34:14–15; Ps 104:29–30).

The premise of this self-distinction on man's part is the fact that only he is able to "cultivate the earth" (see Gen 2:5) and to "subdue it" (Gen 1:28). One can say that from the very beginning the awareness of "superiority" inscribed in the definition of humanity has originated in a typically human praxis or behavior. This awareness brings with it a particular perception of the meaning of one's own body, which emerges precisely from the fact that it is man's task to "cultivate the earth" and to "subdue" it. All of this would be impossible without the typically human intuition of the meaning of one's own body.

2. It seems therefore that we should speak primarily about this aspect, rather than about the problem of anthropological complexity in the metaphysical sense. If the original description of human consciousness reported by the Yahwist text includes also the body in the whole account, if it contains, as it were, the first witness of the discovery of one's own bodiliness (and even, as we said, the perception of the meaning of one's own body), all of this reveals itself not on the basis of some primordial metaphysical analysis, but on the basis of man's sufficiently clear concrete subjectivity. Man is a subject not only by his self-consciousness and by self-determination, but also based on his own body. *The structure of this body is such that it permits him to be the author of genuinely human activity.* In this activity, the body expresses the person. It is thus, in all its materiality ("he formed man with dust of the ground"), penetrable and transparent, as it were, in such a way as to make it clear who man is (and who he ought to be) thanks to the structure of his consciousness and self-determination. On this rests the fundamental perception of the meaning of one's own body, which one cannot fail to discover when analyzing man's original solitude.

The Alternative between Death and Immortality

3. And so with this fundamental understanding of the meaning of his own body, as the subject of the ancient covenant with the Creator, man is placed in front of the mystery of the tree of knowledge: "You may eat of every tree of the garden, but of the tree of the knowledge of good and evil you shall not eat, for when you eat of it you shall certainly die" (Gen 2:16–17). The original meaning of man's solitude rests on the experience of the existence he obtained from the Creator.

This human existence is characterized precisely by subjectivity, which also includes the meaning of the body. Yet, could man, who in his original consciousness knows only the experience of existing and thus of life, have understood *what the words, "You shall die," mean*? Would he have been able *to reach an understanding* of the sense of these words through the complex structure of the life given to him, when "the Lord God...blew into his nostrils the breath of life"? One must suppose that this word, completely new, appeared on the horizon of man's consciousness without his ever having experienced the reality, and that at the same time this word appeared before him as *a radical antithesis of all that man had been endowed with.*

For the first time, man heard the words, "You shall die," without having any familiarity with it in the experience he had up to this point; but on the other hand he could not fail to associate the meaning of death with that dimension of life he had enjoyed up to that point. The words of God-Yahweh addressed to the man confirm a dependence in existing, so that they show man as a limited being and, by his nature, susceptible to nonexistence. These words raised the problem of death in a conditional way, "When you eat of it you shall...die." The man, who had heard these words, had to find their truth in the inner structure of his own solitude. After all, it depended on him, on his decision and free choice, whether he would enter with solitude also into the circle of the antithesis revealed to him by the Creator, together with the tree of the knowledge of good and evil, and would appropriate the experience of dying and of death. When he heard the words of God-Yahweh, the man should have understood that the tree of knowledge had plunged its roots not only into "the garden in Eden," but also into his humanity. In addition, he should have understood that this mysterious tree concealed within itself a dimension of solitude that was unknown to him up to this point, a dimension with which the Creator had endowed him in the midst of the world of living beings, of the animals to which he, the man, had "given names"—in the presence of the Creator himself—so as to come to understand that none of them was similar to him.

4. When the fundamental meaning of his body had thus already been established through distinction from the rest of creatures, when it had become evident thereby that the "invisible" determines man

more than the "visible," then the alternative presented itself before him, strictly and directly linked by God-Yahweh to the tree of the knowledge of good and evil. *The alternative between death and immortality,* which emerges from Genesis 2:17, goes beyond the essential meaning of the human body inasmuch as it picks up the eschatological meaning, not only of the body, but also of humanity itself, distinct from all the living beings, from "bodies." This alternative, however, *regards in a quite particular way the body created from "dust of the ground."*

In order not to prolong this analysis, we limit ourselves to observing that the alternative between death and immortality has entered from the very beginning into the definition of man and that it belongs "from the beginning" to the meaning of his solitude before God himself. This original meaning of solitude, permeated by the alternative between death and immortality, also has a fundamental significance for the whole theology of the body.

With this observation, we conclude for now our reflections on the meaning of man's original solitude. This observation, emerging in a clear and incisive way from the texts of Genesis, leads us to reflect on the texts as much as on man, who has perhaps too little consciousness of the truth that concerns him and that is contained already in the first chapters of the Bible.

3. The Meaning of Original Unity

The Unity of the Two

8 *General Audience of November 7, 1979*
  (Insegnamenti, 2, no. 2 [1979]: 1071–76)

1. THE WORDS OF GENESIS, "It is not good that the man should be alone" (Gen 2:18), are a prelude, as it were, to the account of the creation of woman. Together with this account, the meaning of original solitude enters and becomes part of the meaning of original unity, the key point of which seems to be precisely the words of Genesis 2:24, to which Christ appeals in his dialogue with the Pharisees: "A man will leave his father and his mother and unite with his wife, and the two

will be one flesh" (Mt 19:5). If Christ quotes these words when he appeals to the beginning, we should clarify the meaning of this original unity, which is rooted in the fact of the creation of man as male and female.

The account of Genesis 1 does not mention the problem of man's original solitude: in fact, man is "male and female" from the beginning. The Yahwist text of Genesis 2, by contrast, authorizes us in some way to think first only about man inasmuch as, through the body, he belongs to the visible world while going beyond it; it then lets us think about the same man, but through the duality of sex.* Bodiliness and sexuality are not simply identical. Although in its normal constitution, the human body carries within itself the signs of sex and is by its nature male or female, *the fact that man is a "body" belongs more deeply to the structure of the personal subject than the fact that in his somatic constitution he is also male or female.* For this reason, the meaning of original solitude, which can be referred simply to "man," is substantially prior to the meaning of original unity; the latter is based on masculinity and femininity, which are, as it were, two different "incarnations," that is, two ways in which the same human being, created "in the image of God" (Gen 1:27), "is a body."

2. Following the Yahwist text, in which the creation of woman is described separately (Gen 2:21–22), we should have before our eyes at the same time that "image of God" of the first creation account. In its language and style, the second account keeps all the characteristics of the Yahwist text. The way of narrating fits with the way of thinking of the epoch to which the text belongs. Following contemporary philosophy of religion and of language, one can say that we are dealing with a mythical language. In this case, in fact, the term "myth" does not refer to fictitious-fabulous content, but simply to an archaic way of expressing a deeper content. Without any difficulty, we discover that content under the stratum of the ancient narrative, truly marvelous in the quality and condensation of the truths contained there. Let us add that the second account of the creation of man maintains to some

---

* Translator's note: John Paul II uses the word "sex" consistently to refer to the male "sex" and the female "sex" of the human person, rather than to the act of sexual intercourse (see Index at SEX).

degree the form of a dialogue between man and God the Creator, and this is evident above all in the stage in which the man (ʾādām) is definitively created as male and female (ʾîš / ʾiššāʰ).[12] Creation takes place simultaneously, as it were, in two dimensions: the action of God-Yahweh, who creates, unfolds in correlation with the process of human consciousness.

3. Thus, God-Yahweh says, "It is not good that the man should be alone; I want to make him a help similar to himself" (Gen 2:18). And at the same time the man confirms his own solitude (Gen 2:20). Next we read, "So the Lord God caused torpor [or state of unconsciousness] to fall upon the man, who fell asleep; then he took one of his ribs and closed the flesh again in its place. With the rib that the Lord God had taken from the man he formed a woman" (Gen 2:21–22). Considering the specificity of the language, one must first recognize that this Genesis torpor, in which, by the work of Yahweh-God, the man is immersed in preparation for the new creative act, stimulates much thought. Against the background of contemporary mentality, which is accustomed—by analysis of the subconscious—to link sexual contents with the world of dreams, that torpor may evoke a particular association.[13] The biblical account, however, seems to go beyond the

---

12. The Hebrew term ʾādām expresses the collective concept of the human species, that is, the man who represents humanity. (The Bible names the individual by using the expression "son of man," ben-ʾādām.) The contraposition ʾîš / ʾiššāʰ underlines sexual difference (as in Greek anēr/gynē).

After the creation of the woman, the biblical text continues to call the first man ʾādām (with the definite article), thus expressing his "corporate personality" inasmuch as he became "the father of humanity," its progenitor and representative, just as later Abraham was recognized as "the father of believers" and Jacob was identified with Israel, the Chosen People.

13. Adam's torpor (Hebrew: tardēmāʰ) is a profound sleep (Latin: "*sopor*," Italian: "*sonno*") into which man falls without knowledge or dreams (the Bible has another word to name dreams: ḥălôm); see Gen 15:12; 1 Sam 26:12.

Freud, by contrast, examines the content of dreams (Latin: *somnium*, Italian: *sogno*), which are formed from psychic elements "repressed in the subconscious" and allow one, he holds, to make the unconscious contents emerge from them, contents that are, in the final analysis, always sexual.

This idea is, of course, quite alien to the biblical author.

In the theology of the Yahwist author, the torpor into which God lets the man fall underlines the *exclusiveness of God's action* in the creation of the woman. The man had no conscious part in it. God makes use of his "rib" only to emphasize the common nature of man and woman.

dimension of the human subconscious. If one then supposes that a certain diversity of vocabulary is significant, one can conclude that man (ʾāḏām) falls into that "torpor" in order to wake up as "male" (ʾîš) and "female" (ʾiššāh). In fact, it is here in Genesis 2:23 that we come across the distinction between ʾîš and ʾiššāh for the first time. Perhaps, therefore, the *analogy of sleep* indicates here not so much a passage from consciousness to the subconscious, but a specific return to non-being (sleep has within itself a component of the annihilation of man's conscious existence), or to the moment before creation, *in order that the solitary "man" may by God's creative initiative reemerge from that moment* in his double unity as male and female.[14]

In any case, in the light of the context of Genesis 2:18–20, there is no doubt that man falls into this "torpor" with the desire of finding a being similar to himself. If by analogy with sleep we can speak here also of dream, we must say that this biblical archetype allows us to suppose as the content of this dream a "second I," which is also personal and equally related to the situation of original solitude, that is, to that whole process of establishing human identity in relation to all living beings (*animalia*), inasmuch as it is a process of man's "differentiation" from such surroundings. In this way, the circle of the human

---

14. "Torpor" (tardēmāh) is the term that appears in Sacred Scripture when, during the sleep or immediately after it, extraordinary events are to take place (see Gen 15:12; 1 Sam 26:12; Isa 29:10; Job 4:13; 33:15). The Septuagint translates tardēmāh as "*ekstasis*" (a trance, ecstasy).

In the Pentateuch, tardēmāh appears once more, in a mysterious context: at God's command, Abraham has prepared a sacrifice of animals, driving away birds of prey from them. "As the sun was setting, *torpor* fell on Abraham and a *dark terror* assailed him" (Gen 15:12). It is at this moment that God begins to speak and makes a covenant with him, which is *the summit of the revelation* made to Abraham.

This scene resembles in some way that of the Garden of Gethsemani. Jesus "began to feel fear and distress" (Mk 14:33) and found the apostles *"sleeping from sadness"* (Lk 22:45).

The biblical author admits in the first man a certain sense of lack and solitude, even if not of fear ("it is not good that the man should be alone," "he did not find a help similar to himself"). Perhaps this state causes "sleep from sadness," or perhaps, as in Abraham, *"a dark terror"* of nonexistence, as at the threshold of creation: "the earth was unformed and deserted and darkness covered the abyss" (Gen 1:2).

In any case, according to both texts in which the Pentateuch, specifically Genesis, speaks about deep sleep (tardēmāh), a special divine action takes place, namely, a "covenant" filled with consequences for the whole history of salvation: Adam begins the human race, Abraham the Chosen People.

person's solitude is broken, because the first "man" reawakens from his sleep as "male and female."

Dimensions of Homogeneity

4. The woman is made "with the rib" that God-Yahweh had taken from the man. Considering the archaic, metaphorical, and figurative way of expressing the thought, we can establish that what is meant is the homogeneity of the whole being of both; this homogeneity regards above all the body, the somatic structure, and it is also confirmed by the man's first words to the woman just created: "This time she is flesh from my flesh and bone from my bones" (Gen 2:23).[15] Nevertheless, the words quoted also refer to the humanity of the male human being. They should be read in the context of the statements made before the creation of the woman, in which, though the "incarnation" of man does not yet exist, she is defined as "help similar to himself" (see Gen 2:18, 20).[16] Thus, *the woman is created in a certain sense based on the same humanity.*

---

15. It is interesting to note that for the ancient Sumerians, the cuneiform sign used to indicate the noun "rib" was the same as the one used to indicate the word "life." As for the Yahwist narrative, according to one interpretation of Genesis 2:21, God covers the rib with flesh (rather than closing up the flesh in its place) and in this way "forms" the woman, who thus draws her origin from the "flesh and bones" of the first (male) man.

In biblical language, this is a definition of consanguinity or belonging to the same lineage (e.g., Gen 29:14): the woman belongs to the same species as the man, distinct from other living beings created earlier.

In biblical anthropology, "bones" signify a very important component of the body; given that for the Hebrews there was no precise distinction between "body" and "soul," (the body was considered the outer manifestation of the personality), "bones" signified simply, by synecdoche, the human "being" (e.g., Ps 139:15, "my bones were not hidden from you").

"Bone from my bones" can thus be understood in the relational sense, like "being from being." "Flesh from flesh" signifies that, although she has different physical characteristics, the woman has the same personhood that the man has.

In the first "wedding song" of the first man, the expression, "bone of bones, flesh of flesh" is a form of the superlative, underlined by the threefold repetition: "she, she, she."

16. It is difficult to find an exact translation of the Hebrew expression, ʿēzer kᵊneḡdô, which is differently translated in European languages, e.g., Latin: "*adiutorium ei conveniens sicut oportebat iuxta eum*"; German: "*eine Hilfe, die ihm entspricht*";

Despite the diversity in constitution tied to the sexual difference, *somatic homogeneity* is so evident that the man, on waking up from genetic sleep, expresses it immediately when he says, "This time she is flesh from my flesh and bone from my bones. She will be called woman because from man has she been taken" (Gen 2:23). In this way, for the first time, the man (male) shows joy and even exultation, for which he had no reason before, due to the lack of a being similar to himself. Joy for the other human being, for the second "I," dominates in the words the man (male) speaks on seeing the woman (female). All this helps to establish the full meaning of original unity. The words here are few, but each has great weight. We must therefore take into account—and will do so later—the fact that that first woman "formed with the rib taken from the man" is immediately accepted as a help suited to him.

To this same subject, that is, to the meaning of the original unity of the man and the woman in humanity, we will return in the next meditation.

9 *General Audience of November 14, 1979*
(Insegnamenti, 2, no. 2 [1979]: 1153–57)

1. Following the narrative of Genesis, we observed that the "definitive" creation of man consists in the creation of the unity of two beings. Their *unity denotes* above all *the identity of human nature; duality, on the other hand, shows what, on the basis of this identity, constitutes the masculinity and femininity* of created man. This ontological dimension of unity and duality has, at the same time, an axiological meaning. From the text of Genesis 2:23 and the whole context, it is clear that man has been created as a particular value before God ("God saw everything that he had made, and indeed, it was very good," Gen 1:31), but also as a particular value for man himself: first, because he is "man"; second, because the "woman" is for the man and,

---

French: "*égal vis-à-vis de lui*"; Italian: "*un aiuto che gli sia simile*"; Spanish: "*como él que le ayude*"; English: "a helper fit for him"; Polish: "*odopowicdnia alla niego pomoc.*"

Since the term "*help*" seems to suggest the concept of "complementarity," or, better, of exact correspondence, the term [kʰneḡdô, translated as] "*similar*" is connected rather with that of "similarity," but in a sense that differs from man's likeness with God.

vice versa, the "man" for the woman. While Genesis 1 expresses this value in a purely theological (and indirectly metaphysical) form, Genesis 2, by contrast, *reveals, so to speak, the first circle of experience lived by man as a value.* This experience is inscribed already in the meaning of original solitude, and then in the whole account of the creation of man as male and female. The concise text of Genesis 2:23, which contains the words of the first man on seeing the newly created woman, "taken from him," can be considered the biblical prototype of the Song of Songs. In addition, if it is possible to read impressions and emotions through such remote words, one could even venture to say that the depth and power of this first and "original" emotion of the man before the humanity of the woman, and at the same time before the femininity of the other human being, seems something unique and unrepeatable.

"Communion of Persons"

2. In this way, the meaning of man's original unity through masculinity and femininity expresses itself as an overcoming of the frontier of solitude and at the same time as an affirmation—for both human beings—of everything in solitude that constitutes "man." In the biblical account, solitude is the way that leads to the unity that we can define, following Vatican II, as *communio personarum.*[17] As we observed before, in his original solitude man reaches personal consciousness in the process of "distinction" from all living beings (*animalia*), and at the same time, in this solitude, he opens himself toward a being akin to himself, defined by Genesis as "a help similar to himself" (Gen 2:18, 20). This opening is no less decisive for man as a person; in fact, it is perhaps more decisive than the "distinction" itself. The man's solitude in the Yahwist account presents itself to us not only as the first discovery of the characteristic transcendence proper to the person, but also as the discovery of an adequate relation "to" the person, and thus as opening toward and waiting for a "communion of persons."

---

17. "But God did not create man abandoning him alone, for from the beginning 'male and female he created them' (Gen 1:17), and their union constitutes the first form of the communion of persons [*communionis personarum*]" (GS 12).

One could also use the term "community" here, if it were not so generic and did not have so many meanings. "*Communio*" says more and with greater precision, because *it indicates precisely the "help" that derives in some way from the very fact of existing as a person "beside" a person.* In the biblical account, this fact becomes *eo ipso*—through itself—*existence of the person "for" the person,* given that in his original solitude man existed in some way already in this relation. This is confirmed, in a negative sense, precisely by his solitude. In addition, the communion of persons could form itself only on the basis of a "double solitude" of the man and the woman, or as an encounter in their "distinction" from the world of living beings (*animalia*), which gave to both the possibility of being and existing in a particular reciprocity. The concept of "help" also expresses this reciprocity in existence, which no other living being could have ensured. Indispensable for this solitude was everything that was constitutive in providing the foundation for the solitude of each, and thus also self-knowledge and self-determination, that is, subjectivity and the awareness of the meaning of one's own body.

3. The account of the creation of man in Genesis 1 affirms from the beginning and directly that man was created in the image of God inasmuch as he is male and female. The account in Genesis 2, by contrast, does not speak of the "image of God," but reveals, in the manner proper to it, that the complete and definitive creation of "man" (subject first to the experience of original solitude) expresses itself in giving life to the "*communio personarum*" that man and woman form. In this way, the Yahwist account agrees with the content of the first account. If, vice versa, we want to retrieve also from the account of the Yahwist text the concept of "image of God," we can deduce that *man became the image of God not only through his own humanity, but also through the communion of persons,* which man and woman form from the very beginning. The function of the image is that of mirroring the one who is the model, of reproducing its own prototype. Man becomes an image of God not so much in the moment of solitude as in the moment of communion. He is, in fact, "from the beginning" not only an image in which the solitude of one Person, who rules the world, mirrors itself, but also and essentially the image of an inscrutable divine communion of Persons.

In this way, the second account could also prepare for understanding the trinitarian concept of the "image of God," even if "image" appears only in the first account. This is obviously not without significance for the theology of the body, but constitutes perhaps the deepest theological aspect of everything one can say about man. In the mystery of creation—on the basis of the original and constitutive "solitude" of his being—man has been endowed with a deep unity between what is, humanly and through the body, male in him and what is, equally humanly and through the body, female in him. On all this, right from the beginning, the blessing of fruitfulness descended, linked with human procreation (cf. Gen 1:28).

"Flesh from my Flesh" (Gen 2:23)

4. In this way, we find ourselves within the very bone marrow of the anthropological reality that has the name "body." The words of Genesis 2:23 speak about this directly and for the first time in the following terms, "*flesh from my flesh and bone from my bones.*" The man speaks these words as if it were only at the sight of the woman that he could identify and call by name *that which makes them in a visible way similar, the one to the other,* and at the same time *that in which humanity is manifested.* In the light of the earlier analysis of all the "bodies" man came in contact with and conceptually defined, giving them their names (*animalia*), the expression "flesh from my flesh" takes on precisely this meaning: the body reveals man. This concise formula already contains all that human science will ever be able to say about the structure of the body as an organism, about its vitality, about its particular sexual physiology, etc. In this first expression of the man, "flesh from my flesh" contains also a reference to that by which that body is authentically human and thus to that which determines man as a person, that is, as a being that is, also in all its bodiliness, "similar" to God.[18]

---

18. In the conception of the most ancient biblical books, the dualistic antithesis "body-soul" does not appear. As pointed out already [TOB 8:4], one could speak rather of a complementary combination "body-life." The body is an expression of man's personhood and, though it does not completely exhaust this concept, one should understand it in biblical language as "*pars pro toto*" [the part standing for the whole]; cf. "neither flesh nor blood have revealed this to you, but my Father" (Mt 16:17), that is, no *human being* has revealed it to you.

5. We find ourselves, therefore, within the very bone marrow of the anthropological reality whose name is "body," human body. Yet, as can easily be observed, this marrow is not only anthropological, but also essentially theological. The theology of the body, which is linked from the beginning with the creation of man in the image of God, becomes in some way also a theology of sex, or rather a theology of masculinity and femininity, which has its point of departure here, in Genesis. The original meaning of unity, to which the words of Genesis 2:24 bear witness, was to have a broad and far-reaching perspective in God's revelation. This unity through the body ("and the two will be one flesh") possesses a multiform dimension: an ethical dimension, as is confirmed by Christ's response to the Pharisees in Matthew 19 (see also Mk 10), and also a sacramental dimension, strictly theological, as confirmed by the words of Paul to the Ephesians,[19] that likewise refer to the tradition of the prophets (Hosea, Isaiah, Ezekiel). And this is so because the unity that is realized through the body indicates from the beginning not only the "body," but also the "incarnate" communion of persons—*communio personarum*—and requires this communion right from the beginning. Masculinity and femininity express *the twofold aspect of man's somatic constitution* ("this time she is flesh from my flesh and bone from my bones") and *indicate*, in addition, through the same words of Genesis 2:23, *the new consciousness of the meaning of one's body*. This meaning, one can say, consists in *reciprocal enrichment*. Precisely this consciousness, through which humanity forms itself anew as a communion of persons, seems to constitute the layer in the account of the creation of man (and in the revelation of the body contained in it) that is deeper than the somatic structure as male and female. In any case, this structure is presented from the beginning with a deep consciousness of human bodiliness and sexuality, and this establishes an inalienable norm for the understanding of man on the theological plane.

---

19. "No one, in fact, ever hates his own flesh, but he nourishes and cares for it, as Christ does with the Church, because we are members of his body. For this reason a man will leave his father and his mother and unite with his wife and the two will form one flesh. This mystery is great; I say this with reference to Christ and the Church" (Eph 5:29–32).

10 *General Audience of November 21, 1979*
(Insegnamenti, 2, no. 2 [1979]: 1212–15)

1. LET US RECALL THAT CHRIST, when he was asked about the unity and indissolubility of marriage, appealed to what was "at the beginning." He quoted the words written in the first chapters of Genesis. This is the reason why we are attempting in the present reflections to penetrate into the meaning that truly belongs to these words and these chapters.

The meaning of the original unity of man, whom God has created "male and female," is grasped (particularly in the light of Genesis 2:23) by knowing man in the whole endowment of his being, that is, in the whole wealth of that mystery of creation standing at the basis of theological anthropology. This knowledge, that is, the search for the human identity of the one who, at the beginning, is "alone," must always pass through duality, through "communion."

Let us recall the passage of Genesis 2:23: "Then the man said, 'This time she is flesh from my flesh and bone from my bones. She will be called woman because from man has she been taken.'" In the light of this text we understand that the knowledge of man passes through masculinity and femininity, which are, as it were, two "incarnations" of the same metaphysical solitude before God and the world—*two reciprocally completing ways of "being a body" and at the same time of being human*—as two complementary dimensions of self-knowledge and self-determination and, at the same time, *two complementary ways of being conscious of the meaning of the body*. Thus, as Genesis 2:23 already shows, femininity in some way finds itself before masculinity, while masculinity confirms itself through femininity. Precisely the function of sex [that is, being male or female], which in some way is "constitutive for the person" (not only "an attribute of the person"), shows how deeply man, with all his spiritual solitude, with the uniqueness and unrepeatability proper to the person, is constituted by the body as "he" or "she." The presence of the feminine element, next to the masculine and together with it, signifies an enrichment for man in the whole perspective of his history, including the history of salvation. All this teaching on unity has already been originally expressed in Genesis 2:23.

The Unity of Becoming "One Flesh"

2. The unity about which Genesis 2:24 speaks ("and the two will be one flesh") is without doubt the unity that is expressed and realized in the conjugal act. The biblical formulation, so extremely concise and simple, indicates sex, that is, masculinity and femininity, as that characteristic of man—male and female—that allows them, when they become one flesh, to place their whole humanity at the same time under the blessing of fruitfulness. Yet, the whole context of the lapidary formulation does not allow us to stop on the surface of human sexuality; it does not allow us to treat the body and sex outside the full dimension of man and the "communion of persons," but imposes on us from the "beginning" the obligation to see the fullness and depth proper to this unity, the unity that man and woman must constitute in the light of the revelation of the body.

Before all else, therefore, the future-oriented expression, "the man...will unite with his wife" so intimately that "the two will be one flesh," always leads us to turn to what the biblical text expresses before this with respect to union in humanity, which connects the woman and the man in the very mystery of creation. The words of Genesis 2:23 just analyzed explain this concept in a particular way. When they unite with each other (in the conjugal act) so closely so as to become "one flesh," man and woman rediscover every time and in a special way the mystery of creation, thus returning to the union in humanity ("flesh from my flesh and bone from my bones") that allows them to recognize each other reciprocally and to call each other by name, as they did the first time. This means reliving in some way man's original virginal value, which emerges from the mystery of his solitude before God and in the midst of the world. The fact that they become "one flesh" is a powerful bond established by the Creator through which they discover their own humanity, both in its original unity and in the duality of a mysterious reciprocal attraction. Sex, however, is something more than the mysterious power of human bodiliness, which acts, as it were, by virtue of instinct. On the level of man and in the reciprocal relationship of persons, sex expresses an ever-new surpassing of the limit of man's solitude, which lies within the makeup of his body and determines its original meaning. This surpassing always implies that in a certain way one takes upon oneself the solitude of the body of the second "I" as one's own.

3. For this reason, the assumption is linked with choice. The formulation of Genesis 2:24 itself indicates not only that human beings, created as man and woman, have been created for unity, but also that precisely this *unity, through which they become "one flesh," has from the beginning the character of a union that derives from a choice.* We read, in fact, "A man will leave his father and his mother and unite with his wife." While the man, by virtue of generation, belongs "by nature" to his father and mother, "he unites," by contrast, with his wife (or she with her husband) by choice. The text of Genesis 2:24 defines this character of the conjugal bond in reference to the first man and the first woman, but at the same time it does so also in the perspective of man's earthly future as a whole. In his own time, therefore, Christ was to appeal to this text as equally relevant in his age. Since they are formed in the image of God also inasmuch as they form an authentic communion of persons, the first man and the first woman must constitute the beginning and model of that communion for all men and women who in any period unite with each other so intimately that they are "one flesh." The body, which through its own masculinity and femininity helps the two ("a help similar to himself") from the beginning to find themselves in a communion of persons [see *Gaudium et Spes*, 24:3], becomes in a particular way the constitutive element of their union when they become husband and wife. This takes place, however, through a reciprocal choice. The choice is what establishes the conjugal covenant between the persons,[20] who become "one flesh" only based on this choice.

4. This [role of choice] corresponds to the structure of man's solitude, and concretely to a "twofold solitude." As an expression of self-determination, the choice rests on the foundation of that structure, that is, on the foundation of its self-consciousness. It is only based on the structure proper to man that he "is a body" and that, through the

---

20. "The intimate community of conjugal life and love, established by the Creator and structured by its own laws, is established by the conjugal covenant, that is to say, by irrevocable personal consent" (GS 48).

body, he is also male and female. When both unite so intimately with each other that they become "one flesh," their conjugal union presupposes a mature consciousness of the body. Better yet, this union *carries within itself a particular awareness of the meaning of that body in the reciprocal self-gift of the persons.* In this sense, too, Genesis 2:24 is a future-oriented text. It shows, in fact, that in every conjugal union of man and woman, there is a new discovery of the same original consciousness of the unitive meaning of the body in its masculinity and femininity; the biblical text thereby indicates at the same time that each union of this kind renews in some way the mystery of creation in all its original depth and vital power. "Taken from the man" as "flesh from his flesh," the woman consequently becomes, as "wife" and through her motherhood, mother of the living (Gen 3:20), because her motherhood has its proper origin also in him. Procreation is rooted in creation, and every time it reproduces in some way its mystery.

5. To this subject we will devote a special reflection, "Knowledge and Procreation" [see TOB 20–22]. In it, we will refer to further elements of the biblical text. The analysis of the meaning of original unity carried out so far shows in what way "from the beginning" that unity of man and woman, inherent in the mystery of creation, is also given as a task in the perspective of all future time.

4. The Meaning of Original Nakedness

Introductory Observations about Genesis 2:25

11 *General Audience of December 12, 1979*
(Insegnamenti, 2, no. 2 [1979]: 1378–82)

1. ONE CAN SAY THAT THE ANALYSIS of the first chapters of Genesis forces us in some way to reconstruct the constitutive elements of man's original experience. In this sense, the Yahwist text is by its own character a special source. When we speak of original human experiences, we have in mind not so much their distance in time, as rather their foundational significance. The important thing, therefore, is not that these experiences belong to man's prehistory (to his "theological

prehistory"), but that they are always at the root of every human experience. That is true even though, in the unfolding of ordinary human existence, we pay little attention to these essential experiences. Indeed, they are so interwoven with the ordinary things of life that we generally do not realize their extraordinary character. Based on the analyses carried out so far, we have already been able to realize that what we have previously called "revelation of the body" helps us in some way to discover the extraordinary nature of what is ordinary. That is possible because revelation (the original revelation, which has found expression, first in the Yahwist account of Genesis 2–3 and then in the text of Genesis 1), takes into consideration precisely *such primordial experiences that show in a nearly complete way the absolute originality* of what the male-female human being is inasmuch as he or she is human, that is, also through the body. The human experience of the body, as we discover it in the biblical texts quoted above, is certainly located on the threshold of all later "historical" experience. Nevertheless, this experience also seems to rest on an ontological depth that is so great that man does not perceive it in his own daily life, even if at the same time he presupposes it in some way and postulates it as part of the process of the formation of his own image.

2. Without such an introductory reflection, it would be impossible to define the meaning of original nakedness and to take up the analysis of Genesis 2:25, which says, "Now both were naked, the man and his wife, but they did not feel shame." At first sight, the introduction of this detail, apparently a secondary one, may seem unsuited and misplaced. One might think that this passage cannot compare with what the preceding verses speak about and that it is in some way out of context. Such a judgment, however, cannot stand up to deeper analysis. In fact, Genesis 2:25 presents one of the key elements of the original revelation, just as decisive as the other elements of the text (Gen 2:20, 23) that have already allowed us to determine the meaning of man's original solitude and original unity. To these one must add, as a third element, *the meaning of original nakedness,* which is clearly highlighted in the context; *in the first biblical sketch of anthropology, it is not something accidental.* On the contrary, it is precisely the key for understanding it fully and completely.

Shame—A "Boundary" Experience

3. Precisely this element of the ancient biblical text evidently makes a specific contribution to the theology of the body that absolutely cannot be left out of consideration. Further analyses will confirm this point. Before turning to them, however, I allow myself to observe that precisely the text of Genesis 2:25 expressly demands that we link the reflections on the theology of the body with the dimension of man's personal subjectivity; it is in this sphere, in fact, that consciousness of the meaning of the body unfolds. Genesis 2:25 speaks about this in a much more direct way than other parts of this Yahwist text that we have already defined as the first record of human consciousness. The statement according to which the first human beings, the man and the woman, "were naked" but still "did not feel shame" undoubtedly describes their state of consciousness, or even better, their reciprocal experience of the body, that is, the man's experience of the femininity that reveals itself in the nakedness of the body and, reciprocally, the analogous experience of masculinity by the woman. By affirming "they did not feel shame," the author intends to describe this *reciprocal experience with the greatest precision possible for him.* One can say that this type of precision mirrors a fundamental experience of man in the "common" and pre-scientific sense, but it also corresponds to the demands of anthropology and in particular of contemporary anthropology, which likes to draw on so-called fundamental experiences, such as the feeling of shame.[21]

4. When we allude here to the precision of the account that was possible for the author of the Yahwist text, we are led to consider the degrees of experience of "historical" man, who is burdened by the inheritance of sin, which nevertheless have their point of departure (from the point of view of method) in the state of original innocence. We observed earlier that, by appealing "to the beginning" (which we are here submitting to a series of contextual analyses), Christ indirectly establishes the idea of continuity and connection between the two states, thereby allowing us to go back, as it were, from the threshold of

---

21. See, e.g., M. Scheler, *Über Scham und Schamgefühl* (Halle, 1914); Fr. Sawicki, *Phenomenology of Shame* (Kraków, 1949); K. Wojtyła, *Love and Responsibility* (repr., San Francisco: Ignatius Press, 1993), 174–93.

man's "historical" sinfulness to his original innocence. Precisely Genesis 2:25 asks us in a particular way to cross that threshold. It is easy to see how this passage, together with the meaning of original nakedness expressed in it, fits into the whole context of the Yahwist narrative. In fact, a few verses later the same author writes, "Then the eyes of both were opened, and they realized that they were naked; they sewed fig leaves together and made themselves loincloths" (Gen 3:7). The adverb "then" indicates a new moment and a new situation that followed the breaking of the first covenant; it is a situation that comes after the failure of the test connected with the tree of the knowledge of good and evil, which was at the same time the first test of "obedience," that is, of hearing the Word in all its truth and of accepting Love according to the fullness of the demands of the creative Will. This new moment or new situation also brings with it a new content and a new quality of the experience of the body so that one can no longer say, "they were naked, but did not feel shame." *Thus, shame is not only one of man's original experiences, but is also a "boundary" experience.*

5. The difference of formulations that separates Genesis 2:25 from Genesis 3:7 is thus significant. In the first case, "they were naked, but did not feel shame"; in the second case, "they realized that they were naked." Does this mean that at first "they did not realize that they were naked," that they did not reciprocally see the nakedness of their bodies? The significant transformation witnessed to by the biblical text concerning the experience of shame (about which Genesis speaks again, particularly in 3:10–12), takes place on a level that is deeper than the pure and simple use of the sense of sight. A comparative analysis of Genesis 2:25 and Genesis 3 necessarily leads to the conclusion that it is not a question of passing from "not knowing" to "knowing," but of a *radical change in the meaning of the original nakedness* of the woman before the man and of the man before the woman. This change emerges from their consciousness as a fruit of the tree of the knowledge of good and evil. "Who told you that you were naked? Have you eaten from the tree of which I commanded you not to eat?" (Gen 3:11). This change directly concerns the experience of the meaning of one's own body before the Creator and creatures. That is confirmed later by the man's words, "I heard the sound of your step in the garden, and I was afraid, because I am naked; and I hid myself" (Gen 3:10). In particular, this change, which the Yahwist text outlines in such a concise and dramatic way, concerns directly—perhaps in the most direct way possible—the relation between man and woman, between femininity and masculinity.

6. We will have to return to the analysis of this transformation in other parts of our further analyses. Now that we have reached the boundary that cuts across the sphere of the "beginning," to which Christ appealed, we must ask ourselves *whether we can in some way reconstruct the original meaning of nakedness,* which constitutes the proximate context in Genesis of the doctrine of the unity of the human being as male and female. This seems possible *if we take as a point of reference the experience of shame* as it is clearly presented in the ancient biblical text, namely, as a "threshold" experience.

We will attempt such a reconstruction in the following meditations.

Attempted Reconstruction

12 *General Audience of December 19, 1979*
(Insegnamenti, 2, no. 2 [1979]: 1462–66)

1. WHAT IS SHAME AND HOW CAN ONE explain its absence in the state of original innocence, in the very depth of the mystery of the creation of man as male and female? From the contemporary analyses of shame, and in particular of sexual shame, one can deduce the complexity of this fundamental experience in which man expresses himself as a person according to his own structure. In the experience of shame, the human being experiences fear in the face of the "second I" (thus, for example, woman before man), and this is substantially fear for one's own "I." With shame, the human being manifests "instinctively," as it were, the need for the affirmation and acceptance of this "I" according to its proper value. He experiences this at the same time within himself and toward the outside, in the face of the "other." One can thus say that shame is a complex experience in the sense that, while distancing one human being from another (woman from man), as it were, it seeks at the same time their personal approach toward each other, creating a suitable basis and level for such an approach.

For the same reason, shame has a fundamental significance for the formation of ethos in the relations between human beings who live together, particularly in the relation between man and woman. The analysis of shame clearly indicates how deeply it is rooted precisely in their mutual relations, *how exactly it expresses the essential rules for the "communion of persons,"* and likewise *how deeply it touches the dimension of man's original "solitude."* The emergence of man's original "shame" in the immediately subsequent narrative of Genesis 3 has a meaning with many dimensions, and we must take up its analysis again in due time.

What is the meaning, by contrast, of its original absence in Genesis 2:25, "They were naked, but did not feel shame"?

2. We must establish, first of all, that it is a question of a true non-presence of shame, and not of a lack of it or its insufficient development. Here we can in no way maintain a "primitivization" of its meaning. Thus, the text of Genesis 2:25 decidedly excludes not only the possibility of thinking about a "lack of shame" or about shame-lessness; it excludes even more the possibility of explaining it by analogy with positive human experiences, e.g., those of childhood or those of the life of so-called primitive peoples. Such analogies are not merely insufficient, but they can be entirely misleading. The words of Genesis 2:25, "they did not feel shame," do not express a lack but, on the contrary, they serve to indicate a particular fullness of consciousness and experience, above all the fullness of understanding the meaning of the body connected with the fact that "they were naked."

That one should understand and interpret the text just quoted in this way is witnessed to by the continuation of the Yahwist narrative, in which the emergence of shame, and in particular of sexual shame, is linked with the loss of that original fullness. Presupposing, therefore, that the experience of shame is a "boundary" experience, we must ask ourselves, *To what fullness of consciousness and experience,* and in particular *to what fullness of understanding the meaning of the body, does the meaning of original nakedness correspond,* about which Genesis 2:25 speaks?

Participation in the Visibility of the World

3. To answer this question, one must keep in mind the analytic process conducted so far, which has its basis in the Yahwist passage as a whole. In this context, man's original solitude is portrayed as the "non-identification" of his own humanity with the world of the living beings (*animalia*) that surround him.

This "non-identification" gives way—in consequence of man's creation as male and female—to the happy discovery of his own humanity "with the help" of the other human being; in this way, the man recognizes and finds his own humanity "with the help" of the woman (Gen 2:25). This act of discovery on the part of both brings about at the same time a perception of the world that occurs directly through the body ("flesh of my flesh"). The discovery is the direct and visible source of experience that effectively establishes their unity in humanity. For this reason, it is not difficult to understand that nakedness corresponds to that fullness of consciousness of the meaning of the body that comes from the typical perception of the senses. One can think about this fullness in categories of the truth of being or reality, and one can say that the man and the woman were originally given to each other precisely according to this truth inasmuch as "they were naked." In the analysis of the meaning of original nakedness, one absolutely cannot set aside this dimension. *This participation in the perception of the world*—in its *"exterior"* aspect—is a direct and, as it were, spontaneous fact, before any "critical" complication of knowledge and of human experience, and it seems to be *strictly linked with the experience of the meaning of the body.* Already in this way, one could perceive the original innocence of "knowledge."

The Inner Dimension of Vision

4. Yet, one cannot identify the meaning of original nakedness by considering only man's share in the exterior perception of the world; one cannot determine it without going down into man's innermost [being]. Genesis 2:25 introduces us precisely to this level and wants us to look there for the original innocence of knowing. In fact, it is by the dimension of human interiority that one must explain and measure the particular fullness of interpersonal communion thanks to which man and woman "were naked but did not feel shame."

In our conventional language, the concept of "communication" has been nearly alienated from its deepest, original semantic matrix. It is tied mainly to the realm of the media, that is, for the most part, to products that serve as means for understanding, exchange, and bringing [people] closer together. By contrast, one can rightly assume that in its original and deepest meaning, "communication" was and is directly connected with subjects who "communicate" precisely based on the "common union" that exists between them, both to reach and to express a reality that is proper and pertinent to the sphere of subjects-persons alone. In this way, the human body acquires a completely new meaning, which one cannot place on the same level as the remaining "exterior" perception of the world. In fact, it expresses the person in his or her ontological and essential concreteness, which is something more than "individual," and thus expresses the human, personal "I," which grounds its "exterior" perception from within.

5. The whole biblical narrative, and particularly the Yahwist text, shows that, through its own visibility, the body *manifests* man and, in manifesting him, acts as an intermediary that allows man and woman, from the beginning, to "communicate" with each other according to that *communio personarum* willed for them in particular by the Creator. Only this dimension, it seems, allows us to understand rightly the meaning of original nakedness. In this context, any "naturalistic" criterion is bound to fail, while the "personalistic" criterion can be of great help. Genesis 2:25 certainly speaks about something extraordinary that lies outside the limits of shame known by human experience and that is *decisive for the particular fullness of interpersonal communication,* for the fullness that is rooted in the very heart of the *communio* revealed and developed in this way. In such a relationship, the words "they did not feel shame" can only signify (*in sensu obliquo* [in an indirect sense]) an original depth in affirming what is inherent in the person, that is, what is "visibly" feminine and masculine, through which the "personal intimacy" of reciprocal communication is constituted in all its radical simplicity and purity. To this fullness of *"exterior" perception,* expressed by physical nakedness, *corresponds the "interior" fullness of the vision of man in God,* that is, *according to the measure of the "image of God"* (see

Gen 1:27). According to this measure, man "is" truly naked ("they were naked"),[22] even before becoming aware of it (see Gen 3:7–10).

We must still complete the analysis of this important text in the next meditations.

Intimacy—The Hidden Meaning of Vision

13 *General Audience of January 2, 1980*
(Insegnamenti, 3, no. 1 [1980]: 11–15)

1. WE RETURN TO THE ANALYSIS of the Genesis text (Gen 2:25) begun a few weeks ago.

According to this passage, the man and the woman see each other, as it were, through the mystery of creation; they see each other in this way before knowing "that they were naked." This reciprocal vision of each other is not only a share in the "exterior" perception of the world, but also has an inner dimension of a share in the vision of the Creator himself—in that vision about which the account of Genesis 1 speaks several times, "God saw everything that he had made, and indeed, it was very good" (Gen 1:31). "Nakedness" signifies the original good of the divine vision. It signifies the whole simplicity and fullness of this vision, which shows the "pure" value of man as male and female, the "pure" value of the body and of [its] sex. The situation that is indicated in such a concise, and at the same time suggestive, way by the original revelation of the body as expressed in particular by Genesis 2:25, does not contain an inner break and antithesis between what is spiritual and what is sensible, just as it does not contain a break and antithesis between what constitutes the person as human and what is determined by sex in man, that is, what is male and female.

Seeing each other reciprocally, *through the very mystery of creation, as it were,* the man and the woman *see each other still more fully and clearly* than through the sense of sight itself, that is, through the eyes

---

22. According to the words of Sacred Scripture, God penetrates the creature, who is completely "naked" before him. "There is no creature that can hide before him, but everything is naked (*panta gymna*) and laid bare to his eyes, and to him we must give an account" (Heb 4:13). This character belongs in particular to divine wisdom. "Wisdom...by its purity pervades and penetrates all things" (Wis 7:24).

of the body. They see and know each other, in fact, with all the peace of the interior gaze, which creates precisely the fullness of the intimacy of persons. If "shame" carries with it a specific limitation of vision through the eyes of the body, this happens above all because personal intimacy is, as it were, troubled and "threatened" by such vision. According to Genesis 2:25, the man and the woman "did not feel shame"; seeing and knowing each other in all the peace and tranquility of the interior gaze, they "communicate" in the fullness of humanity, which shows itself in them as reciprocal complementarity precisely because they are "male" and "female." At the same time, they "communicate" based on the communion of persons in which they become a mutual gift for each other, through femininity and masculinity. In reciprocity, they reach in this way a particular understanding of the meaning of their own bodies. The original meaning of nakedness corresponds to the simplicity and fullness of vision in which their understanding of the meaning of the body is born from the very heart, as it were, of their community-communion. We will call this meaning "spousal." The man and the woman in Genesis 2:23–25 emerge, precisely at the very "beginning," with this consciousness of the meaning of their own bodies. This deserves a deepened analysis.

5. Man in the Dimension of Gift

A. THE SPOUSAL MEANING OF THE BODY

Creation as Giving

2. If the account of the creation of man in the two versions, that of Genesis 1 and the Yahwist version in Genesis 2, allows us to establish the original meaning of solitude, unity, and nakedness, by this very fact it allows us also to reach the basis of an adequate anthropology, which seeks to understand and interpret man in what is essentially human.[23]

---

23. The concept of "adequate anthropology" has been explained in the text itself as "an understanding and interpretation of man in what is essentially human." This concept determines the principle of reduction, which is proper to the philosophy of man; it indicates the limits of this principle and indirectly excludes the possibility of going

The biblical texts contain the essential elements of such an anthropology, which become clear in the theological context of the "image of God." This concept contains in a hidden way the very root of the truth about man revealed by the "beginning," to which Christ appeals in the dialogue with the Pharisees (see Mt 19:3–9) when he speaks about the creation of man as male and female. One must remember that all the analyses we are carrying out here are connected, at least indirectly, with precisely these words. Man, whom God created "male and female," bears the divine image impressed in the body "from the beginning"; man and woman constitute, so to speak, two diverse ways of "being a body" that are proper to human nature in the unity of this image.

We should now turn anew to those fundamental words that Christ used, that is, to the word "created" and to the subject, "Creator," introducing into the considerations carried out so far *a new dimension, a new criterion of understanding and of interpretation* that we will call *"hermeneutics of the gift."* The dimension of gift is decisive for the essential truth and depth of the meaning of original solitude-unity-nakedness. It stands also at the very heart of the mystery of creation, which allows us to build the theology of the body "from the beginning," but at the same time demands that we build it in precisely this way.

3. On Christ's lips, the word "created" contains the same truth that we find in Genesis. The first creation account repeats this word several times from Genesis 1:1 ("In the beginning God created the heavens and the earth") to Genesis 1:27 ("God created man in his image").[24] God reveals himself above all as Creator. Christ appeals to this fundamental revelation contained in Genesis. The concept of

---

beyond this limit. "Adequate" anthropology relies on essentially "human" experience. It is opposed to reductionism of the "naturalistic" kind, which often goes hand in hand with the theory of evolution about man's beginnings.

24. The Hebrew term bārāʾ (created), which is used only to determine the action of God, appears in the creation account only in 1:1 (creation of heaven and earth), [in 1:21 (creation of the sea monsters)], and in 1:27 (creation of man). Here, however, [that is, in 1:27], it appears as often as three times. This signifies the fullness and perfection of the act of the creation of man, male and female. Such repetition indicates that here the work of creation reached its high point.

creation has all its depth, not only a metaphysical, but also a fully theological depth, in Genesis. The Creator is he who "calls to existence from nothing" and who establishes the world in existence and man in the world, *because he "is love"* (1 Jn 4:8). We admittedly do not find this word love (God is love) in the creation account; nevertheless, that account often repeats, "God saw everything that he had made, and indeed, it was very good" (Gen 1:31). Through these words we are led to glimpse in love the divine motive for creation, the source, as it were, from which it springs: *only love, in fact, gives rise to the good and is well pleased with the good* (see 1 Cor 13). As an action of God, creation thus means not only calling from nothing to existence and establishing the world's existence as well as man's existence in the world, but, according to the first account, bᵉrēᵓšît bārāᵓ, it also signifies *gift*; a fundamental and "radical" gift, that is, an act of giving in which the gift comes into being precisely from nothing.

Giving and Man

4. Reading the first chapters of Genesis introduces us into the mystery of creation, that is, of the beginning of the world by the will of God, who is omnipotence and love. Consequently, every creature bears within itself the sign of the original and fundamental gift.

Yet, at the same time, the concept of "giving" cannot refer to nothing. It indicates the one who gives and the one who receives the gift, as well as the relation established between them. Now, this relation emerges in the creation account at the very moment of the creation of man. This relation is shown above all by the expression, "God created man in his image; in the image of God he created him" (Gen 1:27). In the account of the creation of the visible world, giving has meaning only in relation to man. In the whole work of creation, it is only about him that one can say, a gift has been granted: the visible world has been created "for him." The biblical creation account offers us sufficient reasons for such an understanding and interpretation: *creation is a gift, because man appears in it, who, as an "image of God," is able to understand the very meaning of the gift* in the call from nothing to existence. He is also able to respond to the Creator with the language of this understanding. When one interprets the creation account precisely with this language, one can deduce from it that creation constitutes the fundamental and original gift: man appears in creation as the one who has received the world as a gift, and vice versa, one can also say that the world has received man as a gift.

At this point, we must interrupt our analysis. What we have said so far stands in the strictest relation with the whole anthropological problematic of the "beginning." Man appears in it as "created," that is, as the one who, in the midst of the "world," has received the other human being as a gift. In what follows, it is precisely this dimension of gift that we must subject to a profound analysis, in order to understand also the meaning of the body in its right measure. This will be the object of our next meditations.

14 *General Audience of January 9, 1980*
 (Insegnamenti, 3, no. 1 [1980]: 88–92)

1. AS WE REREAD AND ANALYZE the second creation account, that is, the Yahwist text, we must ask ourselves whether the first "man" (ᵓādām), in his original solitude, "lived" the world truly as a gift, with an attitude that conforms to the actual condition of someone who has received a gift, as one can gather from the account in Genesis 1. The second account, in fact, shows us man in the garden of Eden (see Gen 2:8); but we must observe that, though man existed in this situation of original happiness, the Creator himself (God-Yahweh) and then also the "man" emphasize that the man is "alone," instead of underlining the aspect of the world as a subjectively beatifying gift created for man (see the first narrative and especially Gen 1:26–29). We have already analyzed the meaning of original solitude; now, however, it is necessary to note that for the first time there clearly appears a certain lack of good, "It is not good that the man" (male) "should be alone," God-Yahweh says, "I want to make him a help..." (Gen 2:18). The same thing is affirmed by the first "man": he, too, after having become completely conscious of his own solitude among all the living beings on the earth, awaits a "help similar to himself" (see Gen 2:20). None of these beings (*animalia*), in fact, offers man the basic conditions that *make it possible to exist in a relation of reciprocal gift*.

Gift—Mystery of a Beatifying Beginning

2. In this way, then, these two expressions, that is, the adjective "alone" and the noun "help," seem truly to be the key for understanding the essence of the gift on the level of man, as the existential content inscribed in the truth of the "image of God." In fact, the gift reveals, so to speak, *a particular characteristic of personal existence,* or even of the very essence of the person. When God-Yahweh says, "It is not good that the man should be alone" (Gen 2:18), he affirms that, "alone," the man does not completely realize this essence. He realizes it only by existing *"with someone"*—and, put even more deeply and completely, by existing *"for someone."* This norm of existing as a person is demonstrated in Genesis as a characteristic of creation precisely by the meaning of these two words, "alone" and "help." They point out how fundamental and constitutive the relationship and the communion of persons is for man. Communion of persons means living in a reciprocal "for," in a relationship of reciprocal gift. And this relationship is precisely the fulfillment of "man's" original solitude.

3. In its origin, such a fulfillment is beatifying. Undoubtedly, it is implicit in man's original solitude, and precisely constitutes the happiness that belongs to the mystery of creation made by love, that is, it belongs to the very essence of creative giving. When the "male" man, awakened from his Genesis sleep, says, "This time she is flesh from my flesh and bone from my bones" (Gen 2:23), these words in some way express the subjectively beatifying beginning of man's existence in the world. Inasmuch as this [expression of joy] was verified at the "beginning," it confirms the process of man's individuation in the world, and is born, so to speak, from the very depth of his human solitude, which he lives as a person in the face of all other creatures and all living beings (*animalia*). This "beginning," too, belongs thus to an adequate anthropology and can always be verified based on that anthropology. This purely anthropological verification brings us, at the same time, to the topic of the "person" and to the topic of "body/sex."

This simultaneity is essential. In fact, if we dealt with sex without the person, this would destroy the whole adequacy of the anthropology that we find in Genesis. Moreover, for our theological study, it would veil the essential light of the revelation of the body, which shines through these first statements with such great fullness.

4. There is a strong link between the mystery of creation, as a gift that springs from Love, and that beatifying "beginning" of man's existence as male and female, in the whole truth of their bodies and of their sexes, which is the simple and pure truth of communion between the persons. When the first man exclaims at the sight of the woman, "she is flesh from my flesh and bone from my bones" (Gen 2:23), he simply affirms the human identity of both. By exclaiming this, he seems to say, *Look, a body that expresses the "person"!* Following an earlier passage of the Yahwist text, one can also say that this "body" reveals the "living soul," which man became when God-Yahweh breathed life into him (see Gen 2:7). His solitude before all other living beings began in virtue of this act. Exactly through the depth of that original solitude, man now emerges in the dimension of reciprocal gift, the expression of which—by that very fact the expression of his existence as a person—is the human body in all the original truth of its masculinity and femininity. The body, which expresses femininity "for" masculinity and, vice versa, masculinity "for" femininity, manifests the reciprocity and the communion of persons. It expresses it through gift as the fundamental characteristic of personal existence. This is *the body: a witness* to creation as a fundamental gift, and therefore a witness *to Love as the source from which this same giving springs.* Masculinity-femininity—namely, sex—is the original sign of a creative donation and at the same time <the sign of a gift that>[*] man, male-female, becomes aware of as a gift lived so to speak in an original way. This is the meaning with which sex enters into the theology of the body.

Discovery of the "Spousal" Meaning of the Body

5. This beatifying "beginning" of man's being and existing as male and female is connected with the revelation and the discovery of the meaning of the body that is rightly called "spousal." If we speak of revelation together with discovery, we do so in reference to the speci-

---

[*] Translator's note: Text in angled brackets supplied from the Polish.

ficity of the Yahwist text, in which the theological guiding thread is also anthropological, or better still, appears as a certain reality that is consciously lived by man. We have already observed that after the words expressing the first joy of man's coming into existence as "male and female" (Gen 2:23) there follows the verse that establishes their conjugal unity (Gen 2:24), and then the one that attests the nakedness of both without reciprocal shame (Gen 2:25). That these verses face each other in such a significant way allows us to speak *of revelation together with the discovery of the "spousal" meaning of the body in the mystery of creation.* This meaning (inasmuch as it is revealed and also consciously "lived" by man) completely confirms the fact that creative giving, which springs from Love, has reached man's original consciousness by becoming an experience of reciprocal gift, as one can already see in the archaic text. A testimony to this fact seems also to be—perhaps even in a very specific way—that nakedness of both our first parents, free from shame.

6. Genesis 2:24 speaks about the ordering of man's masculinity and femininity to an end, in the life of the spouses-parents. Uniting so closely with each other that they become "one flesh," they place their humanity in some way under the blessing of fruitfulness, that is, of "procreation," about which the first account speaks (Gen 1:28). Man enters "into being" with the consciousness that his own masculinity-femininity, that is, his own sexuality, is ordered to an end. At the same time, the words of Genesis 2:25, "Both were naked, the man and his wife, but they did not feel shame," seem to add to this fundamental truth of the meaning of the human body, of its masculinity and femininity, another truth that is not in any way less essential and fundamental. Aware of the procreative power of his own body and of his own sex, man *is at the same time free from the "constraint" of his own body and his own sex.*

The original reciprocal nakedness, which was at the same time not weighed down by shame, expresses such an interior freedom in man. Is this freedom a freedom from "sexual instinct"? The concept of "instinct" already implies an inner constraint, analogous to the instinct that stimulates fruitfulness and procreation in the whole world of living beings (*animalia*). It seems, however, that both Genesis texts, the first and the second account of the creation of man,

sufficiently connect the perspective of procreation with the fundamental characteristic of human existence in the personal sense.
Consequently, the analogy of the human body and of sex in relation
to the world of animals—which we can call analogy "of nature"—is in
both accounts (though in each in a different way) also raised in some
way to the level of "image of God" and to the level of the person and
communion among persons.

To this essential problem, we will have to devote further analyses.
For the consciousness of man—also for that of contemporary man—it
is important to know that in the biblical texts that speak about man's
"beginning" one can find the revelation of the "spousal meaning of
the body." However, it is even more important to establish what this
meaning properly expresses.

"Freedom of the Gift"—Foundation of the Spousal Meaning of the Body

15 *General Audience of January 16, 1980*
(Insegnamenti, 3, no. 1 [1980]: 148–52)

1. WE CONTINUE TODAY THE ANALYSIS of the texts of Genesis we
have undertaken according to the line of Christ's teaching. We recall,
in fact, that in the dialogue about marriage he appealed to the "beginning."

The revelation together with the original discovery of the
"spousal" meaning of the body consists in presenting man, male and
female, in the whole reality and truth of his body and his sex ("they
were naked"), and at the same time in the full freedom from all constraint of the body and of [its] sex. A witness of this seems to be the
nakedness of our first parents, interiorly free from shame. One can say
that, created by Love, that is, endowed in their being with masculinity
and femininity, both are "naked," because they are *free with the very
freedom of the gift*. This freedom lies exactly at the basis of the spousal
meaning of the body. The human body, with its sex—its masculinity
and femininity—seen in the very mystery of creation, is not only a
source of fruitfulness and of procreation, as in the whole natural order,
but contains "from the beginning" the "spousal" attribute, that is, *the
power to express love: precisely that love in which the human person*

becomes a gift and—through this gift—fulfills the very meaning of his being and existence. We recall here the text of the most recent Council in which it declares that man is the only creature in the visible world that God willed "for its own sake," adding that this man cannot "fully find himself except through a sincere gift of self" [*Gaudium et Spes*, 24:3].[25]

2. The root of that original nakedness free from shame, about which Genesis 2:25 speaks, must be sought precisely in the integral truth about man. In the context of their beatifying "beginning," man and woman are free with the very freedom of the gift. In fact, in order to remain in the relation of the "sincere gift of self" and in order to become a gift, each for the other, through their whole humanity made of femininity and masculinity (also in reference to the perspective that Genesis 2:24 speaks about), they must be free in exactly this way. Here we mean freedom above all as *self-mastery* (self-dominion). Under this aspect, self-mastery is indispensable *in order for man to be able to "give himself,"* in order for him to become a gift, in order for him (referring to the words of the Council) to be able to "find himself fully" through "a sincere gift of self" [*Gaudium et Spes*, 24:3]. In this way, the words "they were naked but did not feel shame" can and should be understood as the revelation—together with the discovery—of the freedom that makes possible and qualifies the "spousal" meaning of the body.

---

25. "Indeed, the Lord Jesus, when he prays to the Father, 'that all may be one...as we are one' (Jn 17:21–22) and thus offers vistas closed to human reason, indicates a certain likeness between the union of the divine Persons, and the union of God's sons in truth and love. This likeness shows that man, who is the only creature on earth which God willed for itself, cannot fully find himself except through a sincere gift of self (cf. Lk 17:33)" (*Gaudium et Spes*, 24:3).

The strictly theological analysis of Genesis, in particular Genesis 2:23–25, allows us to refer to this text. This constitutes another step between "adequate anthropology" and "theology of the body," strictly linked with the discovery of the essential characteristics of personal existence in man's "theological prehistory." Although this might meet with resistance from the side of the evolutionistic mentality (as well as among theologians), it would nevertheless be difficult not to realize that the text of Genesis analyzed above, especially Genesis 2:23–25, shows not only the "original" dimension, but also the "exemplary" dimension of the existence of man, in particular of man "as male and female."

The "Spousal Character" of the Body
and the Revelation of the Person

3. Genesis 2:25, however, says even more. In fact, this passage indicates the possibility and the characteristic qualification of such a reciprocal "experience of the body." Further, it allows us to identify that spousal meaning of the body *in actu*. When we read that "both were naked, but did not feel shame," we indirectly touch its root, as it were, and directly already its fruits. Interiorly free from the constraint of their bodies and of sex, free with the freedom of the gift, man and woman *were able to enjoy the whole truth, the whole self-evidence of the human being*, just as God-Yahweh had revealed it to them in the mystery of creation. This truth about man, which the Council's text explains with the words quoted above, has two main emphases. The first affirms that man is the only creature in the world that the Creator willed "for its own sake"; the second consists in saying that this same man, willed in this way by the Creator from the "beginning," can only find himself through a disinterested gift of self [*Gaudium et Spes*, 24:3]. Now, this truth about man, which seems in particular to gather within itself the original condition linked with man's very "beginning" in the mystery of creation, can be reread—on the basis of the Council's text—in both directions. Such a rereading helps us to understand even more the spousal meaning of the body, which is evidently inscribed in the original condition of man and woman (according to Gen 2:23–25) and particularly in the meaning of their original nakedness.

If, as we have noted, the interior freedom of the gift—the disinterested gift of self—lies at the root of nakedness, then precisely this gift allows both the man and the woman *to find each other reciprocally*, inasmuch as the Creator willed each of them *"for his own sake"* (see *Gaudium et Spes*, 24:3). In the first beatifying encounter, the man thus finds the woman and she finds him. In this way he welcomes her within himself (and she welcomes him within herself), welcomes her as she is willed "for her own sake" by the Creator, as she is constituted in the mystery of the image of God through her femininity; and, reciprocally, she welcomes him in the same way, as he is willed "for his own sake" by the Creator and constituted by him through his masculinity. In this consists the revelation and the discovery of the "spousal" meaning of the body. The Yahwist narrative, and in particular Genesis 2:25, allows us to deduce that man, as male and female, enters the world precisely with this consciousness of the meaning of his own body, of his masculinity and femininity.

4. The human body, oriented from within by the "sincere gift" of the person [*Gaudium et Spes*, 24:3], reveals not only its masculinity or femininity on the physical level, but reveals also such a *value* and such a *beauty that it goes beyond the simply physical level of "sexuality."*[26] In this way, the consciousness of the meaning of the body, linked with man's masculinity-femininity, is in some sense completed. On the one hand, this meaning points to a particular power to express the love in which man becomes a gift; what corresponds to this meaning, on the other hand, is power and deep availability for the "affirmation of the person," that is, literally, the power to live the fact that the other—the woman for the man and the man for the woman—is through the body someone willed by the Creator "for his own sake" [*Gaudium et Spes*, 24:3], that is, someone unique and unrepeatable, someone chosen by eternal Love.

The "affirmation of the person" is nothing other than welcoming the gift, which, through reciprocity, creates the communion of persons; this communion builds itself from within, while also taking into itself man's whole "exteriority," that is, all that constitutes the pure and simple nakedness of the body in its masculinity and femininity. At that time—as we read in Genesis 2:25—the man and the woman did not feel shame. The biblical expression "did not feel" directly points to "experience" as a subjective dimension.

The Spousal Meaning of the Body as the Fruit of Rootedness in Love

5. Precisely in this subjective dimension, as two human "I"s determined by their masculinity and femininity, both the man and the

---

26. The biblical tradition reports a distant echo of the physical perfection of the first man: "You were a model of perfection, full of wisdom, perfect in beauty; in Eden, the garden of God" (Ezek 28:12–13).

woman appear in the mystery of their beatifying "beginning" (we see here the state of man's original innocence and at the same time original happiness). This appearance is short, because it includes only a few verses in Genesis; it is, however, full of a surprising content that is theological and anthropological at the same time. *The revelation and discovery of the spousal meaning of the body explain man's original happiness* and, at the same time, they open the perspective of his own earthly history, in which he will never withdraw from this indispensable "theme" of his own existence.

The following verses of Genesis, according to the Yahwist text of Genesis 3, show, one must admit, that this "historical" perspective will be built differently than the beatifying "beginning" (after original sin). It is all the more necessary, however, to penetrate deeply into the mysterious structure, theological and at the same time anthropological, of this "beginning." In fact, in the whole perspective of his own "history," man will not fail to confer a spousal meaning on his own body. Even if this meaning does undergo and will undergo many distortions, it will always remain the deepest level, which demands that it be revealed in all its simplicity and purity and manifested in its whole truth as a sign of the "image of God." Here we also find the road that goes from the mystery of creation to the "redemption of the body" (see Rom 8).

While we remain, for now, on the threshold of this historical perspective, we clearly grasp, based on Genesis 2:23–25, the connection that exists between the revelation-discovery of the spousal meaning of the body and man's original happiness. This *"spousal"* meaning is also *beatifying*, and, as such, it definitively shows the whole reality of the act of giving about which the first pages of Genesis speak to us. Reading them convinces us that the consciousness of the meaning of the body deriving from this [gift]—in particular the consciousness of the "spousal" meaning of the body—constitutes the fundamental component of human existence in the world.

One can understand this "spousal" meaning of the human body only in the context of the person. The body has a "spousal" meaning because the human person, as the Council says, is a creature that God willed for his own sake and that, at the same time, cannot fully find himself except through the gift of self [*Gaudium et Spes*, 24:3].

While Christ reveals to man and woman another vocation, above the vocation to marriage, namely, renouncing marriage in view of the kingdom of heaven, he highlights the same truth about the human person with this vocation. If a man or a woman is capable of making a gift of self for the kingdom of heaven, this shows in turn (and perhaps even more) that the freedom of the gift exists in the human body. This means that this body possesses a full "spousal" meaning.

16 General Audience of January 30, 1980
(*Insegnamenti*, 3, no. 1 [1980]: 218–22)

1. THE REALITY OF THE GIFT and of the act of giving, which is sketched in the first chapters of Genesis as the constitutive content of the mystery of creation, confirms that the irradiation of Love is an integral part of this same mystery. Only Love creates the good, and in the end it alone can be perceived in all its dimensions and its contours in created things and, above all, in man. Its presence is the final result, as it were, of the hermeneutics of the gift we are carrying out here. Original happiness, the beatifying "beginning" of man, whom God created "male and female," the spousal meaning of the body in its original nakedness: all of this expresses rootedness in Love.

This consistent giving, which goes back to the deep roots of consciousness and the subconscious and to the final levels of the subjective existence of both man and woman and which is reflected in their reciprocal *"experience of the body," bears witness to rootedness in Love.* The first verses of the Bible speak of it so much that they remove all doubt. They speak not only about the creation of the world and about man in the world, but also about grace, that is, about the self-communication of holiness, about the irradiation of the Holy Spirit, which produces a special state of "spiritualization" in that first man. In biblical language, that is, in the language of revelation, the qualification *"first" means precisely "of God," "Adam, son of God"* (Lk 3:38).

2. Happiness is being rooted in Love. Original happiness speaks to us about the "beginning" of man, who emerged from love and initiated love. And this happened irrevocably, despite the subsequent sin and death. In his time, Christ was to be a witness to this irreversible love of the Creator and Father, which had already expressed itself in

the mystery of creation and in the grace of original innocence. For this reason, also the common "beginning" of man and woman, that is, the original truth of their body in masculinity and femininity, to which Genesis 2:25 turns our attention, does not know shame. One can define this "beginning" also as the original and beatifying immunity from shame as the result of love.

B. THE MYSTERY OF ORIGINAL INNOCENCE

Gift to the Human Heart

3. This immunity directs us toward the mystery of man's original innocence. Innocence is a mystery of man's existence before the knowledge of good and evil and, as it were, "outside" of that knowledge. The fact that man exists in this way, before the breaking of the first covenant with his Creator, belongs to the fullness of the mystery of creation. If creation is a gift given to man, as we have already said, then *its fullness* and deepest dimension is *determined by grace,* that is, by participation in the inner life of God himself, in his holiness. In man, this holiness is also the inner foundation and source of his original innocence. With this concept—and more precisely with that of "original justice"—theology defines the state of man before original sin. In the present analysis of the "beginning," which paves for us the indispensable ways toward understanding the theology of the body, we must dwell on the mystery of man's original state. In fact, precisely this consciousness of the body—or even better, *consciousness of the meaning of the body*—on which we are trying to throw light through the analysis of the "beginning," *reveals the distinctive character of original innocence.*

What becomes perhaps most of all directly apparent in Genesis 2:25 is precisely the mystery of this innocence, which both the man and the woman bore within themselves from the beginning. The body itself of each is a witness of this characteristic, in some way an "eyewitness." It is significant that the statement contained in Genesis 2:25—about reciprocal nakedness free from shame—is a statement unique in its kind in the whole Bible, so much so that it was never to be repeated. On the contrary, we can quote many texts in which nakedness is linked with shame or even, in a still stronger sense, with "defilement."[27] In this wide context, the reasons are all the more visible for discovering in Genesis 2:25 a particular trace of the mystery of original innocence and a particular factor of its radiation into the human subject. This innocence belongs to the dimension of grace contained in the mystery of creation, that is, to that mysterious *gift made to man's innermost [being]—to the human heart—that allows* both the man and the woman *to exist* from the "beginning" *in the reciprocal relationship of the disinterested gift of self.* Included in this is the revelation together with the discovery of the "spousal" meaning of the body in its masculinity and femininity. One can understand why we speak in this case about revelation together with discovery. From the point of view of our analysis, it is essential that the discovery of the spousal meaning of the body takes place through original innocence; even better: it is this discovery that unveils original innocence and makes it evident.

Original Innocence and Consciousness of the Spousal Meaning of the Body

4. Original innocence belongs to the mystery of man's "beginning," from which he then separated himself by committing the original sin. This does not mean, however, that he is not able to approach this mystery by his theological knowledge. "Historical" man attempts to understand the mystery of original innocence, as it were, through a contrast, that is, by going back also to the experience of his own guilt

---

27. In the ancient Middle East, "nakedness" in the sense of a "lack of clothing" meant the abject state of people deprived of freedom: of slaves, prisoners of war, or condemned criminals, of those who did not enjoy the protection of the law. The nakedness of women was considered a dishonor (see, e.g., the threats of the prophets: Hos 1:2; Ezek 23:26, 29).

A free person, concerned with his or her dignity, had to dress sumptuously: the longer the train of his clothes, the higher was the dignity (e.g., Joseph's coat, which inspired the jealousy of his brothers; or of the Pharisees, who lengthened their fringes).

The second meaning of "nakedness" in the euphemistic sense regarded the sexual act. The Hebrew word ʿerwā[h] can signify an empty place (e.g., of the village), lack of clothing, undressing, but it had nothing in itself shameful.

and of his own sinfulness.[28] He seeks to understand original innocence as a characteristic that is essential for the theology of the body,
taking as his point of departure the experience of shame; in fact, the
biblical text points him in this direction. Original *innocence* is thus
that which "radically," that is, *at its very roots, excludes the shame of the
body* in the relation between man and woman, that which *eliminates
the necessity of this shame in man,* in his *heart* or his *consciousness.*
Although original innocence speaks above all about the gift of the
Creator, about grace, which made it possible for man to live the
meaning of the primary gift of the world and in particular the meaning of reciprocal gift of one person to the other through masculinity
and femininity in this world, nevertheless, this innocence seems to
refer first of all to the interior state of the human "heart," of the
human will. At least indirectly, it includes the revelation and discovery
of human moral consciousness—the revelation and discovery of the
whole dimension of conscience—obviously before the knowledge of
good and evil. In a certain sense, one should understand it as original
righteousness.

5. In the prism of our "historical a posteriori," we are thus trying
to reconstruct in some way the proper character of original innocence,
understood as the content of the reciprocal experience of the body, as
the experience of its spousal meaning (according to the testimony of
Gen 2:23–25). Since happiness and innocence are inscribed in the
frame of the communion of persons, like two converging lines of
man's existence in the very mystery of creation, *the beatifying conscious-*

---

28. "We know, in fact, that the law is spiritual; but I am of flesh, sold as a slave of
sin. I do not even understand what I do: for I do not do what I want, but I do the very
thing I detest.... But in fact it is no longer I that do it, but sin that dwells within me.
For I know that nothing good dwells within me, that is, in my flesh. There is in me
the desire for the good, but not the power to do it. For I do not do the good I want,
but the evil I do not want is what I do. Now if I do what I do not want, it is no longer
I that do it, but sin that dwells within me. So I find it to be a law that when I want
to do what is good, evil lies close at hand. For I joyfully agree with the law of God in
my innermost [being], but I see in my members another law at war with the law of
my mind, making me captive to the law of sin that dwells in my members. Wretched
man that I am! Who will rescue me from this body destined to death?" Rom 7:14–15,
17–24. "*Video meliora proboque, deteriora sequor* [I see and approve what is better, but
follow what is worse]." Ovid, *Metamorphoses,* 7.20.

ness of the meaning of the body—that is, of the spousal meaning of human masculinity and femininity—*is conditioned by original innocence.* There is no obstacle, it seems, against understanding this original innocence as a particular "purity of heart" preserving interior faithfulness to the gift according to the spousal meaning of the body. Consequently, original innocence conceived in this way manifests itself as a tranquil witness of conscience that (in this case) precedes any experience of good and evil; and yet, this serene witness of conscience is something all the more beatifying. One can say, in fact, that consciousness of the spousal meaning of the body in its masculinity and femininity becomes "humanly" beatifying only through this witness.

We will devote the next meditation to this topic, namely, to the link between man's innocence (purity of heart) and his happiness, which becomes evident in the analysis of his "beginning."

Innocence at the Foundation of the Exchange of the Gift

17 *General Audience of February 6, 1980*
(Insegnamenti, 3, no. 1 [1980]: 326–29)

1. WE ARE CONTINUING THE EXAMINATION of the "beginning" to which Jesus appealed in his dialogue with the Pharisees about the topic of marriage. This reflection requires us to go beyond the threshold of man's history and to reach the state of original innocence. To grasp the meaning of this innocence, we base ourselves in some way on the experience of "historical" man, on the witness of his heart, of his conscience.

2. As we follow the line of the "historical a posteriori," we attempt to reconstruct the distinctive character of the original innocence contained in the reciprocal experience of the body and of its spousal meaning as Genesis 2:23–25 attests. The situation described in this text reveals the beatifying meaning of the body, which in the sphere of the mystery of creation man attains, so to speak, in the complementarity of what is masculine and feminine in him. At the roots of this

experience, however, must be the interior freedom of the gift, united above all to innocence; *the human will is originally innocent* and thus *furthers the reciprocity and the exchange of the gift of the body according to its masculinity and femininity as the gift of the person.* Consequently, the innocence attested in Genesis 2:25 can be defined as the innocence of the reciprocal experience of the body. The sentence, "Both were naked, the man and his wife, but they did not feel shame," expresses precisely such innocence in the reciprocal "experience of the body," an innocence that inspires the inner exchange of the gift of the person, which concretely realizes the spousal meaning of masculinity and femininity in their reciprocal relation. Thus, in order to understand the innocence of the mutual experience of the body, we must try to clarify what constitutes the inner innocence of the exchange of the gift of the person. This exchange constitutes, in fact, the true source of the experience of innocence.

3. We can say that inner innocence (that is, the rightness of intention) in the exchange of the gift consists in a reciprocal "acceptance" of the other in such a way that it corresponds to the very essence of the gift; in this way, the mutual gift creates the communion of persons. It is a question, therefore, of "welcoming" the other human being and of "accepting" him or her precisely because in this mutual relationship, about which Genesis 2:23–25 speaks, the man and the woman become a gift, each one for the other, through the whole truth and evidence of their own body in its masculinity and femininity. It is a question, therefore, of such an "acceptance" or "welcome" in reciprocal nakedness that it expresses and sustains the meaning of the gift and thus deepens its reciprocal dignity. This dignity corresponds deeply to the fact that the Creator has willed (and continually wills) man, male and female, "for his own sake" [*Gaudium et Spes*, 24:3]. Innocence "of heart"—and, as a consequence, innocence of experience—signifies a moral participation in the eternal and permanent act of God's will.

The contrary of such "welcoming" or "acceptance" of the other human being as a gift would be a loss of the gift itself and thus a transmutation and even reduction of the other to an "object for myself" (object of concupiscence, of "undue appropriation," etc.).

We will not deal in detail now with this manifold presumable antithesis of the gift. One must, however, note already here, in the context of Genesis 2:23–25, that such extortion of the gift from the other human being (from the woman on the part of the man and vice versa) and his or her inner reduction to a mere "object for me," should mark exactly the beginning of shame. Shame corresponds, in fact, to a threat inflicted on the gift in its personal intimacy and bears witness to the inner downfall of innocence in reciprocal experience.

Exchange of the Gift—Interpretation of Genesis 2:25

4. According to Genesis 2:25, "the man and the woman did not feel shame." This allows us to reach the conclusion that the exchange of the gift, in which their whole humanity, soul and body, femininity and masculinity, participates, is realized *by preserving the inner characteristic (that is, precisely innocence) of self-donation and of the acceptance of the other as a gift.* These two functions of the mutual exchange are deeply connected in the whole process of the "gift of self": giving and accepting the gift interpenetrate in such a way that the very act of giving becomes acceptance, and acceptance transforms itself into giving.

5. Genesis 2:23–25 allows us to deduce that, due to original innocence, the woman, who in the mystery of creation "is given" by the Creator to the man, is "welcomed" or accepted by him as a gift. The biblical text is completely clear and transparent at this point. At the same time, the acceptance of the woman by the man and the very way of accepting her become, as it were, a first gift in such a way that the woman, in giving herself (from the very first moment, in which, in the mystery of creation, she has been "given" by the Creator to the man), at the same time "discovers herself," thanks to the fact that she has been accepted and welcomed and thanks to *the way* in which she has been received by the man. She therefore finds herself in her own gift of self ("through a sincere gift of self," *Gaudium et Spes,* 24:3) when she has been accepted in the way in which the Creator willed her, namely, "for her own sake," through her humanity and femininity; she comes to the innermost depth of her own person and to the full possession of herself when, in this acceptance, the whole dignity of the gift is ensured through the offer of what she is in the whole truth of her humanity and in the whole reality of her body and her sex, of her femininity. We add that this *finding of oneself in one's own gift becomes the source of a new gift of self* that grows by the power of the inner disposition to the exchange of the gift and in the measure in which it encounters the same and even deeper acceptance and welcome as the fruit of an ever more intense consciousness of the gift itself.

6. It seems that the second creation account has assigned to the man "from the beginning" the function of the one who above all receives the gift (see Gen 2:23). The woman has "from the beginning" been entrusted to his eyes, to his consciousness, to his sensibility, to his "heart"; he, by contrast, must in some way ensure the very process of the exchange of the gift, the reciprocal interpenetration of giving and receiving the gift, which, precisely through its reciprocity, creates an authentic communion of persons.

While in the mystery of creation the woman is the one who is "given" to the man, he on his part, in receiving her as a gift in the full truth of her person and femininity, enriches her by this very reception, and, at the same time, he too is enriched in this reciprocal relationship. The man is enriched not only through her, who gives her own person and femininity to him, but also by his gift of self. The man's act of self-donation, in answer to that of the woman, is for him himself an enrichment; in fact, it is here that *the specific essence,* as it were, *of his masculinity is manifested, which, through the reality of the body and of its sex, reaches the innermost depth of "self-possession,"* thanks to which he is able both to give himself and to receive the gift of the other. The man, therefore, not only accepts the gift, but at the same time is welcomed as a gift by the woman in the self-revelation of the inner spiritual essence of his masculinity together with the whole truth of his body and his sex. When he is accepted in this way, he is enriched by this acceptance and welcoming of the gift of his own masculinity. It follows that such an acceptance, in which the man finds himself through the "sincere gift of self," becomes in him a source of a new and more profound enrichment of the woman with himself. The exchange is reciprocal, and the mutual effects of the "sincere gift" and of "finding oneself" reveal themselves and grow in that exchange [*Gaudium et Spes,* 24:3].

In this way, by following the trail of the "historical a posteriori"—
and above all by following the trail of human hearts—we can reproduce and, as it were, reconstruct that reciprocal exchange of the gift of
the person, which is described in the ancient text of Genesis, so rich
and profound.

Theology of Original Innocence

18 *General Audience of February 13, 1980*
(Insegnamenti, 3, no. 1 [1980]: 378–81)

1. TODAY'S MEDITATION PRESUPPOSES what has already been established by our various previous analyses. They sprang from the answer
Jesus gave to his interlocutors (see Mt 19:3–9; Mk 10:1–12), who had
asked him a question about marriage, about its indissolubility and
unity. The Teacher had urged them to consider attentively *what was
"from the beginning."* For this reason, in the cycle of our meditations
up until today, we have attempted to reproduce in some way the reality of union, or better, of the communion of persons, lived "from the
beginning" by man and woman. After this, we tried to penetrate into
the content of the concise verse Genesis 2:25, "Now both were naked,
the man and his wife, but they did not feel shame."

These words refer to the gift of original innocence by revealing its
synthetic character, so to speak. On this basis, theology has built *the
overall image of man's original innocence and justice before original sin* by
applying the method of objectivization specific to metaphysics and
metaphysical anthropology. In the present analysis, we are trying
rather to take into account the aspect of human subjectivity; subjectivity, moreover, seems to be closer to the original texts, especially to
the second creation account, that is, the Yahwist text.

2. A certain diversity of interpretations notwithstanding, it seems
sufficiently clear that the "experience of the body," as we can gather
from the ancient text of Genesis 2:23 and even more so of Genesis
2:25, indicates a degree of spiritualization of man that differs from
the one about which the text speaks after original sin (Gen 3) and
which we know from the experience of "historical" man. It is a different measure of "spiritualization" that implies another composition of
inner forces in man himself, another body-soul relation, as it were,

other inner proportions between sensitivity, spirituality, and affectivity, that is, another degree of inner sensibility for the gifts of the Holy Spirit. All of this conditions the state of man's original innocence and at the same time determines it, allowing us also to understand the account of Genesis. Theology and also the Church's magisterium have given to these fundamental truths a form of their own.[29]

3. When we undertake the analysis of the "beginning" according to the dimension of the theology of the body, we do so by basing ourselves on the words of Christ with which he himself appealed to that "beginning." When he said, "Have you not read that from the beginning the Creator created them male and female?" (Mt 19:4), he ordered us and always orders us to return to the depth of the mystery of creation. And we do so in the full awareness of the gift of original innocence, which belonged to man before original sin. Although an insurmountable barrier divides us from what man was then as male and female, through the gift of grace united to the mystery of creation, and from what both were for each other as a reciprocal gift, we are nevertheless *trying to understand that state of original innocence in its link with man's "historical" state after original sin, "status naturae lapsae simul et redemptae* [the state of fallen and at the same time redeemed nature]."

Through the category of the "historical a posteriori" we are attempting to reach the original meaning of the body and to grasp the link that exists between it and the nature of original innocence in the "experience of the body," which is made evident in such a significant way in the Genesis account. We come to the conclusion that it is important and essential to determine this link with precision, not only with reference to man's "theological prehistory," in which the shared life of man and woman was completely permeated, as it were, by the

---

29. "If anyone does not confess that the first man Adam, when he had transgressed God's commandment *in Paradise,* immediately lost *the holiness and justice in which he was constituted*...let him be anathema." Council of Trent, sess. V, can. 1, 2, DS 788–89.

"The first parents were constituted in the state of holiness and justice.... The state of original justice conferred on the first parents was gratuitous and truly supernatural.... The first parents were constituted in the state of integral nature, that is, immune from concupiscence, ignorance, pain, and death...and enjoyed a unique happiness.... The gifts of integrity conferred on the first parents were gratuitous and preternatural." A. Tanquerey, *Synopsis Theologiae Dogmaticae,* 14th ed. (Paris, 1943), 534–49.

grace of original innocence, but also in relation to the possibility of its revealing to us the permanent roots of the human and especially the theological aspect of the *ethos of the body*.

The Root of the Ethos of the Human Body

4. Man enters into the world and into the innermost guiding thread of his future and his history with the consciousness of the spousal meaning of his own body, of his own masculinity and femininity. Original innocence says that this meaning is conditioned "ethically," and further that, on its part, it constitutes the future of human ethos. This is very important for the theology of the body: it is the reason why we must build this theology "from the beginning," carefully following the indication of Christ's words.

In the mystery of creation, man and woman *were in a particular way "given" to one another by the Creator,* not only in the dimension of that first human pair and of that first communion of persons, but in the whole perspective of the existence of the human race and of the human family. The fundamental fact of this existence of man in every stage of his history is that God "created them male and female"; in fact, he always creates them in this way, and they are always such. The understanding of the fundamental meanings contained in the very mystery of creation, such as the spousal meaning of the body (and of the fundamental conditioning of this meaning), is important and indispensable for knowing who man is and who he ought to be, and therefore how he should shape his own activity. It is something essential and important for the future of human ethos.

5. Genesis 2:24 notes that the two, man and woman, were created for marriage: "For this reason a man will leave his father and his mother and unite with his wife, and the two will be one flesh." In this way, a great creative perspective is opened up, which is precisely the perspective of man's existence, which continually renews itself by means of "procreation" (one could say of "self-reproduction"). This perspective is deeply rooted in the consciousness of humanity (see Gen 2:23) and also in the particular consciousness of the spousal meaning of the body (Gen 2:25). Before they become husband and wife (a little later, Gen 4:1 speaks of it concretely), man and woman *come forth from the mystery of creation* first of all *as brother and sister in the same humanity.* The understanding of the spousal meaning of the body in its masculinity and femininity reveals the innermost point of their freedom, which is the freedom of the gift.

It is from here that the communion of persons begins in which both encounter each other and give themselves reciprocally in the fullness of their subjectivity. In this way, both grow as persons-subjects, and grow reciprocally, one for the other, also through their bodies and through that "nakedness" free from shame. In this communion of persons, the whole depth of the original solitude of man (of the first and of all) is perfectly ensured and, at the same time, this solitude is permeated and enlarged in a marvelous way by the gift of the "other." If man and woman cease being reciprocally a disinterested gift, as they were for one another in the mystery of creation, they recognize that "they are naked" (see Gen 3:7). It is then that shame about that nakedness is born in them, a shame they did not feel in the state of original innocence.

Original *innocence manifests and at the same time constitutes the perfect ethos of the gift.*

We will return to this topic.

19 *General Audience of February 20, 1980* (*Insegnamenti*, 3, no. 1 [1980]: 428–31)

1. GENESIS POINTS OUT THAT MAN AND WOMAN were created for marriage, "A man will leave his father and his mother and unite with his wife, and the two will be one flesh" (Gen 2:24).

This opens the great creative perspective of human existence, which always renews itself through "procreation," that is, "self-reproduction." This perspective is rooted in the consciousness of humanity and also in the particular understanding of the spousal meaning of the body with its masculinity and femininity. In the mystery of creation, man and woman are a reciprocal gift. Original innocence manifests and at the same time determines the *perfect ethos of the gift.*

We spoke about this during the last meeting. The ethos of the gift delineates in part the problem of the "subjectivity" of man, who is a subject made in the image and likeness of God. In the creation account (see Gen 2:23–25), "the woman" is certainly not just "an object" for the man, although both remain before one another in the whole fullness of their objectivity as creatures, as "bone from my bones, flesh from my flesh," as male and female, both of them naked. Only the nakedness that turns the woman into an "object" for the man, or vice versa, is a source of shame. The fact that "they did not feel shame" means that the woman was not an "object" for the man, nor he for her. Inner innocence as "purity of heart" made it impossible somehow for one to be reduced by the other to the level of a mere object. If "they did not feel shame," this means that they were united by the consciousness of the gift, that they had reciprocal *awareness of the spousal meaning of their bodies,* in which the freedom of the gift is expressed and *the whole inner richness of the person as subject is shown.* This reciprocal interpenetration of the "I" of the human persons, of the man and the woman, seems to exclude subjectively any "reduction to an object." What is revealed here is the subjective profile of that love, about which one can say, moreover, that "it is objective" to the very depths, inasmuch as it is nourished by the same reciprocal "objectivity of the gift."

2. After original sin, man and woman were to lose the grace of original innocence. The discovery of the spousal meaning of the body was to cease being for them a simple reality of revelation and of grace. Yet, this meaning was to *remain as a task given to man by the ethos of the gift,* inscribed in the depth of the human heart as a distant echo, as it were, of original innocence. From that spousal meaning, human love was to be formed in its interior truth and authentic subjectivity. And even through the veil of shame, man was continually to discover himself in it as the guardian of the mystery of the subject, that is, of the freedom of the gift, in order to defend this freedom from any reduction to the position of a mere object.

The Foundation of the Primordial Sacrament— The Body as Sign

3. For the present, however, we find ourselves before the threshold of man's earthly history. The man and the woman have not crossed it yet toward the knowledge of good and evil. They are immersed in the

very mystery of creation, and the depth of this mystery hidden in their heart is innocence, grace, love, and justice. "And God saw everything that he had made, and indeed, it was very good" (Gen 1:31). Man appears in the visible world as the highest expression of the divine gift, because he bears within himself the inner dimension of the gift. And with it he carries into the world his particular likeness to God, with which he transcends and also rules his "visibility" in the world, his bodiliness, his masculinity or femininity, his nakedness. A reflection of this likeness is also the primordial awareness of the spousal meaning of the body pervaded by the mystery of original innocence.

4. Thus, in this dimension, a primordial *sacrament* is constituted, understood as a *sign that* efficaciously *transmits in the visible world the invisible mystery hidden in God from eternity.* And this is the mystery of Truth and Love, the mystery of divine life, in which man really participates. In the history of man, it is original innocence that begins this participation and is also the source of original happiness. The sacrament, as a visible sign, is constituted with man, inasmuch as he is a "body," through his "visible" masculinity and femininity. The body, in fact, and only the body, is capable of making visible what is invisible: the spiritual and the divine. It has been created to transfer into the visible reality of the world the mystery hidden from eternity in God, and thus to be a sign of it.

5. In man, created in the image of God, the very sacramentality of creation, the sacramentality of the world, was thus in some way revealed. In fact, through his bodiliness, his masculinity and femininity, man becomes a visible sign of the economy of Truth and Love, which has its source in God himself and was revealed already in the mystery of creation. Against this vast background, we fully understand the words in Genesis 2:24 that are constitutive of the sacrament of Marriage: "For this reason a man will leave his father and his mother and unite with his wife, and the two will be one flesh." Against this vast background we also understand that, through the whole depth of their anthropological meaning, the words of Genesis 2:25 ("Both were naked, the man and his wife, but they did not feel shame") express the fact that, *together with man, holiness has entered the*

visible world, the world created for him. The sacrament of the world, and the sacrament of man in the world, comes forth from the divine source of holiness and is instituted, at the same time, for holiness. Original innocence, connected with the experience of the spousal meaning of the body, is holiness itself, which permits man to express himself deeply with his own body, precisely through the "sincere gift" of self [*Gaudium et Spes,* 24:3]. Consciousness of the gift conditions in this case "the sacrament of the body": in his body as man or woman, man senses himself as a subject of holiness.

6. With this consciousness of the meaning of his own body, man, as male and female, enters into the world as a subject of truth and love. One can say that Genesis 2:23–25 speaks about *the first feast of humanity, as it were,* in the whole original fullness of the experience of the spousal meaning of the body: and it is *a feast of humanity* that draws its origin from the divine sources of Truth and Love in the very mystery of creation. And although over this feast the horizon of sin and death (Gen 3) was very soon to be extended, nevertheless, we draw a first hope already from the mystery of creation: namely, that the fruit of the divine economy of truth and love, which revealed itself "at the beginning," is not Death, but Life, and not so much the destruction of the body <of man made "in the image>* of God," but rather the "call to glory" (Rom 8:30).

6. "Knowledge" and Procreation (Gen 4:1)

Between Poverty of Expression and Depth of Meaning

20 *General Audience of March 5, 1980* (*Insegnamenti,* 3, no. 1 [1980]: 517–21)

1. TO THE WHOLE OF OUR ANALYSES devoted to the biblical "beginning," we wish to add a further brief passage taken from Genesis 4. For this purpose, however, we must always go back to the words spoken by Jesus Christ in the dialogue with the Pharisees (see Mt 19 and

---

*Translator's note: The words in angle brackets are missing in the *Insegnamenti* text, and have been supplied from UD.

Mk 10)[30] within the sphere of which our reflections are unfolding; they concern the context of human existence, according to which death and the destruction of the body connected with it (according to those words, "to dust you shall return," Gen 3:19) have become man's common lot. Christ appeals to the "beginning," to the original dimension of the mystery of creation, when this dimension had already been shattered by the *mysterium iniquitatis* [mystery of iniquity], that is, by sin and, together with sin, also by death: *mysterium mortis* [mystery of death]. Sin and death have entered into man's history *in some way through the very heart of that unity that had from the "beginning" been formed by man and woman,* created and called to become "one flesh" (Gen 2:24). Already at the beginning of our meditations we observed that, by appealing to the "beginning," Christ leads us in some way beyond the limits of man's hereditary sinfulness to his original innocence; he thus allows us to find the continuity and the link that exists between these two situations, the situations by which the drama of the origins was produced as well as the revelation of the mystery of man to historical man.

This authorizes us, so to speak, after the analyses concerning the state of original innocence, to move on to the last of these analyses, namely, to the analysis of "knowledge and generation." Thematically, knowledge is closely tied to the blessing of fruitfulness inserted in the first account of the creation of man as male and female (Gen 1:27–28). Historically, by contrast, it is already inserted into the horizon of sin and death, which, as Genesis 3 teaches, has weighed heavily on the consciousness of the meaning of the human body, as soon as the first covenant with the Creator was broken.

2. In Genesis 4, and thus still within the boundaries of the Yahwist text, we read, "Adam united himself with Eve his wife, who conceived and gave birth to Cain and said, 'I have acquired a man from the Lord.' Then she gave birth also to his brother Abel" (Gen

---

30. One must keep in mind the fact that in the dialogue with the Pharisees (Mt 19:7–9; Mk 10:4–6) Christ takes a position with regard to the practice of the Mosaic Law concerning the so-called "certificate of divorce." The words, "because of the hardness of your heart," spoken by Christ reflect not only "the history of hearts," but also the whole complexity of the positive law of the Old Testament, which always sought "human compromise" in this very delicate area.

4:1–2). If we connect that first fact of the birth of a man on earth with knowledge, we do so on the basis of the literal translation of the text, according to which conjugal "union" is defined precisely as "knowledge." In fact, the translation just quoted says, *"Adam united himself* with Eve his wife," while according to the letter one should translate, *"knew his wife,"* which seems to correspond more exactly to the Semitic term yāḏaᶜ.[31] One can see in this a sign of the poverty of the ancient language, which lacked varied expressions for defining differentiated facts. Nevertheless, it remains significant that *the situation in which husband and wife unite* so intimately among themselves *as to form "one flesh" was defined as "knowledge."* In this way, in fact, from the very poverty of the language there seems to arise a specific depth of meaning that derives from all the meanings analyzed up to this point.

3. Evidently, this depth is also important with respect to the "archetype" of the way we conceive bodily man, his masculinity and femininity, and thus his sex. Thus, the term "knowledge" used in Genesis 4:1–2 and often in the Bible, *raises* the conjugal relation of man and woman, that is, the fact that through the duality of sex they become "one flesh," *and brings it into the specific dimension of the persons.* Genesis 4:1–2 speaks only about "knowledge" of the woman by

---

31. In biblical language, "to know" (yāḏaᶜ) does not signify only a merely intellectual knowledge, but also a concrete experience, such as, for example, the experience of suffering (see Isa 53:3), of sin (Wis 3:13), of war and peace (Judg 3:1; Isa 59:8). From this experience springs also moral judgment: "knowledge of good and evil" (Gen 2:9, 17).

"Knowledge" enters the field of interpersonal relations when it concerns family solidarity (Deut 33:9) and especially conjugal relations. In the case of the conjugal act, the term underlines the fatherhood of illustrious persons and the order of their descendants (see Gen 4:1, 25, 17; 1 Sam 1:19) as valid data for genealogy, to which the Priestly tradition (hereditary in Israel) gave great importance.

"Knowledge" could, however, signify also all other sexual relations, even illicit ones (see Num 31:17; Gen 19:5; Judg 19:22).

In its negative form, the verb denotes abstinence from sexual relations, especially in the case of virgins (see e.g., 1 Kings 1:4; Judg 11:39). In this field, the New Testament uses two Semiticisms when speaking about Joseph (Mt 1:25) and Mary (Lk 1:34).

The aspect of the existential relation of "knowledge" takes on a particular significance when its object is God himself (see e.g., Ps 139; Jer 31:34; Hos 2:22; and also Jn 14:7–9; 17:3).

the man, as if to underline above all the man's activity. One can, however, also speak of the reciprocity of this "knowledge," in which man
and woman participate through their body and their sex. Let us add
that a series of subsequent biblical texts, e.g., the very same chapter of
Genesis (see Gen 4:17.25), speak with the same language. And this
way of speaking goes all the way up to the words spoken by Mary of
Nazareth in the Annunciation, "How is this possible? I do not know
man" (Lk 1:34).

"Knowledge" as Personal Archetype

4. Thus, with that biblical "knew," which appears for the first time
in Genesis 4:1–2, we find ourselves face to face with, on the one hand,
the direct expression of human intentionality (because it is proper to
knowledge) and, on the other hand, the whole reality of conjugal life
and conjugal union, in which man and woman become "one flesh."

When it speaks of "knowledge" here, even if only because of the
poverty of its language, the Bible indicates the deepest essence of the
reality of shared married life. This essence appears as a component
and, at the same time, as a result of the meanings the traces of which
we have been trying to follow from the beginning of our study; it is,
in fact, part of the consciousness of the meaning of one's body. In
Genesis 4:1, when they become one flesh, the man and the woman
experience the meaning of their bodies in a particular way. Together,
they thus become one single subject, as it were, of that act and that
experience, although they remain two really distinct subjects in this
unity. This authorizes us in some sense to affirm that "the husband
knows the wife" or that both "know each other" reciprocally. Thus,
they reveal themselves to one another with *that specific depth of their
own human "I," which precisely reveals itself also through their sex,* their
masculinity and femininity. And thus, in a singular way, the woman
"is given" in the mode of knowledge to the man, and he to her.

5. If we are to keep continuity with the analyses carried out so far
(especially with the final ones interpreting man in the dimension of
gift), we must observe that according to Genesis *datum* [that which is
given] and *donum* [gift] are equivalent.

Nevertheless, Genesis 4:1–2 stresses above all *datum*. In conjugal "knowledge," the woman "is given" to the man and he to her, because the body and [its] sex enter directly into the very structure and content of this "knowledge." Thus, the reality of conjugal union in which man and woman become "one flesh" contains in itself a new and in some way definitive discovery of the meaning of the human body in its masculinity and femininity. Yet, in view of this discovery, is it right to speak only of "sexual life together"? One must keep in mind that each of them, the man and the woman, is not only a passive object, defined by his own body and his own sex, and in this way determined "by nature." On the contrary, precisely through being man and woman, each of them is "given" to the other as a unique and unrepeatable subject, as "I," as person. [His] sex is not only decisive for man's somatic individuality, but at the same time it defines his personal identity and concreteness. And exactly *in this personal identity and concreteness as an unrepeatable feminine or masculine "I," man is "known" when the words of Genesis 2:24 come true*: "the man will unite with his wife, and the two will be one flesh." The "knowledge" about which Genesis 4:1–2 and all subsequent biblical texts speak reaches the innermost roots of this identity and concreteness, which man and woman owe to their sex. Such concreteness means both the uniqueness and unrepeatability of the person.

It was thus worthwhile to reflect about the eloquence of the biblical text quoted and of the word "knew"; despite the apparent lack of terminological precision, it allows us to dwell on the depth and the dimensions of a concept of which our contemporary language, precise though it is, deprives us.

21 General Audience of March 12, 1980
(*Insegnamenti*, 3, no. 1 [1980]: 540–45)

1. IN THE LAST MEDITATION, we analyzed the sentence of Genesis 4:1 and in particular the term "knew," which is used in the original text to define conjugal union. We also pointed out that this biblical "knowledge" establishes a kind of personal archetype[32] of human bodiliness

---

32. As for archetypes, C. G. Jung describes them as "a priori" forms of various functions of the soul: perception of relations, creative imagination. The forms are filled

and sexuality. This seems absolutely fundamental for understanding man, who from the "beginning" is in search of the meaning of his own body. This meaning stands at the very basis of the theology of the body. The term "knew"—"united himself" (Gen 4:1–2)—synthesizes the whole density of the biblical text analyzed so far. According to Genesis 4:1, the "man" who for the first time "knows" the woman,

---

with content by materials of experience. They are not inert, but are charged with feeling and tendency. See esp. "Die psychologischen Aspekte des Mutterarchetypus," *Eranos* 6 (1932): 405–9.

According to this conception, one can encounter an archetype in the mutual relation between man and woman, a relation based on the binary and complementary realization of the human being in two sexes. The archetype will be filled with content through individual and collective experience, and it can bring the imagination into movement, creative of images. One should specify that the archetype (a) neither limits itself to, nor exalts itself in, the physical relation, but includes the relation of "knowing"; (b) it is full of tendency: desire-fear, gift-possession; (c) the archetype as proto-image (*Urbild*) is generator of images (*Bilder*).

The third aspect allows us to pass to hermeneutics, concretely, to that of the texts of Scripture and tradition. Primary religious language is symbolic (see W. Stählin, *Symbolon*, 1958; I. Macquarrie, *God Talk*, 1968; T. Fawcett, *The Symbolic Language of Religion*, 1970). Among symbols, he prefers some that are radical and exemplary, which we can call archetypal. Now, among these, the Bible uses that of the conjugal relation, concretely on the level of the knowing we described.

One of the first biblical poems that applies the conjugal archetype to the relations of God with his people culminates in the verb we are commenting on, "You shall know the Lord" (Hos 2:22, wᵊyādaᶜat ʾet-yhwh, attenuated in, "You will know that I am the Lord" =wᵊyādaᶜat kî-ʾănî yhwh: Isa 49:23; 60:16; Ezek 16:62, which are the three "conjugal poems"). This is the point of departure of a literary tradition that was to culminate in the Pauline application in Ephesians 5 to Christ and the Church; from there it was to pass into the Patristic tradition and that of the great mystics (e.g., *The Living Flame of Love* by St. John of the Cross.)

In the tractate *Grundzüge der Literatur und Sprachwissenschaft*, 4th ed. (Munich, 1976), 1.462, archetypes are defined as follows: "Ancient images and motifs that, according to Jung, form the content of the collective unconscious common to all human beings; they present symbols that, in all times and among all peoples, bring to life by way of images what is decisive for humanity with respect to ideas, representations, and instincts."

Freud, it seems, does not use the concept of archetype. He establishes a symbolism or code of fixed correspondences between present patent images and latent thoughts. The sense of the images is fixed, even if there is not only one; they may be reducible to some final thought that is, on its part, irreducible, usually some childhood experience. These are primary and of a sexual character (he does not, however, call them archetypes). See T. Todorov, *Théories du symbol* (Paris, 1977), 317; J. Jacoby, *Komplex, Archetyp, Symbol in der Psychologie C. G. Jung* (Zürich, 1957).

his wife, in the act of conjugal union is in fact the same one who—in giving names, that is, also by "knowing"—"differentiated" himself from the whole world of living beings or *animalia*, thus affirming himself as a person and subject. The "knowledge" about which Genesis 4:1 speaks does not and cannot distance him from the level of that primordial and fundamental self-consciousness. For this reason—whatever a one-sidedly "naturalistic" mentality may affirm about it—what happens in Genesis 4:1 cannot be a passive acceptance of one's own determination on the part of the body and of [its] sex, precisely because it is a question of "knowledge!"

Genesis 4:1 points, instead, to *a further discovery of the meaning of one's own body*, a common and reciprocal discovery, just as the existence of man, whom "God created male and female," is common and reciprocal from the beginning. The knowledge that stood at the basis of man's original solitude stands now at the basis of this unity of man and woman, the clear perspective of which the Creator included in the very mystery of creation (Gen 1:27; 2:23). In this "knowledge," man confirms the meaning of the name "Eve," given to his wife, "because she was mother of all the living" (Gen 3:20).

Fatherhood and Motherhood as the Human Meaning of "Knowledge"

2. According to Genesis 4:1, the one who knows is the man and the one who is known is the woman, the wife. It seems as if the specific determination of the woman, through her own body and her sex, hides what constitutes the very depth of her femininity. The man, by contrast, is the one who—after sin—was the first to feel the shame of his nakedness and the first to say, "I was afraid, because I am naked, and I hid myself" (Gen 3:10). We will have to return separately to the state of mind of both after the loss of original innocence. Already now, however, we should observe that in Genesis 4:1 *the mystery of femininity manifests and reveals itself in its full depth through motherhood, as the text says, "who conceived and gave birth."* The woman stands before the man as mother, subject of the new human life that is conceived and develops in her and is born from her into the world. In

this way, what also reveals itself is the mystery of the man's masculinity, that is, the generative and "paternal" meaning of his body.[33]

3. The theology of the body contained in Genesis is concise and sparing with words. At the same time, fundamental and in some sense primary and definitive contents find expression in it. All human beings find themselves in their own way in that biblical "knowledge." Woman's constitution differs from that of man; in fact, we know today that it is different even in the deepest bio-physiological determinants. The difference is shown only in a limited measure on the outside, in the build and form of her body. Motherhood shows this constitution from within, as a particular power of the feminine organism, which serves with creative specificity for the conception and generation of human beings with the concurrence of the man. "Knowledge" conditions begetting.

Begetting is a perspective that man and woman insert into their reciprocal "knowledge." Begetting goes thus beyond the limits of the subject-object that man and woman seem to be for each other, given that "knowledge" indicates, on the one hand, he who "knows" and, on the other, she who "is known" (or vice versa). This "knowledge" includes also the consummation of marriage, the specific *consummatum*; in this way one obtains the grasp of the "objectivity" of the body, hidden in the somatic powers of man and woman, and at the same time the grasp of the objectivity of man, who "is" this body. Through the body, the human person is "husband" and "wife"; at the same time, in this particular act of "knowledge" mediated by personal masculinity and femininity, one seems to reach also the discovery of the "pure" subjectivity of the gift: that is, mutual self-realization in the gift.

4. Procreation brings it about that "the man and the woman (his wife)" *know each other reciprocally in the "third," originated by both.* For

---

33. Fatherhood is one of the most prominent aspects of humanity in Sacred Scripture.

The text of Genesis 5:3, "Adam...begot a son *in his image, in his likeness,*" is explicitly connected with the account of the creation of man (Gen 1:27; 5:1) and seems to attribute to the earthly father the participation in the divine work of transmitting life, and perhaps also in the joy present in the statement, "God saw everything that he had made, and indeed, it was very good" (Gen 1:31).

this reason, this "knowledge" becomes in some way a revelation of the new man, in whom both, the man and the woman, again recognize each other, their humanity, their living image. In everything that is determined by both body and sex, "knowledge" inscribes a living and real content. Consequently, "knowledge" in the biblical sense signifies that man's "biological" determination, on the part of his body and his sex, is no longer something passive but reaches a level and content specific to self-conscious and self-determining persons; therefore, it brings with it a particular consciousness of the meaning of the human body bound to fatherhood and motherhood.

5. The whole exterior constitution of woman's body, its particular look, the qualities that stand, with the power of a perennial attraction, at the beginning of the "knowledge" about which Genesis 4:1–2 speaks ("Adam united himself with Eve"), *are in strict union with motherhood.* With the simplicity characteristic of it, the Bible (and the liturgy following it) honors and praises throughout the centuries "the womb that bore you and the breasts from which you sucked milk"(Lk 11:27). These words are a eulogy of motherhood, of femininity, of the feminine body in its typical expression of creative love. And in the Gospel these words refer to the Mother of Jesus, Mary, the second Eve. The first woman, on the other hand, at the moment in which the maternal maturity of her body revealed itself for the first time, when she "conceived and bore," said, "I have acquired a man from the Lord" (Gen 4:1).

6. These words express the whole theological depth of the function of begetting-procreating. The body of the woman becomes a place of the conception of the new human being.[34] In her womb, the human being takes on its characteristic human appearance before being brought into the world. The somatic homogeneity of man and woman, which found its first expression in the words "this...is flesh

---

34. According to the text of Genesis 1:26, the call to existence is at the same time a transmission of the divine image and likeness. Man must proceed to transmitting this image, thus continuing God's work. The account of the generation of Seth underlines this aspect. "When Adam was two hundred and thirty years old, he begot a son in his image, in his likeness" (Gen 5:3).

Given that Adam and Eve were an image of God, Seth inherits this likeness from his parents to pass it on to others.

from my flesh and bone from my bones" (Gen 2:23), is confirmed in turn by the words of the first woman-mother, "I have acquired a man." The first woman to give birth *has full awareness of the mystery of creation, which renews itself in human generation.* She also has full awareness of the creative participation God has in human generation, his work and that of her husband, because she says, "I acquired a man from the Lord."

There cannot be any confusion between the spheres of action of the causes. The first parents transmit to all human parents—even after sin, together with the fruit of the tree of the knowledge of good and evil and on the threshold, as it were, of all "historical" experiences—the fundamental truth about the birth of man in the image of God, according to the laws of nature. In this new man—born from the woman-parent through the work of the man-parent—the same "image of God" is reproduced every time, the image of that God who constituted the humanity of the first man, "God created man in his image...; male and female he created them" (Gen 1:27).

Knowledge and Possession

7. Although there are deep differences between the state of original innocence and the state of man's hereditary sinfulness, that *"image of God" constitutes a basis of continuity and unity.* The "knowledge" about which Genesis 4:1 speaks is *the act that* originates being, or, *in union with the Creator, establishes a new human being in existence.* In his transcendental solitude, the first man took possession of the visible world, created for him, by knowing and giving their names to living beings (*animalia*). Since the same man, as male and female, knows

---

In Sacred Scripture, however, every vocation is united with a mission; the call to existence is, therefore, already predestination for God's work. "Before I formed you in the womb I knew you, and before you were born I consecrated you" (Jer 1:5; see also Isa 44:1; 49:1, 5).

God is the one who not only calls to existence, but sustains and develops life from the first moment of conception. "It is you who drew me from the womb / you have made me rest on my mother's bosom. / At my birth you received me / from my mother's womb you have been my God" (Ps 22:10–11; cf. Ps 139:13–15).

The attention of the biblical author focuses on *the very fact* of the gift of life. Interest in the manner in which it begins is rather secondary and appears only in later books (see Job 10:8.11; 2 Mac 7:22–23; Wis 7:1–3).

himself reciprocally in this specific community-communion of persons, in which man and woman unite so closely with each other that they become "one flesh," he constitutes humanity, that is, he confirms and renews the existence of man as image of God. Every time, both man and woman take this image again, so to speak, from the mystery of creation and transmit it "with the help of God-Yahweh."

The words of Genesis that bear witness to the first birth of man on earth contain, at the same time, everything that one can and should say about the dignity of human generation.

22 General Audience of March 26, 1980
(*Insegnamenti*, 3, no. 1 [1980]: 737–41)

1. WE ARE COMING TO THE END of the cycle of reflections with which we tried to follow the appeal of Christ transmitted by Matthew 19:3–9 and Mark 10:1–12: "Have you not read that from the beginning the Creator *created them male and female* and said, 'For this reason a man will leave his father and his mother and unite with his wife, and the two will be one flesh'?" (Mt 19:4–5). In Genesis, conjugal union is defined as "knowledge." "Adam united with Eve his wife, who conceived and gave birth to Cain and said, 'I have acquired a man from the Lord'" (Gen 4:1). Already in our earlier meditations, we tried to throw light on the content of that biblical "knowledge." By this knowledge, man, both male and female, not only gives the right name, as he did when he gave names to the other living beings (*animalia*), thereby taking possession of them, but he "knows" in the sense of Genesis 4:1 (and other passages of the Bible) and thus *realizes* what the name "man" expresses: he realizes humanity in the new man who is generated. In a certain sense, therefore, he realizes himself, that is, the man-person.

2. *In this way, the biblical cycle of "knowledge-generation" closes.* This cycle of "knowledge" is constituted by the union of persons in love, which allows them to unite so closely with each other that they become one flesh. Genesis fully reveals to us the truth of this cycle. Man, male and female, who, through the "knowledge" about which the Bible speaks, conceives and generates a new being similar to himself, to whom he can give the name "man" ("I have acquired a man"),

takes possession, so to speak, *of humanity itself,* or even better, retakes it into his possession. This retaking, however, occurs in a way that differs from the way he had taken possession of all the other living beings (*animalia*) when he had given each its name. At that time, in fact, he had become their master; he had begun to carry out the content of the Creator's commandment, "Subdue the earth and rule over it" (see Gen 1:28).

3. However, the first part of the commandment, "Be fruitful and multiply, fill the earth" (Gen 1:28), contains a further content and indicates a further component. In this "knowledge," in which they give rise to a being similar to themselves, about which they can say together, "It is flesh from my flesh and bone from my bones" (Gen 2:24), the man and the woman are "carried off" together, as it were, both taken into *possession by* the very humanity which they, in union and reciprocal "knowledge," want to express anew and take possession of anew by drawing it from themselves, from the marvelous masculine and feminine maturity of their bodies and in the end—through the whole sequence of human conceptions and generations from the beginning—from the very mystery of creation.

4. *In this sense one can explain biblical "knowledge" as "possession."* Is it possible to see in this knowledge some biblical equivalent of "eros"? We are dealing here with two conceptual spheres, with two languages: biblical and Platonic; only with great caution can they be interpreted by each other.[35] It seems, however, that in the original revelation one

---

35. According to Plato, "*erōs*" is the love that thirsts for the transcendent Beautiful and expresses the insatiability tending toward its eternal object; it, therefore, always elevates what is human toward the divine, which alone can appease the yearning of the soul imprisoned in matter; it is a love that does not shy away from the greatest effort in order to reach the ecstasy of union; it is therefore an egocentric love; it is desire, though directed toward sublime values. See Anders Nygren, *Agape and Eros,* trans. Philip S. Watson (Philadelphia: The Westminster Press, 1953), 235–40.

With the passing of the centuries, through many transformations, the meaning of "eros" has been lowered to merely sexual connotations. Characteristic of this situation is the following text by P. Chauchard, which even seems to deny to eros the characteristics of human love. "The cerebralization of sexuality does not lie in disagreeable technical tricks, but in the full recognition of its spirituality, of the fact that eros is not human, except when it is animated by agape, and that agape needs the incarnation in eros." P. Chauchard, *Vices des vertus, vertus des vices* (Paris, 1963), 147.

does not find the idea of the possession of the woman by the man, or vice versa, as an object. On the other hand, we know that, due to the tendency toward sin contracted as a consequence of original sin, man and woman must reconstruct the meaning of the reciprocal disinterested gift with great effort. This will be the subject of our further analyses.

Knowledge Stronger than Death

5. The revelation of the body contained in Genesis, particularly in Genesis 3, shows with impressive obviousness that the cycle of "knowledge-generation," rooted so deeply in the power of the human body, has been subjected, after sin, to the law of suffering and death. God-Yahweh says to the woman, "I will multiply your pangs in childbearing; in pain you will bring forth children" (Gen 3:16). *The horizon of death* opens before man together with the *revelation of the generative meaning of the body* in the spouses' act of reciprocal "knowledge." And so the first man, the male, gives to his wife the name Eve, "because she was the mother of all the living" (Gen 3:20), when he had already heard the words of the sentence that determined the whole perspective of human existence "from within" the knowledge of good and evil. This perspective is confirmed by the words, "You will return to the earth, for out of it you were taken; dust you are, and to dust you shall return" (Gen 3:19).

The radical character of this sentence is confirmed by the evidence of the experiences of man's whole earthly history. The horizon of death extends over the whole perspective of human life on earth, a life that has been inserted into that original biblical cycle of "knowl-

---

The comparison of biblical "knowledge" with Platonic "*erōs*" shows the divergence between these two conceptions. The Platonic conception is based on the yearning for the transcendent Beautiful and on the flight away from matter; the biblical conception, by contrast, is directed toward the concrete reality, and the dualism of spirit and matter is alien to it, as is the specific hostility toward matter ("And God saw that it was good," Gen 1:10, 12, 18, 21, 25).

While the *Platonic* concept goes beyond the biblical range of "knowledge," the *contemporary* concept seems *too restricted.* Biblical "knowledge" does not limit itself to the satisfaction of instinct or hedonistic enjoyment, but is a fully human act consciously directed toward procreation and also the expression of interpersonal love (Gen 29:20; 1 Sam 12:24; 2 Sam 12:24).

edge-generation." Man, who has broken the covenant with his Creator, gathering the fruit from the tree of the knowledge of good and evil, is cut off by God-Yahweh from the tree of life. "Now, let him not reach out his hand any more and take also from the tree of life, and eat, and live forever" (Gen 3:21). In this way, the life given to man in the mystery of creation is not taken away, but restricted by the limit of conceptions, of births, and of death, and further worsened by the perspective of hereditary sinfulness; yet it is in some way given to him anew as a task in the same ever-recurring cycle. The sentence, "Adam united himself with" (or "knew") "Eve his wife, who conceived and gave birth" (Gen 4:1) is like a seal impressed in the original revelation of the body at the very "beginning" of man's history on the earth. This history is always formed anew in its most fundamental dimension, from the "beginning," as it were, by the same "knowledge-generation" about which Genesis speaks.

6. And in this way, every man carries in himself the mystery of his "beginning," strictly tied to consciousness of the generative meaning of the body. Genesis 4:1–2 seems to be silent about the relation that runs between the generative and the spousal meaning of the body. It is perhaps not yet the time nor the place to clarify this relation, although this clarification seems indispensable in our further analysis. At that future point, it will be necessary to raise anew the questions tied to the emergence of shame in man, a shame of his masculinity and his femininity that he did not experience before. At present, however, this question moves to a secondary level. On the primary level, by contrast, there remains the fact that "Adam united himself with" ("knew") "his wife, who conceived and gave birth." *This is the precise threshold of* man's *history. It is his "beginning" on the earth. On this threshold, man stands, as male and female, with the consciousness of the generative meaning of his own body: masculinity contains in a hidden way the meaning of fatherhood and femininity that of motherhood.* In the name of this meaning, Christ was one day to give the categorical answer to the question the Pharisees addressed to him (Mt 19; Mk 10). We, on the other hand, when we penetrate the simple content of this answer, are seeking at the same time to shed light on the context of this "beginning," to which Christ appealed. The theology of the body plunges its roots into this [beginning].

7. In man, consciousness of the meaning of the body and consciousness of its generative meaning come into contact with the consciousness of death, whose inevitable horizon they carry, so to speak, within themselves. And yet, in man's history there always returns the "knowledge-generation" cycle, in which life struggles always anew with the inexorable prospect of death, and always overcomes it. *It is as if the reason for this unyielding strength of life, which shows itself in "generation," were always the same "knowledge,"* with which man passes beyond the solitude of his own being, and even more, decides anew to affirm this being in an "other." And both, man and woman, affirm it in the new man whom they generate. In this statement, biblical "knowledge" seems to take on a still greater dimension. It seems to insert itself into that "vision" of God himself, which concludes the first account of the creation of man, concerning "male" and "female" made "in the image of God." "God saw everything that he had made, and indeed, it was very good" (Gen 1:31). Despite all the experiences of his own life, despite the sufferings, the disappointments in himself, his sinfulness, and, finally, despite the inevitable prospect of death, man always continues, however, to place "knowledge" at the "beginning" of "generation"; in this way he seems to participate in that first "vision" of God himself: God, the Creator, "saw everything...and indeed, it was good." And always anew he confirms the truth of these words.

7. [Conclusion: An Integral Vision]*

23 *General Audience of April 2, 1980*
(Insegnamenti, 3, no. 1 [1980]: 788–93)

1. MATTHEW AND MARK REPORT the answer Christ gave to the Pharisees when they asked him about the indissolubility of marriage, appealing to the Law of Moses that allowed in certain cases the practice of the so-called certificate of divorce. Reminding them of the first

---

* Translator's note: This heading has been added. TOB 23 is not found in Wojtyła's original book manuscript.

chapters of Genesis, Christ answered, "Have you not read that from the beginning the Creator created them male and female and said, 'For this reason a man will leave his father and his mother and unite with his wife, and the two will be one flesh?' So it is that they are no longer two, but one single flesh. Therefore what God has joined let man not separate." After this, addressing their question about the Law of Moses, Christ added, "Because of the hardness of your heart Moses allowed you to divorce your wives, but from the beginning it was not so" (Mt 19:3–8; Mk 12:2–9). In his answer, Christ appealed twice to the "beginning" and thus we too, in the course of our analyses, have attempted to clarify as deeply as possible the meaning of this "beginning," which is the first inheritance of every human being in the world, man and woman, the first witness of human identity according to the revealed word, the first source of the certainty of his vocation as a person created in the image of God himself.

2. Christ's answer has a historical meaning, but not only a historical one. Human beings of all times raise the question about the same topic. The same is true about our contemporaries, who in their questions do not, however, appeal to the Law of Moses that allowed the certificate of divorce, but to other circumstances and other laws. Their questions are charged with problems unknown to the interlocutors at the time of Christ. We know what sort of questions about marriage and the family were addressed to the last Council, to Pope Paul VI, and are continuously being formulated in the post-conciliar period, day after day, in the most varied circumstances. They are asked by single persons, by married and engaged couples, by young people, but also by writers, journalists, politicians, economists, demographers, in sum, by contemporary culture and civilization.

I think that among the answers that Christ would give *to the people of our times* and to their questions, often so impatient, *fundamental would still be the one* he gave to the Pharisees. In answering these questions, Christ *would appeal first of all to the "beginning."* He would perhaps do so all the more decidedly and essentially, inasmuch as man's inner and simultaneously cultural situation seems to move away from that beginning and assume forms and dimensions that diverge from the biblical image of the "beginning" to points that are evidently ever more distant.

At any rate, Christ would not be "surprised" by any of these situations, and I suppose that he would continue to refer above all to the "beginning."

3. This is the reason why Christ's answer called for a particularly deep analysis. In fact, this answer recalled fundamental and elementary truths about the human being as man and woman. Through this answer, we gain insight into the very structure of human identity in the dimensions of the mystery of creation and, at the same time, in the perspective of the mystery of redemption. Without this answer, one cannot build a theological anthropology and, in its context, a "theology of the body" from which also the fully Christian vision of marriage and the family originates. Paul VI pointed this out in his encyclical dedicated to the problems of marriage and responsible procreation from the human and Christian point of view, when he appealed to the "integral vision of man" (Paul VI, *Humanae Vitae*, 7). One can say that in the answer to the Pharisees, Christ laid out before his interlocutors also this "integral vision of man," without which no adequate answer can be given to the questions connected with marriage and procreation. Precisely this integral vision of man must be built from the "beginning."

This point is valid for the contemporary mentality just as it was, though in a different way, for Christ's interlocutors. We are, in fact, the children of an age in which, due to the development of various disciplines, this integral vision of man can easily be rejected and replaced by many *partial conceptions* that dwell on one or another aspect of the *compositum humanum* but do not reach man's *integrum* or leave it outside their field of vision. Various cultural tendencies then insert themselves here that are based on these partial truths and on this basis make their proposals and practical suggestions for human behavior and, even more often, about ways of *relating to "man."* Man then becomes more an object of certain technologies than the responsible subject of his own action. It is also the aim of Christ's answer to the Pharisees that man, male and female, be such a subject, that is, a subject who decides his own actions in the light of the integral truth about himself, inasmuch as it is the original or fundamental truth of authentically human experiences. This is the truth Christ makes us seek from the "beginning." It is in this way that we turn to the first chapters of Genesis.

4. The study of these chapters, perhaps more than of others, makes us conscious of the significance and necessity of the "theology of the body." The "beginning" tells us relatively little about the human body in the naturalistic and contemporary sense of the word. From this point of view, we find ourselves in this study on a wholly pre-scientific level. We know almost nothing about the inner structures and regularities that reign in the human organism. Nevertheless, at the same time—perhaps exactly because the text is so ancient—the truth that is important for the integral vision of man reveals itself in a simpler and fuller way. This truth *concerns the meaning of the human body in the structure of the personal subject.* The reflection about these ancient texts allows us as a next step to extend this meaning to the whole sphere of human *intersubjectivity,* especially in the perennial relationship between man and woman. In this reflection we gain a vantage point that we must necessarily place at the basis of the whole contemporary science about human sexuality in the biophysiological sense. This is not to say that we must give up this science or deprive ourselves of its results. On the contrary, if these results are to be useful in teaching us something about the education of man in his masculinity and femininity, and about the sphere of marriage and procreation, we must always arrive—through all the single elements of contemporary science—at what is fundamental and essentially personal, both in every individual, man or woman, and in their reciprocal relations.

And it is exactly here that reflection on the ancient text of Genesis proves to be irreplaceable. It constitutes really the "beginning" of the theology of the body. The fact that *theology also includes the body should not* astonish or surprise anyone who is conscious of the mystery and reality of the Incarnation. Through the fact that the Word of God became flesh, the body entered theology—that is, the science that has divinity for its object—I would say, through the main door. The Incarnation—and the redemption that flows from it—has also become the definitive source of the sacramentality of marriage, which we will deal with more extensively at a suitable time [see TOB 87–117b].

5. The questions raised by contemporary man are also those of Christians: of those who prepare for the sacrament of Marriage or of those who already live in marriage, which is the sacrament of the Church. These are not only the questions of the sciences, but even more so the questions of human life. So many human beings and so many Christians search in marriage for the fulfillment of their vocation. So many want to find in it the way of *salvation* and *holiness*.

For them, the answer Christ gave to the Pharisees, who were filled with zeal for the Old Testament, is particularly important. Those who seek the fulfillment of their own human and Christian vocation in marriage are called first of all to make of this "theology of the body," whose "beginning" we find in the first chapters of Genesis, the content of their lives and behavior. In fact, on the road of this vocation, how indispensable is a deepened consciousness of the meaning of the body in its masculinity and femininity! How necessary is an accurate consciousness of the spousal meaning of the body, of its generative meaning, given that all that forms the content of the life of the spouses must always find its full and personal dimension in shared life, in behavior, in feelings! And this all the more against the background of a civilization that remains under the pressure of a materialistic and utilitarian way of thinking and evaluating. Contemporary bio-physiology can offer much precise information about human sexuality. Nevertheless, the knowledge of the personal dignity of the human body and of sex must still be drawn from other sources. A particular source is God's own word, which contains the revelation of the body, the revelation that goes back to the "beginning."

How significant it is that, in his answer to all these questions, Christ orders man to return in some way to the threshold of his theological history! He orders him to place himself at the boundary between original innocence-happiness and the inheritance of the first fall. By doing so, does he not want to say that the way on which he leads man, male and female, in the sacrament of Marriage, namely, the way of the "redemption of the body," must consist in *retrieving this dignity*, in which the true meaning of the human body, its meaning as personal and "of communion," is fulfilled at the same time?

6. For now we conclude the first part of our meditations devoted to this subject, which is so important. To give a more thorough answer to our questions, at times anxious questions, about marriage—or still more exactly, about the meaning of the body—we cannot dwell only on Christ's answer to the Pharisees, in which he appeals to the "beginning" (see Mt 19:3–9; Mk 10:2–12). We must take into consideration also all his other statements, among which two stand out in a special way as having a particularly rich meaning: *the first*, from the Sermon on the Mount, on the possibilities of the human heart with respect to the concupiscence of the body (see Mt 5:8); and *the second*, when Jesus appealed to the future resurrection (see Mt 22:24–30; Mk 12:18–27; Lk 20:27–36).

We intend to make these two statements the object of our following reflections.

CHAPTER TWO

Christ Appeals to the Human Heart

───────── ❧ ─────────

1. In the Light of the Sermon on the Mount

Matthew 5:27–28—"Whoever Looks to Desire..."

24 *General Audience of April 16, 1980*
(Insegnamenti, 3, no. 1 [1980]: 923–27)

1. AS THE SUBJECT of our future reflections—during the Wednesday meetings—I want to develop the following word of Christ, which is part of the Sermon on the Mount: "You have heard that it was said, 'You shall not commit adultery.' But I say to you: Whoever looks at a woman to desire her [in a reductive way] has already committed adultery with her *in his heart*" (Mt 5:27–28).[*] It seems that this passage has a key significance for the theology of the body, like the one in which Christ appealed to the "beginning," which served as the basis

─────────────

[*] Translator's note: According to John Paul II, sexual desire and sexual pleasure are in themselves good (see Index at DESIRE, FASCINATION, and PLEASURE). "Desire" in a negative sense arises when a man or a woman fails to see this full attractiveness of the other person and reduces it to the attractiveness of sexual pleasure alone. It is this isolation of sexual desire that gives rise to the vice of lust. In lustful or concupiscent desire, one sees the other person in a reductive way as a mere means for sexual pleasure (see esp. TOB 41). It does not matter whether the person one desires in this reductive way is one's spouse or not, because the reduction is in both cases contrary to the full dignity and beauty of the person (see TOB 43). To avoid the impression that Jesus, as John Paul II understands him, condemns sexual desire as such, qualifiers will at times be added as a reminder in square brackets to the word "desire": [lustful], [concupiscent], and [reductive].

of the foregoing analyses. At that time, we were able to realize how vast was *the context of a sentence, or even just of a word, spoken by Christ.* It was a question not only of the immediate context that came out in the course of the dialogue with the Pharisees, but the overall context, which we cannot enter into without going back to the first chapters of Genesis (leaving aside what refers there to the other books of the Old Testament). The foregoing analyses have shown what an extensive content Christ's reference to the "beginning" brings with it.

The statement to which we now turn, namely, Matthew 5:27–28, will certainly lead us not only into the immediate context in which it appears, but also into its overall context, through which the key significance of the theology of the body will gradually become clear to us. This statement is one of the passages of the Sermon on the Mount in which Jesus brings about a *fundamental revision of the way of understanding and carrying out the moral law of the Old Covenant.* This revision applies, in order, to the following commandments of the Decalogue: to the fifth, "You shall not kill" (Mt 5:21–26); to the sixth, "You shall not commit adultery" (Mt 5:27–32)—it is significant that at the end of this passage also the question of the "certificate of divorce" appears, which we discussed already in the last chapter; and to the eighth commandment according to the text of Exodus (see Ex 20:7), "You shall not swear falsely, but carry out the vows you have made to the Lord" (see Mt 5:33–37).

Especially significant are the words that come before these sections of the Sermon on the Mount, and those after them, words by which Jesus declares, "Do not think that I have come to abolish the Law or the Prophets; I have not come to abolish but to fulfill" (Mt 5:17). In the sentences that follow, Jesus explains the meaning of this antithesis and the necessity of the "fulfillment" of the law for the sake of realizing the kingdom of God. "Whoever…carries out [these commandments] and teaches them, will be considered great in the kingdom of heaven" (Mt 5:19; John Paul II's addition). "Kingdom of heaven" means the reign of God in the eschatological dimension. *The fulfillment of the law is the* underlying *condition* for this reign in the temporal dimension of human existence. It is a question, however, of a fulfillment that fully corresponds to the meaning of the law, of the Decalogue, of the single commandments. Only such a fulfillment *builds the justice that God, the Legislator, has willed.* Christ, the Teacher, urges us not to give the kind of human interpretation of the whole law, and of the single commandments contained in it, that does not build the justice willed by God, the Legislator. "Unless your justice surpasses that of the scribes and Pharisees, you will not enter the kingdom of heaven" (Mt 5:20).

Matthew 5:27–28—Ethical Meaning

2. In this context appears Christ's statement according to Matthew 5:27–28, which we intend to take as the basis for the present analyses, because, together with the other statement (Mt 19:3–9; Mk 10), we consider it as key to the theology of the body. This statement, like the other, has an explicitly normative character. It confirms the principle of human morality contained in the commandment "You shall not commit adultery," and, at the same time, it shows a fitting and full understanding of this principle, that is, an understanding of the foundation and at the same time the condition for its adequate "fulfillment"; this fulfillment is to be considered precisely in the light of the words of Matthew 5:17–20 before this text, to which we have just drawn attention. It is a question, on the one hand, of *adhering to the meaning that God, the Legislator, put in the commandment "You shall not commit adultery,"* and, on the other hand, of fulfilling the justice that should "superabound" in man himself, that is, that should reach its specific fullness in him. These are the two aspects, so to speak, of "fulfillment" in the evangelical sense.

3. We thus find ourselves at the heart of ethos, or, as it could be defined, the inner form, the soul, as it were, of human morality. Contemporary thinkers (e.g., Scheler)[36] see in the Sermon on the Mount a great turning point precisely in the area of ethos. A living

---

36. "I know of no more grandiose evidence for such a discovery of a whole realm of values which relativizes an older *ethos* than the Sermon on the Mount, whose very form repeatedly announces evidence of the relativizing of the old values of the 'Law': 'But I say unto you'..." Max Scheler, *Formalism in Ethics and Non-Formal Ethics of Values: A New Attempt toward the Foundation of an Ethical Personalism,* trans. Manfred S. Frings and Roger L. Funk, 5th ed. (Evanston: Northwestern University, 1973), 305, no. 83.

morality in the existential sense is not formed only by the norms that clothe themselves in the form of commandments, precepts, and prohibitions, as in the case of "You shall not commit adultery." The morality in which the very meaning of being human is realized— which is, at the same time, the fulfillment of the law by the "superabounding" of justice through subjective vitality—is formed in the interior perception of values, from which duty is born as an expression of conscience, as an answer of one's own personal "I." Ethos makes us, at one and the same time, enter into the depth *of the norm itself and descend into the interior of man, the subject of morality.* Moral value is connected with the dynamic process of man's innermost [being]. To reach it, it is not enough to stop "on the surface" of human actions, but one must penetrate precisely the interior.

4. In addition to the commandment "You shall not commit adultery," the Decalogue has also, "You shall not desire your neighbor's wife" (see Ex 20:17; Deut 5:21). In his statement in the Sermon on the Mount, Christ in some way connects them with each other: "You have heard that it was said, 'You shall not commit adultery.' But I say to you: Whoever looks at a woman to desire her has already committed adultery with her in his heart." Yet, the point is not so much to distinguish the area covered by these two commandments, but to point out the dimension of interior action also referred to in the words, "You shall not commit adultery." This action finds its visible expression in the "act of the body," the act in which man and woman share, contrary to the law of the exclusivity of marriage. The casuistry of the books of the Old Testament, which was preoccupied with investigating what, according to external criteria, constituted such an "act of the body," and was at the same time oriented toward fighting adultery, opened various legal "loopholes" for adultery.[37] In this way, on the basis of many compromises "because of hardness of...heart" (Mt 19:8), the meaning of the commandment willed by the Legislator suffered deformation. One was concerned with the legalistic observation of the formula, which did not "superabound" in the inner justice of hearts. *Christ shifts the essence of the problem into another dimension* when he says, "Whoever looks at a woman to desire her has

---

37. On this point, see what follows in the present meditations.

already committed adultery with her in his heart." (According to ancient translations, "has already made her an adulteress in his heart," a formula that seems to be more exact.)[38]

Matthew 5:27–28—Anthropological Meaning

Thus, Christ appeals to the inner man. He does so several times and in various circumstances. In this case, it seems particularly explicit and eloquent, not only with respect to the configuration of evangelical ethos, but also with respect to the way of looking at man. Not only ethical, but also anthropological reasons suggest that we dwell longer on this text of Matthew 5:27–28, which contains the words Christ spoke in the Sermon on the Mount.

25 *General Audience of April 23, 1980*
(Insegnamenti, 3, no. 1 [1980]: 971–75)

1. LET US RECALL THE WORDS of the Sermon on the Mount to which we are turning in this present cycle of our Wednesday reflections. "You have heard"—says the Lord—"that it was said, 'You shall not

---

38. The text of the Vulgate offers a faithful translation of the original: *iam moechatus est eam in corde suo.* In fact, the Greek verb *meucheuō* is transitive. In modern European languages, by contrast, "to commit adultery" is an intransitive verb, hence the translation, "has committed adultery *with her.*" And thus, it is translated as follows in:

- Italian: "*ha già commesso adulterio con lei* nel suo cuore" (translation published by the Conference of Italian Bishops, 1971; similarly the translation by the Pontifical Biblical Institute, 1961, and the one edited by S. Garofalo, 1966);
- French: "*a déjà commis, dans son cœur, l'adultère avec elle*" (*Bible de Jérusalem*, [Paris, 1973]; *Traduction Œcuménique* [Paris, 1972]; Crampon); only Fillion translates, "A déjà *commis l'adultère dans son cœur*";
- English: "*hath already committed adultery with her in his heart*" (Douay Version, 1582; analogously the Revised Standard Version and its predecessors from 1611 to 1966; R. Knox; *New English Bible; Jerusalem Bible,* 1966);
- German: "*hat in seinem Herzen schon Ehebruch mit ihr begangen*" (*Einheitsübersetzung der Heiligen Schrift,* published by the Conference of Bishops of the German-speaking area, 1979);
- Spanish: "*ya cometió adulterio con ella en su corazón*" (*Bibl. Societ.,* 1966);
- Portuguese: "*já cometeu adulterio com ela no seu coração*" (M. Soares, São Paulo, 1933);
- Polish: older translations: "*już ją scudzołozył w sercu swoim*"; recent translation: "*już się w swoim sercu dopuścił z nią cudzołóstwa*" (*Biblia Tysiąclecia*).

commit adultery.' But I say to you: Whoever looks at a woman to desire her [in a reductive way] has already committed adultery with her in his heart" (Mt 5:27–28).

The man whom Jesus addresses here is precisely "historical" *man*, the one whose "beginning" and "theological prehistory" we have traced in the earlier series of analyses. Most directly, he is the one who listened with his own ears to the Sermon on the Mount. But together with him, he is also every other man, placed before that moment of history, whether in the immense expanse of the past or in the expanse, equally vast, of the future. To this "future" in front of the Sermon on the Mount belongs our present, our contemporary age as well. This man is in some way "each" man, "every one" of us. Both the man of the past and also the man of the future can be the one who knows the positive commandment "You shall not commit adultery" as "the content of the law" (see Rom 2:22–23), but he can just as well be the one who, according to Romans, has this commandment only "written in (his)* heart" (Rom 2:15).[39] In the light of the foregoing reflections, he is the man *who has from his "beginning" gained a precise sense of the meaning of the body* already, before crossing "the threshold" of his historical experiences, in the very mystery of creation, given that he emerged from it "as man and woman" (Gen 1:27). He is historical man, who at the "beginning" of his earthly drama found himself "inside" the knowledge of good and evil by breaking the covenant

---

* John Paul II's change.

39. In this way, the content of our reflections would in some way shift to the ground of the "natural law." The words quoted from Romans (2:15) have always been considered in revelation as a source that confirms the existence of the natural law. In this way, the concept of the natural law acquires also a theological meaning.

See, among others, D. Composta, *Theologia del diritto naturale, "Status quaestionis"* (Brescia: Civiltà, 1972), 7–22, 41–53; J. Fuchs, S.J., *Lex naturae. Zur Theologie des Naturrechts* (Düsseldorf, 1955), 22–30; E. Hamel. S.J., *Loi naturelle et loi du Christ* (Bruges-Paris: Desclée de Brouwer, 1964), 18; A. Sacchi, "La legge naturale nella Bibbia," in *La legge naturale. Le relazioni del Convegno dei teologi moralisti dell'Italia settentrionale* (11–13 September 1969), (Bologna: Ed. Dehoniane, 1970), 53; F. Böckle, "La legge naturale e la legge cristiana," in ibid., 214–15; A. Feuillet, "Le fondement de la morale ancienne et chretienne d'apres l'Épître aux Romains," *Revue Thomiste* 78 (1970): 357–86; Th. Herr, *Naturrecht aus der kritischen Sicht des Neuen Testaments* (Munich: Schöningh, 1976), 155–64.

with his Creator. He is male man, who "knew (the woman)* his wife" and "knew" her several times, and she "conceived and gave birth" (see Gen 4:1–2) according to the Creator's plan, which went back to the state of original innocence (see Gen 1:28; 2:24).

2. In his Sermon on the Mount, especially in the words of Matthew 5:27–28, Christ turns exactly to this man. He turns to the man of a definite moment in history and, together with him, to all human beings belonging to the same human history. He turns, as we already observed, to the "inner" man. The words of Christ have an explicit *anthropological content*; they touch those perennial meanings that constitute an "adequate" anthropology. Through their ethical content, these words at the same time constitute such an anthropology and demand, so to speak, that man enters into his full image. Man—who is "flesh," and who, as male, remains through his body and his sex in relation with woman (this is, in fact, also what the expression, "You shall not commit adultery," indicates)—must, in the light of these words of Christ, find himself in his interior, in his "heart."[40] The *"heart" is the dimension of humanity with which the sense of the meaning of the human body, and the order of this sense, is* directly *linked.* We are thinking here both of the meaning that we have called "spousal" in the foregoing analyses, as well as the one we called "generative." What order is at issue?

---

* John Paul II's change.

40. "The typically Hebraic usage reflected in the New Testament implies an understanding of man as unity of thought, will and feeling.... It depicts man as a whole, viewed from his intentionality; *the heart as the center of man is thought of as source of will, emotion, thoughts, and affections.*

"The traditional Judaic conception was related by Paul to Hellenistic categories, such as 'mind,' 'attitude,' 'thoughts' and 'desires.' Such a coordination between the Judaic and Hellenistic categories is found in Phil 1:7; 4:7; Rom 1:21.24, where 'heart' is thought of as the center from which these things flow." R. Jewett, *Arbeiten zur Geschichte des antiken Judentums und des Urchristentums [Paul's Anthropological Terms: A Study of Their Use in Conflict Settings]* (Leiden: Brill, 1971), 448.

"The heart...is the secret, inner root of man, and thus of his world...the unfathomable ground and living power of all existential experience and decision." H. Schlier, "Das Menschenherz nach dem Apostel Paulus," *Lebendiges Zeugnis* 27 (1965): 123.

See also F. Baumgärtel and J. Behm, "Kardia," *Theological Dictionary of the New Testament* (Grand Rapids: Eerdmans, 1965), 3.605–14.

Matthew 5:27–28 Indicates a Further Dimension

3. This part of our considerations must provide an answer to pre-cisely this question, an answer that must reach not only the ethical, but also the anthropological reasons; these two remain, in fact, in a reciprocal relation. For now, in a preliminary way, we should establish the meaning of the text of Matthew 5:27–28, the meaning of the expressions used in it and their reciprocal relation. Adultery, which is what the commandment quoted above directly refers to, signifies the violation of the unity in which man and woman can unite only as spouses so closely that they are "one flesh" (Gen 2:24). Adultery is what a man commits if he unites in this way with a woman who is not his wife. Adultery is also what a woman commits if she unites in this way with a man who is not her husband. One must draw the conclu-sion that "adultery in the heart," committed by a man when he "looks at a woman to desire her," signifies a clearly defined interior act. We are dealing with a desire directed, in this case, by the man toward a woman who is not his wife, for the sake of uniting with her as if she were, that is, to use once again the words of Genesis 2:24, in such a way that "the two are one flesh." Such a *desire,* as an interior act, *expresses itself through the sense of sight,* that is, with a look, as in the case of David and Bathsheba, to use an example taken from the Bible (see 2 Sam 11:2).[41] The relation of desire with the sense of sight was particularly emphasized in Christ's words.

4. These words do not say clearly whether the woman—the object of desire—is the wife of another, or simply not the wife of the man who looks at her in this way. She can be the wife of another or also not bound by marriage. We must rather intuit [who she is] by basing ourselves especially on the expression that defines adultery precisely as what the man has committed "in his heart" with his look. One can correctly draw the conclusion from this that such a look of desire directed toward one's own wife is not adultery "in the heart," precisely because the man's relevant interior act refers to the woman who is his wife, in relation to whom adultery cannot take place. If the conjugal

---

41. This is perhaps the best known example; but one can find other examples simi-lar to it (see Gen 34:2; Judg 14:1, 16:1).

act, as an *exterior act* in which "the two unite in such a way that they become one flesh," *is legitimate* in the relationship between the man in question and the woman who is his wife, then also the *interior act* in the same relationship is analogously in conformity with ethics.[*]

5. Nevertheless, that desire indicated by the expression, "whoever looks at a woman to desire her," *has its own biblical and theological dimension,* which we must not neglect to clarify here. Although this dimension is not directly shown by the concrete expression of Matthew 5:27–28, taken by itself, still it is deeply rooted in the overall context, which refers to the revelation of the body. We must go back to this context so that Christ's appeal "to the heart," to the inner man, may ring out in the whole fullness of its truth. The statement quoted from the Sermon on the Mount (Mt 5:27–28) has at root an indicative character. That Christ turns directly to the man as to the one who "looks at a woman to desire her" does not mean that his words, in their ethical sense, do not refer also to the woman. Christ expresses himself in this way to illustrate with a concrete example how one should understand "the fulfillment of the law" in accord with the meaning that God, the Legislator, gave to it and, further, how one must understand that "superabounding of justice" in the man who observes the sixth commandment of the Decalogue. When he speaks in this way, Christ wants us not to dwell on the example in itself, but also to enter into the statement's full ethical and anthropological sense. If the statement has an indicative character, this means that, if we follow its footsteps, we can reach an understanding of the general truth about "historical" man, valid also for the theology of the body. The next stages of our reflections will have the goal of bringing us closer to understanding this truth.

---

[*] Translator's note: As pointed out above (see translator's note on TOB 24:1), the word "desire" can be used in a positive sense. In courtship and marriage, it is not only morally legitimate but good and holy, in conformity with the spousal meaning of the body, for man and woman to desire each other. "Desire" can also be used in a negative sense for a reductive kind of desire in which the other person becomes a mere means for pleasure, contrary to the spousal meaning of the body. Even husband and wife commit "adultery in the heart" if they "desire" each other in this reductive way (see esp. TOB 43:2–4).

2. The Man of Concupiscence

26 General Audience of April 30, 1980
(*Insegnamenti*, 3, no. 1 [1980]: 1026–30)

1. In our last reflection we said that Christ's words in the Sermon on the Mount directly refer to [reductive] "desire" born immediately in the human heart; indirectly, however, these words help us to understand a truth about man that is of universal importance.

This truth about "historical" man, which is of universal importance, and toward which Christ's words in Matthew 5:27–28 direct us, seems to be expressed in the biblical teaching about the threefold concupiscence. We are referring here to the concise statement of 1 John: "All that is in the world, the concupiscence of the flesh, the concupiscence of the eyes, and the pride of life, comes not from the Father but from the world. And the world passes away with its concupiscence; but the one who does the will of God will remain in eternity" (1 Jn 2:16–17). It is evident that to understand these words one must carefully take into account the context in which they are inserted, that is, the context of "Johannine theology" as a whole, about which so much has been written.[42] The same words, however, take their place in the context of the whole Bible; they belong to the whole of revealed truth about man and are important for the theology of the body. *They do not explain concupiscence itself* in its threefold form, because they seem to presuppose that "the concupiscence of the flesh, the concupiscence of the eyes, and the pride of life" are in some way a

---

42. See, for example, J. Bonsirven, *Epîtres de Saint Jean*, 2nd ed; (Paris: Beauchesne, 1954), 113–19; E. Brooke, *Critical and Exegetical Commentary on the Johannine Epistles* (International Critical Commentary; Edingburgh: T.&T. Clark, 1912), 47–49; P. De Ambroggi, Le Epistole Cattoliche (Turin: Marietti, 1947), 216–17; C. H. Dodd, *The Johannine Epistles* (Moffatt New Testament Commentary; London: Hodder and Stoughton, 1946), 41–42; J. Houlden, *A Commentary on the Johannine Epistles* (London: Black, 1973), 73–74; B. Prete, *Lettere di Giovanni* (Rome: Ed. Paoline, 1970), 61; R. Schnackenburg, *Die Johannesbriefe* (Herders Theologischer Kommentar zum Neuen Testament; Freiburg: Herder, 1953), 112–15; J. R. W. Stott, *Epistles of John*, 3rd ed. (London: Tyndale New Testament Commentaries, 1969), 99–101.

On the subject of Johannine theology, see esp. A. Feuillet, *Le mystère de l'amour divin dans la théologie johannique* (Paris: Gabalda, 1972).

clear and well-known concept. Yet, they do explain the coming to be of the threefold concupiscence by indicating its origin, not "from the Father," but "from the world."

2. The concupiscence of the flesh and, together with it, the concupiscence of the eyes and the pride of life, is "in the world" and at the same time "comes from the world," not as a fruit of the mystery of creation, but as a fruit of "the tree of the knowledge of good and evil" (see Gen 2:17) in man's heart. What bears fruit in the threefold concupiscence is not the "world" created by God for man, whose underlying "goodness" we read about several times in Genesis 1: "God saw that it was good...that it was very good." In the threefold concupiscence, what bears fruit, by contrast, is the breaking of the first covenant with the Creator, with God-Elohim, with God-Yahweh. This covenant was broken in man's heart. Here one would have to carry out a careful analysis of the events described in Genesis 3:1–6. However, we are referring only in general to the mystery of sin, to the beginnings of human history. In fact, it is only *as a consequence of sin, as a fruit of the breaking of the covenant with God in the human heart*—in man's innermost [being]—that the "world" of Genesis *became* the "world" of the Johannine words (1 Jn 2:15–16), *the place and source of concupiscence.*

Thus, the statement according to which concupiscence "does not come from the Father, but from the world" seems to direct us once more to the biblical "beginning." The coming to be of the threefold concupiscence presented by John finds in this beginning its first and fundamental clarification, an explanation essential for the theology of the body. To understand this truth contained in Christ's words in the Sermon on the Mount (Mt 5:27–28), which is of universal importance for "historical" man, we must return once more to Genesis, *linger once more "on the threshold"* of the revelation of "historical" man. This is all the more necessary, inasmuch as this threshold of the history of salvation proves to be at the same time a threshold of authentic human experiences, as we will point out in the following analyses. The same fundamental meanings that we drew from the foregoing analyses will come to life again as the constitutive elements of an adequate anthropology and a deep substratum of the theology of the body.

3. The question may still be raised whether it is legitimate to transfer the typical *contents* of "Johannine theology" found in 1 John as a whole (especially in 1 Jn 2:15–16) to the terrain of the Sermon on the Mount according to Matthew, and specifically to *Christ's* statement *taken from Matthew 5:27–28:* "You have heard that it was said, 'You shall not commit adultery.' But I say to you: Whoever looks at a woman to desire her has already committed adultery with her in his heart." We will return to this subject several times. Nevertheless, we appeal right away to the overall biblical context, to the whole of the truth about man that is revealed and expressed in it. It is precisely in the name of this truth that we attempt to achieve a thorough, in-depth understanding of the man whom Christ indicates in the text of Matthew 5:27–28, namely, the man who "looks" at a woman "to desire her." Is such a look, in the end, not explained by the fact that this man is precisely a "man of desire" in the sense of 1 John, or rather, that *both*, namely, the man who looks to desire [lustfully] and the woman who is the object of such a look, *find themselves in the dimension of the threefold concupiscence* that "does not come from the Father, but from the world"? One must, therefore, understand what that concupiscence is, or rather who that "man of desire" is, in order to discover the depth of the words of Christ according to Matthew 5:27–28 and to explain what their reference to the human "heart" means, which is so important for the theology of the body.

A. THE MEANING OF ORIGINAL SHAME

Casting Doubt on the Gift

4. Let us turn afresh to the Yahwist account, in which the same man, male and female, appears at the beginning as the man of original innocence—before original sin—and then as the one who has lost this innocence by breaking the original covenant with his Creator. We do not intend in this place to carry out a complete analysis of the temptation and of sin according to the text of Genesis 3:1–5 itself, the relevant teaching of the Church and of theology. It should only be observed that the biblical description itself *seems to highlight particularly the key moment in which, in man's heart, doubt is cast on the Gift.* The man who picks the fruit of the tree of the knowledge of good and

evil makes at the same time a fundamental choice and carries it through against the will of the Creator, God-Yahweh, by accepting the motivation suggested by the tempter, "You will not die at all. Rather, God knows that when you eat of it your eyes will be opened, and you will become like God, knowing good and evil"; according to some ancient translations, "You will be like gods, knowing good and evil."[43] This motivation clearly implies casting doubt on the Gift and on Love, from which creation takes its origin as gift. As for man, he receives the "world" as a gift and at the same time the "image of God," that is, humanity itself in all the truth of its male and female duality. It is enough to read carefully the whole passage of Genesis 3:1–5, to grasp the mystery *of man in it who turns his back* on the "Father" (even if we do not find this name of God in the account). By casting doubt in his heart on the deepest meaning of the gift, that is, on love as the specific motive of creation and of the original covenant (see Gen 3:5), man turns his back on God-Love, on the "Father." He in some sense casts him from his heart. At the same time, therefore, he detaches his heart and cuts it off, as it were, from that which "comes from the Father": in this way, what is left in him is what "comes from the world."

5. "Then the eyes of both were opened, and they realized that they were naked; they sewed fig leaves together and made themselves

---

43. The Hebrew text can have both meanings, because it says, "Elohim knows that when you eat of it" (of the fruit of the tree of the knowledge of good and evil), "your eyes will be opened and you will become like Elohim, knowing good and evil." The term Elohim (ʾelōhîm) is the plural of ʾelôᵃh (plural of "excellence"). In relation to Yahweh its meaning is singular; it can, however, indicate the plural of other heavenly beings or pagan deities (see e.g., Ps 8:6; Ex 12:12; Judg 10:16; Hos 3:1; and others).

Let us review some *translations*:

Italian: "diverreste *come Dio* [*like God*], conoscendo il bene e il male" (Pontifical Biblical Institute, 1961).

French: "vous serez *comme des dieux* [*like gods*], qui connaissent le bien et le mal" (*Bible de Jérusalem*, 1973).

English: "you will be *like God*, knowing good and evil" (Revised Standard Version, 1966).

Spanish: "seréis *como dioses* [*like gods*], conocedores del bien y del mal" (S. Ausejo, Barcelona, 1964).

Spanish: "seréis *como Dios* [*like God*] en el conocimiento del bien y del mal" (L. Alonso-Schökel, Madrid, 1970).

loincloths" (Gen 3:6). This is the first sentence of the Yahwist account about man's "situation" after sin, and it shows the new state of human nature. *Does not this sentence also suggest the beginning of "concupiscence" in man's heart?* To answer this question more deeply and thoroughly we cannot stop at that first sentence, but must reread the text as a whole. It is, however, worth recalling here what was said in the first analyses about the subject of shame as a "limit" experience [see above, TOB 11:1–13:1]. Genesis refers to this experience to show the "boundary" that runs between man's state of original innocence (see especially Gen 2:25, to which we devoted much attention in the fore-going analyses) and his state of sinfulness at the very "beginning." While Genesis 2:25 underlines that "they were naked...but did not feel shame," Genesis 3:6 speaks explicitly about the birth of shame in connection with sin. That shame is, as it were, the first source of the manifestation in man—in both the man and the woman—of what "does not come from the Father, but from the world."

Man Alienated from Original Love

27 *General Audience of May 14, 1980*
(Insegnamenti, 3, no. 1 [1980]: 1365–69)

1. WE HAVE ALREADY SPOKEN about the shame that arose in the heart of the first man, male and female, together with sin. The first sentence about this beginning of shame in the biblical account is the following. "Then the eyes of both were opened, and they realized that they were naked; they sewed fig leaves together and made themselves loincloths" (Gen 3:6). This passage, which speaks about the recipro-cal shame of the man and the woman as a symptom of the fall (*status naturae lapsae*), should be considered in its context. Shame touches in that moment the deepest level and seems to shake the very founda-tions of their existence. "Then they heard the sound of the Lord God, who was walking in the garden at the time of the evening breeze, and the man and his wife hid themselves among the trees of the garden from the presence of the Lord God" (Gen 3:8). The need to hide shows that, *in the depth of the shame they feel before each other* as the immediate fruit of the tree of the knowledge of good and evil, *a sense of fear before God has matured: a fear previously unknown.* "The

Lord God called to the man and said to him, 'Where are you?' He said, 'I heard the sound of your step in the garden, and I was afraid, because I am naked, and I hid myself'" (Gen 3:9–10). A certain fear is always part of the very essence of shame; nevertheless, original shame reveals its character in a particular way. "I was afraid, because I am naked." We realize that something deeper is at stake here than mere bodily shame connected with the recent birth of the consciousness of being naked. With his shame about his own nakedness, the man seeks to cover the true origin of fear by indicating the effect so as not to name the cause. And it is then that God-Yahweh, instead of the man, names it. "Who told you that you were naked? Have you perhaps eaten from the tree of which I commanded you not to eat?" (Gen 3:11).

2. The precision of this dialogue is overwhelming; the precision of the whole account is overwhelming. It shows the surface of man's emotions in living the events, in such a way that, at the same time, it reveals their depth. In all of this, "nakedness" does not have only a literal meaning: it does not refer only to the body; it is not the origin of a fear related only to the body. In reality, what shows itself through "nakedness" is man deprived of participation in the Gift, man alienated from the Love that was the source of the original gift, the source of the fullness of good intended for the creature. This man, according to the formulas of the Church's theological teaching,[44] was deprived of

---

44. The Church's magisterium dealt in more detail with these problems in three periods, in accord with the needs of the time.

The declarations from the period of the controversies with the Pelagians (fifth and sixth centuries) affirm that the first man, in virtue of divine grace, possessed "a natural power and innocence" (DS 239), also called "freedom" and "freedom of will [or choice]" (DS 371, 242, 383, 622). He remained in a state that the Council of Orange (A.D. 529) calls "integrity."

"Even if human nature had remained *in the integrity in which it was created*, it could not at all have kept this integrity without the help of its Creator" (DS 389).

The concepts of "integrity" and especially "freedom" presuppose freedom from concupiscence, although the Church's documents from that period do not mention it explicitly.

The first man was also free from the necessity of death (DS 222, 372, 1511).

The Council of Trent defines the state of the first man before sin as "holiness and justice" (DS 1511, 1512) or as "innocence" (DS 1521).

The remaining declarations on this subject defend the absolute gratuitousness of the original gift of grace against the claims of the Jansenists. The "integrity of the first

the supernatural and preternatural gifts that were part of his "endowment" before sin; in addition, he suffered damage in what belongs to nature itself, to humanity in the original fullness "of the image of God." The threefold concupiscence does not correspond to the fullness of that image, but rather to the damage, to the deficiencies, to the limitations that appeared with sin. Concupiscence is to be explained as a lack, as a lack, however, that plunges its roots into the original depth of the human spirit. If we want to study this phenomenon at its origins, that is, on the threshold of the experiences of "historical" man, we must take into consideration all the words that God-Yahweh addressed to the woman (Gen 3:16) and to the man (Gen 3:17–19). Furthermore, we must examine the state of consciousness of both: and it is the Yahwist text that expressly enables us to do so. We have already called attention to the specific literary character of the text in this regard [see TOB 3:1].

---

creation" was an "unmerited raising of human nature" and not "a state owed to nature" (DS 1926); God could therefore have created man without these graces and gifts (DS 1955); this would not have violated human nature in its essence, nor would it have deprived it of its fundamental privileges (DS 1903–7, 1909, 1921, 1923, 1924, 1926, 1955, 2434, 2437, 2616, 2617).

In a manner similar to the anti-Pelagian synods, the Council of Trent deals above all with the dogma of original sin, integrating in its teaching the earlier statements on this subject. At this point, however, a certain clarification was introduced that partly changed the content included in the concept of "free will." "Freedom" or "freedom of will" in the anti-Pelagian documents did not mean the possibility of choice that is connected with human nature and thus remains constant, but referred only to the possibility of carrying out meritorious acts, the freedom that springs from grace and that man can lose.

Because of sin, therefore, Adam lost what did not belong to human nature in the strict sense of the word, namely, "integrity, holiness, innocence, and justice." "Free will" was not taken away, but weakened.

"Free will was not at all extinguished...though it grew weak and declined." DS 1521; Council of Trent, sess. VI, can. 1.

Together with sin, concupiscence and inevitable death appeared: "that the first man...when he had transgressed God's commandment, immediately lost the holiness and justice in which he was constituted, and through the offense of such disobedience *incurred* the anger and indignation of God and thus *death*...and, together with death, captivity under the power of him who had the power of death...*and that through the offense of this disobedience the whole Adam was changed for the worse in body and soul.*" DS 1511, Council of Trent, Decree on Original Sin, sess. V, can. 1. See W. Seibel, "Der Mensch als Gottes übernatürliches Ebenbild und der Urstand des Menschen," in *Mysterium Salutis*, vol. 2 (Einsiedeln, Zürich, Cologne: Benziger, 1967), 827–28.

Change in the Meaning of Original Nakedness

3. What state of consciousness can manifest itself in the words, "I was afraid, because I am naked, and I hid myself"? To what interior truth do they correspond? To what meaning of the body do they attest? Certainly, this new state is very different from the original state. *The words of Genesis 3:10 directly attest to a radical change of the meaning of original nakedness.* In the state of original innocence, as we observed earlier, nakedness did not express a lack, but represented the full acceptance of the body in its whole human and thus personal truth. The body, as the expression of the person, was the first sign of the presence of man in the visible world. In that world, from the very beginning, man was able to distinguish himself, to identify himself, as it were—that is, to confirm himself as a person—also through his body. In fact, the body was from the beginning marked, so to speak, as the visible factor of transcendence, in virtue of which man, as person, surpasses the visible world of living beings (*animalia*). In this sense, the human body was from the beginning a faithful witness and a perceptible verification of man's original "solitude" in the world, while becoming at the same time, through masculinity and femininity, a transparent component of reciprocal giving in the communion of persons. Thus, in the mystery of creation, the human body carried within itself an unquestionable sign of the "image of God" and also constituted the specific source of certainty about this image, present in the whole human being. The original acceptance of the body was in some sense the basis of the acceptance of the whole visible world. And in its turn, it was for man the guarantee of his rule over the world, over the earth, which he was to subdue (see Gen 1:28).

4. The words, "I was afraid, because I am naked, and I hid myself" (Gen 3:10), attest to a radical change in this relationship. *Man in some way loses the original certainty of the "image of God"* expressed in his body. He also loses in a certain way the sense of his right *to participate in the perception of the world,* which he enjoyed in the mystery of creation. This right had its foundation in man's innermost [being], in the fact that he himself participated in the divine vision of the world and of his own humanity, which gave him a deep peace and joy in living the truth and value of his body in all its simplicity, transmitted to him

by the Creator. "God saw [that] it was very good" (Gen 1:31). The words of Genesis 3:10, "I was afraid, because I am naked, and I hid myself," confirm the collapse of the original acceptance of the body as a sign of the person in the visible world. Together with this breakdown, the acceptance of the material world in relation to man seems to falter as well. The words of God-Yahweh foretell the hostility, as it were, of the world, the resistance of nature against man and his tasks; they foretell the toil that the human body was then to suffer in contact with the earth subdued by him. "Cursed is the ground because of you; in toil you shall eat of it all the days of your life; thorns and thistles it shall bring forth for you; and you shall eat the plants of the field. By the sweat of your face you shall eat bread until you return to the earth, for from it you were taken" (Gen 3:17–19). The end of this toil, of this struggle of man with the earth, is death. "Dust you are, and to dust you shall return" (Gen 3:19).

In this context, or rather in this perspective, Adam's words in Genesis 3:10, "I was afraid, because I am naked, and I hid myself," *seem to express the awareness of being defenseless,* and the sense of *insecurity* about his somatic structure *in the face of the processes of nature that operate with an inevitable determinism.* In this disturbing statement, one can perhaps find the implication of a certain "cosmic shame" in which the being that is created in the "image of God" and called to subdue the earth and rule over it (see Gen 1:28) expresses itself at the precise moment when, at the very beginning of its historical experiences, that same being is in such an explicit way subjected to the earth, particularly in the "part" of its transcendent constitution represented precisely by the body.

Here we must interrupt our reflections on the meaning of original shame in Genesis. We will take them up again next week.

"Immanent" Shame

28 *General Audience of May 28, 1980*
(Insegnamenti, 3, no. 1 [1980]: 1492–96)

1. WE ARE REREADING the first chapters of Genesis, in order to understand how—with original sin—the "man of concupiscence" took the place of the "man of original innocence." The words in Genesis

3:10, "I was afraid, because I am naked, and I hid myself," which we considered two weeks ago, document man's first experience of shame in the face of his Creator: a shame that could also be called "cosmic."

In the biblical text, however, this "cosmic shame"—if it is possible to grasp its features in man's overall situation after original sin—gives up its place to another form of shame. It is the shame produced in humanity itself, that is, caused by the innermost disorder in that through which man, in the mystery of creation, was "the image of God," in his personal "I" as much as in interpersonal relationship, namely, through the primordial communion of persons constituted by man and woman together. That *shame, whose cause is found in humanity itself,* is both immanent and relative: it manifests itself in the dimension of human interiority and, at the same time, it refers to the "other." This is the shame of woman "with regard to" man, and also of man "with regard to" woman: a reciprocal shame that compels them to cover their nakedness, to hide their own bodies, to withdraw from man's sight what constitutes the visible sign of femininity, and from woman's sight what constitutes the visible sign of masculinity. The shame of both oriented itself in this direction after original sin, when they realized they "were naked," as Genesis 3:7 attests. The Yahwist text seems to indicate explicitly the "sexual" character of this shame. "They sewed fig leaves together and made themselves loincloths." Nevertheless, we can ask ourselves whether the "sexual" aspect has only a "relative" character; in other words, whether it is a question of shame of one's own sexuality only in reference to the person of the other sex.

2. Although in the light of that one decisive phrase in Genesis 3:7, the answer to this question seems to support above all the relative character of original shame; nevertheless, reflection about the whole immediate context allows us to discover its more immanent background. That shame, which shows itself without any doubt in the "sexual" order, reveals *a specific difficulty in sensing the human essentiality of one's own body,* a difficulty man had not experienced in the state of original innocence. In this way, in fact, one can understand the words, "I was afraid, because I am naked," which highlight the consequences of the fruit of the tree of the knowledge of good and evil in man's innermost [being]. These words reveal a certain constitutive

fracture in the human person's interior, *a breakup, as it were, of man's original spiritual and somatic unity.* He realizes for the first time that his body has ceased drawing on the power of the spirit, which raised him to the level of the image of God. Its shame bears within itself the signs of a specific humiliation mediated by the body. Hidden within it is the germ of that contradiction that was to accompany "historical" man in his whole earthly journey, as St. Paul writes, "I joyfully agree with the law of God in my innermost [being], but I see in my members another law at war with the law of my mind" (Rom 7:22–23).

3. Thus, that shame is immanent. It contains such cognitive sharpness that it creates a fundamental disquiet in the whole of human existence, not only in the face of the perspective of death, but also in face of the perspective on which the very value and dignity of the person depend in their ethical meaning. In this sense, the original shame of the body ("I am naked") is already fear ("I was afraid") and pre-announces the unrest of conscience connected with concupiscence. The body is not subject to the spirit as in the state of original innocence, but carries within itself a constant hotbed of resistance against the spirit and threatens in some way man's unity as a person, that is, the unity of the moral nature that plunges its roots firmly into the very constitution of the person. The concupiscence of the body is a specific threat to the structure of self-possession and self-dominion, through which the human person forms itself. And it also constitutes a specific challenge for the person. In any case, *the man of concupiscence does not rule his own body in the same way, with the same simplicity and "naturalness" as the man of original innocence.* The structure of self-possession, which is essential for the person, is in some way shaken in him to its very foundations; he identifies himself anew with this structure in the degree to which he is continually ready to win it.

Sexual Shame

4. It is with such an interior imbalance that immanent shame is connected. And it has a "sexual" character, because the sphere of human sexuality seems to be precisely the one that particularly brings to light the imbalance springing from concupiscence and especially from the "concupiscence of the body." From this point of view, that

first impulse, about which Genesis 3:7 speaks, is very eloquent ("they realized that they were naked; they sewed fig leaves together and made themselves loincloths"); it is as if the "man of concupiscence" (man and woman "in the act of the knowledge of good and evil") experienced that he had simply ceased, also through his body and his sex, to remain above the world of living beings or "*animalia.*" It is as if he had experienced a specific *fracture of the personal integrity of his own body, particularly in that which determines its sexuality* and which is directly linked with the call to that unity in which man and woman "will be one flesh" (Gen 2:24). For this reason, that immanent, and at the same time sexual, shame is always, at least indirectly, relative. It is shame of one's own sexuality "in relation" to another human being. It is in this way that shame is shown in the account of Genesis 3, and so we are in some sense witnesses of the birth of human concupiscence. It is thus sufficiently clear why we go back from Christ's words about the man (male) who "looks at a woman to desire her" (Mt 5:27–28) to that first moment in which shame is explained by concupiscence and concupiscence by shame. In this way we understand better why—and in what sense—Christ speaks about [concupiscent] desire as "adultery" committed in the heart, why he turns to the human "heart."

5. The human heart holds within itself at one and the same time desire and shame. The birth of shame orients us toward the moment in which the inner man, "the heart," by closing itself to what "comes from the Father," opens itself to what "comes from the world." The birth of shame in the human heart goes hand in hand with the beginning of concupiscence, the threefold concupiscence according to Johannine theology (see 1 Jn 2:16), and in particular of the concupiscence of the body. Man has shame of the body because of concupiscence. More exactly, he has shame not so much of the body, but more precisely of concupiscence: *<he has shame of the body motivated by concupiscence.>*[*] He has shame of the body motivated by that state of his spirit to which theology and psychology give the same name: desire or concupiscence, although with a meaning that is not entirely the same.

---

[*] Translator's note: The passage in angled brackets is missing in the *Insegnamenti* text, probably by accidental omission due to the fact that the next clause begins with the same words. It has been supplied from UD.

The biblical and theological meaning of desire and concupiscence differs from the one used in psychology. For psychology, desire springs
from a lack or necessity, which the desired value must appease.
Biblical concupiscence, as we deduce from 1 John 2:16, indicates *the
state of the human spirit distanced from original simplicity and from the
fullness of values* that man and the world possess "in the dimensions of
God." This simplicity and fullness of the value of the human body in
the first experience of its masculinity/femininity, about which Genesis
2:23–25 speaks, later underwent a radical transformation "in the
dimensions of the world." And at that point, together with the concupiscence of the body, shame was born.

6. Shame has a twofold meaning: it indicates the threat to the
value and at the same time it preserves this value in an interior way.[45]
The fact that the human heart, from the moment in which the concupiscence of the body is born in it, holds within itself also shame indicates that one can and must appeal to the heart when it is a question
of guaranteeing those values that concupiscence deprives of their
original and full dimension. If we keep this in mind, we are able to
understand better why Christ, speaking about concupiscence, appeals
to the human "heart."

B. INSATIABILITY OF THE UNION

Corruption of the Consciousness
of the Unitive Meaning of the Body

29 *General Audience of June 4, 1980*
(Insegnamenti, 3, no. 1 [1980]: 1678–81)

1. WHEN WE SPOKE ABOUT THE BIRTH of concupiscence in man, on
the basis of Genesis, we analyzed the original meaning of shame, the
shame which appeared with the first sin. The analysis of shame in the
light of the biblical account allows us to understand even more thoroughly and deeply what meaning it has for all interpersonal relationships between man and woman. Genesis 3 shows without any doubt

---

45. See Wojtyła, "The Metaphysics of Shame," in *Love and Responsibility*, 174–93.

that shame appeared in the reciprocal relationship between man and woman, and that this relationship underwent a radical transformation due to shame in particular. And because shame was born in their hearts together with the concupiscence of the body, the analysis of original shame allows us at the same time to examine *in what relation this concupiscence stands to the communion of persons* that has from the beginning been granted and assigned as a task to man and woman by their being created "in the image of God." Thus, the next stage of our study of concupiscence, which manifested itself "at the beginning" through the shame of the man and the woman, according to Genesis 3, is the analysis of the insatiability of the union, that is, of the communion of persons, that was to be expressed also by their bodies according to their specific masculinity and femininity.

2. Above all, therefore, that shame—which, according to the biblical narrative, makes the man and the woman hide their own bodies before each other, and especially their sexual differentiation—confirms that the original power of communicating themselves to each other, about which Genesis 2:25 speaks, has been shattered. The radical change in the original meaning of nakedness lets us presume negative changes in the whole interpersonal relation between man and woman. That *reciprocal communion in humanity itself through the body* and through its masculinity and femininity, which had such a strong echo in the earlier passage of the Yahwist narrative (see Gen 2:23–25), *is overturned* at this moment, as if the body in its masculinity and femininity ceased to be "free from suspicion" as the substratum of the communion of persons, as if its original function were "called into doubt" in the consciousness of the man and the woman. What disappears is the simplicity and "purity" of their original experience, which helped to bring about a singular fullness of mutual self-communication. Obviously, the first parents did not stop *communicating with each other* through the body and its movements, gestures, and expressions; but what disappeared was the simple and direct self-communion connected with the original experience of reciprocal nakedness. Almost unexpectedly, an insurmountable threshold appeared in their consciousness that limited the original "self-donation" to the other with full trust in all that constituted one's own identity and at the same time diversity, female on the one side, male on the other.

The diversity, or the difference between the male and female sexes, was abruptly sensed and understood as an element of the mutual opposition of persons. This is attested to by the concise expression of Genesis 3:7, "They realized that they were naked," and by its immediate context. All of this is also part of the analysis of the first shame. Genesis not only sketches its origin in the human being, but allows one to show its degrees in both man and woman.

3. *The ending of the power of a full reciprocal communion,* a closure that manifested itself as sexual shame, allows us to understand better the original value of the unifying meaning of the body. It is, in fact, not possible otherwise to understand that closure to each other, or shame, except in reference to the meaning that the body in its femininity and masculinity previously had for man in the state of original innocence. That unifying meaning should be understood not only in reference to the unity that the man and the woman were to constitute as spouses by becoming "one flesh" (Gen 2:24) through the conjugal act, but also in reference to the "communion of persons" itself, which was the proper dimension of the existence of man and woman in the mystery of creation. In its masculinity and femininity, the body was the specific "substratum" of such personal communion. Sexual shame, about which Genesis 3:7 speaks, attests to the loss of the original certainty that through its masculinity and femininity the human body is precisely the "substratum" of the communion of persons, a substratum that simply expresses this communion and serves to realize it (and thus also to complete the "image of God" in the visible world). This state of consciousness of both has strong repercussions in the further context of Genesis 3, with which we will occupy ourselves in a short while. Since after original sin, man had lost the sense, so to speak, of the image of God in himself, that loss manifested itself by shame (see especially Gen 3:10–11). *That shame, invading the man-woman relation as a whole, was manifested through the imbalance of the original meaning of bodily unity, that is, through the imbalance of the body as a specific "substratum" of the communion of persons.* It is as if the personal profile of masculinity and femininity, which before had highlighted the meaning of the body for a full communion of persons, had given up its place to the mere sensation of "sexuality" with regard to the other human being. It is as if sexuality became an "obstacle" in man's

personal relationship with woman. While according to Genesis 3:7 they hide their sexuality from each other, both express it almost instinctively.

A Deeper Dimension of Shame

4. This discovery is at the same time a sort of "second" discovery of sex, which in the biblical narrative differs radically from the first. The whole context of the narrative confirms that this new discovery distinguishes the "historical" man of concupiscence (more precisely, the man of the threefold concupiscence) from the man of original innocence. In what relation does concupiscence, and in particular the concupiscence of the flesh, stand to the communion of persons mediated by the body, by its masculinity and femininity, assigned "from the beginning" to man by the Creator? This is the question that must be asked precisely about "the beginning," about the experience of shame that the biblical text refers to. The narrative of Genesis 3, as we have already observed, manifests shame as the symptom of man's detachment from love, in which he participated in the mystery of creation according to the Johannine expression, that which "comes from the Father." "That which is in the world," *namely, concupiscence,* brings with it an almost constitutive *difficulty in identifying oneself with one's own body,* not only in the sphere of one's own subjectivity, but even more so *in regard to the subjectivity of the other human being,* of woman for man and man for woman.

5. Hence the necessity of hiding oneself before the "other" with one's body, with what determines one's own femininity or masculinity. This necessity shows the fundamental lack of trust, which already in itself points to the collapse of the original relationship "of communion." It is precisely regard for the subjectivity of the other and at the same time for one's own subjectivity that has given rise in this new situation, that is, in the context of concupiscence, to the need for hiding oneself, about which Genesis 3:7 speaks.

And precisely here, it seems to us, we discover a deeper meaning of sexual "shame" and also the full meaning of that phenomenon to which the biblical text appeals to highlight the boundary between the man of original innocence and the "historical" man of concupiscence.

The text of Genesis 3 as a whole provides us with elements to define the deepest dimension of shame; but this calls for a separate analysis. We will begin it in the next reflection.

30 General Audience of June 18, 1980
(Insegnamenti, 3, no. 1 [1980]: 1776–79)

1. WITH SURPRISING PRECISION, Genesis 3 describes the phenomenon of shame, which came on the scene in the first man together with original sin. Careful reflection on this text allows us to conclude from it that shame, which replaced the absolute trust connected with the earlier state of original innocence in the reciprocal relationship between man and woman, has a deeper dimension. On this question, we should *reread* Genesis 3 *to the end* and not limit ourselves to 3:7, nor even to the text of 3:10–11, which contain the testimony about the first experience of shame. After this narrative, the dialogue of God-Yahweh with the man and the woman breaks off and a monologue begins. Yahweh turns to the woman and speaks first about the pains of childbirth that were to accompany her from that point on: "I will multiply your pangs in childbearing; in pain you will bring forth children" (Gen 3:16).

This is followed by the expression that characterizes the future relationship between the two, the man and the woman: "Your desire shall be for your husband, but he will dominate you" (Gen 3:16).

2. Like the words of Genesis 2:24, these words have a future-oriented character. The incisive formulation of Genesis 3:16 seems to concern the whole complex of the facts that in some way came to light already in the original experience of shame, but were later to become clear in the whole inner experience of "historical" man. The history of human consciousness and human hearts was to confirm repeatedly the words contained in Genesis 3:16. The words spoken at the beginning seem to refer to a particular "reduction" of woman in comparison with man. But there is no reason why one should understand this reduction as social inequality. Rather, the expression, "Your desire shall be for your husband, but he will dominate you," immediately indicates another form of inequality that *woman was to feel as a* *lack of full unity precisely in the vast context of union with man* to which both were called according to Genesis 2:24.

3. The words of God-Yahweh "Your desire shall be for your husband, but he will dominate you" do not speak only about the moment of union between man and woman, when both unite so as to become one flesh (see Gen 2:24), but they refer to the wide context of relations of conjugal union as a whole, including indirect relations. For the first time the man is here defined as "husband." In the whole context of the Yahwist narrative, the words of Genesis 3:16 signify above all a breach, a fundamental loss of the primeval community-communion of persons. This communion had been intended to make man and woman mutually happy through the search of a simple and pure union in humanity, through a reciprocal offering of themselves, that is, through the experience of the gift of the person expressed with soul and body, with masculinity and femininity—"flesh of my flesh" (Gen 2:23)—and finally through the subordination of such a union to the blessing of fruitfulness with "procreation."

4. It seems thus that in the words addressed by God-Yahweh to the woman, there is *a deeper echo of the shame* that both began to experience after the breaking of the original covenant with God. Here we find, moreover, a fuller motivation for such shame. In a manner that is very discreet but nevertheless decipherable and expressive enough, Genesis 3:16 attests how that *original beatifying conjugal union of persons was to be deformed in man's heart by concupiscence.* These words are directly addressed to the woman, but they refer to the man, or rather to both together.

The Meaning of "Insatiability of the Union"

5. Already the analysis of Genesis 3:7 carried out before has shown that in the new situation, after the breaking of the original covenant with God, man and woman did not find themselves united with each other, but rather more divided or even set against each other because of their masculinity and femininity. By highlighting the instinctive impulse that had made them cover their bodies, the biblical account describes at the same time the situation in which man as male *or* female—before then it was rather male *and* female—senses himself more estranged from the body as from the source of original union in humanity ("flesh from my flesh"), and more set against the other precisely on the basis of the body and of sex. This antithesis neither destroys nor excludes the conjugal union willed by the Creator (see Gen 2:24), nor its procreative effects; but it confers on the realization of this union another direction that was to be the one proper to the man of concupiscence. This is precisely what Genesis 3:16 speaks about.

The woman, whose "desire shall be for [her] husband" (Gen 3:16), and the man, whose response to this desire, as we read, is to "dominate [her],"* form without any doubt the same human couple, the same marriage as in Genesis 2:24, even *the same community of persons,* but nevertheless they are now something different. They are no longer only called to union and unity, but are also *threatened by the insatiability of that union and unity,* which does not cease to attract man and woman precisely because they are persons, called from eternity to exist "in communion." In the light of the biblical account, sexual shame has its deep meaning, which is connected precisely with the failure to satisfy the aspiration to realize in the "conjugal union of the body" (see Gen 2:24) the reciprocal communion of persons.

6. All of this seems to confirm under various aspects that, at the root of the shame in which "historical" man has become a participant, there lies the threefold concupiscence about which 1 John 2:16 speaks: not only the concupiscence of the flesh, but also "the concupiscence of the eyes and the pride of life." Does not the expression about "domination" ("he will dominate you"), about which we read in Genesis 3:16, indicate that third form of concupiscence? Does not domination "over" the other—of man over woman—essentially change the structure of communion in interpersonal relations? Does it not transpose into the dimension of this structure something that makes an object out of a human being, an object in some sense concupiscible for the eyes?

These are the questions that spring from reflection about the words of God-Yahweh according to Genesis 3:16. Spoken on the

---

* John Paul II's changes.

threshold, as it were, of human history after original sin, these words reveal to us not only the external situation of man and woman, but allow us also to penetrate into the interior of the deep mysteries of their hearts.

Where Does the Insatiability of the Union Come From?

31 *General Audience of June 25, 1980*
(Insegnamenti, 3, no. 1 [1980]: 1831–35)

1. THE ANALYSIS WE CARRIED OUT during the last reflection was centered on the following words of Genesis 3:16, addressed by God-Yahweh to the first woman after original sin: "Your desire shall be for your husband, but he will dominate you" (Gen 3:16). We arrived at the conclusion that these words contain an adequate clarification and *a deep interpretation of original shame* (see Gen 3:7), which became part of man and woman together with concupiscence. The explanation of this shame should *not* be sought *in the body itself, in the somatic sexuality* of both, but it goes back *to the deepest transformations suffered by the human spirit.* Precisely this spirit is particularly aware of how insatiable it is with regard to the mutual union between man and woman. In addition, this consciousness shifts the blame to the body, so to speak; it takes from the body the simplicity and purity of the meaning connected with the original innocence of the human being. In relation to this consciousness, shame is a secondary experience: while, on the one hand, it reveals the moment of concupiscence, at the same time it can provide weapons ahead of time against the consequences of the threefold component of concupiscence. One can even say that, through shame, man and woman almost remain in the state of original innocence. In fact, they continually become conscious of the spousal meaning of the body and intend to protect it, so to speak, from concupiscence, just as they try to maintain the value of communion or of the union of persons in the "unity of the body."

2. Genesis 2:24 speaks with discretion but also clarity about the "union of bodies" in the sense of the authentic union of persons: "The man will...unite with his wife, and the two will be one flesh"; and from the context, it is clear that this union comes from a choice, given that the man "leaves" father and mother to unite with his wife. Such a

union of persons implies that they become "one flesh." Starting from this "sacramental" expression, which corresponds to the communion of persons—of the man and the woman—in their original call to conjugal union, we can understand better the message proper to Genesis 3:16: that is, we can establish *and reconstruct, as it were, what the imbalance consists of,* even better, the special deformation of the *original* interpersonal *relationship of communion,* to which the "sacramental" words of Genesis 2:24 refer.

3. One can therefore say—to show the deeper meaning of Genesis 3:16—that, on the one hand, the "body," which is constituted in the unity of the personal subject, does not cease to arouse the desires for personal union, precisely due to masculinity and femininity ("Your desire shall be for your husband"); on the other hand, concupiscence itself simultaneously directs these desires in its own way; this is confirmed by the expression, "he will dominate you." Now, the concupiscence of the flesh directs these desires toward the appeasement of the body, often at the cost of an authentic and full communion of persons. In this sense, attention should be paid to the manner in which the semantic emphases are distributed in the verses of Genesis 3; in fact, although they are scattered, they reveal an inner coherence. The man seems to feel shame of his body with particular intensity. "I was afraid, because I am naked, and I hid myself" (Gen 3:10); these words highlight the truly metaphysical character of shame. At the same time, the man is the one for whom shame, united with concupiscence, was to become an impulse to "dominate" the woman ("he will dominate you"). Later, the experience of such domination shows itself more directly in the woman as the insatiable desire for a different union. From the moment in which the man *"dominates"* her, *the communion of persons*—which consists in the spiritual unity of the two subjects who gave themselves to each other—*is replaced by a different mutual relationship,* namely, by a relationship *of possession* of the other as an object of one's own desire. If this impulse prevails in the man, the desires that the woman directs toward him, according to the expression of Genesis 3:16, can assume—and do assume—an analogous character. And perhaps, at times, they precede the man's "desire" or even attempt to arouse it and give it impetus.

4. The text of Genesis 3:16 seems to point above all to the man as the one who "desires," analogous to the text of Matthew 5:27–28, which is the point of departure of the present meditations; nevertheless, both the man and the woman have become a "human being" subject to concupiscence. And for this reason the lot of both is shame, whose deep resonance touches the innermost [being] of both the male and the female personality, even though in a different way. What we grasp in Genesis 3 barely allows us to outline this duality, but even the mere hints are already very significant. We add that this text, which is so ancient, is surprisingly eloquent and acute.

C. THE CORRUPTION OF THE SPOUSAL MEANING OF THE BODY

Meaning—"Measure of the Heart"

5. An adequate analysis of Genesis 3 leads thus to the conclusion that the threefold concupiscence, including that of the body, brings with it a limitation of the spousal meaning of the body itself, the spousal meaning in which man and woman shared in the state of original innocence. When we speak about the meaning of the body, we refer above all to the full consciousness of the human being, but we also include every effective experience of the body in its masculinity and femininity, and, in any case, the constant predisposition to such an experience. The "meaning" of the body is not something merely conceptual. We have already sufficiently directed the attention of earlier analyses to this point. *The "meaning of the body" is at the same time what shapes the attitude: it is the way of living the body. It is the measure that the inner man—that is, the heart,* to which Christ appeals in the Sermon on the Mount—applies to the human body with regard to its masculinity or femininity (and thus with regard to its sexuality).

That "meaning" does not modify the reality in itself, that is, that which the human body is and does not cease to be in the sexuality that belongs to it, independently of the states of our consciousness and our experiences. Yet, apart from the system of real, concrete relations between man and woman, the purely objective meaning of the body and of sex is in some sense "a-historical." In the present analysis, we, by contrast, take into account man's historicity—in conformity with the biblical sources—(also because we start from man's theological prehistory). What is evidently at stake here is *an inner dimension* that escapes the outer criteria of historicity, but that can still be considered "historical." Even more: it stands at the root of all facts that constitute man's history—also the history of sin and salvation—and in this way they reveal *the depth and very root of his historicity.*

6. In this vast context, when we speak about concupiscence as a limitation, violation, or complete deformation of the spousal meaning of the body, we go back above all to our earlier analyses regarding the state of original innocence, that is, man's theological prehistory. At the same time, we have in mind the measure that "historical" man, with this "heart," applies to his own body in regard to male and female sexuality. This measure is not something exclusively conceptual: it is what shapes the attitudes and is in general decisive for the way of living the body.

Certainly, the Christ refers to this measure in the Sermon on the Mount. We are trying here to approach the words taken from Matthew 5:27–28 at the very threshold of man's theological history, considering them already in the context of Genesis 3. Concupiscence as a limitation, violation, or complete deformation of the spousal meaning of the body can be observed in a particularly clear way (despite the conciseness of the biblical account) in the two first parents, Adam and Eve; thanks to them, we have been able to find the spousal meaning of the body and to rediscover what it consists of as the measure of the human "heart" such that it shapes the original form of the communion of persons. If in their personal experience (which the biblical text allows us to follow), that original form *suffered imbalance and deformation*—as we tried to show through the analysis of shame—*then what likewise suffered deformation was the spousal meaning of the body, which was the measure of the heart of both,* of the man and of the woman, *in the situation of original innocence.* If we succeed in reconstructing what this deformation consists of, we will also have the answer to our question, namely, what the concupiscence of the flesh consists of and what constitutes its theological and at the same time anthropological specificity. It seems that a theologically and anthropologically adequate answer, important in regard to the meaning of Christ's words in the Sermon on the Mount, can already be drawn from the context of Genesis 3 and from the whole Yahwist account, which has allowed us earlier to clarify the spousal meaning of the human body.

Threat Against the Expression of the Spirit in the Body

32 *General Audience of July 23, 1980*
(Insegnamenti, 3, no. 2 [1980]: 288–91)

1. THE HUMAN BODY in its original masculinity and femininity according to the mystery of creation—as we know from the analysis of Genesis 2:23–25 [see especially TOB 15:1]—is not only a source of fruitfulness, that is, of procreation, but has "from the beginning" a spousal character, that is, it has the power to express the love by which the human person becomes a gift, thus fulfilling the deep meaning of his or her being and existence. In this, its own distinctive character, the body is the expression of the spirit and is called, in the very mystery of creation, to exist in the communion of persons "in the image of God." Now, the concupiscence "that comes from the world"—the concupiscence at stake is directly that of the body—limits and deforms this objective mode of existing of the body, in which man has come to share. *The human "heart" experiences the degree of this limitation or deformation* above all in the sphere of the reciprocal relations between man and woman. Precisely in the experience of the "heart," *femininity and masculinity in their mutual relations seem to be no longer the expression of the spirit that tends toward personal communion* and are left only as an object of attraction, in some sense as it happens "in the world" of living beings, which like man have received the blessing of fruitfulness (see Gen 1).

2. Such a similarity is certainly contained in the work of creation; Genesis 2 also confirms this, especially verse 24. However, already in the mystery of creation, what constituted the "natural," somatic, and sexual substratum of that attraction fully expressed the call of man and woman to personal communion; after sin, on the contrary, in the new situation about which Genesis 3 speaks, this expression grew weak and dark, as if it had been absent in the shaping of reciprocal relations, or as if it had been driven back to another level. The natural

and somatic substrate of human sexuality manifested itself as a quasi self-generating force marked by a certain "constraint of the body" operating according to its own dynamics, which limits the expression of the spirit and the experience of the exchange of the gift of the person. The words of Genesis 3:15 addressed to the woman seem to indicate this quite clearly ("Your desire shall be for your husband, but he will dominate you").

3. The human body in its masculinity and femininity has almost lost the power of expressing this love in which the human person becomes a gift, in conformity with the deepest structure and finality of his or her personal existence, as we have already observed in our earlier analyses [see TOB 15:1; 32:1]. If we do not formulate this judgment here in an absolute way, but add the adverb *"almost (quasi),"* we do so because the dimension of gift—*that is, the power to express the love by which man, through his femininity or masculinity becomes a gift for another*—has in some measure continued to permeate and shape the love born in the human heart. The spousal meaning of the body has not become totally foreign to that heart: *it has not been totally suffocated in it by concupiscence, but only habitually threatened.* The "heart" has become a battlefield between love and concupiscence. The more concupiscence dominates the heart, the less the heart experiences the spousal meaning of the body, and the less sensitive it becomes to the gift of the person that expresses precisely this meaning in the reciprocal relations of man and woman. Certainly, even that "desire" about which Christ speaks in Matthew 5:27–28 appears in many forms in the human heart: it is not always plain and obvious; sometimes it is concealed, so that it passes itself off as "love," although it changes love's authentic profile and obscures the transparent clarity of the gift in the reciprocal relationship of persons. Does this mean that we should distrust the human heart? No! It is only to say that we must remain in control of it.

Loss of the Freedom of the Gift

4. The image of the concupiscence of the body that emerges from the present analysis has a clear reference to the image of the person with which we connected our earlier analyses on the subject of the

spousal meaning of the body. In fact, as a person, man is "the only creature on earth which God willed for itself" and at the same time the one who "cannot fully find himself except through a sincere gift of self" (*Gaudium et Spes*, 24:3).[46] Concupiscence in general—and the concupiscence of the body in particular—attacks precisely this "sincere gift": *it deprives man, one could say, of the dignity of the gift, which is expressed by his body through femininity and masculinity,* and in some sense "depersonalizes" *man, making him an object "for the other."* Instead of being "together with the other"—a subject in unity, or better, in the sacramental "unity of the body"—man becomes an object for man, the female for the male and vice versa. The words of Genesis 3:16— and before them of Genesis 3:7—bear witness to this change with full clarity of contrast when compared to Genesis 2:23–25.

5. By violating the dimension of the mutual gift of the man and the woman, concupiscence also casts doubt on the fact that each of them is willed by the Creator "for himself." The subjectivity of the person gives way in some sense to the objectivity of the body. Because of the body, man becomes an object for man: the female for the male and vice versa. Concupiscence signifies, so to speak, that the personal relations of man and woman are one-sidedly and reductively tied to the body and to sex, in the sense that these relations become almost incapable of welcoming the reciprocal gift of the person. They neither contain nor treat femininity and masculinity according to the full dimension of personal subjectivity; they do not constitute the expression of communion, but remain one-sidedly determined "by sex."

6. Concupiscence brings with it the loss of the interior freedom of the gift. The spousal meaning of the human body is linked exactly to this freedom. Man can become a gift—that is, man and woman can exist in the relationship of the reciprocal gift of self—if each of them

---

46. *Gaudium et Spes*, 24:3: "Indeed, the Lord Jesus, when he prays to the Father, 'that all may be one...as we are one' (Jn 17:21–22) and thus offers vistas closed to human reason, indicates a certain likeness between the union of the divine Persons, and the union of God's sons in truth and charity. This likeness shows that man, who is the only creature on earth which God willed for itself, cannot fully find himself except through a sincere gift of self (cf. Lk 17:33)."

masters himself. *Concupiscence*, which manifests itself as a "*constraint 'sui generis' of the body*," limits and restricts self-mastery from within, and thereby *in some sense makes the interior freedom of the gift impossible.* At the same time, also the beauty that the human body possesses in its male and female appearance, as an expression of the spirit, is obscured. The body is left as an object of concupiscence and thus as a "terrain of appropriation" of the other human being. Concupiscence as such is not able to promote union as a communion of persons. By itself, it does not unite, but appropriates to itself. *The relationship of the gift changes into a relationship of appropriation.*

At this point we interrupt our reflections today. The final problem treated here is of such great importance and subtlety from the point of view of the difference between authentic love (that is, the "communion of persons") and concupiscence that we will have to take it up again in our next meeting.

33 General Audience of July 30, 1980
(*Insegnamenti*, 3, no. 2 [1980]: 311–14)

1. THE REFLECTIONS WE ARE DEVELOPING in the present cycle are concerned with the words that Christ spoke in the Sermon on the Mount about [concupiscent] "desire" for a woman on the part of a man. In the attempt to go on to a thorough, in-depth examination of what characterizes the "man of concupiscence," we went back again to Genesis. There, the situation created in the reciprocal relationship of man and woman is sketched with great acuteness. The single sentences of Genesis 3 are very eloquent. The words of God-Yahweh addressed to the woman in Genesis 3:16, "Your desire shall be for your husband, but he will dominate you," seem to reveal, to deeper analysis, in what way the relationship of reciprocal gift, which existed between them in the state of original innocence, changed after original sin into a relationship of reciprocal appropriation.

If a man relates to a woman in such a way that he considers her only as an object to appropriate and not as a gift, he condemns himself at the same time to become, on his part too, only an object of appropriation for her and not a gift. It seems that the words of Genesis 3:16 deal with this two-sided relationship, although they directly say only, "he will dominate you." Further, in one-sided appropriation (which is indirectly two-sided), the structure of communion among the persons disappears; both human beings become almost incapable of reaching the inner measure of the heart directed toward the freedom of the gift and the spousal meaning of the body, which is intrinsic to that measure. The words of Genesis 3:16 seem to suggest that this happens more at the woman's expense and that in any case she feels it more than the man.

2. It is worth turning our attention to this detail at least. The words of God-Yahweh, according to Genesis 3:16, "Your desire shall be for your husband, but *he will dominate you*," and those of Christ according to Matthew 5:27–28, "Whoever looks at a woman to desire her..." allow us to see a certain parallelism. The main point is perhaps not that it is above all the woman who becomes an object of "desire" on the part of the man, but rather, as we stressed before [see TOB 17:6], that *the man* ought to have been "from the beginning" *the guardian of the reciprocity of the gift and of its true balance.* The analysis of that "beginning" (Gen 2:23–25) shows precisely the man's responsibility in welcoming femininity as a gift [see TOB 15:3] and in receiving it in a mutual, two-sided exchange. It is in open conflict with this exchange to take from the woman her own gift by concupiscence. Although maintaining the balance of the gift seems to be something entrusted to both, the man has a special responsibility, as if it depended more on him whether the balance is kept or violated or even—if it has already been violated—reestablished. Certainly, the diversity of roles, according to these statements, to which we are turning here as the key texts, was also dictated by the social marginalization of women in the conditions of that time (Sacred Scripture both of the Old and the New Testaments gives us sufficient examples); nevertheless, there is a truth contained in it that has its own weight indepen-dent of specific forms of conditioning due to the customs of that determinate historical situation.

The Inner Measure of Belonging

3. Concupiscence has the effect that the body becomes, as it were, a "terrain" of appropriation of the other person. It is easy to understand that this brings with it the loss of the spousal meaning of the body. And together with this loss, another meaning also attaches

to the reciprocal "belonging" of the persons who, uniting in such a way as to be "one flesh" (Gen 2:24), are at the same time called to belong to each other. The particular dimension of the personal union of man and woman through love expresses itself in the word "my." This pronoun, which has always belonged to the language of human love, often recurs in the verses of the Song of Songs and also in other biblical texts (see, e.g., Song 1:9, 13–16; 2:2–3, 8–10, 13–14, 16–17; 3:2, 4–5; 4:1, 10; 5:1–2, 4; 6:2–4, 9; 7:11; 8:12, 14; see also Ezek 16:8; Hos 2:18; Tob 8:7). In its "material" meaning, this pronoun *denotes a relation of possession,* but in our case, *it points to the personal analogy of such a relation. The reciprocal belonging of man and woman,* especially when they belong to each other as spouses "in the unity of the body," *is formed according to this personal analogy.* Analogy—as is well known—indicates at one and the same time similarity and also the lack of identity (that is, a substantial dissimilarity). We can speak of the reciprocal belonging of persons only if we take this analogy into account. In fact, in its original and specific meaning, belonging presupposes the relation of the subject to the object, a relation of possession and property. It is not only an objective relation, but above all "material": the belonging of something, thus of an object to someone.

4. In the eternal language of human love, the term "my" does not—this is certain—have this meaning. It indicates the reciprocity of giving, it expresses the equilibrium of the gift—perhaps precisely this in the first place—that is, the equilibrium of the gift in which the reciprocal *communio personarum* is established. And if this communion is established through the reciprocal gift of masculinity and femininity, the spousal meaning of the body is also preserved in it. Indeed, in the language of love, the word "my" seems to be a radical negation of belonging in the sense in which a material object-thing belongs to the subject-person. The analogy keeps its function as long as it does not fall into the meaning explained above. The threefold concupiscence, and in particular the concupiscence of the flesh, deprives the reciprocal belonging of man and woman of the dimension proper to the personal analogy, in which the term "my" keeps its essential meaning. This essential meaning lies outside the "law of property," outside the meaning of "object of possession"; concupiscence, by contrast, is oriented toward the latter meaning. From possessing, the next step is "enjoyment": the object I possess gains a certain significance for me inasmuch as it is at my disposal and I put it to my service, I use it. It is evident that the personal analogy of belonging is decidedly opposed to such a meaning. And this opposition is a sign that what "comes from the Father" in the reciprocal relation of the man and the woman still persists and continues in the face of what comes "from the world." Concupiscence of itself, however, pushes man toward the possession of the other as an object, pushes him toward "enjoyment," which carries with it the negation of the spousal meaning of the body. In its essence, the disinterested gift is excluded by egotistical "enjoyment." Do not the words of God-Yahweh addressed to the woman in Genesis 3:16 already speak of this?

5. According to 1 John 2:16, concupiscence shows above all the state of the human spirit. The concupiscence of the flesh, too, bears witness in the first place to the state of the human spirit. We should devote a further analysis to this problem.

When we apply Johannine theology to the terrain of the experiences described in Genesis 3 as well as to the words Christ spoke in the Sermon on the Mount (Mt 5:27–28), we find a concrete dimension, so to speak, of the opposition between the spirit and the body that was born—together with sin—in the human heart. Its consequences make themselves felt in the reciprocal relation of persons, whose unity in humanity has from the beginning been determined by the fact that they are man and woman. From the moment in which "another law at war with the law of the mind" (Rom 7:23) installed itself in man, there exists an almost constant danger of a way of seeing, of evaluating, of loving such that "the desire of the body" shows itself stronger than the "desire of the mind." And it is precisely this truth about man, this anthropological component, that we must always keep in mind if we want to gain a thorough and deep understanding of the appeal Christ made to the human heart in the Sermon on the Mount.

3. Commandment and Ethos

34 *General Audience of August 6, 1980*
(Insegnamenti, 3, no. 2 [1980]: 336–39)

1. CONTINUING OUR CYCLE, we take up again today the Sermon on the Mount and in particular the statement, "Whoever looks at a woman to desire her [lustfully] has already committed adultery with her in his heart" (Mt 5:28).

In his dialogue with the Pharisees, Jesus, appealing to the "beginning" (see the earlier analyses [TOB 1:2–2:1]), said the following words about the certificate of divorce: "Because of the hardness of your heart Moses allowed you to divorce your wives, but from the beginning it was not so" (Mt 19:8). This sentence undoubtedly contains an accusation. *"The hardness of heart"*[47] indicates that which, according to the ethos of the people of the Old Testament, *had given rise to the situation contrary* to the original design of God-Yahweh according to Genesis 2:24. And it is there that we must seek the key to interpret the whole legislation of Israel in the area of marriage and, in the broader sense, in all relations between man and woman. When he speaks about "hardness of heart," Christ thus accuses the entire "interior subject," so to speak, which is responsible for the deformation of the law. In the Sermon on the Mount (Mt 5:27–28), he also appeals to the "heart," but the words spoken here do not seem to be only words of accusation.

2. We must reflect on them once again, setting them as far as possible into their "historical" dimension. The analysis carried out so far, which aimed at bringing "the man of concupiscence" into focus in the

---

47. The Greek term *sklērokardia* was formed by the Septuagint to render what was meant in Hebrew by *"uncircumcision of the heart"* (see, e.g., Deut 10:16; Jer 4:4; Sir 3:26); it appears only once in a literal translation in the New Testament (Acts 7:51).

"Uncircumcision" signified "paganism," "shamelessness," and "distance from the covenant with God"; "uncircumcision of the heart" expressed indomitable obstinacy in opposing God. The exclamation of the deacon Stephen shows this: "You obstinate people, pagan in heart [literally: uncircumcised in heart]...you are forever opposing the Holy Spirit: just as your fathers used to do, so do you." Acts 7:51; John Paul II's addition.

One must therefore understand "hardness of heart" in this philological context.

very moment of his coming to be, in the first point, as it were, of his history interwoven with theology, was an extensive and mainly *anthropological* introduction to the work that must still be undertaken. The next stage of our analyses will have to be of an *ethical* character. The Sermon on the Mount, and in particular the passage we have chosen as the center of our analyses, is part of the proclamation of the new ethos: *the ethos of the Gospel*. In the teaching of Christ, it is deeply connected with consciousness of the "beginning," and thus with the mystery of creation in its original simplicity and wealth; and, at the same time, the ethos that Christ proclaims in the Sermon on the Mount is realistically addressed to "historical man," who has become the man of concupiscence. The threefold concupiscence is, in fact, the heritage of all humanity and the human "heart" really participates in it. Christ, who knows "what is in man" (Jn 2:25),[48] cannot speak otherwise than with this awareness. From this point of view, what predominates in the words of Matthew 5:27–28 is not accusation, but judgment: a realistic judgment about the human heart, a judgment that has, on the one hand, an anthropological foundation and, on the other hand, a directly ethical character. For the ethos of the Gospel, it is a constitutive judgment.

3. In the Sermon on the Mount, Christ turns directly to human beings who belong to a definite society. The Teacher, too, belongs to that society, to that people. In the words of Christ, one must, for this reason, look for a reference to the facts, the situations, and the institutions with which he was familiar in everyday life. We must analyze these references at least in a summary way, so that the ethical meaning of the words of Matthew 5:27–28 comes out more clearly. Yet, with these words, Christ turns in an indirect but real way *to every "historical" man* (taking "historical" above all in its theological function). This human being is precisely the "man of concupiscence" whose mystery and heart is known to Christ ("for he himself knew what was in every man," Jn 2:25). The words of the Sermon on the Mount allow us to establish a point of contact *with the inner experience of this man* at every geographical latitude and longitude, as it were, in various epochs, under different social and cultural conditions. The man of our

---

48. Compare "I am the one who searches minds and hearts" (Rev 2:23); "Lord, you know everyone's heart (*kardiognōstēs*)" (Acts 1:24).

time feels himself called by name in this statement of Christ, no less than the man of "that time," whom the Teacher addressed directly.

4. In this resides the universality of the Gospel, which is not at all a generalization. It is perhaps precisely in this statement of Christ, the one we are analyzing here, that this point can be shown in a particularly clear way. In virtue of this statement, the human being of every time and of every place feels himself called in a manner that is adequate, concrete, and unrepeatable, because Christ appeals precisely to the human "heart," which cannot be the subject of any generalization. *With the category of "heart," everyone is identified in a singular manner, even more than by name;* he is reached in that which determines him in a unique and unrepeatable way; he is defined in his humanity "from within."

5. The image of the man of concupiscence concerns above all his innermost [being] (Mt 15:19–20).[49] The history of the human "heart" after original sin is written under the pressure of the threefold concupiscence, with which also the deepest image of ethos is connected in its various historical documents. At any rate, that innermost [being] is also the strength that is decisive for "external" human behavior as well as for the form of the many structures and institutions on the level of social life. If we deduce the content of ethos in its various historical formulations from these structures and institutions, we always encounter this innermost aspect proper *to* man's inner *image.* This image is, in fact, the most essential component. The words of Christ in the Sermon on the Mount, and especially those of Matthew 5:27–28, indicate this fact unmistakably. No study on human ethos can pass by this fact with indifference.

In our next reflections we will therefore try to analyze in a more detailed way Christ's statement, "You have heard that it was said, '*You shall not commit adultery.*' But I say to you: Whoever looks at a woman to desire her has already committed adultery with her in his heart" (or "has already made her an adulteress in his heart").

In order to understand this text better, we will first analyze its *single parts,* with the goal of reaching afterwards a deeper *overall view.*

---

49. "For out of the heart come evil intentions, murder, adultery, prostitution, theft, false witness, slander. These make a man unclean." Mt 15:19–20.

We will take into account not only the listeners of that time, who heard the Sermon on the Mount with their own ears, but also, as far as possible, the listeners of today, the human beings of our time.

A. IT WAS SAID, "DO NOT COMMIT ADULTERY" (MT 5:27)

The History of a People

35 *General Audience of August 13, 1980*
(Insegnamenti, 3, no. 2 [1980]: 396–99)

1. WE MUST CARRY OUT THE ANALYSIS of Christ's statement in the Sermon on the Mount that refers to "adultery" and to [lustful] "desire," which he calls "adultery committed in the heart," by beginning with the first words. Christ says, "You have heard that it was said, 'You shall not commit adultery'" (Mt 5:27). He has in mind the commandment of God, the sixth in the Decalogue; it is part of the so-called second tablet of the law, which Moses received from God-Yahweh.

Let us first take the point of view of the direct listeners of the Sermon on the Mount, of those who heard Christ's words. They are sons and daughters of the Chosen People, the people who had received the "law" from God-Yahweh himself, that had received also the "prophets," who had repeatedly in the course of centuries reproached precisely the people's relation to this law, the many transgressions of the law. Christ, too, speaks about similar transgressions. But even more so, he speaks about a human interpretation of the law that cancels and does away with *the right meaning of good and evil specifically* willed by the Divine Legislator. The law is, in fact, above all a means, an indispensable means in order that "justice may superabound" (the words of Mt 5:20 in the old translation). Christ wants such justice "to exceed"—literally, "abound more than"—"that of the scribes and Pharisees." He does not accept the interpretation they had given in the course of the centuries to the authentic content of the law, inasmuch as they in some measure subjected this content, or the purpose and will of the Legislator, to the various forms of weakness and the limits of the human will that derive precisely from the threefold concupiscence. It was a casuistic interpretation that had superimposed itself on the original vision of good and evil connected with the law of the Decalogue. If Christ strives for a transformation of ethos, he does so above all to recover the fundamental clarity of interpretation. "Do not think that I have come to abolish the Law or the Prophets; I have not come to abolish but to fulfill" (Mt 5:17). The condition for fulfillment is correct understanding. And this applies, among others, to the commandment "You shall not commit adultery."

2. If one follows the history of the Chosen People in the pages of the Old Testament from the time of Abraham, one finds abundant facts that attest to how this commandment was put into practice and how, as a consequence of this practice, *the casuistic interpretation of the law* was worked out. First of all, the history of the Old Testament is clearly the theater of the systematic defection from monogamy, which must have had a fundamental significance for the understanding of the prohibition, "You shall not commit adultery." The abandonment of monogamy, especially at the time of the patriarchs, was dictated by the desire for offspring, for numerous offspring. This desire was so deep, and procreation, as the essential end of marriage, was so evident, that wives who loved their husbands, when they were unable to give them offspring, on their own initiative asked their husbands, who loved them, if they could take "on their own knees" or receive children born of another woman, e.g., those of a serving woman, a slave. This was the case with Sarah and Abraham (see Gen 16:2) or with Rachel and Jacob (see Gen 30:3)

These two narratives reflect the moral climate in which the Decalogue was practiced. They illustrate the way in which Israelite ethos was prepared *to receive the commandment "You shall not commit adultery"* and how this commandment was applied in the most ancient tradition of this people. The authority of the patriarchs was, in fact, the highest in Israel and had a religious character. It was strictly tied to the covenant and the promise.

3. The commandment "You shall not commit adultery" did not change this tradition. Everything indicates that its further development did not limit itself to the (rather exceptional) motives that had guided the behavior of Abraham and Sarah or of Jacob and Rachel. If

we take as an example the most illustrious representatives of Israel after Moses, namely, the kings of Israel, David and Solomon, the description of their lives attests that effective polygamy established itself, and it did so undoubtedly for reasons of concupiscence.

In the story of David, who also had several wives, what is striking is not only the fact that he had taken the wife of one of his subjects, but also the clear consciousness of having committed adultery. This fact as well as the king's repentance are described in a detailed and suggestive way (see 2 Sam 11:2–27). By *adultery* one understood *only the possession of another's wife*, but not the possession of other women as wives next to the first one. The whole tradition of the Old Covenant indicates that the effective necessity of monogamy as an essential and indispensable implication *of the commandment "You shall not commit adultery"* never reached the consciousness and ethos of the later generations of the Chosen People.

4. On this background one must also understand all the efforts that aimed at introducing the specific content of the commandment "You shall not commit adultery" into the framework of promulgated legislation. The books of the Bible in which we find a full account of the whole Old Testament *legislation* confirm this. If one considers the letter of this legislation, it becomes evident that it combats adultery decisively and without hesitation, using radical means, including the death penalty (see Lev 20:10; Deut 22:22). Yet, it does so while actually supporting effective polygamy, fully legalizing it at least in an indirect way. Adultery is thus combated only within definite limits and within the circumference of definite premises that make up the essential form of the Old Testament ethos.

In these laws, adultery is understood above all (and perhaps exclusively) as the violation of the man's property right regarding every woman who was his legal wife (usually one among many); adultery is not understood, by contrast, as it appears from the point of view of the monogamy established by the Creator. We know already that Christ appealed to the "beginning" precisely concerning this matter (see Mt 19:8).

5. Very significant, in addition, is the situation in which Christ takes the side of the woman caught in adultery and defends her from stoning. He says to the accusers, "Let the one among you who is without sin be the first to throw a stone at her" (Jn 8:7). When they drop the stones and go away, he says to the woman, "Go, and from now on, do not sin again" (Jn 8:11). Christ, therefore, clearly identifies adultery as sin. By contrast, when he turns to the ones who wanted to stone the adulteress, he does not appeal to the prescriptions of Israelite law, but only to conscience. The discernment of good and evil inscribed in human conscience can turn out to be deeper and more correct than the content of a legal norm.

As we have seen, the history of the People of God in the Old Covenant (which we tried to illustrate only with a few examples) unfolded to a remarkable degree outside the normative content placed by God in the commandment "You shall not commit adultery"; it bypassed it, so to speak. Christ wants to correct these distortions, hence the words spoken by him in the Sermon on the Mount.

Legislation

36 *General Audience of August 20, 1980*
(Insegnamenti, 3, no. 2 [1980]: 415–19)

1. WHEN CHRIST SAYS in the Sermon on the Mount, "You have heard that it was said, 'You shall not commit adultery'" (Mt 5:27), he refers to something everybody in his audience knew perfectly well and felt himself bound to in virtue of God-Yahweh's commandment. Nevertheless, the history of the Old Testament shows that the life of the people—united to God-Yahweh by a special covenant—as well as the lives of individuals often moved away from this commandment. The same point is shown by a summary glance at the legislation richly documented in the books of the Old Testament.

The prescriptions of the Old Testament law were very severe. They were also very specific and entered into the smallest concrete details of life (see e.g., Deut 21:10–13; Num 30:7–16; Deut 24:1–4; 22:13–21; Lev 20:10–21, etc.). One can presume that, as the legalization of effective polygamy became evident in this law, there was an increased need for fixing its juridical extent and securing its legal limits. Hence the great number of prescriptions and also the severity of the punishments laid down by the lawgiver for breaking such norms.

On the basis of the above analyses of Christ's appeal to the "beginning" in his discourse on the dissolubility of marriage and the "certificate of divorce," it is evident that he clearly sees the fundamental contradiction contained in the marriage law of the Old Testament inasmuch as it accepted effective polygamy, that is, the institution of concubines in addition to legitimate wives, or the right of cohabitation with a slave woman.[50] One can say that this law, while *combating sin, at the same time* contained in itself *the "social structures of sin"*; in fact, it *protected* and legalized them. In these circumstances, the essential ethical meaning of the commandment "Do not commit adultery" necessarily suffered a fundamental revaluation. In the Sermon on the Mount, Christ reveals this meaning again and thus passes beyond its traditional and legal restrictions.

2. It is perhaps useful to add that in the interpretation of the Old Testament, while the prohibition of adultery is marked—one might say—by a compromise with the concupiscence of the body, the opposition to sexual deviations is clearly defined. The relevant prescriptions, which impose capital punishment for homosexuality and bestiality, confirm this opposition. As for the behavior of Onan, son of Judah (whose name is the origin of the modern term "onanism"), Sacred Scripture says that, "What he did was displeasing in the sight of the Lord, and he put him to death also" (Gen 38:10).

Taken in its entirety, the marriage law of the Old Testament places the procreative end of marriage in the foreground. In some cases it tries to implement the equality of women and men before the

---

50. Although the Book of Genesis presents the monogamous marriages of Adam, Seth, and Noah as models to imitate and seems to condemn bigamy, which appears only among the descendants of Cain (see Gen 4:19), the lives of the patriarchs provide counterexamples. Abraham observes the prescriptions of the Code of Hammurabi, which allows marrying a second wife in case the first is barren. Jacob had two wives and two concubines (see Gen 30:1–19).

The Book of Deuteronomy admits the legal existence of bigamy (see Deut 21:15–17) and even polygamy, advising the king not to have too many wives (Deut 17:17); it also confirms the institution of concubines—prisoners of war (Deut 21:10–14) or slaves (Ex 21:7–11). See Roland De Vaux, *Ancient Israel: Its Life and Institutions,* 3rd ed. (London: Darton Longman Todd, 1976), 24–25, 83. In the Old Testament there is no explicit mention of the obligation to monogamy, though the image presented by the later books shows that it was the prevalent social practice (see, e.g., the Wisdom books with the exception of Sir 37:11; Tob).

law—for example, it explicitly says about the punishment for adultery, "If a man commits adultery with the wife of his neighbor, both the adulterer and the adulteress shall be put to death" (Lev 20:10)—but on the whole it judges the woman differently and treats her with greater severity.

3. One should perhaps draw attention to *the language of this legislation,* which is, as always in such cases, an objectifying language of the sexology of that time period. It is also an *important* language for the whole of the *reflections on the theology of the body.* We find in it the explicit confirmation of the character of shame that surrounds what in man belongs to sex. The sexual is even considered in some sense "impure," especially in the case of physiological manifestations of human sexuality. "Uncovering nakedness" (see, e.g., Lev 20:11, 17–21) is stigmatized as the equivalent of performing a complete illicit sexual act. The very phrase seems expressive enough. There is no doubt that the lawgiver sought to use the terminology corresponding to the consciousness and practices of society at that time. In this way, the language of Old Testament legislation should convince us not only that the physiology and the bodily manifestations of sex are known to the lawgiver, but also that they are evaluated in a definite way. It is difficult to avoid the impression that this evaluation has a negative character. This certainly does not cancel the truths we know from Genesis, nor can one accuse the Old Testament—and, among others, also the legislative books—of being a sort of precursor of Manichaeism. The judgment about the body and sex expressed in it is not primarily *"negative"* or even severe, but rather *marked by an objectivism* motivated by the intention of setting this area of human life in order. It is not concerned directly with the order of the "heart" but with the order of social life as a whole, at the basis of which stands, as always, marriage and the family.

4. When one considers the "sexual" problematic as a whole, one should perhaps briefly turn one's attention to another aspect, namely, the link between morality, the law, and medicine as shown in the relevant books of the Old Testament. They contain many practical prescriptions in *the area of hygiene* or medicine, characterized more by experience than science, according to the level reached at that time (see, e.g., Lev 12:1–6; 15:1–28; Deut 21:12–13). In our time, by the way, the link between experience and science is evidently still relevant. In this wide area of problems, medicine always closely accompanies ethics; and ethics, like theology, seeks its collaboration.

The Prophets

5. When in the Sermon on the Mount Christ says, "You have heard that it was said, 'You shall not commit adultery,'" and immediately adds, "But I say to you...," it is clear that he wants to rebuild in the consciousness of his audience the ethical meaning that belongs to this commandment, distancing himself from the "teachers," the official experts of the law. But in addition to the interpretation that comes from tradition, the Old Testament offers us another tradition for understanding the commandment "You shall not commit adultery." It is the tradition of the prophets. When they referred to "adultery," they wanted to remind "Israel and Judah" that their greatest sin was abandoning the one true God in favor of the cult of various idols that had been adopted easily and thoughtlessly by the Chosen People in contact with other peoples. In this way, what is *characteristic of the language of the prophets is the analogy with adultery* rather than adultery itself. Yet, such an analogy also helps one to understand the commandment "You shall not commit adultery" and its interpretation, which (as noted) is absent in the legal texts. In the revelations of the prophets, particularly in Isaiah, Hosea, and Ezekiel, the God of the covenant, Yahweh, is often represented as Bridegroom, and the love with which he joined himself to Israel can and should be equated with the spousal love of a couple. Because of its idolatry and desertion of God, the Bridegroom, Israel commits a betrayal before him that can be compared to that of a woman in relation to her husband: it commits, in fact, "adultery."

6. With eloquent words, and often in extraordinarily drastic images and comparisons, the prophets present the love of Yahweh, the Bridegroom, as well as the betrayal of Israel, the Bride, who throws herself away in adultery. This is a topic that we must take up again in our reflections when we analyze the problem of the "sacrament" [see TOB 104], but already now we should touch upon it as far as neces-

sary for understanding Christ's words in Matthew 5:27–28 and for appreciating the renewal of ethos implied in these words, "But I say to you...." While Isaiah emphasizes in his texts above all the love of Yahweh, the Bridegroom, who in all circumstances goes to meet the Bride, overlooking all her infidelities, Hosea and Ezekiel abound in comparisons that show above all the ugliness and moral evil of the adultery committed by the Bride, Israel.

In the next meditation we will try to enter still more deeply into the texts of the prophets to clarify further the content corresponding to the commandment "You shall not commit adultery" in the consciousness of those who listened to the Sermon on the Mount.

37 General Audience of August 27, 1980
(Insegnamenti, 3, no. 2 [1980]: 451–56)

1. IN THE SERMON ON THE MOUNT, Christ says, "Do not think that I have come to abolish the Law or the Prophets; I have not come to abolish but to fulfill" (Mt 5:17). To show in what this fulfillment consists, he goes on to the individual commandments and comes also to the one that says, "You shall not commit adultery." The last meditation had the aim of showing how the true content of this commandment willed by God was darkened by many compromises in the particular legislation of Israel. The prophets, who often denounce in their teaching the abandonment of the true God-Yahweh by the people, comparing it to "adultery," bring out this content in the most authentic way.

Not only by words, but (as it seems) also by his behavior, *Hosea* seeks to reveal to us (see Hos 1–3) that the people's betrayal is similar to betrayal in marriage, or even more to adultery practiced in the form of prostitution. "Go, take a prostitute for yourself as wife and have children of prostitution, for the land does nothing but prostitute itself by going away from the Lord" (Hos 1:2). The prophet feels this command in himself and accepts it as coming from God-Yahweh: "The Lord said to me again, 'Go, love a woman who is loved by another and is an adulteress'" (Hos 3:1). For, although Israel is as unfaithful toward its God as the Bride who "chased after her lovers and forgot me" (Hos 2:15), nevertheless, *Yahweh does not stop looking for his Bride;* he does not grow tired of waiting for her to turn and come back, and he confirms this attitude by the prophet's words and actions, "And on that day, word of the Lord, you will call me, 'My husband,' and will no longer call me, 'My master (my Baal).'...I will make you my bride for ever, I will make you my bride in righteousness and in justice, in goodness and in love. I will make you my bride in faithfulness, and you shall know the Lord" (Hos 2:18, 21–22). This ardent call for the conversion of the unfaithful bride and wife goes hand in hand with the following threat, "Let her remove from her face the signs of her prostitution and the signs of adultery from between her breasts, or I will strip her all naked and expose her as on the day she was born" (Hos 2:4–5).

2. *The prophet Ezekiel* reminds Israel, the unfaithful Bride, in even greater measure of this image of the humiliating nakedness of birth.

> Like a repugnant object you were thrown out in the open field on the day you were born. I passed near you while you were flailing about in your blood, and I said to you, "Live in your blood and grow up like a plant of the field." You grew up and became tall and arrived at the flower of youth: your breasts blossomed, and you reached puberty, but you were naked and bare. I passed near you again and looked on you; you were at the age for love. I spread the edge of my cloak over you, and covered your nakedness: I swore a covenant with you, says the Lord God, and you became mine.... I put a ring on your nose, earrings in your ears, and a beautiful crown on your head. You were adorned with gold and silver, while your clothing was of fine linen, rich fabric, and embroidered cloth.... Your fame spread among the nations because of your beauty, for it was perfect due to the glory I placed in you.... But you, infatuated with your beauty and profiting from your fame, played the whore and lavished your favors on any passer-by.... How degraded is your heart, says the Lord God, that you did all these things, the deeds of a shameless whore.
>
> Building your high place in every square, you were not like a prostitute in search of payment, but like an adulterous wife, who instead of her husband receives strangers! (Ezek 16:5–8, 12–15, 30–32)

Covenant

3. The quote is somewhat long, but the text is so important that it was necessary to recall it. It expresses *the analogy between adultery and idolatry* in a particularly strong and comprehensive way. *The point of likeness* between the two sides of the analogy consists *in the covenant* *accompanied by love.* Out of love, God-Yahweh makes the covenant with Israel (without any merit on its part); for Israel he becomes a Bridegroom and Husband who is most affectionate, attentive, and generous toward his Bride. For this love, which has accompanied Israel since the dawn of history, Yahweh, the Bridegroom, receives many betrayals in exchange, "the high places"—those places of idolatrous worship in which "the adultery" of Israel, the Bride, is committed [see 1 Kings 11:7; Hos 10:8]. In the analysis we are conducting here, the essential point is the concept of adultery used by Ezekiel. One can say, however, that the situation into which the concept has been inserted (in the framework of the analogy) is on the whole not typical. Here we are not dealing with a mutual choice made by the bride and the bridegroom, which is born from reciprocal love, but with the choice of the bride (which was made already from the moment of her birth), a choice that comes from the Bridegroom's love, which is an act of sheer mercy on the Bridegroom's part. The choice shows itself in this way; it corresponds to the part of the analogy that describes the covenant of Yahweh with Israel; it corresponds less to its second part, which defines the nature of marriage. The mentality of that time was certainly not very sensitive to this reality— for Israelites marriage was rather the result of a one-sided choice, a choice often made by the parents—but such a situation is hard for us to understand.

4. Leaving aside this detail, it is impossible to overlook that the texts of the prophets reveal *a different meaning of adultery* than the legislative tradition gives it. Adultery is sin because it is *the breaking of the personal covenant between the man and the woman.* What is emphasized in the legislative texts is the violation of property rights and, in the first place, of the husband's property right to the woman who, though she is his legal wife, is one among many. In the texts of the prophets, the background of effective and legalized polygamy does not change the ethical meaning of adultery. In many texts, monogamy seems to be the only right analogy of monotheism understood in the categories of the covenant, that is, of faithfulness and trust in the only true God-Yahweh, Israel's Bridegroom. Adultery is the antithesis of this spousal relation and the opposite of marriage (also as an institution) inasmuch as monogamous marriage actualizes in itself the inter-

personal covenant of man and woman and it realizes the covenant that is born from love and welcomed by both parties as a marriage (and recognized as such by society). This sort of covenant between two persons is the foundation of the union by which "the man...unites with his wife, and the two will be one flesh" (Gen 2:24). In the context mentioned above, one can say that this bodily unity is their *"right"* (bilateral), but above all that it is the regular *sign* of the communion of persons, of the unity brought about between the man and the woman inasmuch as they are spouses. Adultery committed by either of them is not only *the violation of this right,* which belongs exclusively to the other spouse, but at the same time a radical *falsification of the sign.* It seems that the oracles of the prophets express precisely this aspect of adultery with sufficient clarity.

5. When we say that adultery is a falsification of this sign, which finds not only its "normativity," but rather its simple inner truth in marriage—that is, in the shared life of man and woman who have become spouses—we go back again in some way to the fundamental statements made above, because we consider them essential and important for the theology of the body from the anthropological as well as ethical point of view. Adultery is a "sin of the body." The whole tradition of the Old Testament attests to this, and Christ confirms it. The comparative analysis of his words in the Sermon on the Mount (Mt 5:27–28) as well as various relevant statements in the Gospels and other passages of the New Testament allow us to find the real reason for the sinfulness of adultery. It is evident that we find this reason for sinfulness or moral evil by relying on the principle of antithesis to the moral good of conjugal faithfulness, that good which can only be adequately realized in the exclusive relation between the two (that is, in the spousal relation between one man and one woman). The need for such a relationship is proper to spousal love, whose interpersonal structure (as we have shown already) is upheld by the inner normativity of the "communion of persons." It is precisely this [communion] that gives the covenant its essential meaning (whether in the relation between man and woman or, by analogy, in the relation between Yahweh and Israel). *One can judge about adultery, about its sinfulness, about the moral evil it contains, on the basis of the principle of antithesis to the conjugal covenant understood in this way.*

6. We must keep all of this in mind when we say that adultery is a "sin of the body"; the body is here considered in the conceptual connection with the words of Genesis 2:24 that speak, in fact, about the man and the woman who unite so intimately with each other that they form "one flesh." Adultery indicates the act by which a man and a woman who are not husband and wife form "one flesh" (that is, those who are not husband and wife in the sense of the monogamy established at the beginning rather than in the sense of the legal casuistry of the Old Testament). The "sin" of the body can be identified only in reference to the relationship between the persons. One can speak of moral good and evil according to whether this relationship makes such a "unity of the body" true and whether or not *it gives to that unity the character of a truthful sign.* In this case, therefore, we can judge adultery as a sin in conformity with the act's objective content.

And this is the content Christ has in mind when he recalls in the Sermon on the Mount, "You have heard that it was said, 'You shall not commit adultery.'" Yet, Christ does not dwell on this aspect of the problem.

B. "WHOEVER LOOKS TO DESIRE..."

Shift in the Center of Gravity

38 General Audience of September 3, 1980
(*Insegnamenti*, 3, no. 2 [1980]: 518–22)

1. IN THE SERMON ON THE MOUNT, Christ limits himself to recalling the commandment "You shall not commit adultery" without evaluating the corresponding behavior of his listeners. What we have said earlier about this topic comes from other sources (above all from Christ's discourse with the Pharisees in which he appeals to the "beginning": Mt 19:8; Mk 10:6). In the Sermon on the Mount, Christ omits this evaluation or rather, he takes it for granted. What he says in the statement's second part, "But I say to you...," is *something more than polemics* against the "teachers of the law" or the moralists of the Torah; and it is *something more than polemics in regard to the evaluation of the ethos* of the Old Testament. It is a direct transition to the new ethos. Christ seems to leave aside all the disputes about the ethical meaning of adultery on the level of legislation and casuistry, in which the essential interpersonal relationship between husband and wife had been considerably obscured by the objective property relation and thus acquired another dimension. Christ says, "But I say to you: Whoever looks at a woman to desire her has already committed adultery with her in his heart" (Mt 5:28; this passage always brings to mind the old translation, "has already made her an adulteress in his heart," a translation that, perhaps better than the Italian translation used now, expresses the fact that here we are dealing with a purely interior and one-sided act). In this way, then, "adultery committed in the heart" is in some sense set over against "adultery committed in the body."

We must ask ourselves, why has the center of gravity of sin shifted? Further, what is the authentic meaning of the analogy? If according to its basic meaning, "adultery" can, in fact, only be a "sin committed in the body," in what sense does what man commits in his heart also deserve to be called adultery? The words with which Christ lays the foundation of the new ethos need to be, on their part, deeply rooted in anthropology. Before we respond to these questions, we will dwell a little on the expression in Matthew 5:27–28 that makes in some sense the transfer or shift *of the meaning of adultery from the "body" to the "heart."* It consists of words about desire.

2. Christ speaks about concupiscence: "Whoever looks to desire." This is the expression that needs to be analyzed in detail to understand the statement as a whole. Here we have to return to the analysis above, the aim of which, I would say, was to reconstruct the image of "the man of concupiscence" at the very beginning of history. The man about whom Christ speaks in the Sermon on the Mount—the man who looks "to desire"—is without doubt the man of concupiscence. Precisely for this reason, because he shares in the concupiscence of the body, he "desires" and "looks to desire." The image of the man of concupiscence, which we reconstructed above, will help us now to interpret the "desire" about which Christ speaks according to Matthew 5:27–28. We are concerned here not only with a *psychological* interpretation, but at the same time with a *theological* interpretation. Christ speaks in the context of human experience and at the same time in the context of the work of salvation. These two contexts in some way

superimpose themselves on each other and interpenetrate: and this has an essential and constitutive meaning for the whole ethos of the Gospel and particularly for the content of the verb "to desire" or "to look to desire."

3. With these expressions, the Teacher appeals first to the experience of those who were his immediate listeners, but he also appeals to the experience and conscience of human beings in every time and place. In fact, although the language of the Gospel has a universal communicative power, Christ's immediate audience, whose conscience was formed by the Bible, most likely saw "desire" as tied to many precepts and admonitions present above all in the Wisdom books, in which we find repeated warnings against the concupiscence of the body as well as counsels for how to preserve oneself from it.

The Wisdom Tradition

4. The Wisdom tradition, as we know, had *a particular interest in the ethics and the morals of Israelite society*. In these warnings and counsels, found, for example, in Proverbs (5:3–6, 15–20; 6:24–7:27; 9:19; 22:14; 30:20) or Sirach (7:19, 24–26; 9:1–9; 23:22–27; 25:13–26; 36:21–25; 42:6, 9–14) and even Ecclesiastes (7:26–28; 9:9), what strikes us immediately is a certain one-sidedness inasmuch as the warnings are above all directed toward men. This could mean that warnings are particularly necessary for them. As for the woman, it is true that in these warnings and counsels she appears more often as an occasion of sin or as a downright seducer of whom to beware. Nevertheless, one should recognize that in addition to warning men to be on guard against women and the seduction of their charm, which pulls men toward sin (see Prov 5:1–6; 6:24–29; Sir 26:9–12), Proverbs and Sirach also deliver eulogies about the woman who is a "perfect" companion for her husband (see Prov 31:10ff.), and they likewise sing the praises of the beauty and charm of a good wife who knows how to make her husband happy.

"A modest wife adds charm to charm, and no balance can weigh the value of a chaste soul. Like the sun rising in the heights of the Lord, so the beauty of a good wife adorns her house. Like the shining lamp on the holy lamp stand, so is a beautiful face on a noble figure.

Like golden pillars on silver bases, so are graceful legs and steadfast feet. A wife's grace delights her husband, and her knowledge strengthens his bones" (Sir 26:15–18).

5. In the Wisdom tradition, *a frequent warning contrasts* with this *eulogy of the woman-wife*, namely, the warning against the beauty and charm of a woman who is not one's own wife and who is thus a motive for temptation and an occasion for adultery. "Do not desire her beauty in your heart" (Prov 6:25). In Sirach (Sir 9:1–9), the same warning is expressed more earnestly: "Turn away your eyes from a shapely woman, and do not look intently at beauty belonging to another. For the beauty of a woman many have perished; on account of it love burns like a fire" (Sir 9:8).

The meaning of the Wisdom texts is primarily pedagogical. They teach virtue and seek to protect the moral order by pointing to the law of God and to experience in a broad sense. In addition, they excel in a particular knowledge of the human "heart." We might say they develop a *specific moral psychology,* though without falling into psychologism. They are in some way close to Christ's appeal to the "heart" reported by Matthew (see 5:27–28) though one cannot say that they show any tendency to transform ethos in a fundamental way. The authors of these books use their knowledge of human interiority to teach morals within the limits of the ethos that prevailed in their historical period and that was substantially confirmed by them. Qoheleth, among others, brings this confirmation together with his own "philosophy" of human existence, which, even if it has an influence on the manner in which he formulates his warnings and counsels, does not change the fundamental structure that undergirds ethical evaluation.

6. Such a transformation of ethos had to await the Sermon on the Mount. Nevertheless the extremely perceptive knowledge of human psychology in the Wisdom tradition was certainly not without significance for the circle of those who listened in person and immediately to this Sermon. Just as in virtue of the prophetic tradition, the audience was in some sense prepared for understanding the concept of "adultery" correctly, so in virtue of the Wisdom tradition, it was prepared for understanding the words about the "concupiscent look" or "adultery in the heart."

We shall have to return to the analysis of concupiscence in the Sermon on the Mount.

The Inner State of the Man of Concupiscence (Sir 23:16–24)

39 *General Audience of September 10, 1980*
(Insegnamenti, 3, no. 2 [1980]: 589–93)

1. WE ARE REFLECTING ON THE FOLLOWING words of Jesus in the Sermon on the Mount. "Whoever looks at a woman to desire her [lustfully] has already committed adultery with her in his heart (has already made her an adulteress in his heart)" (Mt 5:28). Christ says these words to an audience that was in some way prepared for understanding the meaning of a look born from concupiscence. Already last Wednesday we pointed to texts drawn from the Wisdom books.

Here, *for example, is another passage* in which the biblical author analyzes *the state of soul of the man dominated by concupiscence of the flesh.*

> Desire, blazing like a furnace, will not die down until it has been satisfied; the man who is shameless in his body will not stop until the fire devours him; to the impure man, all bread is sweet, he will not grow tired until he dies. The man who is unfaithful to his own marriage bed says to himself, "Who can see me? There is darkness all round me, the walls hide me; no one can see me, why should I be afraid? The Most High will not remember my sins." What he fears are human eyes; he does not realize that the eyes of the Lord are ten thousand times brighter than the sun; they see all the acts of men and penetrate into the most secret corners.... Likewise the woman who abandons her husband, who provides him with heirs received from a stranger" (Sir 23:17–22).

2. Analogous descriptions are not lacking in world literature.[51] Certainly, many of them are distinguished by a more penetrating psychological insight and a more intense suggestiveness and expressive

---

51. See, e.g., St. Augustine: "Bound by the disease of my carnality and its deadly sweetness, I dragged my chain along, fearing to be released from it, rejecting the words of him who counseled me wisely, as if the hand that would have loosed the chain only hurt my wound.... What vehemently gave me most excruciating pain was the habit of satisfying an insatiable concupiscence." *Confessions*, 6.12.21–22.

power. Yet, the biblical description in Sirach (23:17–22) has some elements that can be considered "classical" in the analysis of carnal concupiscence. One such element is, for example, *the comparison between concupiscence of the flesh and fire:* flaring up in the man, it invades his senses, arouses his body, draws the feelings along with itself, and in some way takes possession of the "heart." Such passion, springing from carnal concupiscence, suffocates the deepest voice of conscience in the "heart"; it suffocates the sense of responsibility before God; this suffocation is made especially evident in the biblical text just quoted. There remains, on the other hand, an external modesty in relation to human beings—or rather an appearance of decency—that manifests itself as fear of the consequences rather than of the evil in itself. Suffocating the voice of conscience, passion brings restlessness of the body and of the senses: it is the restlessness of the "outer man." Once the inner man has been reduced to silence and passion has, as it were, gained freedom of action, passion manifests itself as an insistent tendency toward satisfying the senses and the body.

This satisfaction, according to the criteria of the man dominated by passion, ought to extinguish the fire; but, on the contrary, it does not reach the sources of inner peace and only touches the most exter-

---

"Yet I did not stably enjoy my God, but was ravished to you by your beauty, yet soon was torn away from you again by my own weight, and fell again with torment to lower things. Carnal habit was that weight." Ibid., 7:17.

"Thus I was sick at heart and in torment, accusing myself with a new intensity of bitterness, twisting and turning in my chain in the hope that it might be utterly broken, for what held me was so small a thing! But it still held me. And you stood in the secret places of my soul, O Lord, in the harshness of your mercy redoubling the scourges of fear and shame, lest I should give way again and that small chain which remained should not be broken but should grow again to full strength and bind me closer even than before." Ibid., 8:11.

Dante describes this inner break and considers it worthy of punishment. "When they come up against the ruined slope, / then there are cries and wailing and lament, / and there they curse the force of the divine. / I learned that those who undergo this torment / are damned because they sinned within the flesh, / subjecting reason to the rule of lust. / And as, in the cold season, starlings' wings / bear them along in broad and crowded ranks / so does that blast bear on the guilty spirits: / now here, now there, now down, now up, it drives them. / There is no hope that ever comforts them— / no hope for rest and none for lesser pain." *Inferno,* 5:37–43.

"Shakespeare has described the satisfaction of a tyrannous lust as 'something / Past reason hunted and, no sooner had, / past reason hated.'" C. S. Lewis, *The Four Loves* (New York: Harcourt Brace, 1960), 28.

nal levels of the human individual. And here the biblical author rightly observes that the man *whose will is occupied with satisfying the senses*
does not find rest nor does he find himself, but on the contrary "*consumes himself.*" Passion aims at satisfaction; hence it blunts reflective
activity and disregards the voice of conscience; and thus, since it has
in itself no principle of indestructibility, it "wears itself out." What is
connatural to it is the dynamism of use, which tends to exhaust itself.
It is true that, when passion is set into the whole of the spirit's deepest energies, it can also become a creative force; in this case, however,
it must undergo a radical transformation. If, on the other hand, it suffocates the deepest powers of the heart and of conscience (as in the
account of Sir 23:17–22), it "consumes itself" and the man who is
prey to it indirectly consumes himself.

Christ's Call to Halt at the Threshold of the Look

3. When Christ in the Sermon on the Mount speaks about the
man who "desires" and who "looks with desire," one can take it for
granted that he had before his eyes also the images known to his
audience through the Wisdom tradition. Yet, at the same time, he
refers to every human being who *on the basis of his own experience*
knows *what it means "to desire," "to look with desire."* The Teacher does
not analyze this experience, nor does he describe it as, for example,
Sirach 23:17–22 does. He seems to take for granted, I would say, a
sufficient knowledge of that inner fact to which he draws the attention of his listeners, both present listeners then and potential listeners
later. Is it possible that any of them could fail to grasp the issue? If he
truly knows nothing about it, the content of Christ's words would not
apply to him, nor would any analysis or description be able to explain
it to him. If he does know—in this case we are in fact dealing *with
knowledge that is completely interior, located within the heart and conscience*—he will immediately understand when these words refer to
him.

4. Christ, therefore, does not describe or analyze what constitutes
the experience of "desiring," the experience of the concupiscence of
the flesh. One even has the impression that he does not penetrate into
this experience in the whole breadth of its inner dynamism as Sirach,

for example, does, but rather stops on its threshold. The "desire" has not yet transformed itself into an external act, it has not yet become an "act of the body"; it is still an interior act of the heart: it expresses itself in the look, in the way of "looking at the woman." Yet, it allows itself to be understood; it reveals its essential content and quality.

We must now offer such an analysis. *The look expresses what is in the heart.* The look, I would say, expresses man as a whole. If one assumes in general that man "acts in conformity with what he is" (*operari sequitur esse* [operation follows being]), in the present case Christ wants to show that man "looks" in conformity with what he is: *intueri sequitur esse* [looking follows being]. Through the look, man shows himself on the outside and to others; above all he shows what he perceives in his "interior."[52]

5. Christ teaches us thus to see the look as the threshold, as it were, of the interior truth. Already in the look, "in the way one looks," it is possible to grasp fully what concupiscence is. Let us try to explain it. [Lustful] "desiring," "looking to desire," indicates an experience of the value of the body in which its spousal meaning ceases to be spousal precisely because of concupiscence. What also ceases is its procreative meaning (we have spoken about this meaning above), which—when it concerns the conjugal union of man and woman—is rooted in the spousal meaning of the body and comes forth organically, as it were, from it. So then, when man "desires" and "looks to desire" (as we read in Mt 5:27–28), he *experiences* more or less explicitly *the detachment from that meaning of the body* which (as we have already observed in our reflections) stands at the basis of the communion of persons: both outside of marriage and—in a particular way—when man and woman are called to build the union "in the

---

52. Philological analysis confirms the meaning of the expression ho blepōn ("one who looks," Mt 5:28).

"If blepō in Matthew 5:28 has the value of an internal perception, equivalent to 'I think, I fix my attention, I carefully consider,' the evangelical teaching about the interpersonal relations of the disciples of Christ turns out to be more severe and more elevated. According to Jesus, not even a lustful look is necessary to make a person adulterous. Even a mere thought of the heart is sufficient." M. Adinolfi, "Il desiderio della donna in Matteo 5, 28," in *Fondamenti biblici della teologia morale, Atti della XXII Settimana Biblica Italiana* (Brescia: Paideia, 1973), 279.

body" (as the "Gospel of the beginning" says in the classical text of Gen 2:24). The experience of the spousal meaning of the body is particularly subordinated to the sacramental call, but is not limited to it. This meaning is characteristic of the freedom of the gift, which—as we will see in more detail in the analyses below—can realize itself not only in marriage, but also in a different way.

Christ says, "Whoever looks at a woman to desire her," that is, whoever looks with concupiscence, "has already committed adultery with her in his heart" ("has already made her an adulteress in his heart," Mt 5:28). Does he not mean to say thereby that precisely concupiscence—like adultery—is an inner detachment from the spousal meaning of the body? Does he not want to refer his listeners to their inner experiences of such detachment? Is it not for this reason that he defines it as "adultery committed in the heart"?

Concupiscence—Reduction of a Perennial Call

40 *General Audience of September 17, 1980*
(Insegnamenti, 3, no. 2 [1980]: 653–56)

1. IN THE LAST REFLECTION, WE ASKED: What is the [concupiscent] "desire" about which Christ speaks in the Sermon on the Mount (Mt 5:27–28)? We recall that he speaks about it in relation to the commandment "You shall not commit adultery." The very act of "desiring" (more precisely, "looking to desire") is defined as "adultery committed in the heart." This gives us much food for thought. In the preceding reflections, we said that by expressing himself in this way, Christ wanted to point out to his listeners the detachment from the spousal meaning of the body experienced by man (in this case by the male) when he gives in to the concupiscence of the flesh with an interior act of "desire." The detachment from the spousal meaning of the body at the same time brings with it a conflict with its dignity as a person: an authentic conflict of conscience.

At this point it becomes clear that the biblical (and thus also the theological) meaning of "desire" differs from the purely psychological one. The psychologist describes "desire" as an intense orientation toward the object caused by its characteristic value: in the case considered here, it is caused by its "sexual" value. It seems that we find such a definition in the majority of works devoted to these topics. The biblical description by contrast, while not underrating the psychological aspect, emphasizes above all the ethical one, given that there is a value that suffers harm. [Concupiscent] "desire," I would say, is the deception of the human heart with regard to the perennial call of man and woman to communion through a reciprocal gift—a call that has been revealed in the very mystery of creation. Thus, when in the Sermon on the Mount (Mt 5:27–28) Christ refers to "the heart" or to the inner man, his words do not cease to be charged with that truth about the "beginning," to which he had referred the whole problem of man, woman, and marriage in answer to the Pharisees (see Mt 19:8).

2. The perennial call, which we have tried to analyze following Genesis (above all Gen 2:23–25 [see TOB 9–19]), and in some way also the perennial reciprocal attraction of the man to femininity and of the woman to masculinity, is an invitation mediated by the body, but *it is not the desire* signified by the words of Matthew 5:27–28. "Desire" as a realization of concupiscence of the flesh (also and above all in the purely interior act) diminishes the meaning of what this invitation and this reciprocal attraction were—and substantially do not cease to be. The eternal "feminine" (*das Ewig-Weibliche*)—just like, for that matter, the eternal "masculine"—tends even on the level of historicity to free itself from mere concupiscence and seeks a place of affirmation on the level proper to the world of persons. The original shame about which Genesis 3 speaks testifies to this fact. The dimension of the intentionality of thoughts and hearts constitutes one of the main guiding threads of universal human culture. Christ's words in the Sermon on the Mount confirm precisely this dimension.

3. Nevertheless, these words clearly say that "desire" is part of the reality of the human heart. When we say that—in comparison with the original reciprocal attraction of masculinity and femininity—*"desire"* represents a "reduction," what we have in mind is an *intentional "reduction,"* a restriction, as it were, or closure of the horizon of the mind and the heart. It is, in fact, one thing to be aware that the value of sex is part of the whole richness of values with which a feminine being appears to a man; it is quite another thing to "reduce" the whole

personal richness of femininity to this one value, that is, to sex as the fitting object of the satisfaction of one's own sexuality. One can apply the same reasoning to what masculinity is for a woman, although the words of Matthew 5:27–28 refer directly only to the other relation. The intentional "reduction" is, as one can see, above all of an axiological nature. On the one hand, the eternal attraction of the man toward femininity (see Gen 2:23) frees in him—or perhaps it ought to free— a wide range of spiritual-carnal desires that are above all personal and "of communion" in their nature (see the analysis of the "beginning") with a proportional hierarchy of values that corresponds to these desires. On the other hand, [lustful] "desire" *limits* this range and *obscures* the hierarchy of values characteristic of the perennial attraction of masculinity and femininity.

4. [Lustful] desire has the effect that in the interior, in the "heart," in man and woman's interior horizon, the meaning of the body proper to the person itself is obscured. In this way, femininity ceases to be above all a subject for masculinity; it ceases to be a specific language of the spirit; it loses its character as a sign. It ceases, I would say, to bear on itself the stupendous spousal meaning of the body. It ceases to be located in the context of the consciousness and experience of this meaning. The "desire" born precisely from concupiscence of the flesh, from the first moment of its existence in the man's interior—of its existence in his "heart"—bypasses this context in some way (to use an image, one could say it tramples on the ruins of the spousal meaning of the body and of all its subjective components), and, in virtue of its own axiological intentionality, it aims directly toward one and only one end as its precise object: *to satisfy only the body's sexual urge.*

5. According to the words of Christ (Mt 5:27–28), such an intentional and axiological reduction can occur already in the sphere of a look (of "looking") or rather in the sphere of a purely interior act expressed by looking. A look (or rather "looking") is in itself a cognitive act. When concupiscence enters into its inner structure, the look takes on the character of "concupiscent knowledge." The biblical expression "look to desire" can refer either to a cognitive act that the man "makes use of" in desiring (thus giving it the character proper to a desire stretched out toward an object) or to a cognitive act that

arouses desire in the <other>* subject and above all in his will and in his heart. As one can see, it is possible to give an intentional interpretation of an interior act when one has the one or the other pole of man's psychology in mind: knowledge or desire understood as *appetitus*. (*Appetitus* is something broader than "desire," because it indicates everything that manifests itself in the subject as "aspiration" and as such it is always oriented toward an end, that is, toward an object known under the aspect of value). Yet, an adequate interpretation of the words of Matthew 5:27–28 requires that—*through the intentionality proper to knowledge* or "*appetitus*"—we notice something more, namely, *the intentionality of man's very existence in relation to another*, in our case, of the man in relation to the woman and of the woman in relation to the man.

We should return to this topic [see TOB 41]. In concluding today's reflection, one should add that in this "desire," in "looking to desire" as discussed in the Sermon on the Mount, the woman ceases to exist as a subject of the eternal attraction and begins to be only an object of carnal concupiscence for the man who "looks" in this way. The deep inner detachment from the spousal meaning of the body, about which we spoke already in the preceding reflection, is part of this change.

41 General Audience of September 24, 1980
(*Insegnamenti*, 3, no. 2 [1980]: 717–20)

1. IN THE SERMON ON THE MOUNT Christ says, "You have heard that it was said, 'You shall not commit adultery.' But I say to you: Whoever looks at a woman to desire her has already committed adultery with her in his heart" (Mt 5:27–28). For some time we have been trying to enter into the meaning of this statement, analyzing its single components to grasp the totality of the text better.

When Christ speaks about the man who "looks to desire," he points not only to the dimension of the intentionality of "looking," that is, of concupiscent knowledge, the "psychological" dimension, but

---

*Translator's note: The Polish original lacks the word "other (*altro*)." It seems to have entered the Italian translation by mistake, already in the Italian typescript used as the basis of both the *Insegnamenti* text and UD.

he points also to the dimension of the intentionality of man's very existence. He shows in this way who the woman "is" at whom he "looks to desire," or rather who she "becomes" for the man. Thus, the intentionality of knowledge determines and defines the intentionality of existence itself. In the situation described by Christ, this dimension exists one-sidedly between the man, who is a subject, and the woman, who has become an object (this does not mean, however, that this dimension is only one-sided); for the moment we will not turn around the situation we analyzed, nor will we extend it to both parts, to both subjects. Let us dwell on the situation outlined by Christ, underlining that the act is "purely interior," hidden in the heart, standing still on the threshold of the look.

It is enough to point out that the woman—who, due to personal subjectivity, perennially exists "for the man," expecting that for the same reason he also exists "for her"—is deprived of the meaning of her attraction as a person so that this attraction, while belonging to the "eternally feminine," has become a mere object for the man: *that is, she begins to exist intentionally as an object for the possible satisfaction of the man's sexual urge* that lies in his masculinity. Although the act is wholly interior, hidden in the "heart" and expressed only by the "look," a change (subjectively one-sided) <in the very intentionality>[*] of existence takes place in him. If this were not the case, if the change were not so deep, the following words of the sentence would have no meaning, "has already committed adultery with her in his heart" (Mt 5:28).

Concupiscence—"Communion" of Persons Versus "Urge" of Nature

2. This change in the intentionality of existence, by which a certain woman begins to exist for a certain man, not as a subject of the call and of personal attraction or as a subject "of communion," but exclusively as an object for the possible satisfaction of sexual urge,

---

[*] Translator's note: The phrase in angled brackets is missing in the *Insegnamenti* text. It has been supplied from UD.

comes to be in the "heart" to the degree in which it has come to be in the will. Cognitive intentionality as such does not yet mean enslavement of the "heart." It is only when the intentional reduction explained above drags the will into its narrow horizon, when it awakens in it a decision for a relation with another human being (in our case with the woman) according to the scale of values proper to "concupiscence," it is only then that one can say that "desire" has gained mastery over the "heart." It is only when "concupiscence" has gained mastery over the will that one can say, it dominates the subjectivity of the person and stands at the basis of the will and of the possibility of choosing and deciding, by which—in virtue of self-decision or self-determination—the very way of existing in relation to another person is determined. It is then that the intentionality of such an existence acquires a full subjective dimension.

3. Only then—that is, from this subjective moment and its subjective prolongation—is it possible to confirm what we read in Sirach (23:17–22) about the man dominated by concupiscence and what we read in even more eloquent descriptions in world literature. Then we can speak of that *more or less complete "constraint"* which we have called "constraint of the body" and which brings with it *the loss of the "freedom of the gift,"* a freedom connatural with deep consciousness of the spousal meaning of the body, about which we have spoken in the preceding analyses.

4. When we speak of "desire" as a transformation of the intentionality of a concrete existence, e.g., of the man for whom (according to Mt 5:27–28) a certain woman becomes only the object for the satisfaction of the "sexual urge" that lies in his masculinity, we do not in the least call into question that urge as an objective dimension of human nature with the procreative finality that is proper to it. Christ's words in the Sermon on the Mount (in their entire broad context) are far from Manichaeism, and the same holds also for the authentic Christian tradition. In this case, therefore, one cannot raise objections of this sort. What is at issue, instead, is the man and woman's way of existing as persons, or rather this existing in a reciprocal "for" that can and must—also on the basis of what *can be defined as "sexual urge"* according to the objective dimension of human nature—serve the

291

building of the unity "of communion" in their reciprocal relations. Such, in fact, is the fundamental meaning proper to the reciprocal attraction of masculinity and femininity contained in the very reality of man's constitution as a person, body, and sex at the same time.

5. It does not correspond to the personal union or "communion" to which man and woman have been reciprocally called "from the beginning," in fact, it is contrary to it, that one of the two persons should exist only as a subject of the satisfaction of sexual urge and that the other should become exclusively the object for such satisfaction. Further, it does not correspond to this unity of "communion"—in fact, it is contrary to it—that both the man and the woman should mutually exist as objects for the satisfaction of sexual urge, and that each of them on his or her own part should only be a subject of such satisfaction. Such a "reduction" of the rich content of reciprocal and perennial attraction among human persons in their masculinity and femininity does not correspond to the "nature" of the attraction in question. Such a "reduction," in fact, extinguishes the meaning proper to man and woman, a meaning that is personal and "of communion," through which "the man will...unite with his wife and the two will be one flesh" (Gen 2:24). *"Concupiscence" removes* the intentional dimension of the reciprocal existence of man and woman *from the personal perspectives "of communion,"* which are proper to their perennial and reciprocal attraction, reducing this attraction and, so to speak, driving it toward utilitarian dimensions, in whose sphere of influence one human being "makes use" of another human being, *"using her"* only to satisfy his own "urges."

6. It seems that one can find precisely this content, charged with the inner human experience of many different times and environments, in Christ's concise words in the Sermon on the Mount. At the same time, one can in no way lose sight of the meaning that this statement attributes to man's "interiority," to the integral dimension of the "heart" as a dimension of the inner man. Here lies the very core of the transformation of ethos aimed at by Christ's words according to Matthew 5:27–28, words expressed with such great power and, at the same time, wonderful simplicity.

C. "HAS COMMITTED ADULTERY IN THE HEART..."

A "Key" Change of Direction

42 *General Audience of October 1, 1980*
(Insegnamenti, 3, no. 2 [1980]: 744–48)

1. IN OUR ANALYSIS, WE HAVE COME to the third part of Christ's statement in the Sermon on the Mount (Mt 5:27–28). The first part was, "You have heard that it was said, 'You shall not commit adultery.'" The second part, "But I say to you: Whoever looks at a woman to desire her," is grammatically connected with the third part, "has already committed adultery with her in his heart."

The method used here, that *of dividing, of breaking Christ's statement into three parts* that follow each other, may seem artificial. Yet, when we seek the ethical meaning of the whole statement, in its totality, the division of the text that we used can be helpful, as long as we do not merely set the pieces apart but bring them together. And this is what we intend to do. Each of the distinct parts has its own content and connotations that are specific to it, and this is precisely what we want to show by the division of the text; but at the same time one should point out that each of the parts must be explained in direct relation with the others. This point holds in the first place for the main semantic elements through which the statement constitutes a whole. Here are the elements: to commit adultery; to desire; to commit adultery in the body; and to commit adultery in the heart. It would be particularly difficult to identify the ethical meaning of "desire" without the last element, "adultery in the heart." The analysis above has to some degree already considered this element; still, a fuller understanding of the component "to commit adultery in the heart" is possible only after a separate analysis.

2. As we said already at the beginning, the meaning we are looking for is the ethical meaning [see TOB 34:2]. Christ's statement in Matthew 5:27–28 takes as its starting point the commandment "You shall not commit adultery" to show how it is to be understood and put

into practice so that "the justice" willed by God-Yahweh as Legislator might abound in it: so that it might abound in a measure greater than the one resulting from the interpretation and casuistry of the teachers of the Old Testament. If Christ's words intend in this sense *to build the new ethos* (on the basis of the same commandment), the road to this aim passes *through the rediscovery of the values* that had been lost in the general understanding of the Old Testament and in the application of this commandment.

3. From this point of view, the formulation of the text of Matthew 5:27–28 is significant as well. The commandment "You shall not commit adultery" is formulated as a prohibition that categorically excludes a certain moral evil. In addition to "You shall not commit adultery," the same law (the Decalogue) contains also the prohibition "You shall not desire your neighbor's wife" (Ex 20:14, 17; Deut 5:18, 21). Christ does not make one commandment pointless in favor of another. Although he speaks about "desire," he aims at a deeper clarification of "adultery." It is significant that after quoting the prohibition, "You shall not commit adultery," as a prohibition known to his audience, he changes his style and logical structure in what follows in the course of his statement from normative to narrative-affirmative. When he says, "Whoever looks at a woman to desire her has already committed adultery with her in his heart," he describes an inner fact, the reality of which can be easily understood by his audience. At the same time, through the fact described and qualified in this way, he shows how the commandment "You shall not commit adultery" should be understood in order to lead to the "justice" willed by the Legislator.

4. We have thus reached the expression, "has committed adultery in the heart," which seems to be *the key expression* for understanding its correct ethical meaning. This expression is at the same time *the main source for revealing the essential values of the new ethos:* the ethos of the Sermon on the Mount. As is often the case in the Gospel, here too we are faced with a certain paradox. How, in fact, can "adultery" take place without "committing adultery," that is, without an external act that allows one to identify the act prohibited by the law? We have seen to what degree the casuistry of the "teachers of the law" attempted to give an exact account of this problem. Quite apart from casuistry, however, it seems evident that adultery can only be identified "in the flesh," that is, when the two, the man and the woman, who unite with each other in such a way that they become one flesh (see Gen 2:24), are not spouses, that is, husband and wife in the legal sense. What possible meaning can "adultery committed in the heart" thus have? Is this not a merely metaphorical expression used by the Teacher to emphasize the sinfulness of concupiscence?

A First Reading

5. *If we granted such a semantic reading* of Christ's statement (Mt 5:27–28), we would have to reflect deeply about the *ethical consequences* that would follow from it, that is, about the conclusions concerning the ethical order of behavior. Adultery occurs when the man and the woman who unite with each other so as to become one flesh (Gen 2:24), that is, in a manner proper to spouses, are not spouses in the legal sense. The identification of adultery as a sin committed "in the body" is strictly and exclusively tied to the "external" act, to shared conjugal life, which is related also to the state of life of the acting persons recognized by society. In the case before us, this state of life is inappropriate and does not authorize such an act (hence precisely the term "adultery").

6. Moving on to the second part of Christ's statement (in which the configuration of the new ethos begins), one would have to understand the expression, "whoever looks at a woman to desire her," only in reference to persons according to their civil state of life recognized by society, that is, whether they are married or not. Here the questions begin to multiply. Since there is no doubt that Christ points to the sinfulness of the interior act of concupiscence expressed by the act of looking at any woman who is not the wife of the one who looks at her in this way, we can and even must ask if by the same expression he allows and approves such a look, such an interior act of concupiscence when it is directed toward the woman who is the wife of the man who looks at her in this way. An argument in favor of an affirmative answer seems to be the following logical premise: (in our case) only the man who is the potential subject of "adultery in the flesh" can commit "adultery in the heart." Since this subject cannot be a married man in relation to his own legitimate wife, "adultery in the heart"

cannot refer to him, but one can ascribe it as a fault in the case of every other man. If he is the husband, he cannot commit it in relation to his own wife. Only he has the exclusive right to "desire," to "look with concupiscence" at the woman who is his wife and one can never say that on account of such an interior act he deserves being accused of "adultery committed in the heart." If in virtue of marriage he has the right of "uniting with his wife" so that "the two will be one flesh," one can never call this act "adultery"; by analogy, the interior act of desire, which the Sermon on the Mount speaks about, cannot be defined as "adultery committed in the heart" [see TOB 25:4].

7. This interpretation of Christ's words in Matthew 5:27–28 seems to correspond to the logic of the Decalogue, which contains the commandment "You shall not desire your neighbor's wife" (ninth commandment) in addition to the commandment "You shall not commit adultery" (sixth commandment). Besides, the reasoning in support of this interpretation has all the characteristics of objective correctness and accuracy. Nevertheless, there are fundamental doubts whether this reasoning takes into account all the aspects of revelation and of the theology of the body that should be considered, above all when we want to understand Christ's words. We have already seen some time ago the great "specific weight" of these words, the wealth of the anthropological and theological implications of the one sentence in which Christ goes back "to the beginning" (see Mt 19:8). The anthropological and theological implications of the statement in the Sermon on the Mount, in which Christ appeals to the human heart, give also to that statement its own "specific gravity" and make it consistent with the teaching of the Gospel as a whole. For this reason, we must admit that the interpretation presented above, despite all its objective correctness and logical precision, needs to be broadened and above all deepened. We must remember that the reference to the human heart, expressed perhaps in a paradoxical way (Mt 5:27–28), comes from him who "knew what was in every man" (Jn 2:25). And while his words confirm the commandments of the Decalogue (not only the sixth, but also the ninth), they express at the same time *the knowledge about man* that allows us—as we emphasized elsewhere [see TOB 4:3]—to unite the awareness of *human sinfulness with the perspective of "the redemption of the body"* (see Rom 8:23). Precisely such

"knowledge stands at the basis of the new ethos" that emerges from the words of the Sermon on the Mount.

Taking all of this into account, we conclude that, just as in the understanding of "adultery in the flesh" Christ criticizes the erroneous and one-sided interpretation of adultery that stems from the failure to observe monogamy (that is, marriage understood as the indefectible covenant of persons), so also in *understanding* "adultery in the heart," Christ takes into consideration not only the real juridical state of life of the man and the woman in question. Christ makes the moral evaluation of "desire" depend above all *on the personal dignity of the man and the woman*; and this is important both in the case of unmarried persons and—perhaps even more so—in the case of spouses, husband and wife. From this point of view we should complete the analysis of the words from the Sermon on the Mount, and we shall do so next time.

43 *General Audience of October 8, 1980* (*Insegnamenti*, 3, no. 2 [1980]: 807–11)

1. TODAY I WANT TO COMPLETE the analysis of the words Christ spoke in the Sermon on the Mount about "adultery" and "concupiscence" and in particular the last part of the statement, in which the "concupiscence of the look" is specifically defined as "adultery committed in the heart."

We have already shown above that these words are usually understood in the sense of desire for another's wife (that is, according to the spirit of the Decalogue's ninth commandment). It seems, however, that this interpretation—a more restricted one—can and should be extended in the light of the overall context. It seems that the moral evaluation of concupiscence (of "looking to desire"), which Christ calls "adultery committed in the heart," depends above all on the personal dignity of the man and the woman. This holds for those who are not joined in marriage and—perhaps even more so—for those who are husband and wife.

A Second Reading

2. Our earlier analysis of the statement in Matthew 5:27–28, "You have heard that it was said, 'You shall not commit adultery.' But I say to you: Whoever looks at a woman to desire her [in a reductive way]

has already committed adultery with her in his heart," shows that we must extend and above all deepen the interpretation described earlier with respect to the ethical meaning contained in the statement. Let us take a close look at the situation described by the Teacher, in which the one who "commits adultery in the heart" by an interior act of concupiscence (expressed in a look) is the man. It is significant that Christ, when he speaks about the object of this act, does not stress that she is "another's wife," a woman who is not one's own wife, but says generically, a woman. Adultery committed "in the heart" is not circumscribed by the limits of the interpersonal relation that allows one to identify adultery committed "in the flesh." It is not these limits that exclusively and essentially decide the question of adultery committed "in the heart," but the very nature of concupiscence, expressed in this case by a look, that is, by the fact that this man whom Christ uses as an example "looks to desire." Adultery "in the heart" is not committed only because the man "looks" in this way at a woman who is not his wife, but *precisely because he looks in this way at a woman. Even* if he were to look in this way at the woman who is his wife, he would commit the same adultery "in the heart."

3. This interpretation takes into account more comprehensively what was said in our whole analyses about concupiscence, and in the first place about the concupiscence of the flesh as a permanent element of man's sinfulness (*status naturae lapsae* [the state of fallen nature]). The concupiscence that arises as an interior act on this foundation (as we have attempted to show in our analysis above) changes the very intentionality of the woman's existence "for" the man by reducing the wealth of the perennial call to the communion of persons, the wealth of the deep attraction of masculinity and femininity, to the mere satisfaction of the body's sexual "urge" (which is closely related to the concept of "instinct"). Such a reduction has the effect that the person (in this case the woman) becomes for the other person (the man) above all an object for the possible satisfaction of his own sexual "urge." *In this way, a deformation takes place in the reciprocal "for," which loses its character as a communion of persons in favor of the utilitarian function.* The man who "looks" in the way described in Matthew 5:27–28 "makes use" of the woman, of her femininity, to satisfy his own "instinct." Even if he does not use her in an external act, he has already taken such an attitude in his interior when he makes this deci-

sion about a particular woman. Adultery "committed in the heart" consists precisely in this. A man can commit such adultery "in the heart" even with his own wife, if he treats her only as an object for the satisfaction of instinct.*

4. It is not possible to reach this second reading of the words of Matthew 5:27–28 if we limit ourselves to the purely psychological interpretation of concupiscence without taking into account what constitutes its specific theological character, namely, the organic relation between concupiscence (as an act) and the concupiscence of the flesh as, so to speak, a permanent disposition that derives from human sinfulness. It seems that the purely psychological (or "sexological") interpretation of "concupiscence" is not a sufficient basis for understanding our text from the Sermon on the Mount. On the other hand, if we take the theological interpretation as a point of reference—*without undervaluing what remains unchangeable in the first* (psychological) *interpretation—the second* (theological) *interpretation* appears to us *more complete.* In fact, it clarifies the ethical meaning of the key statement from the Sermon on the Mount to which we owe the adequate dimension of the ethos of the Gospel.

Purity of Heart as the Fulfillment of the Commandment

5. In delineating this dimension, Christ remains faithful to the law. "Do not think that I have come to abolish the Law or the Prophets; I have not come to abolish but to fulfill" (Mt 5:17). He consequently shows how deep down it is necessary to go, how the innermost recesses of the human heart must be thoroughly revealed, so that this heart might become a place in which the law is "fulfilled." The statement of Matthew 5:27–28, which shows the inner perspective of adultery committed "in the heart"—and in this perspective points the right way toward fulfilling the commandment

---

* Translator's note: When this statement by John Paul II was first quoted in the Italian press, it led to an uproar that was picked up also in the international press, including major U.S. papers and networks. Most reporters failed to grasp the difference between "desire" in the positive sense and reductive concupiscent "desire" (see Index at DESIRE and translator's notes on TOB 24:1 and TOB 25:4). In the immediately following paragraph (TOB 43:4), John Paul II points out that a merely psychological or sexological understanding of sexuality (which is the dominant understanding in our culture) will not allow one to grasp this difference.

"You shall not commit adultery"—is a singular argument for this conclusion. This statement (Mt 5:27–28) refers in fact to the sphere in which the issue is "purity of heart" (see Mt 5:8) (an expression that has a broad meaning in the Bible). Elsewhere we will have further occasion to consider how the commandment "You shall not commit adultery"—whose mode of expression and contents are a clear and severe prohibition (like the commandment "You shall not desire your neighbor's wife," Ex 20:17)—is fulfilled precisely by purity of heart [see TOB 50–59]. The strictness and power of the prohibition is indirectly attested by a text later in the Sermon on the Mount in which Christ speaks figuratively about "tearing out your eye" and "cutting off your hand" in case these members are a cause of sin (see Mt 5:29–30). We have pointed out earlier that the legislation of the Old Testament, although it contained many harsh punishments, did not contribute toward "fulfilling the law," because its casuistry was marked by many compromises with the concupiscence of the flesh [see TOB 35–36:4]. Christ by contrast teaches that *one fulfills the commandment by "purity of heart,"* in which human beings cannot share *without firmness in facing* everything that has its origin in *concupiscence of the flesh.* "Purity of heart" is gained by the one who knows *how to be consistently demanding* toward his "heart": toward his "heart" and toward his "body."

6. The commandment "You shall not commit adultery" finds its right motive in the indissolubility of marriage, in which man and woman unite with each other in virtue of the original plan of God so that "the two become one flesh" (Gen 2:24). By its essence, adultery conflicts with this unity inasmuch as this unity corresponds to the dignity of the persons. Christ not only confirms this essential ethical meaning of the commandment, but his aim is to anchor it firmly in the very depth of the human person. The new dimension of ethos is always linked with the revelation of the depth that is called "heart" and with the liberation of the heart from "concupiscence" *so that man can shine more fully in this heart*: male and female in all the inner truth of the reciprocal "for." Freed from the constraint and disability of the spirit, which are the result of the concupiscence of the flesh, human beings, male and female, find themselves again in the freedom of the gift, which is the condition of all life together in the truth, and, more particularly, in the freedom of reciprocal self-gift, because both, as husband and wife, must form the sacramental unity willed, as Genesis 2:24 says, by the Creator himself.

7. What Christ demands from all his actual and potential listeners in the Sermon on the Mount clearly belongs to that interior space in which *man*—precisely the one who listens—*must rediscover the lost fullness of his humanity and want to regain it*. This fullness in the reciprocal relation of persons, of man and woman, is what the Teacher demands in Matthew 5:27–28, having in mind above all the indissolubility of marriage but also every other form of shared life of men and women, the shared life that makes up the pure and simple guiding thread of existence. Human life is by its nature "co-educational" and its dignity as well as its balance depend at every moment of history and in every place of geographic longitude and latitude on "who" she shall be for him and he for her.

The words spoken by Jesus in the Sermon on the Mount have without any doubt such a universal and deep reach. Only in this way can they be understood on the lips of him who "knew" to its final depth "what was in every man" (Jn 2:25) and who at the same time carried within himself the mystery of the "redemption of the body," as St. Paul put it. Should we *fear* the severity of these words or rather *have confidence* in their salvific content, in their power?

At any rate, this analysis of the words Christ spoke in the Sermon on the Mount opens the road for further reflections that are indispensable for reaching a full awareness of "historical" man and above all of contemporary man: of his consciousness and of his "heart."

4. The "Heart"—Accused or Called?

44 *General Audience of October 15, 1980*
(Insegnamenti, 3, no. 2 [1980]: 878–82)

1. DURING OUR MANY WEDNESDAY MEETINGS, we analyzed in detail the words in the Sermon on the Mount in which Christ addresses the human "heart." We now realize that his words are demanding. Christ says, "You have heard that it was said, 'You shall not commit adultery.'

But I say to you: Whoever looks at a woman to desire her [in a reductive way] has already committed adultery with her *in his heart*" (Mt 5:27–28). Such a reference to the heart throws light on the dimension of human interiority, the dimension of the inner man proper to ethics and even more to the theology of the body. The [reductive] desire that springs up in the sphere of the concupiscence of the flesh is at one and the same time an inner and a theological reality that is in some way experienced by every "historical" man. It is precisely this man— even if he does not know Christ's words—who continually asks this question about his own "heart." Christ's words make this question particularly explicit: Is the heart accused or called to the good? This is the question we will consider now toward the end of our reflections and analyses about the statement in the Gospel (Mt 5:27–28), connected with this concise and categorical statement, so pregnant with theological, anthropological, and ethical content.

A second question goes hand in hand with it, a more "practical" question: How "can" and "should" someone act who accepts Christ's words in the Sermon on the Mount, someone who accepts the ethos of the Gospel and who accepts it particularly in this area?

2. This person finds in the reflections carried out so far the answer, at least the indirect answer, to the two questions: How "can" he act, that is, on what can he count in his "innermost [being]" at the source of his "interior" and "exterior" acts? And further: How "should" he act, that is, how do the values recognized in accord with the "scale" revealed in the Sermon on the Mount constitute a duty of his will and of his "heart," of his desires and of his choices? In what way do they "oblige" him in action and behavior, if, once they are accepted through knowledge, they commit him already in thought and in some way in "feeling"? These questions are significant for human "praxis," and they indicate an organic link between "praxis" itself and ethos. A living morality is always the ethos of human praxis.

3. One can answer these questions in different ways. Both in the past and today, in fact, people have been and are giving various answers. An abundant literature confirms this point. Beyond the answers that we find in this literature one should take into account the unlimited number of *answers given by concrete human beings* on their own account, answers repeatedly given by the conscience, the moral

awareness, and sensibility of every human being in his or her life. In this area, there is a continual *interpenetration of ethos and praxis*. Here one sees the life (not merely a "theoretical" life) lived by the individual principles, that is, by the norms of morality with their motives, elaborated and popularized by moralists, but also elaborated—certainly not without connection with the work of moralists and scholars—by individual persons as direct authors and subjects of real morality, as co-authors of their history, on which the level of morality itself, its progress or decadence, depends. In all of this, everywhere and always, "historical man" reconfirms himself [as the one] to whom Christ once spoke, announcing the Good News of the Gospel in the Sermon on the Mount in which, among others, he spoke the words we read in Matthew 5:27–28, "You have heard that it was said, 'You shall not commit adultery.' But I say to you: Whoever looks at a woman to desire her has already committed adultery with her in his heart."

4. The statement in Matthew is stupendously concise in comparison with everything written on this topic in world literature. Its power in the history of ethos perhaps lies in this. At the same time one must realize that the history of ethos runs in a riverbed with many forms in which individual currents approach each other and flow apart. "Historical" man always evaluates his own "heart" in his own way, just as he also judges his own "body": and in this way he passes from the pole of pessimism to the pole of optimism, from puritanical strictness to present-day permissiveness. It is necessary to realize this so that the ethos of the Sermon on the Mount can always be sufficiently transparent when it confronts man's actions and behavior. For this purpose some further analyses are necessary.

A. CONDEMNATION OF THE BODY?

Manichaeism

5. Our reflections about the meaning of Christ's words according to Matthew 5:27–28 would not be complete if we did not dwell—at least briefly—on what one could call the echo of these words in the history of human thought and of the evaluation of ethos. *Echo* is always a transformation of the voice and of the words expressed by the voice. We know from experience that such a transformation is

often full of mysterious fascination. In the present case what happened is rather something contrary. In fact, Christ's words were often
stripped of their simplicity and depth, and a meaning was given to
them that is far from the one they expressed, a meaning that in
the end conflicts with them. What we have in mind here is all
that happened on the margins of Christianity under the name of
Manichaeism[53] and that attempted to enter the terrain of Christi-

---

53. Manichaeism contains and brings to maturity the characteristic elements of all
"gnosis," namely, the *dualism* of two coeternal principles radically opposed to each other
and the concept of a *salvation* that is realized only through *knowledge* ("gnosis") or self-
understanding. In the whole Manichaean myth, there is only one hero and only one
situation that always repeats itself: the fallen soul is always imprisoned in matter and is
liberated by knowledge.

The present historical situation is negative for man, because it is a temporary and
abnormal mixture of spirit and matter, of good and evil, which presupposes an earlier, original state, in which the two substances were separate and independent. There
are thus three "times": the "*initium* [beginning]" or primordial separation; the "*medi-
um*" or present mixture; and the "*finis* [end]," which consists in the return to the original division, in a salvation that implies a complete break between spirit and matter.

Matter is, at root, concupiscence, an evil appetite for pleasure, an instinct of death,
comparable if not identical with sexual desire, with "libido." It is a force that attempts
to attack the Light: it is disordered movement, bestial, brutal, and semi-conscious
desire.

Adam and Eve were begotten by two demons; our species was born from a series of
repugnant acts of cannibalism and sexuality, and it always carries the signs of this dia-
bolical origin, namely, the body, which was formed by some "archons of hell," and
"libido," which pushes man to copulate and reproduce and thus to keep the luminous
soul always in prison.

If he wishes to be saved, man must seek to free his "living self" (*nous*) from the flesh
and the body. Since the supreme expression of matter is concupiscence, the capital sin
lies in sexual union (fornication), which is brutality and bestiality, and which turns
men into instruments and accomplices of evil through procreation.

The elect constitute the group of the perfect, whose virtue has an ascetical character, namely, practicing the abstinence commanded by the three "seals": the "seal of the
mouth" prohibits all cursing and commands abstinence from meat, from blood, from
wine and all alcoholic drinks, as well as fasting; the "seal of the hands" commands
respect for the life (the "light") that is enclosed in bodies, in seeds, in trees, and prohibits the gathering of fruit, the tearing of plants, and the taking of the life of men or
animals; the "seal of the womb" commands total continence. See H. C. Puech, *Le
Manichéisme: son fondateur–sa doctrine* (Paris, 1949), 73–88; H. C. Puech, "Le
Manichéisme," *Histoire des Religions* (*Encyclopédie de la Pleiade*) 2 (1972): 522–645; J.
Ries, "Manichéisme," *Catholicisme hier, aujourd'hui, demain* 34 (1977): 314–20.

anity precisely in the area of the theology and ethos of the body. In its original form, Manichaeism, which sprang up in the Orient from Mazdean dualism, that is, outside the biblical sphere, *saw the source of evil in matter, in the body,* and therefore condemned all that is bodily in man. And since in man bodiliness manifests itself above all through [one's] sex, the condemnation was extended to marriage and conjugal life and to all other spheres of being and acting in which bodiliness expresses itself.

6. To an unaccustomed ear, the evident strictness of that system might seem to harmonize with the strict words of Matthew 5:29–30 in which Christ speaks about "tearing out your eye" and "cutting off your hand" if these members are the cause of scandal. By a purely "material" interpretation of these expressions it is even possible to reach a Manichean view of Christ's statement about the man who has "committed adultery in his heart...by looking at a woman to desire her." In this case as well, the Manichaean interpretation tends to condemn the body as the true source of evil, because in it, according to Manichaeism, the "ontological" principle of evil both conceals and manifests itself. People thus tried to discover, and at times they saw, such a *condemnation in the Gospel, finding it where, on the contrary, the only thing expressed is a particular demand addressed to the human spirit.*

Note that the condemnation might—and may always be—a loophole to avoid the requirements set in the Gospel by him who "knew what was in every man" (Jn 2:25). Proofs are not lacking in history. We have already partially had the opportunity (and will certainly have it again) to show to what degree this demand can only spring from an affirmation—and not from a negation or from a condemnation—if it is to lead to a subjectively and objectively even more mature and deep affirmation. And such an affirmation of the human being's femininity and masculinity, as a personal dimension of "being a body," must guide the words of Jesus according to Matthew 5:27–28. This is the correct ethical meaning of these words. They impress on the pages of the Gospel a particular dimension of ethos in order to impress this dimension also within human life.

We will take up this topic again in our next reflections.

The Correct Understanding

45 *General Audience of October 22, 1980*
(Insegnamenti, 3, no. 2 [1980]: 948–52)

1. FOR QUITE A LONG TIME Christ's following statement in the Sermon on the Mount has stood at the center of our Wednesday meetings. "You have heard that it was said, 'You shall not commit adultery.' But I say to you: Whoever looks at a woman to desire her [in a reductive way] has already committed adultery with her" (toward her) "in his heart" (Mt 5:27–28). These words have an essential meaning for the entire theology of the body contained in Christ's teaching. This is why we rightly attribute great importance to their correct understanding and interpretation. Already in our last reflection we observed that Manichaean teaching, both in its earlier and later expressions, conflicts with these words.

In fact, it is not possible to read in the statement from the Sermon on the Mount analyzed here a "condemnation" or accusation of the body. If anything, one could see in it a condemnation of the human heart. Our reflections up to this point, however, show that even if the words of Matthew 5:27–28 contain an accusation, their object is primarily the man of concupiscence. These words do not so much accuse the heart as subject it to a judgment or, better, call it to a critical and, in fact, self-critical examination: whether or not it yields to the concupiscence of the flesh. When we penetrate into the deep meaning of the statement in Matthew 5:27–28, we should note, however, that the implicit judgment about "desire" as an act of the concupiscence of the flesh contains in itself, not the negation, but rather the affirmation of the body as an element that, together with the spirit, determines man's ontological subjectivity and participates in his dignity as a person. To conclude, *the judgment about the concupiscence of the flesh has thus a meaning essentially different from the one that Manichaean ontology is able to presuppose* and that necessarily springs from it.

2. The body in its masculinity and femininity has been called "from the beginning" to become the manifestation of the spirit. It becomes such a manifestation also through the conjugal union of man and woman when they unite with each other so as to form "one flesh." Elsewhere (see Mt 19:5–6) Christ defends the inviolable

rights of this unity, through which the body in its masculinity and femininity takes on the value of a sign, in a certain sense a sacramental sign; and further, when he warns against concupiscence of the flesh, he expresses the same truth about the ontological dimension of the body and confirms its ethical meaning, consistent with his teaching as a whole. This ethical meaning has nothing in common with Manichaean condemnation; rather, it is deeply penetrated by the mystery of the "redemption of the body," about which St. Paul writes in Romans (see Rom 8:23). The "redemption of the body" does not, at any rate, indicate ontological evil as a constitutive attribute of the human body, but points only to *man's sinfulness*, by which *he lost*, among other things, *the clear sense of the spousal meaning of the body*, in which the interior dominion and freedom of the spirit expresses itself. As we have already emphasized above, what is at issue here is a "partial," potential loss in which the sense of the spousal meaning of the body is in some way confused with concupiscence and easily lets itself be absorbed by it.

3. The adequate interpretation of Christ's words (Mt 5:27–28), as well as the "praxis" in which the authentic ethos of the Sermon on the Mount is realized step by step, must be absolutely free from Manichaean elements in thought and attitude. A Manichaean attitude would have to lead to the "annihilation" of the body—if not real, then at least intentional; to a negation of the value of human sex, that is, of the masculinity and femininity of the human person; or at least to their mere "toleration" within the limits of the "need" marked off by procreation. By contrast, on the basis of Christ's words in the Sermon on the Mount, the Christian ethos is characterized by *a transformation of the human person's conscience and attitudes,* both the man's and the woman's, *such as to express and realize the value of the body and of sex* according to the Creator's original plan, placed as they are at the service of the "communion of persons," which is the deepest substratum of human ethics and culture. While for the Manichaean mentality, the body and sexuality constitute, so to speak, an "anti-value," for Christianity, on the contrary, they always remain "a value not sufficiently appreciated," as I will explain in more detail below. The latter attitude shows what should be the form of the ethos in which the mystery of the "redemption of the body" takes root, so to speak, in the

"historical" soil of man's sinfulness. This is expressed by the theological formula that defines the "state" of "historical" man as *status naturae lapsae simul ac redemptae* [the state of fallen and at the same time redeemed nature].

Anti-Value or Value not Sufficiently Appreciated?

4. One must interpret Christ's words in the Sermon on the Mount (Mt 5:27–28) in the light of this complex truth about man. Even if they contain a certain "accusation" of the human heart, *all the more do they turn to it with an appeal.* The accusation of the moral evil that the "desire" born from carnal intemperate concupiscence contains within itself is at the same time a call to overcome this evil. If victory over evil must consist in detachment from it (hence the severe words in the context of Mt 5:27–28), nevertheless one must only *detach oneself from the evil of the act* (in the case at hand, the interior act of "concupiscence") *and one must never transfer the negativity of this act to its object.* Such a transfer would signify—perhaps not in a fully conscious way—a certain acceptance of the Manichaean "anti-value." It would not constitute a real and deep victory over the evil of the act, which is evil by its moral essence, and thus an evil of a spiritual nature; on the contrary, there would be concealed in it the great danger of justifying the act to the detriment of the object (the essential error of the Manichaean ethos consists precisely in this). It is evident that in Matthew 5:27–28, Christ demands detachment from the evil of "concupiscence" (or of the look of inordinate desire), but his statement does not allow us to suppose in any way that the object of this desire, namely, the woman at whom he "looks with [lustful] desire," is an evil. (This clarification seems to be lacking at times in some Wisdom texts.)

5. We must therefore clarify the difference between "accusation" and "appeal." Given that the accusation directed against the evil of concupiscence is at the same time an appeal to overcome it, it follows that this victory must go hand in hand with an effort to discover the authentic value of the object, in order that the Manichaean "anti-value" may not take root in man, in his consciousness and will. In fact, it is a fruit of the evil of concupiscence, that is, of the act about which

Christ speaks in Matthew 5:27–28, that the object to which this act turns is for the human subject "a value not sufficiently appreciated." If in the words analyzed from the Sermon on the Mount (Mt 5:27–28) the human heart is "accused" of concupiscence (or if it is put on guard against that concupiscence), at the same time and by the same words it *is called to discover the full meaning of that which, in the act of concupiscence, constitutes for it "a value not sufficiently appreciated."* As we know, Christ said, "Whoever looks at a woman to desire her has already committed adultery with her in his heart." "Adultery committed in the heart" can and should be understood as a "devaluation" or impoverishment of an authentic value, as an intentional privation of that dignity to which the integral value of her femininity corresponds in the person in question. The words of Matthew 5:27–28 contain a call to discover this value and this dignity and to reaffirm them. It seems that only if one understands the words quoted from Matthew in this way does one respect their semantic content.

To conclude these brief considerations, it should be emphasized once again that the Manichaean way of understanding and evaluating man's body and sexuality is essentially foreign to the Gospel; it does not conform to the exact meaning of the words in the Sermon on the Mount pronounced by Christ. The call to master concupiscence of the flesh springs precisely from an affirmation of the personal dignity of the body and of sex and only serves such dignity. Anyone who wants to see a Manichaean perspective in these words would be committing an essential error.

B. The "Heart" Under Suspicion?

"Masters of Suspicion"

46 *General Audience of October 29, 1980*
(Insegnamenti, 3, no. 2 [1980]: 1011–16)

1. FOR A LONG TIME NOW our Wednesday reflections have centered on the following statement of Jesus Christ in the Sermon on the Mount: "You have heard that it was said, 'You shall not commit adultery.' But I say to you: Whoever looks at a woman to desire her has

already committed adultery with her" (toward her) "in his heart" (Mt 5:27–28). We have just clarified that these words cannot be understood or interpreted in a Manichaean key [see TOB 44:5–45:5]. In no way do they contain a condemnation of the body and of sexuality. They only contain a call to overcome the threefold concupiscence and in particular the concupiscence of the flesh: a call that springs precisely from the affirmation of the personal dignity of the body and of sexuality and only confirms this affirmation.

Clarifying this formulation, that is, determining the proper meaning of the words of the Sermon on the Mount in which Christ appeals to the human heart (see Mt 5:27–28), is important not only because of "deep seated habits" that stem from Manichaeism in the way of thinking and evaluating things, but also because of some *contemporary positions that interpret the meaning of man and of morality*. Ricoeur has called Freud, Marx, and Nietzsche "masters of suspicion"[54] ("*maîtes du soupçon*"), having in mind the whole system each one represents, and perhaps above all the hidden basis and the orientation of each in understanding and interpreting the *humanum* itself.

It seems necessary to take at least a brief look at this basis and orientation. We should do so to discover, on the one hand, a significant convergence with, and, *on the other hand, also* a fundamental *divergence* from, the hermeneutics that has its source in the Bible and that we are attempting to express in our analyses. In what does the convergence consist? It consists in the fact that the thinkers mentioned above, who

---

54. "The philosopher trained in the school of Descartes knows that things are doubtful, that they are not what they appear to be. But he never doubts that consciousness is as it appears to itself.... Since Marx, Nietzsche, and Freud, however, we doubt even this. After doubting the thing, we have begun to doubt consciousness.

"These three masters of suspicion, however, are not three masters of skepticism. They are surely three great 'destroyers'....

"...For the first time comprehension is hermeneutics. Henceforth seeking meaning no longer means spelling out the consciousness of meaning, but rather, *deciphering its expressions*. We are therefore faced not with three types of suspicion but with three types of deception....

"...By the same token, an even deeper relationship is discovered between Marx, Freud, and Nietzsche. All three, as we said, begin with suspicions about the illusions of consciousness and operate by the guile of decipherment." Ricoeur, *Conflict of Interpretations*, 144–46.

have exercised and still exercise a great influence on the way of thinking and evaluating of people of our time, seem in substance also to judge and accuse the human "heart." Even more, they seem to judge and accuse it *due to what* biblical language, especially Johannine language, *calls concupiscence, the threefold concupiscence.*

2. One could distribute the roles as follows. In Nietzschean hermeneutics, the judgment and the accusation of the human heart correspond in some way to what biblical language calls "pride of life"; in Marxist hermeneutics to what it calls "concupiscence of the eyes"; in Freudian hermeneutics, by contrast, to what it calls "concupiscence of the flesh." The convergence of these conceptions with the hermeneutics of man based on the Bible consists in the fact that when we uncovered the threefold concupiscence in the human heart, we too could have limited ourselves to putting this heart in a state of continual suspicion. Yet the Bible does not allow us to stop here. Although Christ's words in Matthew 5:27–28 show the whole reality of desire and concupiscence, they do not allow us to turn such concupiscence into the absolute principle of anthropology and ethics or into the very nucleus of the hermeneutics of man. *In the Bible the threefold concupiscence does not constitute the fundamental* and certainly not the only and absolute *criterion* of anthropology and ethics, although it is without doubt *an important coefficient for understanding man, his actions,* and their *moral value.* Also the analyses we have carried out so far show this.

3. Precisely when we wish to arrive at a complete interpretation of Christ's words about the man who "looks with concupiscence" (cf. Mt 5:27–28), we cannot rest content with just any concept of "concupiscence," even if the fullness of psychological truth accessible to us were reached in this way; we must, rather, draw on 1 John 2:15–16 and on the "theology of concupiscence" contained there. The man who "looks to desire" is, in fact, the man of the threefold concupiscence, he is the man of the concupiscence of the flesh. This is why he "can" look in this way and should even be aware *that when he leaves this interior act at the mercy of the forces of nature he cannot avoid the influence of the concupiscence of the flesh.* In Matthew 5:27–28, Christ speaks about this as well and calls attention to it. His words refer not only to the concrete act of "concupiscence," but indirectly also to the "man of concupiscence."

Essential Divergence

4. Why is it that these words of the Sermon on the Mount, despite the convergence between what they say to the human heart and what is expressed in the hermeneutics of the "masters of suspicion," cannot be considered the basis of the hermeneutics just mentioned or one analogous to it? Why is it that they constitute an expression, a configuration of an ethos that is totally different—different not only from the Manichaean, but also from the Freudian ethos? I think that the whole of the analyses and reflections carried out so far answers this question. Summing up, one can say in brief that Christ's words according to Matthew 5:27–28 do not allow us to stop at the accusation of the human heart and to cast it into a state of continual suspicion, but that they must be understood and interpreted as an appeal addressed to the heart. *This derives from the very nature of the ethos of redemption.* On the foundation of that mystery, which St. Paul defines as "redemption of the body" (Rom 8:23), on the foundation of the reality called "redemption," and, as a consequence, on the foundation of the ethos of the redemption of the body, we cannot stop at the mere accusation of the human heart on the basis of the desire and concupiscence of the flesh. *Man cannot stop at casting the heart into a state of* continual and irreversible *suspicion* due to the manifestations of the concupiscence of the flesh and of the *libido* uncovered, among other things, by a psychoanalyst through analysis of the unconscious.[55] Redemption is a truth, a reality, in the name of which man must feel himself called, and "called with effectiveness." He must become aware of this call also through Christ's words according to

---

55. See, e.g., the characteristic statement in *Freud's* last work. "The core of our being is constituted by the dark 'id,' which does not communicate with the external world and also becomes accessible to our knowledge only through another level. What is at work in this 'id' are the organic *drives,* which are in turn composed in varying measure of mixtures of two primal powers (Eros and Destruction) and differentiated from each other through their relation to organs and systems of organs.

"The only striving of these drives is for satisfaction which is expected from certain changes in the organs with the help of objects of the external world." S. Freud, *Abriß der Psychoanalyse, Das Unbehagen der Kultur,* 4th ed. (Frankfurt and Hamburg: Fischer, 1955), 74–75.

So then, that "core" or "heart" of man would be dominated by the union between erotic and destructive instinct, and life would consist in appeasing them.

Matthew 5:27–28, reread in the full context of the revelation of the body. Man *must feel himself called to rediscover,* or even better, to realize, the spousal meaning of the body and to express in this way the interior freedom of the gift, that is, the freedom of that spiritual state and power that derive from mastery over the concupiscence of the flesh.

5. Man is called to this rediscovery by the word of the Gospel, and so from "outside," but at the same time he is also called from "inside." The words of Christ, who in the Sermon on the Mount appeals to the "heart," lead the listener in some way to such an inner call. If he allows them to work in him he can at the same time hear in his innermost [being] the echo, as it were, of that "beginning," of that good "beginning" to which Christ appealed on another occasion to remind his listeners who man is, who woman is, and who they are reciprocally: one for the other in the work of creation. Christ's words spoken in the Sermon on the Mount are not a call hurled into emptiness. They do not address the man who is completely bound by the concupiscence of the flesh, unable to seek another form of reciprocal relations in the sphere of the perennial attraction that has accompanied the history of man and woman "from the beginning." The words of Christ testify that *the original power* (and thus also the grace) *of the mystery of creation becomes* for each one of them *the power* (that is, the grace) *of the mystery of redemption.* This concerns the very "nature," the very substrate of the humanity of the person, the deepest impulses of the "heart." Does man not sense, together with concupiscence, a deep need to preserve the dignity of the reciprocal relations that find their expression in the body thanks to its masculinity and femininity? Does he not feel the need to impregnate them with everything that is noble and beautiful? Does he not feel the need to confer on them the supreme value, which is love?

6. Rereading this appeal contained in Christ's words in the Sermon on the Mount cannot be an act detached from the context of concrete existence. It always signifies—even if only in the dimension of the act to which it refers—the rediscovery of the meaning of the whole of existence, of the meaning of life, which includes also the meaning of the body that we have called "spousal" here. The meaning of the body is in some way the antithesis of Freudian libido. The

meaning of life is the antithesis of the hermeneutics "of suspicion." Such a *hermeneutics* is very different; *it is radically different* from the one we discover *in Christ's words* in the Sermon on the Mount. These words bring to light not only another ethos, but also another vision of man's possibilities. It is important that precisely in his "heart" he does not feel himself irrevocably accused and given up to the concupiscence of the flesh, but that in the same heart he feels himself called with energy. Called precisely to this supreme value, which is love. Called as a person in the truth of his humanity, and thus also in the truth of his masculinity and femininity, in the truth of his body. Called in that truth which has been his inheritance "of the beginning," the inheritance of his heart, which is deeper than the sinfulness inherited, deeper than the threefold concupiscence. Christ's words, set in the whole reality of creation and redemption, re-activate that deepest inheritance and give it real power in human life.[*]

C. EROS AND ETHOS

Eros as the Source of the "Erotic"

47 *General Audience of November 5, 1980*
(Insegnamenti, 3, no. 2 [1980]: 1066–70)

1. IN THE COURSE OF OUR weekly reflections on Christ's statement in the Sermon on the Mount, in which, in reference to the commandment "You shall not commit adultery," he compares "concupiscence" ("the concupiscent look") to "adultery committed in the heart," we are attempting to answer the question: Do these words only accuse the human "heart" or are they before all else an appeal addressed to it? An appeal, obviously, of an ethical character; an appeal that is important and essential for the very ethos of the Gospel. We answer that the words just quoted are above all an appeal.

At the same time, we are trying to bring our reflections close to the "routes" taken in this sphere by *the consciousness of contemporary human beings*. Already in the preceding cycle of our considerations we mentioned "eros" [see TOB 22:4]. This Greek term, which passed

---

[*] Translator's note: Inheritance: compare the title of the final chapter of TOB: "He Gave Them the Law of Life as Their Inheritance" (TOB 118:1).

from mythology to philosophy, then to literary language, and finally into spoken language, is foreign and unknown to biblical language, in contrast to the word "ethos." If in the present analyses of biblical texts we use the term "ethos," which is <un>known[*] to the Septuagint and the New Testament, we do so because of the general meaning it acquired in philosophy and theology, inasmuch as it embraces in its content the complex spheres of good and evil that depend on the human will and are subject to the laws of conscience and of the sensibility of the human "heart." *The term "eros,"* besides being the proper name of a mythological personage, has a philosophical meaning in the writings of Plato[56] that seems to differ from the common meaning and also from the meaning that is commonly attributed to the term in

---

[*] Translator's note: The *Insegnamenti* text reads "unknown," which does not fit the context. UD reads "known."

56. According to Plato, it is the destiny of man, placed between the world of the senses and the world of the Ideas, to pass from the first to the second. The world of Ideas, however, is not able by itself to overcome the world of the senses: only eros, who is inborn in man, can do this. When man begins to have a presentiment of the existence of the Ideas, thanks to the contemplation of objects existing in the world of the senses, he receives the impulse from eros, that is, from the desire of the pure Ideas. Eros is, in fact, the orientation of the "sensual" or "sensory" man toward the transcendent: the power that directs the soul toward the world of Ideas. In the *Symposium*, Plato describes the stages of eros's influence: it lifts the soul of a human being from the beauty of an individual body to that of all bodies, thus to the beauty of science, and finally to the Idea of Beauty itself (see *Symposium* 211; *Republic* 514).

Eros is neither purely human nor divine: it is something intermediate (*daimonion*) and intermediary. Its main characteristic is permanent aspiration and desire. Even when it seems to give, eros continues to be a "desire to possess," but nevertheless it is different from a purely sensual love in being the love that tends toward the sublime.

According to Plato, the gods do not love, because they do not experience desires, inasmuch as their desires are all satisfied. They can thus only be an object, not a subject of love (*Symposium* 200–1). For this reason they do not have a direct relationship with man; it is only the mediation of eros that allows the connecting of a relationship (*Symposium* 203). Eros is thus the way that leads man to divinity, but not vice versa.

The aspiration for transcendence is thus an element constitutive for the Platonic conception of eros, a conception that overcomes the radical dualism of the world of Ideas and the world of the senses. eros allows a person to pass from one to the other. He is thus a form of flight outside the material world, which the soul must renounce, because the beauty of a sensible subject has value only inasmuch as it leads higher.

Nevertheless, eros remains always, for Plato, an egocentric love: it tends toward conquering and possessing the object that represents a value for man. To love the good signifies to desire to possess it forever. Love is therefore always a desire for immortality, and also this shows the egocentric character of eros. See Nygren, *Agape and Eros,* 166–81.

literature. Obviously, we must consider here the vast range of meanings that differ from each other in a nuanced way with regard to the mythical personage as well as the philosophical content, but above all the "somatic" or "sexual" point of view. Taking such a vast range of meanings into account, one should evaluate in an equally nuanced way what relates to "eros"[57] and is defined as "erotic."

2. According to Plato, "eros" represents the inner power that draws man toward all that is good, true, and beautiful. This "attraction" indicates, in this case, *the intensity of a subjective act of the human spirit.* By contrast, in the common meaning—as also in literature—this *"attraction" seems to be above all of a sensual nature.* It arouses a reciprocal tendency in both the man and the woman to draw near to each other, to the union of their bodies, the union about which Genesis 2:24 speaks. Here we must answer the question whether "eros" connotes the same meaning that is present in the biblical narrative (above all in Gen 2:23–25), which doubtless attests to the reciprocal attraction and the perennial call of the human person—through masculinity and femininity—to that "unity of flesh," which at the same time should realize the union-communion of persons. The way we understand the "concupiscence" discussed in the Sermon on the Mount becomes fundamentally important precisely because of this *interpretation of "eros"* (together with its relation with ethos).

3. It seems that common language considers primarily the meaning of "concupiscence" that we defined as "psychological" and that could also be called "sexological": and this on the basis of premises that limit themselves mainly to a naturalistic, "somatic," and sensualistic interpretation of human eroticism. (The point here is not in any way to diminish the value of scientific research in this field, but to call attention to the danger of reductionism and exclusivism.) In the psychological and sexological sense, then, concupiscence indicates the

---

For Plato, *erōs* is a passage from a more elementary to a deeper science; it is at the very same time the aspiration of passing from "that which is not" and is evil, to that which "exists in fullness" and is the good. See Max Scheler, "Liebe und Erkenntnis," in *Schriften zur Soziologie und Weltanschauungslehre: Gesammelte Werke Band 6* (Bern and Munich: Francke Verlag, 1963), 77–98, here 82.

57. Lewis, "Eros," in *The Four Loves,* 131–33; 152; 159–60. Chauchard, *Vices des vertus,* 147.

subjective intensity of tending toward the object due to its sexual character (sexual value). *This tending has its subjective intensity because of the specific "attraction" that extends its mastery over man's emotive sphere and involves his "bodiliness"* (his somatic masculinity and femininity). When in the Sermon on the Mount we hear about the "concupiscence" of the man who "looks at a woman to desire her," these words—understood in the "psychological" (sexological) sense—refer to the sphere of phenomena that in common language are precisely called "erotic." Within the limits of Matthew 5:27–28, the issue is only the interior act, while the term "erotic" refers above all to ways of acting and reciprocal behavior by man and woman that are an external manifestation proper to such interior acts. Nevertheless, it seems beyond doubt that—if one reasons in this way—one must place the equal sign between "erotic" and that which "derives from desire" (and serves to satisfy the very concupiscence of the flesh). Now, if this were so, Christ's words according to Matthew 5:27–28 would express a negative judgment about what is "erotic" and, when addressed to the human heart, they would at the same time constitute a severe warning against "eros."

Ethos as an Inner Power of Eros

4. Yet, we have already pointed out that the term *"eros" has many semantic nuances.* And so, if one wants to define the relation of the statement in the Sermon on the Mount (Mt 5:27–28) to the wide sphere of "erotic" phenomena, that is, of those actions and reciprocal forms of behavior by which man and woman approach each other and unite so as to be "one flesh" (see Gen 2:24), one must keep in mind this multiplicity of semantic nuances of "eros." It seems in fact possible that in the sphere of the concept of "eros"—keeping its Platonic meaning in mind—one can find room for that ethos, for those ethical and indirectly also theological contents that have been drawn in the course of our analyses from Christ's appeal to the human heart in the Sermon on the Mount. Also our knowledge of the many semantic nuances of "eros" and of that which—in the differentiated experience and description of man in various epochs and at various points of geographic and cultural longitude and latitude—is *defined as "erotic" can help us to understand the specific and complex richness of the "heart" to which Christ appealed* in his statement in Matthew 5:27–28.

5. If we suppose that "eros" signifies the inner power that "attracts" man to the true, the good, and the beautiful, then we also see a road opening up within the sphere of this concept toward what Christ wanted to express in the Sermon on the Mount. While the words of Matthew 5:27–28 are an "accusation" of the human heart, they are at the same time and even more so an appeal addressed to it. This appeal is the category proper to the ethos of redemption. The call to what is true, good, and beautiful means at the same time, in the ethos of redemption, the necessity of overcoming what derives from the threefold concupiscence. It also means *the possibility and the necessity of transforming* what has been weighed down by the concupiscence of the flesh. Further, if the words of Matthew 5:27–28 represent such a call, then this means that in the erotic sphere, "eros" and "ethos" do not diverge, are not opposed to each other, but *are called to meet in the human heart and to bear fruit in this meeting.* What is worthy of the human "heart" is that the form of the "erotic" is at the same time the form of ethos, that is, of that which is "ethical."

6. This statement is very important, for ethos as well as for ethics. In fact, a "negative meaning" is often linked with the latter concept, because ethics brings with it norms, commandments, and also prohibitions. We often have the tendency to consider the words of the Sermon on the Mount about "concupiscence" (about "looking to desire") only as a prohibition, a prohibition in the sphere of "eros," that is, in the "erotic" sphere. And we are often content with this understanding alone, without seeking to *unveil* the truly deep and essential *values* that this prohibition protects, that is, assures. It not only protects them, but makes them accessible and liberates them, provided we learn to open our "hearts" to them.

In the Sermon on the Mount Christ teaches us this and leads man's heart to these values.

The Problem of Erotic Spontaneity

48 *General Audience of November 12, 1980*
(Insegnamenti, 3, no. 2 [1980]: 1131–34)

1. TODAY WE RESUME THE ANALYSIS we began one week ago on the mutual relation between the "ethical" and the "erotic." Our reflections

follow the thread of the words Christ spoke in the Sermon on the Mount by which he referred back to the commandment "You shall not commit adultery" and at the same time defined "concupiscence" (the "concupiscent look") as "adultery committed in the heart." It follows from these reflections that "ethos" is connected with the discovery of a new order of values. It is necessary continually to rediscover the spousal meaning of the body and the true dignity of the gift in what is "erotic." This is the task of the human spirit, and it is by its nature an ethical task. If one does not assume this task, the very attraction of the senses and the passion of the body can stop at mere concupiscence, deprived of all ethical value, and man, male and female, does not experience that fullness of "eros," which implies the upward impulse of the human spirit toward what is true, good, and beautiful, so that what is "erotic" also becomes true, good, and beautiful. It is, therefore, indispensable that ethos becomes the constitutive form of eros.

2. The reflections mentioned above are closely connected with the problem of spontaneity. People often maintain that ethos takes away spontaneity from what is erotic in human life and behavior; and for this reason they often demand detachment from ethos "for the benefit" of eros. The words of the Sermon on the Mount would also seem to prevent this "benefit." Yet this opinion is mistaken and, at any rate, superficial. If we accept it and obstinately maintain it, we will never reach the full dimensions of eros, and this failure will inevitably be echoed in the realm of the corresponding "praxis," that is, in our behavior and also in the concrete experience of values. In fact, the one who accepts the ethos of the statement in Matthew 5:27–28 should know that he or she is also *called to full and mature spontaneity* in relationships that are born from the perennial attraction of masculinity and femininity. Such spontaneity is itself the gradual fruit of the discernment of the impulses of one's own heart.

3. *Christ's words are severe.* They demand that in the sphere in which relationships with persons of the other sex are formed, man has full and deep consciousness of his own acts, and above all of his interior acts, and that he is conscious of the inner impulses of his own "heart" so that he can identify and evaluate them in a mature way. Christ's words demand that in this sphere, which seems to belong

only to the body and the senses (that is, to the exterior man), he should succeed in being really an interior man, able to obey right conscience, able to be the authentic master of his own innermost impulses, like a watchman who watches over a hidden spring, and finally able to draw from all these impulses what is fitting for "purity of the heart" by building with conscience and consistency the personal sense of the spousal meaning of the body, which opens the interior space of the freedom of the gift.

4. Thus, if man wants to respond to the call expressed by Matthew 5:27–28, he must *learn* with perseverance and consistency *what* the meaning of the body *is*, the meaning of femininity and masculinity. He must learn it not only through an objectifying abstraction (though this is needed as well), but above all in the sphere of the interior reactions of his own "heart." This is a "science" that cannot really be learned only from books, because it consists primarily of deep "knowledge" of human interiority.

Within the sphere of this knowledge, man learns to distinguish between what, on the one hand, makes up the manifold richness of masculinity and femininity in the signs that spring from their perennial call and creative attraction and what, on the other hand, bears only the sign of concupiscence. And although within certain limits these variants and nuances of inner movements of the "heart" can be confused with each other, it should nonetheless be said that the inner man is *called by Christ to reach a more mature and complete evaluation that allows him to distinguish and judge the various movements of his own heart.* One should add that this task *can* be carried out and that it is truly worthy of man.

In fact, the discernment we are speaking about is by its essence related to spontaneity. Man's subjective structure shows, in this area, a specific richness and a clear differentiation. Thus, a noble pleasure is one thing, [mere] sexual desire another; when sexual desire is connected with a noble pleasure, it differs from desire pure and simple. Analogously, as far as the sphere of immediate reactions of the "heart" is concerned, sensual arousal is quite different from the deep emotion with which not only inner sensibility but also sexuality itself reacts to the integral expression of femininity and masculinity. The argument cannot be further developed here. But it is certain that, if we claim that Christ's words according to Matthew 5:27–28 are severe, they are severe also in the sense that they contain deep demands in regard to human spontaneity.

5. There cannot be such spontaneity in all the movements and impulses that spring from mere carnal concupiscence, deprived as it is of choice and of an adequate hierarchy. At the price of mastery over these impulses, man reaches that *deeper and more mature spontaneity* with which his "heart," by mastering the instincts, rediscovers the spiritual beauty of the sign constituted by the human body in its masculinity and femininity. Inasmuch as this discovery becomes firm in conscience as conviction and in the will as the orientation both of possible choices and of simple desires, the human heart comes to share, so to speak, in another spontaneity of which the "carnal man" knows nothing or very little. There is no doubt that by Christ's words according to Matthew 5:27–28, we are called precisely to such spontaneity. And perhaps the most important sphere of "praxis"—with respect to the most "interior" acts—is the one that traces the road step by step toward such spontaneity.

This topic is vast, and we will have to take it up once again later when we focus on showing the true nature of "purity of heart" according to the Gospel [see TOB 50–59]. For now, we conclude by saying that the words with which Christ calls the attention of his audience— then and today—to "concupiscence" ("the concupiscent look") indirectly indicate the road toward a mature spontaneity of the human "heart" that does not suffocate its noble desires and aspirations, but on the contrary liberates and helps them.

Let what we have said about the mutual relation between the "ethical" and the "erotic" according to the ethos of the Sermon on the Mount suffice for now.

5. The Ethos of the Redemption of the Body

49 *General Audience of December 3, 1980*
(Insegnamenti, 3, no. 2 [1980]: 1575–79)

1. AT THE BEGINNING OF OUR CONSIDERATIONS about Christ's words in the Sermon on the Mount (Mt 5:27–28), we observed that they

contain a deep ethical and anthropological meaning. In this passage, Christ recalls the commandment "You shall not commit adultery," and adds, "Whoever looks at a woman to desire her has already committed adultery with her" (or toward her) "in his heart." We are speaking about the ethical and anthropological meaning of these words because they allude to the two strictly connected dimensions of ethos and "historical" man. In the course of the preceding analyses, we have sought to follow these two dimensions, always keeping in mind that Christ's words address the "heart," that is, the inner man. The inner man is the specific subject of the ethos of the body, and it is with this [ethos] that the Christ wants to impregnate the consciousness [or conscience] and will of his audience and his disciples. It is without doubt *a "new" ethos. It is "new" in comparison with the ethos of the men of the Old Testament,* as we already tried to show in more particular analyses. It is also "new" in comparison with the state of "historical" man *after original sin, that is, in comparison with the "man of concupiscence."*

It is, therefore, a new ethos in a universal sense and extent. It is "new" in relation to every human being, in a manner independent from any geographical longitude and latitude and from any historical situation.

2. Several times already, we have called this "new" ethos, which emerges from the perspective of Christ's words in the Sermon on the Mount, the "ethos of redemption" and, more precisely, the ethos of the redemption of the body. In this we followed St. Paul, who in Romans contrasts "the slavery of corruption" (8:21) and the submission "to transitoriness" (8:20)—in which the whole creation has come to share because of sin—to the desire for the "redemption of our bodies" (8:23). In this context, the Apostle speaks about the groans of "the whole creation," which "cherishes the hope that it itself will be set free from the slavery of corruption to enter into the freedom of the glory of the children of God" (8:20–21). In this way St. Paul reveals the situation of all that is created and, in particular, that of man after sin. What is significant for this situation is the aspiration that *tends*— together with the new "adoption as sons" (8:23)—precisely *toward the "redemption of the body,"* presented as the end, as the eschatological and mature fruit of the mystery of the redemption of man and the world achieved by Christ.

3. In what sense, then, can we speak of the ethos of redemption and especially of the ethos of the redemption of the body? We must recognize that in the context of the words of the Sermon on the Mount we have analyzed (Mt 5:27–28), this meaning does not yet appear in all its fullness. It will become clearer when we analyze other words of Jesus, namely, those in which he refers to the resurrection (see Mt 22:30; Mk 12:25; Lk 20:35–36).

Yet, there is no doubt that also in the Sermon on the Mount *Christ speaks in the perspective of the redemption* of man and the world (and thus precisely of the "redemption of the body"). This is, in fact, the perspective of the whole gospel, of the whole teaching, even more, of the whole mission of Christ. And although the immediate context of the Sermon on the Mount indicates the Law and the Prophets as the historical point of reference proper to the People of God of the Old Covenant, nevertheless, we can never forget that in the teaching of Christ the fundamental reference to the question of marriage and the problem of the relations between man and woman appeals to the "beginning." Such an appeal can be justified only by the reality of the redemption; outside of it there would, in fact, remain only the three-fold concupiscence or that "slavery of corruption" about which the Apostle Paul writes (Rom 8:21). Only the perspective of the redemption justifies the appeal to the "beginning" or the perspective of the mystery of creation in the whole of Christ's teaching about the problems of marriage, of man and woman, and their reciprocal relation. The words of Matthew 5:27–28 adopt definitely the same theological perspective.

4. In the Sermon on the Mount, Christ does not invite man to return to the state of original innocence, because humanity has left it irrevocably behind, but *he calls him to find*—on the foundation of the perennial and, one might say, indestructible meanings of what is "human"—the *living forms of the "new man."* In this way a connection is formed, even a continuity, between the "beginning" and the perspective of redemption. In the ethos of the redemption of the body, the original ethos of creation was to be taken up anew. Christ does not change the law, but confirms the commandment "You shall not commit adultery"; at the same time, however, he leads the minds and hearts of his listeners toward that "fullness of justice" willed by God the Creator and Legislator that is contained in this commandment. This fullness must be discovered, first with an interior vision "of the heart" and then with an appropriate way of being and of acting. The form of the "new man" can come forth from this way of being and of acting in the measure in which the ethos of the redemption of the body dominates the concupiscence of the flesh and the whole man of concupiscence. Christ shows clearly that the way to attain this goal must be the way of temperance and of mastery of desires, already at the very root, already in the purely interior sphere ("whoever looks to desire..."). The ethos of redemption contains in every context—and directly in the sphere of the concupiscence of the flesh—the imperative of self-mastery, the necessity of immediate continence and habitual temperance.

5. Yet, *temperance and continence do not mean*—if one may put it this way—*being left hanging in the void: neither in the void of values nor in the void of the subject.* The ethos of redemption is realized in self-mastery, that is, in the continence of desires. In this behavior, the human heart remains bound to the value, from which it would otherwise distance itself through its desire, orienting itself toward mere concupiscence deprived of ethical value (as we said in the analysis above). On the ground of the ethos of redemption, an even deeper power and firmness confirms or restores *the union with this value* through an act of mastery. The value in question is that of the body's spousal meaning, the value of a transparent sign by which the Creator—together with the perennial reciprocal attraction of man and woman through masculinity and femininity—has written into the heart of both the gift of communion, that is, the mysterious reality of his image and likeness. This is the value that is at stake in the act of self-dominion and temperance to which Christ calls us in the Sermon on the Mount (Mt 5:27–28).

6. This act can give the impression that one is left hanging "in the void of the subject." It can give this impression particularly when one has to decide to perform it for the first time or, even more so, when one has created a contrary habit, when one has habituated oneself to yield to the concupiscence of the flesh. Yet, already the first time, and all the more so later when he has gained the ability, man gradually experiences his own dignity and through temperance attests to his

own self-dominion and demonstrates that *he fulfills what is essentially personal in him*. In addition, he gradually experiences the freedom of the gift, which is, on the one hand, the condition for, and, on the other hand, the subject's response to, the spousal value of the human body in its femininity and masculinity. Thus, the ethos of the redemption of the body is realized through self-dominion, through temperance of the "desires," when the human heart makes an alliance with this ethos, or rather *when it confirms this alliance through its own integral subjectivity*: when the person's deepest and yet most real possibilities and dispositions show themselves, when the deepest layers of his potentiality acquire a voice, layers that the concupiscence of the flesh would not allow to show themselves. These layers cannot emerge when the human heart is fixed in permanent suspicion, as is the case in Freudian hermeneutics. They also cannot manifest themselves if the Manichaean "anti-value" is dominant in consciousness. The ethos of redemption, by contrast, is based on a strict alliance with these layers.

7. Further reflections will give us other proofs of this. Concluding our analyses of Christ's momentous statement according to Matthew 5:27–28, we see that in this statement the human "heart" is above all the object of a call and not of an accusation. At the same time, we must admit that *the awareness of sinfulness* is not only a necessary point of departure in "historical" man, but also an indispensable *condition of his aspiration* to virtue, to "purity of heart," to perfection. The ethos of the redemption of the body remains deeply rooted in the anthropological and axiological realism of revelation. When he appeals in this case to the "heart," Christ formulates his words in the most concrete way: man, in fact, is unique and unrepeatable above all by reason of his "heart," which is decisive for him "from within." The category of "heart" is in some way the equivalent of personal subjectivity. The way of the call to purity of heart as expressed in the Sermon on the Mount is at any rate a reminiscence of original solitude, from which the man-male was freed by opening to the other human being, to the woman. Purity of heart is explained, in the end, by the relation to the *other subject, who is originally and perennially "co-called."*

Purity is a requirement of love. It is the dimension of the inner truth of love in man's "heart."

6. Purity as "Life according to the Spirit"

"Purity" and "Heart"

50 *General Audience of December 10, 1980*
(Insegnamenti, 3, no. 2 [1980]: 1640–44)

1. THE ANALYSIS OF PURITY is an indispensable completion of the words Christ spoke in the Sermon on the Mount on which we have focused the cycle of our present reflections. When in explaining the correct meaning of the commandment "You shall not commit adultery" Christ appealed to the inner man, he specified at the same time the fundamental dimension of purity by which the reciprocal relations between man and woman must be marked in marriage and outside of marriage. The words, "But I say to you: Whoever looks at a woman to desire her has already committed adultery with her in his heart" (Mt 5:27–28), express the opposite of purity. At the same time, these words demand purity, which in the Sermon on the Mount is included in the statement of the beatitudes, *"Blessed are the pure in heart, because they will see God"* (Mt 5:8). In this manner Christ directs an appeal to the human heart: he invites it, he does not accuse it, as we have already shown above.

2. Christ sees in the heart, in man's innermost [being], the wellspring of purity—but also of moral impurity—in the fundamental and most generic sense of the word. This is confirmed, for example, by the response given to the Pharisees, who are scandalized by the fact that his disciples "break the tradition of the elders, because they do not wash their hands before they eat" (Mt 15:2). Jesus then says to those present, "Not what goes into the mouth defiles a man, but what comes out of the mouth defiles a man" (Mt 15:11). To the disciples, by contrast, he explains these words in answer to Peter's question as follows. "What comes out of the mouth proceeds from the heart, and this is what makes a man unclean. For out of the heart come evil intentions, murder, adultery, prostitution, theft, false witness, blasphemy. These make a man unclean, but to eat with unwashed hands does not make a man unclean" (Mt 15:18–20; see Mk 7:20–23).

When we say *"purity"* and *"pure,"* in the first meaning of these terms *we indicate the opposite of dirty.* "To dirty" means "to make unclean," "to pollute." This pertains to the various spheres of the physical world. One speaks, for example, about a "dirty street," about a "dirty room"; one also speaks about "polluted air." In the same way, man can also be "unclean" when his body is not clean. To remove filth from the body one must wash it. In the tradition of the Old Testament, great importance was attributed to ritual washings, for example, to washing one's hands before eating, which is mentioned in the text just quoted. Many specific types of washing were prescribed in relation to sexual impurity, understood in an exclusively physiological way (see Lev 15), which we already mentioned above [see TOB 36:4]. According to the state of medical science at the time, the various washings could correspond to hygienic prescriptions. Inasmuch as they were imposed in the name of God and included in the sacred books of Old Testament legislation, their observance acquired indirectly a religious meaning; they were ritual washings and in the life of people in the Old Testament served ritual *"purity."*

3. In connection with this juridical and religious tradition of the Old Covenant, *a wrong way of understanding moral purity* developed.[58] Moral purity was often understood in an exclusively external and "material" way. At any rate, an explicit tendency toward such an interpretation became widespread. Christ opposed it in a radical manner: nothing makes a man unclean "from the outside"; no "material" dirti-

---

58. Next to a complex system of prescriptions regarding ritual purity, on the basis of which legal casuistry was unfolded, the Old Testament contains the concept of *moral purity*, which was transmitted in two currents.

The *prophets* called for a behavior in conformity with God's will, which presupposes the conversion of the heart, inner obedience, and complete uprightness before him (see, e.g., Isa 1:10–20; Jer 4:14; 24:7; Ezek 36:25–27). A similar attitude is required by the psalmist. "Who shall ascend the mountain of the Lord...? / The one with innocent hands and *a pure heart...* / He will receive the Lord's blessing" (Ps 24(23):3–5).

According to the *Priestly tradition,* man is aware of his profound sinfulness and, not being able to achieve purification with his own forces, begs God to realize that transformation of the heart, which can only be the work of his creative act. "Create a pure heart in me, O God... / wash me and I shall be whiter than snow... / a broken and humbled heart, O God, you will not spurn" (Ps 51(50):10, 7, 17).

Both currents of the Old Testament come together in the beatitude about the "pure of heart" (Mt 5:8), although its verbal formulation seems to be closer to Psalm 24. See J. Dupont, *Les Béatitudes, vol. III: Les Évangélistes* (Paris: Gabalda, 1973), 603–4.

ness makes a man impure in the moral sense. No washing, not even ritual washing, is by itself suited to produce moral purity. Moral purity has its wellspring exclusively in man's interior: it comes from the heart. The Old Testament prescriptions in question (those found, for example, in Lev 15:16–24; 18:1ff.; 12:1–5) probably served, in addition to hygiene, also to attribute a certain dimension of interiority to what is bodily and sexual in the human person. In any case, Christ thoroughly guarded himself against connecting purity in the moral (ethical) sense with physiology and the organic processes in question. In the light of the words of Matthew 15:18–20 quoted above, none of the aspects of sexual "uncleanness" in the strictly somatic, biological-physiological sense enters per se into the definition of purity or impurity in the moral (ethical) sense.

4. The statement just mentioned (Mt 15:18–20) is important above all for semantic reasons. When we speak about *purity in the moral sense,* that is, about the virtue of purity, *we are using an analogy* according to which moral evil is compared with being dirty. Certainly, this analogy entered and became part of the realm of ethical concepts from earliest times. Christ takes it up and confirms it in all its extension. "What comes out of the mouth proceeds from the heart, and this is what makes a man unclean." Here Christ speaks *about every moral evil,* every sin, that is, about the violations of the various commandments, and he lists "evil intentions, murder, adultery, fornication, theft, false witness, blasphemy" *without limiting himself to a particular kind of sin.* It follows that the concept of "purity" and of "impurity" in the moral sense is a rather general concept, not a specific one: thus, every moral good is a manifestation of purity and every moral evil a manifestation of impurity. The statement in Matthew 15:18–20 does not restrict purity to only one sector of morality, such as the one connected with the commandment "You shall not commit adultery" and "You shall not desire your neighbor's wife," that is, the one that concerns the reciprocal relations between man and woman connected with the body and the corresponding concupiscence. In an analogous way, we can also understand the beatitude of the Sermon on the Mount addressed to those who are "pure in heart," whether in the generic or the more specific sense. Only the context allows one in each case to define and specify this meaning.

"Body" and "Spirit" according to St. Paul

5. The broadest and most general sense of purity is also present in the letters of St. Paul, in which we will identify step by step the contexts that explicitly restrict the meaning of purity to the "somatic" and "sexual" sphere, that is, *to the meaning that can be gathered from Christ's words* in the Sermon on the Mount *about concupiscence,* which expresses itself already in "looking at a woman" and is equated with "adultery committed in the heart" (Mt 5:27–28).

The author of the words about the threefold concupiscence is not Paul. As we know, they are found in 1 John. Yet, one can say that in a manner analogous to what for John (1 Jn 2:16–17) is an antithesis within man between God and the world (between what comes "from the Father" and what comes "from the world")—an antithesis that is born in the heart and penetrates into human actions as the "concupiscence of the eyes, the concupiscence of the flesh, and the pride of life"—St. Paul observes another contradiction in the Christian, namely, the opposition and at the same time the tension *between the "flesh" and the "Spirit"* (written with a capital "S," that is, the Holy Spirit): "I say to you, live by the Spirit and do not satisfy the desires of the flesh; for the flesh has desires contrary to the Spirit, and the Spirit has desires contrary to the flesh; for these are opposed to each other, so that you do not do what you want" (Gal 5:16–17). It follows that life "according to the flesh" stands in opposition to life "according to the Spirit." "For those who live according to the flesh set their minds on the things of the flesh, but those who live according to the Spirit on the things of the Spirit" (Rom 8:5).

In the following analyses we will try to show that purity—purity of heart, about which Christ speaks in the Sermon on the Mount—is realized precisely in life "according to the Spirit."

51 *General Audience of December 17, 1980* (*Insegnamenti,* 3, no. 2 [1980]: 1706–12)

1. "THE FLESH HAS DESIRES CONTRARY to the Spirit, and the Spirit has desires contrary to the flesh." Today we wish to devote further study to these words of St. Paul in Galatians (Gal 5:17), with which we ended our reflections on the topic of the true meaning of purity last week. Paul has in mind the tension that exists in man's innermost [being], in his "heart." The issue is not just the body (matter) and spirit (the soul) as two essentially distinct anthropological components that have from the "beginning" constituted man's very essence. What is presupposed is, rather, that disposition of powers formed in man together with original sin, the sin in which every "historical" human being shares. In this disposition, which was formed in man's innermost [being], the body sets itself against the spirit and easily gains the upper hand over it.[59] The Pauline terminology, however, signifies something more: here the predominance of the "flesh" seems to coincide with what, according to Johannine terminology, is the threefold concupiscence that "comes from the world." The "flesh," in the language of the Letters of St. Paul,[60] *indicates not only the "outer" man,*

---

59. "Paul never, like the Greeks, identified 'sinful flesh' with the physical body....

"Flesh, then, in Paul is not to be identified with sex or with the physical body. It is closer to the Hebrew thought of the physical personality—the self including physical and psychical elements as vehicle of the outward life and the lower levels of experience.

"It is man in his humanness with all the limitations, moral weakness, vulnerability, creatureliness, and mortality, which being human implies....

"Man is vulnerable both to evil and to good; he is a vehicle, a channel, a dwelling place, a temple, a battlefield (Paul uses each metaphor) for good and evil.

"Which shall possess, indwell, master him—whether sin, evil, the spirit that now worketh in the children of disobedience, or Christ, the Holy Spirit, faith, grace—it is for each man to choose.

"That he *can* so choose, brings to view the other side of Paul's conception of human nature, man's conscience and the human *spirit*." R. E. O. White, *Biblical Ethics* (Exeter: Paternoster Press, 1979), 135–38.

60. The interpretation of the Greek word *sarx* (flesh) in the letters of Paul depends on the context of the letter. In Galatians, for example, one can identify at least two distinct meanings of *sarx*.

When he wrote to the Galatians, Paul was battling against two dangers that threatened the young Christian community.

On the one hand, the converts from Judaism attempted to convince the converts from paganism to accept circumcision, which was obligatory in Judaism. Paul reproaches them for "boasting in the flesh," that is, for placing hope again in the circumcision of the flesh. In this context (Gal 3:1–5, 12; 6:12–18), "flesh" thus signifies "circumcision" as *a symbol for a new submission to the laws of Judaism.*

The second danger in the young Galatian church came from the influence of the "Pneumatics" [the Spiritual], who understood the work of the Holy Spirit as man's divinization rather than as a power that is at work in the ethical sense. This led them to underemphasize moral principles. In writing to them, Paul calls "flesh" all that *brings man close to the object of his concupiscence and entices him with the seductive promise of an apparently fuller life* (Gal 5:13–6:10).

but also the man "interiorly" subjected to the "world,"[61] in some way closed in the sphere of the values that belong only to the world and of those ends that the world is able to impose on man: values, therefore, to which man as "flesh" is sensitive. In this way Paul's language seems to connect with the essential contents of John, and the language of both denotes what is defined by various terms of contemporary ethics and anthropology, as for example, "humanistic autarchy," "secularism," or also, in a general sense, "sensualism." The man who lives "according to the flesh (*sarx*)" is the man disposed only to that which comes "from the world": he is the man of the "senses," the man of the three-fold concupiscence. His actions confirm it, as we will say shortly.

"Flesh" thus "boasts" equally in the "law" and in breaking the law, and in both cases it promises what it cannot keep.

Paul explicitly distinguishes between the object of the action and *sarx*. The center of decision does not lie in the "flesh": "Walk according to the Spirit and do not satisfy the desires of the flesh" (Gal 5:16).

Man falls into the slavery of the flesh when he entrusts himself to the "flesh" and to what it promises (in the sense of the "law" or of breaking the law). F. Mussner, *Der Galaterbrief,* Herders theolog. Kommentar zum NT (Freiburg: Herder, 1974), 367; Jewett, *Paul's Anthropological Terms,* 95–106.

61. Paul underlines in his letters the dramatic character of what *is unfolding in the world.* Because human beings, by their own fault, have forgotten God, "for this reason God abandoned them to impurity according to the desires of their heart" (Rom 1:24), from which comes also the whole moral disorder that deforms both sexual life (Rom 1:24–27) and the functioning of *social, economic* (Rom 1:28–32), and even cultural *life:* "Although they knew the judgment of God, that those who do such things deserve death, they not only continue to do them, but also approve those who do them" (Rom 1:32).

From the moment when, because of one man, sin entered the world (Rom 5:12), "the god of this world has blinded the minds of the unbelievers, to keep them from seeing the light of the gospel of the glory of Christ" (2 Cor 4:4), and for this reason also "the wrath of God is revealed from heaven against all ungodliness and injustice of those who suffocate the truth in injustice" (Rom 1:18).

For this reason, "creation itself waits with eager longing for the revelation of the sons of God...and cherishes the hope that it itself will be set free from the slavery of corruption to enter into the freedom of the glory of the children of God" (Rom 8:19–21), the freedom for which "Christ has freed us" (Gal 5:1).

The concept of "world" in *St. John* has many different meanings: in the First Letter of John the world is the place in which the threefold concupiscence manifests itself (1 Jn 2:15–16); and in which the false prophets and the enemies of Christ try to seduce the faithful, but Christians conquer the world thanks to their faith (1 Jn 5:4); the world, in fact, is passing away with its desires, and the one who does the will of God lives forever (see 1 Jn 2:17).

See P. Grelot, "Monde," *Dictionnaire de Spiritualité,* 1628ff. J. Mateos, J. Barreto, *Vocabolario teológico del Evangelio de Juan* (Madrid: Edic. Cristiandad, 1980), 211–15.

2. This man lives, as it were, at the pole opposite to what "the Spirit wants." The Spirit of God wants a reality that differs from that willed by the flesh: it strives for a reality that differs from the one the flesh strives for, already in man's interior, already at the inner well-spring of man's aspirations and actions, "so that you do not do what you want" (Gal 5:17).

Paul expresses this point even more explicitly when he writes else-where about the evil he does, although he does not will it, and about the impossibility—or rather the limited possibility—of accomplishing the good he "wills" (see Rom 7:19). Without entering into a detailed exegesis of this text, one could say that the tension between the "flesh" and the "spirit" is, first, immanent, although it is not reducible to this level. It manifests itself in man's heart as a "combat" between good and evil. The desire that Christ speaks about in the Sermon on the Mount (see Mt 5:27–28), though it is an "interior" act, remains cer-tainly—according to Pauline language—a manifestation of life "according to the flesh." At the same time, that desire allows us to verify *how, within man, life "according to the flesh" is opposed to life "according to the Spirit"* and how the latter, in man's present state, given his hereditary sinfulness, is constantly exposed to the weakness and insufficiency of the former, to which he often yields, unless he is strengthened within, in order to do "what the Spirit wants." We can conclude from this that Paul's words that deal with life "according to the flesh" and "according to the Spirit" are simultaneously a synthesis and a program; and one needs to understand them in this key.

3. We find the same antithesis between life "according to the flesh" and life "according to the Spirit" in Romans. Here too (as in Galatians) it is set in the context of the Pauline teaching about *justifi-cation* by faith, that is, by *the power of Christ* himself *working in man's innermost [being] through the Holy Spirit.* In this context, Paul carries his antithesis to its ultimate consequences when he writes:

> For those who live according to the flesh set their minds on the things of the flesh, but those who live according to the Spirit on the things of the Spirit. But the desires of the flesh lead to death while the desires of the Spirit lead to life and peace. In fact, the desires of the flesh are in revolt against God because they do not submit to God's law *nor are they able to.* Those who live according to the flesh cannot please God.

But you are not under the dominion of the flesh but of the Spirit from the moment that the Spirit of God dwells in you. If anyone does not have the Spirit of Christ, he does not belong to him. And if Christ is in you, your body is dead because of sin, but the Spirit is life because of justification. (Rom 8:5–10)

4. One can clearly see the *horizons* Paul sketches in this text: he *goes back to the "beginning"*—that is, in this case, to the first sin, which was the origin of life "according to the flesh" and which created in man the inheritance of a predisposition for living such a life, together with the heritage of death. *At the same time Paul looks ahead toward the final victory over sin and over death*, of which Christ's resurrection is a sign and pre-announcement: "The one who raised Jesus from the dead will give life also to your mortal bodies by his Spirit, which dwells in you" (Rom 8:11). In this eschatological perspective, Paul stresses the *"justification in Christ" intended already for "historical" man*, for every human being of "yesterday, today, and tomorrow" in the history of the world and also the history of salvation: a justification that is essential for the inner man and is intended precisely for that "heart" to which Christ appealed when he spoke about "purity" and "impurity" in the moral sense. This "justification" by faith does not constitute simply a dimension of the divine plan of salvation and of man's sanctification, but according to St. Paul it is *a real power at work in man that reveals and affirms itself in his actions.*

"Works of the Flesh" and "Fruit of the Spirit"

5. Here again are the words of Galatians, "Now the works of the flesh are obvious: fornication, impurity, licentiousness, idolatry, sorcery, enmities, strife, jealousy, anger, quarrels, dissensions, factions, envy, drunkenness, orgies, and things like these.... The fruit of the Spirit is love, joy, peace, patience, kindness, generosity, faithfulness, gentleness, and self-mastery" (Gal 5:19–23). In Paul's teaching, life "according to the flesh" opposes life "according to the Spirit" not only in man's interior, in his "heart," but as one can see, it finds a wide and differentiated *field for translating itself into works.* Paul speaks, on the one hand, about "works" born from the "flesh"—one could say works in which the man who lives "according to the flesh" manifests himself—and, on the other hand, about the *"fruit of the Spirit,"* that is, about actions,[62] modes of behavior, and virtues, in which the man who lives "according to the Spirit" manifests himself. While in the first case we are dealing with the man abandoned to the threefold concupiscence, about which John says that it comes "from the world," in the second case we are faced with what we have already called the ethos of redemption. Only now are we able to clarify fully *the nature and the structure of this ethos*. It expresses itself through that which in man, in all his "working," in actions and behavior, is the fruit of mastery over the threefold concupiscence: of the flesh, of the eyes, and of the pride of life (of all that the human heart can rightly be "accused" of and that man and his interiority can continually be "suspected" of).

6. If mastery in the sphere of ethos manifests and realizes itself as "love, joy, peace, patience, kindness, generosity, faithfulness, gentleness, and self-mastery"—as we read in Galatians—then behind each of these realizations, these forms of behavior, these moral virtues,

---

62. Exegetes point out that, even if for Paul the concept of "fruit" is applied also to the "works of the flesh" (e.g., Rom 6:21; 7:5), nevertheless "the fruit of the Spirit" is never called "work."

For Paul, "works" are the acts proper to man (or that in which Israel, without reason, places its hope), for which he will be answerable before God.

Paul also avoids the term "virtue," *aretē*; it is found only once, in a very general sense, in Phil 4:8. In the Greek world, this word had an excessively anthropocentric meaning; the Stoics in particular emphasized the self-sufficiency or *autarchia* of virtue.

By contrast, the term "fruit of the Spirit" underlines *God's action* in human beings. This "fruit" grows in them as *the gift* of a life whose only Author is God; man can, at the most, provide for favorable circumstances that the fruit may grow and mature.

The fruit of the Spirit, in the singular form, corresponds in some way to the "*righteousness*" of the Old Testament, which embraces the whole of a life in conformity with God's will; it also corresponds in some way to the "virtue" of the Stoics, which was indivisible. We see it, for example in Ephesians 5:9–11: "the *fruit* of the light is found *in all that is good and right and true*...take no part *in the unfruitful works* of darkness." Nevertheless, the fruit of the Spirit differs from both "justice" and "virtue," because (in all its manifestations and differentiations observable in the catalogues of virtues) it contains the effect of the action of the Spirit, who, in the Church, is the foundation and realization of the life of a Christian.

H. Schlier, *Der Brief an die Galater*, Meyer's Kommentar, 5th ed. (Göttingen: Vandenhoeck-Ruprecht, 1971), 255–64; O. Bauernfeind, "*aretē*," *Theological Dictionary of the New Testament*, 1:460; W. Tatarkiewicz, *Historia Filozofii*, vol. 1 (Warszawa: PWN, 1970) 121; E. Kamlah, *Die Form der katalogischen Paränese im Neuen Testament*, Wissenschaftliche Untersuchungen zum Neuen Testament 7 (Tübingen: Mohr-Siebeck, 1964), 14.

stands a *specific choice,* that is, an effort of the will, a *fruit of the human spirit* permeated by the Spirit of God, which manifests itself in choosing the good. To speak in Paul's language, "The Spirit has desires contrary to the flesh" (Gal 5:17), and in these "desires" it proves to be stronger than the "flesh" and the desires brought into being by the threefold concupiscence. In this struggle between good and evil, man proves to be *stronger thanks to the power of the Holy Spirit, who,* working within the human spirit, causes *its desires to bear fruit in the good.* These are therefore not only—and not so much—"works" of man, but more a "fruit," that is, an effect, of the action of the "Spirit" in man. This is why Paul speaks about "the fruit of the 'Spirit,'" understanding this word with a capital letter.

Without entering into the structures of human interiority by means of the subtle distinctions provided for us by systematic theology (especially beginning with Thomas Aquinas), we limit ourselves to a synthesis of biblical teaching that allows us to grasp in an essential and sufficient way the distinction and antithesis between "flesh" and the "Spirit."

We observed that among the fruits of the Spirit the Apostle also mentions "self-mastery." We should not forget this point, because in our further reflections we will take up this subject again to discuss it in more detail.

52 General Audience of January 7, 1981
(*Insegnamenti*, 4, no. 1 [1981]: 29–33)

1. WHAT IS THE MEANING OF THE STATEMENT: "The flesh has desires contrary to the Spirit, and the Spirit has desires contrary to the flesh" (Gal 5:17)? This question seems important, in fact fundamental, in the context of our reflections about the purity of heart mentioned in the Gospel. In this regard, however, the author of Galatians opens horizons before us that are even vaster. This antithesis of the "flesh" to the Spirit (Spirit of God), and of life "according to the flesh" to life "according to the Spirit," contains the Pauline theology of justification, that is, the expression of faith in *the anthropological and ethical realism of the redemption brought about by Christ,* which Paul, in a context already known to us, also calls "redemption of the

body." According to Romans (8:23), the "redemption of the body" also has a "cosmic" dimension (with respect to the whole of creation), but at its center stands man: man constituted in the personal unity of spirit and body. It is precisely in this man, in his "heart" and thus in all his behavior, that the redemption of Christ bears fruit, thanks to the powers of the Spirit that bring about "justification," that is, that cause justice to "abound" in man, as the Sermon on the Mount insistently teaches (Mt 5:20), that is, to "abound" in the measure God himself wills and expects.

2. It is significant that in speaking about the "works of the flesh" (Gal 5:11–21) Paul mentions not only "fornication, impurity, licentiousness...drunkenness, orgies"—thus, according to an objective way of understanding, everything that possesses the character of "sins of the flesh" and of sensual enjoyment connected with the flesh—but mentions other sins as well to which we would not be inclined to attribute a "carnal" and "sensual" character: "idolatry, sorcery, enmities, strife, jealousy, anger, quarrels, dissensions, factions, envy..." (Gal 5:20–21). According to our anthropological (and ethical) categories, we would tend *to call* all the works in this list *"sins of the human spirit" rather than "sins of the flesh."* Not without reason we could see in them the effects of the "concupiscence of the eyes" or of the "pride of life." Nevertheless, Paul describes all of them as "works of the flesh." One can only understand this way of speaking on the background of that broader (and in some way metonymical) meaning that the term "flesh" takes on in the Pauline letters, since it is used as the antithesis not only of the human "spirit," but also of the Holy Spirit, who works in man's soul (in his spirit).

3. There is thus a significant analogy between Paul's definition of "works of the flesh" and the words with which Christ explains to his disciples what he had first said to the Pharisees about ritual "purity" and "impurity" (see Mt 15:2–20). According to Christ's words, true "purity" (as well as "impurity") has its seat in the "heart" and proceeds "from" the human "heart." He defines as "impure works" in the same sense not only "adultery" and "prostitution," that is, the "sins of the flesh" in the restricted sense, but also "evil intentions...theft, false witness, curses." As we observed above, Christ uses *the general as well as* *the specific sense of "impurity"* (and thus indirectly also of "purity"). *St. Paul expresses himself in an analogous manner:* he understands the works of the "flesh" in the general as well as in the specific sense. All sins *are expressions of life "according to the flesh"* in contrast to "life according to the Spirit." What we consider a "sin of the flesh," in accord with our linguistic convention (partly justified, by the way), is in the Pauline list one of the many manifestations (or species) of what he calls "works of the flesh" and thus one of the symptoms, that is, one of the actualizations of life "according to the flesh" and not "according to the Spirit."

"Flesh" and "The Freedom for Which Christ Set Us Free"

4. Paul's words to the Romans, "So then, brothers, we are debtors, not to the flesh, to live according to the flesh; for if you live according to the flesh, you will die; but if by the Spirit you put to death the deeds of the body, you will live" (Rom 8:12–13), introduce us in a new way into the rich and differentiated sphere of meanings that the terms "body" and "spirit" have for him. The definitive meaning of this statement, however, is parenetic, exhortative, and thus valid for the ethos of the Gospel. When Paul speaks about the necessity of putting to death deeds of the body with the help of the Spirit, he expresses precisely what Christ spoke about in the Sermon on the Mount when he appealed to the human heart and exhorted it to mastery over desires, including those that express themselves in a man's "look" directed toward a woman with the purpose of satisfying the concupiscence of the flesh. Such *mastery*, or, as Paul writes, *"putting to death the deeds of the body by the Spirit," is an indispensable condition of "life according to the Spirit,"* that is, of the "life" that is the antithesis of the "death" about which he speaks in the same context. Life "according to the flesh" bears fruit, in fact, in "death," that is, it brings with it the "death" of the Spirit.

The term "death," therefore, does not signify only bodily death, but also the sin that theology was to call mortal. In Romans and Galatians, the Apostle continually extends the horizon of "sin-death," both toward the "beginning" of human history and toward its end.

And thus, after listing the many forms of "works of the flesh," he says, "those who do such things will not inherit the kingdom of God" (Gal 5:21). Elsewhere he will write with the same firmness: "Be sure of this, that no fornicator or impure person, or one who is greedy," that is, an idolater, "has any inheritance in the kingdom of Christ and of God" (Eph 5:5). Also in this case, *the works that exclude one from sharing "in the kingdom of Christ and of God"*—that is, the "works of the flesh"—are listed as an example and in a general sense, though in the first place one finds here the sins against "purity" in the specific sense (see Eph 5:3–7).

5. To complete the picture of the antithesis between the "body" and the "fruit of the Spirit" one must observe that in all that is a manifestation of life and behavior according to the Spirit, Paul sees at the same time the manifestation of that freedom for which Christ "has set us free" (Gal 5:1). And so he writes, "For you were called to freedom, brothers; only do not use your freedom as a pretext for living according to the flesh, but through love serve one another. For the whole law finds its fullness in a single commandment, 'You shall love your neighbor as yourself'" (Gal 5:13–14). As we pointed out above, the antithesis between "body" and "Spirit," between life "according to the flesh" and life "according to the Spirit," profoundly permeates the whole Pauline doctrine of justification. With exceptional force of conviction, the Apostle to the Gentiles proclaims that man's justification is achieved in Christ and for Christ. Man reaches *justification in "faith that works through love"* (Gal 5:6), and not only by observing individual precepts of the Old Testament law (in particular that of circumcision). Justification thus comes *"from the Spirit"* (of God) *and not "from the flesh."* He therefore exhorts the recipients of his letter to free themselves from the false "carnal" understanding of justification to follow the true one, that is, the "spiritual" understanding; in this sense he exhorts them to consider themselves free from the law, and even more so to be free with the freedom for which Christ "has set us free."

In this way, following the Apostle's thought, we should consider and above all realize evangelical purity, that is, purity of the heart, according to the measure of that freedom for which Christ "has set us free."

53 General Audience of January 14, 1981
(*Insegnamenti*, 4, no. 1 [1981]: 72–76)

1. ST. PAUL WRITES IN GALATIANS, "For you were called to freedom, brothers; only do not use your freedom as a pretext for living according to the flesh, but through love serve one another. For the whole law finds its fullness in a single commandment, 'You shall love your neighbor as yourself'" (Gal 5:13–14). Already a week ago, we dwelt on this statement; nevertheless, we are taking it up again in connection with the main topic of our reflections.

Although the passage just quoted refers above all to the topic of justification, nevertheless the Apostle explicitly intends to make us understand the ethical dimension of the antithesis between "body" and "Spirit," between life according to the flesh and life according to the Spirit. In fact, it is precisely here that he touches the essential point, revealing the very anthropological roots, as it were, of the ethos of the Gospel. If, in fact, "the whole law" (the moral law of the Old Testament) "finds its fullness" *in the commandment of love,* the dimension of the new ethos of the Gospel is nothing other than an *appeal to human freedom,* an appeal for its fullest realization and in some way for the fullest "use" of the powers of the human spirit.

2. It might seem that Paul is only setting freedom against the law, and the law against freedom. A deeper analysis shows, however, that in Galatians St. Paul underlines above all the ethical subordination of freedom to that element in which the whole law is fulfilled, namely, love, which is the content of the greatest commandment in the Gospel. "*Christ* has set us free that we might remain free," precisely inasmuch as he showed us the ethical (and theological) subordination of freedom to love and *linked freedom with the commandment of love.* Understanding the vocation to freedom in this way ("You were called to freedom"—Gal 5:13) means forming the ethos in which life "according to the Spirit" is realized. There is, in fact, also the danger of understanding freedom wrongly, and Paul clearly points to it by writing in the same context, "Only do not use your freedom as a pretext for living according to the flesh, but through love serve one another" (Gal 5:13).

3. In other words, Paul warns us of the possibility of making bad use of freedom, a use that conflicts with the liberation of the human spirit achieved by Christ and contradicts that freedom with which "Christ set us free." In fact, Christ realized and showed the freedom that finds its fullness in love, the freedom thanks to which we "serve one another"; in other words: the *freedom that becomes the source of new "works" and of "life" according to the Spirit.* The antithesis and in some way the negation of this freedom takes place when it becomes "a pretext for living according to the flesh." In that case, freedom becomes a source of "works" and of "life" according to the flesh. It ceases to be the authentic freedom for which "Christ set us free" and becomes "a pretext for living according to the flesh," a source (or instrument) of a specific subjugation under the pride of life, the concupiscence of the eyes, and the concupiscence of the flesh. The one who *lives* in this way, *"according to the flesh,"* that is, who subjects himself—even if not altogether consciously, nevertheless effectively—to the threefold concupiscence, particularly to the concupiscence of the flesh, *ceases to be capable of this freedom* for which "Christ has set us free"; he also ceases to be suitable *for the true gift* of self, which is the fruit and expression of such freedom. He further ceases to be capable of the gift organically linked with the spousal meaning of the human body, which we discussed above in the analyses of Genesis (see Gen 2:23, 25).

Purity—"Keeping the Passions Away" or "Keeping the Body with Holiness and Reverence"?

4. In this way, the Pauline doctrine about purity, a doctrine in which we find the faithful and authentic echo of the Sermon on the Mount, allows us to see Christian "purity of heart" according to the Gospel in a broader perspective and allows us above all to link it with love, in which "the whole law finds its fullness." In a way analogous to Christ, Paul knows a twofold meaning of "purity" and "impurity": a generic and a specific sense. In the first meaning, everything that is morally good is "pure," while everything that is morally bad is "impure." This is clear in Christ's words according to Matthew 15:18–20 quoted above. In Paul's statements about the "works of the flesh," which he contrasts with the "fruit of the Holy Spirit," we find the basis for understanding the problem in an analogous way. Among the "works of the flesh," Paul locates *what is morally evil*, while *every moral good* is linked with life "according to the Spirit." Thus, one of the manifestations of life "according to the Spirit" is behavior in conformity with the virtue that Paul seems to define rather indirectly in Galatians, but which he discusses directly in 1 Thessalonians.

5. In the passages from Galatians discussed in detail above, the Apostle lists in the first place among "works of the flesh," "fornication, impurity, licentiousness" (Gal 5:19); nevertheless, when he contrasts the "fruit of the Spirit" to these works, he does not directly speak about "purity," but only mentions "*self-mastery*," Greek *enkrateia* (Gal 5:22). One can recognize this "mastery" as a virtue that concerns continence in the area of all desires of the senses, above all in the sexual sphere, and thus in antithesis to "fornication, impurity, licentiousness" and also to "drunkenness" and "orgies." One could thus suppose that the Pauline "self-mastery" contains what is expressed in the term "continence" or "temperance," which corresponds to the Latin term *temperantia*. In that case we would find ourselves faced with the well-known system of virtues that later theology, especially Scholasticism, in some way borrows from Aristotle's ethics. Certainly, Paul himself does not use this system in his text. Since "purity" should be understood as the right way of treating the sexual sphere, depending on one's personal state of life (and not necessarily absolute abstinence from sexual life), such "purity" is doubtlessly included in the Pauline concept of "mastery" or *enkrateia*. For this reason, within the Pauline text we find only a generic and indirect mention of purity inasmuch as the author contrasts such "works of the flesh" as "fornication, impurity, licentiousness" with the "fruit of the Spirit," that is, with new works, in which "life according to the Spirit" manifests itself. One can deduce that one of these new works is precisely "purity," the purity that is the opposite of "impurity" as well as of "fornication" and "licentiousness."

6. Already in 1 Thessalonians, however, Paul writes explicitly and unequivocally about this topic. There we read, "For this is the will of God, your sanctification: that you abstain from unchastity; that each one of you knows how to keep his own body[63] with holiness and rev-

---

63. Without entering into the particular discussions of the exegetes, it should nevertheless be pointed out that the Greek expression *to heautou skeuos* can refer also to the wife (see 1 Pet 3:7).

erence, not as the object of lustful passions, like the Gentiles who do not know God." And then, "For God did not call us to impurity but to sanctification. Therefore whoever rejects these norms rejects not a human being but God, who gives his Holy Spirit to you" (1 Thess 4:3–5). Even though also in this text we are dealing with the general meaning of "purity," identified in this case with "sanctification" (inasmuch as "impurity" is named as the antithesis of "sanctification"), nevertheless the *whole* context clearly indicates *what the "purity" or "impurity" in question is, that is, what* the "impurity" mentioned here by Paul *consists in and how "purity" contributes* to man's *"sanctification."*

For this reason, we should take up again this passage from 1 Thessalonians in our future reflections.

54 *General Audience of January 28, 1981* *(Insegnamenti, 4, no. 1 [1981]: 177–80)*

1. ST. PAUL WRITES IN 1 Thessalonians, "For this is the will of God, your sanctification: that you abstain from unchastity; that each one of you knows how to keep his own body with holiness and reverence, not as the object of lustful passions" (1 Thess 4:3–5). And one verse later he continues, "For God did not call us to impurity but to sanctification. Therefore whoever rejects these norms rejects not a man but God, who gives his Holy Spirit to you" (1 Thess 4:7–8). We spoke about these words of the Apostle during our last meeting, on January 14. Today we take them up again because they are particularly important for the topic of our meditations.

2. The purity about which Paul speaks in 1 Thessalonians (see 1 Thess 4:3–5, 7–8) shows itself in the fact that man "knows how to keep his own body with holiness and reverence, not as the object of lustful passions." In this formulation, every word has a particular meaning and calls for an adequate comment.

In the first place, purity is an "ability" or, in the traditional language of anthropology and ethics, an attitude. And in this sense it is a virtue. When this ability, that is, virtue, leads to abstaining "from unchastity," it does so because the man who possesses it knows "how to keep his own body with holiness and reverence, not as the object of lustful passions." What we have here is *a practical ability that enables man to act* in a definite way and at the same time *not to act* in a contrary way. Purity must obviously take root in the will, in the very foundation of man's conscience and acting, if it is to be such an ability or attitude. In his teaching on the virtues, Thomas Aquinas sees the object of purity even more directly in the power of sense-desire, which he calls "*appetitus concupiscibilis*." This power in particular must be "mastered," ordered, and enabled to act in a manner conforming to virtue, if "purity" is to be attributed to a human being. According to this view, purity consists above all in holding back the impulses of sense-desire, which has as its object what is bodily and sexual in man. Purity is a variant of the virtue of temperance.

3. The text from 1 Thessalonians (see 1 Thess 4:3–5) shows that the virtue of purity in Paul's view consists also in mastering and overcoming "lustful passions"; this means that the ability to hold back the impulses of desires, that is, the virtue of *temperance,* belongs necessarily to its nature. At the same time, however, the Pauline text turns our attention to another function of the virtue of purity, to another dimension—one could say—that is more positive than negative.

The task of purity emphasized by the author of the letter is not only (and not so much) abstaining from "unchastity" and from what leads to it, that is, abstaining from "lustful passions," but, at the same time, keeping one's body, and indirectly that of the other, in "holiness and reverence."

These two functions, "*abstaining*" and "*keeping,*" are strictly connected and *dependent on each other.* Since it is in fact impossible to "keep the body with holiness and reverence" without this abstinence "from unchastity" and what it leads to, one can assume as a consequence that keeping the body (one's own and that of the other) "with holiness and reverence" gives an appropriate meaning and value to this abstinence. This abstinence requires by its essence the overcoming of something that exists in man and that is born spontaneously in him as an inclination, as attraction, and also as a value that acts above all in the sphere of the senses, but very often not without repercussions in the other dimensions of human subjectivity, particularly in the affective-emotive sphere.

4. Considering all this, it seems that the Pauline image of the virtue of purity—an image that emerges from the very eloquent placement of the function of "abstinence" (that is, temperance) next to that of "keeping the body with holiness and reverence"—is deeply *right, complete, and adequate.* We owe this completeness perhaps to nothing other than the fact that Paul considers purity not only as an ability (or aptitude) of man's subjective faculties, but at the same time as a concrete manifestation of life "according to the Spirit" in which human ability is made fruitful from within and enriched by what Paul calls the "fruit of the Spirit" (Gal 5:22). *The reverence* born in man for everything bodily and sexual, both in himself and in every other human being, male and female, turns out to be the most essential power for keeping the body "with holiness." In order to understand the Pauline teaching about purity, one must enter deeply into the meaning of the term "reverence," obviously understood here as a power belonging to the spiritual order. It is precisely this interior power that gives full dimension to purity as a virtue, that is, as an ability to act in that whole sphere in which man discovers, in his own innermost [being], the many impulses of "lustful passions" and at times, for various reasons, surrenders to them.

Analysis of the Pauline "Description of the Body" (1 Cor 12:18–27)

5. For a better understanding of the thought of the author of 1 Thessalonians, it will be good to have one further text present to us, which we find in 1 Corinthians. In this text, Paul sets forth his great *ecclesiological teaching* according to which the Church is the body of Christ; he uses the occasion to formulate the following argument about the human body. "God arranged the members in the body, each one of them, as he willed" (1 Cor 12:18); and a little further, "On the contrary, the members of the body that seem weaker are more necessary, and those members of the body that we think less honorable we clothe with greater reverence, and our unpresentable members are treated with greater modesty; whereas our more presentable members do not need this. But God has so arranged the body, giving the greater honor to the member that lacked it, so that there may be no disunion within the body, but the members may have care for one another" (1 Cor 12:22–25).

6. Although the topic of the text just quoted is the theology of the Church as the body of Christ, one can nevertheless note in the mar-

gin of this passage that with his great ecclesiological analogy (which recurs in other letters and which we will take up again in due course) Paul contributes at the same time to a *deeper understanding of the theology of the body.* While in 1 Thessalonians he writes about keeping the body "with holiness and reverence," in the passage just quoted from 1 Corinthians he wants to show this human body as deserving reverence or respect; one could also say that he wants to teach the recipients of his letter the right understanding of the human body.

Thus, this Pauline description of the human body in 1 Corinthians seems to be strictly tied to the recommendations of 1 Thessalonians, "that each one of you knows how to keep his own body with holiness and reverence" (1 Thess 4:4). This is an important line of thought, perhaps the essential one of the Pauline teaching on purity.

55 *General Audience of February 4, 1981* (*Insegnamenti*, 4, no. 1 [1981]: 225–29)

1. IN OUR CONSIDERATIONS last Wednesday about purity according to the teaching of St. Paul, we called attention to the text from 1 Corinthians. In this text, the Apostle presents the Church as the body of Christ, and this offers him the occasion for the following argument about the human body: "God arranged the members in the body, each one of them, as he willed.... The members of the body that seem to be weaker are more necessary, and those members of the body that we think less honorable we clothe with greater reverence, and our unpresentable members are treated with greater modesty; whereas our more presentable members do not need this. But God has so arranged the body, giving the greater honor to the member that lacked it, that there may be no disunion within the body, but the members may have care for one another" (1 Cor 12:18, 22–25).

2. The Pauline "description" of the human body corresponds to the reality that constitutes the body; it is thus a "realistic" description. At the same time, the description weaves into its realism a very subtle thread of evaluation that gives it a deeply evangelical, Christian value. It is certainly possible to "describe" the human body, to express its truth with the objectivity proper to the natural sciences; but such a description—with all its precision—cannot be adequate (that is, com-

mensurate with its object), given that *what is at issue is not only the body* (understood as an organism in the "somatic" sense) but also *man who expresses himself by means of that body,* and in this sense, I would say, "is" that body. In this way, since it is a question of man as a person, *that thread of evaluation* is indispensable for describing the human body. One should also remark how right this evaluation is. This is one of the perennial tasks and themes of all culture: of literature, sculpture, painting, as well as dancing, theater, and finally of the culture of daily life, private or social. This is a subject that would be worth discussing separately.

3. The Pauline description in 1 Corinthians (12:18–25) does not, of course, have a "scientific" meaning: it does not present a biological study on the human organism or human "*somatology.*" From this point of view, it is a simple "pre-scientific" description, concise, consisting only of a few phrases. It has all the characteristics of common realism and is without doubt sufficiently "realistic." However, what shapes its specific character, what particularly justifies its presence in Sacred Scripture, is precisely this evaluation woven into the description and expressed in its "narrative-realistic" plot. One can certainly say that *this description would not be possible without the whole truth of creation;* nor without the truth of the "*redemption of the body,*" which Paul professes and proclaims. One can also say that the Pauline description of the body *corresponds precisely to the* spiritual *attitude of "reverence"* for the human body that is due to the "holiness" (see 1 Thess 4:3–5, 7–8) that wells up from the mysteries of creation and redemption. The Pauline description is equally far from Manichaean contempt for the body and the various manifestations of a naturalistic "cult of the body."

4. The author of 1 Corinthians (12:18–25) has before his eyes the human body in all its truth: the body, therefore, permeated above all (if one may express it this way) by the whole reality of the person and its dignity. At the same time, it is the body of "historical" man, male and female, that is, of that man who, after sin, was conceived, so to speak, within and from the reality of the man who had shared in the experience of original innocence. In Paul's expressions about "unpresentable members" of the human body as well as about those that "seem to be weaker" or those "that we think less honorable," we find,

it seems to us, *the testimony of the same shame* that the first human beings, male and female, had experienced after original sin. This shame impressed itself on them and on all generations of "historical" man as the fruit of the threefold concupiscence (with particular reference to the concupiscence of the flesh). And what impressed itself at the same time—as we emphasized in our earlier analyses—is a certain "echo" of the same original innocence of man: a photographic "negative," as it were, the "positive" of which was precisely original innocence.

5. The Pauline "description" of the human body completely confirms our earlier analyses, it seems. In the human body there are "unpresentable members," not by reason of their "somatic" nature (for a scientific physiological description treats all members and organs of the human body in a "neutral" way, with the same objectivity), but only and exclusively because *in man himself there exists the shame* that *perceives* some members of the body as *"unpresentable"* and leads to considering them as such. This same shame seems to be at the same time the basis of what the Apostle says in 1 Corinthians: "Those members of the body that we think less honorable we clothe with greater reverence, and our unpresentable members are treated with greater modesty" (1 Cor 12:23). Thus, one can say that *from shame is born "reverence"* for one's own body, a reverence that Paul asks us to keep (1 Thess 4:4). Precisely this keeping of the body "with holiness and reverence" is to be considered essential for the virtue of purity.

6. Returning to the Pauline "description" of the body in 1 Corinthians (12:18–25), we wish to call attention to the fact that according to the author of the letter the particular effort to reach reverence for the human body and especially for its "weaker" or "unpresentable" members corresponds to the Creator's original plan or to the vision about which Genesis speaks: "God saw everything that he had made, and indeed, it was very good" (Gen 1:31). Paul writes, "God has so arranged the body, giving the greater honor to the member that lacked it, that there may be no disunion within the body, but the members may have care for one another" (1 Cor 12:24–25). *"Disunion within the body,"* the result of which is that some members are considered "weaker," "less honorable," and thus "unpresentable," is a further

expression of the *vision of man's*—that is, *historical man's*—interior *state* after original sin. The man of original innocence, male and female, about whom we read, "both were naked...but they did not feel shame" (Gen 2:25), did not feel that "disunion within the body" either. An analogous harmony in man's innermost [being], the harmony of the "heart," corresponded to the objective harmony that the Creator gave to the human body, which Paul explains as reciprocal care of the various members (1 Cor 12:25). This harmony, or precisely "purity of heart," allowed man and woman in the state of original innocence to experience in a simple way (in a way that made both of them originally happy) the unitive power of their bodies that was, so to speak, the "unsuspectable" substratum of their personal union or *communio personarum*.

7. As one can see, in 1 Corinthians (12:18–25) the Apostle ties his description of the human body to the state of "historical" man. At the threshold of the history of this man stands the experience of shame connected with "disunion in the body," with the sense of modesty for this body (and especially for those of its members that determine masculinity and femininity in somatic terms). Nevertheless, in the same "description," Paul also indicates *the way that* leads (precisely on the basis of the sense of shame) to the transformation of this state, to the *gradual victory over this "disunion in the body,"* a victory that can and should be realized in the human heart. This is precisely the road of purity or of keeping the body "with holiness and reverence." In 1 Corinthians (12:18–25), Paul takes up again the "reverence" he discussed in 1 Thessalonians (4:3–5) by using some equivalent expressions, when he speaks about "reverence" or esteem toward the "less honorable," "weaker" members of the body and when he commends greater "modesty" in regard to what is considered "unpresentable" in man. These ways of speaking characterize that "reverence" more closely, above all in the sphere of human relationships and behavior with regard to the body, which is important both with regard to "one's own" body and evidently also in reciprocal relations (especially between man and woman, but not limited to them).

We have no doubt that the "description" of the human body in 1 Corinthians has a fundamental significance for the Pauline teaching about purity as a whole.

56 *General Audience of February 11, 1981*
(*Insegnamenti*, 4, no. 1 [1981]: 258–61)

1. DURING OUR RECENT Wednesday meetings [see TOB 53:4–55] we analyzed two passages, one from 1 Thessalonians (4:3–5), the other from 1 Corinthians (12:18–25), to show what seems to be essential in St. Paul's teaching about purity, understood in the moral sense, that is, as a virtue. If in the text quoted from 1 Thessalonians one can observe that purity consists in temperance, nevertheless in this text and also in 1 Corinthians, the aspect of "reverence" is emphasized as well. Through such reverence, which is owed to the human body (and we add that according to 1 Corinthians reverence is seen in relation to its component of modesty), purity as a Christian virtue is revealed in the Pauline letters as an effective way of detaching oneself from what is a fruit of the concupiscence of the flesh in the human heart. Abstaining "from unchastity," which implies keeping the body "with holiness and reverence," allows us to deduce that according to the Apostle's teaching, purity is an *"ability" centered on the dignity of the body*, that is, on the *dignity of the person* in relation to his or her own body, to the masculinity or femininity that shows itself in that body. Understood as "ability," purity is precisely an expression and fruit of life "according to the Spirit" in the full sense of the term, that is, as a new ability of the human being in whom the gift of the Holy Spirit bears fruit. These two dimensions of purity—the moral dimension or *virtue* and the charismatic dimension or *gift* of the Holy Spirit—are present and strictly connected in Paul's message. This connection is emphasized by the Apostle in 1 Corinthians, where he calls the body the "*temple* (and thus dwelling place and sanctuary) *of the Holy Spirit*" (6:19).

Purity as a Virtue and a Gift

2. "Or do you not know that your body is a temple of the Holy Spirit within you, which you have from God, and that you do not belong to yourselves?" Paul asks the Corinthians (1 Cor 6:19) after having instructed them with much severity about the moral demands of purity. "Flee from prostitution! Any sin that a man commits is outside his body; but the one who gives himself to fornication sins

against his own body" (1 Cor 6:18). The particular mark of the sin stigmatized here by the Apostle is that this *sin*, in contrast to all others, is "*against the body*" (while the other sins are "outside the body"). Thus, we find in Pauline terminology the reason for the expressions "sins of the body" or "sins of the flesh." These are the antithesis of the virtue by the power of which man keeps "his own body with holiness and reverence" (1 Thess 4:3–5).

3. Such sins bring with themselves the "*profaning*" *of the body*: they deprive the woman's or man's body of the reverence that is its due because of the dignity of the person. The Apostle, however, goes further: according to him, a sin against the body is also a "*profaning of the temple*." What is decisive for the dignity of the human body, in Paul's eyes, is not only the human spirit, thanks to which man is constituted as a personal subject, but much more so the supernatural reality of the indwelling and continuous presence of the Holy Spirit in man—in his soul and in his body—as the fruit of the redemption accomplished by Christ. It follows from this that man's "body" is no longer only "his own." Not only because it is the body of a person does it merit that reverence the manifestation of which in the reciprocal behavior of human beings, male and female, constitutes the virtue of purity. When the Apostle writes, "Or do you not know that your body is a temple of the Holy Spirit within you, which you have from God" (1 Cor 6:19), he means to show *a further source of the dignity of the body*, namely, the Holy Spirit, who is also the source of the *moral duty* that derives from such dignity.

4. What constitutes this source is the reality of redemption, which is also "redemption of the body." For Paul, this mystery of faith is a living reality, directly oriented to every human being. Through redemption, every human being has received himself and his own body anew, as it were, from God. Christ inscribed in the human body—in the body of every man and of every woman—a new dignity, because he himself has taken up the human body together with the soul into union with the person of the Son-Word. From this new dignity, through the "redemption of the body," a new obligation was born at the same time, about which Paul writes in a concise but very moving way: "You were bought at a great price" (1 Cor 6:20). *The fruit of redemption* is indeed the *Holy Spirit*, who dwells in man and his body as in a temple. In this Gift, which makes every human being holy, the Christian receives himself anew as a gift from God. And this new twofold gift gives rise to an obligation. The Apostle refers to this dimension of obligation when he writes to believers, who are aware of the Gift, to convince them not to commit "unchastity," not to "sin against their own bodies" (1 Cor 6:18). "The body is not for unchastity but for the Lord, and the Lord for the body" (1 Cor 6:13). It is difficult to express more concisely what the mystery of the Incarnation implies for every believer. For this reason, the fact that in Jesus Christ the human body became the body of the God-Man has the effect of a new supernatural elevation in every human being, which every Christian must take into account in his behavior toward "his own" body and obviously also toward another's body: man toward woman and woman toward man. *The redemption of the body* brings with it the establishment in Christ and for Christ of a new *measure of the holiness of the body*. Paul appeals precisely to this holiness when he writes in 1 Thessalonians that one should "keep one's own body with holiness and reverence" (1 Thess 4:4).

5. In 1 Corinthians 6, Paul explains the truth about the holiness of the body in more detail, when he stigmatizes "unchastity" with drastic words as a sin against the holiness of the body, as the sin of impurity. "Do you not know that your bodies are members of Christ? Should I therefore take the members of Christ and make them members of a prostitute? Never! Or do you not know that whoever is united to a prostitute becomes one body with her? For it is said, 'The two will be one flesh.' But anyone united to the Lord forms one spirit with him" (1 Cor 6:15–17). If purity, according to Paul's teaching, is an aspect of "life according to the Spirit," this is to say that what bears fruit in it is *the mystery of the redemption of the body* as part of the mystery of Christ begun in the Incarnation and already by the Incarnation addressed to every human being. This mystery *bears fruit also in purity, understood as a particular commitment based on ethics*. The fact that we "were bought at a great price" (1 Cor 6:20), the price of Christ's act of redemption, makes precisely a new special commitment spring forth, namely, the duty of "keeping one's own body with holiness and reverence." The awareness of the redemption of the body is at work in the human will in favor of abstaining from "unchastity";

in fact, it acts for the end of letting the person gain an appropriate ability or capacity called the virtue of purity.

The words of 1 Corinthians 6:15–17 show that Paul's teaching about the Christian virtue of purity as a realization of life "according to the Spirit" is particularly profound and has the power of the supernatural realism of faith. We will have to come back to this topic more than once.

57 General Audience of March 18, 1981
(*Insegnamenti*, 4, no. 1 [1981]: 682–86)

1. IN OUR MEETING a few weeks ago, we focused attention on the passage in 1 Corinthians in which St. Paul calls the human body "temple of the Holy Spirit." He writes, "Or do you not know that your body is a temple of the Holy Spirit within you, which you have from God, and that you do not belong to yourselves? For you were bought at a great price" (1 Cor 6:19–20). "Do you not know that your bodies are members of Christ?" (1 Cor 6:15). The Apostle shows how the mystery of the "redemption of the body" achieved by Christ is the source of a particular moral duty that commits Christians to purity, to the virtue that Paul defines elsewhere as the need to "keep one's own body with holiness and reverence" (1 Thess 4:4).

2. Yet, we would not discover the full depth of the richness of thought contained in the Pauline texts if we did not notice that the mystery of redemption bears fruit in man *also in a charismatic way*. The Holy Spirit, who according to the Apostle's words enters into the human body as into his own "temple," dwells there and works with his spiritual gifts. Among these gifts, known to the history of spirituality as the seven gifts of the Holy Spirit (see Isa 11:2), the one most congenial to the virtue of purity seems to be *the gift of "piety"* (*eusebeia; donum pietatis*).[64] If purity disposes man to "keep his own body with

---

64. In the Greco-Roman period, *eusebeia* or *pietas* generally referred to the veneration of the gods (as "devotion"), but it still preserves its original and wider meaning of reverence for the *vital* structures of life.

Eusebeia expressed the mutual behavior of relatives, relations between spouses, and also the attitude owed by the legions to Caesar or of slaves to their master.

In the New Testament, only the later writings apply *eusebeia* to Christians; in the earlier writings, this term characterizes the "good pagans" (Acts 10:2, 7; 17:23).

holiness and reverence," as we read in 1 Thessalonians 4:3–5, piety as a gift of the Holy Spirit seems to serve purity in a particular way by making the human subject sensitive to the dignity that belongs to the human body in virtue of the mystery of creation and of redemption. Thanks to the gift of piety, Paul's words "Or do you not know that your body is a temple of the Holy Spirit within you...and that you do not belong to yourselves?" (1 Cor 6:19) take on the convincing power of an experience and become a living and lived truth in actions. They also open fuller access to the experience of the spousal meaning of the body and of the freedom of the gift connected with it, in which the deep face of purity and its organic link with love reveals itself.

3. Although keeping one's own body "with holiness and reverence" is formed *by abstaining from "unchastity"*—and this way is indispensable—nevertheless it always bears fruit in the deeper experience of the love that has from the "beginning" been inscribed in the whole human being and thus also in his body according to the image and likeness of God himself. For this reason, Paul ends his argument in 1 Corinthians 6 with a significant exhortation: "Therefore glorify God in your body" (v. 20). Purity as a virtue or ability of "keeping one's own body with holiness and reverence," allied with the gift of piety as a fruit of the Holy Spirit's dwelling in the "temple" of the body, causes in the body such a fullness of dignity in interpersonal relations that *God himself is thereby glorified.* Purity is the glory of the human body before God. It is the glory of God in the human body, through which masculinity and femininity are manifested. From purity springs that singular beauty that permeates every sphere of reciprocal common life between human beings and allows them to express in it the simplicity and depth, the cordiality and unrepeatable authenticity of personal trust. (There will perhaps be a later occasion to deal with this topic more fully. The link of purity with love, and the link of the same purity in love with piety as gift of the Holy Spirit, is a little known guiding thread of the theology of the body, but nevertheless deserves particularly deep study. This will be possible in the course of analyses about the sacramentality of marriage [see TOB 89 and 131–32].)

Although the Hellenistic *eusebeia*, like the *"donum pietatis,"* refers undoubtedly to the veneration of the divine, it has a wide base in connoting interhuman relationships. See W. Forester, "Eusebeia," *Theological Dictionary of the New Testament,* 2:177–82.

Purity and Wisdom

4. And now a short reference to the Old Testament. The Pauline teaching about purity understood as "life according to the Spirit" seems to suggest a certain *continuity* with the *Wisdom books of the Old Testament.* We find, for example, the following prayer for purity in thoughts, words, and deeds: "O Lord, Father and God of my life, ...let neither sensuality nor lust overcome me, and do not hand me over to shameful desires" (Sir 23:4–6). Purity is, in fact, a condition for finding wisdom and for following her, as we read in the same book. "Toward her," that is, wisdom, "I turned my desire and I found her in purity" (Sir 51:20). One could also consider the text of Wisdom 8:21, known by the liturgy in the Vulgate translation, "*Scivi quoniam aliter non possum esse continens, nisi Deus det; et hoc ipsum erat sapientiae, scire, cuius esset hoc donum.* [I knew that I could only be continent if God granted it, and that this also was part of wisdom, to know whose gift this was.]"[65]

According to this concept, it is not so much *purity that is a condition for wisdom,* but *wisdom that is a condition for purity as a particular gift of God.* It seems that already in the Wisdom texts just quoted the twofold meaning of purity takes shape: as virtue and as gift. The virtue stands at the service of wisdom, and wisdom disposes one to receive the gift that comes from God. This gift strengthens the virtue and allows one to enjoy in wisdom the fruits of a pure behavior and life.

5. Just as Christ, in the beatitude of the Sermon on the Mount that refers to the "pure in heart," highlights the "vision of God" as the fruit of purity *in an eschatological perspective,* so Paul on his part sheds light on its *radiation into the dimensions of temporality* when he writes, "To the pure all things are pure, but to the defiled and unbelieving nothing is pure. Their very minds and consciences are defiled. They profess to know God, but deny him by their actions" (Tit 1:15–16). These words can also refer to purity in the general as well as specific sense, as the characteristic mark of every moral good. What seems to

---

65. This Vulgate translation, preserved by the Neo-Vulgate and the liturgy, quoted a number of times by Augustine (*De S. Virg.,* par. 43; *Confess.* 6:11; 10:29; *Serm.,* CLX,7), *changes* the meaning of the original Greek, which should be translated as follows: "Knowing that I would not otherwise obtain her [that is, wisdom] if God did not grant her to me" (John Paul II's addition).

be fundamental for the Pauline understanding of purity in the sense in which 1 Thessalonians 4:3–5 and 1 Corinthians 6:13–20 speak about it, that is, in the sense of "life according to the Spirit,"—this is the conclusion of our considerations as a whole—is *the anthropology of rebirth in the Holy Spirit* (cf. Jn 3:5ff.). This anthropology grows from roots that plunge down into the reality of the redemption of the body achieved by Christ, a redemption whose final expression is the resurrection. There are deep reasons for linking the whole topic of purity with the words of the Gospel in which Jesus appeals to the resurrection. (This will be the topic of the next stage of our considerations [see TOB 64-85].) Here we have set it in relation above all with the ethos of the redemption of the body.

6. The way of understanding and presenting purity—as inherited from the tradition of the Old Testament and characteristic of the Wisdom books—was certainly an indirect but nonetheless real *preparation for the Pauline teaching* about purity understood as "life according to the Spirit." Without any doubt, that way of understanding also enabled many who listened to the Sermon on the Mount to understand the words of Christ when he appealed to the human heart in his explanation of the commandment "You shall not commit adultery!" Our reflections as a whole have thus been able to show, at least in some measure, how rich and deep the teaching on purity is in its biblical and evangelical sources.

7. The Gospel of Purity of Heart— Yesterday and Today

Theology of the Body

58 *General Audience of April 1, 1981* *(Insegnamenti, 4, no. 1 [1981]: 845–50)*

1. BEFORE CONCLUDING THE CYCLE of considerations about the words of Jesus in the Sermon on the Mount, we should recall these words once more and take up again in summary form the thread of

ideas whose basis they constitute. Here is the tenor of Jesus' words: "You have heard that it was said, 'You shall not commit adultery.' But I say to you: Whoever looks at a woman to desire her has already committed adultery with her in his heart" (Mt 5:27–28). These are *words of synthesis* that call for deep reflection, *analogous to* the words in which Christ *appealed to the "beginning."* When the Pharisees asked him—going back to the Law of Moses that allowed the so-called certificate of divorce—"Is it lawful for a man to divorce his wife for any reason?" he answered, "Have you not read that from the beginning the Creator created them male and female? 'For this reason a man will leave his father and his mother and unite with his wife, and the two will be one flesh.'... Therefore what God has joined let man not separate" (Mt 19:3–6). Also these words called for deep reflection to draw from them all the wealth contained in them. A reflection of this kind enabled us to outline the authentic *theology of the body.*

2. Following Christ's appeal to the beginning, we devoted a series of reflections to the relevant texts of Genesis that deal precisely with this "beginning." What emerged from these analyses was not only an image of the situation of man—male and female—in the state of original innocence, but also *the theological basis of man's truth,* the truth about his particular vocation that springs from the eternal mystery of the person as the image of God, incarnated in the visible and bodily fact *of the masculinity and femininity* of the human person. This truth stands at the basis of the answer given by Christ about the character of marriage and in particular about its indissolubility. It is the truth about man, a truth that plunges its roots deeply into the state of original innocence, a truth therefore that one must understand in the context of that situation before sin, as we attempted to do in the preceding cycle of our reflections.

3. At the same time, however, one must consider, understand, and interpret the same fundamental truth about man, his being male and female, in the prism of another situation, namely, the situation that came to be through the breaking of the first covenant with the Creator, that is, through original sin. One must see this truth about man—male and female—in the context of his hereditary sinfulness. And it is precisely *here that we encounter Christ's statement in the*

Sermon on the Mount. It is obvious that in the Sacred Scriptures of the Old and the New Covenant there are many stories, sentences, and words that confirm the same truth, namely, that "historical" man carries in himself the inheritance of original sin; nevertheless the words of Christ spoken in the Sermon on the Mount seem to have—in all their concise formulation—a particularly rich eloquence. This is shown by the analyses carried out earlier that gradually revealed what these words contain. To clarify the statements about concupiscence, one must grasp the biblical meaning of concupiscence itself—of the threefold concupiscence—and mainly of that of the flesh. One then comes to understand little by little why Jesus defines that concupiscence (precisely, "looking to desire" [in a reductive way]) as "adultery committed in the heart." When we carried out the analyses of this topic, we tried at the same time to grasp what meaning Christ's words had for his *immediate listeners,* educated in the tradition of the Old Testament, that is, in the tradition of the legislative texts, as well as Prophetic and Wisdom literature, and finally what meaning Christ's words can have for human beings of every other epoch and in particular for *contemporary man,* considering the various ways in which he is culturally conditioned. In fact, we are convinced that in their essential content these words refer to man in every place and at every time. In this consists also their value as a concise synthesis: to all they announce the truth that is valid and substantial for them.

4. What is this truth? Without any doubt, it is a *truth of an ethical character* and therefore, in the end, a normative truth, as normative as the truth contained in the commandment "You shall not commit adultery." Christ's interpretation of this commandment indicates the evil that must be avoided and defeated—the evil of the concupiscence of the flesh—and at the same time it points out the good for which the way is opened by overcoming [reductive] desires. This good is the "purity of heart" about which Christ speaks in the same context of the Sermon on the Mount. From the biblical point of view, "purity of heart" signifies being free from *every kind* of sin or guilt, not only from the sins that concern the "concupiscence of the flesh." Here, however, we are concerned particularly with one of the aspects of that "purity," namely, the contrary of adultery "committed in the heart." If

this *"purity of heart"* discussed by us is understood according to the thought of St. Paul *as "life according to the Spirit,"* then the Pauline context offers us a complete image of the content of the words Christ spoke in the Sermon on the Mount. These words contain a truth of an ethical nature, warning us to guard against evil and pointing out the moral good of human behavior; indeed, they direct the listeners to avoid the evil of concupiscence and to acquire purity of heart. These words, therefore, have a normative meaning, and at the same time they serve as a pointer. While they direct the listeners toward the good of "purity of heart," at the same time they point out the values to which the human heart can and should aspire.

5. Hence the question: what truth valid for every human being is contained in Christ's words? We must answer that what is contained in them is *not only an ethical truth, but also* the essential truth about man, *the anthropological truth.* This is precisely the reason why we return to these words in formulating the theology of the body, in strict relation with, and, so to speak, in the perspective of, the earlier words in which Christ appealed to the "beginning." One can affirm that with their expressive evangelical eloquence these words recall the man of original innocence to the conscience of the man of concupiscence. Yet, Christ's words are realistic. They do not attempt to make the human heart return to the state of original innocence, which man left behind in the moment in which he committed the original sin; rather, they point out to him *the path toward a purity of heart that is possible and accessible* for him even in the state of hereditary sinfulness. It is the purity of the "man of concupiscence," who is nevertheless inspired by the word of the Gospel and open to "life according to the Spirit" (in conformity with St. Paul's words), that is, the purity of the man of concupiscence who is completely enveloped by the "redemption of the body" achieved by Christ. This is precisely why we find in the words of the Sermon on the Mount the appeal to the "heart," that is, to the inner man. The inner man must open himself to life according to the Spirit, in order to share in evangelical purity of heart: in order to find again and realize the value of the body, freed by redemption from the bonds of concupiscence.

The normative meaning of Christ's words is deeply rooted in their anthropological meaning, in the dimension of human interiority.

6. According to the Gospel teaching developed so stupendously in the Pauline letters, purity is not only abstinence from unchastity (see 1 Thess 4:3), not only temperance, but at the same time it opens the way toward an ever more perfect discovery of the dignity of the human body, which is organically connected with the freedom of the gift of the person in the integral authenticity of its personal subjectivity, male or female. In this way, *purity in the sense of temperance* matures in the heart of the human being who cultivates it and who *seeks to discover and affirm the spousal meaning of the body* in its integral truth. Precisely this truth must be known in an interior way; it must in some way be "felt with the heart," so that the reciprocal relations between man and woman—and even mere looks—may regain that authentically spousal content of their meanings. And it is precisely this content that is pointed out in the Gospel by "purity of heart."

7. While in the inner experience of man (that is, of the man of concupiscence), "temperance" appears, so to speak, as a *negative* function, the analysis of Christ's words in the Sermon on the Mount linked with the texts of St. Paul allows us to shift this meaning *toward the positive* function of purity of the heart. In mature purity, man enjoys the fruits of victory over concupiscence, a victory about which St. Paul writes when he exhorts everyone to "keep his own body with holiness and reverence" (1 Thess 4:4). Even more, such maturity partly shows the efficaciousness of the gift of the Holy Spirit, whose "temple" the human body is (see 1 Cor 6:19). This gift is above all that of piety (*"donum pietatis"*), which gives back to the experience of the body—especially in the case of the sphere of reciprocal relations between man and woman—all *its simplicity, its lucid clarity,* and also *its interior joy.* This is evidently a very different spiritual climate than the "lustful passion" Paul writes about (which we know also from earlier analyses; it is enough to recall Sirach 26:13, 15–18). The satisfaction of the passions is, in fact, one thing, quite another is the joy a person finds in possessing himself more fully, since in this way he can also become more fully a true gift for another person.

The words Christ spoke in the Sermon on the Mount direct the human heart precisely toward this joy. We must entrust ourselves, our thoughts, and our actions to Christ's words in order to find joy and give it to others.

Theology and Pedagogy

59 *General Audience of April 8, 1981*
(Insegnamenti, 4, no. 1 [1981]: 903–8)

1. IT IS NOW TIME TO CONCLUDE the reflections and analyses based on the words Christ spoke in the Sermon on the Mount by which he appealed to the human heart, exhorting it to purity: "You have heard that it was said, 'You shall not commit adultery.' But I say to you: Whoever looks at a woman to desire her has already committed adultery with her in his heart" (Mt 5:27–28). We have said repeatedly that these words, though spoken once to the limited audience of this Sermon, apply to man at all times and in all places. They appeal to the human heart, in which *the innermost,* and in some way the most essential, *guiding thread of history* is inscribed. It is the history of good and evil (the beginning of which is linked in Genesis with the mysterious tree of the knowledge of good and evil), and, at the same time, it is the history of salvation whose word is the Gospel and whose power is the Holy Spirit, given to those who accept the Gospel with a sincere heart.

2. If Christ's appeal to the human "heart" and, before that, his appeal to the "beginning" allow us to construct or at least to outline an anthropology that we can call "theology of the body," *this theology is at the same time a pedagogy.* Pedagogy seeks to educate man by setting the requirements before him, giving reasons for them, and indicating the ways that lead to their fulfillment. Christ's statements have this end as well; they are "pedagogical" statements; they contain a pedagogy of the body expressed in a concise and, at the same time, remarkably complete way. Both the answer given to the Pharisees about the indissolubility of marriage and the words of the Sermon on the Mount about mastery over concupiscence show—at least indirectly—that the *Creator has assigned the body to man as a task, the body in its masculinity and femininity,* and that in masculinity and femininity he assigned to him in some way his own humanity as a task, that is, the dignity of the person and also the transparent sign of interpersonal "communion" in which man realizes himself through the authentic gift of self. While setting before man the requirements that corre-

spond to the tasks entrusted to him, the Creator at the same time points out to man—male and female—the ways that lead to accepting them and carrying them out.

3. When we analyze these key texts of the Bible, penetrating to the very root of the meanings they contain, we discover precisely the anthropology that can be called "theology of the body." And this *theology* of the body is the basis of the most appropriate method of the *pedagogy of the body,* that is, of man's education (or rather, self-education). This takes on particular importance for contemporary man, whose science in the fields of bio-physiology and bio-medicine is very advanced. Yet, this science deals with man under a certain "aspect" and is thus partial rather than comprehensive. We know well the functions of the body as an organism, the functions linked with the masculinity and the femininity of the human person. But in and of itself such *science does not yet develop* the consciousness of the body as a sign of the person, as a manifestation of the spirit. The whole development of contemporary science of the body as organism has rather the character of biological knowledge, because it is based on the disjunction between what is bodily and what is spiritual in man. When one uses such one-sided knowledge of the body's functions as an organism, it is not difficult to reach the point of treating the body more or less systematically as an *object of manipulations*; in this case, man no longer identifies himself subjectively, so to speak, with his own body, because it is deprived of the meaning and dignity that stem from the fact that this body is proper to the person. Here we touch problems that often need fundamental solutions, which are impossible without an integral vision of man.

4. Precisely here, it becomes clear that the theology of the body, which we are drawing from those key texts of Christ's words, becomes the fundamental method of pedagogy or of man's education from the point of view of the body in the full consideration of its masculinity and femininity. This *pedagogy can be understood* under the aspect of a specific "*spirituality of the body*"; in fact, the body in its masculinity or femininity is given as a task to the human spirit (this has been expressed stupendously by St. Paul in his own language), and, through an adequate maturity of the spirit, [the body] too becomes a sign of

the person, of which the person is conscious, and an authentic "matter" of the communion of persons. In other words, through spiritual maturity, man discovers the spousal meaning that is proper to the body.

Christ's words in the Sermon on the Mount indicate that in itself concupiscence does not reveal that meaning to man, but on the contrary darkens and obscures it. Purely "biological" knowledge of the functions of the body as organism, connected with the masculinity and femininity of the human person, can help to discover the authentic spousal meaning of the body *only if it goes hand in hand with an adequate spiritual maturity of the human person.* Without this, such knowledge can have effects that are quite the opposite; and this is confirmed by many experiences of our time.

5. From this point of view, one must consider the pronouncements of the contemporary Church in a clear-sighted way. Grasping and interpreting them adequately, and also applying them in practice (that is, pedagogy), requires that deepened theology of the body which we draw in its definitive form above all from the key words of Christ. As for the contemporary pronouncements of the Church, one must come to know the chapter entitled "The Dignity of Marriage and the Family and its Appreciation" in the pastoral constitution of Vatican II, *Gaudium et Spes* (Part 2, Chapter 1), and after it of Paul VI's encyclical *Humanae Vitae.* Without any doubt, the words of Christ to which we have devoted a lengthy analysis had no other goal than *the appreciation of the dignity of marriage and the family;* this is the reason for the fundamental convergence between them and the content of both above-mentioned teachings of the contemporary Church. Christ spoke to man at all times and in all places; the teachings of the Church intend to apply Christ's words and must therefore be reread according to the key of that theology and that pedagogy, which is rooted in and supported by Christ's words.

It is difficult to go through an overall analysis of the teachings of the Church's supreme magisterium to which we just referred. We will limit ourselves to quoting some passages. This is how Vatican II—which places "the appreciation of the dignity of marriage and the family" among the most urgent problems of the Church in the contemporary world—*characterizes the situation in this area:* "It is not everywhere that the dignity of this institution (that is, of marriage and the family)* shines with the same brightness, because it is obscured by polygamy, the plague of divorce, so-called free love, and other deformations. In addition, conjugal love is often profaned by egoism, hedonism, and illicit practices against generation" (*Gaudium et Spes*, 47). When Paul VI explains this final problem in *Humanae Vitae*, he writes among other things, "It is also to be feared that the man, growing used to the use of contraceptive practices, may finally lose reverence for woman and...may come to the point of considering her as a mere instrument of selfish enjoyment, and no longer as his respected and beloved companion" (Paul VI, HV 17).

Do we not find ourselves *in the orbit of the same concern* that had once *dictated Christ's words* about the unity and indissolubility of marriage, and likewise those in the Sermon on the Mount about purity of heart and mastery of the concupiscence of the flesh, words developed later with such clear-sightedness by the Apostle Paul?

6. In the same spirit, when he speaks about the demands of Christian morality, the author of *Humanae Vitae* also presents *the possibility of fulfilling them.*

> Mastery over instinct by one's reason and free will undoubtedly requires ascesis (Paul VI uses this term)** so that the affective manifestations of conjugal life may be in accord with the right order, in particular with regard to observing periodic continence. Yet this discipline, which is proper to the purity of married couples, far from harming conjugal love, rather confers on it a higher human value. It demands continual effort (above, this effort was called *ascesis*)† yet, thanks to its beneficent influence, husband and wife *develop* their personalities integrally, enriching each other with spiritual values.... It favors attention to one's partner, helps both parties to drive out egoism, the enemy of true love, and deepens their sense of responsibility. (Paul VI, HV 21)

7. Let us dwell on these few texts. They—especially the last one—show that the theology of the body, whose bases we sought above all in the words of Christ himself, is quite indispensable for an adequate understanding of the magisterial teaching of the contemporary Church. It is precisely this theology—as we said already—that becomes the fundamental method of the whole Christian pedagogy

---

* John Paul II's change.
** John Paul II's change.
† John Paul II's change.

of the body. In view of the words just quoted one can say that the goal of the *pedagogy of the body* lies in ensuring that "*affective manifestations*"—above all those that "belong specifically to conjugal life"—*conform to the moral order* or, in the end, to the dignity of the persons. In these words, we come back to the problem of the reciprocal relation between "eros" and "ethos," which we already discussed earlier. Theology, understood as a method of the pedagogy of the body, prepares us also for further reflections about the sacramentality of human life and, in particular, of married life.

The Gospel of the purity of heart, yesterday and today: as we conclude the present cycle of our considerations with this phrase—before going on to the next cycle, in which the basis of analysis will be Christ's words about the resurrection of the body—we want to devote some attention to the "need to create a climate favorable to education in chastity," which Paul VI's encyclical mentions, and we want to focus these observations on the problem of the ethos of the body in art and media with particular attention to the situations we encounter in contemporary life.

Appendix:
The Ethos of the Body in Art and Media

60 General Audience of April 15, 1981
(*Insegnamenti*, 4, no. 1 [1981]: 942–46)

1. IN OUR EARLIER REFLECTIONS—both in the context of Christ's words in which he appeals to the "beginning" and in the context of the Sermon on the Mount, when he appeals to the human heart—we have attempted to show in a systematic way how the dimension of man's personal subjectivity is an indispensable element present in theological hermeneutics, which we must discover and presuppose at the basis of the problem of the human body. Thus, not only the objective reality of the body, but far more so, as it seems, the subjective consciousness as well as the subjective "experience" of the body, enter at each step into the structure of the biblical texts and therefore require that one considers and reflects them in theology. Consequently, theological hermeneutics must always consider these two aspects. We can-

not consider the body as an objective reality outside of man's personal subjectivity, the personal subjectivity of human beings, male and female. Practically all *the problems of the "ethos of the body" are* at the same time *linked with the body's ontological identification* as the body of the person and with the content and quality of subjective *experience*, that is, at the same time *"living"* both *one's own body* and in interhuman relations, particularly in the perennial "man-woman" relation. Also the words of 1 Thessalonians, in which the author exhorts men and women to keep their own bodies "with holiness and reverence" (that is, the whole problem of "purity of heart"), point without any doubt to these two dimensions.

2. These are dimensions that directly concern concrete, living human beings, their attitudes, and behavior. *Works of culture*, especially works of art, allow those dimensions of "being body" and of "experiencing the body" to extend in some way beyond these living persons. Man encounters the "reality of the body" and "experiences the body" also when it becomes *a subject of creative activity*, a work of art, a content of culture. Although one must recognize as a matter of general principle that this contact comes about on the level of aesthetic experience, which is a matter of looking at the work of art (in Greek, *aisthanomai*: "look," "observe")—and thus, in the case at hand, it is a matter of the objectified body outside its ontological identity, in a different way and according to the criteria proper to artistic activity— nevertheless, the man who is enabled to take such a look is from the beginning too deeply tied to the meaning of the prototype or model, which in this case is he himself—the living human being and the living human body—to be able to detach and to separate completely that substantially aesthetic act, of the work in itself and its viewing, from the behavioral dynamisms or reactions as well as the value judgments that direct that primary experience and the primary way of living. This kind of *look*, which is by its nature *"aesthetic," cannot be* completely *isolated* in man's subjective consciousness *from the "look" about which Christ speaks* in the Sermon on the Mount when he puts us on guard against concupiscence.

3. Thus, the whole sphere of aesthetic experiences lies at the same time within the realm of the ethos of the body. It is, therefore, quite right also to think here about the necessity of creating a climate

favorable to purity. In fact, this climate can be threatened not only in the manner in which the relationships and the common life of living human beings unfold, but also in the realm of the objectifications proper to works of culture, in the realm of social communications, when the spoken or written word is involved; in the realm of images, that is, of representation and looking, whether in the traditional or contemporary sense of the term. In this way we come to the various fields and products of art, of sculpture, of drama, and of the art based on contemporary audiovisual technologies. In this area, which is vast and much diversified, we should ask ourselves a question about the human body as an object of culture, in the light of the ethos of the body outlined in the analyses carried out so far.

4. Before all else it should be observed that the human body is a perennial *object of culture in the widest sense of the term,* for the simple reason that man himself is a subject of culture and employs his humanity in his cultural and creative activity, thus also including his own body in this activity. In the present reflections we must, however, restrict the concept of "object of culture," limiting ourselves to the concept understood as a "subject" of the works of culture and in particular of works of art. In sum, the issue is the thematic representation or "objectification" of the body in such works. One should, however, immediately make some distinctions, at least in the form of an example. The living human body, man's and woman's body, which creates the object of art and the work of art out of itself (as in theater, in ballet, and, up to a point, also at a concert) is one thing; another thing is *the body as the model of the work of art* as in modeling arts, sculpture or painting. Is it possible to put film or the art of photography in the wide sense on the same level? It does seem so, although from the point of view of the body as object or subject we find in this case quite an essential difference. In painting or sculpture, man/body always remains a model that is subjected to a specific reworking by the artist. In film and even more in the art of photography, there is no transfiguration of the model, but the living human being is reproduced: and in this case the human body is not a model for the work of art, but *the object of a reproduction* achieved by appropriate technologies.

5. One should note right away that the distinction just made is important from the point of view of the ethos of the body in the

works of culture. And one should immediately add that artistic reproduction, when it becomes the content of representation and transmission (television or cinema), loses in some way its fundamental contact
with man/body, whose reproduction it is, and very often becomes an
"anonymous" object such as, for example, an anonymous photographic
nude published in an illustrated magazine, or an image spread to TV
screens all over the world. Such *anonymity is the effect of the "spreading"
of the image-*reproduction of the human body, objectified first with the
help of technologies of reproduction, which seems—as pointed out
above—to be essentially different from the transfiguration of a model
typical of a work of art, above all in the figurative arts. Such anonymity (which, by the way, is a way of "veiling" or "hiding" the identity of
the person reproduced), also constitutes a specific problem from the
point of view of the ethos of the human body in works of culture, particularly in contemporary works of so-called mass culture.

Let us limit ourselves today to these preliminary considerations,
which have a fundamental significance for the ethos of the human
body in works of art. A little later, these considerations will make us
aware how closely they are *tied* to Christ's words in the Sermon on
the Mount that compare "looking to desire" with "adultery committed
in the heart." The extension of these words to the sphere of art is particularly important for "*creating a climate favorable to chastity,*" which
Paul VI speaks about in his encyclical *Humanae Vitae.* Let us try to
understand this issue in a very deep and essential way.

61 General Audience of April 22, 1981
(*Insegnamenti*, 4, no. 1 [1981]: 986–90)

1. WE ARE REFLECTING—with reference to Christ's words in the
Sermon on the Mount—on the problem of the ethos of the body in
works of art. The roots of this issue are very deep. Here one should
recall the series of analyses carried out about Christ's appeal to the
"beginning" and then about his appeal to the human "heart" in the
Sermon on the Mount. The human body—the naked human body in
all the truth of its masculinity and femininity—has *the meaning of a
gift* of the person to the person. Due to the dignity of the personal
subject, the ethos of the body, that is, the ethical *order* of its *nakedness,*
is closely related to that system of reference, understood as a *spousal*

system, in which giving by one party encounters the appropriate and adequate response to the gift by the other. This response is decisive for the reciprocity of the gift. Artistic objectification of the human body in its male and female nakedness for the sake of making of it first a model and then a subject of a work of art is always a certain transfer outside of this configuration *of interpersonal gift* that belongs originally and specifically to the body. It constitutes in some way an uprooting of the human body from this configuration and a transfer of it to the dimension of artistic objectification specific to the work of art or to the reproduction typical for film and photographic technologies of our time.

In each of these dimensions, and in each of them in a different way, the human body loses that deeply subjective meaning of the gift and becomes an object destined for the knowledge of many, by which those who look will assimilate or even take possession of something that evidently exists (or rather should exist) by its very essence on the level of gift—of gift by the person to the person, no longer of course in the image, but in the living man. To tell the truth, this act of "*taking possession*" happens already on another level, that is, *on the level of the object of artistic transfiguration or reproduction.* It is, however, impossible not to realize that from the point of view of the *ethos of the body,* understood deeply, a *problem* arises here. It is a very delicate problem that has various levels of intensity depending on various motives and circumstances, both on the side of artistic activity and on the side of knowledge of the work of art or its reproduction. From the fact that this issue arises, it does not at all follow that the human body in its nakedness cannot become the subject of works of art, only that this issue is neither merely aesthetic, nor morally indifferent.

2. In our earlier analyses (especially those regarding Christ's appeal to the "beginning"), we devoted much space to the meaning of shame and tried to understand the difference between the situation (and state) of original innocence, in which "both were naked...but they did not feel shame"(Gen 2:25), and the later situation (and state) of sinfulness, in which the specific *need for intimacy*[*] *with regard to*

---

[*] Translator's note: "Intimacy" in the sense of an interior space protected from the outside (see Index at INTIMATE).

their bodies arose between man and woman *together with shame.* In man's heart subject to concupiscence, this necessity serves also indirectly to ensure the gift and the possibility of reciprocal self-giving. This necessity forms also man's way of acting as an "object of culture" in the widest meaning of the term. When culture shows an explicit tendency to cover the nakedness of the human body, it certainly does not do so only for climatic reasons, but also in relation to the process of the growth of man's personal sensibility. The anonymous nakedness of the man-object contrasts with the progress of an authentically human culture of morality. It is probably possible to confirm this point also in the life of so-called primitive peoples. The process of *sharpening personal human sensibility* is certainly a factor and fruit of culture.

Behind the need for shame, that is, for the intimacy of one's own body (about which the biblical sources inform us with such precision in Genesis 3), a deeper norm lies hidden: that of the gift oriented toward the very depths of the personal subject or toward the other person, especially in the man-woman relation according to the perennial order of reciprocal self-giving. Thus, in the processes of human culture understood in the broad sense, we observe—even in the state of man's hereditary sinfulness—a rather explicit *continuity of the spousal meaning of the body* in its masculinity and femininity. Original shame, known already from the first chapters of the Bible, is a permanent element of culture and morality. It belongs to the very origins of the ethos of the human body.

3. A person of developed sensibility crosses the limit of that shame only with difficulty and inner resistance. This is clear even in situations that otherwise justify the necessity of undressing the body, for example, in the case of medical examinations or operations.

In a group by themselves, one should also recall other circumstances, e.g., those of concentration camps or places of extermination where the violation of bodily shame is a method used consciously to destroy personal sensibility and the sense of human dignity. Everywhere—though in different ways—the same line of order is reconfirmed. Following his personal sensibility, man *does not want to become an object* for others through his own anonymous nakedness, *nor does he want the other to become an object for him* in a similar way. It is evident that he "does not want to" to the degree in which he lets himself be guided by the sense of the dignity of the human body. There are, in fact, various reasons that can induce, incite, and even press man to act contrary to what the dignity of the human body, connected with personal sensibility, demands. One cannot forget that the fundamental inner "situation" of "historical" man is the state of the three-fold concupiscence (see 1 Jn 2:16). This state—and in particular the concupiscence of the flesh—makes itself felt in various ways, in the inner impulses of the human heart as well as in the whole climate of relationships between human beings, and in social morality.

4. We cannot forget this point, not even when we consider the issue of the wide sphere of art, above all when it has the character of a visual image or show, and likewise when one is dealing with *"mass" culture*, which is so significant in our times because it is connected with the broadcasting technology of audiovisual communication. The question arises when and in what case this sphere of man's activity—from the point of view of the ethos of the body—should be accused of *"pornovision"* just as some writing has been and is being accused of *"pornography"* (that second term is older). The one as well as the other happens when one oversteps the limit of shame or of personal sensibility with regard to what is connected with the human body, with its nakedness, when in a work of art or by audiovisual media *one violates* the body's *right to intimacy in its masculinity and femininity* and—in the final analysis—when one violates that deep *order of the gift and of reciprocal self-giving*, which is inscribed in femininity and masculinity across the whole structure of being human. This deep inscription—or rather incision—is decisive for the spousal meaning of the human body, that is, for the fundamental call it receives, that of forming the "communion of persons" and of participating in it.

If we now break off our consideration, which we intend to continue next Wednesday, we should note that the observance or violation of this order, which is so closely connected with man's personal sensibility, cannot be indifferent for the problem of "creating a climate favorable to chastity" in life and social education.

62 *General Audience of April 29, 1981*
(Insegnamenti, 4, no. 1 [1981]: 1064–68)

1. WE HAVE ALREADY DEVOTED a series of reflections to the meaning of the words Christ spoke in the Sermon on the Mount in which he exhorts his listeners to purity of heart and calls their attention even to the "concupiscent look." We cannot forget these words of Christ when we consider the issue of the vast sphere of art, above all when it has the character of a visual image or show, and likewise when one is dealing with the sphere of "*mass*" culture, which is so significant in our times because it is connected with the broadcasting technology of audiovisual communication. We said last time that this sphere of man's activity is at times accused of "pornovision" just as in the case of literature the accusation is that of "pornography." The one as well as the other takes place when the limit of shame or of personal sensibility is overstepped with regard to what is connected with the human ·body, with its nakedness, when in a work of art by audiovisual media *one violates the body's right to intimacy* in its masculinity and femininity and—in the final analysis—when one violates the intimate and constant *order of the gift and of reciprocal self-giving,* which is inscribed in femininity and masculinity across the whole structure of being human. This deep inscription—or rather incision—is decisive for the spousal meaning of the human body, that is, for the fundamental call it receives, that of forming the "communion of persons" and of participating in it.

2. It is obvious that in works of art or in the products of audiovisual artistic reproduction this constant directedness toward the <gift>,* that is, that deep inscription of the meaning of the human body, can be violated only in the intentional order of reproduction and representation. As we said before, here we are dealing with the human body as model or subject. Nevertheless, if the sense of shame and personal sensibility are offended in such cases, this happens because of their transfer into the *dimension of "social communication"* and thus because of the fact that one turns into public property, as it

---

* Translator's note: The *Insegnamenti* text reads "after (*dopo*)"—probably a typographical error—while UD reads "gift (*dono*)."

were, what does and should strictly belong (in man's right feeling) to an interpersonal relation, what is *bound*—as we emphasized before—to the very "*communion of persons*" and corresponds in its own realm to man's inner truth and thus also to the integral truth about man.

It is not possible to agree on this point with the representatives of so-called naturalism who appeal to the right to "everything that is human" in works of art and in the products of artistic reproduction, and who claim that in this way they act in the name of the realistic truth about man. It is precisely this truth about man—the *whole* truth about man—that requires us to consider the sense of the intimacy of the body and the consistency of the gift connected with the masculinity and femininity of the body itself, which reflects the mystery of man proper to the inner structure of the person. We must consider this truth about man also in the artistic order, if we want to speak of a full realism.

3. One notices here that the order proper to the "communion of. persons" agrees profoundly with the vast and differentiated area of "communication." As we said already in our earlier analyses (where we turned to Genesis 2:25 [see TOB 13–19]), the human body in its nakedness—understood as a manifestation of the person and as the person's gift or sign of trust in, and of giving to, another person, who is aware of the gift, who has chosen and decided to respond to it in an equally personal way—becomes the source of a particular interpersonal "communication." As we said already, this is a particular communication in humanity itself. This interpersonal communication penetrates deeply into the system of communion (*communio personarum*) and at the same time grows from it and develops correctly in its context. Precisely *because of the great value of the body in this system of* interpersonal *"communion," making the body* in its nakedness—which expresses precisely "the element" of the gift—the object or subject of a work of art or an audiovisual reproduction is a problem that is by nature not only aesthetic, but also ethical. In fact, that "element of the gift" is, so to speak, suspended in the dimension of an unknown reception and of an unforeseen response, and thereby it is in some way "threatened" in the intentional order in the sense that it can become an anonymous object of "appropriation," an object of abuse. This is why the integral truth about man constitutes in this matter the basis of the norm according to which the good or evil of determinate actions, of behavior, of morality, and situations is formed. Precisely because of his body and his sex (femininity/masculinity), the truth about man, the truth about what is particularly personal and interior in him, creates precise limits that one must not overstep.

4. These limits must be recognized and observed by the artist who makes the human body the model or subject of a work of art or audiovisual reproduction. Neither he nor others who carry responsibility in this field have the right to demand, propose, or allow other human beings whom they invite, exhort, or admit to seeing and looking at the image to violate these limits together with them or because of them. What in itself constitutes the content and deep personal value of the order of gift and of the mutual self-giving of the person in the image is, as a subject, uprooted from its own authentic substratum in order to become an object and, what is more, in some way an anonymous object by means of "social communication."

5. The whole problem of "pornovision" and of "pornography," as it appears on the basis of what was said above, *is not the effect of a puritanical mentality* or of a *narrow moralism,* nor is it the product of a way of thinking burdened by Manichaeism. What is at issue is rather an *extremely important* and fundamental *sphere of values* to which man cannot remain indifferent because of the dignity of humanity, because of the personal character and eloquence of the human body. Through works of art and the activity of audiovisual media, this whole content and these values can be formed and deepened, but they can also be deformed and destroyed *"in man's heart."* We can see that we find ourselves continually within the orbit of the words Christ spoke in the Sermon on the Mount. The problems we are dealing with here should also be examined in the light of the words that speak about "looking" born from concupiscence as "adultery committed in the heart."

And so it seems that reflection about these problems, which are important for "creating a climate favorable to education in chastity," is an indispensable appendix to all preceding analyses, which we have devoted to this topic in the course of many Wednesday meetings.

63 *General Audience of May 6, 1981*
(Insegnamenti, 4, no. 1 [1981]: 1105–10)

1. In the Sermon on the Mount, Christ spoke the words to which we have devoted a series of reflections *in the course of almost a whole year.* When he explains to his listeners the true meaning of the commandment "You shall not commit adultery," Christ expresses himself in this way, "But I say to you: Whoever looks at a woman to desire her has already committed adultery with her in his heart" (Mt 5:28). It seems that these words refer also to the vast spheres of human culture, especially to those of artistic activity, which we have recently discussed in several Wednesday meetings. Today we will devote the final part of these reflections to the problem of the relation between the ethos of the image—or of the description—and the ethos of viewing or listening, of reading or of other forms of cognitive reception by which one encounters the content of the work of art or of audiovision understood in the broad sense.

2. Here we return once again to the problem already noted: whether, and in what measure, the human body in all the visible truth of its masculinity and femininity can be a subject of works of art and thus a subject of that specific social "communication" for which such a work is intended. This question concerns even more the contemporary "mass" culture connected with audiovisual technology. Can the human body be such a model or subject, given that this is connected, as we know, with objectivity "without choice," which a little earlier we called anonymity and which seems to bring with it a serious potential threat to the whole sphere of meanings that belong to the body of man and woman due to the personal character of the human subject and the character of "communion" of interpersonal relations?

One can add at this point that the expressions "pornography" or "pornovision"—despite their ancient etymology—appeared in language relatively late. The traditional Latin terminology used the word *obscaena,* thereby indicating everything that must not find itself before the eyes of spectators, that must be surrounded by fitting discretion, that *cannot be presented without any choice to human view.*

3. When we ask the above question, we realize that, de facto, in the course of whole epochs of human culture and artistic activity, the human body *has been and is such a model or subject* of works of visual art—just as the whole sphere of love between man and woman and also, connected with it, the "reciprocal self-giving" of masculinity and femininity in their bodily expression, has been, is, and will be the subject of literary narrative. Such a narrative found its place also in the Bible, above all in the text of the Song of Songs, which we will have to take up on another occasion [see TOB 108–13]. Indeed, one must note that in the whole history of literature or art, in the history of human culture, this *subject seems to be particularly frequent* and is *particularly important.* In fact, it concerns a problem that is in itself *great and important.* We have shown this from the beginning of our reflections, following the footsteps of the biblical texts, which reveal to us the right dimension of this problem, namely, the dignity of man in his male and female bodiliness, and the spousal meaning of femininity and masculinity inscribed in the whole interior—and at the same time visible—structure of the human person.

4. Our earlier reflections did not intend to cast doubt on the right to this subject. Their goal is simply to show that its treatment is connected with a particular responsibility whose nature is not only artistic, but also ethical. *The artist* who takes up this subject in any sphere of art or by audiovisual technologies *must be conscious* of the full truth of the object, of the whole *scale of values* connected with it; he must not only take them into account *abstractly,* but also live them rightly himself. This requirement corresponds also to that principle of "purity of heart," which must in determinate cases be carried over from the existential sphere of attitudes and forms of behavior to the intentional sphere of artistic creation or reproduction.

It seems that the process of such creation intends not only an objectification of the model (and in some way a new process of "materializing") but at the same time *an expression in such an objectification* of what one can call the artist's *creative idea,* in which his *inner world of values* and thus also his way of living the truth of his object manifests itself. In this process, there is a characteristic transfiguration of the model or the matter and particularly of that which man is, namely, the human body in the whole truth of its masculinity or femininity. (From this point of view, there is a very important difference, for example, between painting or sculpture and photography or film).

The viewer, who is invited by the artist to look at his work, communicates not only with the objectification and thus in some way with a new process of "materializing" the model or the matter, but at the same time he communicates with the truth of the object that the author in his artistic materializing has successfully expressed with his own specific media.

5. In the course of the various epochs from antiquity down—and especially in the great period of classical Greek art—there are works of art whose subject is the human body in its nakedness, the contemplation of which allows one to concentrate in some way on the whole truth of man, on the dignity and beauty—even "suprasensual" beauty—of his masculinity and femininity. These works *bear within themselves in a hidden way, as it were, an element of sublimation* that leads the viewer through the body to the whole personal mystery of man. In contact with such works, we do not feel pushed by their content toward "looking to desire," as the Sermon on the Mount puts it; in some way we learn the spousal meaning of the body, which corresponds to and provides the measure for "purity of heart." But there are also works of art, and perhaps still more often reproductions, that stir up objections in the sphere of man's personal sensibility—not because of their object, because in itself the human body always has its own inalienable dignity—but because of the quality or the way of its artistic reproduction, depiction, and representation. Decisive for this mode and for this quality can be the various coefficients of the work or reproduction, as well as many circumstances often of a more technical than artistic nature.

Through all of these elements, as we know, *the same fundamental intentionality* of the work of art or the product of the technologies involved becomes in some way accessible to the viewer, the reader, or the listener. If our personal sensibility reacts with objection and disapproval, the reason is that in this fundamental intentionality, together with the objectification of man and his body, we discover, as something inseparable from the work of art or its reproduction, the simultaneous reduction [of the human person] to the rank *of an object, of an object of "enjoyment" intended for the satisfaction of mere concupiscence.* And this is opposed to man's dignity also in the intentional order of art and reproduction. By analogy, one should apply the same point to the various fields of artistic activity—in each case according to its specific character—and likewise to the various audiovisual technologies.

6. Paul VI's encyclical *Humanae Vitae* underlines the necessity of "creating a climate favorable to education in chastity." And he thereby intends to affirm that living the human body in the whole truth of its masculinity and femininity must correspond to the dignity of that body and to its meaning in building the communion of persons. One can say that this is one of the fundamental dimensions of human culture, understood as an *affirmation that ennobles everything that is human*. This is why we have devoted this brief sketch to the problem, which can, in synthesis, be called the ethos of the image. The image in question serves in a singular way to make man "visible," understanding that phrase in the more or less direct sense. The sculpted or painted image "expresses" man "visually"; a play or ballet "expresses" him "visually" in another way, film in yet another; even a literary work intends in its own way to arouse inner images by making use of the wealth of human imagination or memory. What we have called *"ethos of the image"* cannot be considered in abstraction from the correlative component, which one would have to call *"ethos of seeing."* The whole process of communication is contained between these two components, regardless of the vastness of the circles described by this communication, which in this case is always "social."

7. The creation of the climate favorable to education in chastity contains *these two components*: it concerns, so to speak, a reciprocal *circuit* that takes place between the image and the act of seeing, between the ethos of the image and the ethos of seeing. Just as the creation of the image, in the wide and differentiated sense of the term, imposes on the author, artist, or reproducer obligations not only of an aesthetic, but also of an ethical nature, so also "looking," understood in the same broad analogy, imposes obligations on the recipient of the work.

Authentic and responsible artistic activity tends to overcome the anonymity of the human body as an object "without choice," seeking (as has already been said) through its creative effort such an artistic expression of the truth about man in his male and female bodiliness, that this truth is, so to speak, *assigned as a task to the viewer* and, in the widest radius, to every *recipient of the work*. It depends upon him, in turn, whether he decides to make his own effort by drawing near to such truth, or whether he remains only a superficial "consumer" of the impressions, that is, one who exploits the encounter with the anonymous subject-body only on the level of sensuality, which by its nature reacts to its object precisely "without choice."

Here we conclude this important chapter of our reflections on the theology of the body, the point of departure of which were the words Christ spoke in the Sermon on the Mount, words that are valid for man at all times and in all places, for "historical" man, and for every one of us.

The reflections on the theology of the body would not be complete, however, if we did not consider other words of Christ, namely, those in which he appeals to the future resurrection. To these, therefore, we propose to devote the next cycle of our considerations.

CHAPTER THREE

Christ Appeals to the Resurrection

───────── ∾ ─────────

1. The Resurrection of the Body as a Reality of the "Future World"

A. THE SYNOPTICS: "HE IS NOT GOD OF THE DEAD BUT OF THE LIVING"

The Third Part of the Triptych

64 *General Audience of November 11, 1981*
(Insegnamenti, 4, no. 2 [1981]: 600–603)

1. TODAY WE TAKE UP AGAIN, after a rather long pause, the meditations we have been presenting for quite a while, which we have defined as reflections on the theology of the body.

As we continue, we should go back to the words of the Gospel in which Christ appeals to the resurrection, words that have a fundamental importance for understanding marriage in the Christian sense and also "the renunciation" of conjugal life "for the kingdom of heaven."

The complex casuistry of the Old Testament in the field of marriage moved not only the Pharisees to go to Jesus, to set before him the problem of the indissolubility of marriage (see Mt 19:3–9; Mk 10:2–12), but on another occasion the Sadducees, to ask him about the law of so-called levirate marriage.[66] This dialogue is reported in similar ways by the Synoptics (see Mt 22:24–30; Mk 12:18–27; Lk 20:27–40). Although the three redactions are nearly identical, one nevertheless notices some differences between them that are slight but at the same time significant. A deeper analysis is required since the dialogue is reported in three versions, those of Matthew, Mark, and Luke, and inasmuch as its contents have an essential meaning for the theology of the body.

Next to the two other important dialogues, namely, the one in which Christ appeals to the "beginning" (see Mt 19:3–9; Mk 10:2–12) and the other in which he appeals to man's innermost [being] (to the "heart") while indicating the [reductive] desire and concupiscence of the flesh as a source of sin (see Mt 5:27–32), the dialogue that we propose to analyze now is, I would say, *the third component of the triptych* of Christ's own statements, the triptych of words that are essential and constitutive for the theology of the body. In this dialogue, Jesus appeals to the resurrection, thereby revealing a completely new dimension of the mystery of man.

2. The revelation of this dimension of the body, stupendous in its content—and yet connected with the Gospel reread as a whole and in depth—emerges in the dialogue with the Sadducees, "who say there is no resurrection" (Mt 22:23);[67] they came to Jesus to present to him an argument that—in their judgment—showed the reasonableness of

---

66. This law, contained in Deuteronomy 25:7–10, concerned brothers who lived under the same roof. If one of them died without leaving children, the brother of the deceased had to take the widow of his dead brother as his wife. The child born from this marriage was recognized as the son of the deceased, so that his bloodline would not become extinct and that his heredity would be preserved in the family (see Gen 38:8).

67. In the time of Christ, the Sadducees formed a distinct group within Judaism tied to the circle of the priestly aristocracy. In opposition to the oral tradition and the theology elaborated by the Pharisees, they held to the literal interpretation of the Pentateuch, which they considered the main source of Yahwist religion. Since there is no mention of life after death in the oldest biblical books, the Sadducees rejected the eschatology proclaimed by the Pharisees and affirmed that "souls die together with the body" (see Flavius Josephus, *Antiquitates Iudaicae*, 17.4.16).

The views of the Sadducees, however, are not directly known to us since all of their writings were lost after the destruction of Jerusalem in A.D. 70, when the group disappeared. The information about the Sadducees is meager: we gather it from the writings of their ideological adversaries.

their position. This argument was supposed to contradict "the hypothesis of the resurrection." The reasoning of the Sadducees is the following: "Teacher, Moses wrote for us that if a man's brother dies, leaving a wife but no child, the man shall marry the widow and raise up children for his brother" (Mk 12:19). Here the Sadducees appeal to the so-called levirate law (see Deut 25:5–10), and by attaching themselves to the prescription of this ancient law *they present the following case:* "There were seven brothers; the first married and, when he died, left no children; and the second married her and died, leaving no children; and the third likewise; none of the seven left children. Last of all the woman herself died. In the resurrection, when they will rise, whose wife will she be? For the seven had married her" (Mk 12:20–23).[68]

3. Christ's answer is one of the key answers of the Gospel, in which—taking purely human arguments as a point of departure and in contrast to them—he reveals another dimension of the question, one that corresponds to the wisdom and power of God himself. In a similar way, the Gospel presents the case of the tax coin with Caesar's image and the correct relation between what is divine and what is human in the realm of power ("belonging to Caesar") (see Mt 22:15–22). This time *Jesus answers as follows:* "Is not this the reason you are wrong, that you know neither the Scriptures nor the power of God? For when they rise from the dead, they take neither wife nor husband, but are like angels in heaven" (Mk 12:24–25). This is the fundamental reply to the "case," that is, to the problem contained in it. Since he knew the ideas of the Sadducees and saw their real intentions, Christ immediately afterward takes up again *the problem of the possibility of the resurrection* denied by the Sadducees. "And as for the dead being raised, have you not read in the book of Moses, in the story about the bush, how God said to him, 'I am the God of Abraham, the God of Isaac, and the God of Jacob?' He is not God of the dead, but of the living" (Mk 12:26–27). As one can see, Christ quotes the same Moses to whom the Sadducees appealed, and he ends by saying, "You are quite wrong" (Mk 12:27).

---

68. By turning to Jesus with a purely theoretical "case," the Sadducees simultaneously attack the primitive view of the Pharisees about life after the resurrection of the body; they insinuate, indeed, that faith in the resurrection of the body leads to allowing polyandry, contrary to the law of God.

4. Christ makes this concluding statement a second time. In fact, the first time he makes it at the beginning of his explanation. He says at that point, "You are wrong, because you know neither the Scriptures nor the power of God." This is the version in Matthew (22:29). In Mark we read, "Is not this the reason you are wrong, that you know neither the Scriptures nor the power of God?" (Mk 12:24). In Luke 20:27, 36, by contrast, Christ's corresponding answer lacks the polemical tone of "You are quite wrong." On the other hand, he proclaims the same thing inasmuch as he introduces into the answer some elements found neither in Matthew nor in Mark: "Jesus said to them, 'The sons of this age take wife and take husband; but those who are considered worthy of the other world and the resurrection from the dead take neither wife nor husband. Indeed they cannot die anymore, because they are equal to the angels and, being sons of the resurrection, they are sons of God'" (Lk 20:34–36). With respect to the very possibility of the resurrection, Luke—like the other two Synoptics—*appeals to Moses, that is, to the passage in Exodus 3:2–6*, which tells the story that the great legislator of the Old Covenant had heard the following words from the bush that "burned with fire, but was not consumed": "I am the God of your father, the God of Abraham, the God of Isaac, the God of Jacob" (Ex 3:6). In the same place, when Moses asked the name of God, he heard the reply, "I am who am" (Ex 3:14).

In this way, when he speaks about the future resurrection of the body, Christ appeals to the very power of the living God. In our next meetings we will have to consider this point in more detail.

65   *General Audience of November 18, 1981*
 (Insegnamenti, 4, no. 2 [1981]: 656–61)

1. "YOU ARE WRONG, because you know neither the Scriptures nor the power of God" (Mt 22:9), Christ said to the Sadducees, who—rejecting faith in the future resurrection of the body—had presented the following case to him: "There were seven brothers among us; the first married, and died childless, leaving the widow to his brother" (according to the Mosaic Law of the "levirate"). "The second did the same, so also the third, down to the seventh. Last of all, the woman herself died. In the resurrection, then, of the seven whose wife will she be?" (Mt 22:25–28).

Christ answers the Sadducees by stating at the beginning and at the end of his answer that they are quite wrong, because they know neither the Scriptures nor the power of God (see Mk 12:24; Mt 22:29). Since the dialogue with the Sadducees is reported in all three Synoptic Gospels, we should briefly compare the parallel texts.

Witness to the Power of the Living God

2. Although it does not refer to the bush, Matthew's version (Mt 22:24–30) agrees almost entirely with Mark's (Mk 12:18–25). Both versions contain two essential elements: (1) the statement about the future resurrection of the body; (2) the statement about the state of the bodies of risen human beings.[69] These two elements are also found in Luke 20:27–36.[70] The first element, concerning the future resurrection of the body, is joined, especially in Matthew and Mark, with the words addressed to the Sadducees that they "know neither the Scriptures nor the power of God." This statement deserves special attention, because in it Christ points to the very basis of faith in the resurrection, to which he had appealed in answering the question posed by the Sadducees with the concrete example of the Mosaic Law of the levirate.

3. Without any doubt, the Sadducees treat the question of the resurrection as a type of theory or hypothesis that can be refuted.[71]

---

69. Although the New Testament does not know the expression "resurrection of the body" (which appears for the first time in St. Clement, 2 Clem 9:1, and in Justin, *Dial.* 80:5), but uses the expression "resurrection of the dead," intending by it man in his integrity, it is nevertheless possible to find in many texts of the New Testament faith in the immortality of the soul and its existence also apart from the body (see, e.g., Lk 23:43; Phil 1:23–24; 2 Cor 5:6–8).

70. The text of Luke contains some new elements around which a discussion among the exegetes is taking place.

71. We know that in the Judaism of that period there was no clearly formulated doctrine about the resurrection; there were only the different theories launched by the individual schools.

The Pharisees, who cultivated theological speculation, strongly developed the doctrine of the resurrection, seeing allusions to it in all the books of the Old Testament. Yet, they understood the future resurrection in an earthly and primitive way, predicting, for example, an enormous increase of crops and of fertility after the resurrection.

The Sadducees, by contrast, polemicized against this view, starting with the premise that the Pentateuch does not speak about eschatology. One must also keep in mind that in the first century, the canon of the books of the Old Testament had not yet been determined.

The case presented by the Sadducees directly attacks the Pharisaic view of the resurrection. In fact, the Sadducees held that Christ was a follower of the Pharisaic view. Christ's answer equally corrects the views of the Pharisees and those of the Sadducees.

Jesus first shows them a mistake in their method: *they do not know the Scriptures*; and then an error of substance: they do not accept what is revealed by the Scriptures—*since they do not know the power of God*—they do not believe in the one who revealed himself to Moses in the burning bush.

It is a very significant and very precise answer. Here Christ meets men who consider themselves experts and competent interpreters of the Scriptures. Jesus responds to these men—the Sadducees—that mere literal knowledge of Scripture is not enough. Scripture is in fact and above all a means for knowing the power of the living God, who reveals himself in it, just as he revealed himself to Moses in the bush. In this revelation, he called himself "the God of Abraham, the God of Isaac, and of Jacob"[72]—of those, therefore, who were the ancestors of Moses in the faith that springs from the revelation of the living God. All of them have been dead for a long time; nevertheless, Christ completes the reference to them with the statement that God "is not God of the dead, but of the living." One can only understand this key statement, in which Christ interprets the words addressed to Moses from the burning bush, if *one admits the reality of a life that does not end with death.* Moses' fathers in the faith, Abraham, Isaac, and Jacob, are living persons for God ("for all live for him," Lk 20:38) although according to human criteria they should be numbered among the dead. Correctly rereading Scripture, and particularly God's words just quoted, means knowing and welcoming with faith the power of the Giver of life, who is not bound by the law of death, which rules over man's earthly history.

---

72. This expression does *not* mean, "God *who was honored* by Abraham, Isaac, and Jacob," but, "God who *took care* of the patriarchs and freed them."

This formula returns in Exodus 3:6, 15–16, and 4:5, always in the context of the promise of the liberation of Israel: the name of the God of Abraham, Isaac, and Jacob is a pledge and guarantee of this liberation.

"God of X is synonymous with help, support, and shelter for Israel." A similar sense is found in Genesis 49:24: "God of Jacob—Shepherd and Rock of Israel, the God of your father, who will help you" (see Gen 49:24–25; see also Gen 24:27; 26:24; 28:13; 32:10; 46:3). F. Dreyfus, O.P., "L'argument scripturaire de Jésus en faveur de la résurrection des morts (Mc 12:26–27)," *Revue Biblique* 66 (1959): 218.

In Jewish exegesis at the time of Jesus, the formula, "God of Abraham, Isaac, and Jacob," in which all three of the names of the patriarchs are quoted, indicated *God's relationship with the people of the covenant as a community.* See E. Ellis, "Jesus, the Sadducees and Qumran," *New Testament Studies* 10 (1963–1964): 275.

4. It seems to be in this way that one must interpret Christ's answer given to the Sadducees about the possibility of the resurrection,[73] according to the version of all three Synoptics. The moment was to come when Christ would give an answer to this question by his own resurrection; meanwhile, however, he appeals to the testimony of the Old Testament by showing how to find in it the truth about immortality and resurrection. In order to find it, one must not stop at the mere sound of the words, but go up also to the power of God revealed by these words. The reference to Abraham, Isaac, and Jacob in that theophany granted to Moses, about which we read in Exodus 3:2–6, constitutes a testimony that the living God gives to those who live "for him," to those who, thanks to his power, have life, even if according to the dimensions of history one would have to number them among those long dead.

5. The full meaning of this testimony, to which Jesus appeals in his dialogue with the Sadducees, could be gathered (still in the light of the Old Testament alone) in the following way. He who is—he who lives and is Life—constitutes the inexhaustible fountain of existence and of life, just as he revealed himself at the "beginning" in Genesis (see Gen 1–3). Although, due to sin, bodily death has became man's lot[74] and access to the tree of Life (this great symbol of Genesis) was denied to him (see Gen 3:22), nevertheless, *when the living God enters his covenant with man* (Abraham, the patriarchs, Moses, Israel), *he continually renews* in this covenant *the very reality of Life,* reveals again its prospects, and in some way opens up again the access to the tree of Life. Together with the covenant, a share in this life, whose fountain is God himself, is given to the same human beings who, as a consequence of breaking the first covenant, had lost

---

73. In our contemporary way of understanding this Gospel text, Jesus' reasoning concerns only immortality; if, in fact, the patriarchs are alive after their death already now, before the eschatological resurrection of the body, then Jesus' statement regards the immortality of the soul and does not speak about the resurrection of the body.

Jesus' reasoning, however, was directed toward the Sadducees who did not know the dualism of body and soul and accepted only the biblical psycho-physical unity of man, who is "body and breath of life." And so, according to them, the soul dies together with the body. To the Sadducees, Jesus' statement that the patriarchs are alive could only signify the resurrection with the body.

74. We are not pausing here to examine the purely Old Testament understanding of death, but take into account theological anthropology as a whole.

access to the tree of Life and, in the dimensions of their earthly history, were subjected to death.

6. Christ is God's final word on this subject; in fact, the covenant established with him and through him between God and humanity opens an infinite prospect of Life: and access to the tree of Life—according to the original plan of the God of the covenant—is revealed to every man in its definitive fullness. This will be the meaning of Christ's death and resurrection; this will be the testimony of the paschal mystery. The dialogue with the Sadducees, however, takes place *in the pre-paschal phase of Christ's messianic mission.* The course of the conversation according to Matthew 22:24–30, Mark 12:19–25, and Luke 20:28–36 shows that Christ—who, particularly in the dialogues with his disciples, had spoken a number of times about the future resurrection of the Son of Man (see Mt 17:9, 23; 20:19)—does not refer to this topic in the dialogue with the Sadducees. The reasons are obvious and clear. The discussion takes place with the Sadducees, "who say there is no resurrection" (as the evangelist stresses), that is, who cast doubt on its very possibility, and at the same time consider themselves experts on the Scripture of the Old Testament and its qualified interpreters. For this reason Jesus appeals to the Old Testament and shows on its basis that "they do not know the power of God."[75]

---

75. This is the decisive argument, which confirms the authenticity of the discussion with the Sadducees.

If the pericope were "*a post-paschal addition by the Christian community*" (as Bultmann, for example, held), faith in the resurrection would be supported by the resurrection of Christ, which imposed itself as an irresistible force, as St. Paul, for example, makes us understand (see 1 Cor 15:12).

See J. Jeremias, *Neutestamentliche Theologie*, pt. 1 (Gütersloh: Mohn, 1971); see also I. H. Marshall, *The Gospel of Luke* (Exeter: The Paternoster Press, 1978), 738.

The reference to the Pentateuch—while in the Old Testament there were texts that dealt directly with the resurrection (e.g., Isa 26:19 or Dan 12:2)—attests that the dialogue was truly with the Sadducees, who considered the Pentateuch the only decisive authority.

The structure of the controversy shows that this was a rabbinic discussion according to the classical models in use in the academies at that time.

Cf. J. Le Moyne, O.S.B., *Les Sadducéens* (Paris: Gabalda, 1972), 124f.; E. Lohmeyer, *Das Evangelium des Markus* (Göttingen: Vandenhoeck & Ruprecht, 1959), 257; D. Daube, *New Testament and Rabbinic Judaism* (London: Athlone Press, 1956), 158–63; J. Rademakers, S.J., *La bonne nouvelle de Jésus selon St Marc* (Brussels: Institut d'Etudes Théologiques, 1974), 313.

7. Regarding the possibility of the resurrection, Christ appeals precisely to that power that goes hand in hand with the testimony of the living God, who is the God of Abraham, of Isaac, of Jacob, and the God of Moses. The God whom the Sadducees "deprive" of this power, is no longer the true God of their Fathers, but the God of their hypotheses and interpretations. Christ, on the other hand, has come to bear witness to the God of Life in the whole truth of his power that unfolds over man's life.

The New Meaning of the Body

66 *General Audience of December 2, 1981*
(Insegnamenti, 4, no. 2 [1981]: 805–9)

1. "WHEN THEY RISE from the dead, they take neither wife nor husband" (Mk 12:25). Christ speaks these words, *which have a key meaning for the theology of the body*, after having affirmed in the dialogue with the Sadducees that the resurrection conforms to the power of the living God. All three Synoptic Gospels report the same statement, except that Luke's version differs in some details from Matthew's and Mark's. Essential for all three of them is the observation that in the future resurrection human beings, having regained their bodies in the fullness of the perfection proper to the image and likeness of God—having regained them in their masculinity and femininity—"will take neither wife nor husband." Luke 20:34–35 expresses the same idea with the following words: "The sons of this age take wife and take husband; but those who are considered worthy of the other world and the resurrection from the dead take neither wife nor husband" (Lk 20:34–35).

2. As is clear from these words, *marriage*—the union in which, as Genesis says, "the man will...unite with his wife, and the two will be one flesh" (Gen 2:24), a union proper to man from the "beginning"—belongs *exclusively "to this world."* Marriage and procreation do not constitute man's eschatological future. In the resurrection they lose, so to speak, their *raison d'être.* That "other world" about which Luke speaks (Lk 20:35) means the definitive fulfillment of the human race, the quantitative closure of that circle of beings created in the image

and likeness of God in order that, multiplying through the conjugal "unity of the body" of men and women, they would subdue the earth to themselves. That "other world" is not the world of the earth, but the world of God, who, as we know from 1 Corinthians, will completely fill it, becoming "all in all" (1 Cor 15:28).

3. At the same time, that "other world," which according to revelation is "the kingdom of God," is also man's definitive and eternal "fatherland" (see Phil 3:20); it is "the Father's house" (Jn 14:2). That "other world" as *man's new fatherland comes forth* definitively from the present world—which is temporal, subjected to death or the destruction of the body (cf. "to dust you will return," Gen 3:19)—*through the resurrection*. The resurrection, according to Christ's words reported by the Synoptics, means not only the recovery of bodiliness and the reestablishment of human life in its integrity, through the union of body and soul, but also a wholly new state of human life itself. We find the confirmation of this new state of the body in Christ's resurrection (see Rom 6:5–11). After Christ's resurrection, the words reported by the Synoptics (Mt 22:30; Mk 12:25; Lk 20:35–36) must have sounded with, I would say, new demonstrative power for those who had heard them, and at the same time they must have acquired the character of a convincing promise. For now, however, we will dwell on these words in their "pre-paschal" phase, basing ourselves only on the situation in which Christ spoke them. There is no doubt that already in the answer given to the Sadducees, Christ reveals the new condition of the human body in the resurrection, and he does so precisely by proposing a reference to and a comparison with the condition in which man shared from the "beginning."

4. The words "take neither wife nor husband" seem to affirm, at one and the same time, that human bodies, which are recovered and also renewed in the resurrection, will preserve their specific masculine or feminine character and that *the meaning of being male or female in the body* will be *constituted and understood differently* in the "other world" than it had been "from the beginning" and then in its whole earthly dimension. The words of Genesis, "a man will leave his father and his mother and unite with his wife, and the two will be one flesh" (Gen 2:24), have from the beginning constituted the condition and relation

of masculinity and femininity, extending also to the body, which must rightly be defined as "conjugal" and at the same time as "procreative" and "generative"; in fact, it is connected with the blessing of fruitfulness pronounced by God (Elohim) at man's being created "male and female" (Gen 1:27). The words Christ spoke about the resurrection allow us to deduce that the dimension of masculinity and femininity—that is, being male and female in the body—will be newly constituted in the resurrection of the body in that "other world."

Spiritualization

5. Is it possible to say something in more detail about this topic? Without any doubt, Christ's words reported by the Synoptics (Lk 20:27–40) authorize us to do so. There we read, in fact, that "those who are considered worthy of the other world and the resurrection from the dead...cannot die anymore, because they are equal to the angels and, being sons of the resurrection, they are sons of God" (Matthew and Mark report only the words "they will be like angels in heaven"). This statement allows us above all to deduce *a spiritualization of man according to a dimension that is different from that of earthly life* (and even different from that of the very "beginning"). It is obvious that we are not dealing here with a transformation of man's nature into an angelic, that is, purely spiritual nature. The context indicates clearly that in the "other world" man will keep his own psychosomatic nature. If it were otherwise, it would be meaningless to speak about the resurrection.

Resurrection means restoration to the true life of human bodiliness, which was subjected to death in its temporal phase. In Luke's expression just quoted (Lk 20:36; compare Mt 22:30; Mk 12:25) we are certainly dealing with human (that is, psychosomatic) nature. The comparison with heavenly beings used in this context is nothing new in the Bible. Already Psalm 8, when it exalts man as a work of the Creator, says, "You have made him little less than the angels" (Ps 8:6). One must suppose that in the resurrection this likeness will be greater: not through a disincarnation of man, but by another kind (one could also say, another degree) of spiritualization of his somatic nature, that is, by another "system of powers" within man. The resurrection signifies a new submission of the body to the spirit.

6. Before we begin to develop this topic, one should recall that the truth about the resurrection had a *key meaning for the formation of the-ological anthropology as a whole,* which could simply be considered *"anthropology of the resurrection."* Reflection about the resurrection led Thomas Aquinas in his metaphysical (and simultaneously theologi-cal) anthropology to abandon Plato's philosophical conception on the relation between the soul and the body and to draw near to Aristotle's view.[76] In fact, the resurrection attests, at least indirectly, that in the whole of the human composite, the body is not, contrary to Plato, only temporarily linked with the soul (as its earthly "prison," as Plato maintained),[77] but that together with the soul it constitutes the unity and integrity of the human being. This is precisely what Aristotle taught,[78] in contrast to Plato. When St. Thomas in his anthropology accepted Aristotle's conception, he did so because he considered the truth about the resurrection. In fact, the truth about the resurrection clearly affirms that man's eschatological perfection and happiness cannot be understood as a state of the soul alone, separated (according to Plato, liberated) from the body, but must be understood as *the definitively and perfectly "integrated" state of man* brought about by such a union of the soul with the body that it definitively qualifies and assures this perfect integrity.

---

76. See, e.g., "The soul, however, has one mode of being when it is united to the body and another when it is separated from the body, while the nature of the soul remains the same; *not in such a way that being united to the body is accidental to it, but by reason of its nature it is united to the body.*" St. Thomas Aquinas, *Summa Theol.* (ST hereafter), 1.89.1.

"If this [that is, being able to know only through sensible phantasms] is not from the nature of the soul, but belongs to it accidentally from the fact that it is *tied to a body, as the Platonists held...the soul would return to its nature after the removal of the impediment consisting of the body....* But, according to this view, the soul would not be united to the body for the greater good of the soul...; but this would only be for the greater good of the body: which is irrational, since matter is for the sake of form and not the other way around." Ibid.; John Paul II's addition.

"It belongs to the soul according to itself to be united with a body.... The human soul remains in its existence when it is separated from the body, having a natural fit-ness and inclination for union with the body." Ibid., 1.76.1 ad. 6.

77. *To men sōma hēmin estin sēma* [the body (*sōma*) is a grave (*sēma*) for us]. Plato, *Gorgias,* 493a; see also *Phaedo,* 66b; *Cratylus,* 400c.

78. Aristotle, *De Anima,* 412a19–22; see also *Metaphysics,* 1029b11 to 1030b14.

At this point we interrupt our reflection on the words Jesus spoke about the resurrection. The great richness of contents hidden in these words leads us to take them up again in further considerations.

67 General Audience of December 9, 1981 (*Insegnamenti*, 4, no. 2 [1981]: 880–83)

1. "In the resurrection they take neither wife nor husband, but are like angels in heaven" (Mt 22:30; cf. Mk 12:25). "They are equal to the angels, and, being sons of the resurrection, they are sons of God" (Lk 20:36).

Let us attempt to understand these words of Christ about the future resurrection in order to draw a conclusion from them about man's *spiritualization,* different from that of earthly life. Here one could speak also about a perfect system of powers in the reciprocal relations between what is spiritual and what is bodily in man. Following original sin, "historical" man experiences many imperfections of this system of powers as expressed in the well-known words of St. Paul, "I see in my members another law at war with the law of my mind" (Rom 7:23).

"Eschatological" man will be free from this "opposition." In the resurrection, the body will return to perfect unity and harmony with the spirit: man will no longer experience the opposition between what is spiritual and what is bodily in him. "*Spiritualization*" signifies not only that the spirit will master the body, but, I would say, that *it will also fully permeate the body and the powers of the spirit will permeate the energies of the body.*

2. In earthly life, the mastery of the spirit over the body—and the simultaneous subordination of the body to the spirit—can, as the fruit of persevering work on oneself, express a spiritually mature personality; nevertheless, the fact that the energies of the spirit succeed in mastering the forces of the body does not take away the possibility of their reciprocal opposition. The "spiritualization" to which the Synoptic Gospels allude (Mt 22:30; Mk 12:25; Lk 20:35–36) in the texts analyzed here lies beyond this possibility. It is thus a perfect spiritualization, in which *the possibility* of "another law at war with the law of my mind" (Rom 7:23) is completely eliminated. Nevertheless,

this state, which—as is evident—is essentially (and not only in degree) different from what we experience in earthly life, does not signify any "disincarnation" of the body nor, consequently, man's "dehumanization." On the contrary, it signifies his perfect "realization." In fact, in the composite, psychosomatic being that is man, perfection cannot consist in a reciprocal opposition of the spirit and the body, but *in a deep harmony between them, in safeguarding the primacy of the spirit.* In the "other world," this primacy will be realized, and it will be manifested in a perfect spontaneity without any opposition on the part of the body. Nevertheless, this should not be understood as a definitive "victory" of the spirit over the body. The resurrection will consist in the perfect participation of all that is bodily in man in all that is spiritual in him. At the same time, it will consist in the perfect realization of what is personal in man.

Divinization

3. The words of the Synoptics attest that man's state in the "other world" will not only be a state of perfect spiritualization, but also of the fundamental "divinization" of his humanity. The "sons of the resurrection"—as we read in Luke 20:36—are not only "equal to the angels," but also "sons of God." One can draw the conclusion that the degree of spiritualization proper to "eschatological" man will have its source in the degree of his "divinization," incomparably superior to what can be reached in earthly life. One should add that here we are not dealing only with a different degree, but in some way with another kind of "divinization." Participation in the divine nature, participation in the inner life of God himself, penetration and permeation of what is essentially human by what is essentially divine, will then reach its peak, so that the life of the human spirit will reach a fullness that was absolutely inaccessible to it before. This new spiritualization will thus be a *fruit of grace,* that is, *of God's self-communication in his very divinity,* not only to the soul, but *to the whole of man's psychosomatic subjectivity.* We speak here about "subjectivity" (and not only about "nature"), because that divinization should be understood not only as an "interior state" of man (that is, of the subject) able to see God "face to face," but also as a new formation of man's entire personal subjectivity according to the measure of union with God in his trinitarian

mystery and of intimacy with him in the perfect communion of persons. This intimacy—with all its subjective intensity—will not absorb man's personal subjectivity, but, quite on the contrary, will make it emerge in an incomparably greater and fuller measure.

4. The "divinization" in the "other world" indicated by Christ's words will bring to the human spirit such a "range of experience" of truth and of love that man would never have been able to reach it in earthly life. When Christ speaks about the resurrection, he shows at the same time that even the human body will participate, in its own way, in this eschatological experience of truth and love, united with the vision of God "face to face." When Christ says that those who will participate in the future resurrection "take neither wife nor husband" (Mk 12:25), his words—as we observed earlier—affirm not only the end of earthly history, tied to marriage and procreation, but seem also to unveil the new meaning of the body. Is it possible, in this case—*on the level of biblical eschatology*—to think *of the discovery of the "spousal" meaning* of the body above all as the *"virginal"* meaning of being male and female in the body? To answer this question, which emerges from the words reported in the Synoptics, we should penetrate more deeply into the very essence of what will be the beatific vision of the Divine Being, the vision of God "face to face" in the future life. We should also let ourselves be guided by that "range of experience" of truth and love that surpasses the limits of man's cognitive and spiritual possibilities in temporality, and in which he will come to share in the "other world."

5. This "eschatological experience" of the Living God will not only concentrate in itself all of man's spiritual energies, but at the same time reveal to him in a living and experiential way the *"self-communication"* of God to everything created and, in particular, *to man, [a self-communication] that is God's most personal "self-giving": in his very divinity to man,* to that being who has from the beginning borne his image and likeness within himself. Thus, in the "other world," the object of "vision" will be that mystery hidden from eternity in the Father, a mystery that has in time been revealed in Christ to be fulfilled unceasingly by the work of the Holy Spirit; that mystery will become, if one may express it in this way, the content of eschatological experience and the "form" of human existence as a whole in the dimension of the "other world." Eternal life should be understood in

an eschatological sense, that is, as the full and perfect experience of the grace (*charis*) of God in which man can share through faith during his earthly life and which, by contrast, will not only be revealed to those who will participate in the "other world" in all its penetrating depth, but will also be experienced in its beatifying reality.

Here we interrupt our reflection focused on the words of Christ about the future resurrection of the body. In this "spiritualization" and "divinization" in which man will participate in the resurrection, we discover—in an eschatological perspective—the same characteristics that mark the "spousal" meaning of the body; we discover them in the encounter with the mystery of the living God, which reveals itself through the face-to-face vision of him.

68 *General Audience of December 16, 1981* (*Insegnamenti*, 4, no. 2 [1981]: 1136–39)

1. "IN THE RESURRECTION THEY TAKE neither wife nor husband, but are like angels in heaven" (Mt 22:30; cf. Mk 12:25). "They are equal to the angels, and, being sons of the resurrection, they are sons of God" (Lk 20:36).

The eschatological communion (*communio*) of man with God, which is constituted thanks to the love of a perfect union, will be nourished by the vision "face to face," by the *contemplation* of the most perfect communion—because it is purely divine—which is, namely, the *trinitarian communion of the divine Persons* in the unity of the same divinity.

2. The words of Christ reported by the Synoptic Gospels allow us to deduce that those who participate in the "other world" will keep—in this union with the living God that springs from the beatific vision of his unity and trinitarian communion—not only their authentic subjectivity, but will acquire it in a much more perfect measure than in earthly life. This acquisition will confirm the law of the integral order of the person, according to which the perfection of communion is not only conditioned by the spiritual perfection or maturity of the subject, but also in turn determines it. Those who will participate in the "future world," that is, in the perfect communion with the living God, will enjoy a perfectly mature subjectivity. If in this perfect sub-

jectivity, while keeping masculinity and femininity in their risen (that is, glorious) bodies, "they will take neither wife nor husband," then *this is explained* not only by the end of history, but also—and above all—by the "eschatological *authenticity" of the response* to that "self-communication" of the Divine Subject that will constitute the beatifying experience of God's gift of self, an experience absolutely superior to every experience proper to earthly life.

3. The reciprocal gift of oneself to God—a gift in which man will concentrate and express all the energies of his own personal and at the same time psychosomatic subjectivity—will be the response to God's gift of himself to man.[79] In this reciprocal gift of self by man, a gift that will become completely and definitively beatifying as the response worthy of a personal subject to God's gift of himself, the "virginity" or rather the virginal state of the body will manifest itself completely as the eschatological fulfillment of the "spousal" meaning of the body, as the specific sign and authentic expression of personal subjectivity as a whole. In this way, then, the eschatological situation in which "they will take neither wife nor husband" has its solid foundation in the future state of the personal subject when, as a consequence of the vision of God "face to face," *a love of such depth and power of concentration on God himself* will be born in the person that it *completely absorbs the person's whole psychosomatic subjectivity.*

4. This concentration of knowledge ("vision") and love on God himself—a concentration that cannot be anything but full participation in God's inner life, that is, in trinitarian Reality itself—will at the same time be the discovery in God of the whole "world" of relations that are constitutive of the world's perennial order ("cosmos"). This concentration will above all be man's rediscovery of himself, not only

---

79. "[Biblical faith] treats immortality in a 'dialogical' way [=being raised], that is, immortality is not simply derived from the evident impossibility of death in the indivisible, but from the saving act of one who loves and who has the power to bestow immortality. Man no longer faces the prospect of utter dissolution, because God knows him and loves him. All love desires eternity; God's love not only desires it, but also effects it and is it.... Because immortality as it is biblically presented does not proceed from intrinsic indestructibility, but comes instead from being included in a dialogue with the Creator, it must be called 'being raised.'" Joseph Ratzinger, "Resurrection, Theological," *Sacramentum Mundi* (English ed.), 5:341a; translation altered.

in the depth of his own person, but also in that union that is proper to the world of persons in their psychosomatic constitution. Certainly this is a union of communion. The concentration of knowledge and love on God himself in the trinitarian communion of Persons can find a beatifying response in those who will become sharers in the "other world" only *through realizing reciprocal communion commensurate with created persons*. And for this reason we profess faith in the "communion of saints" (*communio sanctorum*) and profess it in organic connection with faith in the "resurrection of the body." The words with which Christ affirms that in the "other world...they will take neither wife nor husband" stand at the basis of these contents of our faith, and at the same time they require an adequate interpretation precisely in its light. We should think of the reality of the "other world" in the categories of the rediscovery of a new, perfect subjectivity of each person and at the same time of the *rediscovery* of a new, *perfect intersubjectivity of all*. In this way this reality means the true and definitive fulfillment of human subjectivity and, on this basis, the definitive fulfillment of the "spousal" meaning of the body. The total concentration of created, redeemed, and glorified subjectivity on God himself will not take man away from this fulfillment, but—on the contrary—will introduce him into it and consolidate him in it. One can say, finally, that in this way the eschatological reality will become the source of the perfect realization of the "trinitarian order" in the created world of persons.

5. The words with which Christ appeals to the future resurrection—words confirmed in a singular manner by his own resurrection—complete what in the present reflections we are used to calling "the revelation of the body." This revelation penetrates in some way to the very heart of the reality we experience, and this reality is above all man, his body, the body of "historical" man. At the same time, this revelation allows us to pass beyond the sphere of this experience in two directions: before all else, in the direction of that "beginning" to which Christ appeals in his dialogue with the Pharisees about the indissolubility of marriage (Mt 19:3–9); in the second place in the direction of the "other world" to which the Teacher calls the attention of his listeners in the presence of the Sadducees who "say there is no resurrection" (Mt 22:23). These two "extensions of the sphere" of the

experience of the body (if one may say so) are not completely beyond the reach of our (obviously theological) understanding of the body. *What the human body is in the realm of man's historical experience is not completely cut off from these two dimensions of his existence* revealed by Christ's word.

6. It is clear that what is at issue here is not the "body" in the abstract, but man, who is both spiritual and bodily. When we continue in the two directions indicated by Christ's word and attach ourselves to the experience of the body in the dimension of our earthly existence (that is, in the historical dimension), we can make a certain theological reconstruction of what might have been the experience of the body on the basis of man's revealed "beginning" and also what it will be in the dimension of the other world. The possibility of such a reconstruction, which extends our experience of man/body, indicates, at least indirectly, *the coherence of the theological image of man in these three dimensions,* which come together in constituting the theology of the body.

69 *General Audience of January 13, 1982*
(Insegnamenti, 5, no. 1 [1982]: 81–85)

1. "IN THE RESURRECTION they will take neither wife nor husband, but will be like angels in heaven" (Mk 12:25; cf. Mt 22:30). "They are equal to the angels, and, being sons of the resurrection, they are sons of God" (Lk 20:36).

The words with which Christ appeals to the future resurrection—words confirmed in a unique way by his own resurrection—complete what in the present reflections we are used to calling "revelation of the body." This revelation penetrates, so to speak, to the very heart of the reality we experience, and this reality is above all man, his body, the body of "historical" man. At the same time, this revelation allows us to pass beyond the sphere of this experience in two directions: first in the direction of that "beginning" to which Christ appeals in his dialogue with the Pharisees about the indissolubility of marriage (Mt 19:3–8); then in the direction of the "future world" to which the Teacher directs the minds of his listeners in the presence of the Sadducees who "say there is no resurrection" (Mt 22:23).

2. Neither the truth about this "beginning" about which Christ speaks, nor the eschatological truth can be reached by empirical and rationalist methods alone. Yet, is it not possible to affirm that man carries these two dimensions in some way in the depth of the experience of his being, or, rather, that he is in some way on the way toward them as toward dimensions that fully justify the very meaning of his being body, that is, of his being "carnal" man? Then with regard to the eschatological dimension, is it not true that death itself and the destruction of the body can give to man an eloquent meaning in reference to the experience in which the personal meaning of existence is realized? When Christ speaks about the future resurrection, his words do not fall into emptiness. The experience of humanity and especially the experience of the body allow the listener to unite with these words the image of the new existence in the "future world," for which earthly experience provides the substratum and basis. A corresponding *theological reconstruction* is possible.

3. For the construction of this image—which corresponds in its content to the article of our profession of faith, "I believe in the resurrection of the body"—a great contribution is provided by the awareness that there is a connection between earthly experience and the whole dimension of man's biblical "beginning" in the world. If in the beginning God "created them male and female" (Gen 1:27), if in this duality with respect to the body he also planned in his foresight such a unity by which "they will be one flesh" (Gen 2:24), if he joined this unity to the blessing of fruitfulness or of procreation (see Gen 1:29), and if now, speaking before the Sadducees about the future resurrection, Christ explains that in the "other world" ... "they will take neither wife nor husband"—then it is clear that here we are dealing with a development of the *truth about the same man.* Christ points out man's identity, although this identity *is realized in a different way in eschatological experience than* in the experience of the very "beginning" and of all history. And nevertheless, man will always be the same, just as he came forth from the hand of his Creator and Father. Christ says, "They will take neither wife nor husband," but he does not affirm that this man of the "future world" will no longer be male and female as he was "from the beginning." It is thus evident that the meaning of being, with respect to the body, male or female in the

"future world" should be sought outside of marriage and procreation, but there is no reason to seek it outside of that which (independently from the blessing of procreation) derives from the very mystery of creation and thereafter also forms the deepest structure of man's history on earth, given that this history was deeply co-penetrated by the mystery of redemption.

4. In his original situation, man *is thus alone,* and at the same time, he *comes to be* as male and female: the unity of the two. In his solitude "he reveals himself" to himself as person to "reveal" at the same time the communion of persons in the unity of the two. In the one as well as the other state, the human being constitutes himself as image and likeness of God. From the beginning, man *is* also a body among bodies and in the unity of the two, he *comes to be* as male and female, discovering the "spousal" meaning of his body in the measure of his being a personal subject. Subsequently, the meaning of being a body and, in particular, of being male and female in the body, is linked with marriage and procreation (and thus with fatherhood and motherhood). Yet, *the original* and fundamental *meaning of being a body,* as also of being, as a body, male and female—that is, precisely that "spousal" meaning—*is united to the fact that man is created as a person and is called to a life "in communione personarum."* Marriage and procreation do not definitively determine the original and fundamental meaning of being a body nor of being, as a body, male and female. Marriage and procreation only give concrete reality to that meaning in the dimensions of history. The resurrection indicates the closure of the historical dimension. And so it is that the words "when they rise from the dead, they will take neither wife nor husband" (Mk 12:25) not only express clearly what meaning the human body will not have in the "future world," but allow us also to deduce that the "spousal" meaning of the body in the resurrection to the future life will perfectly correspond both to the fact that man as male-female is a person, created in the "image and likeness of God," and to the fact that this image is realized in the communion of persons. That "spousal" meaning of being a body will, therefore, be realized as a *meaning that is perfectly personal and communitarian at the same time.*

5. When we speak about the body glorified through the resurrection to new life, what we have in mind is man, male and female, in all

the truth of his humanity, who *together with the eschatological experi-ence of the living God* (with the vision "face to face") *will experience pre-cisely this meaning of his body.* This will be a completely new experi-ence, and yet, at the same time, it will not be alienated in any way from the experience man shared "from the beginning" nor from that which, in the historical dimension of his existence, constituted in him the source of the tension between the spirit and the body, mainly and precisely with reference to the procreative meaning of the body and of [its] sex. The man of the "future world" will find in this new experi-ence of his own body *the fulfillment* of what he carried in himself perennially and historically, in some sense, as an inheritance and even more so as a task and objective, as the content of ethos.

6. *The glorification of the body,* as the eschatological fruit of its divinizing spiritualization, will reveal the definitive meaning of what was from the beginning to be a distinctive sign of the created person in the visible world, as well as a means for reciprocal self-communica-tion between persons and an authentic expression of truth and love by which the *communio personarum* is built up. That perennial meaning of the human body, to which the existence of every man, burdened by the heritage of concupiscence, has necessarily brought a series of limi-tations, struggles, and sufferings, will then be revealed again and will be revealed at once in such *simplicity and splendor* that everyone who shares in the "other world" will find in his glorified body the fountain of the freedom of the gift. The perfect "freedom of the sons of God" (Rom 8:21) will nourish with this gift also all the communions that will constitute the great community of the communion of saints.

7. It is all too clear that—on the basis of man's experiences and knowledge in temporality, that is, in "this world"—*it is difficult to con-struct a fully adequate image* of the "future world." Nevertheless, at the same time, there is no doubt that with the help of Christ's words at least a certain approximation to this image is possible and reachable. We make use of this theological approximation, professing our faith in the "resurrection of the body" and "eternal life," as well as faith in the "com-munion of saints," which belongs to the reality of the "future world."

8. In concluding this part of our reflections, we should note once again that Christ's words reported by the Synoptic Gospels (Mt

22:30; Mk 12:25; Lk 20:35–36) have a decisive meaning, not only for what concerns the words of Genesis (to which Christ appeals in another context), but also in what concerns the whole Bible. These words allow us in some way to reread in a new way—that is, in all its depth—the whole revealed meaning of the body, the meaning of being man, that is, an "incarnated" person, of being, as a body, male or female. These words allow us to understand the meaning, in the eschatological dimension of the "other world," of that unity in humanity which was constituted "in the beginning" and which the words of Genesis 2:24 ("The man will...unite with his wife and the two will be one flesh"), pronounced in the act of man's creation as male and female, seem to direct, if not completely, at least, in any case, especially towards "this world."* Given that the words of Genesis were the threshold, as it were, of the whole theology of the body—a threshold on which Christ based himself in his teaching about marriage and its indissolubility—one must admit that his words reported by the Synoptics are like a new threshold of this integral truth about man, which we find again in the revealed Word of God. It is indispensable for us to dwell on this threshold if we wish our theology of the body—and also our Christian "spirituality of the body"—to be able to use it as a complete image.

B. PAULINE INTERPRETATION OF THE RESURRECTION IN 1 CORINTHIANS 15:42–49

Final Victory over Death

70 *General Audience of January 27, 1982*
(Insegnamenti, 5, no. 1 [1982]: 227–31)

1. DURING THE PRECEDING AUDIENCES we reflected about Christ's words about the "other world" that will emerge together with the resurrection of the body.

---

* Translator's note: The "skeleton" of this sentence is: These words allow us to understand the meaning...of that unity in humanity which was constituted "in the beginning" and which the words of Genesis 2:24...seem to direct...toward "this world."

These words had a singularly intense echo in St. Paul's teaching. Between the answer given to the Sadducees as transmitted by the Synoptic Gospels (see Mt 22:30; Mk 12:25; Lk 20:35–36) and Paul's apostolate, the event that took place first of all was Christ's own resurrection and a series of encounters with the Risen One, among which one should number as the last link in the chain the event that occurred near Damascus. Saul or Paul of Tarsus, who after his conversion became the Apostle to the Gentiles, also had *his own post-paschal experience,* analogous to that of the other apostles. At the basis of his faith in the resurrection, which he expresses above all in 1 Corinthians 15, certainly stands that encounter with the Risen One that became the beginning and foundation of his apostolate.

2. It is difficult at this point to summarize and comment adequately on the stupendous and far-ranging argument of 1 Corinthians 15 in all its particulars. It is significant that, while in the words reported by the Synoptic Gospels, Christ replied to the Sadducees, who "deny there is a resurrection" (Lk 20:27), Paul himself also responds or rather polemicizes (in conformity with his temperament) against those who contest it.[80] In his (pre-paschal) response, Christ did not refer to his own resurrection, but appealed to the fundamental reality of the covenant of the Old Testament, to the reality of the living God, who is the basis of the conviction about the possibility of the resurrection: the living God "is not a God of the dead but of the living" (Mk 12:27). In his post-paschal argument about the future resurrection, Paul appeals above all to the reality and truth of Christ's resurrection. In fact, he defends this truth even as the foundation of the faith in its integrity. "If Christ has not been raised, our preaching is in vain and also your faith is in vain.... But now Christ has been raised from the dead" (1 Cor 15:14, 20).

3. Here we find ourselves on the same line of revelation: *the resurrection of Christ is the final* and fullest word *of the self-revelation* of the

---

80. The Corinthians were probably troubled by currents stamped by Platonic dualism and a religious form of Neo-Pythagoreanism, as well as by Stoicism and Epicureanism; all Greek philosophies, moreover, denied the resurrection of the body. In Athens, Paul had already experienced the reaction of the Greeks to the doctrine of the resurrection during his speech at the Areopagus (see Acts 17:32).

living God as "*God* not of the dead, but *of the living*" (Mk 12:27). It is the final and fullest confirmation of the truth about God, who from the beginning has expressed himself through this revelation. The resurrection is also the answer given by the God of life to the historical inevitability of death, to which man was subjected after breaking the first covenant and which entered his history together with sin. First Corinthians 15 illustrates this answer about the victory won over death with extraordinary clear-sightedness by a presentation of the resurrection of Christ as the beginning of that eschatological fulfillment in which through him and in him everything will return to the Father, everything will be subjected to him (that is, handed back to him definitively) so that "God may be all in all" (1 Cor 15:28). And so—in this definitive victory over sin, over what sets the creature against the Creator—death is vanquished as well, "The last enemy to be destroyed will be death" (1 Cor 15:26).

4. In this context one finds words that can be considered a synthesis of *Pauline anthropology* concerning *the resurrection*. We should dwell a little longer on these words. We read in 1 Corinthians 15:42–46, "What is sown is perishable, what is raised is imperishable. It is sown in dishonor, it is raised in glory. It is sown in weakness, it is raised full of power. It is sown a natural[*] body, it is raised a spiritual body. If there is a natural body, there is also a spiritual body. Thus, it is written, that the first man, Adam, became a living being, but the last Adam became a life-giving spirit. But it is not the spiritual that is first, but the natural, and then the spiritual."

The First Adam and the Last Adam

5. Between this Pauline anthropology of the resurrection and the anthropology that emerges from the text of the Synoptic Gospels (Mt 22:30; Mk 12:25; Lk 20:35–36), there is consistency in essentials,

---

* Translator's note: The translation "natural" adopted by many English translations is an attempt to render the much-discussed Greek term *psychikon* (see footnote 82 below), from *psyche* (soul) as opposed to *pneumatikon*, from *pneuma* (spirit). The Vulgate and, following it, the CEI version of the Bible used by John Paul II read "animal" from "*anima*" (soul). "Animal body," however, could be misleading in English, because the connection with the Latin *anima* is no longer evident.

except that the text of 1 Corinthians is more developed. Paul shows the depth of what Christ had proclaimed, penetrating at the same time into the various aspects of this truth, which had been expressed concisely and substantially in the words written in the Synoptics. It is also significant for the Pauline text that the *eschatological perspective* on man, based on faith in "the resurrection of the body," *is united with the reference to the "beginning"* as well as the deep consciousness *of man's "historical" situation.* The man to whom Paul turns in 1 Corinthians and who opposes the possibility of the resurrection (like the Sadducees) has also his ("historical") experience of the body, and from this experience he sees clearly that the body is "perishable," "weak," "natural," "in dishonor."

6. Paul brings this man, the recipient of his letter—whether in the community of Corinth or also, I would say, at all times—face to face with the risen Christ, "the last Adam." By doing so, he invites him in some way to follow in the footsteps of his own post-paschal experience. At the same time, he reminds him of "the first Adam," that is, he leads him to turn toward the "beginning," to that first truth about man and the world that stands at the basis of the revelation of the mystery of the living God. *In his synthesis,* Paul thus *reproduces* everything *Christ had proclaimed* when he appealed at three different moments to the "beginning" in the dialogue with the Pharisees (see Mt 19:3–8; Mk 10:2–9); to the human "heart" as a place of struggle with concupiscent desires in man in the Sermon on the Mount (see Mt 5:27); and to the resurrection as a reality of the "other world" in the dialogue with the Sadducees (see Mt 22:30; Mk 12:25; Lk 20:35–36).

7. It belongs to the style of Paul's synthesis that it plunges its roots deeply into the whole of the revealed mystery of creation and redemption, from which it is developed and in the light of which alone it can be explained. The creation of man, according to the biblical account, is an act of enlivening matter by the spirit, thanks to which "the first man Adam became a living being" (1 Cor 15:45). Here the Pauline text repeats the words of Genesis 2:7, that is, of the second creation account (the so-called Yahwist account). The same source tells us that this original "animation of the body" suffered corruption because of sin. Although at this point in 1 Corinthians the author does not speak directly about original sin, nevertheless the

series of definitions that he attributes to the body of historical man, namely, that it is "perishable...weak...natural...in dishonor," indicates sufficiently what revelation portrays as a consequence of sin, what the same Paul elsewhere will call "slavery of corruption" (Rom 8:21). To this *slavery of corruption" the whole creation is* indirectly *subjected because of the sin of man,* who had been placed by the Creator in the midst of the visible world that he might "dominate" it (see Gen 1:28). In this way, man's sin has not only an interior but also a "cosmic" dimension. And according to this dimension, the body—which Paul (in conformity with his experience) characterizes as "perishable... weak...natural...in dishonor"—expresses in itself the state of creation after sin. This creation, in fact, "groans and suffers labor pains until now" (Rom 8:22). Nevertheless, just as labor pains are united to the desire for birth, to the hope of a new human being, so also the whole creation "waits with eager longing for the revelation of the sons of God...and cherishes the hope that it itself will be set free from the slavery of corruption to enter into the freedom of the glory of the children of God" (Rom 8:19–21).

8. Through this "cosmic" context of the statement contained in Romans—in a certain sense through the "body of all creatures"—we are attempting to understand the Pauline interpretation of the resurrection in its true depth. If this image of the body of historical man, which is so realistic and adequate to the universal experience of human beings, *conceals within itself,* according to Paul, *not only the "slavery of corruption"* but also hope, similar to the hope that accompanies "labor pains," the reason is that the Apostle captures in this image also *the presence of the mystery of redemption.* The consciousness of this mystery breaks out of all the experiences of man that can be defined as "slavery of corruption"; it breaks out, because redemption is at work in man's soul through *the gifts of the Spirit.* "We ourselves, who have the first fruits of the Spirit, groan inwardly while we wait for adoption as sons, the redemption of our bodies" (Rom 8:23). Redemption is the way to the resurrection. The resurrection constitutes the definitive accomplishment of the redemption of the body.

We will come back to the analysis of the Pauline text in 1 Corinthians in our further reflections.

71 *General Audience of February 3, 1982*
(Insegnamenti, 5, no. 1 [1982]: 288–91)

1. FROM CHRIST'S WORDS about the future resurrection from the dead reported by all three Synoptic Gospels (Matthew, Mark, and Luke), we have passed to the Pauline anthropology of the resurrection. We are analyzing 1 Corinthians 15:42–49.

In the resurrection, the human body will show itself—according to the words of the Apostle—"imperishable, glorious, full of power, spiritual." The resurrection is not, therefore, only a manifestation of life that conquers death—a final return, as it were, to the tree of Life, which man was distanced from at the moment of original sin—but also a revelation of man's destiny in all the fullness of his psychosomatic nature and of his personal subjectivity. Paul of Tarsus—who, following the footsteps of the other apostles, has experienced the state of Christ's glorified body in the encounter with the risen Christ—bases himself on this experience when, in Romans 8:23, he announces *"the redemption of the body"* and (in 1 Cor 15:42–49) *the completion* of this *redemption in the future resurrection.*

2. The literary method Paul uses here corresponds perfectly to his style. His style is to use antitheses that at the same time bring closer together what they contrast. In this way, they are useful for allowing us to understand Pauline thought about the resurrection, both its "cosmic" dimension and what concerns the characteristics of the inner structure of "earthly" and "heavenly" man. By contrasting Adam and (the risen) Christ—or the first Adam and the last Adam—the Apostle in fact shows in some way the two poles in the mystery of creation and redemption between which *man is situated* in the cosmos. One could even say that man is "set in tension" between these two poles *in the perspective of eternal destiny* that concerns from the beginning to the end his same human nature. When Paul writes, "The first man taken from the earth consists of earth, the second man comes from heaven" (1 Cor 15:27), he has in mind both Adam-man and Christ as man. Between these two poles—between the first and the last Adam—the process unfolds that he expresses in the words, "Just as we have borne the image of the man of earth, we will bear the image of the heavenly man" (1 Cor 15:49).

3. This "heavenly man"—the man of the resurrection, whose prototype is the risen Christ—is not so much the antithesis and negation
of the "man of earth" (whose prototype is the "first Adam") but above
all his fulfillment and confirmation. He is the fulfillment and confirmation of what corresponds to the psychosomatic constitution of
humanity in the realm of eternal destiny, that is, in the thought and
plan of the one who created man from the beginning in his image and
likeness. The humanity of the "first Adam," the "man of earth," carries
within itself, I would say, *a particular potentiality* (which is capacity
and readiness) *for receiving* all *that the "second Adam" became,* the heavenly Man, namely, Christ: what he became in his resurrection. It is
the same humanity, which all human beings, sons of the first Adam,
participate in. It is "perishable"—since it is fleshly—while being burdened with the heritage of sin, and yet it carries in itself at the same
time the potentiality of "incorruptibility."

It is the same humanity, which in all its psychosomatic constitution seems to be "in dishonor" and which nevertheless carries within
itself the desire for glory, that is the tendency and capacity to become
"glorious" in the image of the risen Christ. Finally, it is the same
humanity, which the Apostle—in conformity with the experience of
all human beings—calls "weak" and a "natural body," which nevertheless carries in itself the aspiration to become "full of power" and
"spiritual."

4. We are speaking here about human nature in its integrity, that
is, about humanity in its psychosomatic constitution. Paul, by contrast, speaks about the "body." Nevertheless, on the basis of the immediate and remote context, we can assume that what is at issue for him
is not only the body, but the whole man in his bodiliness, therefore
also in his ontological complexity. Without any doubt, if in the whole
visible world (cosmos) only this body, which is *the* human *body,* carries
in itself the "potentiality of the resurrection," that is, the aspiration
and the capacity of becoming definitively "imperishable, glorious, full
of power, spiritual," the reason is that, persisting from the beginning
in the psychosomatic unity of its personal being, *it can gather and
reproduce in this "earthly" image and likeness of God also the "heavenly"
image of* the last Adam, *Christ.* The Pauline anthropology of the resurrection is cosmic and universal together: everyone bears in himself

the image of Adam, and everyone is also called to bear in himself the image of Christ, the image of the Risen One. This image is the reality of the "other world," the eschatological reality (Paul writes "we will bear"), but at the same time it is already in some way a reality of this world, given that it was revealed in it through the resurrection of Christ. It is a reality implanted in the man of "this world," maturing in him toward the final fulfillment.

5. All the antitheses that follow each other in Paul's text help to draw a valid sketch of the anthropology of the resurrection. This sketch is at the same time more detailed than the one that emerges from the text of the Synoptic Gospels (Mt 22:30; Mk 12:25; Lk 20:35–36), but on the other hand, it is in some way more one-sided. The words of Christ reported by the Synoptics open before us the prospect of the body's eschatological perfection fully submitted to the divinizing depth of the vision of God "face to face," which is the inexhaustible source of both perpetual "virginity" (united with the spousal meaning of the body) and perpetual "intersubjectivity" of all human beings who will share (as male and female) in the resurrection. *The Pauline sketch* of the eschatological perfection of the glorified body seems to remain *rather in the sphere of the* same *inner structure of the man-person.* His interpretation of the future resurrection would seem to link itself again with the body-spirit "dualism" that constitutes the source of the inner "system of powers" in man.

6. This "system of powers" will undergo a radical change in the resurrection. Paul's words that explicitly suggest this change can, at any rate, not be understood and interpreted in the spirit of dualist anthropology,[81] as we will attempt to show in the continuation of our analysis. In fact, we should devote one more reflection to the anthropology of the resurrection in the light of 1 Corinthians.

---

81. "Paul takes absolutely no account of the Greek 'soul and body' dichotomy.... The apostle has recourse to a kind of trichotomy in which the totality of man is body, soul, and spirit.... All these terms are in movement and the division itself does not have fixed boundaries. There is insistence on the fact that body and soul are capable of being 'pneumatic,' spiritual." B. Rigaux, *Dieu l'a ressuscité. Exégèse et théologie biblique* (Gembloux: Duculot, 1973), 406–8.

72 General Audience of February 10, 1982 (Insegnamenti, 5, no. 1 [1982]: 336–39)

1. FROM CHRIST'S WORDS about the future resurrection of the body reported by all three Synoptic Gospels (Matthew, Mark, and Luke) we have passed in our reflections to what Paul writes about this subject *in 1 Corinthians 15*. Our analysis focuses above all on what one could call the "anthropology of the resurrection" according to St. Paul. The author of the letter contrasts the state of the man "of earth" (that is, historical man) with the state of the risen man, characterizing in a lapidary and simultaneously penetrating way the inner "system of powers" specific to each of these states.

2. That this inner system of powers must undergo a radical transformation in the resurrection seems indicated first of all by the contrast between the "weak" body and the body "full of power." Paul writes, "What is sown is perishable, what is raised is imperishable. It is sown in dishonor, it is raised glorious. It is sown in weakness, it is raised full of power" (1 Cor 15:42–43). "Weak" is thus the body that rises—to use metaphysical language—from the temporal soil of humanity. Paul's metaphor [of the seed] corresponds also to scientific terminology, which defines the beginning of man as a body by the same term ("*semen*" [seed]). If to the Apostle's eyes the human body that rises from the earthly seed seems "weak," this signifies not only that it is "perishable," subject to death and to all that leads to it, but also that it is a "natural body."[82] The body "full of power," on the other hand, which man will inherit from the last Adam, Christ, inasmuch as he is a sharer in the future resurrection, will be a "spiritual" body. It will be imperishable, no longer threatened by death. In

---

82. The original Greek uses the term *psychikon*. In St. Paul, it appears only in 1 Corinthians (2:14; 15:44, 46) *and nowhere else*, probably due to the pre-Gnostic tendencies of the Corinthians, and *it has a pejorative sense*; with regard to its content, it corresponds to the term "carnal" (see 2 Cor 1:12; 10:4).

However, in the other Pauline letters, *psychē* and its derivatives signifies man's earthly existence in its manifestations, the individual's way of living, and even the human person itself, *in a positive sense*—e.g., to indicate the ideal of the ecclesial community's life: *mia psychē*, in one spirit (Phil 1:27); *sympsychoi*, with the union of your spirits, (Phil 2:2); *isopsychon*, with equal mind (Phil 2:20). See Jewett, *Paul's Anthropological Terms*, 448–49.

this way, the antithesis "weak/full of power" refers explicitly not so much to the body considered apart, but to the whole constitution of man considered in his bodiliness. It is only within the framework of such a constitution that the body can become "spiritual"; and *this spiritualization of the body will be the source of its power and imperishability* (or immortality).

3. This theme has its origins already in the first chapters of Genesis. One can say that St. Paul sees the future resurrection as a certain *restitutio in integrum,* that is, as the reintegration and at the same time as the attainment of the fullness of humanity. It is not only a restitution, because in this case the resurrection would be, in a certain sense, a return to the state the soul shared in before sin, outside the knowledge of good and evil (see Gen 1–2). Yet, such a return does not correspond to the inner logic of the whole economy of salvation, to the deepest meaning of the mystery of redemption. *Restitutio in integrum,* linked with the resurrection and the reality of the "other world," can only be *an introduction to a new fullness.* It will be a fullness that presupposes man's whole history, formed by the drama of the tree of the knowledge of good and evil (see Gen 3) and at the same time permeated by the mystery of redemption.

4. According to the words of 1 Corinthians, the man in whom concupiscence prevails over spirituality, that is, the "natural body" (1 Cor 15:44), is condemned to death; instead, he should rise as a "spiritual body," as the man in whom the spirit will gain a just supremacy over the body, spirituality over sensuality. It is easy to understand that what Paul has in mind here is sensuality as the sum of the factors that constitute the limitation of human spirituality, that is, as a power that "binds" the spirit (not necessarily in the Platonic sense) by hindering its own power of knowing (seeing) the truth and also the power to will freely and to love in the truth. However, what cannot be at issue here is the fundamental function of the senses that serves to liberate spirituality, namely, the simple power of knowing and loving that belongs to the psychosomatic *compositum* of the human subject. Since the subject of discussion is the resurrection of the body, that is, of man in his authentic bodiliness, "spiritual body" should signify precisely *the perfect sensitivity of the senses, their perfect harmonization with the activ-*

ity of the human *spirit* in truth and in freedom. The "natural body," which is the earthly antithesis of the "spiritual body," by contrast indicates sensuality as a force that often undermines man inasmuch as, by living "in the knowledge of good and evil," he is often urged or pushed, as it were, toward evil.

5. One cannot forget that what is at issue here is not anthropological dualism, but a basic antinomy. What is part of it is not only the body (as Aristotelian *"hylē"*), but also the soul, or man as "a living soul" (see Gen 2:7). Its constituents are, on the one hand, man as a whole, the sum total of his psychosomatic subjectivity, inasmuch as he remains under the influence of the life-giving Spirit of Christ, and, on the other hand, the same man inasmuch as he resists and opposes this Spirit. In the second case, man is "a natural body" (and his works are "works of the flesh"). By contrast, *if he remains under the influence of the Holy Spirit,* man is "spiritual" (and produces the "fruit of the Spirit," Gal 5:22).

6. One can, therefore, say that we are dealing with the anthropology of the resurrection not only in 1 Corinthians 15, but that St. Paul's entire anthropology (and ethics) are permeated by the mystery of the resurrection, by which we have definitively received the Holy Spirit. First Corinthians 15 constitutes the Pauline interpretation of the "other world" and of man's state in that world, in which, with the resurrection of the body, everyone will share fully in the gift of the life-giving Spirit, that is, in the fruit of Christ's resurrection.

7. To conclude the analysis of the "anthropology of the resurrection" we should *turn our minds* once again *to Christ's words* about the resurrection and about the "other world," words reported by the evangelists Matthew, Mark, and Luke. We recall that in his answer to the Sadducees, Christ linked faith in the resurrection with the whole revelation of the God of Abraham, Isaac, Jacob, and Moses, who "is not God of the dead, but of the living" (Mt 22:32). And at the same time, rejecting the difficulty raised by his interlocutors, he spoke these significant words, "When they rise from the dead, they will take neither wife nor husband" (Mk 12:25). To these words—in their immediate context—we devoted our previous considerations, passing on from there to the analysis of 1 Corinthians 15.

These reflections have a fundamental significance for the whole theology of the body, *for understanding both marriage and celibacy "for the kingdom of heaven."* Our next analyses *will be* devoted *to the latter topic.*

2. Continence for the Kingdom of Heaven

A. THE WORDS OF CHRIST IN MATTHEW 19:11–12

Christ's Word and the Rule for Understanding

73 *General Audience of March 10, 1982*
(Insegnamenti, 5, no. 1 [1982]: 789–93)

1. TODAY WE BEGIN TO REFLECT about virginity or celibacy "for the kingdom of heaven."

The question of the call to an exclusive gift of self to God in virginity and celibacy plunges its roots deeply into the evangelical soil of the theology of the body. To show the dimensions proper to it, one must keep in mind the words by which Christ appealed to the "beginning," and those by which he appealed to the resurrection of the body. The statement "When they rise from the dead, they will take neither wife nor husband" (Mk 12:25) indicates that there is a condition of life without marriage, in which man, male and female, finds at one and the same time the fullness of personal giving and of the intersubjective communion of persons, thanks to the glorification of his whole psychosomatic being in the eternal union with God. When the call to continence "for the kingdom of heaven" finds an echo in the human soul, in the conditions of temporality and thus in the conditions under which persons "take a wife and take a husband" (Lk 20:34), it is not difficult to perceive *a particular sensibility of the human spirit* that *seems to anticipate,* already in the conditions of temporality, what man will share in the future resurrection.

2. Christ, however, did not speak about this particular vocation in the immediate context of his dialogue with the Sadducees (see Mt 22:23–30; Mk 12:18–25; Lk 20:27–36) when he appealed to the resurrection of the body. He had spoken about it (already earlier) in the context of the dialogue with the Pharisees about marriage and its indissol-

ubility, as an extension, as it were, of that dialogue (see Mt 19:3–9). His concluding words are about the so-called certificate of divorce allowed by Moses in some cases: "Because of the hardness of your heart Moses allowed you to divorce your wives, but from the beginning it was not so. Therefore I say to you, Whoever divorces his wife, except in the case of concubinage, and marries another commits adultery" (Mt 19:8–9). Then the disciples, who—as one can deduce from the context—were attentively listening to that dialogue and particularly to the final words spoken by Jesus, say to him, "If this is the condition of man in relation to woman, it is not advantageous to marry" (Mt 19:10). Christ gives them the following answer. "Not all can understand it, *but only those to whom it has been granted. For there are eunuchs who were born this way from their mother's womb; there are some who were made eunuchs by men, and there are others who *made themselves eunuchs for the kingdom of heaven.* Let anyone understand this who can" (Mt 19:11–12).

3. About this dialogue reported by Matthew one can raise the question: What did the disciples think when, after having heard the answer Jesus had given to the Pharisees about marriage, they expressed their observation, "If this is the condition of man in relation to woman, it is not advantageous to marry"? At any rate, Christ considered the circumstance fitting for talking to them about voluntary continence for the kingdom of heaven. In saying these things, he does not directly take a position about the disciples' statement, nor does he remain in the line of their reasoning.[83] Thus, he does not answer, "It is advantageous to marry," or, "It is not advantageous to marry." The question of continence for the kingdom of heaven is not set in opposition to marriage, nor is it based on a negative judgment about the importance of marriage. After all, when speaking earlier about the indissolubility of marriage, he had appealed to the "beginning," that is, to the mystery of creation, thus indicating the first and fundamental source of the value of marriage. Consequently, to answer the question of the disciples, or rather to clarify the problem raised by them,

---

83. On the more detailed problems of the exegesis of this passage, see L. Sabourin, *Il Vangelo di Matteo: Teologia e Esegesi* (Rome: Ed. Paoline, 1977), 2.834–36; "The Positive Values of Consecrated Celibacy," *The Way (Supplement)* 10 (1970): 51; J. Blinzler, "Eisin eunuchoi: Zur Auslegung von Mt 19, 12," *Zeitschrift für die Neutestamentliche Wissenschaft* 48 (1957): 268.

Christ *appeals to another principle.* It is not because "it is not advantageous to marry," nor because of a supposedly negative value of marriage that continence is observed by those who make such a choice
"for the kingdom of heaven" in their lives, but in view of the particular
value which is connected with this choice and which one must discover and welcome as one's own vocation. For this reason Christ says,
"Let anyone understand this who can" (Mt 19:12). Immediately
before this, he says, "Not all can understand it, but only those to
whom it has been granted" (Mt 19:11).

4. As one can see, in his response to the problem raised by the disciples, Christ *precisely and clearly states a rule for understanding* his
words. In her teaching, the Church is convinced that these words do
not express *a commandment* that is binding for all, but *a counsel* that
regards only some persons,[84] namely, those who are able to "understand it." And "able to understand it" are those "to whom it has been
granted." The quoted words clearly indicate the importance of the personal choice together with the importance of the particular grace, that
is, of the gift that man receives to make such a choice. One can say
that the choice of continence for the kingdom of heaven is a charismatic orientation toward that eschatological state in which human
beings "take neither wife nor husband": nevertheless, between man's
state in the resurrection of the body and the voluntary choice of continence for the kingdom of heaven in earthly life and in the historical
state of fallen and redeemed man, there is an essential difference. The
eschatological state of "will not marry" will be a "state," that is, the proper
and fundamental mode of the existence of human beings, men and
women in their glorified bodies. *Continence* for the kingdom of heav-
en, *as the fruit of a charismatic choice,* is an exception with respect to the
other state, that is, the state in which man came to share "from the
beginning" and still does share during his whole earthly existence.

---

84. "Likewise, the holiness of the Church is fostered in a special way by the observance of the counsels proposed in the Gospel by our Lord to his disciples. An emi-
nent position among these is held by virginity or the celibate state (cf. 1 Cor 7:32–34).
This is a precious gift of divine grace given by the Father to certain souls (cf. Mt
19:11; 1 Cor 7:7), whereby they may devote themselves to God alone the more easily, due to an undivided heart, in virginity or celibacy." Vatican II, *Lumen Gentium,* 42.

5. It is very significant that Christ does not directly link his words about continence for the kingdom of heaven with his announcement of the "other world" in which "they will take neither wife nor husband" (Mk 12:25). His words are found instead—as we have already said—in the continuation of the dialogue with the Pharisees in which Jesus appealed "to the beginning," indicating the institution of marriage by the Creator and recalling its indissoluble character, which corresponds in God's plan to the conjugal unity of husband and wife.

The counsel and, therefore, the charismatic choice of continence for the kingdom of heaven are linked in Christ's words, with the maximum recognition of the "historical" order of human existence with respect to soul and body. On the basis of the immediate context of the words about continence for the kingdom of heaven in man's earthly life, one must see in the vocation to such continence *a kind of exception to what is, by contrast, a general rule of this life.* This is what Christ emphasizes above all. Christ does not directly speak here about the fact that such an exception contains within itself the anticipation of eschatological life without marriage and proper to the "other world" (that is, to the final stage of the "kingdom of heaven"). It is indeed not a question of continence *in* the kingdom of heaven, but of continence *"for* the kingdom of heaven." The idea of virginity or celibacy as an eschatological anticipation and sign (see, e.g., *Lumen Gentium,* 44; *Perfectae Caritatis,* 12) derives from linking the words spoken here with the words Jesus was to speak in other circumstances, namely, in the dialogue with the Sadducees when he proclaims the future resurrection of the body.

We will come back to this topic in the course of the next Wednesday reflections.

Three Kinds of "Eunuchs"—Why?

74 *General Audience of March 17, 1982*
(Insegnamenti, 5, no. 1 [1982]: 878–81)

1. WE ARE CONTINUING THE REFLECTION about virginity or celibacy for the kingdom of heaven, an important topic also for a complete theology of the body.

In the immediate context of the words about continence for the kingdom of heaven, Christ makes a very significant comparison; and this confirms us still more in the conviction that he wants to root the vocation to such continence deeply in the reality of earthly life by opening a way for himself into the mentality of his audience. He lists, in fact, three categories of eunuchs.

This term [eunuch] refers to the physical defects that make the procreative power of marriage impossible. These defects explain the first two categories, when Jesus speaks about both congenital defects, "eunuchs who were born this way from their mother's womb," and defects acquired and caused by human intervention, "there are some who were made eunuchs by men" (Mt 19:12). Both cases involve *a state of external necessity*, that is, they are not voluntary. In his comparison, when Christ goes on to speak about those "who made themselves eunuchs for the kingdom of heaven" (Mt 19:12) as a third category, *he certainly makes this distinction to emphasize* even more *its voluntary and supernatural nature*: voluntary, because those who belong to this category "*made themselves* eunuchs," and supernatural, because they did it "for the kingdom of heaven."

2. The distinction is very clear and very forceful. Equally forceful and eloquent, however, is the comparison. Christ is speaking to men to whom the tradition of the Old Testament had not handed down the ideal of celibacy or virginity. Marriage was so common that only physical impotence could constitute an exception. The answer given to the disciples in Matthew 19:10–12 is at the same time directed *in some way to the whole Old Testament tradition*. Let us confirm this point by a single example taken from the Book of Judges, to which we appeal not so much for the particular plot, but for the sake of the significant words that accompany it. "Grant me...that I may go...and bewail my virginity" (Judg 11:37), says the daughter of Jephthah to her father after finding out from him that she had been destined to be sacrificed by a vow made to the Lord (in the biblical text we find the explanation of how things came to this point). "Go," we read a little later, "and he sent her away.... So she departed, she and her companions, and bewailed her virginity on the mountains. At the end of two months, she returned to her father, who did to her what he had promised with a vow" (Judg 11:38–39).

3. In the tradition of the Old Testament there is evidently no room for the meaning of the body that Christ wants to show and reveal to his disciples by speaking about continence for the kingdom of God. Among the personages known to us as spiritual leaders of the people of the Old Covenant, there is none who proclaimed such continence by word or deed.[85] Marriage was at that time not only a common state, but, even more, it had acquired in that tradition a meaning *consecrated by the promise made by the Lord to Abraham:* "As for me, my covenant is with you, and you will be the father of a multitude of nations.... I will make you very, very fruitful; and I will make nations of you, and kings shall be born from you. I will establish my covenant with you and your offspring after you from generation to generation, for an everlasting covenant, to be your God and the God of your descendants after you" (Gen 17:4.6–7). For this reason, in the tradition of the Old Testament marriage was *a religiously privileged state,* privileged by revelation itself, inasmuch as it is a source of fruitfulness and of the procreation of descendants. On the background of this tradition, according to which the Messiah was to be "son of David" (Mt 20:30), it was difficult to understand the ideal of continence. Everything spoke in favor of marriage: not only reasons arising from human nature, but also those from the kingdom of God.[86]

4. In this context, the words of Christ bring about a decisive change of direction. When he speaks to his disciples for the first time about continence for the kingdom of heaven, he clearly realizes that,

---

85. It is true that, at God's explicit command, Jeremiah had to observe celibacy (see Jer 16:1–2), but this was a "prophetic sign" that symbolized the coming abandonment and destruction of the land and the people.

86. It is true, as we know from sources other than the Bible, that celibacy was maintained within Judaism by some members of the group called Essenes (see Josephus, *Bell. Iud.* 2.8.2 120–21; Philo, *Hypothet.* 11, 14), but this occurred on the margins of official Judaism and probably did not continue beyond the beginning of the second century.

In the community of Qumran, celibacy was not binding for all, but some of its members observed it until death because they transferred to the area of common life in peacetime the prescriptions of Deuteronomy 23:10–14 about ritual purity, which was binding during holy war. According to the beliefs of people at Qumran, such a war was always taking place "between the sons of light and the sons of darkness." Thus, celibacy was for them the expression of being always ready for battle (see 1 Qm 7:5–7).

as sons of the tradition of the Old Law, they must associate celibacy and virginity with the situation of individuals, especially those of the male sex, who cannot marry due to defects of a physical nature ("eunuchs"), and for this reason he refers to them directly. This reference has a varied background: historical as well as psychological, ethical as well as religious. With this reference, *Jesus in some way touches upon all of these backgrounds,* as if he wanted to say, I know that what I am going to tell you now will raise great difficulties in your consciousness, in your way of understanding the meaning of the body; I shall speak to you, in fact, about continence, and this will undoubtedly be associated in you with a state of physical deficiency, inborn or acquired by human cause. I want to tell you, by contrast, that continence can also be voluntary and chosen by man "for the kingdom of heaven."

5. Matthew does not report any immediate reaction of the disciples in chapter 19. We find it later, only in the writings of the apostles, especially in Paul (see 1 Cor 7:25–40; see also Rev 14:4). This fact confirms that these words impressed themselves in the consciousness of the first generation of the disciples of Jesus and then bore fruit repeatedly and in many ways in the generations of his confessors in the Church (and perhaps also outside her). From the point of view of theology—that is, of the revelation of the meaning of the body, which is entirely new in comparison with the tradition of the Old Testament—these *words* are thus a *turning point.* Their analysis shows how precise and substantial they are, although they are so very concise. (We will see this even better when we analyze the Pauline text of 1 Corinthians 7.) Christ speaks about continence "for" the kingdom of heaven. In this way he wants to underline that this state, when it is consciously chosen by man in temporal life, the life in which human beings "take wife and take husband" has a single supernatural finality. Even if it is consciously chosen and personally decided, continence without this finality does not enter into the content of Christ's statement quoted above. By speaking of those who have consciously chosen celibacy or virginity for the kingdom of heaven (that is, "made themselves eunuchs"), Christ emphasizes—at least indirectly—that, in earthly life, this choice is connected *with renunciation* and also with a determined *spiritual effort.*

Continence for the Kingdom of Heaven and "Fruitfulness from the Spirit"

6. The same *supernatural finality*—"for the kingdom of heaven"—*allows a series of* more detailed *interpretations,* which Christ does not go through one by one in this passage. Nevertheless, one can say that through the lapidary formula that he uses he indicates indirectly all that has been said about this topic in revelation, in the Bible, and in tradition; all that has become the spiritual wealth of the Church's experience, in which celibacy and virginity for the kingdom of heaven have in many ways born fruit in the various generations of the Lord's disciples and followers.

75 *General Audience of March 24, 1982*
(Insegnamenti, 5, no. 1 [1982]: 978–81)

1. WE CONTINUE OUR REFLECTIONS on celibacy and virginity "for the kingdom of heaven."

Continence *"for"* the kingdom of heaven is certainly related to the revelation of the fact that *"in"* the kingdom of heaven "they take neither wife nor husband" (Mt 22:30). *It is a charismatic sign.* To be a living human being (male and female) who—in the earthly situation, in which "they take wife and take husband" (Lk 20:34)—of his own free will chooses continence "for the kingdom of heaven" shows that in this reign, that is, the "other world" of the resurrection, "they will take neither wife nor husband" (Mk 12:25), because God will be "all in all" (1 Cor 15:28). This way of existing as a human being (male and female) points out the eschatological "virginity" of the risen man, in which, I would say, the absolute and eternal spousal meaning of the glorified body will be revealed in union with God himself, by seeing him "face to face," glorified moreover through the union of a perfect intersubjectivity that will unite all the "sharers in the other world," men and women, in the mystery of the communion of saints. Earthly continence "for the kingdom of God" is without doubt a sign that *indicates* this truth and this reality. It is a sign that the body, whose end is not death, tends toward glorification; already by this very fact it is, I would say, a testimony among men that anticipates the future resurrection. Yet, *this* charismatic *sign* of the "other world" *expresses the most authentic power and dynamics* of the mystery of the "redemption of the body": a mystery Christ inscribed in man's earthly history and deeply rooted in this history. Thus, continence "for the kingdom of heaven" carries *above all the imprint of likeness to Christ* who himself, in the work of redemption, made this choice "for the kingdom of heaven."

2. In fact, from the very beginning, Christ's whole life was a discreet but clear detachment from what had so deeply determined the meaning of the body in the Old Testament. Against the expectations, as it were, of the whole Old Testament tradition, Christ was born from Mary, who at the moment of the Annunciation clearly says about herself, "How is this possible? I do not know man" (Lk 1:34), and thus professes her virginity. And although he is born from her like every man, as a son from his mother, although this coming into the world was accompanied also by the presence of a man who was Mary's betrothed and [then], before the law and men, her husband, still Mary's motherhood was virginal; and to this virginal motherhood corresponded the virginal mystery of Joseph, who, following the voice from above, did not hesitate to "take Mary...because what is begotten in her comes from the Holy Spirit" (Mt 1:20). Although *Jesus Christ's virginal conception and birth into the world* were hidden from men, although before the eyes of his fellow countrymen in Nazareth he was considered "son of the carpenter" (Mt 13:55; "*ut putabatur filius Joseph* [as it was thought, the son of Joseph]," Lk 3:23), nevertheless, the same reality and essential truth of his conception and birth distance themselves from what in the tradition of the Old Testament was exclusively in favor of marriage and made continence incomprehensible as well as socially unacceptable. Thus, how could "continence for the kingdom of heaven" be understood if the expected Messiah was to be a "descendant of David" and therefore, as was thought, was to be a son of the royal stock "according to the flesh"? Only Mary and Joseph, who lived the mystery of his birth, became the first witnesses of a fruitfulness different from that of the flesh, that is, the fruitfulness of the Spirit. "What is begotten in her comes from the Holy Spirit" (Mt 1:20).

3. The history of the birth of Jesus is certainly in line with the revelation of the "continence for the kingdom of heaven," about which Christ was to speak one day to his disciples. This event, how-ever, remained hidden from the men of that time and also from the disciples. It was to be revealed only gradually before the eyes of the Church on the basis of the testimonies and texts of the Gospels of Matthew and Luke. *The marriage of Mary with Joseph* (in which the Church honors Joseph as Mary's spouse and Mary as his spouse) *con-ceals within itself*, at the same time, *the mystery* of the perfect com-munion of persons, of Man and Woman in the conjugal covenant and at the same time the mystery of this *singular "continence for the kingdom of heaven"*: a continence that served the most perfect *"fruit-fulness of the Holy Spirit"* in the history of salvation. Indeed, it was in some way the absolute fullness of that spiritual fruitfulness, because precisely in the Nazarene conditions of Mary and Joseph's covenant in marriage and continence, the gift of the Incarnation of the Eternal Word was realized: the Son of God, consubstantial with the Father, was conceived and born as a Man from the Virgin Mary. The grace of the hypostatic union is connected, I would say, precisely with this absolute fullness of supernatural fruitfulness, fruitfulness in the Holy Spirit, shared by a human creature, Mary, in the order of "continence for the kingdom of heaven." Mary's divine motherhood is also in some way a superabundant revelation of that fruitfulness in the Holy Spirit to which man submits his spirit when he freely chooses conti-nence "in the body," specifically, continence "for the kingdom of heaven."

4. This image had to reveal itself gradually before the Church's consciousness in the continuously new generations of those who con-fess Christ, when the infancy Gospels firmly established in them the certainty of the divine motherhood of the Virgin, who had conceived by the Holy Spirit. Though only in an indirect way—and yet in an essential and fundamental way—this certainty *was to help in under-standing*, on the one hand, the holiness of marriage and, on the other hand, disinterestedness in view "of the kingdom of heaven," about which Christ had spoken to his disciples. Nevertheless, when he had spoken about it for the first time (as Matthew 19:10–12 attests), the great mystery of his conception and of his birth was completely unknown to them; it was hidden from them as it was from all the lis-teners and interlocutors of Jesus of Nazareth. When Christ spoke

about those who "made themselves eunuchs for the kingdom of heaven" (Mt 19:12), the disciples were able to understand it *only on the basis of his* personal *example.* Such continence must have impressed itself on their consciousness as a particular trait of likeness to Christ, who had himself remained celibate "for the kingdom of heaven." The detachment from the tradition of the Old Covenant, in which marriage and procreative fruitfulness "in the body" were a religiously privileged condition, must have been brought about above all on the basis of the example of Christ himself. Only little by little did it consciously take root that *for "the kingdom of heaven"* a special significance attaches to *man's spiritual and supernatural fruitfulness—which comes from the Holy Spirit* (the Spirit of God), and which, in a specific sense and in determined cases, *is served* precisely *by continence—*and that this is precisely continence "for the kingdom of heaven."

We find more or less all of these elements of evangelical consciousness (that is, of the consciousness proper to the New Covenant in Christ) in Paul. We shall seek to show this at a suitable time [see TOB 82–85].

To sum up, we can say that the main topic of today's reflection was the relation between continence "for the kingdom of God" proclaimed by Christ and the supernatural fruitfulness of the human spirit, which comes from the Holy Spirit.

Change in Direction—Motivation "For the Kingdom of Heaven"

76 *General Audience of March 31, 1982*
(Insegnamenti, 5, no. 1 [1982]: 1047–50)

1. WE CONTINUE TO REFLECT about the topic of celibacy and virginity for the kingdom of heaven, basing ourselves on the text of Matthew 19:10–12.

Speaking of continence *for* the kingdom of heaven and founding it on the example of his own life, Christ undoubtedly wanted his disciples to understand it above all in relation to the "kingdom" that he had come to announce and for which he indicated the right ways. The continence about which he spoke is precisely one of these ways and, as is clear from the context of Matthew, it is a particularly valid and privileged way. In fact, that *preference given to celibacy and virginity "for the kingdom"* was *an absolute novelty* in comparison with the tradition of the Old Covenant and had a decisive importance both for the ethos and the theology of the body.

2. In his statement, Christ stressed above all the finality of continence. He says that the way of continence, to which he himself gives testimony with his own life, not only exists and is not only possible, but is particularly valid and important "for the kingdom of heaven." It must be so, given that Christ himself chose it for himself. And if this way is so valid and important, *a particular value* must belong to continence for the kingdom of heaven. As we already pointed out, Christ does not face the problem on the same level and in the same line of reasoning in which the disciples had placed it when they said, "If this is the condition...it is not advantageous to marry" (Mt 19:10). Their words implied at root a certain utilitarianism. In his response, by contrast, Christ indirectly indicated that if *marriage* possesses its full fittingness and value for the kingdom of heaven, a *fundamental,* universal, and ordinary *value,* faithful to its original institution by the Creator (recall that precisely in this context the Teacher appealed to the "beginning"), then continence on its part possesses *a particular and "exceptional" value* for this kingdom. It is obvious that we are dealing here with continence chosen consciously for supernatural reasons.

3. In his statement, when Christ emphasizes before all else the supernatural finality of this continence, he does so not only in an objective, but also in an explicitly subjective sense, that is, he indicates *the need for a motivation* corresponding in an adequate and full way to the objective finality declared in the expression "for the kingdom of heaven." To realize the end in question—that is, to discover in continence that particular spiritual fruitfulness that comes from the Holy Spirit—one must will it and choose it in the power of a deep faith that not only shows us the kingdom of God in its future fulfillment, but also allows and enables us in a particular way *to identify ourselves with the truth and the reality of this kingdom,* precisely as it is revealed by Christ in his evangelical message and above all by the personal example of his life and actions. This is why it was said above that continence "for the kingdom of heaven"—inasmuch as it is an indubitable sign of the "other world"—bears within itself above all the inner dynamism of the mystery of the redemption of the body (see Lk 20:35), and in this meaning it also possesses the characteristic of a particular likeness with Christ. The one who consciously chooses such continence chooses in some sense a particular *participation in the mystery of the redemption (of the body)*; he wishes to complete it in a particular way in his own flesh (see Col 1:24), finding thereby also the imprint of a likeness with Christ.

4. All of this refers to the motivation of the choice (or to its end in the subjective sense): in choosing continence for the kingdom of heaven, man "should" let himself be guided exactly by such motivation. In the case in question, Christ does not say that man has an obligation to it (in any case, it is certainly not a question of a duty that springs from a commandment); still, without any doubt, his concise *words about continence* "for the kingdom of heaven" *strongly highlight* precisely *its motivation.* They highlight the motive (that is, they indicate the finality of which the subject is aware) both in the first part of the whole statement and in the second, by indicating that what is at stake is a particular choice, a choice proper to a rather exceptional vocation that is not universal and ordinary. At the beginning of the first part of his statement, Christ speaks about understanding ("Not all can understand it, but only those to whom it has been granted," Mt 19:11); and it is not a question of an "understanding" in the abstract, but an understanding that influences the decision, the personal choice in which the "gift," that is, the grace, must find an adequate resonance in the human will. Such an *"understanding"* thus *involves motivation.* Motivation then influences the choice of continence, which is accepted after one has understood its meaning "for the kingdom of heaven." In the second part of his statement, Christ declares that man "makes himself" a eunuch when he chooses continence for the kingdom of heaven and makes it the fundamental situation or state of his whole earthly life. *In a decision that is consolidated in this way,* the supernatural *motive,* from which the decision itself took its origin, *subsists.* It subsists by *renewing itself,* I would say, continually.

5. We have already turned our attention to the particular meaning of the final statement. When Christ speaks in this case about "making oneself" a eunuch, he not only highlights the specific weight of this decision, which is explained by the motivation born from a deep faith, but he does not even attempt to hide *the travail* that such a decision and its long-lasting consequences can have for man, for the normal (and also noble) inclinations of his nature.

The appeal to "the beginning" in the problem of marriage allowed us to discover the whole original beauty of this vocation of man, male and female, a vocation that comes from God and corresponds to man's twofold constitution as well as to the call to the "communion of persons." By proposing continence for the kingdom, Christ not only makes a pronouncement against the whole tradition of the Old Covenant, according to which, as we have said, marriage and procreation were religiously privileged, but he makes a pronouncement in some sense also in contrast with that "beginning" to which he himself had appealed, and it is perhaps also for this reason that he nuances his words with that particular "rule of understanding" we discussed above [see TOB 73:4]. The analysis of the "beginning" (especially on the basis of the Yahwist text) had, in fact, shown that, although it is possible to conceive man as solitary before God, nevertheless God himself drew him from this "solitude" when he said, "It is not good that the man should be alone; I want to make him a help similar to himself" (Gen 2:18).

6. Thus, the male-female duality proper to the very constitution of humanity and the unity of the two that is based on it remain "from the beginning," that is, to their very ontological depth, a work of God. And Christ, when he speaks about continence "for the kingdom of heaven," has this reality before him. Not without reason does he speak about it (according to Matthew) in the more immediate context, in which he appeals precisely "to the beginning," that is, to the divine beginning of marriage in man's very constitution.

On the background of the words of Christ one can assert not only that marriage helps us to understand continence for the kingdom of heaven, but also that continence itself throws a particular light on marriage viewed in the mystery of creation and redemption.

Continence and Marriage—
Vocation of "Historical" Man

77 *General Audience of April 7, 1982*
(Insegnamenti, 5, no. 1 [1982]: 1126–31)

1. WITH OUR EYES TURNED TO CHRIST, the Redeemer, we now continue our reflections on celibacy and virginity "for the kingdom of heaven" according to Christ's words reported in Matthew 19:10–12.

When he proclaims continence "for the kingdom of heaven," Christ fully accepts all that the Creator wrought and instituted from the beginning. Consequently, on the one hand, that continence must demonstrate that man, in his deepest constitution, is not only "dual," but also (in this duality) "alone" before God with God. Nevertheless, on the other hand, that which, in the call to continence for the kingdom of heaven, is an invitation to *solitude for God,* respects at the same time both the "dual nature of humanity" (that is, its masculinity and femininity) and also that *dimension of the communion* of existence that is *proper to the person.* The one who, in conformity with the words of Christ, adequately "grasps" the call to continence for the kingdom of heaven, follows this call and in this way preserves the integral truth of his humanity without losing along the way any of the essential elements of the vocation of the person created "in the image and likeness of God." This is important for the idea itself, or rather for the idea of continence, that is, for its objective content, which appears in the teaching of Christ as a radical novelty. It is equally important for realizing that ideal, that is, in order that the concrete decision made by man to live in celibacy or virginity for the kingdom of heaven (by the one who "makes himself" a eunuch, to use Christ's words) might be fully authentic in its motivation.

2. From the context of Matthew 19:10–12, it is sufficiently clear that the point is not to diminish the value of marriage to the advantage of continence, nor to eclipse one value with another. It is rather a question of "breaking away from," with full awareness, *that within man which, by the will of the Creator himself, leads to marriage and to go toward continence,* which reveals itself before the concrete man, male or female, as a call and gift of particular eloquence and of a particular meaning "for the kingdom of heaven." Christ's words (Mt 19:11–12)

begin with the whole realism of man's situation and with the same realism they *lead* him out, toward the call in which, in a new way, though he remains by his nature a "dual" being (that is, directed as a man toward woman, and as a woman toward man), he is able to discover in this solitude of his, which never ceases to be a personal dimension of everyone's dual nature, a new and even *fuller form of intersubjective communion with others*. This orientation of the call explains in an explicit way the expression "for the kingdom of heaven"; in fact, the realization of this kingdom must be found along the line of the authentic development of the image and likeness of God, in its trinitarian meaning, that is, in its meaning precisely "of communion." When he chooses continence for the kingdom of heaven, man has the awareness that in this way he can realize himself "differently," and in some sense "more" than in marriage, by becoming "a sincere gift for others" (*Gaudium et Spes*, 24:3).

3. Through the words reported by Matthew 19:11–12, Christ makes us understand clearly that this "going" toward continence for the kingdom of heaven is joined with a voluntary renunciation of marriage, of the state in which man and woman (according to the meaning the Creator gave "in the beginning" to their unity) become a reciprocal gift through their masculinity and femininity, also through bodily union. Continence means *a conscious and voluntary renunciation* of this union and all that is connected with it in the full dimension of human life and the sharing of life. The one who renounces marriage also renounces generation as the foundation of the community of the family composed of parents and children. The words of Christ to which we refer indicate undoubtedly this whole sphere of renunciation, although they do not dwell on particulars. And the way these words were spoken allows us to suppose that Christ understands the importance of such a renunciation and that he understands it not merely in view of the opinions on this subject dominant in Jewish society at that time. He understands *the importance of this renunciation also in relation to the good* that marriage and the family constitute in themselves because of their divine institution. Therefore, by the way he speaks the words in question, he makes us understand that this breaking away from the circle of the good, a break which he himself calls "for the kingdom of heaven," is connected with a certain self-sacrifice. This break also becomes the beginning of

further renunciations and voluntary self-sacrifices that are indispensable if the first and fundamental choice is to be consistent in the breadth of one's entire earthly life; and it is only thanks to such consistency that the choice is interiorly reasonable and not contradictory.

4. In this way, *the call to continence* as Christ expressed it—concisely and at the same time with great precision—outlines *the profile of the mystery of redemption together with its dynamism,* as already said before. It is the same profile under which Jesus, in the Sermon on the Mount, said the words about the need to keep watch over the concupiscence of the body, over the desire that begins to "look" and becomes already in that moment "adultery in the heart." Behind the words of Matthew, both in 19:11–12 and in 5:27–28, *one finds the same anthropology and the same ethos.* The invitation to voluntary continence for the kingdom of heaven enlarges the perspectives of this ethos: in the horizon of the words in the Sermon on the Mount, one finds the anthropology of "historical" man; in the horizon of the words about voluntary continence, it remains essentially the same anthropology, but irradiated by the perspective of "kingdom of heaven" or, at the same time, by the future anthropology of the resurrection. Nevertheless, on the ways of this voluntary continence in earthly life, the anthropology of the resurrection does not replace the anthropology of "historical" man. It is precisely this man, in any case "historical" man, in whom there remains at one and the same time the heritage of the threefold concupiscence, the heritage of sin, as well as the heritage of redemption; it is this man who makes the decision about continence "for the kingdom of heaven": he must *make this decision by subordinating the sinfulness of his own humanity to the powers that flow from the mystery of the redemption of the body.* He must do so just as every other person does who does not make a similar decision and whose way remains marriage. What is different is only the kind of responsibility for the chosen good, just as the kind of good chosen is different.

Right Understanding of the "Superiority" of Continence for the Kingdom of Heaven

5. In his statement, does Christ highlight the superiority of continence for the kingdom of heaven over marriage? He certainly says that it is an "exceptional" vocation, not "ordinary." He affirms, further,

that it is particularly important and necessary for the kingdom of heaven. If we understand superiority over marriage in this sense, we must admit that Christ points to it implicitly; still, he does not express it in a direct way. Only Paul was to say about those who choose marriage that they do "well" and about those who are willing to live in voluntary continence that they do "better" (see 1 Cor 7:38).

6. This is also the opinion of the whole tradition, both doctrinal and pastoral. The *"superiority" of continence to marriage never means, in the authentic tradition of the Church, a disparagement of marriage* or a belittling of its essential value. It does not even imply sliding, even merely implicitly, toward Manichean positions, or a support for ways of evaluating or acting based on a Manichean understanding of the body and of sex, of marriage and procreation. The evangelical and genuinely Christian superiority of virginity, of continence, is thus dictated by the motive of the kingdom of heaven. In the words of Christ reported by Matthew 19:11–12, we find a solid basis for admitting only such superiority, while we do not find any basis whatsoever for the disparagement of marriage that could be present in the recognition of that superiority.

We will return to this problem in our next reflection.

78 General Audience of April 14, 1982
(*Insegnamenti*, 5, no. 1 [1982]: 1176–79)

1. WE NOW CONTINUE THE REFLECTION of the last few weeks on the words about continence "for the kingdom of heaven," which, according to Matthew 19:11–12, Christ addressed to his disciples.

We say once more that these words, concise as they are, are wonderfully rich and precise, rich with a set of implications both doctrinal and pastoral in nature, and at the same time they point to the right limit in this matter. Thus, any sort of *Manichean interpretation* remains decidedly *outside that limit,* just as much as the concupiscent desire "in the heart" remains outside the limit according to what Christ said in the Sermon on the Mount (see Mt 5:27–28).

In Christ's words about continence "for the kingdom of heaven," there is not a hint of an "inferiority" of marriage related to the "body" or to the essence of marriage consisting in the fact that man and woman unite with each other in such a way as to become "one flesh."

Christ's words reported in Matthew 19:11–12 (like Paul's words in 1 Cor 7) give us no reason for holding either the "inferiority" of marriage or the "superiority" of virginity or celibacy on the grounds that by their very nature the latter consists in abstaining from conjugal "union in the body." On this point Christ's words are decidedly clear. He proposes the ideal of continence and the call to it to his disciples, *not by reason of the inferiority of,* or of prejudices against, *conjugal "union in the body,"* but *only for the "kingdom of heaven."*

2. In this light, a deeper clarification of the expression "for the kingdom of heaven" becomes particularly useful; and this is what we will try to do, at least in summary form in what follows. However, for the right understanding of the relation between marriage and continence, about which Christ speaks, and for an understanding of this relation as the whole tradition conceived it, it is worth adding that *"superiority" and "inferiority" are held within the limits of the complementarity of marriage and continence* for the kingdom of God. Marriage and continence are neither opposed to each other, nor do they divide the human (and Christian) community into two camps (let us say, of those who are "perfect" because of continence, and those who are "imperfect" or less perfect because of the reality of conjugal life). But these two fundamental situations, or, as one used to say, these two "states," in some sense explain or complete each other with respect to the existence and (Christian) life of this community, which as a whole and in all its members is realized in the dimension of the kingdom of God and has an eschatological orientation proper to that kingdom. Now, with regard to this dimension and orientation—in which the whole Christian community, all those who belong to it, must participate in faith—continence "for the kingdom of heaven" has a particular importance and particular eloquence for those who live a conjugal life. In any case, the latter obviously are the majority.

3. It seems, therefore, that *complementarity understood in this way finds its basis in the words of Christ according to Matthew* 19:11–12 (and also 1 Cor 7). There is no basis, by contrast, for a supposed opposition according to which celibates (or unmarried people) would constitute the class of the "perfect" on the mere basis of continence, and, on the opposite side, that married persons would constitute the class of the

"imperfect" (or the "less perfect"). If, according to a certain theological tradition, one speaks about the state of perfection (*status perfectionis*), one does not do so on the basis of continence by itself, but in view of the whole formed by a life based on the evangelical counsels (poverty, chastity, and obedience), because this life corresponds to Christ's call to perfection ("If you wish to be perfect...," Mt 19:21). *The perfection of Christian life is measured*, rather, *by the measure of love.* It follows that a person who does not live in the "state of perfection" (that is, in an institution that bases its plan of life on the vows of poverty, chastity, and obedience) or in a religious institute, but in the "world," can "de facto" reach a higher degree of perfection—the measure of which is love—than a person who lives in the "state of perfection" with a lesser degree of love. Still, the evangelical counsels undoubtedly help one to reach a fuller love. Therefore, whoever attains such a love, even if he does not live in an institutionalized "state of perfection," reaches the perfection that flows from love *through faithfulness to the spirit of those counsels.* Such perfection is possible and accessible for every human being, whether in a "religious institute" or in the "world."

4. What adequately corresponds to Christ's words reported in Matthew 19:11–12 seems thus to be the complementarity of marriage and continence for "the kingdom of heaven" in their meaning and manifold importance. In the life of an authentically Christian community, the attitudes and the values proper to the one and the other state—that is, to the one and the other essential and conscious choice as the vocation for one's whole earthly life and in the perspective of the "heavenly Church"—*complete each other and in some sense interpenetrate.* Perfect conjugal love must be marked by the faithfulness and the gift to the one and only Bridegroom (and also by the faithfulness and gift of the Bridegroom to the one and only Bride) on which religious profession and priestly celibacy are based. In sum, the nature of the one as well as the other love is "spousal," that is, expressed through the complete gift of self. The one as well as the other love tends to express that spousal meaning of the body, which has been inscribed "from the beginning" in the personal structure of man and woman.

We will take up this subject in what follows.

5. On the other hand, spousal love that finds its expression in continence "for the kingdom of heaven" must lead in its normal development to "fatherhood" or "motherhood" in the spiritual sense (that is, precisely to that "fruitfulness of the Holy Spirit" we have already spoken about), in a way analogous to conjugal love, which *matures in physical fatherhood and motherhood* and is confirmed in them precisely as spousal love. On its part, physical generation also fully corresponds to its meaning only if it is completed by fatherhood and motherhood *in the spirit*, whose expression and fruit is the whole educational work of the parents in regard to the children born of their bodily conjugal union.

As one can see, there are many aspects and spheres of the complementarity between the vocation, in the evangelical sense, of those who "take wife and take husband" (Lk 20:34) and those who consciously and voluntarily choose continence "for the kingdom of heaven."

In 1 Corinthians (which we will analyze later in our considerations [see TOB 82–85]), Paul wrote on this topic: "Each has his own gift from God, one in one way and another in another" (1 Cor 7:7).

Continence for the Kingdom— Between Renunciation and Love

79 *General Audience of April 21, 1982*
(Insegnamenti, 5, no. 1 [1982]: 1270–74)

1. WE CONTINUE OUR REFLECTIONS on the words of Christ about continence "for the kingdom of heaven."

It is impossible to understand fully the meaning and character of continence, if the last phrase of Christ's statement, "for the kingdom of heaven" (Mt 19:12), is not filled with its appropriate, concrete, and objective content. We said earlier [see TOB 76:3] that this phrase expresses the motive or highlights in a certain sense the subjective finality of Christ's call to continence. Nevertheless, in itself the expression has an objective character; it indicates in fact an objective reality for which individual persons, men or women, can "make themselves" (as Christ says) eunuchs. *The reality of the "kingdom" in Christ's statement according to Matthew 19:11–12 is defined in a precise and at the same time general way* so that it can include all the particular deter-minations and meanings that are proper to it.

2. The "kingdom of heaven" signifies the "kingdom of God," which Christ preached in its final, that is, eschatological fulfillment. Christ *preached* this kingdom in its temporal realization or establish-ment and at the same time *foretold* it in its eschatological fulfillment. The temporal establishment of the kingdom of God is at the same time its beginning and the preparation for its definitive fulfillment. Christ calls us to this kingdom and in some sense invites all to it (cf. the parable of the wedding banquet, Mt 22:1–14). If he calls some to continence "for the kingdom of heaven," it follows from the content of this expression that he calls them to participate uniquely in the establishment of the kingdom of God on earth, through which the definitive stage of the "kingdom of heaven" is begun and prepared.

3. In this sense, we said that this call carries within itself the par-ticular sign of the dynamism proper to the mystery of the redemption of the body [see TOB 76:3]. What is thus highlighted in continence for the kingdom of God, as we have already said, is denying oneself, taking up one's cross every day, and following Christ (cf. Lk 9:23), which can go as far as renouncing marriage and a family of one's own. All of this derives from the conviction that it is possible in this way to contribute more to the realization of the kingdom of God in its earth-ly dimension with the prospect of eschatological fulfillment. In his statement according to Matthew 19:11–12, Christ says in a general sense that the voluntary renunciation of marriage has this end, but he does not spell out this statement. In his first statement about this sub-ject, he does not yet specify *for what concrete tasks* such continence *is needed* or indispensable in the realization of the kingdom of God on earth and in preparing for its future fulfillment. We will hear some-thing further on this question from Paul of Tarsus (see 1 Cor), and the rest was to be completed by the Church's life in its historical development, carried by the stream of the authentic tradition.

4. In Christ's statement about continence "for the kingdom of heaven," we do not find any more detailed indication about *how to understand* that same *"kingdom"*—both with respect to its earthly realization and its definitive fulfillment—in its specific and *"excep-*

tional" relation with those who voluntarily "make themselves eunuchs" for it.

Nor is it said by what particular aspect of the reality that constitutes the kingdom those who have freely made themselves "eunuchs" are associated with it. In fact, it is evident that the kingdom of heaven is for all: also those who "take wife and take husband" are in relation with it on earth (and in heaven). For all, it is "the Lord's vineyard" in which they are to work here on earth, and later it is the "Father's house," in which they are to find themselves in eternity. What then is that kingdom for those who choose voluntary continence in view of it?

5. To these questions *we do not find* an answer, *for now*, in Christ's statement reported by Matthew 19:11–12. It seems that this corresponds to the character of the whole statement. Christ answers his disciples in such a way that he does not stay in line with their thought and evaluations, in which, at least indirectly, a utilitarian attitude about marriage lay hidden ("If this is the condition...it is not advantageous to marry," Mt 19:10). The Teacher distances himself explicitly from this way of setting up the problem, which is why, when he speaks about continence "for the kingdom of heaven," he does not point out why it is worthwhile to give up marriage in this manner, so that "advantageous" would not have a utilitarian note in the ears of the disciples. He only says that such continence is at times called for, if not indispensable, for the kingdom of God. He thereby points out that in the kingdom that he preaches and to which he calls, it constitutes *a particular value in itself*. Those who choose it voluntarily must choose it out of appreciation of its value and not on the basis of any other calculation whatsoever.

6. This essential tone of Christ's response, which directly concerns continence "for the kingdom of heaven," can also be linked indirectly with the earlier problem of marriage (see Mt 19:3–9). Therefore, if we consider the statement as a whole (see Mt 19:3–11) according to Christ's underlying intention, the answer would be the following. If someone chooses marriage, he must choose it exactly as it was instituted by the Creator "from the beginning"; he must seek in it those values that correspond to the plan of God; if on the other hand someone decides to follow continence for the kingdom of heaven, he must seek in it the values proper to such a vocation. In other words, *he must act in conformity with his chosen vocation*.

7. The "kingdom of heaven" is certainly the definitive fulfillment of the aspirations of all human beings, to whom Christ addresses his message: it is the fullness of the good that the human heart desires beyond the limits of all that can be its portion in earthly life; it is the greatest fullness of God endowing man with the gift of grace. In the dialogue with the Sadducees (see Mt 22:24–32; Mk 12:18–27; Lk 20:27–40), which we analyzed earlier [see TOB 64–69], we find other particulars about this "kingdom" or about the "other world." There are still others in the whole New Testament. It seems, nevertheless, that to clarify what the kingdom of heaven is for those who choose voluntary continence for its sake, *the revelation of the spousal relationship between Christ and the Church* has particular significance. Among the other texts, therefore, the decisive one is *Ephesians 5:25–33,* on which we should base ourselves above all when we consider the question of the sacramentality of marriage [see TOB 87–117b].

This text is equally valid both for the theology of marriage and for the theology of continence "for the kingdom," the theology of virginity or celibacy. It seems that it is precisely in this text that we find concretized, as it were, what Christ had said to his disciples when he invited them to voluntary continence "for the kingdom of heaven."

8. In this analysis, we have already sufficiently highlighted that Christ's words—in all their great conciseness—are fundamental, full of essential content, and also characterized by a certain severity. There is no doubt that Christ issues his call to continence in the perspective of the "other world," but he places the emphasis in this call on everything that expresses the temporal realism of the decision for such continence, a decision joined with the will to participate in the redeeming work of Christ.

Thus, in the light of Christ's words reported by Matthew (19:11–12), what emerges above all are the depth and seriousness of the decision to live in continence "for the kingdom" and what finds expression is the momentousness of the renunciation that such a decision implies.

Without any doubt, through all this, through the seriousness and depth of the decision, through the severity and responsibility it brings with it, what shines and gleams is love: *love as the readiness to make the exclusive gift of self for the "kingdom of God."* In the words of Christ, however, such love seems veiled by what is put in the foreground instead. Christ does not hide from his disciples the fact that the choice of continence "for the kingdom of heaven"—*seen in the categories of the temporal order*—is a renunciation. That way of speaking to his disciples, which formulates clearly the truth of his teaching and of the demands contained in it, is significant for the whole Gospel; and it is precisely this way of speaking that gives to the Gospel, among other things, such a convincing stamp and strength.

9. It is a characteristic feature of the human heart to accept even difficult demands in the name of love, for an ideal, and above all *in the name of love for a person* (love is, in fact, oriented by its very nature toward the person). And so, in this call to continence "for the kingdom of heaven," first the disciples and then the whole living tradition of the Church quickly discovered the love for *Christ himself as the Bridegroom of the Church, Bridegroom of souls,* to whom he has given himself to the end (cf. Jn 13:1; 19:30) in the mystery of his Passover and of the Eucharist.

In this way, continence "for the kingdom of heaven," the choice of virginity or celibacy for one's whole life, has become in the experience of the disciples and followers of Christ the act of *a particular response to the love* of the Divine Bridegroom, and therefore *acquired the meaning of an act of spousal love,* that is, of a spousal gift of self with the end of answering in a particular way the Redeemer's spousal love; a gift of self understood as a *renunciation,* but realized above all *out of love.*

80 General Audience of April 28, 1982
(Insegnamenti, 5, no. 1 [1982]: 1344–48)

1. "THERE ARE OTHERS WHO MADE themselves eunuchs for the kingdom of heaven." This is how Christ expresses himself according to Matthew 19:12.

It is a characteristic feature of the human heart to accept even difficult demands in the name of love, for an ideal, and above all *in the name of love for a person* (love is, in fact, oriented by its very nature toward the person). And so, in this call to continence "for the kingdom of heaven," first the disciples and then the whole living tradition of the Church quickly discovered the love *for Christ himself as the*

Bridegroom of the Church, Bridegroom of souls, to whom he has given himself to the end (cf. Jn 13:1; 19:30) in the mystery of his Passover and in the Eucharist. In this way, continence "for the kingdom of heaven," the choice of virginity or celibacy for one's whole life, has become in the experience of the disciples and followers of Christ an act of *particular response to the love* of the Divine Bridegroom, and therefore *acquired the meaning of an act of spousal love,* that is, of a spousal gift of self with the end of answering in a particular way the Redeemer's spousal love; a gift of self understood as a *renunciation,* but realized above all *out of love.*

The Spousal Meaning of the Body as the Foundation of Christ's Call to Continence

2. In this way we uncovered all the wealth of the meaning contained in the very concise but at the same time very profound statement of Christ about continence "for the kingdom of heaven"; but now we should direct our attention to the meaning these words have for the theology of the body, the biblical foundations of which we have tried to present and reconstruct "from the beginning." Exactly the analysis of that biblical "beginning" to which Christ appealed in his conversation with the Pharisees on the subject of marriage, on its unity and indissolubility (cf. Mt 19:3–9)—*shortly before* addressing the words about continence for the kingdom of heaven (cf. Mt 19:11–12) to his disciples—allows us to recall *the profound truth about the spousal meaning of the human body* in its masculinity and femininity, which we deduced then *from the analysis* of the first chapters of Genesis (especially from 2:23–25). It was exactly in this way that we had to formulate and specify what we find in those ancient texts [see TOB 13–19].

3. Contemporary mentality has become accustomed to think and speak above all about sexual instinct, thereby transferring to the terrain of human reality what is proper to the world of living beings, to the *animalia.* Now, a deepened reflection on the concise text of Genesis 1–2 allows us to show with certainty and conviction that "from the beginning" a clear and unambiguous boundary is drawn between the world of the animals (*animalia*) and man created in the image and likeness of God. In that text, though it is relatively short,

there is nevertheless enough room to show that man has a clear consciousness of what distinguishes him essentially from all living beings (*animalia*) [see esp. TOB 5–7].

4. Thus, *the application to man* of this *category*, a substantially naturalistic one, which is contained in the concept and expression of *"sexual instinct,"* is not entirely appropriate and adequate. Of course, one can apply this term on the basis of a certain analogy; in fact, man's particularity in comparison with the whole world of living beings (*animalia*) is not such that, understood from the point of view of species, he cannot be qualified in a fundamental way as an *animal* as well, but as an *animal rationale* [rational animal]. For this reason, despite this analogy, the application of the concept of "sexual instinct" to man—given the dual nature in which he exists as male and female—nevertheless greatly limits and in some sense "diminishes" what the same masculinity-femininity is in the personal dimension of human subjectivity. It limits and "diminishes" also that for which both, the man and the woman, unite so as to be one flesh (see Gen 2:24). To express this appropriately and adequately, one must also use *an analysis different from the naturalist one.* Precisely the study of the biblical "beginning" puts us under the obligation to do this in a convincing way. The truth about the spousal meaning of the human body in its masculinity and femininity, deduced from the first chapters of Genesis (see especially Gen 2:23–24), or *the simultaneous discovery of the spousal meaning of the body* in the personal structure of the subjectivity of man and woman, seems to be a key concept in this area and at the same time the only appropriate and adequate concept.

5. Now, it is precisely in relation to this concept, to this truth about the spousal meaning of the human body, that one must reread and understand the words of Christ about continence "for the kingdom of heaven," which he spoke in the immediate context of that appeal to the "beginning," on which he based his teaching about the unity and indissolubility of marriage. At the basis of Christ's call to continence there stands not only "sexual instinct" as a category of, I would say, naturalistic necessity, but also *the awareness of the freedom of the gift, which is* organically connected with the deep and mature *consciousness of the spousal meaning of the body* in the structure of man's and woman's personal subjectivity as a whole. Only in relation to such a

meaning of the masculinity and femininity of the human person does *the call to voluntary continence* "for the kingdom of heaven" *find a full guarantee and motivation.* Only and exclusively in such a perspective does Christ say, "Let anyone understand this who can" (Mt 19:12). He thereby indicates that such continence—although in every case it is above all a "gift"—can also be "understood," that is, it can be drawn and deduced from the concept man has of his psychosomatic "I" in its wholeness, and, more specifically, of the masculinity and femininity of this "I" in the reciprocal relationship that is as though "by nature" inscribed in all human subjectivity.

6. As we recall from the earlier analyses carried out on the basis of Genesis 2:23–25, that reciprocal relation of masculinity and femininity, that reciprocal "*for*" of man and woman, can be understood appropriately and adequately only within the dynamic whole of the personal subject. Christ's words in Matthew 19:11–12 show accordingly that this "*for,*" which has been present "from the beginning" at the basis of marriage, *can also stand at the basis of continence "for" the kingdom of heaven!* Relying on the same disposition of the personal subject, thanks to which man fully finds himself through a sincere gift of self (see *Gaudium et Spes,* 24:3), man (male and female) is able to choose the personal gift of self to another person in the conjugal covenant, in which they become "one flesh," and he is also able to *renounce freely* such a gift of self to another person, in order that by choosing continence "for the kingdom of heaven" he may give himself totally to Christ. On the basis of the same disposition of the personal subject and on the basis of the same spousal meaning of being, as a body, male and female, there can be formed the love that commits man to marriage for the whole duration of his life (see Mt 19:3–9), but there can be formed also the love that commits man for his whole life to continence "for the kingdom of heaven" (see Mt 19:11–12). This is what Christ speaks about in his whole statement addressed to the Pharisees (Mt 19:3–9) and then to the disciples (see Mt 19:11–12).

7. It is evident that the choice of marriage as it was instituted by the Creator "from the beginning" presupposes the consciousness and inner acceptance of the spousal meaning of the body, which is connected with the masculinity and femininity of the human person. Exactly this, in fact, is what is expressed in lapidary fashion in the

verses of Genesis. As we listen to Christ's words addressed to the disciples about continence "for the kingdom of heaven" (see Mt 19:11–12), we cannot think that this second kind of choice can be made in a free and conscious manner without a reference to one's own masculinity or femininity and to that spousal meaning proper to man precisely in the masculinity or femininity of his being a personal subject. Even more, in the light of the words of Christ, we must admit that *this second kind of choice,* namely, *continence for the kingdom of God,* is made also in relation to the masculinity and femininity proper to the person who makes this choice; it is made *on the basis of the full consciousness* of the *spousal meaning,* which masculinity and femininity contain in themselves. If this choice were made by artificially "prescinding" from this real richness of every human subject, it would not correspond appropriately and adequately to the content of Christ's words in Matthew 19:11–12.

In these words, Christ explicitly calls for full understanding when he says, "Let anyone understand this who can" (see Mt 19:12).

81 General Audience of May 5, 1982
(*Insegnamenti*, 5, no. 1 [1982]: 1405–8)

1. IN RESPONDING TO THE QUESTIONS of the Pharisees about marriage and its indissolubility, Christ appealed to the "beginning," that is, to its original institution by the Creator. Given that his interlocutors appealed to the Law of Moses that provided for the possibility of the so-called "certificate of divorce," he answered, "Because of the hardness of your heart Moses allowed you to divorce your wives, but from the beginning it was not so" (Mt 19:8).

After the dialogue with the Pharisees, the disciples of Christ turned to him with the following words, "If this is the condition of man in relation to woman, it is not advantageous to marry." He answered them, "Not all can understand it, but only those to whom it has been granted. For there are eunuchs who were born this way from their mother's womb; there are some who were made eunuchs by men, and there are others who made themselves eunuchs for the kingdom of heaven. Let anyone understand this who can" (Mt 19:10–12).

2. Christ's words allude doubtlessly to a conscious and voluntary renunciation of marriage. Such a renunciation is possible only when one admits an authentic consciousness of the value constituted by the spousal disposition of masculinity and femininity for marriage. In order for man to be fully *aware of what he is choosing* (continence for the kingdom), he must also be fully aware *of what he is renouncing* (the consciousness at stake here is exactly the consciousness of the value in the "ideal" sense; nevertheless this consciousness is completely "realistic"). In this way, Christ certainly calls for a mature choice. The form in which he expresses the call to continence for the kingdom of heaven proves it without a doubt.

Yet, a fully conscious renunciation of the value mentioned above is not enough.

Renunciation in the Service of Affirmation

3. In the light of Christ's words, and also in the light of the whole authentic Christian tradition, one can deduce that this *renunciation is at the same time a particular form of affirmation of the value* from which the unmarried person consistently abstains by following the evangelical counsel. This may seem like a paradox. We know, however, that paradox goes hand in hand with many statements of the Gospel, and often with the most eloquent and profound. If we accept this meaning of the call to continence "for the kingdom of heaven," we draw a correct conclusion when we maintain that the realization of this call serves also—and in a particular way—to confirm the spousal meaning of the human body in its masculinity and femininity. *The renunciation* of marriage for the kingdom of God at the same time *highlights* that meaning in all its inner truth and in all its personal beauty. One can say that this renunciation on the part of individual persons, men and women, is in some sense indispensable for the clearer recognition of the same spousal meaning of the body in the whole ethos of human life and above all in the ethos of conjugal and family life.

4. Thus, although continence "for the kingdom of heaven" (virginity, celibacy) orients the life of the persons who freely choose it toward a way outside the common way of conjugal and family life,

it nevertheless *does not remain without significance* for this life, for its style, value, and *evangelical authenticity*. We do not forget that the one and only key for understanding the sacramentality of marriage is the spousal love of Christ for the Church (see Eph 5:22–23), of Christ who was son of the Virgin, who himself was a virgin, that is, "a eunuch for the kingdom of heaven" in the most perfect sense of the term. We will have to take up this subject again at a later time.

5. At the end of these reflections one concrete problem still remains. In the person to whom the call to continence for the kingdom "has been granted"—how is such a call formed on the basis of the consciousness of the spousal meaning of the body in its masculinity and femininity, and further, as a fruit of such consciousness? *How is it formed or rather "transformed"?* This question is equally important from the viewpoint of the theology of the body and from the viewpoint of the development of the human personality, which is both personalistic and charismatic in character. If we wanted to answer this question exhaustively—in the dimension of all the aspects and all the concrete problems it includes—one would have to devote a special study to the relation between marriage and virginity, and between marriage and celibacy. This, however, would go beyond the limits of the present considerations.

6. Remaining within the sphere of Christ's words according to Matthew 19:11–12, we should conclude our reflections with the following statement. *First,* while continence "for the kingdom of heaven" undoubtedly signifies a renunciation, this *renunciation* is at the same time an *affirmation that flows from the discovery* of the "gift," that is, at the same time from the discovery of a new perspective of personally realizing oneself "through a sincere gift of self" (*Gaudium et Spes,* 24:3); therefore, this discovery stands in deep inner harmony with the sense of the spousal meaning of the body connected "from the beginning" with the masculinity or femininity of man as a personal subject. *Second,* although continence "for the kingdom of heaven" is a renunciation of marriage—which in the life of a man and a woman gives rise to the family—in no way can one see in it a negation of the essential value of marriage; on the contrary, continence indirectly *serves to high-*

light what is most lasting and most profoundly personal in the conjugal vocation, what *corresponds* in the dimensions of temporality (and at the same time in the perspective of the "other world") *to the dignity of the personal gift* connected with the spousal meaning of the body in its masculinity or femininity.

7. In this way, Christ's call to continence "for the kingdom of heaven," which is correctly associated with the appeal to the future resurrection (see Mt 21:24–30; Mk 12:18–27; Lk 20:27–40), has a capital importance not only for the Christian ethos and spirituality, but also for anthropology and for the whole theology of the body, which we are uncovering at its basis. We recall that when Christ appealed to the resurrection of the body in the "other world," he said, according to the version of the three Synoptic Gospels, "For when they rise from the dead, they will take neither wife nor husband..." (Mk 12:25). These words, which we already analyzed earlier, are part of the whole of our considerations on the theology of the body and contribute to building it.

B. PAUL'S UNDERSTANDING OF THE RELATION BETWEEN VIRGINITY AND MARRIAGE (1 COR 7)

Christ's Statement and the Teaching of the Apostles

82 *General Audience of June 23, 1982*
(Insegnamenti, 5, no. 1 [1982]: 2385–87)

1. HAVING ANALYZED CHRIST'S WORDS reported in Matthew 19:11–12, we should pass on to the Pauline interpretation of virginity and marriage.

Christ's statement about continence for the kingdom of heaven is concise and fundamental. In Paul's teaching, as we will soon be convinced, we can see a correlation of the Teacher's words; however, the meaning of his statement (1 Cor 7) as a whole should be evaluated differently. The greatness of Paul's teaching consists in the fact that, when he presents the truth proclaimed by Christ in all its authenticity and identity, he gives it his own tone, in some sense his own "personal" interpretation, an interpretation, however, arising above all from the experiences of his apostolic and missionary activity and perhaps immediately from the need to answer the concrete questions of those to whom this activity was directed. In this way we encounter in Paul the question of the reciprocal relation between marriage and celibacy or virginity *as a question that troubled the minds of the first generation of the confessors of Christ,* the generation of the disciples of the apostles, of the first Christian communities. This question was raised by the converts from Hellenism, that is, from paganism, more than by those from Judaism; and this may explain the fact that the topic presents itself precisely in a letter to the Corinthians, the first.

2. The <tone> [*] of the whole statement is undoubtedly magisterial; still, the tone, like the language, is also pastoral. Paul teaches the doctrine that the Teacher handed down to the apostles and, at the same time, he enters into a kind of continuous dialogue on this subject with those to whom he writes his letter. He speaks like a classical teacher of morality, facing and resolving questions of conscience, which is why moral theologians love to turn by preference to the clarifications and deliberations of 1 Corinthians 7. It should be remembered, however, that the ultimate basis of these deliberations is to be sought in the life and teaching of Christ himself.

3. The Apostle underlines with great clarity that voluntary virginity or continence *flows only from a counsel and not from a commandment.* "Now concerning virgins, I have no commandment of the Lord, but I give my counsel as one who by the Lord's mercy is trustworthy" (1 Cor 7:25). As one can see from the words just quoted, the Apostle distinguishes, exactly like the Gospel (see Mt 19:11–12), between counsel and commandment. On the basis of the "doctrinal" rule of understanding the proclaimed teaching [see TOB 73:4; 76:5], he wants to counsel, he wishes to give his personal advice to people who turned to him. Thus, *"counsel"* in 1 Corinthians 7 clearly *has two different meanings.* The author affirms that virginity is a counsel and not a commandment, and at the same time he gives his counsels both to married people and to those who still have to make a decision in this

---

[*] Tranlsator's note: The *Insegnamenti* text has "gift (*dono*)." UD reads "tone (*tono*)," which fits the context better.

regard, and finally to those who are in the state of widowhood. The problem is substantially the same as the one we meet in the whole statement of Christ reported by Matthew (see Mt 19:2–12): first about marriage and its indissolubility, and then about voluntary continence for the kingdom of heaven. Nevertheless, *the style* of this problem is very distinctive; it is Paul's.

4. "If anyone thinks that he is not behaving properly toward his virgin, if she is past her prime, and it is fitting that it happen in this way, let him do as he wishes; it is no sin. Let them even marry. But if someone stands firm in his heart, being under no necessity, but being the arbiter of his own will, and has determined in his own mind to keep his virgin, he will do well. So then, he who marries his virgin does well; and he who refrains from marrying her does better" (1 Cor 7:36–38).

5. The one who had asked for counsel could have been a young man who found himself faced with the decision to take a wife, or perhaps a newlywed who, faced with ascetic currents that existed in Corinth, reflected about the direction to give to his marriage; it could also have been a father or guardian of a girl who had raised the question of her marriage. In this case, the issue would have been directly the decision that derived from his rights as a guardian. Paul is, in fact, writing at a time when decisions of this sort were up to the parents or guardians rather than the young people themselves. In answering the question addressed to him in this way, *he attempts to explain very precisely* that *the decision about continence* or the life of virginity *must be voluntary* and that only *such* continence *is better than marriage.* The expressions "does well" and "does better" are in this context completely unambiguous.

6. So then, the Apostle teaches that virginity or voluntary continence, the abstaining of the young woman from marriage, flows exclusively from a counsel and that, in the right circumstances, it is "better" than marriage. The question of sin, on the other hand, does not enter in any way. "Are you bound to a wife? Do not seek to be free. Are you free from a wife? Do not seek a wife. But if you marry, you do not sin, and if the young one marries, she does not sin" (1 Cor 7:27–28). On the basis of these words alone we certainly cannot form a judgment on what the Apostle thought and taught about marriage. This topic will be explained in part already on the basis of the context of 1 Corinthians 7 and more fully in Ephesians 5:21–23. In our case, we are probably dealing with the answer to the question whether marriage is a sin; and one might even think that in such a question there is some influence of dualistic, pre-Gnostic currents that later turned into encratism and Manichaeism. Paul answers that *the question of sin does not come into play here at all.* It is not a question *of discernment between "good" and "evil," but only between "good" and "better."* Later he goes on to explain why the one who chooses marriage "does well," and the one who chooses virginity or voluntary continence "does better."

We will occupy ourselves with Paul's argument during our next reflection.

Paul's Argumentation

83 *General Audience of June 30, 1982*
(Insegnamenti, 5, no. 1 [1982]: 2452–56)

1. WHEN ST. PAUL in 1 Corinthians 7 explains the question of marriage and virginity (or continence for the kingdom of God), *he tries to explain* the reason why the one who chooses marriage does "well," while the one who chooses a life in continence or virginity does "better." He writes, "I say this to you, brothers, the appointed time has grown short; from now on, let those who have wives live as though they had none," and then, "let those who buy as though they had no possessions, and those who make use of the world as though they made no use of it. *For the stage of this world is passing away.* I want you to be free from anxieties" (1 Cor 7:29–32).

2. The final words of the text just quoted show that, in his argumentation, Paul *appeals* also *to his own experience,* which makes his argumentation more personal. Not only does he formulate the principle and try to explain it as such, but he ties it together with personal convictions born from the practice of the evangelical counsel of celibacy. The persuasive power of these convictions is attested by the various expressions and phrases. The Apostle writes to his Corinthians not only, "I wish that all were as I myself am" (1 Cor 7:7), but goes further when he says in reference to those who marry, "Still, those who marry will have troubles in the flesh, and I would spare you that" (1 Cor 7:28). This personal conviction of his, by the way, had already been expressed in the first words of 1 Corinthians 7, when he restates the following opinion of the Corinthians, even if only to modify it. "Now concerning the matters about which you wrote: It is well for a man not to touch a woman" (1 Cor 7:1).

3. One can raise the question: *What "troubles in the flesh"* did Paul have in mind? Christ only spoke about the sufferings (or "afflictions") experienced by a woman when she is about to "give birth to a child," but he underlines the joy (see Jn 16:21) she experiences as a recompense of these sufferings after the child's birth: the joy of motherhood. Paul, by contrast, speaks about "troubles of the body" that the spouses expect. Would this be the expression of a personal aversion of the Apostle against marriage? In this realistic observation one should see a justified warning for those who think—as at times young people do—that conjugal union and life should bring them only happiness and joy. The experience of life shows that spouses are not seldom left disappointed in what they expected most. The joy of the union brings with it also the "tribulations in the flesh" about which the Apostle writes in 1 Corinthians. These are often "troubles" of a moral nature. If he thereby intends to say that *true conjugal love*—exactly the one in virtue of which "the man...will unite with his wife, and the two will be one flesh" (Gen 2:24)—*is also a difficult love,* he certainly remains on the grounds of evangelical truth, and there is no reason to detect any symptoms of the attitude that was later to characterize Manichaeism.

4. In his words about continence for the kingdom of God, Christ does not attempt in any way to direct his listeners to celibacy or virginity by pointing out "the troubles" of marriage. One notices rather that he seeks to highlight various aspects, humanly painful, of the decision for continence: both the social reason and reasons of a subjective nature lead Christ to say about the person who makes such a decision that he makes himself a "eunuch," that is, voluntarily embraces continence. But precisely for this reason, what stands out very clearly is the whole subjective meaning, the greatness and exceptional character of such a *decision*: the significance of a mature answer to a particular gift of the Spirit.

5. Nothing else is intended by Paul's counsel of continence in 1 Corinthians, but he expresses it differently. He writes, "I say this to you, brothers, the time has grown short" (1 Cor 7:29), and a little later, "for the stage of this world is passing away" (1 Cor 7:31). This statement about the futility of human life and the *transitoriness of the temporal world,* in some sense the accidental character of everything created, should cause "those who have wives to live as though they had none" (1 Cor 7:29; cf. 7:31), and should prepare the ground for the teaching about continence. In the center of his reasoning, in fact, Paul places this key sentence, which can be brought together with Christ's statement, unique in its kind, about the subject of continence for the kingdom of God (see Mt 19:12).

6. While Christ highlights the greatness of the renunciation that is inseparable from such a decision, Paul shows above all how one should understand "kingdom of God" in the life of the person who renounced marriage for the sake of that kingdom. And while the triple parallelism of Christ's statement reaches its high point in the verb signifying the greatness of the renunciation voluntarily made ("and there are others who made themselves eunuchs for the kingdom of heaven," Mt 19:12), Paul defines the situation with a single word, the "unmarried (*agamos*)"; a little later, however, he renders the whole content of the expression "kingdom of heaven" in a splendid synthesis. He says, "The unmarried person is anxious about what is the Lord's, how to please the Lord" (1 Cor 7:32).

Every word of this statement deserves special analysis.

7. The context of the verb "be anxious" or "seek" in the Gospel of Luke, disciple of Paul, indicates that one must truly seek only the kingdom of God (see Lk 12:31), what constitutes "the better part," the *unum necessarium* (see Lk 10:41). And Paul himself speaks directly about his "being anxious for all the churches" (2 Cor 11:28), of seeking Christ through solicitude for the problems of the brothers, for the members of the body of Christ (see Phil 2:20–21; 1 Cor 12:25). Already from this context, there emerges the whole vast field of "anxiousness" to which the unmarried man can completely dedicate his thought, his effort, and his heart. Man can, in fact, "be anxious" only about what is truly close to his heart.

8. In Paul's statement, the unmarried is anxious about what is the Lord's (*ta tou kyriou*). With this concise expression, Paul encompasses the entire *objective reality of the kingdom of God.*

"The Lord's is the earth and everything in it," he himself will say a little further on in this letter (1 Cor 10:26; cf. Ps 24:1).

The object of the Christian's solicitude is the whole world! But Paul, when he says "Lord," means first of all Jesus Christ (see, e.g., Phil 2:11), and so "what is the Lord's" signifies in the first place "the Kingdom of Christ," his body, which is the Church (see Col 1:18) and everything that contributes toward its growth. All of this is what the unmarried person is anxious about, and therefore Paul, being in the full sense of the word an "apostle of Jesus Christ" (1 Cor 1:1) and a minister of the Gospel (see Col 1:23), writes to the Corinthians, "I wish that all were as I myself am" (1 Cor 7:7).

9. Still, apostolic zeal and the most fruitful activity do not yet exhaust what is contained in the Pauline motivation for continence. One could even say that their root and source is found in the second part of the phrase, which shows the subjective reality *of the kingdom of God.* "The unmarried man is anxious about...how to please the Lord." This statement embraces the whole field of man's personal relationship with God. "To please God"—the expression is found in ancient books of the Bible (see e.g., Deut 13:19)—is a synonym of life in God's grace and expresses the attitude of the one who seeks God, or who behaves according to his will so as to be pleasing to him. In one of the last books of Sacred Scripture, this expression becomes a theological synthesis of holiness. St. John applies it only once to Christ, "I always do what is pleasing to him" (the Father; Jn 8:29). St. Paul observes in Romans that Christ "did not seek to please himself" (Rom 15:3).

Between these two observations everything is included that constitutes the content of "pleasing to God," which the New Testament understands as following the footsteps of Christ.

10. It seems that the two parts of the Pauline expression overlap: in fact, being anxious about "what is the Lord's," about the "affairs of the Lord," must "please the Lord." On the other hand, the one who pleases God cannot close himself in himself, but opens himself to the world, to everything that is to be led back to Christ. These evidently

are only two aspects of the same reality of God and his kingdom. Paul, nevertheless, had to distinguish them to show more clearly the nature and the possibility of continence "for the kingdom of heaven."

We will return again to this subject.

84 General Audience of July 7, 1982
(Insegnamenti, 5, no. 2 [1982]: 28–32)

1. DURING LAST WEDNESDAY'S meeting, we tried to reach a deeper grasp of the argumentation St. Paul uses in 1 Corinthians to convince his audience that the one who chooses marriage does "well" while the one who chooses virginity (or continence according to the spirit of the evangelical counsel) does "better" (1 Cor 7:38). As we continue this meditation today, let us recall that according to St. Paul "the unmarried man is anxious about…how to please the Lord" (1 Cor 7:32).

"Pleasing the Lord" has love as its background. This background becomes visible in a further comparison: the one who is not married is anxious about how to please God, while the married man must be anxious also about how to satisfy his wife. The spousal character of "continence for the kingdom of God" becomes in some way apparent here. Man always tries to please the person he loves. "Pleasing God" is thus not without that which is distinctive of the interpersonal relationship of spouses. On the one hand, pleasing is an effort on man's part, who tends toward God and seeks how to please him, that is, how to express love in an active way; on the other hand, to this aspiration of pleasing there corresponds the good pleasure of God, who, accepting man's efforts, crowns his own work by giving a new grace: from the beginning, in fact, this aspiration has been his gift. "Being anxious about how to please God" is thus a contribution by man to the continued dialogue of salvation begun by God. It is evident that every Christian who lives by faith takes part in this dialogue.

2. Paul observes, however, that the man who is bound by the marriage bond "finds himself divided" (1 Cor 7:34) because of his family duties (see 1 Cor 7:34). From this observation, it seems thus to follow that the unmarried person should be characterized by an *inner integration*, by a unification that would allow him to devote himself completely to the service of the kingdom of God in all its dimensions.

This attitude presupposes abstention from marriage, exclusively "for the kingdom of God," and a life directed uniquely to this goal. Otherwise "division" can secretly enter also the life of an unmarried person, who, being deprived, on the one hand, of married life and, on the other hand, of a clear goal for which he should renounce marriage, could find himself faced with a certain void.

3. The Apostle seems to know all this well and takes pains to make clear that he does not want to "put a restraint" on the one whom he counsels not to marry, but he does so to direct him to what is *worthy and keeps him united with the Lord without distractions* (1 Cor 7:35). These words bring to mind what Christ said to the apostles according to Luke during the Last Supper. "You are those who stood by me in my trials [literally, "in temptations"]; and I am preparing a kingdom for you, just as the Father has prepared it for me" (Lk 22:28–29; John Paul II's interpolation). The unmarried person, "being united with the Lord," can be certain that his difficulties will be met with understanding, "for we do not have a high priest who is unable to sympathize with our weaknesses, but one who has similarly been tested in every way, yet without sin" (Heb 4:15). This allows the unmarried person, not so much to immerse himself exclusively in possible personal problems, but rather to include them in the great stream of the sufferings of Christ and his body, which is the Church.

4. The Apostle shows how one can be "united with the Lord": one can reach this by aspiring to dwell constantly with him, to rejoice in his presence (*euparedron*), without letting oneself be distracted by nonessential matters (*aperipastōs*) (see 1 Cor 7:35). Paul unfolds this thought even more clearly when he speaks about the situation of the married woman and of the one who has chosen virginity or no longer has a husband. While the married woman must be anxious about "how to please her husband," the unmarried one "is anxious about what is the Lord's, to be holy in body and spirit" (1 Cor 7:34).

5. In order to grasp the whole depth of Paul's thought in an adequate manner, one must observe that "holiness," according to the biblical conception, is a state rather than an action; it has first of all an ontological character and then also a moral one. Especially in the Old Testament, it is a "separation" from what is not subject to God's influ-

ence, from what is *"profanum,"* in order *to belong only to God.* "Holiness in body and in spirit" thus also signifies the sacredness of virginity or celibacy accepted for the "kingdom of God." And at the same time, what is offered to God must distinguish itself by moral purity and thus presupposes a way of acting "without spot or wrinkle...holy and immaculate" according to the virginal model of the Church standing before Christ (Eph 5:27).

In this chapter of 1 Corinthians, the Apostle touches on the problems of marriage and celibacy or virginity in a deeply human and realistic way, realizing the mentality of the recipients of his letter. Paul's argumentation is to some extent *ad hominem.* In the environment of his addressees in Corinth, the new world, the new order of values that he announces, had to encounter another "world" and another order of values, different also from the one to which the words spoken by Christ were first addressed.

6. When Paul, with his teaching about marriage and continence, appeals also to the *transitoriness of the world* and of human life in it, he certainly does so in reference *to the environment* that was in some sense programmatically *oriented* toward *"use of the world."* From this point of view, his appeal to "those who make use of the world" that they might do it "as if they made no use of it" (1 Cor 7:31) is very significant. From the immediate context it is clear that, in this environment, even marriage was understood as *a way of "using the world"*—in a manner different from how it was in the whole Israelite tradition (despite some deformations, which Jesus indicated in his dialogue with the Pharisees and in the Sermon on the Mount). Undoubtedly, all this explains the style of Paul's answer. The Apostle clearly realized that, when he encouraged abstinence from marriage, he had to highlight, at the same time, a way of understanding marriage that would be in agreement with the whole evangelical order of values. And he had to do so with the greatest realism, that is, keeping in mind the environment of those to which he was addressing himself, the ideas and ways of evaluating things that were dominant in it.

7. To people who lived in an environment where marriage was considered above all as one of the ways of "making use of the world," Paul thus expressed himself with significant words both about virginity or celibacy (as we have seen) and about marriage itself. "To the unmarried and the widows I say that it is well for them to remain as I am. But if they do not know how to live in continence, they should marry. For it is better to marry than to be aflame" (1 Cor 7:8–9). Paul expressed almost the same idea a little earlier. "Now concerning the matters about which you wrote: It is well for a man not to touch a woman. Still because of the danger of incontinence, each man should have his own wife and each woman her own husband" (1 Cor 7:1–2).

"Concupiscence" and "Gift from God"

8. Does the Apostle in 1 Corinthians see marriage *only from the point of view of a "remedium concupiscentiae* [remedy for concupiscence]," as one used to say in traditional theological language? The statements quoted a little earlier would seem to attest to this. However, right next to the formulations just quoted, we read a sentence that leads us to see the whole of St. Paul's teaching in 1 Corinthians 7 differently. "I wish that all were as I myself am" (he repeats his favorite argument for abstaining from marriage). "But each has his own gift from God, one in one way and another in another" (1 Cor 7:7). Thus, also those who choose marriage and live in it receive a "gift" from God, "their own gift," that is, the grace proper to this choice, of this way of living, of this state. The gift received by persons who live in marriage is different from the one received by persons who live in virginity and choose continence for the kingdom of God; nevertheless it is a true "gift from God," a gift that is "one's own," destined for concrete persons, and "specific," that is, adapted to their vocation in life.

9. One can therefore say that, while the Apostle in his characterization of marriage from the "human" side (and perhaps even more from the side of the dominant local situation in Corinth) strongly highlights the motivation *in view of the concupiscence of the flesh,* at the same time he brings out, and with no less strength of conviction, also its sacramental and "*charismatic*" character. With the same clarity with which he sees man's situation in relation to the concupiscence of the flesh, he also sees the action of grace in every human being—in the one who lives in marriage no less than in the one who voluntarily chooses continence—keeping in mind that "the stage of this world is passing away."

85 *General Audience of July 14, 1982*
(Insegnamenti, 5, no. 2 [1982]: 70–74)

1. DURING OUR EARLIER CONSIDERATIONS, when we analyzed 1 Corinthians 7, we tried to gather together and understand the teachings and counsels that St. Paul gives to the addressees of his letter on the questions regarding marriage and voluntary continence (or abstaining from marriage). Affirming that the one who chooses marriage "does well" and that the one who chooses virginity "does better," the Apostle refers to the transitoriness of the world—or of everything temporal.

It is easy to grasp that the motive of the transitoriness and instability of what is temporal speaks, in this case, with much greater force than the reference to the reality of the "other world." Although the Apostle's way of expressing himself here is not without difficulty, we can still agree that what lies at the basis of the Pauline interpretation of the subject of "marriage" and "virginity" is not so much the metaphysics of accidental (and thus fleeting) being, but rather *the theology of a great expectation,* whose fervent spokesman Paul was. Not the "world" is man's eternal destiny, but the kingdom of God. Man cannot attach himself too much to the goods that follow the measure of a transitory world.

2. Marriage also is tied to the "stage of this world," which is passing; and here we are in some way quite close to the perspective Christ opened in his statement about the future resurrection (see Mt 22:24–32; Mk 12:18–27; Lk 20:27–40). Thus, according to Paul's teaching, the Christian must live marriage from the point of view of his definitive vocation. And while marriage is tied to the stage of this world, which is passing, and thus imposes *in some way the necessity of "closing oneself" in this transitoriness,* abstaining from marriage, one could say by contrast, liberates from such necessity. Exactly for this reason, the Apostle declares that the one who chooses continence "does better." Although his argument follows this path, nevertheless he decidedly gives first place (as we noted already) to the question of "pleasing the Lord" and "being anxious about what is the Lord's."

3. One can suppose that the same reasons speak in favor of the counsel the Apostle gives to women who are widowed. "The wife is

bound for the whole time in which the husband is alive; but if the husband dies, she is free to marry anyone she wishes, only in the Lord. But in my judgment it is better if she remains as she is. And I think that I too have the Spirit of God" (1 Cor 7:39–40). Thus, she *should remain a widow rather than enter a new marriage.*

4. Through what we discover in a clear-sighted reading of 1 Corinthians, especially chapter 7, we discover the whole realism of the Pauline theology of the body. While the Apostle proclaims in the letter that "your body is a temple of the Holy Spirit within you" (1 Cor 6:19), he is at the same time fully aware of the weakness and sinfulness to which man is subject precisely by reason of the concupiscence of the flesh.

Still, such awareness in no way eclipses for him the reality of the gift of God in which both those who abstain from marriage and those who take husband or wife come to share. In 1 Corinthians 7, we find a clear encouragement to abstain from marriage and the conviction that the one who decides to abstain "does better," but nevertheless we do not find any foundation for considering those who live in marriage "carnal" and those, by contrast, who for religious reasons choose continence "spiritual." In fact, in one as well as the other way of living—today we would say, in one as well as the other vocation—the "gift" is at work that each one receives from God, that is, *grace, which brings it about that the body is "a temple of the Holy Spirit"* and remains such *in virginity* (continence) *as well as in marriage,* if man remains faithful to his own gift and, in conformity with his state or vocation, does not "dishonor" the "temple of the Holy Spirit," which is his body.

5. In Paul's teaching contained above all in 1 Corinthians 7, we do not find any premise for what was later to be called "Manichaeism." The Apostle is fully aware that—even though continence for the kingdom of God is always worthy of recommendation—at the same time grace, that is, "one's own gift of God," helps also spouses in the shared life in which (according to the words of Genesis 2:24) they are so closely united that they become "one flesh." *This shared carnal life* is thus subject to the power of their *"own gift from God."* The Apostle writes about this with the same realism that characterizes his whole reasoning in chapter 7 of this letter. "The husband should carry out his duty toward his wife, and likewise the wife to her husband. For the wife is not arbiter over her own body, but the husband is; likewise the husband is not arbiter over his own body, but the wife is" (1 Cor 7:3–4).

6. One can say that these formulations are a clear comment by the New Testament about the words of Genesis we just recalled (Gen 2:24). Nevertheless, the words used here, in particular the expressions *"due" and "is not arbiter,"* cannot be explained by abstracting from the proper dimension of the marriage covenant, as we tried to show in the analysis of the Genesis texts; we will try to show it more fully when we speak about the sacramentality of marriage on the basis of Ephesians 5:22–33. At the proper time we will have to come back to these significant expressions that passed from St. Paul's vocabulary into the whole theology of marriage [see TOB 101:2–3].

7. For now we will continue to turn our attention to the other sentences in the same passage in 1 Corinthians 7, in which the Apostle addresses the following words to the spouses: "Do not abstain from each other except by common agreement for a set time, to devote yourselves to prayer, and then come together again, so that Satan may not tempt you through lack of self-control. This I say by way of concession, not of command" (1 Cor 7:5–7). This is a very significant passage, to which we will have to return in the context of our meditations on the other topics [see TOB 127–130].

Highly significant is the fact that the Apostle, who, like Christ, makes a clear distinction between commandment and evangelical counsel in his whole argumentation about marriage and continence, senses the need *to refer also to "concession" as a supplementary rule,* above all in particular *reference to the spouses* and their conjugal relations with each other. St. Paul clearly says that both conjugal relations and the voluntary periodic abstinence of the spouses must be a fruit of the "gift of God," which is their "own," and that the spouses themselves, by consciously cooperating with it, can keep up and strengthen their reciprocal personal bond together with the dignity that being "temple[s] of the Holy Spirit who is in [them]" (see 1 Cor 6:19) confers on their bodies.

8. It seems that the Pauline rule of "concession" indicates the need to consider all that in some way corresponds to the subjectivity, so highly differentiated, of man and woman. Everything in this subjec-

tivity, not only what is spiritual, but also what is psychosomatic, man's whole subjective wealth, which expresses itself between his spiritual and material being in the sensibility specific to the man as well as to the woman—all this must remain *under the influence of the gift each of them receives from God, a gift that is* his or her *very own.*

As one can see, in 1 Corinthians 7, St. Paul interprets the teaching of Jesus about continence for the kingdom of heaven in the very pastoral way characteristic of him, not without adding certain emphases on this occasion that are entirely personal to him. He interprets the teaching about continence, about virginity, in parallel with the teaching on marriage, keeping the realism proper to a pastor and, at the same time, the proportions we find in the Gospel, in the words of Christ himself.

9. In Paul's view, one can find the basic supporting structure of revealed teaching about man, who is destined for "future life" with his body. This supporting structure stands at the basis of the entire evangelical teaching about continence for the kingdom of God (see Mt 19:12)—but at the same time it supplies the basis on which the definitive (eschatological) fulfillment of the Gospel teaching about marriage rests (see Mt 22:30; Mk 12:25; Lk 20:35–36). These two dimensions of the human vocation are not opposed to each other, but complementary. Both provide a full answer to one of man's underlying questions: namely, the question about the meaning of "being a body," that is, the meaning of masculinity and femininity, of being "in the body" a man or a woman.

10. What we have customarily defined as theology of the body proves to be something truly fundamental and constitutive *for anthropological hermeneutics* as a whole—and at the same time equally fundamental for ethics and for *the theology of human ethos.* In each of these fields, we must listen attentively not only to the words of Christ in which he appeals to the "beginning" (Mt 19:4) or to the human "heart" as the interior and simultaneously "historical" place (see Mt 5:28) of the clash with the concupiscence of the flesh, but we must also listen attentively to the words in which Christ appealed to the resurrection to implant in the same restless human heart the first seeds of the answer to the question about the meaning of being "flesh" in the perspective of the "other world."

[The Redemption of the Body]*

———— ∽ ————

86 *General Audience of July 21, 1982*
(Insegnamenti, 5, no. 2 [1982]: 92–96)

1. "WE OURSELVES, WHO HAVE the first fruits of the Spirit, groan inwardly while we wait for...the redemption of our bodies" (Rom 8:23). Paul sees this "redemption of the body" *in an anthropological,* and simultaneously *a cosmic, dimension.* Creation in fact "was subjected to transitoriness" (Rom 8:20). The whole visible creation, the whole cosmos, carries the effects of man's sin. "The whole creation groans and suffers until now in labor pains" (Rom 8:22). And at the same time the whole "creation itself waits with eager longing for the revelation of the sons of God...and cherishes the hope that it itself will be set free from the slavery of corruption to enter into the freedom of the glory of the children of God" (Rom 8:19–21).

2. The redemption of the body, according to Paul, is an object of hope. This hope has been implanted in the human heart in some sense immediately after the first sin. It is enough to recall the words of Genesis that have traditionally been defined as the "Protoevangelium" (see Gen 3:15) and thus, we could say, as the beginning of the Good News, the first announcement of salvation. The redemption of the body is tied, according to Romans, precisely to this hope, in which—as we read—"we have been saved" (Rom 8:24). *Through hope,* which goes back to the very beginnings of man, the redemption of the body has its anthropological dimension: it is the redemption

---

* Translator's note: This heading has been added.

of man. At the same time, it irradiates in some way on all creation, which has from the beginning been tied to man in a particular way and subordinated to him (see Gen 2:28–30). The redemption of the body and, therefore, the redemption of the world, has a cosmic dimension.

3. In Romans, when he presents the "cosmic" image of salvation, Paul of Tarsus places man at its very center, just as "in the beginning" he had been placed at the very center of the image of creation. It is man, it is human beings in particular, who possess "the first fruits of the Spirit" and groan inwardly, expecting the redemption of their bodies (see Rom 8:23). Christ, who "came to reveal man fully to man himself and make his supreme vocation clear" (*Gaudium et Spes*, 22:1), *speaks* in the Gospel *about the very divine depth of the mystery of redemption,* which finds its specific "historical" subject precisely in him. Christ, therefore, speaks in the name of that hope that has been implanted in the human heart already in the "Protoevangelium." Christ gives fulfillment to this hope, not only with the words of his teaching, but above all with the testimony of his death and resurrection. Thus, the redemption of the body has already been completed in Christ. In him, the *hope* in which "we were saved" has been *confirmed*. At the same time, that hope *has been re-opened anew* to its definitive eschatological fulfillment. "The revelation of the sons of God" in Christ has been definitively directed toward that "freedom and glory" that is to be definitively shared in by the "children of God."

4. To understand all that "the redemption of the body" implies according to Romans, an authentic theology of the body is necessary. We have attempted to build one, appealing first of all to the words of Christ. The constitutive elements of the theology of the body are contained in what Christ says when he appeals to the "beginning" concerning the question of the indissolubility of marriage (see Mt 19:8), in what he says about concupiscence when he appeals to the human heart in the Sermon on the Mount (see Mt 5:28), and also in what he says when he appeals to the resurrection (see Mt 22:30). Each one of these statements contains in itself a rich content of an anthropological as well as ethical nature. Christ speaks to man—and speaks about man, who is a "body" and is created as male and female in the image

and likeness of God; he speaks about man, whose heart is subjected to concupiscence; and, finally, about man, before whom the eschatological perspective of the resurrection of the body opens up.

The *"body" signifies* (according to Genesis) the visible aspect of man and his belonging to the visible world. For St. Paul, it signifies not only this belonging, but at times also man's alienation from the influence of the Spirit of God. Both the one and the other meaning remain in relation to the "redemption of the body."

5. Since in the texts analyzed earlier Christ speaks about the divine depth of the mystery of redemption, his *words serve* precisely the *hope* that Romans speaks about. According to the Apostle, "the redemption of the body" is in a conclusive manner what we "await." In this way, we await precisely the eschatological *victory over death*, to which Christ gave witness above all with his resurrection. In the light of the paschal mystery, his words about the resurrection of the body and about the reality of the "other world" recorded by the Synoptics have gained their full eloquence. Both Christ and then Paul of Tarsus proclaimed the call to abstinence from marriage "for the kingdom of heaven" precisely in the name of this eschatological reality.

6. The "redemption of the body," however, expresses itself not only in the resurrection as a victory over death. It is present also in the words of Christ addressed to "historical" man, both when they confirm the principle of the indissolubility of marriage as a principle coming from the Creator himself, and when—in the Sermon on the Mount—Christ invites us to overcome concupiscence, even in the exclusively inner movements of the human heart. About both of these key statements one must say that they refer to *human morality* and have an *ethical sense.* Here it is not a question of the eschatological hope of the resurrection, but of the hope of victory over sin, which can be called the hope of everyday.

7. In his everyday life, man must draw from the mystery of the redemption of the body the inspiration and strength to overcome the evil that is dormant in him in the form of the threefold concupiscence. Man and woman, bound in marriage, must daily undertake the task of the indissoluble union of the covenant they made with each other. In addition, men and women who have voluntarily chosen con-

tinence for the kingdom of heaven must give a daily living witness of faithfulness to such a choice, listening to Christ's directives in the Gospel and those of the Apostle Paul in 1 Corinthians. In any case, what is at stake is *the hope of everyday*, which in the measure of normal tasks and difficulties of human life helps to overcome "evil with good" (Rom 12:21). In fact, "in hope we have been saved": the hope of everyday shows its power in human works and even in the very movements of the human heart, clearing a path in some sense for the great eschatological hope tied to the redemption of the body.

8. When it penetrates into daily life with the dimension of human morality, the redemption of the body helps man, above all, *to discover the whole good in which he achieves the victory over sin* and over concupiscence. Christ's words, which flow from the divine depth of the mystery of redemption, allow us to discover and strengthen the bond that exists between the dignity of the human being (of the man or the woman) and the spousal meaning of his body. On the basis of this meaning, they allow us to understand and bring about the mature freedom of the gift, which expresses itself in one way in indissoluble marriage and in another by abstaining from marriage for the kingdom of God. In these different ways, Christ "fully reveals man to man himself and makes his supreme vocation clear" [*Gaudium et Spes*, 22:1]. This vocation is inscribed in man according to his whole psychophysical *compositum* precisely through the mystery of the redemption of the body.

Everything we have tried to do in the course of our meditations in order to understand the words of Christ has its definitive foundation in the mystery of the redemption of the body.

Part Two

THE SACRAMENT

CHAPTER ONE

The Dimension of Covenant and of Grace

---------- ✺ ----------

1. Ephesians 5:21–33

A. INTRODUCTION AND CONNECTION

The Text of Ephesians 5:21–33

87 *General Audience of July 28, 1982*
(Insegnamenti, 5, no. 2 [1982]: 132–35)

1. TODAY WE BEGIN A NEW CHAPTER on the subject of marriage by reading Paul's words to the Ephesians:

> Wives, be subject to your husbands as you are to the Lord. For the husband is the head of the wife as *Christ* is the head of the Church, he who is *the Savior of his body.* And as the Church is subject to Christ, so also wives ought to be subject to their husbands in everything.
>
> And you, husbands, love your wives, as Christ loved the Church and gave himself for her, in order to make her holy by cleansing her with the washing of water accompanied by the word, so as to *present his Church before himself* all glorious, without spot or wrinkle or anything of the kind, but holy and immaculate. In the same way, husbands have the duty to love their wives *as their own body,* for the one who loves his wife loves himself. No one, in fact, ever hates his own flesh, but he nourishes and cares for it, as Christ does with the Church, because we are members of his body. For this reason a man will leave his father and his mother and unite with his wife, and the two will form one flesh. This *mystery is great*; I say this with reference to Christ and the Church. Therefore also you, each one on his part, should love

his wife as himself, and the woman should have reverence toward her husband. (Eph 5:22–33)

Ephesians 5:21–33 and Christ's Words

2. We should now subject the quoted text contained in Ephesians 5 to a thorough and deep analysis, just as earlier we analyzed the different words of Christ that seem to have a key significance for the theology of the body. We treated the words in which Christ appeals to the "beginning" (Mt 19:4; Mk 10:6), to the human "heart" in the Sermon on the Mount (Mt 5:28), and to the future resurrection (Mt 22:30; Mk 12:25; Lk 20:35–36). What is contained in the passage of Ephesians is the *"crowning,"* as it were, of these other comprehensive key words. Since the theology of the body emerged from them in its evangelical outline, simple and at the same time fundamental, *we must in some sense presuppose this theology* in interpreting the passage from Ephesians just quoted. Therefore, if one wishes to *interpret this passage,* one must do so *in the light* of what *Christ* has told us about the human body. By his words he not only appealed to "historical" man (to his "heart")—and by this very fact to the man of concupiscence, who is always "contemporary"—but he also highlighted, on the one hand, the perspective of the "beginning" or of original innocence and justice, and, on the other hand, the eschatological perspective of the resurrection of the body when "they will take neither wife nor husband" (Lk 20:35). All of this is part of the theological perspective of the "redemption of the body" (Rom 8:23).

Ephesians 5:21–33—Two Meanings of "Body"

3. The words of the author of Ephesians[87] too are centered on the body, both in its *metaphorical meaning,* that is, on the body of Christ which is the Church, and *in its concrete meaning,* that is, on the human body in its perennial masculinity and femininity, in its perennial des-

---

87. The Pauline authorship of Ephesians, which is recognized by some exegetes and denied by others, is a problem that can be resolved by *an* intermediate *supposition* that we accept here as *a working hypothesis*: namely, that St. Paul entrusted some concepts to his secretary, who then developed and finished them.

We have in mind this provisional solution of the problem when we speak about the "author of Ephesians," about "the Apostle," and about "St. Paul."

tiny for union in marriage, as Genesis says, "For this reason a man will leave his father and his mother and unite with his wife, and the two will be one flesh" (Gen 2:24).

In what way do these two meanings of the term "body" appear and converge in the passage from Ephesians? And *why* do they appear and converge there? We must ask ourselves these questions, expecting not so much immediate and direct answers, but possibly deeply thought-through and "long-term" answers that our earlier analyses have prepared us for. In fact, that passage from Ephesians cannot be correctly understood except *in the broad biblical context,* considering it as the "crowning" of the themes and truths that ebb and flow like long waves through the Word of God revealed in Sacred Scripture. They are central themes and essential truths. And for this reason the text quoted from Ephesians is also a key text and "classical."

Does Ephesians 5:21–33 Speak about the Sacramentality of Marriage?

4. It is a well-known text in the *liturgy,* where it always appears *in the context of the sacrament of Marriage.* The Church's *lex orandi* [rule of prayer] sees in it an explicit reference to this sacrament: and the *lex orandi* presupposes and at the same time expresses the *lex credendi* [rule of faith]. If we grant this premise, we must immediately ask ourselves: in this "classical" text of Ephesians, how does *the truth about the sacramentality of marriage* come to light? *In what way* is it expressed or confirmed in that text? It will become clear that the answer to these questions cannot be immediate and direct, but gradual and "long term." This is already confirmed by a first glance at this text, which brings us back to Genesis and thus "to the beginning," and which takes up again the well-known *analogy of spousal love* between God and his Chosen People from the writings of the prophets of the Old Testament in its description of the relationship between Christ and the Church. Without examining these relationships, it would be difficult to answer the question about the manner in which Ephesians treats *the sacramentality* of marriage. We will also see how the answer we are seeking must pass through the whole area of problems analyzed earlier, that is, through the theology of the body.

Sacrament and Body

5. The sacrament or sacramentality—in the most general sense of this term—intersects with the body and presupposes the "theology of the body." According to the generally recognized meaning, *the sacrament* is, in fact, a *"visible sign."* "Body" also refers to what is visible; it signifies the "visibility" of the world and of man. In some way, therefore—even if in the most general way—the body enters into the definition of sacrament, which is "a visible sign of an invisible reality," namely, of the spiritual, transcendent, and divine reality. In this sign— and through this sign—God gives himself to man in his transcendent truth and in his love. The sacrament is a sign of grace, and it is *an efficacious sign.* It does not merely *indicate* and express grace in a visible way, in the manner of a sign, but *produces* grace and contributes efficaciously to cause that grace to become part of man and to *realize and fulfill the work of salvation* in him, the work determined ahead of time by God from eternity and fully revealed in Christ.

Direction of the Following Analyses

6. I would say that this first glance at the "classical" text of Ephesians already indicates the direction in which we must develop our further analyses. These analyses must begin with the preliminary *understanding of the text in itself*; they must then lead us, so to speak, beyond the limits of the text, in order that we may understand if possible "to the very depths" what wealth of truth revealed by God is contained within the scope of that stupendous page. Using the well-known expression of the constitution *Gaudium et Spes,* one can say that the passage we chose from Ephesians "reveals —in a particular way—*man to man himself* and makes *his supreme vocation* clear" (*Gaudium et Spes,* 22:1) inasmuch as he participates in the experience of the incarnate person. In fact, when he created him in his image, God created him from the beginning as "male and female" (Gen 1:27).

During the following analyses we will try—above all in the light of the text quoted from Ephesians—to understand the sacrament more deeply (in particular marriage as a sacrament): first in the dimension of the covenant and of grace and then in the dimension of the sacramental sign.

B. DETAILED ANALYSIS

Ephesians 5:21–33 in the Context of Ephesians as a Whole

88 *General Audience of August 4, 1982*
(Insegnamenti, 5, no. 2 [1982]: 160–63)

1. IN OUR CONVERSATION LAST WEDNESDAY, I quoted Ephesians 5:22–33. After the introductory glance at this "classical" text, we should now examine the way in which this passage—which is so important, both for the mystery of the Church and for the sacramentality of marriage—is placed *in the immediate context of the letter as a whole.*

While realizing that biblical scholars discuss a series of problems with reference to the recipients of the letter, its authorship, and its date of composition, one should note that Ephesians has a very significant structure. The author begins this letter by presenting *the eternal plan of man's salvation in Jesus Christ.*

"The God and Father of our Lord Jesus Christ...chose us in Christ...to be holy and immaculate before him in love, predestining us to be his adoptive sons through Jesus Christ, according to the good pleasure of his will, to the praise and glory of his grace, which he has given to us in his beloved Son, in whom we have redemption through his blood, the forgiveness of our sins, according to the riches of his grace...to realize [this design] in the fullness of time: to bring everything together in Christ, as head" (Eph 1:3–7, 10).

Having presented with words full of gratitude the plan that is in God from eternity and that is at the same time already realized in the life of humanity, the author of Ephesians prays to God that all men and women (and directly the addressees of the letter) may fully know Christ as head. "He has set him over all things *as head of the Church, who is his body,* the fullness of him who fills all in all" (Eph 1:22–23). Sinful humanity is called to a new life in Christ, in which Gentiles and Jews are to unite as in a temple (see Eph 2:11–21). The Apostle is a preacher of the ministry of Christ among the Gentiles, to whom he turns, above all, in his letter, bending the "knees before the Father" and asking that he may grant them "according to the riches of his glory, to be powerfully strengthened through his Spirit in the inner man" (Eph 3:14, 16).

The Mystery of Christ and the Vocation of the Christian

2. After this profound and suggestive unveiling of the mystery of Christ in the Church, the author passes in the second part of the letter *to more detailed instructions* that are intended to define Christian life as a vocation flowing from the divine plan, which we spoke about earlier, that is, from the mystery of Christ in the Church. Here too, the author touches on various questions that are always relevant for Christian life. He exhorts us to preserve unity, underlining at the same time that such unity is built upon the multiplicity and diversity of the gifts of Christ. To each is given a different gift, but all, as Christians, must "clothe themselves with *the new man,* created according to God in justice and true holiness." Tied to this is a categorical appeal to overcome the vices and acquire the virtues that correspond to the vocation all have received in Christ (see Eph 4:25–32). The author writes, "Therefore be *imitators of God,* as beloved children, and walk in love, as Christ loved us and gave himself for us...in sacrifice" (Eph 5:1–2).

The Atmosphere of the Christian Community's Life

3. In Ephesians 5, these appeals become even more detailed. The author severely condemns pagan abuses and writes, "While once you were darkness, now in the Lord you are light. Live therefore as children of the light" (Eph 5:8). And then, "Do not be thoughtless, but understand what is the will of the Lord. Do not get drunk with wine [see Prov 23:31]...but *be filled with the Spirit,* conversing among yourselves with psalms, hymns and spiritual songs, singing and making hymns to the Lord with all your heart" (Eph 5:17–19; John Paul II's addition). With these words, the author of the letter wants to illustrate the climate of spiritual life that should animate every Christian community. At this point *he goes on* to the domestic community, that is, *to the family.* He writes, "Be filled with the Spirit...giving thanks to God the Father at all times and for everything in the name of our Lord Jesus Christ. Be subject to one another in the fear of Christ" (Eph 5:18, 20–21). We thus enter the passage of the letter that will be the subject of our particular analysis. We can easily observe that the essential content of this "classical" text appears at the intersection of

the *two main guiding lines* of the whole letter to the Ephesians: the first is the mystery of Christ, which is realized in the Church as an expression of the divine plan for man's salvation; the second is the Christian vocation as the model of life of baptized persons and particular communities, corresponding to the mystery of Christ or to the divine plan for the salvation of man.

Indications for the Community of the Family

4. In the immediate context of the passage quoted, the author of the letter tries to explain in what way the Christian vocation understood in this way must be realized and shown in the relationships *between all the members of a family*; thus not only between husband and wife (the precise subject of the passage chosen by us, Eph 5:22–33), but also between parents and children. "Children, obey your parents in the Lord, for this is just. Honor your father and mother: this is the first commandment with a promise: so that you may be happy and enjoy a long life on the earth. And you, fathers, do not embitter your children, but bring them up in the education and discipline of the Lord" (Eph 6:1–4). After this, the text speaks about the duties of servants in regard to their masters and vice versa of masters in relation to servants, that is, slaves (see Eph 6:5–9), which should also be referred to directives about the family in the wider sense. The family, in fact, consists not only of the parents and children (as one generation follows another), but in the wider sense also of servants of both sexes, male and female slaves.

5. Thus, the text of Ephesians we are proposing as the object of a deeper and more thorough analysis is found *in the immediate context of teachings about the* moral *obligations of the society of the family* (the so-called "*Haustafeln*" or domestic codes, according to Luther's definition). We find analogous instructions also in other letters (see, e.g., Col 3:18–4:1; 1 Pet 2:13–3:7). In addition, our passage fits into this immediate context inasmuch as the "classical" text we have chosen discusses the reciprocal duties of husbands and wives. Still, one should note that Ephesians 5:22–33 focuses as such only *on the spouses and on marriage*, while points regarding the family in the wider sense are found nearby. Before we begin a deeper and more detailed analysis of the text, we should add that the whole letter ends with a stupendous encouragement to spiritual battle (see Eph 6:10–20), with short recommendations (see Eph 6:10–20) and a final greeting (see Eph 6:23–24). That appeal for spiritual battle seems to be logically based on the argumentation of the whole letter. It is, so to speak, the explicit point of arrival of its main guiding lines.

Having before our eyes in this way the overall structure of the whole letter to the Ephesians, we will try in the first analysis to clarify the meaning of the words, "Be subject to one another in the fear of Christ" (Eph 5:21), addressed to husbands and wives.

The Spouses: "Reciprocally Subject in the Fear of Christ"

89 *General Audience of August 11, 1982*
(Insegnamenti, 5, no. 2 [1982]: 204–7)

1. TODAY WE BEGIN A MORE DETAILED analysis of the passage in Ephesians 5:21–33 in which the author addresses the spouses and calls on them to *"be subject to one another in the fear of Christ"* (Eph 5:21).

What is at issue here is *a relationship* with two dimensions or *on two levels*: reciprocal and communitarian. One specifies and characterizes the other. The reciprocal relations of husband and wife must spring from their common relation with Christ. The author of the letter speaks about the "fear of Christ" in a sense analogous to his words about the "fear of God." In this case, it is not a question of a fear or fright that is a defensive attitude in the face of the threat of an evil, but a question of reverence for holiness, for the *sacrum*; it is a question of *pietas,* which the language of the Old Testament expressed with the term "fear of God" (see, e.g., Ps 103:11; Prov 1:7; 23:17; Sir 1:11–16). In effect, such *pietas, which springs from the* profound *consciousness of the mystery of Christ,* must constitute *the basis* of the reciprocal *relations between the spouses.*

2. Like the immediate context, the text chosen by us also has a "parenetic" character, that is, the character of moral instruction. The author of the letter wants to point out to the spouses how their reciprocal relations and all their behavior should be formed. He draws the

specific indications and directives as a conclusion from the mystery of Christ presented at the beginning of the letter. This mystery must be spiritually present in the reciprocal relation of the spouses. Penetrating their hearts, kindling in them that holy "fear of Christ" (that is, *pietas*), the mystery of Christ must lead them to "be subject to one another": the mystery of Christ, that is, the mystery of the election of each of them from all eternity in Christ "to be adoptive sons" of God.

3. The expression that opens our passage of Ephesians 5:21–33, which we have approached by an analysis of the remote and immediate context, has an utterly unique eloquence. The author speaks about the mutual submission of the spouses, husband and wife, and in this way shows also how to understand *the words* he writes afterward *about the submission of the wife to the husband.* We read, "Wives, be subject to your husbands as you are to the Lord" (Eph 5:22). When he expresses himself in this way, the author does not intend to say that the husband is the "master" of the wife and that the interpersonal covenant proper to marriage is a contract of domination by the husband over the wife. He expresses a different concept instead, namely, that it is in her relationship with Christ—who is for both spouses the one and only Lord—that the wife can and should find the motivation for the relationship with her husband, which flows from the very essence of marriage and the family. This relationship is nevertheless not one-sided submission. According to the teaching of Ephesians, marriage excludes this element of the contract, which weighed on this institution and at times does not cease to weigh on it. Husband and wife are, in fact, "subject to one another," mutually subordinated to one another. *The source* of this reciprocal submission lies in Christian *pietas* and *its expression is love.*

4. The author of the letter underlines this love in a particular way when he turns to husbands. He writes, "And you, husbands, love your wives," and with this way of expressing himself he takes away any fear that could have been created (given the contemporary sensibility) by the earlier sentence, "Wives, be subject to your husbands." Love excludes every kind of submission by which the wife would become a servant or slave of the husband, an object of one-sided submission. Love makes the *husband simultaneously subject* to

the wife, and *subject* in this *to the Lord himself,* as the wife is to the husband. The community or unity that they should constitute because of marriage is realized through a reciprocal gift, which is also a mutual submission. Christ is the source and at the same time the model of that submission—which, being reciprocal "in the fear of Christ," confers on the conjugal union a deep and mature character. Many factors of a psychological and moral nature are so transformed in this source and before this model that they give rise, I would say, to a new and precious "fusion" of the conduct and relations on both sides.

Analogy and Mystery (At the Foundation of the Sacramentality of Marriage)

5. The author of Ephesians is not afraid to accept the concepts that were characteristic of the mentality and customs of that time; he is not afraid of speaking about the submission of the wife to the husband; he is, in addition, not afraid (also in the last verse of the text quoted by us) of recommending to the wife "to have reverence toward her husband" (Eph 5:33). In fact, it is certain that, when husband and wife are subject to one another "in the fear of Christ," everything will find a just balance, that is, such as to correspond to their Christian vocation in the mystery of Christ.

6. Certainly, our contemporary sensibility is different, mentality and customs are different, and the social position of women in comparison with men is different. Nevertheless, the underlying parenetic principle that we find in Ephesians remains the same and bears the same fruits. Reciprocal submission "in the fear of Christ"—a submission born on the foundation of Christian *pietas*—always forms the deep and firm supporting structure of the *community of the spouses,* in which the true *"communion" of persons* is realized.

7. The author of Ephesians, who began his letter with a magnificent vision of the eternal plan of God for humanity, does not limit himself to highlighting only the traditional aspects of morality or the ethical aspects of marriage, but goes beyond the limits of such teaching and, in writing on the reciprocal relation of the spouses, uncovers in it the dimension of the same mystery of Christ, whose herald and

apostle he is. "Wives, be subject to your husbands as you are to the Lord. For the husband is the head of the wife as Christ is the head of the Church, he who is the Savior of his body. And as the Church is subject to Christ, so also wives ought to be subject to their husbands in everything. And you, husbands, love your wives, as Christ loved the Church and gave himself for her" (Eph 5:22–25). In this way, *the teaching* that belongs to this parenetic part of the letter is in some sense *inserted into the very reality of the mystery* hidden from eternity in God and revealed to humanity in Jesus Christ. In the letter to the Ephesians, we are witnesses, I would say, of a particular encounter of this mystery with the very essence of the vocation to marriage. How should this encounter be understood?

8. In the text of Ephesians, the encounter presents itself first of all as a great *analogy*. We read, "Wives, be subject to your husbands *as* you are to the Lord." This is the first component of the analogy. "For the husband is the head of the wife *as* Christ is the head of the Church." This is the second component that clarifies the first and shows its cause. "And *as* the Church is subject to Christ, *so* also wives ought to be subject to their husbands." The relationship of Christ with the Church, which had been presented earlier, is now expressed as a relationship of the Church with Christ, and the next component of the analogy is contained here. Finally, "And you, husbands, love your wives, *as* Christ loved the Church and gave himself for her." This is the final component of the analogy. The remainder of the text of the letter develops the underlying thought contained in the passage just quoted, and the whole text of Ephesians 5:21–23 is permeated by the same analogy: that is, the reciprocal relationship between the spouses, husband and wife, should be understood by Christians *according to the image of the relationship between Christ and the Church.*

90 General Audience of August 18, 1982
(Insegnamenti, 5, no. 2 [1982]: 245–48)

1. WHEN WE ANALYZED the relevant parts of Ephesians last Wednesday, we noted that Christians should understand the reciprocal relationship between spouses, husband and wife, according to the image of the relationship between Christ and the Church.

This relationship is a revelation and realization in time of the mystery of salvation, of the election of love "hidden" from eternity in God. In this revelation and realization, the mystery of salvation includes the particular feature of spousal love in the relationship of Christ with the Church, and for this reason one can express it most adequately by going back to the analogy of the relationship that exists—that should exist—between husband and wife in marriage. This *analogy clarifies the mystery,* at least to a certain degree. Indeed, it seems that, according to the author of Ephesians, this analogy is complementary to that of the "Mystical Body" (see Eph 1:22–23) when we try to express the mystery of the relationship of Christ with the Church and—going back even further—the mystery of God's eternal love for man, for humanity: the mystery that is expressed and realized in time through the relationship of Christ with the Church.

2. If, as has been said, this analogy illuminates the mystery, it itself in turn *is illuminated by that mystery.* The spousal relationship that unites the spouses, husband and wife, must—according to the author of Ephesians—help us to understand the love that unites the Christ with the Church, the reciprocal love of Christ and the Church in which the eternal divine plan of man's salvation is realized. Nevertheless, the meaning of the analogy is not exhausted here. While the analogy used in Ephesians clarifies the mystery of the relationship between the Christ and the Church, at the same time *it reveals the essential truth about marriage,* namely, that marriage corresponds to the vocation of Christians only when it mirrors the love that Christ, the Bridegroom, gives to the Church, his Bride, and which the Church (in likeness to the wife who is "subject," and thus completely given) seeks to give back to Christ in return. This is the redeeming, saving love, the love with which man has been loved by God from eternity in Christ, "In him he chose us before the creation of the world to be holy and immaculate before him" (Eph 1:4).

3. Marriage corresponds to the vocation of Christians as spouses only when precisely that love is mirrored and realized in it. This will become clear if we attempt to *reread the* Pauline *analogy in the opposite direction,* that is, beginning with the relationship of Christ with the Church and turning next to the relationship between husband and wife in marriage. The text uses the tone of exhortation: "Wives, be subject to your husbands...as the Church is subject to Christ." And on the other hand, "You, husbands, love your wives, as Christ loved the Church." These expressions show that what is at issue is a moral obligation. Yet, to be able to recommend such an obligation, one must admit that the very essence of marriage contains *a particle of the same mystery*. Otherwise, this whole analogy would hang in a void. The invitation with which the author of Ephesians addresses the spouses, that they model their reciprocal relationship according to the likeness of Christ's relationship with the Church ("*as—so*"), would be deprived of a real basis, as if it had no ground under its feet. This is the logic of the analogy used in the text quoted from Ephesians.

4. As one can see, this analogy works in two directions. While it allows us, on the one hand, to understand better the relationship of Christ with the Church, it permits us, on the other hand, to penetrate more deeply into the essence of the marriage to which Christians are called. It shows in some sense the way in which this marriage, in its deepest essence, *emerges from the mystery* of God's eternal love for man and humanity: from the salvific mystery that Christ's spousal love fulfills in time for the Church. If we begin with the words of Ephesians 5:22–33, we can develop the thought contained in the great Pauline analogy in two directions: both in the direction of a deeper understanding of the Church, and in the direction of a deeper understanding of marriage. In our considerations, we will follow first the latter direction, keeping in mind that at the basis of the understanding of marriage in its very essence stands Christ's spousal relationship with the Church. We should analyze that relationship even more carefully to establish—presupposing the analogy with marriage—how marriage becomes a *visible sign of the eternal divine mystery*, according to the image of the Church united with Christ. In this way, Ephesians leads us to *the very foundations of the sacramentality* of marriage.

An Additional Aspect of the Analogy—Head and Body

5. Let us, therefore, carry out a detailed analysis of the text. When we read in Ephesians that "the husband is the head of the wife as Christ is the head of the Church, he who is the Savior of his body"

(Eph 5:23), we can assume that the author, who had already explained earlier that the submission of the wife to the husband as head should be understood as a reciprocal submission "in the fear of Christ," goes back to the concept rooted in the mentality of his time, in order to express first of all the truth about the relationship of Christ with the Church, that is, that Christ is the head of the Church. He is head as "Savior of his body." The Church is precisely that body, which—being subject in everything to Christ as her head—receives from him everything by which she becomes and is his body, that is, the fullness of salvation as a gift of Christ, who "gave himself for her" to the end. Christ's "gift of self" to the Father through obedience to the point of death on the cross takes on a strictly ecclesiological character here. *"Christ loved the Church and gave himself for her"* (Eph 5:25). Through a total gift that springs from love, he *formed* the Church *as his body* and continually builds her, thus becoming her head. As head, he is the Savior of his body and, at the same time, as Savior, he is the head. As head and Savior of the Church, he is also Bridegroom of his Bride.

6. The Church is herself in the degree to which she, as body, receives from Christ her head the whole gift of salvation as a fruit of Christ's love and of his giving for the Church: fruit of Christ's giving to the end. That gift of self to the Father through obedience to the point of death (see Phil 2:8) is at the same time, according to Ephesians, an act of "giving himself for the Church." In this expression, *redeeming love* transforms itself, I would say, *into spousal love*: by giving himself for the Church, with the same redeeming act, Christ united himself once and for all with her as the Bridegroom to the Bride, as the husband with the wife, giving himself through all that is included once and for all in his "giving himself" for the Church. In this way, the mystery of the redemption of the body conceals within itself in some sense the mystery "of the marriage of the Lamb" (see Rev 19:7). Because Christ is the head of the body, the whole salvific gift of redemption penetrates the Church as the body of that head, and continually forms the deepest essential substance of her life. He forms her in the spousal way, given that in the quoted text the analogy of body and head passes over into the analogy of bridegroom and bride, or rather of husband and wife. This is shown by the immediately following passages of the text, to which we will turn next.

91 General Audience of August 25, 1982
(Insegnamenti, 5, no. 2 [1982]: 284–88)

1. In our earlier considerations of Ephesians 5:21–33, we drew attention particularly to the analogy of the relationship that exists between Christ and the Church, and the one that exists between bridegroom and bride, that is, between husband and wife united by the spousal bond. Before we begin to analyze the next passages of the text we are studying, we must be conscious of the fact that in the sphere of the fundamental Pauline analogy of Christ and the Church on the one hand, and man and woman as spouses on the other, there is also *a supplementary analogy,* namely, *the analogy of the head and the body.* And it is precisely this analogy that gives a chiefly ecclesiological meaning to the statement we have been analyzing: the Church, as such, is formed by Christ; she is constituted by him in her essential part as the body by its head. The union of the body with the head is above all of an organic nature; it is, to put it simply, the somatic union of the human organism. Biological union is directly built on this organic union, inasmuch as one can say, "the body has life from the head" (even if at the same time, although in another way, the head has life from the body). Further, if we are dealing with man, psychic union, understood in its integrity and in the end as the integral union of the human person, builds on this organic union.

2. As was already said (at least in the passage just analyzed), the author of Ephesians has introduced the supplementary analogy of the head and the body into the sphere of the analogy of marriage. It even seems that he conceived the first analogy, namely "head and body," in a more central way from the point of view of the truth about Christ and the Church proclaimed by him. Nevertheless, one must also affirm that he did not *place this analogy next to or outside of the analogy of marriage* as a spousal bond. Quite the contrary is true, in fact. In the whole text of Ephesians 5:22–33, and especially in its first part, with which we are now dealing (Eph 5:22–23), the author speaks as if in marriage also the husband were "head of his wife" and the wife "body of her husband," as if spouses also formed an organic union. This perspective can find its basis in the text of Genesis that speaks about "one flesh" (Gen 2:24), that is, in the very text to which the author of Ephesians refers a little later in the context of his great anal-

ogy. Nevertheless, the text of Genesis clearly highlights that man and woman are two distinct personal subjects who make a conscious decision about their conjugal union, which is defined in this ancient text by the terms "one flesh." This is equally clear in Ephesians. The author uses a twofold analogy, head-body and husband-wife, in order to illustrate clearly *the nature of the union between Christ and the Church*. In some sense, especially in this passage at the beginning of Ephesians 5:22–33, the ecclesiological dimension seems decisive and predominant.

3. "Wives, be subject to your husbands as you are to the Lord. For the husband is the head of the wife as Christ is the head of the Church, he who is the Savior of his body. And as the Church is subject to Christ, so also wives ought to be subject to their husbands in everything. And you, husbands, love your wives, as Christ loved the Church and gave himself for her" (Eph 5:22–25). This supplementary analogy of "head and body" shows that in the sphere of the whole passage of Ephesians 5:22–23 we are dealing with two distinct subjects who, in virtue of a particular reciprocal relation, *become in some sense a single subject*: together with the body, the head constitutes one subject (in the physical and metaphysical sense), one organism, one human person, one being. There is no doubt that Christ is a subject distinct from the Church; still, in virtue of a particular relationship, he makes himself one with her in an organic union of head and body: the Church is so strongly, so essentially herself in virtue of a union with the (mystical) Christ. Is it possible to say the same thing about the spouses, about man and woman united in a marriage bond? If the author of Ephesians sees *the analogy of the union of the head with its body* also in marriage, this analogy seems to apply in some sense to marriage in consideration of the union of Christ with the Church and of the Church with Christ. For this reason, the analogy regards above all marriage itself as that union through which "the two will form one flesh" (Eph 5:31; cf. Gen 2:24).

4. Still, this analogy *does not blur the individuality of the subjects*, that of the husband and that of the wife, that is, the essential bi-subjectivity that stands at the basis of the image of "one body," more precisely, the essential bi-subjectivity of the husband and the wife in

marriage, which makes them in a certain sense "one body," passes in the whole text we are examining (Eph 5:22–33) into the image of the Church as body united with Christ as head. One sees this especially in the later part of the text where the author describes the relationship of Christ with the Church precisely by means of the image of the relationship of husband and wife. In this description, the Church, the body of Christ, clearly appears as the second subject of conjugal union, to whom the first subject, Christ, shows the love of one who has loved by giving "himself for her." This love is the image and above all the model of the love which a husband must show his wife in marriage, when both are subject to one another "in the fear of Christ."

Two Subjects or One?

5. We read, "And you, husbands, love your wives, as Christ loved the Church and gave himself for her, in order to make her holy by cleansing her with the washing of water accompanied by the word, so as to present his Church before himself all glorious, without spot or wrinkle or anything of the kind, but holy and immaculate. In the same way, husbands have the duty to love their wives as their own bodies, for the one who loves his wife loves himself. No one, in fact, ever hates his own flesh, but he nourishes and cares for it, as Christ does with the Church, because we are members of his body. For this reason a man will leave his father and his mother and unite with his wife, and the two will form one flesh" (Eph 5:25–31).

6. It is easy to realize that in this part of Ephesians 5:22–33 *bi-subjectivity* clearly "*is predominant*": it is highlighted both in the relationship between Christ and the Church and in the relationship between husband and wife. This is not to say that the image of a single subject disappears: the image of "one body." It is kept also in this passage of our text, and in some sense it is explained there even better. One will see this with greater clarity when we submit the passage just quoted to a detailed analysis. In this way, then, the author of Ephesians speaks about the love of Christ for the Church so as to explain the way in which this love expresses itself and to present, at the same time, both this love and its expressions as the model the husband must follow in regard to his wife. The essential goal of the love of

Christ for the Church is her *sanctification*. "Christ loved the Church and gave himself for her, in order to make her holy" (Eph 5:25–26). At the *beginning* of this sanctification stands *Baptism,* the first and essential fruit of Christ's gift of self for the Church. In this text, Baptism is not called by its own name, but is defined as a purification "with the washing of water accompanied by the word" (Eph 5:26). This washing, with the power that flows from the redemptive gift of self Christ made for the Church, brings about the fundamental purification through which his love for the Church gains, in the eyes of the author of the letter, a spousal character.

7. It is obviously an individual in the Church who participates in the sacrament of Baptism. Still, through this individual subject, the author of the letter sees the whole Church. The spousal love of Christ refers to her, to the Church, every time that a single person receives in her the fundamental purification by Baptism. The one who receives Baptism becomes at the same time—by virtue of the redemptive love of Christ—a participant in his spousal love for the Church. "The washing of water accompanied by the word" is, in our text, *the expression of spousal love* in the sense that it prepares the Bride (the Church) for the Bridegroom, it makes the Church the Bride of Christ, I would say, "*in actu primo* [in first act]." Some biblical scholars observe here that in the text we quoted the "the washing of water" recalls the ritual washing that preceded the wedding and was an important religious rite also among the Greeks.

8. As the sacrament of Baptism, the "washing of water accompanied by the word" (Eph 5:26) makes the Church a Bride not only "*in actu primo,*" but also *in the* more distant or *eschatological perspective.* This perspective opens before our eyes when we read in Ephesians that "the washing of water" serves the Bridegroom "to present his Church before himself all *glorious,* without spot or wrinkle or anything of the kind, but holy and immaculate" (Eph 5:27). The expression, "present before himself," seems to indicate that moment of the wedding when the bride is led to the bridegroom already clothed in the wedding dress and adorned for the wedding. The quoted text highlights that the same Bridegroom, Christ, takes care to adorn the Bride, the Church, in order that she might be beautiful with the beauty of grace, beautiful in virtue of the gift of salvation in its full-

ness, already granted from the moment of the sacrament of Baptism. Yet, Baptism is only the beginning, from which the figure of the Church should emerge glorious (as we read in the text) as the definitive fruit of redemptive and spousal love, only with the final coming of Christ (*parousia*).

We see how deeply the author of Ephesians looks into sacramental reality when he proclaims the great analogy: both the union of Christ with the Church and the spousal union of man and woman in marriage are in this way illuminated by a particular supernatural light.

92 *General Audience of September 1, 1982*
(Insegnamenti, 5, no. 2 [1982]: 350–54)

1. PROCLAIMING THE ANALOGY between the spousal bond that unites Christ and the Church and the bond that unites husband and wife in marriage, the author of Ephesians writes, "And you, husbands, love your wives, as Christ loved the Church and gave himself for her, in order to make her holy by cleansing her with the washing of water accompanied by the word, so as *to present* his Church *before himself* all glorious, without spot or wrinkle or anything of the kind, but holy and immaculate" (Eph 5:25–27).

2. It is significant that *the image of the glorious Church* is presented, in the text quoted, *as a bride all beautiful in her body.* Certainly, this is a metaphor, but it is a very eloquent one and testifies how deeply important the body is in the analogy of spousal love. The "glorious" Church is the one "without spot or wrinkle." "Spot" can be understood as a sign of ugliness, "wrinkle" as a sign of growing old and senile. In the metaphorical sense, both one and the other expression indicate moral defects, sin. One can add that in St. Paul the "old man" signifies the man of sin (Rom 6:6). Christ, therefore, with his redemptive and spousal love brings it about that the Church not only becomes sinless, but remains "eternally young."

3. The sphere of the metaphor is, as one can see, quite vast. The expressions that refer directly and immediately to the human body, characterizing it in reciprocal relations between bridegroom and bride, between husband and wife, indicate at the same time attributes and qualities of the moral, spiritual, and supernatural order. This is

essential for this analogy. For this reason, the author of the letter can define the "glorious" state of the Church in terms of the bride's body, free from all signs of ugliness and old age ("or anything of the kind"), simply as holiness and absence of sin: such is the "*holy and immaculate*" Church. It is therefore evident what kind of beauty of the Bride is in question, in what sense the Church is the body of Christ and in what sense that body-Bride receives the gift of the Bridegroom who "loved the Church and gave himself for her." It is nevertheless significant that St. Paul explains this whole reality, which is essentially spiritual and supernatural, through the likeness of the body and of the love by which the spouses, husband and wife, become "one flesh."

"... As Their Own Body" (Eph 5:28)

4. The whole passage quoted above very clearly preserves the principle of *bi-subjectivity*: Christ-Church, Bridegroom-Bride (husband-wife). The author presents the love of Christ for the Church—the love that makes the Church the body of Christ, whose head he is—as the model of the love of the spouses and as the model of the wedding feast of bridegroom and bride. Love binds the bridegroom (husband) to be concerned for the good of the bride (wife); it commits him to desire her beauty and at the same time to sense this beauty and care for it. What is at stake here is also visible beauty, physical beauty. The bridegroom examines his bride attentively, as though in a creative loving restlessness, to find all that is good and beautiful in her and that he desires for her. The good that the one who loves creates with his love in the beloved is like a test of that same love and its measure. Giving himself in the most disinterested way, the one who loves does not do so outside the limits of this measure and this verification.

5. When the author of Ephesians—in the next verses of the text (Eph 5:28–29)—turns his attention wholly to the spouses themselves, the analogy of the relationship of Christ with the Church resonates still more deeply and impels him to express himself as follows: "In the same way, husbands have the duty *to love their wives as their own body*" (Eph 5:28). Here we see the return of the motif of "one flesh," which is not only taken up again but also clarified in the sentence just quoted and in the sentences after it. If husbands should love their wives as

their own bodies, this means that this uni-subjectivity is built on the base of bi-subjectivity and does not have a real, but an intentional, character: the body of the wife is not the husband's own body, but should be loved as his own body. It is a question of unity, not in the ontological, but in the moral sense: *of unity through love.*

6. "The one who loves his wife loves himself" (Eph 5:28). This sentence confirms that character of unity even more. In some sense, love makes the "I" of another person one's own "I": the wife's "I," I would say, becomes through love the husband's "I." The body is the expression of this "I" and the foundation of its identity. The union of husband and wife in love expresses itself also through the body. It expresses itself in the reciprocal relationship, although the author of Ephesians indicates it above all from the husband's side. This is a result of the structure of the image as a whole. Although the spouses should be "subject to one another in the fear of Christ" (this point is already highlighted in the first verse of Ephesians 5:21–33), nevertheless in what follows, *the husband* is above all *the one who loves* and the wife, by contrast, is *the one who is loved.* One might even venture the idea that the wife's "submission" to the husband, understood in the context of the whole of Ephesians 5:22–23, means above all "the experiencing of love." This is all the more so, because this "submission" refers to the image of the submission of the Church to Christ, which certainly consists in experiencing his love. The Church as Bride, being the object of the redemptive love of Christ, the Bridegroom, becomes his body. The wife, being the object of the spousal love of her husband, becomes "one flesh" with him: in some sense, his "own" flesh. The author repeats this idea once more in the last sentence of the passage we are analyzing. "Therefore also you, each one on his part, should love his wife as himself" (Eph 5:33).

7. This is the moral unity conditioned and constituted by love. Love not only unites the two subjects, but allows them to interpenetrate each other, belonging spiritually to one another, to the point that the author of the letter can affirm, "The one who loves his wife loves himself" (Eph 5:28). The "I" becomes in some way the "you," and the "you" the "I" (in the moral sense, of course). And for this reason, the continuation of the text we are analyzing reads as follows: "No one, in fact, ever hates his own flesh, but he nourishes and cares for it, as Christ does with the Church, because we are members of his body" (Eph 5:29–30). The sentence, which at the beginning still refers to the relationship between the spouses, explicitly returns in the next clause to the relationship between Christ and the Church and thus, in the light of that relationship, leads us to define the meaning of the whole sentence. After explaining the character of the relationship of the husband to the wife in forming "one flesh," the author wishes to strengthen even more his earlier statement ("the one who loves his wife loves himself") and *to uphold it in some sense by the negation and exclusion of the opposite possibility* ("no one, in fact, ever hates his own flesh," Eph 5:29). In union through love, the body "of the other" becomes "one's own" in the sense that one is moved by concern for the good of the body of the other as for one's own. One might say that the above-mentioned words, which characterize the "bodily" love that should unite the spouses, express the most general and, at the same time, most essential content. They seem to speak above all with the language of "*agape.*"

8. The expression according to which man "nourishes and cares" for his own flesh—that is, the husband nourishes and cares for his wife's flesh as for his own—might seem to indicate the concern of parents, the relationship of custody over children, rather than conjugal tenderness. One should look for the reason for this character of the relationship in the fact that here the author clearly passes on from the relationship that unites spouses to the relationship between Christ and the Church. The expressions referring to care for the body, and above all for its *nourishment,* to *providing food for it,* suggest to a number of Scripture scholars a reference *to the Eucharist,* with which *Christ, in his spousal love, "feeds" the Church.* If these expressions, though only in a muted tone, indicate the specific character of conjugal love, especially of the love by which the spouses become "one flesh," they help us at the same time to understand, at least in a general way, the dignity of the body and the moral imperative to care for its good, the good that corresponds to its dignity. The comparison with the Church as the body of Christ, the body of his redemptive and simultaneously spousal love, must leave in the consciousness of the recipients of Ephesians 5:22–33 a profound sense of the *"sacrum" of the*

human *body* in general, and especially in marriage as the "place" in which such a sense of the "sacrum" determines in a particularly deep way the reciprocal relationships of persons, and above all those of man with the woman as wife and mother of their children.

"This Mystery Is Great"

93 *General Audience of September 8, 1982*
(Insegnamenti, 5, no. 2 [1982]: 389–94)

1. THE AUTHOR OF EPHESIANS writes, "No one, in fact, ever hates his own flesh, but he nourishes and cares for it, as Christ does with the Church, because we are members of his body" (Eph 5:29–30). After this verse, the author considers it fitting to quote the text that can be considered the fundamental text on marriage in the whole Bible, Genesis 2:24. "For this reason a man will leave his father and his mother and unite with his wife, and the two will form one flesh" (Eph 5:31; Gen 2:24). It is possible to infer from the immediate context in Ephesians that quoting Genesis 2:24 is necessary here, not so much to recall the unity of the spouses, defined "from the beginning" in the work of creation, but to present the mystery of Christ with the Church, from which the author deduces the truth about the unity of the spouses. This is the most important point of the whole text, *in some sense its keystone.* The author of Ephesians includes in these words everything he said earlier, when he traced the analogy and presented the likeness between the unity of spouses and the unity of Christ with the Church. By quoting the words of Genesis 2:24, the author emphasizes that the bases of this analogy should be sought *in the line that unites, in God's salvific plan, marriage* as *the most ancient revelation* (and "manifestation") of that plan in the created world *with the definitive revelation* and "manifestation," namely, the revelation that "Christ loved the Church and gave himself for her" (Eph 5:25), endowing his redemptive love with a spousal nature and meaning.

2. Thus, the analogy that permeates Ephesians 5:22–33 has its ultimate basis in God's saving plan. This point will become still clearer and more evident when we locate the passage of the text we are analyzing in the overall context of Ephesians. Then we will grasp

more easily the reason why, after quoting the words of Genesis 2:24, the author writes, "This mystery is great; I say this with reference to Christ and the Church" (Eph 5:32).

In the overall context of Ephesians and further in the wider context of the words of Sacred Scripture, which reveal God's salvific plan "from the beginning," one can see that here the term *"mysterion"* signifies the mystery first hidden in God's mind and later revealed in man's history. Given its importance, the mystery is *"great"* indeed: as God's salvific plan for humanity, that mystery is in some sense the central theme of the whole of revelation, its central reality. It is what God as Creator and Father wishes above all to transmit to mankind in his Word.

3. The point is not only to transmit the "good news" about salvation, but to *begin at the same time the work of salvation,* as the fruit of grace that sanctifies man for eternal life in union with God. Precisely on the path of this revelation and realization, St. Paul highlights the continuity between the most ancient covenant, which God established by constituting marriage already in the work of creation, and the definitive covenant in which Christ, having loved the Church and given himself for her, unites with her in a spousal way, that is, corresponding to the image of spouses. This *continuity of God's salvific initiative* constitutes the essential basis of the great analogy contained in Ephesians. The continuity of God's salvific initiative signifies the continuity and even the sameness of the mystery, of the "great mystery," in the different phases of its revelation—and thus in some sense of its "manifestation"—and at the same time the sameness of its realization: in the *"most ancient"* phase from the point of view of human history and of salvation, and in the phase of the "fullness of time" (Gal 4:4).

4. Is it possible to understand that "great mystery" as a "sacrament"? In the text we quoted, does the author of Ephesians speak about the sacrament of Marriage? If he does not speak about it directly and in the strict sense—here one must agree with the rather widespread opinion of scholars and theologians—it seems nevertheless that in this biblical text he speaks *about the bases of the sacramentality* of the whole of Christian life and in particular about the bases of the sacramentality of marriage. *In an indirect way,* and yet at the same time in the most fundamental way possible, he speaks about

the sacramentality of all Christian existence in the Church and especially about the sacramentality of marriage.

5. "Sacrament" is not synonymous with "mystery."[88] The mystery remains, in fact, "hidden"—concealed in God himself—in such a way that even after its proclamation (or revelation) it does not cease to be called "mystery," and it is also preached as a mystery. The sacrament presupposes the revelation of the mystery and presupposes that man also accepts it by faith. Still, it is at the same time something more than the proclamation of the mystery and the acceptance of the mystery by faith. The sacrament consists in *"manifesting"* that *mystery in a sign* that serves not only to proclaim the mystery but also *to accomplish it* in man. The sacrament is a visible and efficacious sign of grace. It is a means for accomplishing in man the mystery hidden from eternity in God, about which Ephesians speaks immediately at the beginning (see Eph 1:9)—the mystery of God calling man to holiness in Christ and the mystery of man's predestination to become an adoptive son. The mystery is accomplished in a mysterious way, under the veil of a

---

88. "Sacrament," a central concept for our considerations, has traveled a long way in the course of the centuries. The semantic history of "sacrament" must begin with the Greek word " *mystērion*," which, to tell the truth, still refers to the king's military plans in Judith ("the mystery of his will"—Jud 2:2), but already in the Wisdom of Solomon (2:22) and the prophecy of Daniel (2:27) signifies God's creative plans and the end he assigns to the world, which are revealed only to those who are faithful confessors.

In this sense *"mystērion"* appears only once in the Gospels, "To you has been entrusted the mystery of the kingdom of God" (Mk 4:11 and its parallels, Mt 13:11; Lk 8:10). In the great letters of St. Paul, this term returns seven times, with the high point in Romans: "according to my gospel and the proclamation of Jesus Christ, according to the revelation of the *mystery* that was kept secret for long ages but is now disclosed" (Rom 16:25–26).

In the later letters, the *"mystērion"* is identified with the Gospel (see Eph 6:19) and even with Jesus Christ himself (see Col 2:2; 4:3; Eph 3:4), which is a turning point in the understanding of the term: *"mystērion"* is no longer merely God's eternal plan, but *the realization* of this plan on earth, revealed in Jesus Christ.

For this reason, in the patristic period, the term *"mystērion"* was applied also to the historical events that show God's will to save man. Already in the second century, in the writings of St. Ignatius of Antioch, St. Justin, and Melito, the mysteries of the life of Jesus, the prophecies, and the symbolical figures of the Old Testament are defined by the term "mystery."

In the third century the oldest Latin translations begin to appear in which the Greek term is translated both as *"mysterium"* and *"sacramentum"* (e.g., Wis 2:22; Eph 5:32), perhaps as a way of explicitly distancing oneself from the pagan mystery rites and from Neoplatonic Gnostic mystagogy.

sign; nevertheless, that sign always "makes visible" the supernatural mystery that is at work in man under its veil.

6. When one considers the passage of Ephesians analyzed here and in particular the words, "This mystery is great; I say this with reference to Christ and the Church," one must observe that the author

---

Originally, however, "*sacramentum*" signified the military oath taken by Roman legionaries. Given that in that oath one could observe the aspect of "initiation to a new form of life," of "unreserved commitment," and "faithful service even at the risk of death," Tertullian shows that these dimensions are present in the Christian sacraments of Baptism, of anointing, and of the Eucharist. Thus, in the third century, the term "*sacramentum*" is applied both to the mystery of God's salvific plan in Christ (see e.g., Eph 5:32) and to its concrete realization through the seven fountains of grace, today called "sacraments of the Church."

St. Augustine, using the various meanings of this term, applied "sacrament" to the religious rites of both the Old and the New Testaments, to the biblical symbols and figures, and also to the revealed Christian religion. All of these "sacraments," according to St. Augustine, belong to the great sacrament, namely, the mystery of Christ and the Church. St. Augustine had much influence on the further specification of the term "sacrament" by underlining that the sacraments are sacred signs, that they have in themselves a likeness with what they signify and that they confer what they signify. With his analyses, he thus contributed to the working out of the concise Scholastic definition of "sacrament": "*signum efficax gratiae,* an efficacious sign of grace."

St. Isidore of Seville (seventh century) underlined another aspect: the mysterious nature of a sacrament, which, under the veil of material appearances, conceals the action of the Holy Spirit in man's soul.

The theological summas of the twelfth and thirteenth centuries already formulated the systematic definition of the sacraments, but St. Thomas's definition has particular importance: "*Non omne signum rei sacrae est sacramentum, sed solum ea quae significant perfectionem sanctitatis humanae.* [Not every sign of a sacred thing is a sacrament, but only those that signify the perfection of human holiness]" (ST, III, qu. 60 a. 2).

From this point on, "sacrament" was understood exclusively in the sense of the seven sources of grace, and theological studies focused on delving into the essence and the action of the seven sacraments, thereby working out in a systematic way the main lines contained in the Scholastic tradition.

Only in the last century was attention paid to the aspects of "sacrament" that had not received attention in the course of centuries, for example, to its ecclesial dimension and to the personal encounter with Christ, which has found expression in the *Constitution on the Liturgy* (*Sacrosanctum Concilium,* 59). Above all, however, Vatican II returns to the original meaning of "*sacramentum-mysterium*" when it calls the Church "the universal sacrament of salvation" (*Lumen Gentium,* 48), a sacrament, or "a sign and instrument of intimate union with God and of the unity of all the human race" (*Lumen Gentium,* 1).

In conformity with its original meaning, "sacrament" is here understood as the realization of the eternal divine plan for the salvation of humanity.

of the letter writes not only about the great mystery hidden in God, but also, and above all, about the mystery that is brought into being by the fact that Christ, who in an act of redemptive love has loved the Church and given himself for her, united in the same act in a spousal way with the Church, as husband and wife are reciprocally united in marriage instituted by the Creator. It seems the words of Ephesians are a sufficient reason for what we read at the very beginning of *Lumen Gentium: "The Church is in Christ like a sacrament* or a sign and instrument of intimate union with God and of the unity of the whole human race" (*Lumen Gentium,* 1). This text of Vatican II does not say, "The Church is a sacrament," but, "it is like a sacrament," thereby indicating that when we speak about the sacramentality of the Church we must speak analogously, not in a manner identical to what we mean when we speak about the seven sacraments administered by the Church on the basis of their institution by Christ. If there are reasons for speaking about the Church as a sacrament, these reasons are for the most part indicated precisely in Ephesians.

7. One can say that this sacramentality of the Church is constituted by all the sacraments, through which she fulfills her sanctifying mission. One can say in addition that the sacramentality of the Church is the source of the sacraments, and in particular of Baptism and the Eucharist, as is clear from Ephesians 5:25–30, which we already analyzed. One must say, finally, that *the sacramentality of the Church remains in a particular relationship with marriage,* the most ancient sacrament.

2. Sacrament and Mystery

The Mystery Hidden from Ages
Revealed and Active in Christ

94 *General Audience of September 15, 1982*
   (Insegnamenti, 5, no. 2 [1982]: 459–63)

1. WE HAVE BEFORE US the text of Ephesians 5:21–33, which we have been analyzing for some time because of its importance for the issue of marriage and the sacrament. In its content as a whole, beginning

with the first chapter, the letter treats above all the mystery *"hidden from ages in God"* *as a gift* eternally *destined for man.* "Blessed be God, the Father of our Lord Jesus Christ, who has blessed us in Christ with every spiritual blessing in the heavens. In him he has chosen us before the foundation of the world to be holy and immaculate in his sight in love, predestining us to be his adoptive sons through Jesus Christ, according to the good pleasure of his will, to the praise and glory of his grace that he gave us in his beloved Son" (Eph 1:3–6).

2. Up to this point Ephesians speaks about the mystery hidden "from ages" (Eph 3:9) in God.

The sentences immediately following introduce the reader to the phase of the realization of this mystery in man's history: *the gift* destined for him "from ages" in Christ *becomes a real part of man in the same Christ,* "in whom we have the redemption through his blood, the forgiveness of sins, according to *the riches of his grace.* He has abundantly poured it out on us with all wisdom and insight, because he has made known to us the mystery of his will, according to the design that, in his benevolence, he had preestablished in him, to realize it in the fullness of time: the plan of gathering up all things in him as head, those in heaven and those on earth" (Eph 1:7–10).

3. In this way, the eternal mystery has passed from the state of "hiddenness in God" to the phase of revelation and realization. Christ, in whom humanity has "from ages" been chosen and blessed "with every spiritual blessing" of the Father—Christ, who was destined according to God's eternal "plan" to be the one in whom, as the head, *in the eschatological perspective* "all things would be gathered up, those in heaven and those on earth"—*reveals* the eternal mystery and *accomplishes it* among men and women. For this reason, in the remainder of the letter, the author of Ephesians exhorts those to whom this revelation has come and who have received it in faith to model their lives in the spirit of the truth they have come to know. He exhorts Christian spouses, husband and wife, in a particular way to the same thing.

4. The remainder of the letter becomes for the most part instruction or parenesis. The author seems to speak above all about moral aspects of the vocation of Christians, always, however, referring *back to the mystery that is already at work in them* in virtue of the redemption

of Christ and that works with efficaciousness, above all in virtue of Baptism. "In him you also, when you had heard the word of truth, the gospel of your salvation, and had believed in him, have received the seal of the Holy Spirit who had been promised" (Eph 1:13). In this way, *the moral aspects* of the Christian vocation remain linked not only with the revelation of the eternal divine mystery in Christ, and with its acceptance in faith, but also *with the sacramental order,* which, though it does not occupy the first floor of the whole letter, seems nevertheless to be discreetly present in it. It cannot be otherwise, by the way, given that the Apostle is writing to Christians, who had become members of the ecclesial community through Baptism. For this point of view, the passage of Ephesians 5:22–33 analyzed here seems to have a particular importance. In fact, it throws a special light on the essential relationship of the mystery with the sacrament and especially on the sacramentality of marriage.

5. *At the center of the mystery is Christ.* In him—precisely in him—humanity has been eternally blessed "with every spiritual blessing." In him—in Christ—humanity has been chosen "before the creation of the world," chosen "in love" and predestined to adoption as sons. When later, with the "fullness of time," this eternal mystery is realized in time, this is brought about also in him and through him; in Christ and through Christ. Through Christ the mystery of divine Love is revealed. Through him and for him it is accomplished: in him "we have the redemption through his blood, the forgiveness of sins" (Eph 1:7). In this way, the men and women who accept through faith the gift offered to them in Christ really become sharers in the eternal mystery, although it is at work in them under the veils of faith. According to Ephesians 5:22–33, this supernatural *gift of the fruits of the redemption* accomplished by Christ gains the features of a spousal gift of self by Christ himself to the Church according to the likeness of the spousal relationship between husband and wife. Thus, not only the fruits of redemption are a gift, but above all Christ himself is a gift: he gives himself to the Church as to his Bride.

The Analogy of Spousal Love

6. We must raise the question whether at this point this *analogy does not allow us to penetrate* more deeply and with greater precision

into *the essential content of the mystery.* We must raise this question all the more because this "classical" passage, Ephesians 5:22–33, does not appear in the abstract and in isolation, but stands in continuity with, in some sense as a *consequence of, the statements* of the Old Testament that present the love of God-Yahweh for the people Israel, chosen by him according to the same analogy. In the first place, we are thinking of the texts of the prophets that had introduced the likeness of spousal love to characterize in a particular way the love Yahweh has for Israel, the love that, on the part of the Chosen People, does not find understanding and requital, but, on the contrary, unfaithfulness and betrayal. The expression of unfaithfulness and betrayal was first of all idolatry, worship rendered to foreign gods.

7. To tell the truth, in most cases the prophets dramatically highlighted precisely that betrayal and unfaithfulness, which were called Israel's "adultery." *Yet at the basis of* all *these statements* of the prophets stands the explicit *conviction* that the love of Yahweh for the Chosen People can and must be compared to the love that unites bride and bridegroom, the love that should unite spouses. It would be good to quote many passages from Isaiah, Hosea, and Ezekiel. (Some of these were quoted earlier, when we analyzed the concept of "adultery" on the background of Christ's words spoken in the Sermon on the Mount [see TOB 36:5–37:5]). One cannot forget that part of the heritage of the Old Testament is also the Song of Songs, in which the image of spousal love is outlined—it is true—without the analogy typical of the prophetic texts that presented in this love the image of Yahweh's love for Israel, but also without the negative element constituted by the motif of "adultery" or unfaithfulness in the other texts. In this way, *the analogy of bridegroom and bride,* which allowed the author of Ephesians to define the relationship of Christ with the Church, has *a rich tradition* in the books of the Old Covenant. As we analyze this analogy in the "classical" text of Ephesians, we cannot fail to go back to that tradition.

8. To illustrate this tradition, we will limit ourselves for the moment to quoting a text from Isaiah. The prophet says:

> Do not fear, for you will no longer blush;
> do not be ashamed, for you will no longer be dishonored;
> for you will forget the shame of your youth,
> and the dishonor of your widowhood you will remember no more.

For your Creator is your husband,
Lord of hosts is his name;
the Holy One of Israel is your Redeemer,
the God of the whole earth he is called.
For like a wife forsaken and grieved in spirit the Lord
has called you.
Is the wife of one's youth cast off, says your God?
For a brief moment I abandoned you,
but with immense love I will take you again....
my steadfast affection shall not depart from you,
and my covenant of peace shall not waver,
says the Lord, who has compassion on you. (Isa 54:4–10)

During our next meeting we will begin the analysis of this text
from Isaiah.

95 General Audience of September 22, 1982 (*Insegnamenti*, 5, no. 2 [1982]: 517–22)

1. BY COMPARING THE RELATIONSHIP between Christ and the
Church with the spousal relationship of husband and wife, Ephesians
refers to the tradition of the prophets of the Old Testament. To illustrate this, we quote the following text of Isaiah:

Do not fear, for you will no longer blush;
do not be ashamed, for you will no longer be dishonored;
for you will forget the shame of your youth,
and the dishonor of your widowhood you will remember no more.
For your Creator is your husband,
Lord of hosts is his name;
the Holy One of Israel is your Redeemer,
the God of the whole earth he is called.
For like a wife forsaken and grieved in spirit the Lord has called you.
Is the wife of one's youth cast off, says your God?
For a brief moment I abandoned you,
but with immense love I will take you again.
In overflowing wrath for a moment I hid my face from you,
but with everlasting affection I have had compassion on you,
says the Lord, your Redeemer.
This is like the days of Noah for me,
when I swore that the waters of Noah would never again go
over the earth,
so I swear now that I will not be angry with you

and will not threaten you.
For even if the mountains depart
and the hills are removed,
my steadfast affection shall not depart from you,
and my covenant of peace shall not waver,
says the Lord, who has compassion on you. (Isa 54:4-10)

2. *The text of Isaiah* does not, in this case, contain any of the reproaches against Israel as the unfaithful spouse echoing so forcefully through other texts, especially Hosea and Ezekiel. As a consequence, the essential content of the biblical analogy becomes more transparent: the love of God-Yahweh for Israel, the Chosen People, is expressed as the love of a human bridegroom for the woman chosen to be his wife through the conjugal covenant. In this way, Isaiah explains the events that make up the course of Israel's history, by going back to the mystery hidden, as it were, in the very heart of God. He leads us in some way *in the same direction* in which many centuries later the author of Ephesians was to lead us, who—basing himself on the redemption already brought about in Christ—was to reveal the depth of the same mystery much more fully.

3. The prophet's text has all the color of the tradition and mentality of the people of the Old Testament. Speaking in the name of God and, as it were, with God's own words, the prophet turns to Israel as the bridegroom to his chosen bride. These words overflow with the authentic ardor of love and at the same time highlight the whole specificity of the situation and the mentality proper to that period. They underline that *being chosen by a man* takes away a woman's "dishonor," which, according to the opinion of that society, seemed to be connected with the single state, whether original (virginity), or secondary (widowhood), or due to the divorce of an unloved wife (Deut 24:1), or in some cases of an unfaithful wife. Still, the text quoted does not mention unfaithfulness, but highlights instead the motive of "merciful love,"[89] thereby indicating not only the social *nature* of marriage in the Old Covenant, but also the true *character of the gift* that God's love is for Israel, a gift coming entirely from God's initiative; in other words, by indicating *the dimension of grace*, which is contained in this love

---

89. In the Hebrew text, we have two words that appear together more than once: ḥeseḏ, faithfulness, love, and raḥămîm, bowels, mercy.

from the beginning. This is perhaps the strongest "declaration of love" by God, joined with a solemn oath of faithfulness forever.

Isaiah and Ephesians

4. The analogy with the love that unites spouses is strongly highlighted in this passage. Isaiah says:

> For your Creator is your husband,
> Lord of hosts is his name;
> the Holy One of Israel is your Redeemer,
> the God of the whole earth he is called. (Isa 54:5)

Thus, in this text, God himself in all his majesty as Creator and Lord of creation is explicitly called "husband" of the Chosen People. This "husband" speaks about his great "affection," which will not "depart" from Israel, his wife, but will constitute a stable foundation of the "covenant of peace" with him. In this way, the motif of *spousal love and of marriage* is linked with the motif of the *covenant*. In addition, the "Lord of hosts" calls himself not only "Creator" but also "Redeemer." The text has a theological content of extraordinary richness.

5. When we compare the text of Isaiah with Ephesians and observe the continuity with regard to the analogy of spousal love and marriage, we must at the same time highlight a certain difference of theological perspective. Even in the first chapter, the author of the letter speaks about the mystery of love and election, with which "God, the Father of our Lord Jesus Christ" embraces men and women in his Son, above all as a mystery "hidden in God's mind." It is the mystery of fatherly love, the mystery of election to holiness ("to be holy and immaculate in his sight," Eph 1:4), and of the adoption as sons in Christ ("predestining us to be his adopted sons through Jesus Christ," Eph 1:5). In this context, the deduction of the analogy about marriage, which we found in Isaiah ("Your Creator is your husband, Lord of hosts is his name," Isa 54:5), seems to be a foreshortened view that is part of the theological perspective. *The first dimension of love and election,* as a mystery hidden from ages in God, *is a fatherly dimension and not a "conjugal" one.* According to Ephesians, the first characteristic mark of that mystery remains connected with the very fatherhood of God, which is particularly brought out by the prophets (see Hos 11:1–4; Isa 63:8–9; 64:7; Mal 1:6).

6. The analogy of spousal love and of marriage appears only when the "Creator" and the "Holy One of Israel" manifests himself as "Redeemer." Isaiah says,

> For your Creator is your husband,
> Lord of hosts is his name;
> the Holy One of Israel is your Redeemer. (Isa 54:5)

Already in this text one can in some sense see the parallelism between "husband" and "Redeemer." Going on to Ephesians, we must observe that precisely this thought is fully developed there. The figure of the Redeemer[90] is outlined already in Ephesians 1 as a characteristic proper to him who is the first "beloved Son" of the Father (Eph 1:6), *beloved from eternity,* proper to him in whom we have been loved "from ages" by the Father. It is the Son, one in being with the Father, "*in whom we have redemption* through his blood, the forgiveness of our sins, according to the riches of his grace" (Eph 1:7). The same Son, as Christ (or as "Messiah") "loved the Church and gave himself for her" (Eph 5:25).

This splendid formulation of Ephesians summarizes and highlights the elements of the Song of the Suffering Servant of Yahweh and the Canticle of Zion (see, e.g., Isa 42:1; 53:8–12; 54:8).

And thus the gift of self for the Church is equivalent to the fulfillment of the work of redemption. In this way, the "Creator, the Lord of hosts" of Isaiah becomes "the Holy One of Israel" of the "new Israel" inasmuch as he is Redeemer. In Ephesians, the theological perspective of the prophetic text is preserved and at the same time

---

90. Although in the most ancient biblical books the term "redeemer" (Hebrew: gōʾēl) signified the person who was bound by ties of kinship to avenge a relative who had been killed (see, e.g., Num 35:19), to provide help for a relative fallen into misfortune (see, e.g., Ruth 4:6), and especially to redeem him from slavery (see, e.g., Lev 25:48), in the course of time, this analogy was applied to Yahweh "who redeemed you from the house of slavery, from the hand of Pharaoh, king of Egypt" (Deut 7:8).

Particularly in Deutero-Isaiah, the accent shifts from the action of redemption to the person of the Redeemer, who personally saves Israel, by his sheer presence, as it were, "without money and without gifts."

For this reason, the application of the "Redeemer" of the prophecy of Isaiah 54 ["your Creator is your husband...the Holy One of Israel is your Redeemer"] to Ephesians has the same reason as the application of the texts of the Song of the Suffering Servant of Yahweh in the same letter (see Isa 53:10–12; Eph 5:23, 25–26).

deepened and transformed. New revealed aspects enter: the trinitarian, christological,[91] and finally eschatological aspects.

7. Thus, St. Paul, writing the letter to the People of God of the New Covenant and in particular to the Church of Ephesus, no longer repeats, "Your Creator is your husband," but shows how the "Redeemer," who is the firstborn Son and from ages "the beloved of the Father," reveals at the same time that his *saving love,* which consists in his gift of self for the Church, is *a spousal love by which he marries the Church* and makes her his own Body. In this way, the analogy of the prophetic texts of the Old Testament (in this case above all Isaiah) is preserved in Ephesians and at the same time in an evident manner transformed. To the analogy corresponds the mystery, which is expressed and in some way explained through it. In Isaiah, this mystery is barely outlined, "half open," as it were; in Ephesians, by contrast, it is fully unveiled (without ceasing to be a mystery, of course). In Ephesians, the eternal dimension of the mystery as hidden in God ("Father of our Lord Jesus Christ") is clearly distinct from the dimension of its historical realization according to its christological as well as ecclesiological dimension. The analogy of marriage refers above all to the second dimension. Also in the prophets (in Isaiah), the analogy referred directly *to a historical dimension*: it was linked with the history of the Chosen People of the Old Covenant, with the history of Israel; however, in the realization of the mystery in the Old Testament, *the christological and ecclesiological dimension* was present only in embryonic form, as something merely foreshadowed.

Nevertheless, it is clear that the text of Isaiah helps us to reach a better understanding of Ephesians and of the great analogy of the spousal love of Christ and the Church.

---

91. In place of the relationship "God-Israel," Paul introduces the relationship "Christ-Church," applying to Christ all that referred in the Old Testament to Yahweh (*Adonai-Kyrios*). Christ is God, but Paul also applies to him everything that refers to the Servant of Yahweh in the four songs (Isa 42; 49; 50; 52–53) that were interpreted in the intertestamental period in a messianic sense.

The motif of the "Head" and the "Body" is not biblical in origin, but probably Hellenistic (Stoic?). In Ephesians, this theme has been used in the context of marriage (while in 1 Corinthians the theme of the "Body" serves to show the order that reigns in society).

From the biblical point of view, the introduction of this motif is an absolute *novelty.*

The Reality of the Gift, The Meaning of Grace

95b *General Audience of September 29, 1982*
(Insegnamenti, 5, no. 2 [1982]: 626–30)

1. IN EPHESIANS (Eph 5:22–33)—as in the prophets of the Old Testament (e.g., Isaiah)—we find the great analogy of the marriage or spousal love between Christ and the Church.

What function does this analogy have in relation to the mystery revealed in the Old and New Covenants? One must answer this question step by step. First of all, the analogy of conjugal or spousal love helps us to penetrate into the very essence of the mystery. It helps us to understand the mystery up to a certain point, by way of analogy, of course. It is obvious that the analogy of earthly human love, of the husband for his wife, of human spousal love, cannot offer an adequate and complete understanding of that absolutely transcendent Reality, the divine mystery, both as hidden from ages in God and in its "historical" realization in time when "Christ loved the Church and gave himself for her" (Eph 5:25). *The mystery* remains *transcendent with respect to this analogy* as with respect to any other analogy with which we try to express it in human language. At the same time, however, this analogy offers the possibility of a certain cognitive "penetration" into the very essence of the mystery.

2. The analogy of spousal love allows us in some way to understand the mystery, which was hidden from ages in God and is realized in time by Christ as the love proper to a total and irrevocable gift of self by God to man in Christ. What is at stake is "man" in the personal as well as communitarian dimensions (this communitarian dimension is expressed in Isaiah and the other prophets as "Israel," in Ephesians as "the Church"; one can say, the People of God of the Old and New Covenants). Let us add that in both conceptions the communitarian dimension is placed in some sense on the first level, but not in a way that would completely hide the personal dimension, which after all belongs simply to the very essence of spousal love. In both cases we are dealing, rather, with a significant *"reduction of the community to the person"*.[92] Israel and the Church are considered as a

---

92. It is not only a question of the personification of human society, which is a rather common phenomenon in world literature, but a *"corporate personality"* specific

Bride-person by the Bridegroom-person ("Yahweh" and "Christ"). Every concrete "I" must find itself in that biblical "we."

3. Thus, the analogy we are discussing allows us to understand to a certain degree the revealed mystery of the living God, who is Creator and Redeemer (and as such at the same time God of the covenant); it allows us to understand this mystery in the manner of spousal love, just as it allows us also to understand it (according to Isaiah) in the manner of "merciful" love, or in the manner of "fatherly" love (according to Ephesians, especially chapter 1). These ways of understanding the mystery are doubtless also analogical. The analogy of spousal love contains a characteristic of the mystery that is not directly emphasized by the analogy of merciful love, nor by the analogy of fatherly love (nor by any other analogy used in the Bible to which we could have appealed).

4. The analogy of the love of spouses (or spousal love) seems *to emphasize* above all *the aspect of* God's *gift of himself* to man who is chosen "from ages" in Christ (literally, his gift of self to "Israel," to the "Church"); a gift that is in its essential character, or as gift, total (or rather "radical") and irrevocable. This gift is certainly "radical" and therefore "total." One cannot speak here of totality in the metaphysical sense. As a creature, man is in fact not capable of "receiving" the gift of God in the transcendental fullness of his divinity. Such a "total gift" (an uncreated gift) is shared only by God himself in the "trinitarian communion of persons." By contrast, God's gift of himself to man, which is what the analogy of spousal love speaks about, *can only have the form of a participation in the divine nature* (see 2 Pet 1:4) as theology has made clear with great precision. Nevertheless, according to such a measure, the gift given by God to man in Christ is a "total" or "radical" gift, which is precisely what the analogy of spousal love indicates: it is in some sense "all" that God "could" give of himself to man, considering the limited faculties of man as a creature. In this way the analogy of spousal love indicates the "radical" character of grace: of the whole order of created grace.

---

to the Bible, marked by a continuous reciprocal relationship between the individual and the group. See H. Wheeler Robinson, "The Hebrew Conception of Corporate Personality," *BZAW* 66 (1936): 49–62; see also J. L. McKenzie, "Aspects of Old Testament Thought," *New Jerome Biblical Commentary* (Englewood Cliffs, NJ: Prentice Hall, 1990), 1296.

5. What was said before seems to be what can be said about the first function of our great analogy, which passed from the writings of the prophets of the Old Testament to Ephesians, where, as we noted already, it underwent significant transformation. The analogy of marriage, as a human reality in which spousal love is incarnated, helps in some way to *understand the mystery of grace* as an eternal reality in God and as a "historical" fruit of the redemption of humanity in Christ. Yet, we said earlier that this biblical analogy not only "explains" the mystery, but also, conversely, the mystery defines and determines the adequate way of understanding the analogy and precisely that component of it in which the biblical authors see *"the image and likeness"* of the divine mystery. Thus, the comparison of marriage (due to spousal love) with the relationship between "Yahweh and Israel" in the Old Covenant, and between "Christ and the Church" in the New, is at the same time decisive *for the way of understanding marriage* itself and determines this way.

6. This is *the second function* of our great analogy. And in the perspective of this function we approach the problem of "sacrament and mystery," or, in a general and fundamental sense, the problem of the sacramentality of marriage. This seems particularly justified in the light of the analysis of Ephesians 5:22–33. By presenting the relationship of Christ with the Church according to the image of the spousal union of husband and wife, the author of this letter speaks in the most general and fundamental way not only about the realization of the eternal divine mystery, but also about the way in which that *mystery* has expressed itself in the visible order, about the way it has *become visible* and thereby *entered into the sphere of the Sign.*

7. By the term "sign" we mean here simply the "visibility of the Invisible." The mystery hidden from ages in God, that is, the Invisible, became visible first of all *in the historical event itself of Christ.* The relationship of Christ with the Church, which is defined in Ephesians as *"mysterium magnum,* the great mystery," constitutes the fulfillment and concretization of the visibility of the same mystery. Moreover, the fact that the author of Ephesians compares the indissoluble relationship of Christ and the Church with the relationship between husband and wife, that is, with marriage—at the same time appealing to the words of Genesis 2:24 that together with God's cre-

ative act originally instituted marriage—turns our reflection toward what we presented previously—in the context of the very mystery of creation—as the "visibility of the Invisible," toward the very "origin" of man's theological history.

One can say that the visible sign of marriage "in the beginning," inasmuch as it is linked to the visible sign of Christ and the Church on the summit of God's saving economy, *transposes* the eternal plan of love *into the "historical" dimension* and makes it *the foundation of the whole sacramental order.* It is a particular merit of the author of Ephesians that he brought these two signs together, making of them *the single great sign,* that is, *a great sacrament ("sacramentum magnum").*

Marriage as the Primordial Sacrament

96 *General Audience of October 6, 1982*
(Insegnamenti, 5, no. 2 [1982]: 697–701)

1. WE ARE CONTINUING THE ANALYSIS of the classical text of Ephesians 5:22–33. For this purpose it is useful to quote some sentences in one of the earlier analyses devoted to this subject. "Man appears in the visible world as the highest expression of the divine gift, because he bears within himself the inner dimension of the gift. And with it he carries into the world his particular likeness to God, with which he transcends and also rules his 'visibility' in the world, his bodiliness, his masculinity or femininity, his nakedness. A reflection of this likeness is also the primordial awareness of the spousal meaning of the body pervaded by the mystery of original innocence" [TOB 19:3]. These sentences summarize in few words the result of the analyses that focused on the first chapters of Genesis in relation to the words with which Christ, in his dialogue with the Pharisees about the subject of marriage and its indissolubility, appealed to the "beginning." Other sentences of the same analysis raise *the issue of the primordial sacrament.* "Thus, in this dimension, a primordial sacrament is constituted, understood as a sign that efficaciously transmits in the visible world the invisible mystery hidden in God from eternity. And this is the mystery of Truth and of Love, the mystery of divine life, in which man really participates.... It is original innocence that begins this participation" [TOB 19:4].

2. One must look again at the content of these statements *in the light of the Pauline teaching expressed in Ephesians,* keeping present above all Ephesians 5:22–33, set in the overall context of the letter as a whole. The letter, moreover, authorizes us to do this, because in 5:31 the author himself appeals to the "beginning" and precisely to the words of the institution of marriage, Genesis 2:24. In what sense can we glimpse in these words a statement about the sacrament, about the primordial sacrament? The earlier analyses of the biblical "beginning" have led us step by step to an answer to this question, in consideration of man's original endowment in existence and in grace, which was the state of original innocence and justice. Ephesians leads us to approach this situation—man's state before original sin—from the point of view of the mystery hidden from eternity in God. In fact, at the beginning of the letter we read, "*God, the Father* of our Lord Jesus Christ...*has blessed us with* every *spiritual blessing* in the heavens in Christ. *In him he has chosen us before the creation of the world* to be *holy and immaculate* before him in love" (Eph 1:3–4).

3. Ephesians opens before us the supernatural world of the eternal mystery, of the eternal plans of God the Father in regard to man. These plans precede the "creation of the world" and thus also the creation of man. At the same time, these divine plans begin to be realized already in the whole reality of creation. If also the state of original innocence of man created, as male and female, in the image of God belongs to the mystery of creation, this means that the primordial gift given to man by God already included within itself *the fruit of election,* about which we read in Ephesians: "He has chosen us...*to be holy and immaculate* before him" (Eph 1:4). This, indeed, is what the words of Genesis seem to highlight, when the Creator, Elohim, finds in man—male and female—who appears "before him" a good worthy of his being well pleased. "God saw everything that he had made, and indeed, it was very good" (Gen 1:31). Only after sin, after the breaking of the original covenant with the Creator, does man feel the need of hiding "from the Lord God": "I heard the sound of your step in the garden, and I was afraid, because I am naked, and I hid myself" (Gen 3:10).

4. Before sin, by contrast, man carried in his soul the fruit of eternal election in Christ, the eternal Son of the Father. Through the

grace of this election, man, male and female, was "holy and immaculate" before God. This primordial (or original) holiness and purity expressed itself also in the fact that, though both were "naked...they did not feel shame" (Gen 2:25), as we tried to show in the earlier analyses. When we compare the testimony of the "beginning" reported in the first chapters of Genesis with the testimony of Ephesians, we must deduce that *the reality of the creation of man* was already *permeated* by the perennial election of man in Christ: *called to holiness through the grace of adoption as sons,* "predestining us to be his adopted sons through Jesus Christ, according to the good pleasure of his will, to the praise and glory of his grace, which he has given to us in his beloved Son" (Eph 1:5–6).

5. From the "beginning," man, male and female, shared in this supernatural gift. This endowment was given in view of him, who from eternity was "beloved" as Son, although—according to the dimensions of time and history—it preceded the Incarnation of this "beloved Son" and also the "redemption" we have in him "through his blood" (Eph 1:7).

Redemption was to become the source of man's supernatural endowment after sin and, in a certain sense, despite sin. This supernatural endowment, which took place before original sin, that is, the grace of original justice and innocence—an endowment that was the fruit of man's election in Christ before the ages—was brought about precisely *out of regard for him, that one and only Beloved,* while chronologically anticipating his coming in the body. In the dimensions of the mystery of creation, election to the dignity of adoptive sonship was proper only to the "first Adam," that is, to man created in the image and likeness of God as male and female.

6. *In what way can one verify the reality of the sacrament,* of the primordial sacrament, in this context? In the analysis of the "beginning," from which we quoted a passage a little earlier, we said, "The sacrament, as a visible sign, is constituted with man, inasmuch as he is a 'body,' through his 'visible' masculinity and femininity. The body, in fact, and only the body, is capable of making visible what is invisible: the spiritual and the divine. It has been created to transfer into the visible reality of the world the mystery hidden from eternity in God, and thus to be a sign of it" [TOB 19:4].

This sign has, in addition, its own efficaciousness, as I likewise said, "Original innocence, connected with the experience of the spousal meaning of the body," has the effect that "in his body as man or woman, man senses himself as a subject of holiness" [TOB 19:5]. "He senses himself" and he is from "the beginning." This holiness, which the Creator conferred on man from the "beginning," belongs to the reality of the "sacrament of creation." *The words of Genesis 2:24,* "the man will...unite with his wife, and the two will be one flesh," spoken on the background of this original reality in the theological sense, *constitute marriage as an integral part* and in some sense the central part of the *"sacrament of creation."* They constitute—or perhaps, rather, they simply confirm—the character of its origin. According to these words, marriage is a sacrament inasmuch as it is an integral part—and, I would say, the central point—of the "sacrament of creation." In this sense, it is the primordial sacrament.

7. *The institution of marriage,* according to the words of Genesis 2:24, expresses not only the beginning of the fundamental human community, which by the "procreative" power proper to it ("be fruitful and multiply," Gen 1:28) serves to continue the work of creation, but at the same time *it expresses the Creator's salvific initiative,* which corresponds to man's eternal election spoken about in Ephesians. This salvific initiative comes forth from God, the Creator, and its supernatural efficaciousness is identical with the very act of the creation of man in the state of original innocence. In this state, already beginning with the act of the creation of man, his eternal election in Christ has borne fruit. In this way, one must recognize that the original sacrament of creation *draws its efficaciousness from the "beloved Son"* (see Eph 1:6, where the author speaks about "his grace, which he has given to us in his beloved Son"). As for marriage, one can deduce that—instituted in the context of the sacrament of creation in its totality, or in the state of original innocence—it was to serve not only to extend the work of creation, or procreation, but also to spread the same sacrament of creation to further generations of human beings, that is, to spread the supernatural fruits of man's eternal election by the Father in the eternal Son, the fruits man was endowed with by God in the very act of creation.

Ephesians seems to authorize us to understand Genesis in this way, and the truth about the "beginning" of man and marriage contained in it.

97 General Audience of October 13, 1982
(*Insegnamenti*, 5, no. 2 [1982]: 810–14)

1. IN OUR LAST CONSIDERATION, we tried to gain a deeper grasp—in the light of Ephesians—of the sacramental "beginning" of man and of marriage in the state of original justice (or innocence).

It is clear, however, that the heritage of grace was driven out of the human heart when man broke the first covenant with the Creator. *Instead of being illumined by the heritage of original grace,* which was given by God as soon as he infused the rational soul, the perspective of procreation was darkened by the *heritage of original sin.* One can say that marriage, as the primordial sacrament, was deprived of the supernatural efficaciousness it drew at the moment of its institution from the sacrament of creation in its totality. Nevertheless, also in this state, that is, in the state of man's hereditary sinfulness, *marriage never ceases to be the figure of the sacrament, about which we read in Ephesians* 5:22–33 and which the author of the same letter does not hesitate to call a "great mystery." Can we not deduce that marriage has remained the platform for the realization of God's eternal plans, according to which the sacrament of creation had come near to human beings and prepared them for the sacrament of redemption, introducing them into the dimension of the work of salvation? The analysis of Ephesians, and in particular the "classical" text of Ephesians 5:22–33, seems to lead toward such a conclusion.

"The Sacrament of Redemption"

2. In Ephesians 5:31, when the author appeals to the words of the institution of marriage in Genesis 2:24 ("For this reason a man will leave his father and his mother and unite with his wife, and the two will be one flesh"), and immediately after this declares, "This mystery is great; I say this with reference to Christ and the Church" (Eph 5:32), he seems to point out not only the identity of the Mystery

hidden in God from eternity, but also the continuity of its realization between the primordial sacrament connected with man's supernatural gracing [that is, endowment with grace] in creation itself and the new gracing—which was brought about when "Christ loved the Church and gave himself for her, in order to make her holy" (Eph 5:25–26)— *an endowment with grace that can be defined in its entirety as the sacrament of redemption.* This redemptive gift of self "for" the Church also includes—according to Pauline thought—Christ's gift of self to the Church, in the image of the spousal relation that unites husband and wife in marriage. In this way, the sacrament of redemption clothes itself, so to speak, in the figure and form of the primordial sacrament. To the marriage of the first husband and wife, as a sign of the supernatural endowment of man with grace in the sacrament of creation, corresponds the marriage, or rather the analogy of the marriage, of Christ with the Church, as the fundamental "great" sign of man's supernatural gracing in the sacrament of redemption, of the gracing in which the covenant of the grace of election that was broken in the "beginning" by sin is renewed in a definitive way.

3. The image contained in the passage quoted from Ephesians seems to speak above all about the sacrament of redemption as *the definitive realization of the Mystery hidden from eternity in God.* Indeed, in this *mysterium magnum,* everything that Ephesians talks about in chapter 1 is definitively realized. It says, in fact, as we remember, not only that "in him [that is, Christ] he has chosen us before the creation of the world to be holy and immaculate before him" (Eph 1:4; John Paul II's addition), but also, "in whom we have redemption through his blood, the forgiveness of our sins, according to the riches of his grace. He has abundantly poured it out on us" (Eph 1:7–8). Man's new supernatural endowment with the gift of grace in the "sacrament of redemption" is also a new realization of the Mystery hidden from eternity in God, new in comparison with the sacrament of creation. At this moment, endowment with grace is in some sense a "new creation." It differs, however, from the sacrament of creation inasmuch as the original gracing, united with the creation of man, constituted that man "from the beginning" through grace in the state of original innocence and justice. Man's new gracing in the sacrament of redemption, by contrast, gives him above all the "for-

giveness of sins." Still, even here "grace" can "superabound" as St. Paul expresses himself elsewhere: "Where sin abounded, grace super-abounded" (Rom 5:20).

4. *On the basis of Christ's spousal love* for the Church, the sacrament of redemption—fruit of Christ's redeeming love—becomes *a permanent dimension of the life of the Church herself,* a fundamental and life-giving dimension. It is the *"mysterium magnum"* of Christ and the Church, the eternal mystery realized by Christ, who "gave himself for her" (Eph 5:25), uniting with her with an indissoluble love, just as spouses, husband and wife, unite in marriage. In this manner, the Church lives from the sacrament of redemption and on her part completes this sacrament, just as the wife, in virtue of spousal love, completes her husband, which was in some way already brought out "at the beginning" when the first man found in the first woman "a help similar to himself" (Gen 2:20). Although Ephesians does not specify it, we can nevertheless add that the Church too, united with Christ as the wife with her husband, draws from the sacrament of redemption her whole spiritual fruitfulness and motherhood. A testimony of this fruitfulness is offered in some way by 1 Peter, where he writes that we were "reborn not from a corruptible, but from an immortal, seed, from the living and eternal word of God" (1 Pet 1:23). In this way the Mystery hidden from all eternity in God—a mystery that in the beginning in the sacrament of creation became *a visible reality through the union* of the first man and the first woman in the perspective of marriage—becomes in the sacrament of redemption *a visible reality in the indissoluble union of Christ with the Church,* which the author of Ephesians presents as the spousal union of the two, husband and wife.

5. The "sacramentum magnum" of Ephesians (the Greek text says, *"to mystērion touto mega estin"*) speaks about the new realization of the Mystery hidden from eternity in God; a definitive realization from the point of view of the earthly history of salvation. It speaks, further, about "making visible" the mystery, about the visibility of the Invisible. This visibility does not make the mystery cease to be a mystery. This point applies to marriage as constituted in the "beginning" in the state of original innocence in the context of the sacrament of creation. It also applies to the union of Christ with the Church as the "great mystery" of the sacrament of redemption. The visibility of the

Invisible does not mean—if one may put it this way—a total clearing of the mystery. As an object of faith, it remains veiled even by that in which it is, indeed, expressed and realized. The visibility of the Invisible belongs thus to the order of signs, and the "sign" merely indicates the reality of the mystery, but does not "unveil" it. Just as the "first Adam"—man, male and female—who was created in the state of original innocence and called in this state to conjugal union (in this sense we speak about the sacrament of creation) was a sign of the eternal Mystery, so also the "second Adam," Christ, who is united with the Church through the sacrament of redemption in an indissoluble bond analogous to the indissoluble covenant of spouses, is the definitive sign of the same eternal Mystery. Thus, when we speak about the realization of the eternal mystery, we are speaking also about the fact that it becomes visible with the visibility of the sign. For this reason we are also speaking about the sacramentality of the whole heritage of the sacrament of redemption in reference to the entire work of creation and redemption, and all the more so in reference to marriage, which was instituted in the context of the sacrament of creation, yet also in reference to the Church as Bride of Christ, who is endowed with a quasi-conjugal covenant with him.

Marriage as Figure and as Sacrament of the New Covenant

98 *General Audience of October 20, 1982*
(Insegnamenti, 5, no. 2 [1982]: 857–61)

1. LAST WEDNESDAY, WE SPOKE about the integral heritage of the covenant with God and about the grace originally united to the divine work of creation. Part of this integral heritage—as one can deduce from Ephesians 5:22–33—was marriage as the primordial sacrament, instituted from the "beginning" and linked with the sacrament of creation in its totality. The sacramentality of marriage is not only a *model and figure* of the sacrament of the Church (of Christ and the Church), but also constitutes an *essential part* of the new heritage, that of the sacrament of redemption with which the Church is endowed in Christ. Here one must go back once more to Christ's words in

Matthew 19:3–9 (cf. Mk 10:5–9), in which *Christ*, in responding to the question of the Pharisees about marriage and its specific character, *appeals only and exclusively to* its *original institution* by the Creator at the "beginning." As we reflect about the meaning of this answer in the light of Ephesians, especially Ephesians 5:22–33, we end up with a somehow double relation of marriage to the whole sacramental order that emerges from the very sacrament of redemption in the New Covenant.

2. As the primordial sacrament, marriage constitutes, on the one hand, *the figure* (and thus the likeness, the analogy) according to which the underlying, weight-bearing structure of the new economy of salvation and the sacramental order is built, which springs from the spousal gracing that the Church receives from Christ with all the goods of redemption (one could say, using words from the beginning of Ephesians, "with all spiritual blessings," Eph 1:3). Thus, as the primordial sacrament, marriage is assumed and inserted into the integral structure of the new sacramental economy, which has arisen from redemption *in the form, I would say, of a "prototype."* It is assumed and inserted, as it were, from its very basis. In the dialogue with the Pharisees (Mt 19:3–9), Christ himself confirms first of all its existence. If we reflect deeply on this dimension, we have to conclude that all the sacraments of the New Covenant find their prototype in some way in marriage as the primordial sacrament. This seems to be what comes into view in the classical passage quoted from Ephesians, as we shall say again soon.

3. However, the relation of marriage to the whole sacramental order, which has arisen from the Church's endowment with the benefits of redemption, is not limited only to the dimension of model. In his dialogue with the Pharisees (see Mt 19), Christ not only confirms the existence of marriage instituted from the "beginning" by the Creator, but he declares *also that it is an integral part of the new sacramental economy,* of the new order of salvific "signs" that draws its origin from the sacrament of redemption, just as the original economy emerged from the sacrament of creation; and in fact, Christ limits himself to the one and only sacrament, which was marriage instituted in the state of original justice and innocence of man, created as male and female "in the image and likeness of God."

4. The new sacramental economy, which is constituted on the basis of the sacrament of redemption, coming forth from the spousal gracing of the Church by Christ, *differs from the original economy.* It is, in fact, directed, not toward the man of original justice and innocence, but toward the man burdened by the heritage of original sin and the state of sinfulness (*status naturae lapsae*). It is directed *toward the man of the threefold concupiscence* according to the classical words of 1 John 2:16, toward the man in whom "the flesh has desires contrary to the Spirit, and the Spirit has desires contrary to the flesh" (Gal 5:17) according to Pauline theology (and anthropology), to which we have devoted much space in our earlier reflections.

5. Following a deeper and more thorough analysis of the meaning of Christ's statement in the Sermon on the Mount about the "concupiscent look" as "adultery of the heart," these considerations prepare us to understand marriage as an integral part of the new sacramental order that draws its origin from the sacrament of redemption, or from the "great mystery," which, as the mystery of Christ and the Church, determines the sacramentality of the Church herself. These considerations also prepare us to understand *marriage as a sacrament of the New Covenant,* whose saving work is to be organically linked with the ethos we defined in our earlier analyses as the *ethos of redemption* [see TOB 46:4; 47:5; 49:2–7]. Ephesians in its own way expresses the same truth: it speaks, in fact, about marriage as a "great" sacrament in a broad parenetic context, namely, in the context of moral exhortations about the ethos that should characterize the life of Christians, that is, of those who are aware of their election, which is realized in Christ and the Church.

The Sacraments of the Church

6. Against this vast background of reflections emerging from reading Ephesians (especially 5:22–33) one can and must still touch upon the matter of the sacraments of the Church. The text quoted from Ephesians speaks about them in an indirect, and, I would say, secondary though sufficient, way so that this matter too can find a place in our considerations. Yet, we should clarify at least briefly *the meaning we are adopting in using the term "sacrament,"* which is significant for our considerations.

7. Up till now, in fact, we have been using the term "sacrament" (in agreement with the whole biblical and patristic tradition)[93] in a wider sense than the one characteristic of traditional and contemporary theological terminology, which uses the word "sacrament" to indicate the signs instituted by Christ and administered in the Church, which express and confer divine grace on the person who receives particular sacraments. In this sense, each of the seven sacraments of the Church is characterized by a definite liturgical action constituted by the word (form) and the specific sacramental "matter"—according to the widespread hylomorphic account that comes down to us from Thomas Aquinas and the whole Scholastic tradition.

8. In comparison with this restricted meaning, we used a *wider and perhaps an older and more fundamental meaning of the term* "sacrament" in our considerations [see TOB 93:5, with footnote]. Ephesians, and especially *5:22–33*, seems to authorize us specifically in this use. Here "sacrament" means the very mystery of God, which is hidden from eternity, yet not in an eternal concealment, but first in its very revelation and realization (also: in its revelation through realization). In this sense, we also spoke about the sacrament of creation and the sacrament of redemption. On the basis of the sacrament of creation one must understand the original sacramentality of marriage (the primordial sacrament). In a further step, on the basis of the sacrament of redemption, one can understand the sacramentality of the Church or rather the sacramentality of Christ's union with the Church, which the author of Ephesians presents in the likeness of marriage, of the spousal union of husband and wife. An attentive analysis of the text shows that in this case, what is at stake is not only a comparison in the sense of a metaphor, but a real *renewal* (or "re-creation," that is, a new creation) *of what constituted the salvific content* (in a certain sense the "salvific substance") of the primordial sacrament. This observation has an essential significance, both for clarifying the sacramentality of the Church (the very significant words of *Lumen Gentium*, 1, appeal to this) and for understanding the sacramentality of marriage understood as one of the sacraments of the Church.

---

93. See Leo XIII, *Acta Apostolicae Sedis* 2 (1881): 22.

99 *General Audience of October 27, 1982*
(Insegnamenti, 5, no. 2 [1982]: 936–39)

1. THE TEXT OF EPHESIANS 5:22–33 speaks about the sacraments of the Church—and in particular about Baptism and the Eucharist—but only indirectly and in some sense by allusion, when it develops the analogy of marriage in reference to Christ and the Church. And thus we read first that Christ, who "loved the Church and gave himself for her" (Eph 5:25), has done so "in order to make her holy by cleansing her with the washing of water accompanied by the word" (Eph 5:26). This text without any doubt speaks about the *sacrament of Baptism,* which has been conferred since the beginning according to the instruction of Christ on those who convert. The words quoted show in a very impressive way how Baptism draws its essential significance and sacramental strength from the Redeemer's spousal love through which above all the sacramentality of the Church herself is constituted, the *sacramentum magnum.* One can perhaps say the same thing also about the *Eucharist,* which seems to be indicated by the following words about the nourishment of one's own body: everyone nourishes and cares for his body "as Christ does with the Church, because we are members of his body" (Eph 5:29–30). In fact, Christ nourishes the Church with his Body precisely in the Eucharist.

2. One can see, however, that neither in the first nor the second case can we speak about a sacramental theology developed in much detail. One cannot speak about such a theology even in the case of the *sacrament of Marriage as one of the sacraments of the Church.* When it expresses Christ's spousal relationship with the Church, Ephesians allows us to understand that, on the basis of this relationship, the Church herself is the "great sacrament," the new sign of the covenant and of grace that draws its roots from the depths of the sacrament of redemption, just as marriage came forth from the depths of the sacrament of creation as the primordial sign of the covenant and of grace. The author of Ephesians proclaims that this primordial sacrament is realized in a new way in the "sacrament" of Christ and the Church. It is also for this reason that, in the same "classical" text of Ephesians 5:21–33, the Apostle turns to the spouses so that they might be "subject to one another in the fear of Christ" (Eph 5:21) and model their conju-

gal life, setting it on the foundation of the sacrament instituted in the "beginning" by the Creator, a sacrament that found its definitive greatness and holiness in the spousal covenant of grace between Christ and the Church.

3. Although Ephesians *does not speak directly and immediately* about marriage as one of the sacraments of the Church, it nevertheless particularly *confirms and deeply explains* the sacramentality of marriage. In the "great sacrament" of Christ and the Church, Christian spouses are called to shape their life and vocation on the sacramental foundation.

3. Sacrament and "Redemption of the Body"

A. THE GOSPEL

The Words of Christ and the Mystery of Redemption

4. After the analysis of the classical text of Ephesians 5:21–33, addressed to Christian spouses, in which Paul sets forth for them the "great mystery" (*sacramentum magnum*) of the spousal love of Christ and the Church, we should return to those significant words of the Gospel analyzed earlier in which we saw the key statements for the theology of the body. *Christ speaks these words, so to speak, from the divine depth of the "redemption of the body"* (Rom 8:23). All of these words have a fundamental significance for man precisely inasmuch as he is a body—as male and female. They have significance for marriage, in which man and woman unite in such a way that the two become "one flesh," according to the expression of Genesis 2:24, though at the same time Christ's words also indicate the vocation to continence "for the kingdom of heaven" (Mt 19:12).

5. In each of these ways, "the redemption of the body" is not only a great expectation for those who have "the first fruits of the Spirit" (Rom 8:23), but also a permanent source of hope that the creation will be "set free from the slavery of corruption to enter into the freedom of the glory of the children of God" (Rom 8:21). Christ's words, which he spoke from the divine depth of the mystery of redemption

and of the "redemption of the body," carry in themselves the leaven of this hope: they open the perspective on it, both in the eschatological dimension and the dimension of daily life. In fact, the words addressed to the immediate listeners are at the same time addressed to "historical" man in various times and places. Indeed, the man *who possesses "the first fruits of the Spirit* groans...waiting for...the redemption of the body" (Rom 8:23). In him, there is concentrated also the "cosmic" hope of creation as a whole, which in him, in man, "waits with eager longing for the revelation of the sons of God" (Rom 8:19).

The Sacrament of Redemption and the Indissolubility of Marriage

6. Christ speaks with the Pharisees, who ask him, "Is it lawful for a man to divorce his wife for any reason?" (Mt 19:3); they ask him in this way precisely because the law attributed to Moses allowed the so-called "certificate of divorce" (Deut 24:1). Christ's response is, "Have you not read that from the beginning the Creator created them male and female and said, 'For this reason a man will leave his father and his mother and unite with his wife, and the two shall be one flesh?' So it is that they are no longer two, but one single flesh. Therefore what God has joined let man not separate" (Mt 19:4–6). With respect to the "certificate of divorce" Christ answers, "Because of the hardness of your heart Moses allowed you to divorce your wives, but from the beginning it was not so. Therefore I say to you: Whoever divorces his wife, except in the case of concubinage, and marries another commits adultery" (Mt 19:8–9). "The one who marries a woman divorced by her husband commits adultery" (Mt 5:32).

7. The horizon of "the redemption of the body" opens up with these words, which are the answer to a concrete juridical-moral question; it opens first of all by the fact that *Christ takes a stand on the level of* that *primordial sacrament,* which his interlocutors inherit in a unique way, given that they also inherit the revelation of the mystery of creation contained in the first chapters of Genesis.

At the same time, these words give an all-embracing answer to "historical" man of all times and places, because they are decisive for marriage and for its indissolubility; in fact, they appeal to what man is, male and female, what he has irreversibly come to be by virtue of being created "in the image of God": man who does not cease to be such even after original sin, although this sin deprived him of original innocence and justice. Christ, who appeals to the "beginning" in his answer to the question of the Pharisees, seems in this way to underline particularly the fact that he speaks from the depth of the mystery of redemption and the redemption of the body. *Redemption* means, in fact, a *"new creation,"* as it were, it means *taking up all that is created* to express in creation the fullness of justice, equity, and holiness planned for it by God and to express that fullness above all in man, created male and female "in the image of God."

In the perspective of the words of Christ to the Pharisees about what marriage was "from the beginning," we also reread the classical text of Ephesians 5:22–33 as a testimony of the sacramentality of marriage based on the "great mystery" of Christ and the Church.

100 *General Audience of November 24, 1982* (*Insegnamenti*, 5, no. 2 [1982]: 1431–35)

1. WE HAVE ANALYZED EPHESIANS, and above all 5:22–33, from the point of view of the sacramentality of marriage. We are now examining still the same text in the perspective of the words of the Gospel.

Christ's words to the Pharisees (see Mt 19) appeal to marriage as a sacrament, or to the primordial revelation of God's salvific will and action "at the beginning" in the very mystery of creation. In virtue of God's salvific will and action, man and woman, uniting with each other in such a way as to become "one flesh" (Gen 2:24), were at the same time destined to be united "in truth and love" as sons of God (see *Gaudium et Spes*, 24:3), adoptive sons in the firstborn Son, beloved from eternity. To such unity and such a communion of persons, according to likeness with the union of divine Persons (see *Gaudium et Spes*, 24:3), are dedicated Christ's words referring to marriage as the primordial sacrament and confirming that sacrament at the same time on the basis of the mystery of redemption. In fact, the original "unity in the body" of man and woman does not cease to shape man's history on earth, although it lost the lucid clarity of the sacrament, of the sign of salvation, which it possessed "at the beginning."

2. When Christ, in the presence of his interlocutors in Matthew and Mark (see Mt 19; Mk 10) *confirms marriage* as *a sacrament instituted by the Creator "at the beginning"*—when he accordingly requires its indissolubility—he thereby *opens* marriage to the salvific action of God, *to the powers flowing "from the redemption of the body,"* which help to overcome the consequences of sin and to build the unity of man and woman according to the Creator's eternal plan. The salvific action deriving from the mystery of redemption takes into itself God's original sanctifying action in the very mystery of creation.

3. The words of Matthew 19:3–9 (cf. Mk 10:2–12) have at the same time a very expressive ethical eloquence. On the basis of the mystery of redemption, these words confirm the primordial sacrament and at the same time *establish an adequate ethos* that we called "ethos of redemption" in our earlier reflections. In its theological essence, the evangelical and Christian ethos is *the ethos of redemption*. We can certainly find a rational interpretation for this ethos, a philosophical interpretation of a personalistic sort; nevertheless, in its theological essence, it is an ethos of redemption, even better, *an ethos of the redemption of the body*. Redemption becomes at the same time the basis for understanding the particular dignity of the human body, which is rooted in the personal dignity of man and woman. The reason for this dignity is precisely what stands at the root of the indissolubility of the conjugal covenant.

4. Christ appeals to the indissoluble character of marriage as the primordial sacrament and, by confirming this sacrament on the basis of the mystery of redemption, at the same time draws from it conclusions of an ethical nature: "Whoever divorces his wife and marries another commits adultery against her; and if the woman divorces her husband and marries another, she commits adultery" (Mk 10:11–12). One can say that in this way *redemption is given* to man *as the grace* of the New Covenant with God in Christ—and at the same time it is *assigned to him as ethos,* as the form of morality that corresponds to the action of God in the mystery of redemption. If marriage as a sacrament is an efficacious sign of God's salvific action "from the beginning," then at the same time—in the light of the words of Christ meditated upon—this *sacrament* is also *an exhortation* addressed to man, *male and female, that they might conscientiously share in the redemption of the body.*

Sacrament—Given as Grace and Assigned as an Ethos

5. The ethical dimension of the redemption of the body shows its outlines with particular depth when we meditate on the words Christ spoke in the Sermon on the Mount about the commandment "You shall not commit adultery": "You have heard that it was said, 'You shall not commit adultery.' But I say to you: Whoever looks at a woman to desire her has already committed adultery with her in his heart" (Mt 5:27–28). Previously we commented at length on this lapidary statement by Christ, in the conviction that it has a fundamental significance for the whole theology of the body, above all in the dimension of "historical man." And although these words do not refer directly and immediately to marriage as a sacrament, nevertheless *it is impossible to separate them from the whole sacramental substratum* in which, as far as the conjugal covenant is concerned, man's existence as male and female has been set, both in the original context of the mystery of creation and also, later, in the context of the mystery of redemption. This sacramental substratum always concerns concrete persons; it penetrates into what man and woman are (or rather into who the man and the woman are) in their own original dignity as image and likeness of God due to creation, and at the same time in the same dignity inherited despite sin, which is continuously "assigned" to man as a task through the reality of redemption.

6. Christ, who *in the Sermon on the Mount* gives his own *interpretation of the commandment "You shall not commit adultery"*—an interpretation constitutive of the new ethos—with the same lapidary words assigns the dignity of every woman as a task to every man; at the same time (although this conclusion follows only indirectly from the text) he assigns also the dignity of every man to every woman.[94] Finally, he assigns to each—both to the man and to the woman—his or her own dignity, *in some sense the "sacrum" of the person, specifically with respect to* the person's femininity or masculinity, *with respect to the "body."* It is not difficult to show that Christ's words in the Sermon on the Mount are about ethos. At the same time, it is not difficult to

---

94. The text in Mark about the indissolubility of marriage clearly affirms that the woman also becomes a subject of adultery if she divorces her husband and marries another (see Mk 10:12).

affirm after deeper reflection that such words flow from the very depth of the redemption of the body. Although they do not refer directly to marriage as a sacrament, it is not difficult to observe that they reach their own and full meaning in relation with the sacrament, both with the primordial sacrament, which is united with the mystery of creation, and with the one in which "historical" man, after sin and due to his hereditary sinfulness, must find again the dignity and holiness of conjugal union "in the body" on the basis of the mystery of redemption.

7. In the Sermon on the Mount—as also in the dialogue with the Pharisees about the indissolubility of marriage—Christ speaks from the depth of that divine mystery. At the same time, *he penetrates into the very depth of the human mystery.* For this reason, he appeals to the "heart," to that "intimate place," in which good and evil, sin and justice, concupiscence and holiness fight each other in man. Speaking about concupiscence (about the concupiscent look, see Mt 5:28), Christ makes his listeners aware that everyone carries within himself, together with the mystery of sin, the inner dimension of the "man of concupiscence" (which is threefold: "concupiscence of the flesh, concupiscence of the eyes, and the pride of life," 1 John 2:16). Precisely *to this man of concupiscence* there is given in marriage *the sacrament* of redemption *as grace* and sign of the covenant with God—and *it is assigned* to him *as an ethos.* At the same time, in relation with marriage as a sacrament, it is assigned as ethos to every man, male and female: it is assigned to his "heart," to his conscience, to his looks, and to his behavior. Marriage—according to Christ's words (see Mt 19:4)—is a sacrament from the "beginning" itself, and at the same time, on the basis of man's "historical" sinfulness, it is a sacrament that arose from the mystery of the "redemption of the body."

101   *General Audience of December 1, 1982*
 (Insegnamenti, 5, no. 2 [1982]: 1485–90)

1. WE HAVE ANALYZED EPHESIANS, and above all 5:22–33, in the perspective of the sacramentality of marriage. Now we will try to consider the same text once again in the light of the words of the Gospel and the Letters of Paul to the Corinthians and the Romans.

As a sacrament born of the mystery of the redemption and in some sense reborn from the spousal love of Christ and the Church, marriage is an efficacious expression of the saving power of God, who realizes his eternal plan also after sin and despite the threefold concupiscence hidden in the heart of every man, male and female. As a sacramental *expression of that saving power, marriage is also an exhortation to gain mastery over concupiscence* (as Christ speaks about in the Sermon on the Mount). A fruit of this mastery is the unity and indissolubility of marriage and, in addition, the deepened sense of the woman's dignity in the man's heart (as also the man's dignity in the woman's heart), in conjugal life together and in every other sphere of reciprocal relations.

Sacrament—Call to "Life according to the Spirit"

2. The truth according to which marriage, as sacrament of redemption, is given "to the man of concupiscence" as a grace and at the same time as an ethos, has found particular expression in the teaching of St. Paul as well, especially in *1 Corinthians 7*. When he compares marriage with virginity (or "continence for the kingdom of heaven") and declares the "superiority" of virginity, he still observes, "each has his own gift from God, one in one way and another in another" (1 Cor 7:7). Thus, based on the mystery of redemption, *a particular "gift," that is, grace, corresponds to marriage.* In the same context, when the Apostle gives advice to the recipients of his letter, he recommends marriage "because of the danger of incontinence" (1 Cor 7:2), and a little later he recommends to the spouses that "the husband should give to his wife her due, and likewise the wife to her husband" (1 Cor 7:3). And he continues, "It is better to marry than to be aflame" (1 Cor 7:9).

3. On the basis of these Pauline statements, the opinion was formed that marriage is a specific *remedium concupiscentiae*, remedy of concupiscence. St. Paul, however, who explicitly teaches, as we were able to observe, that a particular "gift" corresponds to marriage and that in the mystery of redemption marriage is given to the man and the woman as grace, simply expresses the thought in his words, suggestive and paradoxical as they are, that marriage is assigned to the

spouses as an ethos. In the Pauline words, "It is better to marry than to be aflame," the word *"aflame" signifies the disorder of the passions* springing from concupiscence of the flesh (concupiscence is presented in an analogous way in the Old Testament by Sir 23:17 [see TOB 39:1]). "Marriage," by contrast, signifies *the ethical order,* which is consciously introduced in this context. One can say that marriage is the place of the encounter of eros and ethos and of their reciprocal interpenetration in the "heart" of man and woman, and likewise in all their reciprocal relations.

4. In addition, this truth—namely, that marriage, as a sacrament springing from the mystery of redemption, is given to "historical" man as both a grace and an ethos—determines the character of marriage as one of the sacraments of the Church. *As a sacrament of the Church,* marriage is by nature indissoluble. As a sacrament of the Church, it is also a word of the Spirit exhorting man and woman to shape their whole life together by drawing strength from the mystery of the "redemption of the body." In this way, they are called to chastity as to the state of life "according to the Spirit" proper to them (see Rom 8:4–5; Gal 5:25). The redemption of the body also signifies in this case the hope that can be defined in the dimension of marriage as the everyday hope, the hope of temporality. *On the basis of such a hope, one can master the concupiscence of the flesh* as the source of the tendency toward an egotistical satisfaction, and in the sacramental covenant of masculinity and femininity, "flesh" itself becomes the specific "substratum" of a lasting and indissoluble communion of persons (*communio personarum*) in a manner worthy of persons.

5. Those who unite with each other as spouses according to the eternal divine plan so as to *become* in some sense "one flesh" are in turn *called by the sacrament* to a *life* "according to the Spirit," such that this life corresponds to the "gift" received in the sacrament. In virtue of this "gift," by leading a life as spouses "according to the Spirit," they are able to discover the particular gratuitous gift in which they have come to share. Just as "concupiscence" darkens the horizon of interior vision and deprives hearts of the lucid clarity of desires and aspirations, so life "according to the Spirit" (or the grace of the sacrament of Marriage) allows man and woman to find the true freedom of the gift

together with the awareness of the spousal meaning of the body in its masculinity and femininity.

6. Thus life "according to the Spirit" expresses itself also in the reciprocal "union" or "knowledge" (see Gen 4:1) by which the spouses, when they become "one flesh," submit their femininity and masculinity to the blessing of procreation. "Adam united himself with Eve his wife, who conceived and gave birth...and said, 'I have acquired a man from the Lord'" (Gen 4:1).

Here too, *life "according to the Spirit"* expresses itself in the awareness of the gratuitous gift, which corresponds to the dignity of the spouses themselves as parents, that is, it expresses itself *in the deep awareness of the holiness of the life (sacrum)* to which both give rise, thereby participating in the powers of the mystery of creation—like the first parents. In the light of that hope, which is connected with the mystery of the redemption of the body (see Rom 8:19–23), this new human life, the new human being conceived and born from the conjugal union of his father and mother, opens himself to the "first fruits of the Spirit" (Rom 8:23) "to enter into the freedom of the glory of the children of God" (Rom 8:21). And if "the whole creation groans and suffers until now in labor pains" (Rom 8:22), a particular hope accompanies the mother's labor pains, namely, the hope of the "revelation of the sons of God," a hope of which every newborn who comes into the world carries a spark with himself.

Sacrament and the Eschatological Hope of the "Redemption of the Body"

7. This hope, which is "in the world," penetrating—as St. Paul teaches—the whole of creation, is at the same time not "from the world." Even more: it must fight in the human heart against what is "from the world," with what is "in the world." "For all that is in the world, the concupiscence of the flesh, the concupiscence of the eyes, and the pride of life, comes not from the Father but from the world" (1 Jn 2:16). *As the primordial sacrament* and at the same time as the sacrament born in the mystery of the redemption of the body from the spousal love of Christ and the Church, *marriage* "comes from the

Father." It is not "from the world," but "from the Father." Consequently, as a sacrament, marriage also constitutes the basis of hope for the person, for the man and the woman, for the parents and the children, for the human generations. On the one hand, "the world passes away with its concupiscence," and on the other, "the one who does the will of God will remain in eternity" (1 Jn 2:17). Man's origin in the world is linked with marriage as a sacrament, and his coming to be is inscribed in marriage, not only in the historical but also in the eschatological dimensions.

8. This is what *the words in which Christ appeals to the resurrection of the body* refer to, words reported by the three Synoptics (see Mt 22:23–32; Mk 12:18–27; Lk 20:34–39). "In the resurrection they take neither wife nor husband, but are like angels in heaven," as Matthew puts it, and Mark likewise, while Luke has, "The sons of this age take wife and take husband; but those who are considered worthy of the other world and of the resurrection from the dead take neither wife nor husband. Indeed they cannot die anymore, because they are equal to the angels and, being sons of the resurrection, they are sons of God" (Lk 20:34–36). We analyzed these texts earlier in detail.

9. Christ affirms that *marriage—the sacrament of the origins* of man in the visible temporal world—*does not belong* to the eschatological reality of the "future world." Nevertheless, the man who is called to participate in this eschatological future through the resurrection of the body is the same man, male and female, whose origin in the visible temporal world is linked with marriage as the primordial sacrament of the very mystery of creation. Even more, every man, called to share in the reality of the future resurrection, carries this vocation in the world because he has his *origin in the visible temporal world through the marriage of his parents*. Thus, Christ's words, which exclude marriage from the reality of the "future world," at the same time indirectly reveal the meaning of this sacrament for *the participation* of human persons, sons and daughters, *in the future resurrection*.

10. Marriage, which is the primordial sacrament, reborn in some sense from the spousal love of Christ and the Church, does not belong to the "redemption of the body" in the dimension of eschatological hope (see Rom 8:23). The same marriage, which is given to man as a grace, as a "gift" destined by God precisely for the spouses, and at the same time assigned to them by Christ's words as an ethos—that sacramental marriage *is fulfilled* and realized *in the perspective of the eschatological hope*. It has an essential meaning for the "redemption of the body" in the dimension of this hope. It comes, in fact, from the Father and owes its origin in the world to him. And if this "world passes away," and if the concupiscence of the flesh, the concupiscence of the eyes, and the pride of life, which come "from the world," also pass away with it, marriage as a sacrament immutably serves the purpose that man, male and female, by mastering concupiscence, does the will of the Father. And the one who "does the will of God will remain in eternity" (1 Jn 2:17).

11. In this sense, marriage as a sacrament also bears within itself the germ of man's eschatological future, that is, the perspective of the "redemption of the body" in the dimension of eschatological hope, to which Christ's words about the resurrection correspond: "In the resurrection they take neither wife nor husband" (Mt 22:30); moreover, those who, "being sons of the resurrection...are equal to the angels and...sons of God" (Lk 20:36), owe their origin in the visible temporal world to the marriage and procreation of man and woman. As a sacrament of the human "beginning," *as a sacrament of the temporality* of historical man, marriage thus performs an irreplaceable service with regard to man's extra-temporal future, with regard to the mystery of the "redemption of the body" in the dimension of eschatological hope.

B. EPHESIANS

The Spousal and Redemptive Meaning of Love

102 *General Audience of December 15, 1982*
(*Insegnamenti*, 5, no. 2 [1982]: 1602–06)

1. AS WE HAVE ALREADY SEEN, the author of Ephesians speaks about a "great mystery" linked with the primordial sacrament through the continuity of God's salvific plan. He too goes back to the "beginning," as Christ had in the dialogue with the Pharisees (see Mt 19:8), quoting the same words: "For this reason a man will leave his father and

his mother and unite with his wife, and the two will be one flesh" (Gen 2:24). That "great mystery" is above all the mystery of the union of Christ with the Church, which the Apostle presents in the likeness of the unity of spouses. "I say this with reference to Christ and the Church" (Eph 5:32). We find ourselves in the sphere of the great analogy, in which *marriage as a sacrament* is, on the one hand, *presupposed* and, on the other, *rediscovered.* It is presupposed as the sacrament of the human "beginning," united with the mystery of creation. It is rediscovered, by contrast, as the fruit of the spousal love of Christ and the Church, linked with the mystery of redemption.

2. Turning directly to the spouses, the author of Ephesians exhorts them to shape their reciprocal relationship on the model of the spousal union of Christ and the Church. One can say—presupposing the sacramentality of marriage in its primordial meaning—that he orders them to *learn this sacrament anew* from the spousal relationship of Christ and the Church. "And you, husbands, love your wives, as Christ loved the Church and gave himself for her, in order to make her holy" (Eph 5:25–26). This invitation, which the Apostle addresses to Christian spouses, has its full motivation inasmuch as, through marriage as a sacrament, they participate in the salvific love of Christ, which at the same time expresses itself as his spousal love for the Church. In the light of Ephesians—precisely *through participation in this salvific love of Christ—marriage is confirmed and simultaneously renewed as the sacrament of the human "beginning,"* that is, as the sacrament in which man and woman, called to become "one flesh," share in the creative love of God himself. They share in it both by the fact that, created in the image of God, they have been called in virtue of this image to a particular union (*communio personarum,* the communion of persons), and because this union has itself been blessed from the beginning with the blessing of fruitfulness (see Gen 1:28).

3. This whole original and stable structure of marriage as the sacrament of the mystery of creation—according to the "classical" text of Ephesians 5:21–33—is renewed in the mystery of redemption, when that mystery takes on the aspect of the Church's spousal endowment by Christ. That original and stable form of marriage is renewed when the spouses receive it as the sacrament of the Church, drawing on the new depth of man's endowment by God, which is revealed and

opened with the mystery of redemption, when "Christ loved the Church and gave himself for her, in order to make her holy" (Eph 5:25–26). That original and stable image of marriage as a sacrament *is renewed* when Christian spouses—aware of the authentic depth of the "redemption of the body"—unite "in the fear of Christ" (Eph 5:21).

4. The Pauline image of marriage, inscribed in the "great mystery" of Christ and the Church, brings together the redemptive dimension of love with its spousal dimension. In some sense it unites these two dimensions in a single one. Christ has become the Church's Bridegroom, he married the Church as his Bride because "he gave himself for her" (Eph 5:25). Through marriage as a sacrament (as one of the sacraments of the Church), *both of these dimensions of love, the spousal and the redemptive,* penetrate together with the grace of the sacrament into the life of the spouses. The spousal meaning of the body in its masculinity and femininity, which manifested itself for the first time in the mystery of creation on the background of man's original innocence, is united in the image of Ephesians with the redemptive meaning, and in this way it is confirmed and in some sense "created anew."

Redemption of the Body and "The Sacrament of Man"

5. This is important with regard to marriage and the Christian vocation of husbands and wives. The text of Ephesians 5:21–33 turns directly to them and speaks above all to them. Still, that linking of the spousal meaning of the body with its "redemptive" meaning is equally essential and *valid for the hermeneutics of man* in general: for the fundamental problem of understanding him and for the self-understanding of his being in the world. It is obvious that we cannot exclude from this problem the question about the meaning of being a body, about the meaning of being, as a body, man and woman. We first raised these questions in relation to the analysis of the human "beginning" in the context of Genesis. It was that context itself that in some sense demanded that they should be raised. The "classical" text of Ephesians demands the same thing. And if the "great mystery" of Christ's union with the Church obliges us to link *the spousal meaning of the body with its redemptive meaning,* in this link the spouses find the answer to the question about the meaning of "being a body," and not only they, although this text of the Apostle's letter is addressed above all to them.

6. The Pauline image of the "great mystery" of Christ and the Church indirectly speaks also about "continence for the kingdom of heaven," in which both dimensions of love, the spousal and the redemptive, are united with each other in a way that differs from that of marriage, in accord with different proportions. *Is* not the spousal *love with which Christ "loved the Church,"* his Bride, *"and gave himself for her"* equally the fullest *incarnation* of the ideal of *"continence for the kingdom of God"* (see Mt 19:12)? Is it not precisely in this love that support is found for all those—both men and women—who choose the same ideal and thus desire to link the spousal dimension of love with the redemptive dimension, according to the model of Christ himself? They desire to confirm with their lives that the spousal meaning of the body—of its masculinity and femininity—a meaning deeply inscribed in the essential structure of the human person has been opened in a new way by Christ and with the example of his life to the hope united with the redemption of the body. Thus, the grace of the mystery of redemption also bears fruit—even more: bears fruit in a particular way—with the vocation to continence "for the kingdom of heaven."

7. The text of Ephesians 5:22–33 does not speak about this explicitly. It is addressed to spouses and constructed according to the image of marriage, which by this analogy explains the union of Christ with the Church: a union in redemptive and spousal love together. Is it not this love itself as a living and life-giving expression of the mystery of redemption that *passes beyond the circle of the addressees of this letter circumscribed by the analogy of marriage?* Does it not embrace every human being and, in some sense, everything created, as the Pauline text on the "redemption of the body" in Romans indicates (see Rom 8:23)? In this sense, the *sacramentum magnum* is indeed *a new* sacrament of man in Christ and in the Church: *the sacrament "of man and of the world,"* just as the creation of man, male and female, in the image of God was the original sacrament of man and of the world [see TOB 19:5]. Marriage is organically inscribed in this new sacrament of redemption, just as it was inscribed in the original sacrament of creation.

8. Man, who is "from the beginning" male and female, must seek the meaning of his existence and the meaning of his humanity by reaching all the way to the mystery of creation through the reality of redemption. There he finds also the essential answer to the question about the meaning of the human body, about the meaning of the masculinity and femininity of the human person. The union of Christ with the Church allows us to understand in what way the spousal meaning of the body is completed by the redemptive meaning on the different roads of life and in different situations: not only in marriage or "continence" (or virginity, celibacy), but also, for example, in the many kinds of *human suffering*, indeed, in man's very *birth and death*. Through the "great mystery" discussed in Ephesians, through the New Covenant of Christ with the Church, marriage is inscribed anew in the "sacrament of man," which embraces the universe; it is inscribed in the sacrament of man and of the world, which, thanks to the "redemption of the body," is formed according to the model of the spousal love of Christ and the Church, until the measure of definitive fulfillment is reached in the kingdom of the Father.

Marriage as a sacrament remains a living and life-giving part of this salvific process.

CHAPTER TWO

The Dimension of Sign

---

1. *"Language of the Body" and the Reality of the Sign*

The Marital Promise

103 *General Audience of January 5, 1983*
(Insegnamenti, 6, no. 1 [1983]: 41–45)

1. "I...TAKE YOU...AS MY WIFE"; "I...take you...as my husband." These words stand at the center of the liturgy of marriage as a sacrament of the Church. The engaged couple speak these words, inserting them in the following formula of consent: "I promise to be faithful to you always, in joy and in sorrow, in sickness and in health, and to love you and honor you all the days of my life." With these words the engaged couple contract marriage, and at the same time they receive it as a sacrament of which both are the ministers. *Both, the man and the woman, administer the sacrament.* They do so before witnesses. The authorized witness is the priest, who at the same time blesses the marriage and presides over the whole liturgy of the sacrament. Further witnesses are, in a certain sense, all the participants in the wedding rite and in an "official" way some of them (usually two) who are specifically called as witnesses. They must witness that the marriage is contracted before God and confirmed by the Church. In the normal course of events, sacramental marriage is a public act before society and the Church by which two persons, a man and a woman, become husband and wife, that is, the actual subject of the married vocation and life.

2. Marriage as a sacrament is contracted by means of *the word*, which is *a sacramental sign in virtue of its content*, "I take you as my wife/as my husband, and I promise to be faithful to you always, in joy and in sorrow, in sickness and in health, and to love you and honor you all the days of my life." However, this sacramental word is, of itself, only a sign of the coming to be of marriage. And the coming to be of marriage is distinct from its consummation, so much so that without this consummation, marriage is not yet constituted in its full reality. The observation that a marriage is juridically contracted but not consummated (*ratum, non consummatum*) corresponds to the observation that it has not been fully constituted as a marriage. In fact, the words themselves, "I take you as my wife/as my husband," do not only refer to a determinate reality, but they can only be fulfilled by the *copula conjugale* (conjugal intercourse). This reality (the *copula conjugale*), moreover, has been defined from the very beginning by institution of the Creator. "A man will leave his father and his mother and unite with his wife, and the two will be one flesh" (Gen 2:24).

3. Thus, *from the words* with which the man and the woman express their readiness to become "one flesh" according to the eternal truth established in the mystery of creation, we pass *to the reality* that corresponds to these words. Both the one and the other element are important *with regard to the structure of the sacramental sign,* to which we should devote what follows in the present considerations. Given that the sacrament is the sign by means of which the saving reality of grace and the covenant is expressed and realized, we must now consider it under the aspect of sign, while the preceding reflections were devoted to the reality of grace and the covenant.

As a sacrament of the Church, marriage is contracted by the words of the ministers, that is, of the new spouses, words that signify and indicate in the intentional order what (or rather who) both have decided to be from now on, for and with one another. The words of new spouses are part of the integral structure of the sacramental sign, not only *by what* they signify, but also in some sense *with what* they signify and determine. The sacramental sign is constituted in the intentional order inasmuch as it is simultaneously constituted in the real order.

4. Consequently, the sign of the sacrament of Marriage is constituted by the words of the new spouses inasmuch as the "reality" that they themselves constitute corresponds to them. *Both of them, as man and woman,* being ministers of the sacrament at the moment of contracting marriage, at the same time *constitute the full and real visible sign* of the sacrament itself. The words spoken by them would not of themselves constitute the sacramental sign if the human subjectivity of the engaged man and woman and at the same time the consciousness of the body linked with the masculinity and the femininity of the bride and the bridegroom did not correspond to them. Here one must call to mind again the whole series of analyses of Genesis 1–2 carried out earlier. The structure of the sacramental sign remains, in fact, in its essence the same as "in the beginning." What determines it is *in some sense "the language of the body,"* inasmuch as the man and the woman, who are to become one flesh by marriage, express in this sign the reciprocal gift of masculinity and femininity as the foundation of the conjugal union of the persons.

5. The sign of the sacrament of Marriage is constituted by the fact that the words spoken by the new spouses take up again the same "language of the body" as at the "beginning" and, at any rate, give it a concrete and unrepeatable expression. They give it an intentional expression on the level of intellect and will, of consciousness and the heart. The words, "I take you as my wife/as my husband," bear within themselves precisely that perennial and ever unique and unrepeatable "language of the body," and they place it at the same time in the context of the communion of persons. "I promise to be faithful to you always, in joy and in sorrow, in sickness and in health, and to love you and honor you all the days of my life." In this way the perennial and ever new "language of the body" *is not only the "substratum,"* but *in some sense also the constitutive content of the communion of persons.* The persons—the man and the woman—become a reciprocal gift for each other. They become this gift in their masculinity and femininity while they discover the spousal meaning of the body and refer it reciprocally to themselves in an irreversible way: in the dimension of life as a whole.

6. Thus, the sacrament of Marriage as a sign allows one to understand the words of the new spouses, words that confer a new aspect on their life in the strictly personal (and interpersonal, *communio personarum*) dimension on the basis of the "language of the body." The administration of the sacrament consists in this, that at the moment

of contracting marriage the man and the woman, with the suitable words and in rereading the perennial "language of the body," form a sign, an unrepeatable sign, which also has a future-oriented meaning, "all the days of my life," that is, until death. This is the visible and efficacious *sign* of the covenant with God in Christ, that is, of *grace, which is to become their portion in this sign as "their own gift"* (according to the expression of 1 Cor 7:7).

7. If one formulates the question in socio-juridical terms, one can say that between the new spouses a conjugal contract is stipulated that has a clearly determined content. One can say, in addition, that in consequence of this contract, they have become spouses in a socially recognized way, and that in this way the family as the fundamental social cell is constituted. This way of understanding it agrees obviously with the human reality of marriage, and, indeed, it is fundamental in the religious and religious-moral sense. Yet, from the point of view of the theology of the sacrament, *the key for understanding* marriage remains *the reality of the sign* with which marriage is constituted on the basis of man's covenant with God in Christ and in the Church: it is constituted in the supernatural order of the sacred bond requiring grace. In this order, marriage is a visible and efficacious sign. Having originated in the mystery of creation, it draws its new origin from the mystery of redemption in order to serve the "union of the sons of God in truth and love" (*Gaudium et Spes*, 24:3). The liturgy of the sacrament of Marriage gives a form to that sign: directly, during the sacramental rite on the basis of the ensemble of its eloquent expressions; indirectly, throughout the whole of life. As spouses, the man and the woman bear this sign throughout the whole of their lives, and they remain this sign until death.

"Prophetism of the Body"

104 *General Audience of January 12, 1983*
(Insegnamenti, 6, no. 1 [1983]: 100–4)

1. WE ARE ANALYZING the sacramentality of marriage under the aspect of sign.

When we affirm that the "language of the body" also enters essentially into the structure of marriage as a sacramental sign, we appeal *to a long biblical tradition.* This tradition has its origin in Genesis 2:23–25 and finds its definitive crowning in Ephesians 5:21–33. The prophets of the Old Testament had an essential role in forming this tradition. When we analyzed the texts of Hosea, Ezekiel, Deutero-Isaiah, and other prophets [see TOB 36:5–37:6, 94:6–95b:2], we found ourselves on the road of that great analogy whose ultimate expression is the New Covenant under the form of a marriage between Christ and the Church (Eph 5:21–33). On the basis of this long tradition, it is possible to speak *about a specific "prophetism of the body,"* both because we find this analogy above all in the prophets and also in regard to its very contents. Here the "prophetism of the body" signifies precisely the "language of the body."

2. It seems to be a *two-level analogy. On the first level,* the fundamental level, the prophets *portray the covenant as a marriage* established between God and Israel (which in turn allows us to understand marriage itself as a covenant between husband and wife; see Prov 2:17; Mal 2:14). In this case the covenant comes from the initiative of God, the Lord of Israel. The fact that, as Creator and Lord, he makes a covenant first with Abraham and then with Moses attests a particular election. And for this reason, the prophets, who presuppose the whole juridical-moral content of the covenant, go into greater depth, revealing an incomparably deeper dimension than that of a mere "contract." By choosing Israel, God united himself with his people through love and grace. He bound himself with a particular bond, which is deeply personal, and thus Israel, although it is a people, is presented in this prophetic vision of the covenant as "Bride" or "wife" and thus in some sense as a person.

> For your Creator is your husband,
> Lord of hosts is his name;
> the Holy One of Israel is your Redeemer,
> the God of the whole earth he is called....
> my steadfast affection shall not depart from you,
> and my covenant of peace shall not waver,
> says the Lord, who has compassion on you. (Isa 54:5–6, 10)

3. *Yahweh is the Lord of Israel, but he also became its Bridegroom.* The books of the Old Testament attest the complete originality of Yahweh's "lordship" over his people. To the other aspects of the lord-

ship of Yahweh, Lord of the covenant and Father of Israel, a new one is added that is revealed by the prophets, namely, the stupendous dimension of this "lordship," which is the spousal dimension. In this manner, the absolute of lordship turns out to be the absolute of love. In relation to this absolute, breaking the covenant signifies not only an infraction of the "covenant" connected with the authority of the Supreme Legislator, but unfaithfulness and betrayal: a blow that directly pierces his heart as Father, Bridegroom, and Lord.

4. If one can speak of levels in the analogy used by the prophets, this is in some sense the first and fundamental level. Given that the covenant of Yahweh with Israel has the character of a spousal bond like a conjugal covenant, that *first level of the analogy reveals its second level*, which is *precisely the "language of the body."* Here we have in mind in the first place *the language in the objective sense*: the prophets compare the covenant to marriage, they go back to that primordial sacrament about which Genesis 2:24 speaks, in which man and woman by free choice become "one flesh." Nevertheless, it is characteristic of the way the prophets express themselves that, presupposing the "language of the body" in the objective sense, they go on at the same time to *its subjective meaning*: that is, they allow *the body itself*, as it were, *to speak*. In the prophetic texts about the covenant based on the analogy of the spousal union of the couple, it is the body itself that "speaks"; it speaks with its masculinity or femininity, it speaks with the mysterious language of the personal gift, it speaks finally—and this happens more often—both in the language of faithfulness, that is, of love, and in the language of conjugal unfaithfulness, that is, of "adultery."

5. It was, as we know, the different sins of the Chosen People— and above all the frequent infidelities in the worship of the one God, that is, various forms of idolatry—that offered the prophets the occasion for these statements. *The prophet of Israel's "adultery"* was in a particular way Hosea, who stigmatizes this adultery not only with words, but also with acts of symbolic meaning. "Go, take a prostitute for yourself as wife and have children of prostitution, for the land does nothing but prostitute itself by going away from the Lord" (Hos 1:2). Hosea highlights the whole splendor of the covenant, of the wedding in which Yahweh shows himself as a sensitive Bridegroom or husband ready to forgive and at the same time demanding and severe. The "adultery" and "prostitution" of Israel form an evident *contrast with the spousal bond*, on which the covenant is based, just as, by analogy, the marriage of a man with a woman is based on the same bond.

6. In a similar way *Ezekiel* stigmatizes idolatry by using the symbol of the adultery of Jerusalem (see Ezek 16) and, in another passage, that of Jerusalem and Samaria (see Ezek 23). "I passed near you again and looked on you; you were at the age for love.... I swore a covenant with you, says the Lord God, and you became mine" (Ezek 16:8). "But you, infatuated with your beauty and profiting from your fame, played the whore, and lavished your favors on any passerby" (Ezek 16:15).

7. In the prophetic texts, the human body speaks a *"language"* of which it is not the author. *Its author is man,* as male or female, as bridegroom or bride: man with his perennial vocation to the communion of persons. Yet, man is *in some sense unable to express* this singular language of his personal existence and vocation *without the body.* He is constituted in such a way from the "beginning" that the deepest words of the spirit—words of love, gift, and faithfulness—call for an appropriate "language of the body." And without this language, they cannot be fully expressed. We know from the gospel that this point applies both to marriage and to continence "for the kingdom of heaven."

8. Through this "language of the body," the prophets, as the inspired spokesmen of Yahweh's covenant with Israel, attempt to express both the spousal depth of that covenant and all that contradicts it. They sing the praises of faithfulness and stigmatize unfaithfulness as "adultery": they speak thus according to ethical categories, setting moral good and evil in mutual opposition. The antithesis of good and evil is essential for ethos. The prophetic texts have in this sphere an essential significance, as we emphasized already in our earlier reflections [see TOB 36:5–37:6, 94:6–95b:2]. It seems, however, that the "language of the body" according to the prophets is not only a language of ethos, not only a song of praise for faithfulness and purity as well as a condemnation of "adultery" and "prostitution." In fact,

inasmuch as every language is an expression of knowledge, the categories of truth and untruth (or falsity) are essential for it. In the texts of the prophets, who see in marriage the analogy of Yahweh's covenant with Israel, *the body tells the truth* through faithfulness and conjugal love, and, when it commits "adultery" it tells a lie, *it commits falsehood.*

9. The point is not to replace ethical differentiations by logical ones. When the prophetic texts point to conjugal faithfulness and chastity as "truth" and to adultery, by contrast, as un-truth, as "falsity" in the language of the body, they do so because in the first case the subject (Israel as a bride) agrees with the spousal meaning that corresponds to the human body (because of its masculinity or femininity) in the integral structure of the person; in the second case, by contrast, the same subject finds itself in contradiction against, and in collision with, that meaning.

We can say that the essential element for marriage as a sacrament is the "language of the body" reread in the truth. It is precisely through this that the sacramental sign is constituted.

"Language of the Body" Reread in the Truth

105 *General Audience of January 19, 1983*
(Insegnamenti, 6, no. 1 [1983]: 155–59)

1. THE TEXTS OF THE PROPHETS have great importance for understanding marriage as a covenant of persons (in the image of Yahweh's covenant with Israel) and particularly for understanding the sacramental covenant of man and woman in the dimension of sign. The "language of the body" enters—as we saw earlier—into the integral structure of the sacramental sign, whose main subject is man, male and female. The words of conjugal consent *constitute this sign,* because the spousal meaning of the body in its masculinity and femininity finds expression in them. This meaning is expressed above all by the words, "I...take you...as my wife / as my husband." In addition, these words *confirm* the essential "*truth*" of the language of the body and (at least indirectly, *implicitly*) they also *exclude* the essential "*untruth*," the falseness of the language of the body. The body speaks the truth through

conjugal love, faithfulness, and integrity, just as untruth or falsity is expressed through all that negates conjugal love, faithfulness, and integrity. One can thus say that when they pronounce the words of conjugal consent, the new spouses *set themselves on the line of the same "prophetism of the body,"* whose spokesmen were the ancient prophets. The "language of the body," expressed by the lips of the ministers of marriage as a sacrament of the Church, institutes the same visible sign of the covenant and of grace, which—though its origin goes back to the mystery of creation—is continually nourished with the power of the "redemption of the body" offered by Christ to the Church.

2. According to the prophetic texts, the human body speaks a "language" of which it is not the author. Its author is *man* who, as male or female, as bridegroom or bride, correctly rereads the meaning *of this "language."* He thus rereads that spousal meaning of the body as integrally inscribed in the structure of the masculinity or femininity of the personal subject. A correct rereading "in the truth" is an indispensable condition for proclaiming this truth or instituting the visible sign of marriage as a sacrament. The spouses proclaim exactly this "language of the body," reread in the truth, as the content and principle of their new life in Christ and in the Church. On the basis of the "prophetism of the body," the ministers of the sacrament of Marriage *perform an act of prophetic character.* They confirm in this way their share in the prophetic mission of the Church. A "prophet" is one who expresses with human words the truth that comes from God, one who speaks this truth in the place of God, in his name and in some sense with his authority.

3. All of this refers to the new spouses who, as ministers of the sacrament, institute with the words of conjugal consent the visible sign, proclaiming the "language of the body" reread in the truth as the content and principle of their new life in Christ and the Church. This "prophetic" *proclamation has a complex character.* Conjugal consent is both the announcement and the cause of the fact that from now on the two are husband and wife before the Church and society (We mean this announcement as an "indication" in the ordinary sense of the term). Nevertheless, conjugal consent has above all *the character of a reciprocal profession* of the new spouses before God. It is

enough to examine the text attentively to become convinced that this prophetic proclamation of the language of the body, reread in the truth, is immediately and directly addressed by the "I" to the "you": by the man to the woman and by her to him. The central position in conjugal consent belongs precisely to the words that indicate the personal subject, the pronouns "I" and "you." By the words of the new spouses, the "language of the body," reread in the truth of its spousal meaning, constitutes the union-communion of persons. If conjugal consent has a prophetic character, if it is *the proclamation of the truth that comes from God* and in some sense the act of stating this truth in the name of God, then this comes about above all *in the dimension of interpersonal communion* and only indirectly "before" others and "for" others.

4. On the background of the words spoken by the ministers of the sacrament of Marriage, there stands the perennial "language of the body," to which God himself "gave its beginning" by creating man male and female: a language that was renewed by Christ. This perennial "language of the body" bears within itself the whole richness and depth of the Mystery: first of creation, then of redemption. When they bring into being the visible sign of the sacrament through the words of their conjugal consent, they express in this sign "the language of the body" with the whole depth of the mystery of creation and of redemption (the liturgy of the sacrament of Marriage offers a rich context of this expression). When they reread "the language of the body" in this way, the spouses not only include in the words of conjugal consent the subjective fullness indispensable for bringing the sign of precisely this sacrament into being, but *they also reach in some sense the very sources* from which this sign each time draws its prophetic eloquence and sacramental strength. One must not allow oneself to forget that before being spoken by the lips of the spouses, the ministers of the sacrament as a sacrament of the Church, "the language of the body" was spoken by the word of the living God, from the beginning in Genesis through the prophets of the Old Covenant all the way to the author of Ephesians.

5. Here we are using again and again the expression "language of the body," in which we go back to the prophetic texts. In these texts, as we said already, the human body speaks a "language" of which it is not the author in the proper sense of the term. The author is man—male and female—who rereads the true sense of that "language," thereby bringing to light again the spousal meaning of the body as integrally inscribed in the very structure of the masculinity and femininity of the personal subject. Already through itself (per se), *this rereading of the language of the body "in the truth" gives a prophetic character* to the words of conjugal consent, through which man and woman bring into being the visible sign of marriage as a sacrament of the Church. These words, however, contain something more than a simple rereading in the truth of the language that the femininity and masculinity of the new spouses speaks of in their reciprocal relation, "I take you as my wife/as my husband." The words of conjugal consent contain within themselves: the intention, the decision, and the choice. Both of the spouses *decide* to act in conformity with the language of the body, reread in the truth. If man, male and female, is the author of that language, he is so above all inasmuch as he wants to give, and effectively does give, to his behavior and to his actions the meaning in conformity with the reread eloquence of the truth of masculinity and femininity in the reciprocal conjugal relationship.

6. In this area, *man* is the causal origin of actions that have through themselves (per se) clearcut meanings. He is thus *the causal origin of actions and at the same time the author of their meanings.* The sum of these meanings constitutes in some sense the whole of the "language of the body" with which the spouses decide to speak to each other as ministers of the sacrament. The sign they bring into being with the words of the conjugal consent is not merely an immediate and fleeting sign, but a sign that looks toward the future and produces a lasting effect, namely, the conjugal bond, one and indissoluble ("all the days of my life," that is, until death). *In this perspective, they must fill that sign with the manifold contents* offered by the conjugal and familial communion of persons, and also with the content that springs from the language of the body and is continually reread in the truth. In this way, the essential "truth" of the sign will remain organically linked with the ethos of conjugal conduct. Into this truth of the sign, and consequently into the ethos of conjugal conduct, there is

inserted, in a future-related perspective, *procreative meaning of the body*, that is, fatherhood and motherhood, which we discussed earlier. To the question, "Are you ready to accept children lovingly from God and bring them up according to the Law of Christ and his Church?" the man and the woman answer, "Yes."

We now postpone further in-depth discussion of the subject to other meetings.

"Language of the Body" and the Concupiscence of the Flesh

106 *General Audience of January 26, 1983* (*Insegnamenti*, 6, no. 1 [1983]: 247–49)

1. THE SIGN OF MARRIAGE AS A SACRAMENT of the Church is consti-tuted each time according to the dimension that is proper to it from the "beginning," and at the same time it is constituted on the founda-tion of the spousal love of Christ and the Church as the unique and unrepeatable expression of the covenant between "this" man and "this" woman, who are ministers of the sacrament as the sacrament of their vocation and their life. In saying that the sign of marriage as a sacra-ment of the Church is constituted on the basis of the *"language of the body," we are using analogy ("analogia attributionis" [analogy of attribu-tion])*, which we tried to clarify earlier [see TOB 104:7]. It is obvious that the body as such does not "speak," but the one who speaks is man, who rereads what needs to be expressed precisely on the basis of the "body," of the masculinity or femininity of the personal subject, or, even better, on the basis of what can be expressed by man only through the body.

In this sense, man—male and female—does not merely speak with the language of the body, but in some sense he allows the body to speak "for him" and "on his behalf": I would say, in his name and with his personal authority. Also the concept of "prophetism of the body" seems to be founded in this way: the "prophet," in fact, is one who speaks "for" and "on behalf": in the name and with the authority of a person.

2. The new spouses are aware of this when, in contracting marriage, they institute its visible sign. In the perspective of a shared life and of the conjugal vocation, that initial sign of marriage as a sacrament of the Church will be continually filled with the "prophetism of the body." The body of each spouse *will speak "for" and "on behalf of"* each of them; the body will speak *in the name and with the authority of the person,* of each of the persons, thus carrying out the conjugal dialogue, which is proper to their vocation and based on the language of the body, continually reread on the right occasion and at the proper time: and it is necessary that it is reread in the truth! The couple are called to form their lives and their living together as a "communion of persons" on the basis of this language. Given that *a complex of meanings corresponds to the language,* the couple—through their conduct and behavior, actions and gestures ("gestures of tenderness," see *Gaudium et Spes,* 49)—are called to become the authors of these meanings of the "language of the body," from which they then build and continually deepen love, faithfulness, conjugal integrity, and the union that remains indissoluble until death.

3. The sign of marriage as a sacrament of the Church is formed precisely through those meanings, of which the couple are the authors. All of these meanings are initiated and in a certain sense "programmed" in a comprehensive way in conjugal consent, for the sake of then building the same sign—in a more analytic way, day by day—so that the spouses identify with it in the dimension of the whole of life. *There is an organic link between rereading* the integral meaning of the "language of the body" in the truth and the consequent *use* of that language in conjugal life. In the latter sphere, the human being—male and female—is the author of the meanings of the "language of the body." This implies that this language, of which he is the author, corresponds to the truth that has been reread. On the basis of the biblical tradition we speak here about the "prophetism of the body." If the human being—male and female—in marriage (and indirectly also in all spheres of mutual life together) *gives to* his *behavior a meaning in conformity with the* fundamental *truth of the language of the body,* then *he too "is in the truth."* In the opposite case, he commits lies and falsifies the language of the body.

4. If we place ourselves in the future-oriented perspective of conjugal consent, which—as we have said already—offers the spouses a particular share in the prophetic mission of the Church handed down from Christ himself, one can in this regard also use the biblical distinction between "true" and "false" prophets. Through marriage as a sacrament of the Church, man and woman are explicitly called to bear witness—by correctly using the "language of the body"—to spousal and procreative love, *a testimony worthy of "true prophets."* In this consists the true significance and the greatness of conjugal consent in the sacrament of the Church.

5. The problematic of the sacramental sign has a highly anthropological character. We build it on the basis of theological anthropology and in particular on what from the very beginning of the present considerations we have defined as "theology of the body." Thus, in continuing these analyses, we must always have before our eyes the earlier considerations referring to the analysis of the key words of Christ. (We call them "key words," because they open—like a key— the various dimensions of theological anthropology, especially of the theology of the body). When we build on this basis the analysis of the sacramental sign of marriage, in which—even after original sin— man and woman always share as "historical" man, we must always recall the fact that that "historical man," man and woman, *is at the same time the "man of concupiscence"*; as such, every man and woman enters into the history of salvation and is drawn into it by the sacrament, which is a visible sign of the covenant and of grace.

For this reason, in the context of the present reflections about the sacramental structure of the sign, we must take into account not only what Christ said about the unity and indissolubility of marriage when he appealed to the "beginning," but also (and even more so) what he expressed in the Sermon on the Mount when he appealed to the "human heart."

107 *General Audience of February 9, 1983* *(Insegnamenti, 6, no. 1 [1983]: 365–68)*

1. WE SAID EARLIER [see TOB 106:5] that in the context of the present reflections on the structure of marriage as a sacramental sign we

must take into account not only what Christ solemnly taught about its unity and indissolubility by appealing to the "beginning," but also (and even more so) to what he said in the Sermon on the Mount when he appealed to the "human heart." Going back to the commandment "You shall not commit adultery," Christ spoke about "adultery in the heart": "Whoever looks at a woman to desire her has already committed adultery with her in his heart" (Mt 5:28).

Thus, when we affirm that the sacramental sign of marriage—the *sign of the conjugal covenant* of man and woman—is formed on the basis of the "language of the body," once reread in the truth (and continuously reread), we realize that *the one who rereads this "language" and then expresses it* not according to the needs proper to marriage as a covenant and sacrament, is naturally and morally the man of concupiscence: male and female, both understood as the "man of concupiscence." The prophets of the Old Testament certainly have before their eyes this man when they use an analogy to stigmatize the "adultery of Israel and of Judah." The analysis of Christ's words in the Sermon on the Mount leads us to understand "adultery" itself more deeply. At the same time, it carries us to the conviction that the human "heart" is not so much "accused and condemned" by Christ because of concupiscence (*concupiscentia carnis* [the concupiscence of the flesh]), but first of all "called." Here we find a decisive divergence between the anthropology (or anthropological hermeneutics) of the Gospel and some influential representatives of the contemporary hermeneutics of man (the so-called masters of suspicion) [see TOB 46:1–3].

2. Continuing on the terrain of our present analysis, we can observe that although man naturally remains the man of concupiscence, despite the sacramental sign of marriage, despite conjugal consent and its realization, still he is at the same time *the man of the "call."* He is "called" through the mystery of the redemption of the body, a divine mystery that is at the same time—in Christ and for Christ in every man—a human reality. That mystery implies, further, a definite ethos that is by its essence "human," which we earlier called the ethos of redemption [see TOB 46:4; 47:5; and especially 49:2–7].

"Language of the Body" and
"Hermeneutics of the Sacrament"

3. In the light of the words Christ spoke in the Sermon on the Mount, in the light of the whole Gospel and the New Covenant, the threefold *concupiscence* (and in particular the concupiscence of the flesh) *does not destroy the capacity to reread the "language of the body" in the truth*—and to reread it in an ever more mature and full way—for which the sacramental sign is constituted both in its first liturgical moment and later in the dimension of the whole of life. In this light, one must observe that, while concupiscence through itself (per se) brings about many "errors" in rereading the "language of the body" and at the same time it also brings about "sin"—moral evil contrary to the virtue of chastity (be it conjugal or extra-conjugal)—nevertheless, in the sphere of the ethos of redemption there is always the possibility of passing from "error" to the "truth" as well as the possibility of return, or of conversion, from sin to chastity as an expression of life according to the Spirit (see Gal 5:16).

4. In this way, from the evangelical and Christian perspective on the problem, "historical" man (after original sin)—as male and female—is able, on the basis of the "language of the body" reread in the truth, *to constitute the sacramental sign of* conjugal *love*, faithfulness, and integrity, and this as *an enduring sign*: "To be faithful to you always, in joy and in sorrow, in sickness and in health, and to love you and honor you all the days of my life." This means that in a real way man is the author of the meanings whereby, after having reread the "language of the body" in the truth, he is also capable of forming that language in the truth in the conjugal and familial communion of persons. He is capable of it even as the "man of concupiscence," since he is at the same time "called" by the reality of the redemption of Christ (*simul lapsus et redemptus* [simultaneously fallen and redeemed]).

5. The dimension of the sign, which is proper to marriage as a sacrament, confirms the specific theological anthropology, the specific hermeneutics of man, which in this case could also be called

"*hermeneutics of the sacrament*," because it allows us *to understand man on the basis of the analysis of the sacramental sign.* As the minister of the sacrament and author (co-author) of the sacramental sign, man—male and female—is a conscious subject capable of self-determination. Only on this basis can he be the author of the "language of the body," can he also be the author (co-author) of marriage as a sign: a sign of the divine creation and "redemption of the body." The fact that man (male and female) is the man of concupiscence does not utterly undermine his capacity to reread the language of the body in the truth. He is the "man of concupiscence," but at the same time he is able to distinguish the truth from falsity in the language of the body and can be the author of the true (or false) meanings of that language.

6. He is the man of concupiscence, *but he is not* completely determined by "libido" (in the sense in which that term is often used). Such a determination would mean that the whole of man's behavior, even, for example, the choice of continence for religious reasons, would be explained only through the specific transformations of that "libido." In this case, man would be condemned—in the sphere of the language of the body—to essential falsifications: he would only be the one who expresses a specific determination by "libido," but he would not express the truth (or the falsity) of spousal love and the communion of persons, even though he might think that he manifest it. Consequently, he would be condemned to suspecting himself and others in regard to the truth of the language of the body. Because of the concupiscence of the flesh, he could only be "accused," but he could not be truly "called."

The "hermeneutics of the sacrament" allows us to draw the conclusion that man is always *essentially "called" and not merely "accused,"* even inasmuch as he is precisely the "man of concupiscence."

2. The Song of Songs

Resuming Genesis: Wonder

108
Not delivered
(Text: *Uomo e donna*, 411–16)[*]

1. IN RELATION TO THE REREADING of the language of the body in the truth, and thus also in relation to the reality of the sacramental sign of marriage, we should analyze, even if only in summary fashion, also that entirely special book of the Old Testament, namely, the Song of Songs. The theme of the spousal love that unites man and woman connects this part of the Bible in some way with the whole tradition of the "great analogy," which flows through the writings of the prophets into the New Testament and especially into Ephesians (cf. Eph 5:21–33). One should immediately add, however, that in the Song of Songs the theme is not treated within the sphere of the analogy of the love of God toward Israel (or the love of Christ for the Church in Ephesians). *The theme of spousal love* in this singular biblical "poem" lies *outside that great analogy.*[95] The love of bridegroom and bride in the Song of Songs is a theme by itself, and in this lies the singularity and originality of that book.[96]

---

[*] Translator's note: The catecheses on the Song of Songs and Tobit originally prepared by John Paul II are printed on the left-hand pages, the shorter catecheses he actually delivered are found on the right, marked by shading. For details, see pp. 731–2. UD contains five footnotes on the Song of Songs, the *Insegnamenti* text only the first three. Since John Paul II omitted this paragraph in the shorter version, he relocated footnotes 95 and 96 and pushed footnote 97 to a later position.

95. "The Song of Songs is thus to be taken simply as what it manifestly is: a song of human love." This sentence by J. Winandy, O.S.B., expresses the conviction of a growing number of exegetes. J. Winandy, *Le Cantique des Cantiques: Poéme d'amour mué en écrit de Sagesse* (Tournai, Paris, and Maredsous: Casterman/Maredsous, 1960), 26.

M. Dubarle adds: "Catholic exegesis, which has at times appealed to the obvious sense of the biblical texts in the case of passages of great dogmatic importance, should not lightly abandon it in the case of the Song of Songs." Recalling a sentence of G. Gerlemann, Dubarle continues, "The Song of Songs celebrates the love between man and woman without adding to it any mythological element, but considering it simply on its own level and in its specificity. Implicit in the poem, without didactic insistence, is the equivalent of the Yahwist faith (because the sexual powers were not placed under the patronage of foreign gods and were not attributed to Yahweh himself, who appears as transcendent in this sphere). The poem was thus in tacit harmony with the fundamental convictions of Israel's faith.

General Audience of May 23, 1984
(*Insegnamenti*, 7, no. 1 [1984]: 1471–75)

1. DURING THE HOLY YEAR, I interrupted the treatment of the subject of human love in the divine plan. I want to conclude this subject now with some considerations, above all, on the teaching of *Humanae Vitae*—proposing first, however, some reflections on the Song of Songs and Tobit. It seems to me, in fact, that what I want to set forth in the coming weeks is, as it were, the crowning of what I have explained.

The theme of the spousal love that unites man and woman connects this part of the Bible in some way with the whole tradition of the "great analogy," which flows through the writings of the prophets into the New Testament and especially into Ephesians (cf. Eph 5:21–33), the explanation of which I interrupted at the beginning of the Holy Year.

"The same open, objective, and not expressly religious attitude in relation to physical beauty and sexual love is found in some narratives of the Yahwist document. These similarities show that the little book is not as isolated in the whole of biblical literature as was once claimed." A. M. Dubarle, "Le Cantique des Cantiques dans l'exégèse récente," in *Aux grands carrefours de la Révélation et de l'exégèse de l'Ancien Testament* (Paris: Desclée de Brouwer, 1967), 149, 151.

96. This does not, of course, exclude the possibility of speaking about a "fuller meaning" of the Song of Songs.

See, e.g., the remarks of L. Alonso-Schökel, "In the ecstasy of love, the lovers seem to occupy and fill the whole book as its only protagonists.... For this reason, when Paul reads the words of Genesis, 'For this reason a man will leave his father and his mother and unite with his wife, and the two will form one flesh' (Eph 5:31), he does not deny the real and immediate sense of the words that refer to human marriage; however to this first sense he adds another with a mediated [the *Insegnamenti* text reads: "immediate"] reference, 'I say this with reference to Christ and the Church,' confessing that 'this mystery is great' (Eph 5:32)....

"Some readers of the Song of Songs have jumped immediately to reading a disincarnate love into its words. They have forgotten the lovers or have petrified them into pretence, into an intellectual key,... they have multiplied the most minute allegorical correspondences in every sentence, word, or image.... This is not the right way. He who does not believe in the human love of the spouses, he who must ask forgiveness for the body, does not have the right to rise higher.... With the affirmation of human love, by contrast, it is possible to discover the revelation of God in it." L. Alonso-Schökel, "Cantico dei Cantici, Introduzione," in *La Bibbia: Parola di Dio scritta per noi*, Official text of the Conference of Italian Bishops (Turin: Marietti, 1980), 2.425–27.

2. It has become the object of many exegetical studies, commentaries, and hypotheses. With regard to its content, apparently "profane," the positions have varied. On the one hand, it has been placed among books forbidden to read, and, on the other hand, it has been the source of the inspiration of the greatest mystical writers, and the verses of the Song of Songs have been inserted into the Church's liturgy.[97]

3. Although the analysis of the text of this book obliges us to situate its content outside the sphere of the great prophetic analogy, *it is not possible to separate it from the reality of the primordial sacrament.* It is not possible to reread it except along the lines of what is written in the first chapters of Genesis, as a testimony of the "beginning"—of that beginning—to which Christ appealed in his decisive conversation with the Pharisees (cf. Mt 19:4).[98] The Song of Songs is certainly found in

---

97. To explain the inclusion of a love song in the biblical canon, Jewish exegetes, already from the first centuries after Christ, have seen in the Song of Songs an allegory of Yahweh's love for Israel or an allegory of the history of the Chosen People, in which love is manifested, and in the Middle Ages the allegory of Divine Wisdom and of human beings who seek it.

Since the first Fathers, Christian exegesis extended such an idea to Christ and the Church (Hippolytus and Origen), or of the individual soul of the Christian (St. Gregory of Nyssa), or to Mary (St. Ambrose) and also her Immaculate Conception (Richard of St. Victor). St. Bernard saw in the "Song of Songs" a dialogue of the Word of God with the soul, and this led to St. John of the Cross's concept of the mystical marriage.

The only exception in this long tradition was Theodore of Mopsuestia in the fourth century, who saw in the Song of Songs a poem that sings about Solomon's human love for the daughter of Pharaoh.

Luther, by contrast, referred the allegory to Solomon and his reign. In recent centuries, new hypotheses have appeared. Some have seen the Song of Songs, for example, as a drama of a bride's faithfulness kept toward a shepherd, despite all temptations, or as a collection of songs performed during popular rites at weddings or mythical ritual ceremonies that reflected the cult of Adonis-Tammuz. Some have even seen in the Song of Songs the description of a dream, appealing either to ideas about dreams in antiquity or to psychoanalysis.

In the twentieth century, a return was made to the most ancient allegorical traditions (Bea), again seeing the history of Israel in the Song of Songs (Joüon, Ricciotti) and a developed *midrash* (as Roberts calls it in his commentary, which constitutes a "summa" of the interpretation of the Song).

At the same time, however, one has begun to read the book in its more evident meaning as a poem that exalts natural human love (Rowley, Young, Laurin).

The first to show in what way this meaning is linked with the biblical context of Genesis 2 was Karl Barth. Dubarle proceeds from the hypothesis that a faithful and happy human love reveals to human beings the attributes of divine love, and Van den

It has become the object of many exegetical studies, commentaries, and hypotheses. With regard to its content, apparently "profane," the positions have varied. On the one hand, its reading was often discouraged, and, on the other hand, the greatest mystical writers have drawn from this source, and the verses of the Song of Songs have been inserted into the Church's liturgy.[95]

Although the analysis of the text of this book obliges us to situate its content outside the sphere of the great prophetic analogy, *it is not possible to detach it from the reality of the primordial sacrament*. It is not possible to reread it except along the lines of what is written in the first chapters of Genesis, as a testimony of the "beginning"—of the beginning that Christ referred to in his decisive conversation with the Pharisees (cf. Mt 19:4).[96] The Song of Songs is certainly found in the

---

Oudentrijn sees in the Song of Songs the antitype of the typical sense that appears in Ephesians 5:23. Murphy, excluding all allegorical and metaphorical explanations, underlines that human love, created and blessed by God, can be the theme of an inspired biblical book.

D. Lys observes that the content of the Song of Songs is at the same time sexual and sacred. When one prescinds from the second characteristic, one ends up treating the canticle as a purely secular erotic composition; and when one ignores the first, one falls into allegorism. It is only by putting these two aspects together that one can read the book in the right way.

Besides the works of the authors mentioned above, and especially with a view to a sketch of the history of the exegesis of the canticle, see H. H. Rowley, "The Interpretation of the Song of Songs," in *The Servant of the Lord and Other Essays on the Old Testament* (London: Lutterworth, 1952), 131–233; Dubarle, "Cantique des Cantiques," 139–51; D. Lys, *Le plus beau chant de la création—Commentaire du Cantique des Cantiques* (Paris: du Cerf, 1968), 31–35; M. H. Pope, *Song of Songs* (Anchor Bible; Garden City, NY: Doubleday, 1977).

98. [Translator's note: The following note is found only in *Uomo e donna*.] K. Barth was probably the first in the history of exegesis to discover the strict connection between the Song of Songs and Genesis 2, and he explains it as follows: "Here [in the Song of Songs], but only here—and this exception confirms the rule—Genesis 2 is unfolded. Here it becomes apparent that the comparison of Genesis 2 did not enter the Old Testament by mere chance or as a foreign element, but played a precise though normally invisible role in the thought of Israel: pleasure—not merely that of a possible father or head of a family, but simply that of the man as such—not pleasure in the possible mother of his children, but simply in the woman as such, eros, for which precisely according to Genesis 2:25 no shame is necessary." K. Barth, *Kirchliche Dogmatik*, vol. 3, pt. 1, 2nd ed. (Zollikon and Zürich: Evangelischer Verlag, 1947), 358; John Paul II's addition.

the wake of this sacrament, in which, through the "language of the body," the visible sign of man and woman's participation in the covenant of grace and love offered by God to man is constituted. The Song of Songs demonstrates the richness of this language, whose first sketch is already found in Genesis 2:23–25.

4. *Here are the first verses of the Song:*

> Let him kiss me with the kisses of his mouth!
> For your love is better than wine....
> Draw me after you, let us make haste....
> We will exult and rejoice for you;
> we will remember your tender caresses. (Song 1:1–2, 4)

These words lead us immediately into the atmosphere of the whole "poem," in which the bridegroom and the bride seem to move in the circle traced by the inner irradiation of love. The words, movements, and gestures of the spouses, their whole behavior, correspond to the inner movement of their hearts. It is only through the prism of this movement that one can understand the "language of the body." In this impulse, which penetrates from one person to the other, *that discovery* occurs (one does not know how often, but certainly in a unique and unrepeatable way) *which the first* male *man expressed* in front of her who had been created as "a help like himself" (cf. Gen 2:20, 23) and who had been created—as the biblical text reports, from his "ribs" ("rib" also seems to indicate the heart).

5. This discovery—already analyzed on the basis of Genesis 2— clothes itself in the Song of Songs with all the richness of the language of human love. What was barely expressed in the second chapter of Genesis (vv. 23–25) in just a few simple and essential words is developed here in a full dialogue, or rather in a duet, in which the bridegroom's words are interwoven with the bride's, and they complete each other. On seeing the woman created by God, man's first words express wonder and admiration, or even better, the sense of fascination (cf. Gen 2:23). *And a similar fascination—which is wonder and admiration—*runs in fuller form through the verses of the Song of Songs. It runs, to tell the truth, in a peaceful and even wave from the beginning to the end of the poem.

wake of that sacrament in which, through the "language of the body," the visible sign of man and woman's participation in the covenant of grace and love offered by God to man is constituted. The Song of Songs demonstrates the richness of this language, whose first expression is already found in Genesis 2:23–25.

2. Already the first verses of the "Song" lead us immediately into the atmosphere of the whole "poem," in which the bridegroom and the bride seem to move in the circle traced by the irradiation of love. The words, movements, and gestures of the spouses correspond to the inner movement of their hearts. It is only through the prism of such a movement that one can understand the "language of the body" in which *that discovery* occurs *which the first man expressed* in front of her who had been created as "a help similar to himself" (cf. Gen 2:20, 23) and who had been drawn—as the biblical text reports, from one of his ribs ("rib" seems to also indicate the heart).

This discovery—already analyzed on the basis of Genesis 2—clothes itself in the Song of Songs with all the richness of the language of human love. What was barely expressed in the second chapter of Genesis (vv. 23–25) in just a few simple and essential words is developed here in a full dialogue, or rather in a duet, in which the bridegroom's words are interwoven with the bride's, and they complete each other. On seeing the woman created by God, man's first words express wonder and admiration, or better more, the sense of fascination (cf. Gen 2:23). *And a similar fascination—which is wonder and admiration—*runs in fuller form through the verses of the Song of Songs. It runs in a peaceful and even wave from the beginning to the end of the poem.

It is a voice and a duet; it is speaking and conversing. One can say that it is precisely this reciprocal "language of the body" that testifies—through all the richness of meanings of which it is composed—in what way in the prism of human hearts the sign of spousal union is formed and develops, which has become a sacramental sign in the eternal economy of the covenant and of grace, a sign of marriage as a sacrament.

6. Even a summary analysis of the text of the Song of Songs allows one to sense in that reciprocal fascination the "language of the body." The point of departure as well as the point of arrival for this fascination—reciprocal wonder and admiration—are in fact the bride's femininity and the bridegroom's masculinity, in the direct experience of their visibility. The words of love spoken by both of them are therefore concentrated on the "body," not so much because in itself it constitutes the source of reciprocal fascination, but above all because the *attraction toward the other person*—toward the other "I," female or male, which in the inner impulse of the heart gives rise to love—lingers directly and immediately on it.

In addition, *love unleashes a special experience of the beautiful,* which focuses on what is visible, although at the same time it involves the entire person. The experience of beauty gives rise to pleasure, which is reciprocal.

"O most beautiful among women" (Song 1:8), the bridegroom says, and the bride's words echo back to him, "I am black but beautiful, O daughters of Jerusalem" (Song 1:5). The words of the enchanted man are repeated continually, and they return in all five songs of the poem.

> Your cheeks are beautiful between pendants
> your neck between strings of pearls. (Song 1:10)
> How beautiful you are, my beloved, how beautiful you are!
> Your eyes are doves. (Song 1:15)

And immediately we hear her answer: "How beautiful you are, my beloved, how graceful" (Song 1:16).

In the second song we return to the same words, enriched by new themes.

> Arise, my friend,
> my beautiful one, and come away.

3. Even a summary analysis of the text of the Song of Songs allows one to sense in that reciprocal fascination the "language of the body." The point of departure as well as the point of arrival for this fascination—reciprocal wonder and admiration—are in fact the bride's femininity and the bridegroom's masculinity, in the direct experience of their visibility. The words of love uttered by both of them are therefore concentrated on the "body," not only because in itself it constitutes the source of reciprocal fascination, but above all because the *attraction toward the other person*—toward the other "I," female or male, which in the inner impulse of the heart generates love—lingers directly and immediately on it.

In addition, *love unleashes a special experience of the beautiful*, which focuses on what is visible, but at the same time it involves the entire person. The experience of beauty gives rise to pleasure, which is reciprocal.

"O most beautiful among women" (Song 1:8), the bridegroom says, and the bride's words echo back to him, "I am black but beautiful, O daughters of Jerusalem" (Song 1:5). The words of the enchanted man are repeated continually, and they return in all five songs of the poem.

Similar expressions of the bride echo these words.

O my dove...
let me see your face,
let me hear your voice;
for your voice is sweet,
and your face is lovely. (Song 2:13–14)

7. The same image—at once *an image of experience and an image of the person who is present in the experience*—reappears even more fully in the fourth song.

How beautiful you are, my friend,
how beautiful you are!
Your eyes are doves
behind your veil.
Your hair is like a flock of goats,
moving down the slopes of Gilead.
Your teeth are like a flock of shorn ewes
that have come up from the washing,
all of which come in pairs,
and not one among them is without companion.
Your lips are like a crimson thread,
and your mouth is suffused with grace.
Your cheeks are like halves of a pomegranate
behind your veil.
Your neck is like the tower of David,
built like a fortress.
. . . .
Your two breasts are like two fawns,
twins of a gazelle,
that feed among the lilies.
. . . .
You are altogether beautiful, my friend,
there is no flaw in you. (Song 4:1–4a, 5, 7)

8. *The metaphors* of the Song of Songs can surprise us today. Many of them were taken from the life of shepherds; others seem to indicate the royal status of the bridegroom.[99] The analysis of that poetic lan-

---

99. Although there is an extensive series of divergent hypotheses about the literary genre (allegory, drama, collection of wedding songs, or even ritual and mystical songs), there is no doubt about the artistic value of the Song of Songs. The author used a classical language with the highest literary art underlined by a wealth of idyllic and courtly metaphors. It is thus not surprising to us that the metaphors, which belong to an environment that stretches from the end of the second millennium to the fifth and fourth centuries B.C., is far from modern schemes.

4. The *metaphors* involved can surprise us today. Many of them were taken from the life of shepherds; others seem to indicate the royal status of the bridegroom.[97]* The analysis of that poetic language

---

* Translator's note: For the text of footnote 97, see TOB 108:2.

guage should be left to the experts. The very fact of adopting metaphors shows how much, in our case, the *"language of the body" seeks support and confirmation in the whole visible world.*

This is without doubt a "language" reread at one and the same time with the heart and eyes of the bridegroom, in the act of a special concentration on the whole female "I" of the bride. This "I" speaks to him through every feminine trait, giving rise to that state of mind that can be defined as fascination, enchantment. This female "I" expresses itself without words; nevertheless, the "language of the body," expressed without words, finds a rich echo in the bridegroom's words, in his speech full of poetic transport and of metaphors bearing witness to the experience of beauty, to a love filled with pleasure. While the metaphors of the Song search for an analogy of this beauty in the various things of the visible world (in this world, which is the bridegroom's "own world"), at the same time they seem to indicate the insufficiency of each of these particular analogies.

"You are all-beautiful, my friend, and there is no spot in you" (Song 4:7). The bridegroom ends his song with this word, leaving all metaphors behind, in order to turn to the only one, through whom the "language of the body" seems to express the "*integrum*" of femininity and the "*integrum*" of the person.

On her part, the bride speaks a similar language:

> Return, my beloved,
> be like a gazelle or a young stag
> on the mountain of fragrances. (Song 2:17)

Another time by contrast she confides to her companions:

> His appearance is like Lebanon,
> choice as the cedars.
> Sweetness is his palate
> and he is all delights.
> This is my beloved, this is my friend,
> O daughters of Jerusalem. (Song 5:15–16)

109 *Not delivered*
(Text: *Uomo e donna*, 417–19)

1. BOTH THE FEMININITY of the bride and the masculinity of the bridegroom speak without words: *the language of the body* is a language

should be left to the experts. The very fact of adopting metaphors shows how much, in our case, the *"language of the body" seeks support and confirmation in the whole visible world.*

This is without doubt a "language" reread at one and the same time with the heart and eyes of the bridegroom, in the act of special concentration on the *whole* female "I" of the bride. This "I" speaks to him through every feminine trait, giving rise to that state of mind that can be defined as fascination, enchantment. This female "I" expresses itself almost without words; nevertheless, the "language of the body," expressed without words, finds a rich echo in the bridegroom's words, in his speech full of poetic transport and of metaphors bearing witness to the experience of beauty, to a love filled with pleasure. While the metaphors of the "Song" search for an analogy of this beauty in the various things of the visible world (in this world, which is the bridegroom's "own world"), at the same time they seem to indicate the insufficiency of each of these particular analogies.

"You are all-beautiful, my friend, and there is no spot in you" (Song 4:7). The bridegroom ends his song with this word, leaving all metaphors behind, in order to turn himself to the only one, through whom the "language of the body" seems to express what is most proper to femininity and the whole of the person.

We will continue the analysis of the Song of Songs in the next general audience.

General Audience of May 30, 1984
(*Insegnamenti*, 7, no. 1 [1984]: 1560–1614)

1. WE TAKE UP AGAIN OUR analysis of the Song of Songs in order to understand more adequately and exhaustively the sacramental sign of

without words. At the same time that language becomes in her—and also in him—a source of inspiration for the words, *for* that *singular language of love,* which seeks means of expression in poetic metaphor. For us today, the metaphors of the Song of Songs sound archaic, but nevertheless that which they express as well as the very force with which they are expressed have kept their value. The "language of the body" is interpreted as a language of the heart by both the bride and the bridegroom. It is possible that the bridegroom-man expresses more directly the beauty of the bride and her own attractiveness, being aware of it above all with the eyes of the body; the bride by contrast looks rather with the eyes of the heart through her affection. Both, at any rate—he and she—together *express* in the verses of the Song wonder and *amazement* not only *for the "I" of the other* in his or her feminine or masculine "revelation," but also *for the love* by which this "revelation" is realized.

2. The words of the bridegroom are therefore a language about love and at the same time a language about the femininity of the bride, which "appears," on account of love, so worthy of amazement and admiration. In the same way, the words of the bride also express admiration and amazement since they are a language about love and a language about the masculinity of the bridegroom. What the words of both express is, therefore, a particular *experience of values that irradiates over everything* that stands in relation to the beloved person.

> Your lips distill honey, my bride;
> honey and milk are under your tongue;
> and the scent of your garments
> is like the scent of Lebanon. (Song 4:11)

We find here—always with a special coloring—the themes that fill the literature of the whole world. The presence of these elements in this book that enters into the canon of Sacred Scripture shows that they and the related "language of the body" contain a primordial and essential sign of holiness.

"My Sister, My Bride"

3. To pursue under another aspect our analysis of this—apparently uniform—rhythm of the duet of love between the bridegroom and

marriage, which is a singular language of love generated by the heart, as the language of the body manifests it.

At a certain point the bridegroom, expressing a particular *experience of values* that irradiates over everything that stands in relation to the beloved person, says,

the bride, let us quote the words on which we should dwell in a particular way.

The bridegroom says:

You have ravished my heart, my sister, my bride;
you have ravished my heart with one glance of your eyes,
with one bead of your necklace.
How sweet are your caresses, my sister, my bride. (Song 4:9–10)

For the theology of the body—and in this case for the theology of the sacramental sign—it is a matter of essential importance to know in this duet—dialogue of love—*who the feminine "you" is for the male "I"* and vice versa [see TOB 43:7]. The bridegroom in the Song of Songs says first, "You are all-beautiful, my friend" (Song 4:7) and in the same context addresses her as "my sister, my bride" (Song 4:9). He does not call her by her proper name (only twice does the name "Shulamite" appear), but uses expressions that say more than the proper name. Under a certain aspect, the name and appellation of the bride as "sister" seems to be more eloquent and more rooted in the Song of Songs as a whole in comparison with calling her "friend."

4. *The term "friend"* indicates what is always essential for love, which puts *the second "I" beside one's own "I."* "Friendship"—the love of friendship (*amor amicitiae*)—signifies in the Song a particular approach of the bride's feminine "I," a mutual approach felt and experienced as an interiorly unifying power.

The fact that in this approach the feminine "I" is revealed for the bridegroom as "sister"—and that *she is bride* precisely *as sister*—has a particular eloquence. The expression "sister" speaks of union in humanity and at the same time of feminine diversity, of the originality of this humanity. This difference and originality exists not only with regard to sex, but to the very way of "being a person." If "being a person" means both "being a subject," but also "being in relation," the term "sister" seems to express in the simplest way *the subjectivity of the feminine "I"* in its personal relation, that is, *in its openness* toward others, toward the neighbor the particular addressee of this openness becomes *the man understood as "brother."* The "sister" in some sense helps the man to define and conceive himself, she becomes, I would say, a challenge in this direction.

You have ravished my heart, my sister, my bride;
you have ravished my heart with one glance of your eyes,
with one bead of your necklace.
How sweet are your caresses, my sister, my bride. (Song 4:9–10)

From these words it becomes clear that it is of essential importance for the theology of the body—and in this case for the theology
of the sacramental sign of marriage—to know *who the feminine "you" is
for the male "I" and vice versa* [see TOB 43:7]. The bridegroom in the
Song of Songs exclaims, "You are all-beautiful, my friend" (Song 4:7)
and calls her "My sister, my bride." He does not call her by her proper
name, but uses expressions that say more.

Under a certain aspect, in comparison with the address "friend," the
name and appellation of the bride as "sister" seems to be more eloquent
and more rooted in the Song of Songs as a whole that shows how love
reveals the other.

2. The *term "friend"* indicates what is always essential for love,
which puts *the second "I" beside one's own "I."* "Friendship"—the love of
friendship (*amor amicitiae*)—signifies in the Song a particular movement near each other, felt and experienced as an interiorly unifying
power.

The fact that in this approach the feminine "I" is revealed for the
bridegroom as "sister"—and that *she is bride* precisely *as sister*—has a
particular eloquence. The expression "sister" speaks of union in
humanity and at the same time of the feminine diversity and originality of the same humanity, not only with regard to sex, but to the very
way of "being a person," which means both "being a subject" and
"being in relation." The term "sister" seems to express in the simplest
way the subjectivity of the feminine "I" in its personal relation to the
man, that is, *in its openness* toward others who are *understood and perceived as brothers.* The "sister" in some sense helps the man to define and
conceive himself, becoming a kind of challenge in this direction.

One can say that the bridegroom of the Song accepts this challenge and gives a spontaneous answer to it.

5. When the bridegroom in the Song of Songs addresses the bride with the word "sister," this expression signifies also *a specific rereading of the "language of the body."* This rereading is unfolded explicitly in the duet of the spouses.

O that you were a brother to me,
who nursed at my mother's breast!
If I met you outside, I could kiss you,
and no one could despise me.
I would lead you and bring you
into the house of my mother. (Song 8:4)

The bridegroom responds:

Do not stir up, do not awaken the beloved
until she wants it! (Song 8:4)

And a little further on:

We have a little sister,
and she still has no breasts.
What shall we do for our sister,
on the day when she is spoken for? (Song 8:8)

And again the words of the bride:

I am a wall
and my breasts are towers.
Thus I am in his eyes
as the one who has found peace! (Song 8:10)

6. The passages just quoted are sufficient proof that the bridegroom of the Song accepts the challenge in relation to the feminine "I" contained in the term "sister." These passages also clarify what it means that the man turns to this "sister" as to his "bride," because the "bride" remains for him "sister." This is the reason for *the convergence (and not divergence) of both expressions and both references.* The term "sister" used in the Song belongs certainly to the "language of the body" (this is also evident in the verses quoted above), to the "language of the body" reread in the truth of reciprocal spousal love. At the same time, in a simple but firm way, this term seems to overcome *the* original *determination* of this "language" (and of this love) *by*

3. The bridegroom of the Song accepts the challenge,

"libido" alone and to open its entire content in a wholly original manner to the expression "bride" when this expression is joined in the mouth of the bridegroom with the term "sister."

110 Not delivered
(Text: *Uomo e donna*, 420–23)

1. THE WORDS OF THE BRIDEGROOM addressed to the bride as "sister" as well as her words in the same relation are impregnated with a particular content. Love—as we see in the verses quoted above—pushes both to seek the common past as though they descended from the same family circle, as though from infancy they had been united by memories of the common hearth. In this way, they reciprocally feel as close as brother and sister who owe their existence to the same mother. A specific sense of common belonging follows from this. The fact *that they feel like brother and sister allows them to live their reciprocal closeness in security and to manifest it* ("I could kiss you..."), finding support in this closeness, and not fearing the negative judgment of other men ("...and no one could despise me"). The one who calls attention to this aspect of the fraternal relation is, above all, the bride.

2. Through the appellation "sister," the bridegroom's words tend to reproduce, I would say, the history of the femininity of the beloved person; they see her still in the time of girlhood ("We have a little sister, and she still has no breasts")—and by means of this vision that goes back to the past, these words embrace her entire "I," soul and body, *with a disinterested tenderness. From here,* consequently, *arises the peace* that the bride speaks of. It is the "peace of the body," which in appearance resembles sleep ("Do not rouse, do not stir up the beloved until she wants it"). It is above all *the peace of the encounter* in humanity as the image of God—and the encounter *by means of a reciprocal and disinterested gift.* ("Thus am I in his eyes, as the one who has found peace," Song 8:10).

3. At this point those *sentences of Genesis 2:23–25* can come to mind that seem to reveal for the first time the experience of the masculine and feminine "I," born from the common sense of belonging to the Creator as their common Father. Before him, in all the truth of their masculinity and femininity, they were above all "brother" and

and seeks the common past as though he and his woman descended from the same family circle, as though from infancy they had been united by memories of the common hearth. In this way they recipro-cally feel as close as brother and sister who owe their existence to the same mother. A specific sense of common belonging follows from this. The fact that they feel like brother and sister allows them to live their reciprocal closeness in security and to manifest it, finding sup-port in this closeness, and not fearing the negative judgment of other men.

Through the appellation "sister," the bridegroom's words tend to reproduce, I would say, the history of the femininity of the beloved person; they see her still in the time of girlhood and embrace her entire "I," soul and body, *with a disinterested tenderness*. From here *arises the peace* that the bride speaks of. It is the "peace of the body," which in appearance resembles sleep ("Do not rouse, do not stir up the beloved until she wants it"). It is above all the *peace of the encounter* in humanity as the image of God—and the encounter *by means of a reciprocal and disinterested gift*. ("Thus am I in his eyes, as the one who has found peace," Song 8:10).

"sister" in the union of the same humanity ("they were both naked, but did not feel shame," Gen 2:25). And this reciprocal relation of "brother" and "sister" is constituted in them as the first foundation of the communion of persons—in a certain sense as the constitutive condition of their reciprocal destiny, also in the dimension of the vocation by which they were to become "husband and wife." This prototypical beginning of the "language of the body" in Genesis 2:23–25 is wonderfully developed in the Song of Songs. It seems to delineate *the dimension of the experience of femininity*—or rather of the reciprocal experience of the male and female "I"—*that should consolidate its essential content in every experience* in order that this experience might not detach itself from the richness of the "primordial sacrament." In fact, we are carrying out our present reflection under the aspect of sign—the sign of marriage—which is constituted on the basis of the "language of the body" reread in truth.

4. According to a rather widespread opinion, the verses of the Song of Songs are wide open to all that *the concept of "eros"* includes. In another context, we already dealt with the various meanings of this concept [see TOB 22:4; 46:4; 47:1–6; 48:1–2]. If "eros" expresses itself in subjective transport, in the reciprocal ecstasy, as it were, of the good and the beautiful in love—and through love of the good and the beautiful of the male and female "I"—the duet of the spouses in the Song of Songs bears witness precisely to this. It is a fully authentic and original testimony: authentic and original with *the authenticity and originality of Scripture.* The terms "my sister, my bride" seem to arise precisely from this deep level and only on the basis of that level can they be interpreted adequately.

> My only one is my dove, my perfect one,
> she is the only one of her mother,
> the darling of the one who gave birth to her. (Song 6:9)

"A Garden Closed, A Fountain Sealed"

5. In relation to the preceding theme, which could be called a "fraternal" theme, another theme emerges in the loving duet of the Song of Songs, let us say, another deep layer of content. We can examine it by starting from certain phrases that seem to have a key

4. In relation to the preceding theme, which could be called a "fraternal" theme, another theme emerges in the loving duet of the Song of Songs, let us say, another deep layer of content. We can examine it by starting from certain phrases that seem to have a key

significance in the poem as a whole. This theme (or layer) is never presented explicitly in the Song of Songs. One should rather observe that it passes through the whole poem, though it expressly manifests itself only in a few poetical cadences.

This is what the bridegroom says:

> *A garden closed* you are, my sister, bride,
> a garden closed, *a fountain sealed.* (Song 4:12)

6. We cannot limit ourselves to a summary glimpse of the poetic beauty of these metaphors. It is not only a beauty of language, but a beauty of the truth expressed by this language. Just as the name "sister" carries with itself the whole simplicity of the depth the bridegroom and the bride place in the reciprocal rereading of the "language of the body," so the metaphors just quoted seem simultaneously to confirm and surpass what was expressed by the name "sister." In the phrase "my sister, bride," the man unites spousal love, which is just being formed, with a rereading of the "language of the body" which is such that the feminine "I" speaks to him with its "sisterly" content. The metaphors just quoted, "a garden closed, a fountain sealed," reveal *the presence of another vision of the same feminine "I."*

7. From the "beginning," in fact, femininity determines the mystery about which Genesis speaks in relation to the man's "knowledge," that is, to "union" with the man. ("Adam united with Eve, his wife, who conceived and gave birth," Gen 4:1). Although the Song of Songs in its content as a whole does not directly speak about this "knowledge" or "union," nevertheless the metaphors just quoted remain in indirect, but at the same time very strict, relation with it. The bride appears to the eyes of the bridegroom as a "garden closed" and "fountain sealed," or she speaks to him with what seems most profoundly hidden in the entire structure of her feminine "I," which also constitutes the strictly personal mystery of femininity. The bride *presents herself to the eyes of the man as the master of her own mystery.* One can say that both metaphors, "garden closed" and "fountain sealed," express the whole *personal dignity of the sex*—of that femininity which belongs to the personal structure of self-possession and can consequently decide not only the metaphysical depth, but also the essential truth and authenticity, of the personal gift. This gift of self has its dimension

significance in the little poem. This theme never emerges explicitly but passes through the whole composition, and it expressly manifests itself only in a few passages.

This is what the bridegroom says:

A garden closed you are, *my sister, bride,*
a garden closed, a fountain sealed. (Song 4:12)

The metaphors just read, "garden closed, fountain sealed," *reveal the presence of another vision of the same feminine "I," master of its own mystery.* One can say that both metaphors express the personal dignity of the woman, who, as a spiritual subject, possesses herself and can decide not only the metaphysical depth, but also the essential truth when, in view of spousal love, that "knowledge" of which the Book of Genesis speaks must reveal itself.

8. In the Song of Songs, we find ourselves at any rate in the vestibule of that "union" and precisely for this very reason, the expressions that allow us to grasp its profoundly personal dimension and meaning take on great value. The language of metaphors—poetic language—seems to be especially appropriate and precise in this sphere. The "sister bride" is for the man the master of her own mystery as a "garden closed" and a "fountain sealed." The "language of the body" reread in the truth goes hand in hand *with the discovery of the inner inviolability of the person.* At the same time, precisely this discovery expresses the authentic depth of the reciprocal belonging of the spouses, the beginning and growing *consciousness of belonging to each other,* of being destined for each other: "My beloved is mine and I am his" (Song 2:16).

And the same elsewhere:

I am my beloved's and my beloved is mine;
he pastures his flock among the lilies. (Song 6:3)

9. This consciousness of reciprocal belonging resounds especially on the lips of the bride. In a certain sense, with these words she responds to the bridegroom's words with which he acknowledged her as the master of her own mystery. When the bride says, "My beloved is mine," she means at the same time, "It is he to whom I entrust myself," and therefore she says, "and I am his" (Song 2:16). The apposition "my" affirms here the whole *depth of the trust* that corresponds to the inner truth of the person. It likewise corresponds to the spousal meaning of femininity in relation to the male "I," that is, to the "language of the body" reread in the truth of personal dignity. The bridegroom states this truth with the metaphor of the "garden closed" and the "fountain sealed." The bride answers him with the words of the gift, that is, of entrusting herself. As the master of her own choice, she says, "I am for my beloved" (or "I am my beloved's"). The Song of Songs subtly reveals the inner truth of this response. The freedom of the gift is the response to the deep consciousness of the gift expressed in the bridegroom's words. Through this truth and freedom, the love is built up that thus becomes authentic love.

and authenticity of the gift of self that tends toward the union about which Genesis speaks.

The language of metaphors—poetic language—seems to be especially appropriate and precise in this sphere. The "sister bride" is for the man the master of her own mystery as a "garden closed" and a "fountain sealed." The "language of the body" reread in the truth goes hand in hand *with the discovery of the inner inviolability of the person.* At the same time, precisely this discovery expresses the authentic depth of the reciprocal belonging of the spouses, who are conscious of belonging to each other, of being destined for each other: "My beloved is mine and I am his" (Song 2:16).

5. This consciousness of reciprocal belonging resounds especially on the lips of the bride. In a certain sense, with these words she responds to those of the bridegroom with which he acknowledged her as the master of her own mystery. When the bride says, "My beloved is mine," she means at the same time, "It is he to whom I entrust myself." Therefore she says, "and I am his" (Song 2:16). The word "my" affirms here the whole *depth of trust* that corresponds to the inner truth of the person.

It likewise corresponds to the spousal meaning of femininity in relation to the male "I," that is, to the "language of the body" reread in the truth of personal dignity.

The bridegroom states this truth with the metaphors of the "garden closed" and the "fountain sealed." The bride answers him with the words of the gift, that is, of entrusting herself. As the master of her own choice, she says, "I am for my beloved" (or "I am my beloved's"). The Song of Songs subtly reveals *the* inner *truth* of this response. The freedom of the gift is the response to the deep consciousness of the gift expressed by the bridegroom's words. Through this truth and freedom, the love is built up that one must call authentic love.

111 *Not delivered*
(Text: *Uomo e donna*, 424–27)

1. THE TRUTH OF LOVE, which is proclaimed by the Song of Songs, cannot be separated from the "language of the body." The truth of love *enables the same "language of the body" to be reread in the truth*. This is also the truth of the increasing *closeness of the spouses*, which grows through love: and closeness means also initiation into the mystery of the person. However, it in no way signifies the violation of that mystery.

> My beloved is for me a bag of myrrh,
> resting between my breasts.
> My beloved is to me a cluster of henna blossoms
> in the vineyards of En-gedi.
> . . . .
> Our couch is green. (Song 1:13–14, 16)

And elsewhere:

> As an apple tree among the trees of the wood,
> so is my beloved among young men.
> I sit in his shadow, for which I longed,
> and sweet is his fruit to my taste.
> He brought me into the wine cellar,
> and his banner over me is love.
> Sustain me...
> . . . .
> for I am sick with love.
> His left hand is under my head
> and his right hand embraces me. (Song 2:3–6)

2. The truth of the increasing closeness of the spouses through love develops in the subjective dimension "of the heart," of affection and sentiment. In the same dimension, this is equally *the discovery within oneself of the gift of the other*, in some sense, of "tasting him" within oneself. This discovery and taste is confirmed by the words of the bride quoted above, and they are attested also by the further words of the bridegroom, which explain at the same time how one should understand these words, "my beloved is mine [or for me]" (Song 6:3), in the subjective dimension of experience. These words cannot be separated from the "language of the body"—especially on

General Audience of June 6, 1984
(*Insegnamenti*, 7, no. 1 [1984]: 1615–19)

1. TODAY WE WILL REFLECT again on the Song of Songs with the goal of understanding the sacramental sign of marriage better.

The truth of love, which is proclaimed by the Song of Songs, cannot be separated from the "language of the body." The truth of love, in fact, *enables the same "language of the body" to be reread in the truth*. This is also the truth of the *increasing closeness of the spouses,* which grows through love: and closeness means also initiation into the mystery of the person, without, however, implying its violation.

The truth of the increasing closeness of the spouses through love develops in the subjective dimension "of the heart," of affection and sentiment, and this truth allows one to discover the other in oneself as a gift and, in some sense, to "tasting him" within oneself.

the lips of the bride—is no longer a rereading of the same "language of the body." The reciprocal closeness expressed through the body (the words of the bride are a proof of such closeness) is above all a source of the *growth* of the intimate *"language of the heart."* The verses spoken by the man-bridegroom, by contrast, have another shade of color. One can say that they concentrate above all on the specific "revelation of femininity," the visible expression of which more and more dominates the eyes and heart of the bridegroom.

> **3.** You are beautiful, my friend, as Tirzah,
> lovely as Jerusalem,
> terrible as an army with banners unfurled.
> Turn away your eyes from me:
> their gaze confuses me. (Song 6:4–5)
> . . . .
> What do you admire in the Shulammite,
> during the dance in two rows?
> How beautiful are your feet in sandals,
> O daughter of a prince!
> Your rounded thighs are like jewels,
> the work of a master hand.
> Your navel is a rounded bowl
> that never lacks spiced wine.
> Your belly is a heap of wheat,
> encircled with lilies.
> Your two breasts are like two fawns,
> twins of a gazelle.
> Your neck is like an ivory tower.
> Your eyes are like the pools in Heshbon,
> by the gate of Bath-rabbim.
> Your nose is like a tower of Lebanon,
> that keeps guard over Damascus.
> Your head crowns you like Carmel,
> and your flowing locks are like purple;
> a king has been held captive by your tresses.
> How beautiful and gracious you are,
> O love, daughter of delights!
> You are stately as a palm tree,
> and your breasts are like its clusters. (Song 6:13–7:7)

4. The metaphors of this poetic language authorize various comments about the origin, the author, and the character of the poem. Although modern readers *do not associate many of these metaphors* with

things familiar to them in the visible "world," nevertheless the "language of the body" expressed and reread by them in the truth of increasing spousal closeness remains fully comprehensible. The verses quoted above evoke that circle of closeness in which *the "garden closed" opens up in some way before the eyes of the bridegroom's soul and body.* Through this circle of closeness, the bridegroom lives more fully the experience of the gift that is united on the part of the female "I" with the spousal expression and meaning of the body. His words quoted earlier contain not only a poetic description of the beloved, of her feminine beauty, on which the senses dwell, but these words *speak about gift and self-gift.* In them we always hear the echo of the very first words of Genesis (2:23) by which the sign of the primordial sacrament was constituted. When one reads the Song of Songs, it even seems that its verses—with all their poetic wealth—are a weaker expression of the same "language of the body" than the statement—so simple and apparently poor—of Genesis. Therefore, one should interpret this poverty by this wealth—but also vice versa, this wealth by this poverty and in its light. In the meantime, the "masculine eros" continues to express itself in the words of the bridegroom.

> I said I will climb the palm tree
> and lay hold of its clusters of dates.
> Oh, may your breasts be for me like clusters of grapes,
> and the scent of your breath like apples.
> Your palate is like exquisite wine
> that flows directly to my beloved,
> and glides over lips and teeth. (Song 7:8–9)

And immediately the response of the bride:

> I am my beloved's [or for my beloved],
> and his desire is for me.
> Come, my beloved,
> let us go into the fields,
> and pass the night in the villages.
> Let us go out early in the morning to the vineyards;
> we will see whether the vines have budded,
> whether the flowers have opened
> and the pomegranates are in bloom:
> there I will give you my caresses. (Song 7:10–13)

Through this closeness, the bridegroom lives more fully the experience of the gift that is united on the part of the female "I" with the spousal expression and meaning of the body. The man's words contain not only a poetic description of the beloved, of her feminine beauty on which the senses dwell, but they speak *about the gift and the person's self-gift.*

5. *The "language of the body" speaks to the senses.* The words of the bridegroom quoted earlier confirm this particularly clearly. The bride knows that *"his desire" is for her.* She goes to meet him with the readiness of the gift of self. The love that unites them is of a spiritual and sensual nature together. On the basis of this love, the rereading of the spousal meaning of the body in the truth is achieved, because the man and the woman together must constitute the sign of the reciprocal gift of self, which *sets the seal on their whole life.*

The bride says:

> Set me as a seal upon your heart,
> as a seal upon your arm;
> for love is strong as death,
> jealousy relentless as the netherworld.
> Its flashes are flashes of fire,
> a flame of the LORD!
> The great waters cannot quench love,
> neither can the rivers drown it.
> If one were to give all the wealth of his house
> in exchange for love,
> he would have nothing but scorn from it. (Song 8:6–7)

6. Here we reach in a certain sense the peak of a declaration of love. These words about love deserve suitable reflection, and at the same time they seem to be final chords in the "language of the body." In the light of these words about love, which is "strong as death," we find the closure and crowning of everything in the Song of Songs that begins with the metaphor of the "garden closed" and of the "fountain sealed." In the moment in which the bride of the Song of Songs, the bride-sister, inviolate in the deepest experience of the man-bridegroom, herself master of the intimate mystery of her own femininity, asks, *"set me as a seal upon your heart,"* the whole delicate structure of spousal love *closes,* so to speak, in its own inner interpersonal circle. It is in this closure that the visible sign of the perennial sacrament matures, born of the "language of the body," reread, so to speak, to the end in the truth of the spousal love between man and woman.

In an extraordinary way worthy of the greatest works of human genius, the Song of Songs delineates the structure—so extremely rich—of this sign.

The bride knows that the bridegroom's "desire" is for her and she goes to meet him with the readiness of the gift of self (see Song 7:8–13) because the love that unites them is of a spiritual and sensual nature together. And it is also on the basis of this love that the rereading of the meaning of the body in the truth is achieved, because the man and the woman together must constitute that sign of the reciprocal gift of self which *sets the seal on their whole life.*

Eros or Agape?

112 *Not delivered*
(Text: *Uomo e donna*, 428–30)

1. ACCORDING TO A RATHER WIDESPREAD opinion, the verses of the Song of Songs are wide open to all that we are accustomed to define by the concept of "eros" [see TOB 110:4]. One can say that this biblical poem reproduces the human face of eros, its subjective dynamism as well as its limits and its end, with authenticity free from defects. The "language of the body" is inserted in the singular process of the reciprocal tendency of the persons, of the bridegroom and of the bride, to one another that runs through the whole Song of Songs and is expressed in the frequent refrains that speak of the search full of longing and of the spouses' reciprocal rediscovery. This brings them joy and calm, and at the same time seems to lead them to a new search, a continual search. One has the impression that *in reaching each other,* in experiencing closeness to each other, *they ceaselessly continue to tend toward something*: they yield to the call of something that goes beyond the transitory content and seems to surpass the limits of *eros* reread in the words of the reciprocal "language of the body."

> Tell me, O love of my soul,
> where you are going to pasture your flock...? (Song 1:7)

exclaims the bride at the beginning of the Song, and the bridegroom responds:

> If you do not know,
> O most beautiful among women,
> follow the tracks of the flock. (Song 1:8)

2. Still, this is only a distant prelude. That *process of tension and search* is expressed more fully in the following songs and verses.

> Before the day breathes
> and the shadows lengthen,
> return, my beloved, like a gazelle
> or a young stag over the mountains of perfumes. (Song 2:17)

> Upon my bed at night
> I sought him whom my soul loves;
> I sought him, but found him not....
> I will rise now and go about the city,

2. In the Song of Songs, the "language of the body" is inserted in the singular process of the reciprocal attraction of the man and the woman, which is expressed in frequent refrains speaking of the search full of longing, of affectionate care (see Song 2:7), and of the spouses' mutual rediscovery (see Song 5:2). This brings them joy and calm, and seems to lead them to a continual search. One has the impression that in encountering each other, reaching each other, experiencing closeness to each other, *they ceaselessly continue to tend toward something:* they yield to the call of something that goes beyond the transitory content of the moment and seems to surpass the limits of *eros* reread in the words of the mutual "language of the body" (see Song 1:7–8; 2:17).

through the streets and through the squares;
I will seek the beloved of my heart.
I sought him, but found him not.
The sentinels found me,
as they made their rounds in the city.
Have you seen the beloved of my heart?
Scarcely had I passed them,
when I found the beloved of my heart.
I held him tight, and will not let him go
until I have brought him into my mother's house,
into the chamber of her that conceived me. (Song 3:1–4)

In the words of the bridegroom, by contrast, when he seems to be speaking from afar, what finds voice is *not so much longing, but affectionate concern.*

I adjure you, O daughters of Jerusalem,
by the gazelles or the wild does:
do not stir up or awaken the beloved
until she wants it. (Song 2:7)

And the spouses approach each other,

I sleep, but my heart is awake.
Listen! my beloved is knocking.
Open to me, my sister, my friend,
my dove, my perfect one. (Song 5:2)

3. The search-aspiration has its interior dimension: "the heart is awake" even in sleep. The term "perfect" on the lips of the bridegroom belongs to this dimension. The male aspiration born from love on the basis of the "language of the body" is a search for integral beauty, for purity free from every stain; it is a search for perfection that contains, I would say, *the synthesis of human beauty, beauty of soul and body.* And if the words of the bridegroom just quoted seem to contain the distant echo of the "beginning"—that first search-aspiration of the male man for a being still unknown—they resound much nearer in Ephesians where Christ, as Bridegroom of the Church, desires to see his Bride without "spot," desires to see her "holy and immaculate" (Eph 5:27).

4. In the Song of Songs, human eros reveals the face of *love* ever *in search* and, as it were, *never satisfied.* The echo of this restlessness runs through the verses of the poem:

The search-aspiration has its interior dimension, "the heart is awake" even in sleep. This aspiration born from love on the basis of the "language of the body" is a search for integral beauty, for purity free from every stain; it is a search for perfection that contains *the synthesis of human beauty, beauty of soul and body.*

In the Song of Songs, human eros reveals the face of love ever *in search* and, as it were, *never satisfied.* The echo of this restlessness runs through the verses of the little poem:

I opened to my beloved,
but my beloved had departed, he was gone.
My soul failed me, I did not find him;
I called for him but he did not answer me. (Song 5:6)
. . . .
I adjure you, daughters of Jerusalem,
if you find my beloved,
What shall you tell him?
That I am sick with love. (Song 5:8)

The chorus of young women answers,
What has your beloved different than another,
O most beautiful among women?
What has your beloved different than another,
that you thus implore us? (Song 5:9)

5. The "language of the body" that runs through the verses of the Song of Songs seems to have its limits. *Love* shows itself *as greater than what the "body" is able to express.* And it is at this point that its weakness becomes in some way a "language of the body." "I am sick with love," says the bride, as if she wanted to bear witness to the fragility of the subject that bears the love of both. Eros—as we have seen before [see TOB 111:4]—takes on the aspect of desire in which the bride finds again the proof of spousal love. "I am for my beloved [or I am my beloved's], and his desire is for me" (Song 7:11). The "language of the body," finding its expression in desire, leads to the loving union of the spouses, in which they belong one to the other. *It is from the depth of this union* that the words come forth, *"love is strong as death"* (Song 8:6). These words express the power of love, the force of eros in loving union, but they also say (at least indirectly) that in the "language of the body" this love finds its conclusive end in death.

113 *Not delivered* (Text: *Uomo e donna*, 431–33)

1. THE BODY CONCEALS WITHIN itself the prospect of death, to which love does not want to submit. In fact—as we read in the Song of Songs—love is "a flame of the Lord" that "the great waters cannot quench... / neither can the rivers drown it" (Song 8:6–7). Among words written in all of world literature, these seem particularly fitting and beautiful. They show at the same time what love is in its subjec-

I opened to my beloved,
but my beloved had departed, he was gone.
My soul failed me, I missed him but I did not find him;
I called him, he did not answer me. (Song 5:6)
. . . .
I adjure you, daughters of Jerusalem,
if you find my beloved,
What shall you tell him?
That I am sick with love. (Song 5:8)

tive dimension as a bond that unites the feminine and masculine "I." According to these verses of the Song, love is not only "strong as death"; it is also jealous, *"jealousy relentless as the netherworld"* (Song 8:6). Jealousy confirms in a certain sense *the exclusivity and indivisibility of love*—it indicates at least indirectly the irreversibility and subjective depth of one's spousal choice. It is nevertheless difficult to deny that jealousy manifests still another limitation of love, a spiritual kind of limitation. The bride repeats continually, "his desire is for me" (Song 7:11), so that the reciprocal belonging of both, "my beloved is mine [for me] and I am his [for him]" (Song 2:16), seems to be *generated from desire*, above all from masculine desire, to which there corresponds on the part of the bride the desire and the acceptance of this desire. The desire itself is not able to pass beyond the threshold of jealousy.

2. Thus, the verses of the Song of Songs present eros as the form of human love in which the energies of desire are at work, and it is in them that one finds the root of the consciousness or the subjective certainty of reciprocal belonging. At the same time, however, many verses of the poem lead us to reflect on the cause of the search and the restlessness accompanying the consciousness of reciprocal belonging. Is this restlessness also part of the nature of eros? If it is, such restlessness would indicate at the same time *the need for [eros] to surpass itself.* The truth of love expresses itself in the consciousness of reciprocal belonging, which is the fruit of the reciprocal aspiration and search, and at the same time this truth of love expresses itself in the necessity of the aspiration and search, which springs from the experience of reciprocal belonging. Love demands from both that they take a further step on the staircase of such belonging, always seeking a new and more mature form of it.

3. What becomes apparent in this inner necessity, in this dynamic of love, is *the impossibility*, as it were, *of one person being appropriated and mastered by the other.* The person is someone who stands above all staircases of appropriation and domination, of possession and satisfaction emerging from the same "language of the body." If the bridegroom and the bride reread this "language" in the full truth of the person and of love, they arrive at the ever deeper conviction that the limit of their belonging constitutes that reciprocal gift in which love is

3. Thus, some verses of the Song of Songs present eros as the form of human love in which the energies of desire are at work. And it is in them that one finds the root of the consciousness or the subjective certainty of reciprocal, faithful, and exclusive belonging. At the same time, however, many other verses of the poem lead us to reflect on the cause of the search, and the restlessness accompanying the consciousness of the person being the other's. Is this restlessness also part of the nature of eros? If it is, such restlessness would indicate also *the need for [eros] to surpass itself.* The truth of love expresses itself in the consciousness of reciprocal belonging, the fruit of the mutual aspiration and search, and in the necessity of the aspiration and search—the outcome of reciprocal belonging.

What becomes apparent in this inner necessity, in this dynamic of love, is *the impossibility*, as it were, *of one person being appropriated and mastered by the other.* The person is someone who stands above all the measures of appropriation and domination, of possession and satisfaction emerging from the same "language of the body." If the bridegroom and the bride reread this "language" in the full truth of the person and of love, they arrive at the ever deeper conviction that the fullness of their belonging constitutes that reciprocal gift in which revealed "strong as death," that is, it goes back, so to speak, to the furthest limits of the "language of the body" to overcome even those limits. The truth of inner love and the truth of the reciprocal gift, in a certain sense, *continually call* the bridegroom and the bride—through the means of expressing the reciprocal belonging, and even by breaking away from those means—*to reach* what constitutes *the very nucleus of the gift of person to person.*

4. Following the paths of the words marked out by the verses of the Song of Songs, it seems we are approaching the dimension in which "eros" seeks to integrate itself by means of a further truth of love. At a certain moment, in the light of the death and resurrection of Christ, Paul of Tarsus was to proclaim this truth in the words of 1 Corinthians: "Love is patient; love is kind. Love is not envious; it does not put on airs; it is not snobbish. Love is never rude; it is not self-seeking; it is not prone to anger; neither does it brood over injuries, it does not rejoice in what is wrong but is well pleased in the truth. It covers all, it believes all, it hopes all, it endures all. Love will never end" (1 Cor 13:4–8).

5. Is the truth about love expressed in the verses of the Song of Songs *confirmed in the light of these Pauline words?* In the Song we read about love, for example, that its "jealousy" is "relentless as the nether world" (Song 8:6), and in the Pauline letter we read that "love is not envious." What is the relation between these two expressions about love? What is the relation between the love that is "strong as death," according to the Song of Songs, and the love "that will never end," according to the Pauline letter? We will not multiply these questions; we will not begin a comparative analysis. Nevertheless, it seems that love here opens up before us, I would say, in two perspectives, as though that in which human eros closes its own horizon were opened further, through Paul's words, in another horizon of love that speaks another language, the love that seems to emerge from another dimension of the person, and which calls, invites, to another communion. *This love has been called agape.*

love is revealed "strong as death," that is, it goes to the furthest limits of the "language of the body" to overcome them. The truth of inner love and the truth of the reciprocal gift, in a certain sense, continually call the bridegroom and the bride—through the means of expressing the reciprocal belonging, and even by breaking away from those means—to *reach* what constitutes the very nucleus of the gift from person to person.

4. Following the paths of the words marked out by the verses of the Song of Songs, it seems that we are approaching the dimension in which "eros" seeks to integrate itself by means of a further truth of love. Centuries later, in the light of the death and resurrection of Christ, Paul of Tarsus was to proclaim this truth in the words of 1 Corinthians: "Love is patient; love is kind. Love is not envious; it does not put on airs; it is not snobbish. Love is never rude; it is not self-seeking; it is not prone to anger; neither does it brood over injuries, it does not rejoice in what is wrong but is well pleased in the truth. It covers all, it believes all, it hopes all, it endures all. Love will never end" (1 Cor 13:4–8).

5. Is the truth about love expressed in the verses of the Song of Songs *confirmed in the light of these Pauline words?* In the Song we read about love, for example, that its "jealousy" is "relentless as the nether world" (Song 8:6), and in the Pauline letter we read that "love is not envious." What is the relation between these two expressions about love? What is the relation between the love that is "strong as death," according to the Song of Songs, and the love "that will never end," according to the Pauline letter? We will not multiply these questions; we will not begin a comparative analysis. Nevertheless, it seems that love here opens up before us in two perspectives, as though that in which human eros closes its own horizon were opened further, through Paul's words, to another horizon of love that speaks another language, the love that seems to emerge from another dimension of the person, and which calls, invites, to another communion. *This love has been called "agape,"* and agape brings eros to fulfillment while purifying it.

6. The Song of Songs is a rich and eloquent text of the truth about human love. Many are the forms possible for a commentary on this particular and deeply original book. The analysis offered here *is not a commentary* in the proper sense of this term. It is only a little fragment of reflections on the sacrament of Marriage, whose visible sign is constituted through rereading in the truth the "language of the body." For such reflections, the Song of Songs has an altogether singular significance.

3. When the "Language of the Body" Becomes the Language of the Liturgy (Reflections on Tobit)

The Marriage of Tobias and Sarah

114 *Not delivered* (Text: *Uomo e donna*, 434–36)

1. "Blessed are you, O God of our fathers,
and blessed for all generations is your name.

"Let the heavens and the whole creation bless you for all ages.
You created Adam, and you created his wife Eve
to be a help and support for him.

"From the two of them the whole human race was born.
You said, 'It is not good that the man should be alone;
let us make him a help similar to himself.'

"Now it is not out of lust that I take this kinswoman of mine, but
with rightness of intention. Grant that she and I may find mercy
and that we may grow old together."

And they both said, "Amen, Amen." (Tob 8:5–8)

2. Tobit, which belongs to a particular category (the so-called "didactic tale" of the genre Midrash) in the biblical literature of the Old Testament, does not have features similar to the Song of Songs. Nevertheless, when we read the description of the wedding of young Tobias with Sarah, daughter of Raguel, we find a word that attracted our attention already in the analysis of the Song of Songs. Tobias *calls his bride "kinswoman"* (Tob 8:7). This is what he calls her in the prayer they say together in the first night after the wedding, the prayer we

We have thus concluded these short meditations about the Song of Songs that are intended to offer a deeper understanding of the subject of the "language of the body." In this area, the Song of Songs has an altogether singular significance.

quoted at the beginning. "I take this kinswoman of mine" (Tob 8:7); "sister" (Tob 7:11), which is what her father Raguel also calls her when he agrees to give her as a wife to Tobias. Here are his words: "She is given to you in accordance with the decree in the book of Moses, and as it has been decreed from heaven that she be given to you. Take your cousin; from now on you are her brother, and she is your sister. She is given to you from today for ever" (Tob 7:12).

3. These words could simply confirm the blood relation between the new spouses. In fact, Raguel, whom young Tobias meets during his trip, is a brother by blood of his father Tobit (see Tob 5:9; [7:2]), from whom he had been separated for many years due to the Babylonian slavery. Still, when Raguel gives Sarah as a wife to young Tobias, he not only says, "take...your cousin," but also, *"from now on you are* her *brother, and she is* your *sister"* (Tob 7:12). This means that between the young people also a reciprocal relation should be formed through marriage similar to the one that unites brother and sister. Here the words come to mind, "my sister, bride" (Song 4:10), spoken by the bridegroom of the Song of Songs. These words from the poetical context of the Song sound different in Tobit; yet, despite this difference, they seem to indicate in both texts a particular link of reference: in fact, through marriage man and woman become brother and sister in a special way. The fraternal character seems to be rooted in spousal love.

4. In the story of the wedding of Tobias and Sarah, besides the expression "sister," we find a further relationship that evokes an analogy with the Song of Songs.

We recall that in the duet of the spouses, their mutually declared *love is "strong as death"* (Song 8:6). In Tobit we do not find such a declaration, just as, besides, we do not find there any of the typical confessions of love that make up the Song of Songs. It only says that young Tobias loved Sarah "to the point of no longer being able to draw his heart away from her" (Tob 6:19): nothing except this sentence. In the story of the wedding of Tobias with Sarah, however, we *face a situation,* it seems, that strikingly confirms the truth of the words about love, "strong as death."

General Audience of June 27, 1984
(*Insegnamenti*, 7, no. 1 [1984]: 1939–42)

1. IN COMMENTING ON THE SONG OF SONGS, in the last few weeks I underlined how the sacramental sign of marriage is constituted on the basis of the "language of the body," which man and woman express in its proper truth. Under this aspect I will analyze today some passages of Tobit.

In the story of the wedding of Tobias and Sarah—besides the expression "sister," which indicates that a fraternal character is rooted in spousal love—there is another expression analogous to those in the Song of Songs.

As you will recall, in the duet of the spouses, the *love* they mutually declare to each other is "strong as death" (Song 8:6). In Tobit we find the statement that he loved Sarah "to the point of no longer being able to draw his heart away from her" (Tob 6:19), which presents a situation that confirms the truth of the words about love, "strong as death."

5. We must go back to some details that can be explained on the background of the specific character of Tobit. We read there that Sarah, daughter of Raguel had already "been given in marriage to seven men" (Tob 6:14), but that each one of them had died before uniting with her. This had happened through the work of the evil spirit Asmodeus, as he is called in Tobit. Young Tobias too had reasons to fear a similar death. When he asks for Sarah's hand, Raguel gives her to him with the significant words, "May the Lord of heaven help you tonight, my child, and grant you his mercy and peace" (Tob 7:12).

6. Thus, from the very first moment, Tobias's love had *to face the test of life-or-death.* The words about love, "strong as death," spoken by the spouses of the Song of Songs in the transport of their hearts, here take on the character of a real test. If love proves to be strong as death, this happens above all in the sense that Tobias (and Sarah with him) go without hesitating toward this test. They are later verified, because in this test of life-or-death, *life has the victory,* that is, during the test of the wedding night, love is revealed as stronger than death.

7. This *happens on account of the prayer* we quoted at the beginning of the chapter, which sprang from the admonitions of the young bride's father, but above all from the instructions given by the archangel Raphael who had accompanied Tobias on his whole journey under the name of Azariah. (This fact doubtless constitutes the uniqueness of Tobit, which allows one to classify this biblical book in a distinct category.) Azariah-Raphael gives young Tobias various pieces of advice about how to free himself from the action of the evil spirit, of that Asmodeus, who had caused the death of the seven men to whom Sarah had been married before. Finally, the angel himself takes the initiative in this matter (see Tob 6:17; 8:3). Above all, however, he recommends prayer to Tobias and Sarah: "Then, before you unite yourself with her, first stand up, both of you, and pray. *Implore the Lord of heaven that his grace* and salvation *may come over you.* Do not be afraid; she was destined for you from eternity, and you are the one to save her. She will follow you, and I pledge my word she will give you children who will be like brothers to you. Do not worry" (Tob 6:18).

2. For a better understanding, we must go back to some details that can be explained on the background of the specific character of Tobit. We read there that Sarah, daughter of Raguel, had already "been given in marriage to seven men" (Tob 6:14), but all had died before uniting with her. This had happened through the work of the evil spirit, and young Tobias too had reasons to fear a similar death.

Thus, from the very first moment, Tobias's love had *to face the test of life-or-death*. The words about love, "strong as death," spoken by the spouses of the Song of Songs in the transport of their hearts, here take on the character of a real test. If love proves to be strong as death, this happens above all in the sense that Tobias (and Sarah with him) go without hesitating toward this test. But in this test of life-or-death, *life has the victory*, because, during the test of the first wedding night, *love supported by prayer is revealed as stronger than death*.

8. The content of Raphael's words is different from that of Raguel's, Sarah's father. Raguel's words express affliction, Raphael's the promise. With this promise, it was easier for both to face the test of life-or-death awaiting them on the wedding night.

When the parents "had gone out and had closed the door of the wedding chamber," Tobias got up from the bed and called Sarah to pray together, according to the advice of Raphael-Azariah, "Sister," he said, "get up. Let us pray and ask the Lord to give us his mercy" (Tob 8:4). This was the origin of the prayer we quoted at the beginning. One can say that in this prayer (which we will analyze presently) *the dimension of the liturgy* proper to the sacrament is outlined against the horizon of the "language of the body." Everything, in fact, happens during the couple's wedding night.

Love as a Test

115 *Not delivered*
(Text: *Uomo e donna*, 437–39)

1. We said earlier that the sacramental sign of marriage is constituted on the basis of the "language of the body," which the man and the woman express in the truth proper to it. It is under this aspect that we are analyzing Tobit right now.

When one compares Tobit with the Song of Songs or the prophets, it is right to raise the question as to whether or not the text we are examining speaks about this "language." While the Song offers us the whole richness of the "language of the body," reread with the eyes and hearts of the couple, in the same measure the Book of Tobit falls short from this point of view, because it is extremely spare and sober.

The fact that Tobias loves Sarah "to the point of no longer being able to draw his heart away from her" (Tob 6:19) finds its expression above all *in his readiness to share in her lot* and to remain together "for better or worse," whatever their lot. It is not eros that characterizes Tobias's love for Sarah, but from the beginning this love is confirmed and *validated by ethos*, that is, by the will and the choice of values. On the very threshold of marriage, the criterion of these values becomes the test of life-or-death that both must face already during their first

night. Both. Even if the demon's victim is to be Tobias alone, it is nevertheless easy to imagine what sacrifice of heart also Sarah would have had to undergo.

2. That test of life-or-death—as Tobit speaks of it—has another meaning as well that helps us understand the love and the marriage of the new spouses. And so, when they unite as husband and wife, they must find themselves in the situation in which *the powers of good and evil fight against each other and measure each other.* The duet of the spouses in the Song of Songs seems not to perceive this dimension of reality at all. The spouses of the Song live and express themselves in an ideal or "abstract" world in which it is as if the struggle of objective powers between good and evil did not exist. Is it perhaps precisely the inner strength and truth of love that mitigates the struggle in man and around him?

On the contrary, the fullness of this truth and strength proper to love seems to be different and seems to tend rather where the experience of Tobit leads us. The truth and strength of love show themselves in the ability to place oneself between the forces of good and of evil that fight within man and around him, because love is confident in the victory of good and is ready to do everything in order that good may conquer.

3. Consequently, the truth of the love of the spouses in Tobit is not confirmed by the words expressed in the language of loving transport, but by the choices and acts that take on the whole weight of human existence in the union of the two.

The sign of marriage as a sacrament is brought into being on the basis of the "language of the body" reread in the truth of love. In the Song of Songs, this is the truth of love absorbed by looks and by the heart: the truth of experience and of loving affection. In Tobit, the distressing situation of the "limit" together with the test of life-or-death brings *the loving dialogue of the spouses in some way to silence.* What emerges instead is *another dimension of love:* the "language of the body" that seems to dialogue with the words of choices and acts springing from this dimension.

Is not the touchstone of a test of life-or-death also part of the "language of the body"? Is not the word "death," so to speak, the last word of that language which speaks of the accidental character of the human

3. This test of life-or-death also has another meaning that helps us understand the love and the marriage of the new spouses. In fact, when they unite as husband and wife, they find themselves in the situation in which *the powers of good and evil fight against each other and measure each other.* The duet of the spouses in the Song of Songs seems not to perceive this dimension of reality at all. The spouses of the Song live and express themselves in an ideal or "abstract" world in which it is as if the struggle of objective forces between good and evil did not exist. Is it perhaps precisely the inner strength and truth of love that mitigates the struggle in man and around him?

On the contrary, the fullness of this truth and strength proper to love seems to be different and seems to tend rather where the experience of Tobit leads us. The truth and strength of love show themselves in the ability to place between the forces of good and of evil that fight within man and around him, because love is confident in the victory of good and is ready to do everything in order that good may conquer.

Consequently, the truth of the love of the spouses in Tobit is not confirmed by the words expressed in the language of loving transport, as in the Song of Songs, but by the choices and acts that take on the whole weight of human existence in the union of the two.

Here the "language of the body" seems to use the words of choices and acts that spring from a love that is victorious because it prays.

being and of the corruption of the body, a word to which Tobias and Sarah must refer at the very beginning of their marriage? What depth does their love acquire in this way, and their loving "language of the body" reread in the truth of such love? For, in fact, in the sacramental sign of conjugal unity, in its masculinity and femininity, the body expresses itself also through *the mystery of life and death*. It expresses itself through this mystery more eloquently perhaps than ever.

4. From this vast and, I would say, "metaphysical" background, we should pass on to the dimension of the liturgy that belongs to the sign of marriage as a sacrament and plays a defining role for this sign.

The dimension of the liturgy *takes up into itself* the "language of the body" reread in the truth of human hearts—as we know this language from the Song of Songs. At the same time, however, it seeks to set this "language" into the context of the integral truth of man, reread in the word of the living God. This is what the prayer of the new spouses in Tobit expresses, which we quoted at the beginning.

In Tobit there is neither a dialogue nor a duet between the spouses. On the wedding night, they decide above all *to speak in unison*—and this unison is nothing other than prayer. In that unison, which is prayer, man and woman are united not only through the communion of hearts, but also through the union of both in facing the great test, the test of life-or-death.

5. Before we submit *the text of Tobias's and Sarah's prayer* to a more detailed analysis, we say once again that precisely this prayer becomes the one and only word in virtue of which the new spouses meet the test, which is at the same time a test of good and evil, of a good or bad lot—in the dimension of life as a whole. They realize that the evil that threatens them on the part of the demon can strike as suffering, as death, destruction of the life of one of them. But *in order to repel the evil* threatening to kill the body, one must *prevent the evil spirit from having access to the soul,* one must free oneself within oneself from his influence.

6. In this dramatic moment of the history of both, Tobias and Sarah, when on the wedding night it was their due, as new spouses, to speak reciprocally with the "language of the body," they transform this "language" into a single voice. That unison is prayer. This voice, this act of speaking in unison, allows both of them to pass beyond the

"limit situation," beyond the threat of evil and death, inasmuch as they open themselves totally, in the unity of the two, to the living God.

The prayer of Tobias and Sarah becomes in some way the deepest *model of the liturgy*, whose word is *a word of power*. It is a word of power drawn from the sources of the covenant and of grace. It is the power that frees from evil and purifies. In this word of the liturgy, the sacramental sign of marriage is brought into being, built in the unity of man and woman on the basis of the "language of the body" reread in the integral truth of the human being.

The Prayer of the New Spouses

116 *Not delivered* (Text: *Uomo e donna*, 440–42)

1. THE PRAYER OF TOBIAS AND SARAH—quoted in full in the preceding chapters [see TOB 114:1]—has above all the character of praise and thanksgiving; and it is only thereafter that it gradually becomes a prayer of petition. "Grant that she and I may find mercy and that we may grow old together" (Tob 8:7). When they praise the God of the covenant, "God of our fathers," the new spouses speak in some sense the language of all visible and invisible creatures. "Let the heavens and the whole creation bless you for all ages" (Tob 8:5).

On this vast, one can say *"cosmic," background*, both *recall with gratitude the creation of man*, "male and female he created them" (Gen 1:27).

Two traditions are present in the words of the prayer—both the Levite tradition (Gen 1:27–28), the creation of man, male and female, and the gratuitous gift of the blessing of fruitfulness, "From the two of them the whole human race has sprung" (Tob 8:6); and, perhaps in even fuller form, the Yahwist tradition. Thus, the prayer speaks about the distinct creation of woman with the words, "let us make him a help similar to himself" (Gen 2:18). Tobias and Sarah highlight this point twice in their prayer. "You said, 'It is not good that the man should be alone; let us make him a help similar to himself,'" and before this, "You made Adam, and you made his wife Eve to be a help and support for him" (Tob 8:6).

2. One can infer that the truth expressed in precisely these words of Genesis occupies the place at the center of Tobias and Sarah's reli-

4. The prayer of Tobias (Tob 8:5–8), which is above all a prayer of praise and thanksgiving, then of petition,

gious consciousness, *as the very bone marrow of their conjugal "creed,"* and that at the same time this truth is particularly close to them. By means of this truth they turn to God-Yahweh, not only with the words of the Bible, but they go further in expressing fully what fills their hearts. Their desire is to become a new link in the chain that goes back up to man's very beginnings. In that moment, in which, since they just married each other, they should be "one flesh" as husband and wife, they commit themselves together to rereading the *"language of the body"* proper to their state in its divine source. In this way, the "language of the body" becomes the language of the liturgy: it is anchored in the deepest way possible, namely, by being set into the mystery of the "beginning."

3. The need for a full purification goes hand in hand with this anchoring. As they approach the divine source of the "language of the body," the new spouses sense this need and express it. Tobias says, "Now it is not out of lust that I take this kinswoman of mine, but with rightness of intention" (Tob 8:7). In this way, he points to *the moment of purification* to which the "language of the body" must be subjected when a man and a woman prepare themselves to express the sacramental sign of the covenant in this language. In this sign, marriage must serve to build the reciprocal communion of persons, by reproducing the spousal meaning of the body in its inner truth. Tobias's words, "not out of lust," should be reread in the integral text of the Bible and of the tradition.

4. The prayer in Tobit sets the "language of the body" on the terrain of the essential themes of the theology of the body. It is an "objectivized" language, filled throughout not so much with the emotive strength of experience (as in the case of the Song of Songs, but also, in a different way, of some prophetic texts), but rather with the depth and weight of the truth of existence itself.

The spouses profess this truth together before the God of the covenant, "God of our fathers." One can say that under this aspect the "language of the body" becomes the language of the liturgy. Tobias and Sarah *speak the language of the ministers of the sacrament,* who are aware that in the conjugal covenant of man and woman—precisely through the "language of the body"—the mystery, which has its

sets the "language of the body" on the terrain of the essential themes of the theology of the body. It is an "objectivized" language, filled throughout not so much with the emotive strength of experience, but rather with the depth and weight of the truth of existence itself.

The spouses profess this truth together, in unison, before the God of the covenant, "God of our fathers." One can say that under this aspect the "language of the body" becomes *the language of the ministers of the sacrament,* who are aware that in the conjugal covenant the mystery, which has its source in God himself, is expressed and brought into being. Their conjugal covenant is in fact the image—and

source in God himself, is expressed and brought into being. Their conjugal covenant is in fact the image—and the primordial sacrament of the covenant of God with man, with the human race—of the covenant that draws its origin from eternal Love.

Tobias and Sarah end their prayer with the following words, "Grant that she and I may find mercy and that we may grow old together" (Tob 8:7).

One may suppose (on the basis of the context) that they have before their eyes the prospect of standing fast in communion to the end of their days—a prospect that opens up before them with the test of life-or-death already during their wedding night. At the same time, they see with the eyes of faith the holiness of this vocation, in which—through the unity of the two built on the reciprocal truth of the "language of the body"—*they must respond to the call of God himself*, contained in the mystery of the "beginning." And for this they ask, "Grant that she and I may find mercy."

5. The spouses of the Song of Songs mutually declare their human love with ardent words. The new spouses in Tobit ask God that they may know how to respond to love. Both aspects find their place in what constitutes the sacramental sign of marriage. Both share in the formation of this sign.

One can say that *through one as well as the other*, the "language of the body," reread both in the subjective dimension of the truth of human hearts and in the objective dimension of the truth of living in communion, *becomes the language of the liturgy*. The prayer of the new spouses in Tobit seems certainly to confirm this in a manner different from the Song of Songs, and also in a manner that is undoubtedly more deeply moving.

the primordial sacrament of the covenant of God with man, with the human race—of the covenant that draws its origin from eternal Love.

Tobias and Sarah end their prayer with the following words, "Grant that she and I may find mercy and that we may grow old together" (Tob 8:7).

One may suppose (on the basis of the context) that they have before their eyes the prospect of standing fast in communion to the end of their days—a prospect that opens up before them with the test of life-or-death already during their wedding night. At the same time, they see with the eyes of faith the holiness of this vocation, in which—through the unity of the two built on the reciprocal truth of the "language of the body"—they must *respond to the call of God himself*, contained in the mystery of the Beginning. And for this they ask, "Grant that she and I may find mercy."

5. The spouses of the Song of Songs mutually declare their human love with ardent words. The new spouses in Tobit ask God that they may know how to respond to love. Both aspects find their place in what constitutes the sacramental sign of marriage. Both share in the formation of this sign.

One can say that *through one as well as the other*, the "language of the body," reread both in the subjective dimension of the truth of human hearts and in the objective dimension of the truth of living in communion, *becomes the language of the liturgy*.

The prayer of the new spouses in Tobit seems certainly to confirm this in a manner different from the Song of Songs, and also in a manner that is undoubtedly more deeply moving.

When the Language of the Liturgy
Becomes the "Language of the Body"

117 *Not delivered
(Text: *Uomo e donna*, 443-45)

1. LET US RETURN to the "classical" fifth chapter of Ephesians. This text is, besides, always present in our considerations of marriage as a sacrament—in the first place (and above all) in the dimension of the covenant and of grace. We should consider this text again in the treatment of the dimension of the sacramental sign.

Like the texts of the prophets, Tobit obviously makes use of references to the Old Covenant, above all, however, of references to the original covenant, to the "beginning," with which marriage is united as the primordial sacrament. *Ephesians* reveals the eternal sources of the covenant in the love of the Father and at the same time its new and definitive institution in Jesus Christ.

This connection explains the sacramentality of marriage to the disciples and followers of Christ, who *participate in the New Covenant* (see especially Eph 3:6). This obviously refers to marriage *also in the dimension of the sacramental sign.* Also from this point of view, the words of the "classical" text of Ephesians (Eph 5:21–33) seem very eloquent. We have already shown this indirectly in the earlier analyses of this text. Still, now we should again consider it exclusively under the aspect of the sacramental sign of marriage.

2. "Be subject to one another in the fear of Christ" (Eph 5:21), writes the author of Ephesians. "Husbands have the duty to love their wives *as their own bodies,* for the one who loves his wife loves himself. No one, in fact, ever hates his own flesh, but he nourishes and cares for it, as Christ does with the Church.... Therefore also you, each one on his part, should love his *wife as himself,* and the woman should have reverence toward her husband" (Eph 5:29, 33).

---

* Translator's note: Both 117 and 117b are present in the original pre-papal work (see above, pp. 7–11) and in the Polish edition, while only the first is present in UD and only the second in the *Insegnamenti.* For further details, see pp. 731–2.

If the sign of marriage as a sacrament is built on the basis of the "language of the body" reread in the truth of love, Ephesians is certainly a stupendous expression of it. One can say, "definitive." In this letter we find (also in this respect) the traditions of the prophets of the Old Covenant and in addition the echo of the Song of Songs.

The short passage from Ephesians does not, as does the Song of Songs, contain the "language of the body" in all the richness of its subjective meaning. One can say that it contains *the "objective" confirmation of this language* in its entirety, a solid and complete confirmation.

3. The words of the author of Ephesians seem to be *above all a commentary* on those older, original *biblical words*, in which the nature of the sacramental sign of marriage finds its expression. "The two will be one flesh" (Gen 2:24). This commentary is personalistic in the full meaning of the word, which was already shown in the earlier analyses of this text. The language of the liturgy is equally personalistic—both when we consider Tobit and when we consider the present liturgy of the Church.

Tobias says, "I take this kinswoman of mine.... Grant that she and I may find mercy" (Tob 8:7). The present liturgy of the Latin Church has the new spouses say, "I take you as my wife/as my husband.... I promise to be true to you.... I will love you and honor you all the days of my life."

From the commentary of Ephesians, it is clear that the "language" of masculinity and femininity connected with the sign of "unity of the flesh" must be understood *in a fully personalistic way*.

4. It is sufficient to recall briefly what was already established about the text of Ephesians, "Husbands have the duty to love their wives as their own bodies" (Eph 5:28). The wife's body is not the husband's own body, but should be loved like his own. The unity at issue is not ontological but moral, a unity through love. "The one who loves his wife loves himself" (Eph 5:28).

Love makes the other "I" in a certain sense one's own "I." Through love, the wife's "I" becomes, so to speak, the husband's "I." The body is the expression of this "I," it is the basis of its identity. The union of husband and wife also expresses itself through the body, through the mutual relationship. Love not only unites the two subjects, but it allows them to penetrate each other so mutually, thereby belonging spiritually to each other, that the author of Ephesians can affirm, "The one who loves his wife loves himself" (Eph 5:28). The "I" becomes in a certain sense "you" and the "you" becomes "I." (Cf. marriage as a sacrament, in the first place in the dimension of covenant and grace [TOB 87–107].)

5. In this way the *"language of the body"—precisely with this personalistic commentary of Ephesians*—becomes the *language of the liturgy,* because it is on its basis, on its foundation, that the sacramental sign of marriage is built.

The liturgy reveals above all how in this sign the dimension of the covenant and of grace is realized. In the prayer of Tobias and Sarah, this is evident in the language of the Old Covenant. It is also evident in the rite of the sacrament of Marriage in the manifold richness and differentiation characteristic of the Church's liturgy.

This liturgy models itself for the most part on Ephesians, its definitive biblical model. In the prism of this model, one can see distinctly and with particular clarity that through the "language of the body" reread in the truth—the truth of love, which is at the same time the integral truth of the persons-subjects—the sacramental sign of marriage is built up in the language of the liturgy and in the whole liturgical ritual.

6. In the prism of the same text one also sees the way in which *the language and ritual* of the liturgy *are modeled after the "language of the body"* as the text authentically inscribed in the conjugal life of man and woman on the level of the communion of persons. They model it through the covenant and grace that the liturgy proclaims and realizes in the sacrament. Is this not shown by the words in which the author of Ephesians explains how husbands must love their wives ("as their own bodies"!) and what the Christian "style" of reciprocal relations and of the shared life of the spouses should be? Do not the words of the letter, in the specific context of the personalist commentary on Genesis (2:23–25), reveal, *so to speak, the "absolute" sense* of this *"language of the body,"* which it can reach only in the analogy of the love of Christ with the Church?

The Sacramental Sign—*"Mysterium"* and "Ethos"

117b *General Audience of July 4, 1984*
(Insegnamenti, 7, no. 2 [1984]: 7–10)

1. TODAY WE RETURN to the classical text of Ephesians 5, which reveals the eternal sources of the covenant in the Father's love and, at the same time, its new and definitive institution in Jesus Christ.

This text brings us to a dimension of the "language of the body" that could be called "mystical." It speaks in fact about marriage as a "great mystery." "This mystery is great" (Eph 5:32). And although this mystery is realized in the spousal union of Christ, the Redeemer, with the Church, and of the Church as Bride with Christ ("I say this with reference to Christ and the Church," Eph 5:32), although it is definitively realized in the eschatological dimensions, still the author of Ephesians does not hesitate to extend the analogy of Christ's union with the Church in spousal love, outlined in such an "absolute" and "eschatological" way, to the sacramental sign of the spousal covenant between man and woman, who are "subject to one another in the fear of Christ" (Eph 5:21). He does not hesitate to *extend that mystical analogy to the "language of the body,"* reread in the truth of spousal love and of the conjugal union of the two.

2. One must recognize the logic of this wonderful text, which radically frees our way of thinking from Manichaean elements or from a non-personalist way of thinking about the body, and at the same time brings the "language of the body," which is contained in the sacramental sign of marriage, closer to the dimension of *real holiness.*

The sacraments infuse holiness into the terrain of man's humanity: they penetrate the soul and body, the femininity and masculinity of the personal subject, with the power of holiness. All of this is expressed in the language of the liturgy: there it is expressed, and there it is realized.

The liturgy, liturgical language, *elevates the conjugal covenant* of man and woman, which is based on the "language of the body" reread in the truth, *to the dimensions of the "mystery,"* and at the same time enables that covenant to be realized in these dimensions through the "language of the body."

It is precisely about this that the sign of the sacrament of Marriage speaks, which expresses in liturgical language an interpersonal event full of intense personal content, assigned as a task to the two "until death." The sacramental sign signifies not only the *"fieri* [coming to be]" or birth of marriage, but builds its *"esse* [being]," its duration: both the one and the other as a sacred and sacramental reality rooted in the dimension of the covenant and of grace, in the dimension of creation and redemption. In this way, the liturgical language assigns love, faithfulness, and conjugal integrity to both man and woman through the "language of the body." It assigns them the unity and indissolubility of marriage in the "language of the body." *It assigns them as a task the whole "sacrum" of the person and of the communion of persons,* and in the same way their masculinity and femininity, *precisely in this language.*

3. In this sense, we affirm that liturgical language becomes the "language of the body." This signifies a series of acts and tasks that form the *"spirituality"* of marriage, its "ethos." In the daily life of the couple, these acts become tasks, and the tasks acts. These acts—likewise also the obligations—are by nature spiritual, but they are still at the same time expressed by the "language of the body."

The author of Ephesians writes in this regard, "husbands have the duty to love their wives as their own bodies" (Eph 5:28; "as himself," Eph 5:33), "and the woman should have reverence toward her husband" (Eph 5:33). Both, moreover, should "be subject to one another in the fear of Christ" (Eph 5:21).

The "language of the body," as an uninterrupted continuity of liturgical language, expresses itself not only with the *reciprocal fascination and pleasure* of the Song of Songs, but also as a deep experience of the *"sacrum"* that seems to be *infused* in masculinity and femininity itself through *the dimension of "mystery,"* the *"mysterium magnum"* of Ephesians, whose roots plunge precisely into the "beginning," that is, into the mystery of the creation of man, male and female, in the image of God, called "from the beginning" to be the visible sign of God's creative love.

4. Thus, that "fear of Christ" and "reverence," about which the author of Ephesians speaks, is nothing other than *a spiritually mature*

form of that reciprocal *fascination,* that is to say, of the man for femininity and of the woman for masculinity, which reveals itself for the first time in Genesis 2:23–25. Later, the same fascination seems to run like a wide torrent through the verses of the Song of Songs to find, under wholly different circumstances, its concise and concentrated expression in Tobit.

The spiritual maturity of this fascination is nothing but *the fruit born of the gift of fear,* one of the seven gifts of the Holy Spirit, which St. Paul spoke about in 1 Thessalonians 4:4–7.

Besides, Paul's teaching about chastity as "life according to the Spirit" (see Rom 8:5) allows us (particularly on the basis of 1 Corinthians 6) to interpret that *"reverence"* in the charismatic sense, that is, as a gift of the Holy Spirit.

5. By calling on the couple to submit to one another "in the fear of Christ" (Eph 5:21) and then by stirring their desire for "reverence" in conjugal relations, Ephesians seems to highlight chastity as a virtue and as a gift—in keeping with the Pauline tradition.

In this way, *the reciprocal fascination* of masculinity and femininity *matures spiritually through the virtue* and even more so *through the gift* ("life according to the Spirit"). Both the man and the woman, provided they turn away from concupiscence, find the proper dimension of the freedom of the gift, united with femininity and masculinity in the true spousal meaning of the body.

Thus, liturgical language, that is, the language of the sacrament and of the "mystery," becomes in their life and living together the "language of the body" in a depth, simplicity, and beauty hitherto altogether unknown.

6. This seems to be *the integral meaning of the* sacramental *sign* of marriage. In this way, through the "language of the body," man and woman encounter the great *"mysterium"* in order to transfer the light of this mystery, a light of truth and of beauty expressed in liturgical language, into the "language of the body," that is, into the language of the praxis of love, of faithfulness, and of conjugal integrity, or into the ethos rooted in the "redemption of the body" (see Rom 8:23). On this road, conjugal life in some sense becomes liturgy.

He Gave Them the Law of Life as Their Inheritance

1. *The Ethical Problem*

The Moral Norm and the Truth of the "Language of the Body"

118 *General Audience of July 11, 1984*
(Insegnamenti, 7, no. 2 [1984]: 85–88)

1. THE REFLECTIONS ABOUT HUMAN LOVE in the divine plan carried out so far would remain in some way incomplete if we did not try to see their concrete application in the area of conjugal and familial morality. We want to take this further step, which will bring us to the conclusion of our, by now, long journey, under the guidance of an important pronouncement of the recent magisterium, the encyclical *Humanae Vitae*, which Pope Paul VI published in July 1968. We will reread this significant document in the light of the conclusions we reached when we examined the original divine plan and Christ's words referring to it.

2. "*The Church...teaches* that each and every marriage act (*quilibet matrimonii usus*) must remain through itself open to the transmission of life. That teaching, often set forth by the magisterium, is founded upon the inseparable connection, willed by God and unable to be broken by man on his own initiative, between *the two meanings of the*

conjugal act: the unitive meaning and the procreative meaning" (HV 11–12).*

3. The considerations I am about to propose will refer particularly to the passage of the encyclical that deals with the "two *meanings* of the conjugal act" and their "inseparable connection." I do not intend to present a commentary on the whole encyclical, but rather to explain one passage at greater depth. From the point of view of moral doctrine contained in the document quoted, that passage has a central significance. At the same time, it is a text strictly linked with our earlier reflections about *marriage in the dimension of the (sacramental) sign.*

Since—as I said—it is a central passage of the encyclical, it is obviously inserted very deeply in its structure: thus the analysis of this passage must point us toward the various parts of that structure, even if we do not intend to comment on the whole text.

4. In the reflections about the sacramental sign, we already said several times that this sign is based on the *"language of the body" reread in the truth.* The truth at stake here is affirmed for the first time at the beginning of marriage, when the new spouses, by promising "to be faithful to [each other] always...and to love and honor [each other] all the days of [their lives]," become ministers of marriage as a sacrament of the Church.

---

* Translator's note: The English translation offered above follows the official Italian text of *Humanae Vitae* quoted by John Paul II. In particular, the phrase, "must remain through itself *open* to the transmission of life," corresponds to the Italian, "*deve rimanere per sé* aperto *alla trasmissione della vita* (emphasis added)." The Latin text is considerably stronger: "must remain through itself *destined* to the procreation of human life, *ad vitam humanam procreandam per se* destinatus *permaneat* (emphasis added)." Throughout TOB, John Paul II quotes the Italian text of *Humanae Vitae* without mentioning any of the differences between it and the Latin text. In the original Polish of TOB, John Paul II quotes the official Polish translation of *Humanae Vitae,* which follows the Latin text rather than the Italian.

The key point of the Latin text (sexual intercourse is *"through itself"* or essentially *"destined"* or ordered to the end of procreation) is reflected in John Paul II's teaching that procreation is the "essential" end of marriage (see TOB 35:2) and that the traditional hierarchy of the ends of marriage is re-confirmed by Vatican II in *Gaudium et Spes* (see TOB 127:3 and Index at entry for END). For a discussion of various English translations of this passage, see Janet Smith, "Appendix: *Humanae Vitae,*" in Janet Smith, ed., *Why Humanae Vitae Was Right: A Reader* (San Francisco: Ignatius Press, 1993) 533–67, here 549.

We are also dealing with a truth that is, so to speak, always affirmed anew. In fact, as man and woman live in marriage "until death," in some sense they continuously re-propose the sign they themselves gave—through the liturgy of the sacrament—on the day of their wedding.

The words of Paul VI's encyclical quoted above concern the moment in the common life of the couple in which the two, by being united in the conjugal act, become "one flesh," according to the biblical expression (Gen 2:24). Precisely *in this moment, so rich in meaning,* it is also particularly important that the "language of the body" be reread in the truth. This reading becomes an indispensable condition for *acting in the truth* or for behaving *in conformity with the value and the moral norm.*

5. The encyclical does not merely recall this norm, but also tries to give its *adequate foundation.* In order to clarify more deeply that "inseparable connection, willed by God...between the two meanings of the conjugal act," Paul VI writes in the sentence after this as follows: "By its intimate structure, the conjugal act, while most closely uniting husband and wife, capacitates them for the generation of new lives, according to laws inscribed in the very being of man and of woman" (HV 12).

We observe that in the preceding sentence the text just quoted deals above all with "*meaning*" and in the sentence after this with the "*innermost structure*" (that is, nature) of conjugal relations. When it defines this "innermost structure," the text refers to "laws inscribed in the very being of man and woman."

The transition from the sentence expressing the moral norm to the sentence explaining it and giving its reasons is particularly significant. The encyclical leads one to look for the foundation of the norm determining the morality of the actions of man and woman in the conjugal act, in the nature of this act itself and more deeply still in the nature of the acting *subjects themselves.*

6. In this way, the "*innermost structure*" (or *nature*) of the conjugal act constitutes *the necessary basis for an adequate reading and discovery of the meanings* that must be carried over into the conscience and the decisions of the acting persons. It also constitutes the necessary basis for grasping the adequate relationship of these meanings, namely, their inseparability. Since "the conjugal act"—at one and the same time—"deeply unites husband and wife" and together "makes them able to generate new lives," and since the one as well as the other thing comes about "by its innermost structure," it follows (with the necessity proper to reason, logical necessity) that the human person "should" read, *at one and the same time,* the "*two meanings* of the conjugal act" and also the "*inseparable connection* between the two meanings of the conjugal act."

Nothing else is at stake here than reading the "language of the body" in the truth, as has been said several times in the earlier biblical analyses. The moral norm, constantly taught by the Church in this sphere, recalled and reconfirmed by Paul VI in his encyclical, springs from reading the "language of the body" *in the truth.*

What is at stake here is the *truth,* first *in the ontological dimension* ("innermost structure") and then—as a consequence—in the *subjective and psychological dimension* ("meaning"). The text of the encyclical underlines that in this case we are dealing with a norm of the natural law.

119 General Audience of July 18, 1984
(Insegnamenti, 7, no. 2 [1984]: 101–4)

1. IN HUMANAE VITAE WE READ, "Calling human beings back to the observance of the norms of the natural law, as interpreted by her constant doctrine, the Church teaches that each and every marriage act must remain through itself open to the transmission of life" (HV 11).

At the same time the same text considers and even highlights the subjective and psychological dimension when it speaks about "meaning" and, in particular, of the "two meanings of the conjugal act."

"*Meaning*" is born in consciousness *with the rereading of the* (ontological) *truth of the object.* Through this rereading, the (ontological) truth enters, so to speak, into the cognitive, that is, subjective and psychological dimension.

Humanae Vitae seems to turn our attention particularly to this latter dimension. This is indirectly confirmed, among other things, also by the next sentence: "We believe that the human beings of our day are particularly capable of seeing the deeply reasonable and human character of this fundamental principle" (HV 12).

2. This "reasonable character" concerns not only the truth in the ontological dimension, that is, what corresponds to the real structure of the conjugal act. It concerns also the same truth in the subjective and psychological dimension, that is to say, *the right understanding* of the innermost structure of the conjugal act, that is, the adequate rereading of the meanings that correspond to this structure and their inseparable connection in view of morally right behavior. In this consist the moral norm and the corresponding ordering of human acts in the sphere of sexuality. In this sense, we say that the norm is identical with rereading the "language of the body" in the truth.

The Rightness of the Norm and Its "Practicability"

3. *Humanae Vitae* thus contains the moral norm and its reason, or at least a deeper understanding of what constitutes the reason of the norm. Since, in addition, the moral value is expressed in the norm in a binding way, acts that conform to the norm are thus morally right, while acts contrary to it are intrinsically illicit. The author of the encyclical underlines that this norm *is part of the "natural law,"* that is, that it conforms to reason as such. The Church teaches this norm even though it is not formally (that is, literally) expressed in Sacred Scripture, and she does so in the conviction that the interpretation of the precepts of the natural law belongs to the competence of the magisterium.

We can say more, however. Even if the moral norm, formulated in this way in *Humanae Vitae,* is not found literally in Sacred Scripture, nevertheless from the fact that it is contained in the tradition and, as Pope Paul VI writes, has been "often set forth by the magisterium" (HV 12) to the faithful, it follows that this norm *corresponds to revealed teaching as a whole* as contained *in the biblical sources* (see HV 4).

4. The issue is not simply the whole moral teaching contained in Sacred Scripture, its essential premises, and the general character of its content, but the fuller whole to which we earlier devoted many analyses when we discussed the "theology of the body."

Precisely on the background of such a full whole it becomes evident that the moral norm just mentioned is not only part of the natural law, but also of the *moral order revealed by God*: also from this point of view it could not be different, but only as it has been handed down by tradition and the magisterium and, in our days, by *Humanae Vitae* as a contemporary document of this magisterium.

Paul VI writes, "We believe that the human beings of our day are particularly capable of seeing the deeply reasonable and human character of this fundamental principle" (HV 12). One can add that they are also able to grasp its deep conformity with all that is transmitted by the tradition flowing from the biblical sources. The bases of this conformity should be sought particularly in biblical anthropology. We know what importance anthropology has for ethics, that is, for moral teaching. It seems to be entirely reasonable to look in the "theology of the body" for *the foundation of the truth of the norms* concerning such a fundamental issue of man as "body": "the two will be one flesh" (Gen 2:24).

5. The norm of *Humanae Vitae* concerns all men and women inasmuch as it is a norm of the natural law and is based on conformity with human reason (evidently when reason is seeking the truth). It concerns even more all the believing members of the Church, given that the reasonable character of this norm finds an indirect confirmation and solid support in the whole of the "theology of the body." From this point of view, we spoke in our earlier analyses about the *"ethos" of the redemption of the body.*

Based on this "ethos," the norm of the natural law finds not only a new expression, but also *a full* anthropological and ethical *foundation* in the word of the Gospel as well as in the purifying and strengthening action of the Holy Spirit.

These are all good reasons why every believer, and in particular every theologian, should reread and understand ever more deeply the moral teaching of the encyclical in this integral context.

The reflections we have been carrying out for a long time constitute precisely an attempt at such a rereading.

120 *General Audience of July 25, 1984*
(Insegnamenti, 7, no. 2 [1984]: 121–24)

1. WE TAKE UP AGAIN the reflections that had the purpose of linking *Humanae Vitae* with the theology of the body as a whole.

The encyclical does not limit itself to recalling the moral norm concerning conjugal life, reconfirming it in the face of new circumstances. When Paul VI made a pronouncement of the authentic magisterium through the encyclical (1968), he had before his eyes the authoritative statement of Vatican II contained in the constitution *Gaudium et Spes* (1965).

Not only is the encyclical aligned with the conciliar teaching, but it also constitutes *the development and completion* of the issues raised there, particularly in regard to the question of the "harmony between human love and reverence for life" (*Gaudium et Spes*, 51). On this point, we read the following words in *Gaudium et Spes*: "The Church issues the reminder that a true contradiction cannot exist between the divine laws pertaining to the transmission of life and those pertaining to fostering authentic conjugal love" (ibid.).

2. The pastoral constitution of Vatican II *excludes any "true contradiction"* in the normative order, which Paul VI confirms on his part while seeking at the same time to throw light on this "non-contradiction" and thus to offer reasons for the relevant moral norm by showing its conformity with reason.

Humane Vitae does not, however, speak so much about "*noncontradiction*" in the normative order, but rather about the "*inseparable connection*" between the transmission of life and authentic conjugal love from the point of view of "the two meanings of the conjugal act: the unitive meaning and the procreative meaning" (HV 12), which we have already discussed.

3. One could dwell for a long time on the analysis of the norm itself, but the character of both documents leads rather to reflections that are, at least indirectly, pastoral. In fact, *Gaudium et Spes* is a pastoral constitution, and Paul VI's encyclical—with all its doctrinal value—tends to have the same orientation. It is intended, in fact, to be *a response to the questions of contemporary men and women.* There are questions of a demographic and consequently socio-economic and political nature, in relation to population growth throughout the world. These are questions that come from the field of particular sciences and hand in hand with them questions of contemporary moralists (moral theologians). They are above all questions of spouses, who already stand at the center of the attention of the conciliar constitu-

tion, which the encyclical takes up again with all desirable precision. We read there, in fact, "Granted the conditions of life today, and granted the meaning that conjugal relations have with respect to the harmony between husband and wife and to their mutual faithfulness, *would not a revision* of the ethical norms, in force up to now, *seem to be advisable,* especially when it is considered that they cannot be observed without sacrifices, sometimes heroic sacrifices?" (HV 3).

4. In the formulation above, it is evident with what concern the author of the encyclical tries to face the questions of contemporary man in all their weightiness. The importance of these questions calls for a proportionately weighed and deep answer. If, therefore, it is right on the one hand to expect a penetrating treatment of the norm, one can also expect that no less weight *be given to pastoral arguments* concerning more directly the life of concrete human beings, of precisely those who raise the questions mentioned at the beginning.

Paul VI always had these persons before his eyes. The following passage, among others, is an expression of this concern. "The teaching of the Church on the regulation of birth, which promulgates the divine law, will easily appear to many to be difficult or even impossible to observe. And indeed, like all great beneficent realities, it *demands* serious engagement and much effort—individual, family, and social effort. More than that, it would be impossible to observe without the help of God, who upholds and strengthens the good will of men. Yet, to anyone who reflects well, it cannot but be clear that such efforts *ennoble man* and are beneficial to the human community" (HV 20).

5. At this point, the text no longer speaks about "non-contradiction" on the level of norms, but rather about the *"possibility of observing the divine law,"* that is, about an at least indirectly pastoral topic. That it should be possible to carry out the law belongs directly to the very nature of law and is therefore contained in the framework of "non-contradiction on the level of the norm." Still, the "possibility" *understood as the "feasibility"* of the norm belongs also to the practical and pastoral sphere. In the text quoted, my Predecessor speaks precisely from this point of view.

6. One can add a consideration here: the fact that the whole *biblical background* called "theology of the body" offers us, even if indirectly, the confirmation of the truth of the moral norm contained in *Humanae Vitae* and prepares us *to consider the practical and pastoral aspects* of the problem as a whole *at greater depth*. Did we not draw all the principles and general presuppositions of the "theology of the body" from the answers Christ gave to the questions of his concrete interlocutors? Are Paul's texts—such as 1 Corinthians—not a little manual about the problems of the moral life of the first followers of Christ? And in these texts, we certainly find the *"rule of understanding"** present in *Humanae Vitae* that seems so indispensable in the face of the problems treated in this encyclical.

Those who believe that the Council and the encyclical do not sufficiently take into account the difficulties of concrete life do not understand the pastoral concern that stood at the origin of these documents. Pastoral concern means seeking the *true* good of man, promoting the values impressed by God in the human person; that is, it signifies applying the "rule of understanding," which aims at the ever clearer discovery of God's plan for human love, in the certainty that the *one and only true* good of the human person consists in putting this divine plan into practice.

Responsible Parenthood

One could say that precisely in the name of the "rule of understanding" quoted above [see TOB 120:1], the Council raised the question of the "harmony between human love and reverence for life" (*Gaudium et Spes*, 51), and *Humanae Vitae* recalls not only the moral norms binding in this area, but is broadly concerned with the problem of the "possibility of observing the divine law."

The present reflections about the character of the document *Humanae Vitae* prepare us to take up next the topic of "responsible parenthood."

---

* Translator's note: The "rule of understanding" is contained in the statement, "a true contradiction cannot exist between the divine laws pertaining to the transmission of life and those pertaining to authentic conjugal love" (*Gaudium et Spes*, 51). Arguments in favor of contraception are often based on a perceived conflict between conjugal love (which calls for sexual union) and the transmission of life, or rather the non-transmission, that is, the need to limit the number of children (which requires at least periodic abstinence from sexual union unless contraceptives are used).

121 General Audience of August 1, 1984
(*Insegnamenti*, 7, no. 2 [1984]: 144–47)

1. FOR TODAY WE HAVE CHOSEN the topic of "responsible fatherhood and motherhood" in light of *Gaudium et Spes* and *Humanae Vitae*.

In facing this question, *the conciliar constitution* limits itself to recalling the fundamental premises; *the papal document*, by contrast, goes further and gives more concrete contents to these premises.

The Council text reads as follows: "When there is question of harmonizing conjugal love with the responsible transmission of life, the moral aspects of any procedure do not depend solely on sincere intentions or on an evaluation of motives, but must be determined by objective standards. These, based on the nature of the human person and his acts, preserve the full sense of mutual self-giving and human procreation in the context of true love. Such a goal cannot be achieved unless *the virtue of conjugal chastity* is sincerely practiced."

And the Council adds, "Relying on these principles, children of the Church *may not undertake methods of birth control* which are found blameworthy by the teaching authority of the Church" (*Gaudium et Spes*, 51).

2. Before this passage, the Council teaches: "Thus they will fulfill their task with human and Christian *responsibility*, and with docile reverence toward God." This means that they "will make decisions by common counsel and effort. Let them thoughtfully take into account both their own welfare and that of their children, those already born and those which the future may bring. For this accounting they need to reckon with both the material and the spiritual conditions of the times as well as of their state in life. Finally, they should consult the interests of the family group, of temporal society, and of the Church herself."

At this point, words follow that are of particular importance in determining with greater precision *the moral character of "responsible fatherhood and motherhood."* We read, "The parents themselves and no one else should ultimately make this judgment in the sight of God."

And continuing, "But in their manner of acting, spouses should be aware that they cannot proceed at will, but must always be governed according to a conscience dutifully conformed to the divine law itself, and should be docile toward the Church's teaching office, which authentically interprets that law in the light of the Gospel. That divine law reveals and protects the integral meaning of conjugal love and impels it toward a truly human fulfillment" (*Gaudium et Spes*, 50).

3. While limiting itself to recalling the premises needed for "responsible fatherhood and motherhood," the conciliar constitution highlighted them *without any ambiguity* by clarifying *the constitutive elements* of this fatherhood and motherhood, namely, the mature judgment of personal conscience in its relation to the divine law authentically interpreted by the magisterium of the Church.

4. Basing itself on the same premises, *Humanae Vitae* goes further by offering concrete indications. One can see this first *in the way of defining "responsible parenthood"* (HV 10). Paul VI attempts to clarify this concept by going back to its various aspects and excluding before-hand its reduction to one of the "partial" aspects, a reduction found among those who speak exclusively about birth control. From the very beginning, in fact, Paul VI is guided in his argumentation by an integral conception of man (see HV 7) and of conjugal love (see HV 8–9).

5. One can speak about responsibility in the exercise of fatherhood and motherhood under various aspects. Thus he writes, "In relation to *biological processes*, responsible parenthood means the knowledge of *and reverence* for their functions; the human intellect discovers in the power of giving life biological laws which are part of the human person" (HV 10). When the psychological dimension is at issue and the "*tendencies of instinct or passion*, responsible parenthood means that necessary dominion which reason and will must exercise over them" (HV 10).

Taking the above-mentioned aspects within the person as given and adding "economic...and social conditions," one must recognize that "responsible parenthood is exercised, either by the prudent and generous decision to raise a numerous family, or by the decision, made for serious reasons and with due respect for the moral law, to avoid for the time being, or even for an indeterminate period, a new birth" (HV 10).

It follows from this that the concept of "responsible parenthood" contains *the disposition, not only to avoid "a new birth," but also to increase the family according to the criteria of prudence.* In this light, in which one must examine and decide the question of "responsible parenthood," what remains central is *"the objective moral order* established by God, of which a right conscience is the faithful interpreter" (HV 10).

6. The couple observe in this area "their own duties towards God, towards themselves, towards the family, and towards society, in a correct hierarchy of values" (HV 10). Thus, one cannot speak here of "proceeding at will." On the contrary, the couple must "conform their activity to the creative intention of God" (HV 10).

Beginning with this principle, the encyclical builds its argumentation on the "innermost structure of the conjugal act" and on the "inseparable connection between the two meanings of the conjugal act" (HV 12), which was already presented earlier. The relevant principle of conjugal morality is thus faithfulness to the divine plan manifested in the "innermost structure of the conjugal act" and in the "inseparable connection between the two meanings of the conjugal act."

122 *General Audience of August 8, 1984*
(Insegnamenti, 7, no. 2 [1984]: 169–226)

1. WE SAID EARLIER that the principle of conjugal morality taught by the Church (Vatican II, Paul VI) is the criterion of faithfulness to the divine plan.

In conformity with this principle, *Humanae Vitae strictly distinguishes* between that which constitutes the *morally illicit* method of the regulation of births, or more precisely of fertility, and what constitutes a *morally correct* method.

In the first place, the following are morally illicit: "the direct interruption of the generative process already begun" ("abortion," HV 14), "direct sterilization," and "every action which, either in anticipation of the conjugal act, or in its accomplishment, or in the development of its natural consequences, proposes, whether as an end or as a means, to render procreation impossible" (HV 14), and thus all contraceptive means. Morally permitted, by contrast, is *"recourse to the infertile periods"* (HV 16). "If, then, there are serious motives to space out births, which derive from the physical or psychological conditions of husband and wife, or from external circumstances, the Church teaches that it is then licit to take into account the natural rhythms immanent in the generative functions, for the use of marriage in the infertile periods only, and in this way to regulate birth without offending the moral principles" (HV 16).

2. The encyclical highlights especially that "there is an essential difference," that is, a *difference of an ethical nature,* between the two cases. "In the former [that is, "making use of the infertile period"], the married couple make legitimate use of a natural disposition; in the latter [that is, "the use of means which directly prevent conception"], they impede the development of natural processes" (HV 16).

Two actions flow from this difference that have, in fact, completely opposite ethical qualifications: the natural regulation of fertility is morally right; contraception is not morally right. This essential difference between the two actions (or ways of acting) concerns their intrinsic ethical qualification, even though my Predecessor Paul VI affirms that "in the one and the other case, the married couple are concordant in the positive will of avoiding children *for plausible reasons*" and even writes, "seeking the certainty that offspring will not arrive" (HV 16). In these words, the document admits that, although those who make use of contraceptive practices can also be inspired by "plausible reasons," still this does *not change the moral qualification founded on the very structure of the conjugal act* as such.

3. One could observe at this point that the couple who have recourse to the natural regulation of fertility can lack the valid reasons spoken about earlier: this, however, constitutes *a separate ethical problem* when one treats of the moral sense of "responsible fatherhood and motherhood."

If we assume that the reasons for deciding not to procreate are morally right, the *moral* problem of the way of acting in such a case remains, and this mode expresses itself in an act that—according to the Church's teaching transmitted in the encyclical—possesses its own intrinsic moral qualification, positive or negative. The first, positive, corresponds to the "natural" regulation of fertility; the second, negative, corresponds to "artificial contraception."

The Truth of the "Language of the Body" and the Evil of Contraception

4. The whole argument presented above can be *summarized in the exposition of the teaching* contained in *Humanae Vitae*, bringing out the normative and simultaneously pastoral character of the encyclical. In the normative dimension, the point is to specify and clarify the moral principles of action; in the pastoral dimension, the concern is to throw light on the possibility of acting according to these principles ("possibility of observing the divine law," HV 20).

We should spend some more time on the interpretation of the encyclical's content. For the sake of such an interpretation, one must see this content, this normative-pastoral whole, in the light of the theology of the body that emerges from the analysis of the biblical texts.

5. The theology of the body is not merely a theory, but rather a specific evangelical, Christian pedagogy of the body. This pedagogic character comes from the character of the Bible and above all of the Gospel as a salvific message revealing *what man's true good is* for the sake of shaping—according to the measure of this good—his life on earth in the perspective of the hope of the future world.

Following this line, *Humanae Vitae* answers the question about man's true good as a person, inasmuch as he is male and female, about what corresponds to the dignity of man and woman when one is dealing with the important problem of the transmission of life in conjugal life.

To this problem we will devote further reflections.

123 General Audience of August 22, 1984
(Insegnamenti, 7, no. 2 [1984]: 227–30)

1. WHAT IS THE ESSENCE of the teaching of the Church about the transmission of life in the conjugal community, the essence of the teaching recalled for us by the Council's pastoral constitution *Gaudium et Spes* and the encyclical *Humanae Vitae* by Pope Paul VI?

The problem lies in maintaining *the adequate relationship* between that which is defined as *"domination...of the forces of nature"* (HV 2) and *"self-mastery"* (HV 21), which is indispensable for the human person. Contemporary man shows the tendency of transferring the methods proper to the first sphere to those of the second. "Finally and above all, man has made stupendous progress in the domination and rational organization of the forces of nature," we read in the encyclical, "such that he tends to extend this domination to his own total being: to the body, to psychical life, to social life and even to the laws which regulate the transmission of life" (HV 2).

This extension of the sphere of the means of "the domination...of the forces of nature" threatens the human person for whom the method of "self-mastery" is and remains specific. It—that is, self-mastery—corresponds in fact to the fundamental constitution of the person: it is a perfectly "natural" method. The transposition of "artificial means," by contrast, *breaks* the constitutive dimension of the person, deprives man of the subjectivity proper to him, and turns him into *an object of manipulation.*

2. The human body is not only the field of reactions of a sexual character, but it is at the same time the means of the expression of man as an integral whole, of the person, which reveals itself through the "language of the body." This "language" has an important interpersonal meaning, especially in the area of the reciprocal relations between man and woman. In addition, our earlier analyses show that in this case the "language of the body" should *express,* at a determinate level, *the truth of the sacrament.* By participating in the eternal plan of love, "*Sacramentum absconditum in Deo*" [the mystery hidden in God], the "language of the body" becomes in fact a "prophetism of the body," as it were.

One can say that *Humanae Vitae* carries this truth about the human body in its masculinity and femininity to its final consequences, not only its logical and moral, but also its practical and pastoral, consequences.

3. The unity of the two aspects of the problem—of the *sacramental* (or theological) and the *personalistic dimension*—corresponds to the overall "revelation of the body." From this derives also the connection of the strictly theological vision with the ethical vision, which appeals to the "natural law."

In fact, the subject of the natural law is man, not only in the "natural" aspect of his existence, but also in the integral truth of his personal subjectivity. He is shown to us in revelation as male and female in his full temporal and eschatological vocation. He is called by God to be a witness and interpreter of the eternal plan of love by becoming the minister of the sacrament, which has "from the beginning" been constituted in the sign of the "union of the flesh."

4. As ministers of a sacrament that is constituted through consent and perfected by conjugal union, man and woman are called *to express the mysterious "language" of their bodies in all the truth that properly belongs to it.* Through gestures and reactions, through the whole reciprocally conditioned dynamism of tension and enjoyment—whose direct source is the body in its masculinity and femininity, the body in its action and interaction—through all this *man, the person,* "speaks."

In the "language of the body," man and woman carry on the dialogue that—according to Genesis 2:24–25—began on the day of creation. Precisely on the level of this "language of the body"—which is something more than mere sexual reactivity, and which, as an authentic language of the persons, is subject to the demand for truth, that is, to objective moral norms—man and woman reciprocally express *themselves* in the fullest and most profound way made possible for them by the somatic dimension itself of their masculinity and femininity. Man and woman express themselves in the measure of the whole truth of their persons.

5. Man *is person precisely because he is master of himself and has dominion over himself.* Indeed, inasmuch as he is master over himself he can "give himself" to another. And it is this dimension—the dimension of the freedom of the gift—that becomes essential and decisive for the "language of the body" in which man and woman express themselves reciprocally in conjugal union. Given that this union is a communion of persons, the "language of the body" must be judged according to the criterion of truth. This is exactly the criterion *Humanae Vitae* recalls, as the passages quoted before confirm.

6. *According to the criterion of this truth,* which must be expressed in the "language of the body," the conjugal act "means" not only love, but also potential fruitfulness, and thus it cannot be deprived of its full and adequate meaning by means of artificial interventions. In the conjugal act, it is not licit to separate artificially the unitive meaning from the procreative meaning, because the one as well as the other

belong to the innermost truth of the conjugal act. The one is realized together with the other and, in a certain way, the one through the other. This is what the encyclical teaches (see HV 12). Thus, in such a case, when the conjugal act is *deprived of its inner truth* because it is deprived artificially of its procreative capacity, it also *ceases to be an act of love.*

7. One can say that in the case of an artificial separation of these two meanings in the conjugal act, a real bodily union is brought about, but it does not correspond to the inner truth and dignity of personal communion, *"communio personarum."* This communion demands, in fact, that the "language of the body" be expressed reciprocally in the integral truth of its meaning. If this truth is lacking, one can speak neither of the truth of the reciprocal gift of self nor of the reciprocal acceptance of oneself by the person. Such a violation of the inner order of conjugal communion, a communion that plunges its roots into the very order of the person, *constitutes the essential evil of the contraceptive act.*

8. The interpretation just offered of the moral teaching set forth in *Humanae Vitae* is situated on the vast background of the reflections connected with the theology of the body. Especially important for this interpretation are the reflections about "sign" in connection with marriage understood as a sacrament. And the essence of the violation that disturbs the inner order of the conjugal act cannot be understood in a theologically adequate way without the reflections on the topic of the "concupiscence of the flesh."

Ethical Regulation of Fertility (The Primacy of Virtue)

124 *General Audience of August 29, 1984*
(Insegnamenti, 7, no. 2 [1984]: 271–74)

1. WHILE SHOWING THE MORAL EVIL of contraception, *at the same time* Humanae Vitae *fully approves the natural regulation of fertility,* and, in this sense, it approves of *responsible fatherhood and motherhood.* Here one must refuse to apply the term "responsible" from the ethical point of view to procreation in which one has recourse to contraception in order to regulate fertility. The true concept of "responsible

fatherhood and motherhood" is rather connected with the regulation of fertility that is honorable from the ethical point of view.

2. We read in this regard, "The honorable practice of regulating birth rate demands first of all that husband and wife acquire and possess solid convictions concerning *the true values of life and of the family*, and that they strive to acquire perfect self-mastery. Dominion over instinct by means of one's reason and free will undoubtedly requires an ascesis, so that the affective manifestations of conjugal life may observe the correct order, in particular with regard to the observance of periodic continence. Yet this discipline, which is proper to the purity of married couples, far from harming conjugal love, rather confers on it a higher human value. It demands continual effort yet, thanks to its beneficent influence, husband and wife fully develop their personalities, being enriched with spiritual values" (HV 21).

3. The encyclical then illustrates the consequences of such behavior not only for the couple themselves, but also for the whole family understood as a communion of persons. We shall have to take up this issue again. The encyclical underlines that the ethically upright regulation of fertility demands from the couple above all a certain *behavior with respect to the family and procreation,* that is, it demands that they "acquire and possess solid convictions concerning the true values of life and of the family" (HV 21). Beginning with this premise, it was necessary to take the next step by considering the question as a whole, which *the 1980 Synod of Bishops* did (*De muneribus familiae christianae*). After the synod, the teaching about this particular issue of conjugal and family morality treated in *Humanae Vitae* found its proper place and fitting perspective in the larger context of the apostolic exhortation *"Familiaris Consortio."* The theology of the body, particularly as a pedagogy of the body, *in some way plunges its roots into the theology of the family and, at the same time, leads to it.* This pedagogy of the body, whose key today is *Humanae Vitae,* can be explained only in the full context of a correct vision of the values of life and the family.

4. In the text quoted above, Paul VI refers to conjugal chastity when he writes that observing periodic continence is the form of self-mastery in which "the purity of married couples" is shown (HV 21).

As we prepare to carry out a deeper analysis of this problem, we should keep in mind the whole teaching about purity understood as life according to the Spirit (see Gal 5:25), which we considered earlier [see TOB 51–57], in order to understand in this way the relevant statements of the encyclical about the topic of "periodic continence." That doctrine remains, in fact, *the true reason in terms of which* Paul VI's teaching defines the ethically upright regulation of births and *responsible fatherhood and motherhood.*

Although the "periodic" character of continence is in this case applied to the so-called "natural rhythms" (HV 16), still, *continence* itself is a definite and permanent moral attitude, *it is a virtue*, and thus the whole mode of behavior guided by it becomes virtuous. The encyclical underlines rather clearly that here it is *not* merely a question of a certain "*technique*," but of *ethics* in the strict sense of the term as *the morality of a certain behavior.*

For this reason, the encyclical is right to highlight, on the one hand, the need in such behavior for reverence in relation to the order established by the Creator and, on the other hand, the need for an immediate motivation of an ethical character.

5. *In regard to the first aspect* we read, "To make use of the gift of conjugal love with reverence for the laws of the generative process means to acknowledge oneself not to be the arbiter of the sources of human life, but rather the minister of the plan established by the Creator" (HV 13). "Human life is sacred"—as our Predecessor Pope John XXIII recalled—"from its very beginning it directly involves the creative action of God" (John XXIII, *Mater et Magistra*, 194; see HV 13). *As regards the immediate motivation, Humanae Vitae* requires that "in order to space births there must be serious reasons that stem either from the physical or psychological condition of the couple or from external circumstances" (HV 16).

6. In the case of a morally right regulation of fertility brought about by periodic continence, the point is clearly to *practice conjugal chastity*, that is, a certain ethical attitude. In biblical language, we would say that the point is to live by the Spirit (see Gal 5:25).

The morally right regulation is also called "*natural* regulation *of fertility*," which can be explained as conformity with the "natural law."

By "natural law" we understand here the "order of nature" in the field of procreation inasmuch as it is understood by right reason: this order is the expression of the Creator's plan for the human person. And it is exactly this that the encyclical, together with the whole tradition of Christian teaching and practice, particularly underlines: the virtuous character of the attitude expressing itself in the "natural" regulation of fertility is determined, *not so much* by faithfulness to an impersonal *"natural law," but to the personal Creator,* the source and Lord of the order that is shown in this law.

From this point of view, the reduction to mere biological regularity, detached from the "order of nature," that is, from the "Creator's plan," deforms the authentic thought of *Humanae Vitae* (see HV 14).

The document certainly presupposes that *biological regularity,* even more, it urges competent persons to study it and apply it in a more thorough way, but it always understands such regularity *as the expression of the "order of nature," that is, of the Creator's providential plan,* in the faithful realization of which consists the true good of the human person.

Ethical Regulation of Fertility: Person, Nature, and Method

125 *General Audience of September 5, 1984*
(Insegnamenti, 7, no. 2 [1984]: 320–23)

1. WE SPOKE EARLIER about the honorable regulation of fertility according to the teaching contained in *Humanae Vitae* (HV 9) and the exhortation *Familiaris Consortio.* The qualifier "natural," which is attributed to the morally right regulation of fertility (following "the natural rhythms," HV 16), is to be explained by the fact that the way of behaving in question corresponds to the truth of the person and thus to the person's dignity: a dignity that belongs "by nature" to man as a rational and free being. As a rational and free being, man can and should reread with insight the biological rhythm that belongs to the natural order. He can and should conform himself to it for the sake of exercising "responsible fatherhood and motherhood," which is inscribed according to the Creator's plan in the natural order of human fruitfulness. The concept of a morally right regulation of fer-

tility is nothing other than rereading the "language of the body" in the truth. The same "natural *rhythms* immanent in the generative functions" *belong to the objective truth of this language,* which the persons involved should reread in its full objective content. One should keep in mind that the "body speaks" not only with the whole outer expression of masculinity and femininity, but also with the inner structures of the organism, of somatic and psychosomatic reactivity. All this should find its fitting place in the language with which the spouses dialogue as persons called to communion in the "union of the body."

2. All efforts directed toward an ever more precise knowledge of the "natural rhythms" that become apparent in relation to human procreation, all consequent efforts of family counselors and finally of the couple themselves do not have the goal of "biologizing" the language of the body (of "biologizing ethics" [that is, of reducing ethics to biology], as some mistakenly hold), but only of *ensuring the integral truth* of the "language of the body" with which the couple should express themselves in a mature way, face to face with the requirements of responsible fatherhood and motherhood.

Humanae Vitae underlines several times that "responsible parenthood" is connected with a continual effort and commitment and that it can be realized only at the price of a precise ascesis (see HV 21). All these and similar expressions show that in the case of "responsible parenthood," or the morally right regulation of fertility, the question is, *What is the true good of human persons and what corresponds to the true dignity of the person?*

3. The use of "infertile periods" in conjugal shared life can become a source of abuses if the couple thereby attempt to evade procreation without just reasons, lowering it below the morally just level of births in their family. This just level needs to be set by taking into account not only the good of one's family and the state of one's health as well as the means of the spouses themselves, but also the good of the society to which they belong, the good of the Church, and even of humanity as a whole.

Humanae Vitae presents "responsible parenthood" as an expression of a high ethical value. *In no way* does it *aim one-sidedly* at limiting, even less at excluding, children; it means also the willingness to welcome a greater number of children. Above all, according to *Humanae*

Vitae, "responsible parenthood" brings about "a more profound relationship to the objective moral order established by God, of which a right conscience is a faithful interpreter" (HV 10).

4. The truth of responsible fatherhood and motherhood as well as its realization is linked with the moral maturity of the person, and it is here that a divergence can very often be seen between what the encyclical explicitly gives *primacy* to and what the common mentality gives it to.

The encyclical places the ethical dimension of the *problem* in the foreground, underlining the role of the *virtue of temperance rightly understood.* In the area of this dimension, there is also an adequate "method" of acting. In the common way of thinking, it often happens that the "method," detached from the ethical dimension proper to it, is applied in a merely functional and even utilitarian way. When one separates the "natural method" from the ethical dimension, one no longer sees the difference between it and the other "methods" (artificial means), and one ends up speaking about it as if it were just another form of contraception.

5. From the point of view of the authentic teaching expressed by *Humanae Vitae*, it is thus important to present the method itself correctly, and the same document alludes to this need (HV 16); it is above all important *to have a deep grasp of the ethical dimension*, in whose area the method, as a "natural" method, acquires its meaning as an honorable or "morally right" method. And thus, in the context of the present analysis, we should turn our attention mainly to what the encyclical says about the topic of self-mastery and *continence.* Without a penetrating interpretation of this topic, we will not reach the core of the moral truth nor the core of the anthropological truth of the problem. We pointed out earlier that the roots of this problem plunge into the theology of the body: it is this theology (provided it becomes a pedagogy of the body as it should) that in reality constitutes the morally honorable "method" of the regulation of births understood in the deepest and fullest sense.

6. When he goes on to characterize the specifically moral values of the "natural" (that is, honorable or morally right) regulation of births, the author of *Humanae Vitae* writes as follows: "Such discipline bestows upon family life fruits of serenity and peace, and facilitates

the solution of other problems; it favors attention to one's partner, helps the spouses to drive out selfishness, the enemy of true love; and deepens their sense of responsibility. By its means, parents acquire the capacity of having a deeper and more efficacious influence in the education of their offspring; little children and youths grow up with a just appraisal of human values, and in the serene and harmonious development of their spiritual and sensitive faculties" (HV 21).

7. The sentences quoted *complete the picture* of what *Humanae Vitae* means by "honorable practice of the regulation of births." This [honorable practice] is, as one can see, not only a "way of behaving" in a certain field, but an attitude that builds *on the integral moral maturity of the persons* and at the same time completes that maturity.

2. Outline of Conjugal Spirituality

The Power that Flows from Sacramental "Consecration"

126 *General Audience of October 3, 1984*
(Insegnamenti, 7, no. 2 [1984]: 728–31)

1. TAKING THE TEACHING contained in *Humanae Vitae* as a point of reference, we will try to outline further the spiritual life of the spouses.
Here are the encyclical's great words:

> The Church, while teaching inviolable demands of the divine law, announces the tidings of salvation, and by means of the sacraments flings wide open the channels of grace, which makes man a new creature, capable of corresponding with love and true freedom to the design of his Creator and Savior, and of finding the yoke of Christ to be sweet.
>
> Christian married couples, then, docile to [Christ's] voice, must remember that their Christian vocation, which began at Baptism, is further specified and reinforced by the sacrament of Marriage. *By it husband and wife are strengthened and as it were consecrated* for the faithful accomplishment of their proper duties, for the carrying out of their proper vocation even to perfection, and for the Christian witness which is proper to them before the whole world. To them the Lord entrusts the task of making visible to men the holiness and sweetness of the law which unites the mutual love of husband and wife with their cooperation with the love of God the author of human life. (HV 25)

2. By showing the moral evil of the contraceptive act and outlining at the same time as complete as possible a picture of the "honorable" practice of the regulation of fertility, or of responsible fatherhood and motherhood, *Humanae Vitae* creates the premises that allow us to trace the main lines of the *Christian spirituality of the conjugal life and vocation,* and likewise that *of parents and of the family.*

One can even say that the encyclical presupposes the whole tradition of this spirituality, which plunges its roots into the biblical sources analyzed earlier, thus offering us the occasion to reflect anew about these sources and to build an adequate synthesis.

One should recall here what was said about the organic relation between the theology of the body and the pedagogy of the body [see TOB 59:2–5]. Indeed, such a "theology-pedagogy" constitutes already by itself the essential core of conjugal spirituality. And this is indicated also by the sentences from the encyclical quoted above.

3. Certainly, one would reread and interpret *Humanae Vitae* in a mistaken way if one saw in it only the reduction of "responsible fatherhood and motherhood" to mere "biological rhythms of fertility." The author of the encyclical energetically disapproves of and contradicts every form of reductive (and thus "partial") interpretation and with insistence proposes the integral understanding. *Responsible fatherhood and motherhood understood integrally* are nothing other than an important *component of conjugal and familial spirituality as a whole,* that is, of the vocation that the text of *Humanae Vitae* quoted above speaks about when it affirms that the spouses should realize "their proper vocation even to perfection" (HV 25). It is the sacrament of Marriage that strengthens and, as it were, consecrates them to reach such perfection.

In the light of the teaching expressed in the encyclical, one should be more aware of the "strengthening power" that comes with the "consecration s*ui generis*" of the sacrament of Marriage.

Since the analysis of the ethical problematic of Paul VI's document focused above all on the correctness of the *norm that is involved,* the sketch of conjugal spirituality found there intends to highlight precisely these "powers," which allow the authentic Christian witness of conjugal life.

4. "We do not at all intend to hide the sometimes serious difficulties inherent in the life of Christian married persons; for them as for everyone else, 'the gate is narrow and *the way is hard that leads to life.*' But *the hope of that life* must illuminate their way, as with courage they strive to live with wisdom, justice, and piety in this present time, knowing that the figure of this world passes away" (HV 25).

The view of married life in the encyclical is marked at every step by Christian realism, and it is precisely this that offers greater help to reach the "powers" that allow the formation of the spirituality of spouses and parents in the spirit of an authentic pedagogy of the heart and body.

The very consciousness "of the future life" opens, *so to speak, a wide horizon of the powers* that must guide them along the difficult way (see HV 25) and lead them through the narrow gate of their evangelical vocation.

The encyclical says, "Let married couples, then, face up to the efforts needed, supported by faith and by the hope that 'does not disappoint...because God's love has been poured out in our hearts by the Holy Spirit, who has been given to us' (Rom 5:5)" (HV 25).

5. This, then, is the essential and fundamental "power": *the love planted in the heart* ("poured out in our hearts") *by the Holy Spirit.* The encyclical then goes on to point out how the spouses must implore [God] for such "power" and for every other "divine help" in prayer; how they must draw grace and love from the ever-living fountain of the Eucharist; how "with humble perseverance" they must overcome their own faults and sins in the sacrament of Penance.

These are the means—*infallible and indispensable*—to form the Christian spirituality of conjugal and familial life. With their help, that essential and *spiritually creative "power" of love* reaches human hearts and, at the same time, human bodies in their subjective masculinity and femininity. Indeed, this love allows the spouses to build up their whole life together *according to* the *"truth of the sign,"* by means of which marriage is built up in its sacramental dignity, as the central point of the encyclical shows (HV 12).

127 *General Audience of October 10, 1984*
(Insegnamenti, 7, no. 2 [1984]: 845–47)

1. WE ARE CONTINUING to outline the spirituality of married life in the light of *Humanae Vitae.*

According to the teaching contained in *Humanae Vitae*, in conformity with the biblical sources and the whole tradition, *love is a "power"*—from the subjective point of view—that is, it is a capacity of the human spirit *of a* "theological" (or rather "theologal" [that is, divine]) *character*. It is thus *the power given to the human person to participate* in the love with which God himself loves in the mystery of creation and redemption. It is the love that "rejoices in the truth" (1 Cor 13:6), that is, in which spiritual joy (the Augustinian "*frui*") about every authentic value is expressed: a joy similar to the joy of the Creator himself who saw in the beginning that everything "was very good" (Gen 1:31).

While *the powers of concupiscence* tend to *detach* the "language of the body" from the truth, that is, try to *falsify it, the power of love, by contrast, strengthens it* ever anew in that truth, so that the mystery of the redemption of the body can bear fruit in it.

2. The same love that makes possible and brings about conjugal dialogue according to the full truth of the life of the spouses *is at the same time a power or capacity of a moral character,* actively oriented toward the fullness of the good, and for this reason toward every true good. And thus its task consists in safeguarding the inseparable unity of the "two meanings of the conjugal act" that the encyclical deals with (see HV 12), that is, in protecting both the value of the true union of the spouses (namely, personal communion) and that of responsible fatherhood and motherhood (in the mature form that is worthy of man).

3. According to the traditional language, love, as a superior "power," coordinates the acts of the persons, of the husband and wife, *in the area of the ends of marriage.* Although, in approaching the issue, neither the conciliar constitution nor the encyclical use the language that was at one time customary, they nevertheless speak about that to which the traditional expressions refer.

As a higher power that man and woman receive from God together with the particular "consecration" of the sacrament of Marriage, love involves a right *coordination* of the ends according to which—in the Church's traditional teaching—*the moral* (or rather "theologal and moral") *order* of the life of the spouses *is constituted.*

The teaching of *Gaudium et Spes* as well as that of *Humanae Vitae* clarifies the same moral order in reference to love, understood as a superior power that gives *adequate content and value* to conjugal acts *according to the truth* of the two meanings, the unitive and the procreative, in reverence for their inseparability.

In this renewed orientation, the traditional teaching on the ends of marriage (and on their hierarchy) is confirmed and at the same time deepened from the point of view of the interior life of the spouses, of conjugal and familial spirituality.

Analysis of the Virtue of Continence

4. The task of love, which is "poured out in hearts" (Rom 5:5) as the fundamental spiritual power of their conjugal covenant, consists—as we said above—in protecting both the value of the true communion of the spouses and that of truly responsible fatherhood and motherhood. The power of love—of authentic love in the theological and ethical sense—expresses itself in this: that love *rightly unites "the two meanings of the conjugal act,"* excluding not only in theory, but above all in practice, the "contradiction" that could come about in this area. This "contradiction" is the most frequent reason for objecting to *Humanae Vitae* and the teaching of the Church. A truly thorough analysis, not only theological but also anthropological (we have attempted to provide it in the whole present reflection), is needed to show that one should *not* speak about "*contradiction*" here, *but only about "difficulty."* Now, the encyclical itself underlines this "difficulty" in various passages.

The difficulty derives from the fact that *the power of love is planted in man threatened by concupiscence*: in human subjects, love comes up against the threefold concupiscence (see 1 Jn 2:16), particularly against the concupiscence of the flesh, which deforms the truth of the "language of the body." And for this reason also love is not able to realize itself in the truth of the "language of the body" except through mastery over concupiscence.

5. If the key element of the spirituality of spouses and parents—the essential "power" that the spouses must continually draw from their sacramental "consecration"—is *love,* this love, as the text of the

encyclical makes clear (see HV 20), is by its nature *linked with chastity, which, in turn, manifests itself as self-mastery or continence*: in particular as periodic continence. In biblical language the author of Ephesians seems to allude to this when in his "classical" text he exhorts the spouses to "be subject to one another in the fear of Christ" (Eph 5:21).

One can say that *Humanae Vitae* constitutes precisely the development of this biblical truth about Christian conjugal and familial spirituality. To make this development clearer, however, what is needed is *a more thorough and in-depth analysis of continence* and of its particular meaning for the truth of the mutual "language of the body" in conjugal life and (indirectly) in the wide sphere of the reciprocal relations between man and woman.

We will take up this analysis during the next Wednesday reflections.

128 General Audience of October 24, 1984 (*Insegnamenti*, 7, no. 2 [1984]: 1013–17)

1. IN KEEPING WITH what we announced, today we are taking up the analysis of the virtue of continence. "Continence," which is part of the more general virtue of temperance, consists in the *ability to master, control, and orient the sexual drives* (concupiscence of the flesh) and their consequences in the psychosomatic subjectivity of human beings. As a constant disposition of the will, such an ability deserves to be called virtue.

We know from the earlier analyses that the concupiscence of the flesh—and the corresponding sexual "desire" aroused by it—expresses itself with a specific drive in the sphere of somatic reactivity and further with a psycho-emotive arousal of the sexual impulse.

In order to reach mastery over this drive and arousal, the personal subject must devote himself or herself to a progressive education in self-control of the will, of sentiments, of emotions, which must be developed from the simplest gestures, in which it is relatively easy to put the inner decision into practice. This education obviously presupposes the clear perception of the values expressed in the norm and the consequent maturation of firm convictions that give rise to the corresponding virtue, provided they are accompanied by the *corresponding disposition* of the will. This is precisely the virtue of continence (self-mastery), which reveals itself as the fundamental condition both for the reciprocal language of the body to remain in the truth and for the spouses to "be subject to one another in the fear of Christ," according to the words of the Bible (Eph 5:21). This "reciprocal submission" *signifies the shared concern for the truth of the "language of the body,"* while submission "in the fear of Christ" indicates the gift of the fear of God (a gift of the Holy Spirit), which accompanies the virtue of continence.

2. This is very important for an adequate understanding of the virtue of continence and, in particular, of so-called "periodic continence" discussed in *Humanae Vitae.* The conviction that *the virtue of continence* "opposes" the concupiscence of the flesh is correct, but it is not entirely complete. It is not complete, especially when we consider the fact that this virtue does not appear and act abstractly and thus in isolation, but always in connection with the other virtues (*"nexus virtutum"* [the link between the virtues]), and thus *in connection* with prudence, justice, fortitude, *and above all with love.*

In the light of these considerations, it is easy to understand that continence is not limited to offering resistance against the concupiscence of the flesh, but through this resistance *also opens itself to the deeper and more mature values* that are part of the spousal meaning of the body in its femininity and masculinity, as well as to the authentic freedom of the gift in the reciprocal relationship of persons. Inasmuch as it seeks first of all fleshly and sensual enjoyment, the concupiscence of the flesh makes man in some way blind and insensitive to the deeper values that spring from love and that, at the same time, constitute love in the inner truth proper to it.

3. In this way, the essential character of conjugal chastity also becomes clear in its organic link with the "power" of love, which is poured out in the hearts of the spouses together with the "consecration" of the sacrament of Marriage. It becomes evident, further, that the invitation addressed to the spouses to "be subject to one another in the fear of Christ" (Eph 5:21) seems to open up the interior room in which *both become ever more sensitive to the deeper and more mature values* connected with the spousal meaning of the body and the true freedom of the gift.

If conjugal chastity (and chastity in general) manifests itself at first as an ability to resist the concupiscence of the flesh, it subsequently reveals itself as a *singular ability* to perceive, love, and realize those meanings of the "language of the body" that remain completely unknown to concupiscence itself and progressively enrich the spousal dialogue of the couple by purifying, deepening, and at the same time simplifying it.

For this reason, the ascesis of continence, about which the encyclical speaks (see HV 21), *does not impoverish "affective manifestations"* but, on the contrary, it makes them spiritually more intense and thus *enriches* them.

4. When we analyze continence in this way, in the (anthropological, ethical, and theological) dynamics proper to this virtue, we realize that the apparent "contradiction"—often brought in as an objection against *Humanae Vitae* and against the Church's teaching about conjugal morality—disappears. That is, according to those who raise this objection, there would be a "contradiction" between the two meanings of the conjugal act, the unitive and the procreative meaning (see HV 12), such that, if it were not licit to separate them, the spouses would be deprived of the right to conjugal union when they cannot responsibly allow themselves to procreate.

To this apparent "contradiction," *the encyclical* Humanae Vitae *offers an answer,* if one studies it in depth. Indeed, Pope Paul VI confirms that there is no such "contradiction," but only a "difficulty" linked with the whole inner situation of the "man of concupiscence." Precisely by reason of this "difficulty," *the true order of conjugal life,* with a view to which the spouses are "strengthened and as it were consecrated" (HV 25) by the sacrament of Marriage, *is assigned to their interior and ascetical commitment.*

5. This order of conjugal life signifies, further, the subjective harmony between (responsible) parenthood and personal communion, a harmony created by conjugal chastity. It is, indeed, in this harmony that the inner fruits of continence mature. Through this inner maturation, *the conjugal act itself* acquires the importance and dignity proper to it in its potentially procreative meaning; at the same time, an adequate meaning is given to *all the "affective manifestations"* (HV 21)

that serve to express the personal communion of the spouses in proportion to the subjective richness of femininity and masculinity.

6. In keeping with experience and the tradition, the encyclical points out that the conjugal act is *also* a "manifestation of affection" (HV 16), but a *particular "manifestation of affection,"* because, *at the same time,* it has a potentially procreative meaning. Consequently, it is oriented toward expressing personal union, but *not only* union. At the same time, although only indirectly, the encyclical points out many "manifestations of affection" that are *exclusively* an expression of the personal union of the spouses.

The task of conjugal chastity, and still more specifically of continence, lies *not only* in protecting the importance and the dignity of the conjugal act in relation to its potentially procreative meaning, *but also* in safeguarding the importance and dignity proper to the conjugal act inasmuch as it expresses interpersonal union, by revealing to the consciousness and experience of the spouses all the other possible "manifestations of affection" that are to express their deep communion.

It is indeed a question of *not doing harm to the communion of the spouses* when they should abstain from the conjugal act for right reasons. Still more, it is a question of this communion, which is continually built up day by day through suitable "affective manifestations," constituting, so to speak, *a vast terrain* on which, under suitable conditions, the decision for a morally right conjugal act matures.

129 *General Audience of October 31, 1984* (*Insegnamenti,* 7, no. 2 [1984]: 1069–72)

1. WE ARE CONTINUING the analysis of continence in the light of the teaching contained in *Humanae Vitae.*

It is often thought that continence causes inner tensions from which men and women should free themselves. In the light of the analyses offered earlier, continence, integrally understood, is, on the contrary, the one and only *way to free oneself from such tensions.* Continence means nothing other than the spiritual effort aimed at expressing the "language of the body" not only in the truth, but also in the authentic richness of the "manifestations of affection."

Continence between "Arousal" and "Emotion"

2. *Is this effort possible?* What returns here with other words (and under another aspect) is the question of the "feasibility of the moral norm" recalled and confirmed by *Humanae Vitae*. It is one of the most essential (and right now also one of the most urgent) questions in the area of conjugal spirituality.

The Church is fully convinced of the correctness of the principle affirming responsible fatherhood and motherhood—in the sense explained in previous catecheses—not only on "demographic" grounds, but for more essential reasons. *Responsible is what we call the fatherhood and motherhood that corresponds to the personal dignity of the spouses* as parents, to the *truth* of their person, and of their conjugal *act.* From here stems the strict and direct relationship that links this dimension with the whole conjugal spirituality of marriage.

In *Humanae Vitae,* Paul VI expressed what many authoritative moralists and scientists, including non-Catholics,[100] affirmed elsewhere, namely, precisely that in this field, which is so deeply and essentially human and personal, one must before all else look toward the human being as a person, toward the subject who decides about himself or herself, and not toward the "means" that turn him into an "object" (of manipulations) and "depersonalize" him. What is at stake here is an authentically "humanistic" meaning of the development and progress of human civilization.

3. Is this effort possible? The whole *problematic of the encyclical Humanae Vitae* is not simply reducible to the biological dimension of human fertility (to the question of the "natural rhythms of fertility") *but goes back to the very subjectivity* of the human person, to that personal "I" through which the person is man or woman.

Already *during the discussions at Vatican II* about the chapter of *Gaudium et Spes* on "The Dignity of Marriage and its Promotion," participants spoke about the necessity of *a more thorough and deep*

---

100. See, for example, the declarations of the "Bund für evangelischkatholische Wiedervereinigung," *L'Osservatore Romano* (September 19, 1968): 3, of the Anglican Dr. F. King, *L'Osservatore Romano* (October 5, 1968), and also of the Muslim Mohammed Chérif Zeghoudu (in the same number). Particularly significant is the letter written on November 28, 1968, by Karl Barth to Cardinal Cicognani, in which he praises the great courage of Paul VI.

analysis of the reactions (and also emotions) *connected with the reciprocal influence of masculinity and femininity* on the human subject.[101] This problem belongs not so much to biology, but to psychology: from biology and psychology, it then passes into the sphere of conjugal and family spirituality. In that sphere, indeed, it stands in close connection with how one understands the virtue of continence, that is, of self-mastery and, in particular, of periodic continence.

4. An attentive analysis of human psychology (which is at the same time a subjective self-analysis and then becomes an analysis of an "object" accessible to human science) allows one to reach some essential points. In fact, in interpersonal relations in which the reciprocal influence of masculinity and femininity expresses itself, what is set free *in the psycho-emotive subject,* in the human "I," is not only *a reaction* that can be qualified as "arousal," but also another reaction that can and should be called *"emotion."* Although these two kinds of reactions seem connected, it is possible to distinguish them by experience and to "differentiate" them by their contents or their "object."[102]

The objective difference between one and the other kind of reaction consists in the fact that *arousal* is first of all "bodily" and in this sense *"sexual"*; by contrast, emotion—though it is stirred by the reciprocal reaction of masculinity and femininity—refers above all to the other person understood in his or her "wholeness." One can say that this is an *"emotion caused by the person"* in relation to his or her masculinity or femininity.

5. What we are saying here about the psychology of the reciprocal reactions of masculinity and femininity helps us to understand the function of the virtue of continence, about which we spoke earlier. Continence is not only—nor even mainly—*the ability to "abstain,"* that is, mastery over the many reactions woven together in the reciprocal influence of masculinity and femininity: this sort of function can be defined as "negative." But there exists also another function of self-mastery (which we can call "positive"): and it is *the ability to orient* the respective *reactions* both as to their content and as to their character.

---

101. See interventions of Cardinal Leo Suenens at the General Congregation 138, (September 29, 1965); *Acta Synodalia S. Concilii Oecumenici Vaticani II,* vol. 4, pt. 3, p. 30.

102. In this context one could recall what St. Thomas says in an acute analysis of human love in relation to the "concupiscible" and the will: ST Ia–IIae, q. 26, a. 2.

It has already been said that, in the field of the reciprocal reactions of masculinity and femininity, "arousal" and "emotion" appear not only as two distinct and different experiences of the human "I," but they also often appear together within the same experience as two of its distinct components. The reciprocal proportion in which these two components appear in one determinate experience depends on various circumstances both of an internal and an external nature. At times, one of the components definitely has the upper hand; at other times, there is rather an equilibrium between them.

6. As the ability to orient "arousal" and "emotion" in the sphere of the reciprocal influence of masculinity and femininity, continence *has the essential task of maintaining the equilibrium* between the communion in which the spouses want to express reciprocally only their intimate union and the communion in which they (at least implicitly) welcome responsible parenthood. In fact, "arousal" and "emotion" can jeopardize, on the part of the subject, the orientation and character of the reciprocal "language of the body."

Arousal seeks first of all to express itself in the form of sensual and bodily pleasure, that is, it tends *toward the conjugal act*, which (depending on the "natural rhythms of fertility") brings with it the possibility of procreation. By contrast, *emotion* called forth by another human being as a person, even if it is conditioned in its emotive content by the femininity or masculinity of the "other," does not through itself tend to the conjugal act, but *limits itself* to other "*manifestations of affection*," in which the spousal meaning of the body expresses itself and which nevertheless do not include its (potentially) procreative meaning.

It is easy to understand what consequences arise from this with respect to the problem of responsible fatherhood and motherhood. These consequences are of a moral nature.

130 General Audience of November 7, 1984
(Insegnamenti, 7, no. 2 [1984]: 1173–75)

1. WE ARE CONTINUING the analysis of the virtue of continence in light of the teaching contained in *Humanae Vitae*.

One should recall that the great classics of ethical (and anthropological) thought, both pre-Christian and Christian (Thomas

Aquinas), see in the virtue of continence not only the ability to "contain" bodily and sensual reactions, but even more the ability to control and guide the whole sensual and emotive sphere of the human person. In the case under discussion, it is a question of the *ability both to direct the line of arousal* toward its correct development, *and also* to direct the line *of emotion* by orienting it toward the deepening and inner intensification of its "pure" and, in a certain sense, "disinterested" character.

2. This differentiation between the line of arousal and the line of emotion is not an antithesis. It does not mean that the conjugal act, as an effect of arousal, does not imply at the same time a deep emotional stirring of the other person. This is certainly how it is; or at any rate, *it ought not to be otherwise.*

In the conjugal act, the intimate union should bring with itself a particular intensification of emotion, even more, the deep emotional stirring, of the other person. This is also contained in Ephesians under the form of the exhortation addressed to the spouses: "Be subject to one another in the fear of Christ" (Eph 5:21).

The distinction between "arousal" and "emotion" revealed in this analysis only proves *the subjective reactive-emotive richness* of the human "I"; this richness excludes any one-sided reduction and allows the virtue of continence to be realized as an ability to direct the manifestation of both arousal and emotion stirred by the reciprocal reactivity of masculinity and femininity.

3. The virtue of continence, so understood, plays an essential role in maintaining the inner equilibrium between the two meanings, the unitive and the procreative (see HV 12), in view of truly responsible fatherhood and motherhood.

Humanae Vitae gives due attention to the biological aspect of the problem, that is to say, to the periodic character of human fertility. Although, in the light of the encyclical, this "*periodicity*" can be called a *providential pointer* for responsible fatherhood and motherhood, it is nevertheless *not on this level alone* that a *problem* like this, which has such a deeply personalistic and sacramental (theological) meaning, *can be resolved.*

The encyclical teaches responsible fatherhood and motherhood "as the verification of a mature conjugal love," and thus it contains not only the response to the concrete question raised in the area of the ethics of conjugal life, but, as has been said already, it also indicates a sketch of conjugal spirituality that we want at least to outline.

4. The right way of *understanding and practicing periodic continence as a virtue* (that is, according to HV 21, "self-mastery") is also essentially decisive for the "naturalness" of the method also called "natural method": this is "naturalness" on the level of the person. One cannot, therefore, think of it as a mechanical application of biological laws. By itself, knowledge of the "rhythms of fertility"—though indispensable—does not yet create that interior freedom of the gift that is explicitly spiritual in nature and depends on the maturity of the inner man. This freedom presupposes that one is able to direct sensual and emotive reactions in order to allow the *gift* of self to the other "I" *on the basis of the* mature *possession* of one's own "I" in its bodily and emotive subjectivity.

5. As we know from the biblical and theological analyses carried out earlier, the human body in its masculinity and femininity is oriented from within to the communion of persons ("*communio personarum*"). In this consists its spousal meaning.

Precisely the spousal meaning of the body has been deformed almost at its very roots by concupiscence (in particular by the concupiscence of the flesh in the sphere of the "threefold concupiscence"). In its mature form, the virtue of continence gradually reveals the "pure" aspect of the spousal meaning of the body. In this way, continence develops *the personal communion* of man and woman, a communion that *cannot be formed* and developed in the full truth of its possibilities *on the ground of concupiscence alone*. This is precisely what *Humanae Vitae* affirms. This truth has two aspects: the personalistic and the theological.

The Gift of Reverence

131 General Audience of November 14, 1984
(*Insegnamenti*, 7, no. 2 [1984]: 1208–11)

1. In the light of the encyclical *Humanae Vitae*, the fundamental element of conjugal spirituality is the love poured out in the hearts of

the spouses as a gift of the Holy Spirit (see Rom 5:5). In the sacrament, the spouses receive this gift together with a particular "consecration." Love is united with conjugal chastity, which, manifesting itself as continence, realizes the inner order of conjugal life together.

Chastity means living in the order of the heart. This order allows the development of the "affective manifestations" to the extent and in the meaning proper to them. In this way, *conjugal chastity* is also confirmed *as "life by the Spirit"* (see Gal 5:25), according to St. Paul's expression. What the Apostle had in mind is not only the energies within the human spirit, but above all the sanctifying influence of the Holy Spirit and his particular gifts.

2. At the center of conjugal spirituality, therefore, stands chastity, not only as a moral virtue (formed by love), but equally as a virtue connected with the gifts of the Holy Spirit—*above all with the gift of reverence for what comes from God ("donum pietatis").* This gift is what the author of Ephesians has in mind when he exhorts the spouses to "be subject to one another in the fear of Christ" (Eph 5:21). Thus, the inner order of conjugal life, which allows the "affective manifestations" to develop according to their right extent and meaning, is a fruit not only *of the virtue* in which the spouses *exercise themselves,* but also *of the gifts* of the Holy Spirit *with which they collaborate.*

In some passages (especially HV 21 and 26), when it discusses specifically conjugal ascesis or the commitment to acquire the virtues of love, of chastity, and of continence, *Humanae Vitae* speaks indirectly about the gifts of the Holy Spirit, to which the spouses become sensitive as they mature in virtue.

3. This corresponds to the vocation of the human person to marriage. These "two," who—according to the most ancient expression of the Bible—"will be one flesh" (Gen 2:24), cannot realize such a union on the level of persons (*communio personarum*) *except through the powers that come from the spirit,* and precisely *from the Holy Spirit,* who purifies, enlivens, strengthens, and perfects the powers of the human spirit. "It is the Spirit that gives life; the flesh is useless" (Jn 6:63).

It follows from this that the essential lines of conjugal spirituality are "from the beginning" inscribed in the biblical truth about marriage. This spirituality is also "from the beginning" *open to the gifts of the Holy Spirit.* If *Humanae Vitae* exhorts the spouses to "persevering prayer" and sacramental life (saying, "let them draw from the source of grace and love in the Eucharist"; "let them...have recourse with humble perseverance to the mercy of God, which is poured forth in the sacrament of Penance," HV 25), it does so inasmuch as it is mindful of the Spirit who "gives life" (2 Cor 3:6).

4. The gifts of the Holy Spirit, and in particular the gift of reverence for what is sacred, seem to have a fundamental meaning here. This gift sustains and develops in the spouses a singular *sensibility for all* that in their vocation and shared life carries *the sign of the mystery of creation and redemption*: for all that is a created reflection of God's wisdom and love. For this reason, this gift seems to initiate man and woman particularly deeply into reverence for the two inseparable meanings of the conjugal act, which the encyclical speaks about (see HV 12) in relation to the sacrament of Marriage. Reverence for the two meanings of the conjugal act can fully develop only on the basis of a deep orientation to the *personal dignity* of what is intrinsic to *masculinity and femininity* in the human person, and inseparably in reference to the *personal dignity of the new life* that can spring *from* the conjugal *union* of man and woman. The gift of reverence for what has been created by God expresses itself precisely in such an orientation.

5. Reverence for the twofold meaning of the conjugal act in marriage, which is born from the gift of reverence for God's creation, manifests itself also as a salvific fear: as the fear of violating or degrading what bears in itself the sign of the divine mystery of creation and redemption. It is this fear that the author of Ephesians speaks about. "Be subject to one another in the fear of Christ" (Eph 5:21).

While such *salvific fear* is immediately associated with the "negative" function of continence (that is, with resistance against concupiscence of the flesh), it also manifests itself—and in increasing measure as this virtue gradually matures—as a sensibility full of veneration for *the essential values of conjugal union*: for the "two meanings of the conjugal act" (or, speaking in the language of earlier analyses, for the inner truth of the mutual "language of the body").

Based on a profound orientation to these two essential values, the meaning of the *union* of spouses is harmonized in the subject with the meaning of responsible *fatherhood and motherhood*. The gift of reverence for what God has created makes the apparent "contradiction" in this sphere disappear and gradually overcomes the difficulty stemming from concupiscence, thanks to the maturity of the virtue and the power of the gift of the Holy Spirit.

6. If the issue is the problematic of so-called periodic continence (or the recourse to "natural methods"), the gift of reverence for the work of God helps at the deep level of principle to reconcile human dignity with the *"natural rhythms of fertility,"* that is, with the biological dimension of the femininity and masculinity of the spouses, a dimension that also has its own meaning for the truth of the mutual "language of the body" in conjugal life.

In this way, also what is oriented—not so much in the biblical sense, but directly in the "biological" sense—to "conjugal union of the body" finds its humanly mature form thanks to life "according to the Spirit."

The whole *practice of the honorable regulation of fertility,* which is so strictly tied to responsible fatherhood and motherhood, *is part of* Christian *conjugal and family spirituality;* and only if one lives "according to the Spirit" does it become interiorly true and authentic.

132 *General Audience of November 21, 1984*
 (Insegnamenti, 7, no. 2 [1984]: 1257–59)

1. ON THE BACKGROUND of the teaching of *Humanae Vitae,* we intend to trace an outline of conjugal spirituality. In the spiritual life of the spouses, also the gifts of the Holy Spirit are at work and, in particular, the *"donum pietatis,"* that is, the gift of reverence for that which is God's work.

2. This gift, united with love and chastity, helps one *to identify,* in the whole of conjugal shared life, *the act* in which, at least potentially, the spousal meaning of the body is linked with the procreative meaning. It guides one to understand, among the possible "manifestations of affection," the singular and even exceptional meaning of that act: its dignity and the consequent grave responsibility connected with it. Therefore, the antithesis of conjugal spirituality is constituted in some sense by the subjective lack of such understanding, connected with anti-conceptive practices and mentality. In addition to everything else, this is an enormous harm from the point of view of the inner

culture of the human person. The virtue of conjugal chastity, and even more so the gift of reverence for that which comes from God, shapes the spirituality of the spouses *for the sake of protecting the particular dignity of this act,* of this "manifestation of affection," in which the truth of the "language of the body" can be expressed only by safeguarding the procreative potential.

Responsible fatherhood and motherhood imply the spiritual appreciation—in conformity with the truth—of the conjugal act in the consciousness and the will of both spouses, who, after considering the inner and outer circumstances, in particular the biological ones, express in this "manifestation of affection" their mature readiness for fatherhood and motherhood.

3. Reverence for the work of God contributes to ensuring that the conjugal act is not diminished and deprived of interiority in the whole of conjugal life—*that it does not become "habitual"*—and that there be expressed in it an appropriate fullness of personal and ethical contents, as well as religious contents, that is, veneration for the majesty of the Creator, the only and ultimate depository of the source of life, and for the spousal love of the Redeemer. All of this creates and enlarges, so to speak, the interior space of the mutual freedom of the gift, in which the spousal meaning of masculinity and femininity is fully manifested.

The obstacle against this freedom lies in the inner *constraint of concupiscence* directed toward the other "I" as an object of enjoyment. Reverence for what God has created frees one from this constraint, frees one from all that reduces the other "I" to a simple object: it strengthens the interior freedom of the gift.

4. This can be realized only through a deep *understanding of the personal dignity* of both the feminine and the masculine "I" in reciprocal shared life. This spiritual understanding is the fundamental fruit of the gift of the Spirit that impels the person to reverence for the work of God. It is from this understanding, and thus indirectly from this gift, that all the "affective manifestations" that form the fabric of the stability of conjugal union draw true spousal meaning. This union is expressed through the conjugal act only in some circumstances, but it can and should be manifested continually, every day, through the various "affective manifestations" that are shaped by the power of a

"disinterested" emotion of the "I" in relation to femininity and—reciprocally—in relation to masculinity.

The attitude of *reverence for the work of God*, which the Spirit stirs up in the spouses, has an enormous *significance* for those "affective manifestations," because it goes hand in hand with the capacity for profound pleasure in, admiration for, disinterested attention to the "visible" and at the same time "invisible" beauty of femininity and masculinity, and finally a profound appreciation for the disinterested gift of the "other."

5. All of this is decisive for the spiritual identification of what is male and female, of what is "bodily" and at the same time personal. From this spiritual *identification* emerges *the awareness of union "through the body"* under the guidance of the interior freedom of the gift. Through "affective manifestations," the spouses help each other to remain within the union, and at the same time these "manifestations" protect in each of them that "deep-rooted peace" [see TOB 13:1; 27:4; 110:2], which is in some way the inner resonance of chastity guided by the gift of reverence for what God has created.

This gift brings with it a deep and all-encompassing *attention to the person* in his or her masculinity or femininity, thus creating the interior climate suitable for personal communion. Only in such a climate of personal communion between spouses can the procreation that we qualify as "responsible" mature in the right way.

6. *Humanae Vitae* allows us to draw an outline of conjugal spirituality. This is the human and supernatural climate in which—bearing in mind the "biological" order and, at the same time, on the basis of chastity, sustained by the "*donum pietatis*"—the *inner harmony of marriage* is formed with respect to what the encyclical calls "the twofold meaning of the conjugal act" (HV 12). This harmony means that the spouses live together in the inner truth of the "language of the body." *Humanae Vitae* proclaims the inseparability of the connection between this "truth" and love.

[Conclusion]*

∞

133 General Audience of November 28, 1984
(Insegnamenti, 7, no. 2 [1984]: 1316–20)

1. THE WHOLE OF THE CATECHESES that I began more than four years ago and that I conclude today can be grasped under the title, "Human Love in the Divine Plan," or with greater precision, "The Redemption of the Body and the Sacramentality of Marriage." They are divided into two parts.

The first part is devoted to the *analysis of the words of Christ,* which prove to be suitable for opening the present topic. We analyzed these words at length in the wholeness of the Gospel text: and in the course of a reflection lasting several years, it seemed right to throw into relief the three texts analyzed in the first part of the catecheses.

There is first of all the text in which Christ appeals "to the beginning" in the dialogue with the Pharisees about the unity and indissolubility of marriage (see Mt 19:8; Mk 10:6–9). Continuing on, there are the words Christ spoke in the Sermon on the Mount about "concupiscence" as "adultery committed in the heart" (see Mt 5:28). Finally, there are the words transmitted by all the Synoptics in which Christ appeals to the resurrection of the body in the "other world" (see Mt 22:30; Mk 12:25; Lk 20:35–36).

The second part of the catechesis is devoted to the *analysis of the sacrament* based on Ephesians (Eph 5:22–33), which goes back to the biblical "beginning" of marriage expressed in the words of Genesis, "a

---

* Translator's note: This heading has been inserted. TOB 133 is not found in the original book manuscript.

man will leave his father and his mother and unite with his wife, and the two will be one flesh" (Gen 2:24).

The catecheses of the first and the second part repeatedly use the term "*theology of the body.*" This is in some sense a "working" term. The introduction of the term and concept of "theology of the body" was necessary to set the topic "The Redemption of the Body and the Sacramentality of Marriage" on a wider basis. One must immediately observe, in fact, that the term "theology of the body" goes far beyond the content of the reflections presented here. These reflections do not include many problems belonging, with regard to their object, to the theology of the body (e.g., the problem of suffering and death, so important in the biblical message). One must say this clearly. Nevertheless, one must also recognize explicitly that the reflections on the topic "The Redemption of the Body and the Sacramentality of Marriage" can be correctly developed by taking as one's point of departure the moment in which the light of revelation touches the reality of the human body (that is, on the basis of the "theology of the body"). This is confirmed, among others, by the words of Genesis "the two will be one flesh," words that stand originally and thematically at the basis of our argument.

2. The reflections about the sacrament of Marriage were carried out in the consideration of the *two dimensions* essential to this *sacrament* (as to every other sacrament), namely, the dimension of covenant and grace and the dimension of the sign.

Through these two dimensions, we continually went back to the reflections on the theology of the body that were linked with the key words of Christ. We went back to these reflections also by carrying out, at the end of this whole cycle of catecheses, the analysis of *Humanae Vitae.*

The doctrine contained in this document of the Church's contemporary teaching remains in organic relation both with the sacramentality of marriage and the whole biblical problematic of the theology of the body, which is centered on the "key words" of Christ. In some sense, one can even say that all the reflections dealing with the "Redemption of the Body and the Sacramentality of Marriage" *seem* to constitute *an extensive commentary* on the doctrine contained precisely in *Humanae Vitae.*

Such a commentary seems very necessary. In giving an answer to some questions of today in the sphere of conjugal and family morality, the encyclical, in fact, also raised other questions, as we know, of a bio-medical nature. However, *the questions are* also (and first of all) *of a theological nature*; they belong to the sphere of anthropology and theology that we have called "theology of the body."

The reflections carried out consist in facing the questions raised about *Humanae Vitae*. The reaction the encyclical stirred up confirms the importance and difficulty of these questions. They are reaffirmed also by the further statements of Paul VI, where he emphasized the possibility of deepening the explanation of the Christian truth in this area.

The exhortation *Familiaris Consortio*, fruit of the 1980 Synod of Bishops "*De muneribus familiae christianae*, The Role [or Duties, Gifts, Tasks] of the Christian Family," confirms this. The document contains an appeal addressed particularly to theologians, to work out more completely *the biblical and personalistic aspects of the doctrine* contained in *Humanae Vitae*.

To take up the questions raised by the encyclical means to formulate them and at the same time to seek an answer to them. The teaching contained in *Familiaris Consortio* asks that both the formulation of the questions and the search for an appropriate answer concentrate on the biblical and personalistic aspects. This teaching also indicates the course of the development of the theology of the body, and thus also the direction of its progressive completion and deepening.

3. The analysis of the *biblical aspects* speaks about the way of rooting the teaching proclaimed by the Church in revelation. This is important *for the development of theology*. Development or progress in theology takes place, in fact, through continually taking up again the study of the deposit of revelation.

The rooting of the teaching proclaimed by the Church in the whole tradition and in divine revelation itself is always open to the questions raised by people and also uses the instruments most in keeping with modern science and today's culture. It seems that in this area the intense development of philosophical anthropology (in particular the anthropology that stands at the basis of ethics) *meets very closely with the questions* raised by *Humanae Vitae* regarding theology and especially theological ethics.

The analysis of the *personalistic aspects* contained in this document has an existential meaning for establishing what *true progress* consists in, that is, the development *of the human person*. In contemporary civilization as a whole—especially in Western civilization—there exists, in fact, a hidden and at the same time rather explicit tendency to measure this progress with the measure of "things," that is, of material goods.

The analysis of the personalistic aspects of the Church's teaching contained in Paul VI's encyclical highlights a resolute appeal to measure man's progress with the measure of the "person," that is, of that which is a good of man as man, which corresponds to his essential dignity.

The analysis of the *personalistic aspects* leads to the conviction that *the fundamental problem* the encyclical presents is the viewpoint of the *authentic development of the human person*; such development should be measured, as a matter of principle, by the measure of ethics and not only of "technology."

4. The catecheses devoted to *Humanae Vitae* constitute only one part, the final part, of those that dealt with the redemption of the body and the sacramentality of marriage.

If I draw particular attention precisely to these final catecheses, I do so not only because the topic discussed by them is more closely connected with our present age, but first of all because *it is from this topic that the questions spring* that run in some way through the whole of our reflections. It follows that this final part is not artificially added to the whole, but is organically and homogeneously united with it. In some sense, that part, which in the overall disposition is located at the end, is at the same time found at the beginning of that whole. This is important from the point of view of structure and method.

Also the historical moment seems to have its significance: in fact, the present catecheses were begun in the period of preparations for the *1980 Synod of Bishops* on the topic of marriage and the family ("*De muneribus familiae christianae*"), and they end after the publication of the exhortation *Familiaris Consortio*, which is the fruit of the work of this synod. As everyone knows, the 1980 Synod also referred to *Humanae Vitae* and fully reconfirmed its teaching.

Still, the most important aspect seems to be the essential aspect that, in the whole of the reflections carried out, one can specify as follows: to face the questions raised by *Humanae Vitae* above all in theology, to formulate these questions, and to look for an answer to them, one must find *that biblical, theological sphere* to which we allude when we speak about the "redemption of the body and the sacramentality of marriage." It is in this sphere that one finds the answers to the perennial questions in the conscience of men and women and also to the difficult questions of our contemporary world concerning marriage and procreation.

Bibliography

1. Recommended Studies

Asci, Donald. *The Conjugal Act as Personal Act: A Study of the Catholic Concept of the Conjugal Act in the Light of Christian Anthropology*. San Francisco: Ignatius, 2002.

Ciccone, Lino. *Uomo—Donna: L'amore umano nel piano divino: La grande Catechesi del mercoledì di Giovanni Paolo II*. Turin: Elle Di Ci, 1986.

George, Francis Cardinal, OMI. "Education in Love: The Interior Culture of the Person." *Anthropotes* 14 (1998): 179–83.

Hogan, Richard M., and John M. LeVoir. *Covenant of Love: Pope John Paul II on Sexuality, Marriage, and Family in the Modern World*. Garden City: Doubleday, 1985.

Ide, Pascal. "Le don du corps: Une lecture des catéchèses de Jean-Paul II sur le corps humain." Unpublished commentary on *Man and Woman He Created Them*, 1992.

————. "Une théologie du don: Les occurrences de *Gaudium et spes*, n. 24, §3 chez Jean-Paul II." *Anthropotes* 17 (2001): 149–78, 313–44.

————. "Don et théologie du corps dans les catéchèses sur l'amour dans le plan divin." In *Jean-Paul II face a la question de l'homme: Actes du 6ème Colloque International de la Fondation Guilé*, edited by Yves Semen, 159–212. Boncourt: Guilé Foundation Press, 2004.

Lio, Ermenegildo. *Humanae vitae e coscienza: L'insegnamento del Card. Wojtyła teologo e Papa*. Rome: Libreria Editrice Vaticana, 1980.

————. *Humanae vitae e infallibilità: Paolo VI, il Concilio e Giovanni Paolo II*. Rome: Libreria Editrice Vaticana, 1986.

Mattheeuws, Alain. "De la Bible à *Humanae Vitae*: Les catéchèses de Jean-Paul II." *Nouvelle Revue Théologique* 111 (1989): 228–48.

————. *Les "dons" du mariage : Recherche de théologie morale et sacramentelle*. Bruxelles: Culture et Vérité, 1996.

McAleer, Graham J. *Ecstatic Morality and Sexual Politics: A Catholic and Antitotalitarian Theory of the Body*. New York: Fordham University, 2005.

Schindler, David L. "The 'Nuptial-Sacramental' Body and the Significance of World and Culture for Moral Theology." *Anthropotes* 21 (2005) 35–55.

Schmitz, Kenneth L. *At the Center of the Human Drama: The Philosophical Anthropology of Karol Wojtyła/Pope John Paul II.* Washington, DC: Catholic University of America Press, 1993.

Schwaderlapp, Dominik. *Erfüllung durch Hingabe: Die Ehe in ihrer personalistischen, sakramentalen und ethischen Dimension nach Lehre und Verkündigung Karol Wojtyłas / Johannes Pauls II.* St. Ottilien: Eos, 2002.

Scola, Angelo. *The Nuptial Mystery.* Grand Rapids MI: Eerdmans, 2005.

———. *L'esperienza elementare: La vena profonda del magistero di Giovanni Paolo II.* Genoa: Marietta, 2003.

Shivanandan, Mary. *Crossing the Threshold of Love: A New Vision of Marriage in the Light of John Paul II's Anthropology.* Washington, DC: Catholic University of America Press, 1999.

Styczen, Tadeusz. *Comprendere l'uomo: La visione antropologica di Karol Wojtyła.* Rome: Lateran University Press, 2005.

Waldstein, Michael. "John Paul II and St. Thomas on Love and the Trinity." *Anthropotes* 18 (2002), 113–38, 269–86.

West, Christopher. *Theology of the Body Explained: A Commentary on John Paul II's "Gospel of the Body."* Boston: Pauline Books & Media, 2003.

2. Study Guides and Presentations

Goraieb, Charles. *El Plan de Dios para el Amor Conyugal: La Teologia del Cuerpo de Juan Pablo II.* Two-DVD set. Our Father's Will Communications, 2005.

Hajduk, David. *God's Plan for You: Life, Love, Marriage, and Sex.* Boston: Pauline Books & Media, 2006.

Healy, Mary. *Men and Women Are from Eden: A Study Guide to John Paul II's Theology of the Body.* Cincinnati, OH: Servant Books, 2005.

Kellmeyer, Steven. *Sex and the Sacred City: Meditations on the Theology of the Body.* Peoria, IL: Bridegroom Press, 2003.

Loya, Thomas. *Theology of the Body Teacher Training.* Three-DVD set. Our Father's Will Communications, 2005.

———. *The Theology of the Body and Art: The Naked Truth.* DVD. Our Father's Will Communications, 2005.

Northrop, Anastasia. *The Freedom of the Gift: A Study Guide for John Paul II's Theology of the Body.* Three volumes. Cheyenne, WY: Resurrection Publications, 2004, 2005.

Percy, Anthony. *Theology of the Body Made Simple.* Boston: Pauline Books & Media, 2006.

Torode, Sam. *Pope John Paul II's Theology of the Body in Simple Language: Book 1: Body and Gift: Reflections on Creation.* West Chester, PA: Ascension Press, 2005.

———. *Pope John Paul II's Theology of the Body in Simple Language: Book 2: Purity of Heart: Reflections on Love and Lust.* West Chester, PA: Ascension Press, 2005.

Walsh, Vincent M. *Pope John Paul II: The Theology of the Body: A Simplified Version.* Wynnewood, PA: Key of David Publications, 2002.

West, Christopher. *Theology of the Body for Beginners: A Basic Introduction to John Paul II's Sexual Revolution.* Wynnewood, PA: Ascension Press, 2004.

————. *Good News About Sex & Marriage: Honest Answers to Your Questions about Catholic Teaching*. Cincinnati, OH: Servant Books, 2000.

————. *A Crash Course in the Theology of the Body*. Twelve-part CD series with study guide. Dundee, IL: The Gift Foundation.

————. *Created and Redeemed: A Faith Formation Program Based on Pope John Paul II's Theology of the Body*. Eight-part DVD or CD series with study guide. West Chester, PA: Ascension Press, 2004.

————. *God, Sex, and the Meaning of Life: An Introduction to Pope John Paul II's Theology of the Body*. CD, cassette. West Chester, PA: Ascension Press, 2004.

————. *God's Plan for a Joy Filled Marriage: A Marriage Preparation Supplement*. Six-part DVD or CD series with couples' workbooks and leader's guide. West Chester, PA: Ascension Press.

————. *Introduction to the Theology of the Body*. DVD, CD, cassette, study guide. West Chester, PA: Ascension Press, 2004.

————. *And the Two Became One*. Audio CD. West Chester, PA: Ascension Press, 2003.

————. *Purity in an Impure Age: Discovering God's Glorious Plan for Sexuality*. DVD, CD, VHS, or cassette. West Chester, PA: Ascension Press, 2004.

————. *Winning the Battle for Sexual Purity*. Three-part CD series. West Chester, PA: Ascension Press, 2004.

————. *Woman: God's Masterpiece*. Two-part CD series. West Chester, PA: Ascension Press.

Zeno, Katrina J. *Every Woman's Journey: Answering "Who Am I" for the Feminine Heart*. Steubenville, OH: Women of the Third Millennium, 2005.

3. Selected Studies

Albacete, Lorenzo. "Younger than Sin." *Communio* 22 (1995): 593–612.

Anderson, Carl A., and William J. Gribbin, eds. *The Family in the Modern World: A Symposium on Pope John Paul II's Familiaris Consortio*. Washington, DC: American Family Institute, 1982.

Arregui, Jorge V. "The Nuptial Meaning of the Body and Sexual Ethics." In *Issues for a Catholic Bioethic*, edited by Luke Gormally. London: The Linacre Center, 1999.

Ashley, Benedict M. "John Paul II: Theologian of the Body of the Acting Person." *Josephinum Journal of Theology* 7 (2000): 1–2.

Atkinson, Joseph C. "Nuptiality as a Paradigmatic Structure of Biblical Revelation." In *Dialoghi sul mistero nuziale: Studi offerti al Cardinale Angelo Scola*, edited by Gilfredo Marengo and Bruno Ognibeni, 15–34. Rome: Lateran University Press, 2003.

Böckle, Franz. "Anthropologie und sittliche Weisung nach dem Apostolischen Schreiben *Familiaris Consortio*." In *Die Würde des Menschen: Die theologisch-anthropologischen Grundlagen der Lehre Papst Johannes Pauls II*, edited by Gerhard Höver, Rainer Öhlschläger, Heinz Theo Risse, and Heinz Tiefenbacher, 107–22. Mainz: Grünewald, 1986.

————. "'*Humanae Vitae*' und die philosophische Anthropologie Karol Wojtyłas. Zur päpstlichen Lehrposition zur künstlichen Befruchtung und ihrer Begründung." *Herder-Korrespondenz* 43 (1989): 374–80.

Brinkman, Terence P. "John Paul II's Theology of the Human Person and Technologized Parenting." In *Technological Powers and the Person: Nuclear Energy and Reproductive Technologies*. Boston: Pope John Center, 1983.

Brown, Susan Mader. "*Mulieris Dignitatem*: A New Perspective on the Image of God." *Journal of Dharma* 23 (1998): 501–16.

Burggraf, Jutta. "Juan Pablo II y la vocacion de la mujer." *Scripta Theologica* 31 (1999), 139–55.

Butler, Sara. "Personhood, Sexuality and Complementarity in the Teachings of Pope John Paul II." *Chicago Studies* 32 (1993): 43–53.

Buttiglione, Rocco. *Karol Wojtyła: The Thought of the Man Who Became Pope John Paul II*. Grand Rapids, MI: Eerdmans, 1997.

Caffarra, Carlo. "Conscience, Truth and Magisterium in Conjugal Morality." *Anthropos* 2 (1986): 79–88.

————. "La trasmissione della vita nella *Familiaris Consortio*." *Mater et Magistra* 4 (1983): 391–9.

Cahill, Lisa Sowle. "Accent on the Masculine." In *Considering Veritatis Splendor: The Encyclical Letter of Pope John Paul II on the Church's Moral Teaching*, edited by John Wilkins, 35–40. Cleveland: Pilgrim, 1994.

————. "Catholic Sexual Ethics and the Dignity of the Person: A Double Message." *Theological Studies* 50 (1989): 120–50.

Caldecott, Léonie. "Sincere Gift: The Pope's 'New Feminism.'" In *John Paul II and Moral Theology*, edited by Charles E. Curran and Richard A. McCormick, 216–34. New York: Paulist, 1998.

Caldera, Rafael Tomás. "El don de sí." In *Trinidad y salvacion: Estudios sobre la trilogia trinitaria de Juan Pablo II*, edited by Antonio Aranda, 275–87. Pamplona: Ediciones Universidad de Navarra, 1990.

Callahan, Daniel, ed. *The Catholic Case for Contraception*. New York: Macmillan, 1969.

Calloway, Donald H., ed. *The Virgin Mary and Theology of the Body*. Stockbridge, MA: Marian Press, 2005.

Chiaia, Maria, and Enrica Rosanna. *Le donne per una cultura della vita: Rilettura della Mulieris Dignitatem a cinque anni dalla sua pubblicazione*. Rome: Las, 1994.

Chorpenning, Joseph F. "The Holy Family as Icon and Model of the Civilization of Love: John Paul II's *Letter to Families*." *Communio* 22 (1995): 77–98.

————. "John Paul II's Theology of the Mystery of the Holy Family." *Communio* 28 (2001): 140–66.

Ciccone, Lino. "Per una corretta comprensione della Catechesi di Giovanni Paolo II nelle udienze generali del mercoledì." *Divus Thomas* 84 (1980): 356–80.

Cokeley, Meghan K. "Shame, Lust and the Human Body after the Fall: A Comparison of St. Augustine and Pope John Paul II." *Nova et Vetera (English)* 2 (2004): 249–56.

Connery, John R. "*Familiaris Consortio*: The Family as a Social Institution." In *Catholic Social Thought and the Teaching of John Paul II: Proceedings of the Convention of the Fellowship of Catholic Scholars*, edited by Paul L. Williams, 32–8. Scranton, PA: Northeast Books, 1983.

Connor, Robert A. "The One Truth of Freedom: Gift of Self." *Communio* 21 (1994): 367–71.

Crawford, David. "*Humanae Vitae* and the Perfection of Love." *Communio* 25 (1998): 414–38.

———. "The Nuptial Mystery at the Heart of Freedom: Reflections on the Significance of the States of Life for Moral Action." In *Dialoghi sul mistero nuziale: Studi offerti al Cardinale Angelo Scola,* edited by Gilfredo Marengo and Bruno Ognibeni, 67–82. Rome: Lateran University Press, 2003.

———. *Marriage and the Sequela Christi.* Rome: Lateran University Press, 2004.

Crosby, John F. "John Paul II's Vision of Sexuality and Marriage: The Mystery of 'Fair Love.'" In *The Legacy of Pope John Paul II: His Contribution to Catholic Thought,* edited by Geoffrey Gneuhs, 52–70. New York: Crossroad, 2000.

———. "The Personalism of John Paul II as the Basis of his Approach to the Teaching of *Humanae Vitae.*" In *Why* Humanae Vitae *Was Right: A Reader,* 195–226. San Francisco, 1993.

———. *Personalist Papers.* Washington, DC: Catholic University of America, 2004.

Curran, Charles E. *The Moral Theology of Pope John Paul II.* Washington, DC: Georgetown University Press, 2005.

Curran, Charles E., and Richard A. McCormick, eds. *John Paul II and Moral Theology.* New York: Paulist, 1998.

Del Colle, Ralph. "Theological Dialogue on the 'Full Gospel': Trinitarian Contributions from Pope John Paul II and Thomas A. Smail." *Pneuma* 20 (1998): 141–60.

de Ladurantaye, Paul F. "Irreconcilable Concepts of the Human Person and the Moral Issue of Contraception: An Examination of the Personalism of Louis Janssens and the Personalism of Pope John Paul II." *Anthropotes* 13 (1997): 433–55.

———. "Contraception and the Person: Speaking at Cross-Purposes." *National Catholic Bioethics Quarterly* 3 (2003): 33–43.

DeMarco, Donald. "The Body as Supernatural, Personalistic and Nuptial." *National Catholic Bioethics Quarterly* 3 (2003): 81–93.

DeVille, Adam A. "The Trinity and Contraception." *Homiletic and Pastoral Review* 100 (2000): 30–43.

Dilsaver, G.C. "Karol Wojtyła and the Patriarchal Hierarchy of the Family: His Exegetical Comment on Ephesians 5:21–33 and Genesis 3:16." *Christian Order* (June/July 2002).

Dulles, Avery Robert. *The Splendor of Faith: The Theological Vision of Pope John Paul II.* New York: Crossroad, 1999.

Durkin, Mary G. *Feast of Love: Pope John Paul II on Human Intimacy.* Chicago: Loyola University Press, 1983.

Elshtain, Jean Bethke. "Ethical Equality in a New Feminism." In *Women in Christ: Toward a New Feminism,* edited by Michele M. Schumacher, 285–96. Grand Rapids, MI: Eerdmans, 2004.

Fedoryka, Damian. "Toward a Concept and a Phenomenology of the Gift." In *Values and Human Experience,* edited by Stephen D. Schwarz. New York: Peter Lang, 1999.

Fox-Genovese, Elizabeth. "A Pro-Woman Pope: Why Radical Feminists Can't Hear the Good Words John Paul II Has for Women." *Christianity Today* 27 (1998): 73–75.

Galvin, John. "*Humanae Vitae*: Heroic, Deficient—or Both." *The Latin Mass* 11 (2002): 7–17.

Glick, Daryl J. "Recovering Morality: Personalism and Theology of the Body in John Paul II." *Faith and Reason* 12 (1986): 7–25.

Gneuhs, Geoffrey, ed. *The Legacy of Pope John Paul II: His Contribution to Catholic Thought*. New York: Crossroad, 2000.

Gorevan, Patrick. "Karol Wojtyła in Philosophical Dialogue with Max Scheler." In *The Challenge of Truth: Reflections on Fides et Ratio*, edited by James McEvoy, 134–53. Dublin: Veritas Publications, 2002.

Grabowski, John S. "Theological Anthropology and Gender since Vatican II: A Critical Appraisal of Recent Trends in Catholic Theology." Doctoral Thesis, Marquette University, 1991.

―――. "Mutual Submission and Trinitarian Self-Giving." *Angelicum* 74 (1997): 489–512.

―――. *Sex and Virtue*. Washington, DC: University of America Press, 2003.

Grecco, Richard "La teologia del corpo di Giovanni Paolo II." *Concilium—Italian Edition* 20 (1984): 135–47.

―――. "Recent Ecclesiastical Teaching." In *John Paul II and Moral Theology*, edited by Charles E. Curran and Richard A. McCormick, 137–148. New York: Paulist, 1998.

Hanink, James G. "Karol Wojtyła: Personalism, Intransitivity, and Character." *Communio* 23 (1996): 244–51.

Harper McCarthy, Margaret. "The Body, 'Sacrament of the Person.'" In *Dialoghi sul mistero nuziale: Studi offerti al Cardinale Angelo Scola*, edited by Gilfredo Marengo and Bruno Ognibeni, 97–113. Rome: Lateran University Press, 2003.

Heller, Karin. "The Interpersonal Communion of Trinity, Origin and Aim of Communion between Man and Woman." In *Dialoghi sul mistero nuziale: Studi offerti al Cardinale Angelo Scola*, edited by Gilfredo Marengo and Bruno Ognibeni, 115–29. Rome: Lateran University Press, 2003.

Hellman, John. "John Paul II and the Personalist Movement." *Cross Currents* 30 (1980–81): 409–19.

Hildebrand, Dietrich von. *In Defense of Purity: An Analysis of the Catholic Ideals of Purity and Virginity*. London: Sheed & Ward, 1927 [1931].

―――. *Marriage: The Mystery of Faithful Love*. Manchester, NH: Sophia, 1929 [1997].

Hittinger, Russell. "Making Sense of the Civilization of Love: John Paul II's Contribution to Catholic Social Thought." In *The Legacy of Pope John Paul II: His Contribution to Catholic Thought*, edited by Geoffrey Gneuhs, 71–93. New York: Crossroad, 2000.

Hobbs, Russell Joseph. "Toward a Protestant Theology of Celibacy: Protestant Thought in Dialogue with John Paul II's Theology of the Body." PhD Thesis, Baylor University, 2006.

Hogan, Margaret Monahan. *Finality and Marriage*. Marquette: Marquette University Press, 1993.

Huerga, Alvaro. "Karol Wojtyła, comentador de San Juan de la Cruz." *Angelicum* 56 (1979): 348–66.

Janssens, Louis, and Joseph A. Selling. "Theology and Proportionality: Thoughts about the Encyclical *Veritatis Splendor*." *Bijdragen* 55 (1994): 118–32.

Kaczynski, Edward, ed. *Fede di studioso e obbedienza di pastore: Atti del Convegno sul 50o del dottorato di K. Wojtyła e del 20o del Pontificato di Giovanni Paolo II.* Rome: Millennium Romae, 1999.

Kamykowski, Lukasz. "Karol Wojtyła—Papa Giovanni Paolo II—teologo: Motivi emergenti dallo studio delle opere di S Giovanni della Croce." *Analecta Cracoviensia* 30–31 (1999): 181–90.

Kupczak, Jaroslaw. *Destined for Liberty: The Human Person in the Philosophy of Karol Wojtyła / John Paul II.* Washington, DC: Catholic University of America Press, 2000.

Langan, Janine. "John Paul II's *Letter to Families*: Dead Letter or Good News?" *Communio* 22 (1995): 65–76.

Latkovic, Mark S. "Pope John Paul II's 'Theology of the Body' and the Significance of Sexual Shame in Light of the Body's 'Nuptial Meaning': Some Implications for Bioethics and Sexual Ethics." *Nova et Vetera (English)* 2 (2004): 305–36.

Lawler, Ronald D., ed. *The Christian Personalism of Pope John Paul II.* Chicago: Franciscan Herald, 1982.

Lescoe, Francis J. "Existential Personalism." *Proceedings of the American Catholic Philosophical Association* 60 (1986).

MacIntyre, Alasdair. "How Can We Learn What *Veritatis Splendor* Has to Teach?" *Thomist* 58 (1994): 171–95.

Maheu, Betty Ann. "Commentary on Pope John Paul II's 'A Letter to the Women of the World.'" *Tripod* 89 (1995): 47–51.

Martin, Francis. "Male and Female He Created Them: A Summary of the Teaching of Genesis Chapter One." *Communio* 20 (1993) 240–65.

———. "The Integrity of Christian Moral Activity: The First Letter of John and *Veritatis Splendor*." *Communio* 21 (1994): 265–85.

———. "Radiation of Fatherhood: Some Biblical Reflections." *Josephinum Journal of Theology* 9 (2002): 22–41.

———. "The Holiness of the Church: *Communio Sanctorum* and the *Splendor of Truth*." *Nova et Vetera (English)* 2 (2004): 367–92.

Mattheeuws, Alain. *Union et procréation: Développements de la doctrine des fins du mariage.* Paris: Cerf, 1989.

May, William E. "Christian Marriage and Married Love." *Anthropos* 2 (1986): 95–130.

———. *Contraception, Humanae Vitae, and Catholic Moral Thought.* Chicago: Franciscan Herald, 1984.

———. "The 'New' Evangelization, Catholic Moral Life in Light of *Veritatis Splendor* and the Family." *Nova et Vetera (English)* 2 (2004): 393–402.

———. "The Sanctity of Human Life, Marriage and the Family in the Thought of Pope John Paul II." *Annales Theologici* 2 (1988).

McGovern, Thomas J. "The Christian Anthropology of John Paul II: An Overview." *Josephinum Journal of Theology* 8 (2001): 132–47.

Melina, Livio. "Dimensioni etiche del mistero nuziale: Per una cultura della famiglia." In *Dialoghi sul mistero nuziale: Studi offerti al Cardinale Angelo Scola*, edited by Gilfredo Marengo and Bruno Ognibeni, 175–84. Rome: Pontificia Università Lateranense, 2003.

————. *Sharing in Christ's Virtues: For a Renewal of Moral Theology in Light of* Veritatis Splendor. Washington, DC: Catholic University of America Press, 2001.

Miller, Paula Jean. "The Theology of the Body: A New Look at *Humanae Vitae*." *Theology Today* 57 (2001): 501–8.

Mitchell, Louise M. "A Bibliography for the *Theology of the Body*." *National Catholic Bioethics Quarterly* 3 (2003): 69–77.

Modras, Ronald. "A Man of Contradictions? The Early Writings of Karol Wojtyła." In *The Church in Anguish: Has the Vatican Betrayed Vatican II?*, edited by Hans Küng and Leonard J. Swidler, 39–51. San Francisco: Harper & Row, 1987.

————. "The Moral Philosophy of Pope John Paul II." *Theological Studies* 41 (1980): 683–97.

————. "Pope John Paul II's Theology of the Body." In *John Paul II and Moral Theology*, edited by Charles E. Curran and Richard A. McCormick, 149–56. New York: Paulist, 1998.

————. "The Thomistic Personalism of Pope John Paul II." *Modern Schoolman* 59 (1982): 117–27.

Mohler, R. Albert, Jr. "The Culture of Death and the Gospel of Life: An Evangelical Response to *Evangelium Vitae*." *Ethics & Medicine* 13 (1997): 2–4.

Mumford, Stephen D. *The Pope and the New Apocalypse: The Holy War Against Family Planning*. Center for Research on Population and Security, 1986.

Nachef, Anthony E. *The Mystery of the Trinity in the Theological Thought of Pope John Paul II*. New York: Peter Lang, 1999.

Ognibeni, Bruno. *Dominare la moglie? A proposito di Gn 3,16: Lezione inaugurale Cattedra di Teologia biblica del matrimonio e della famiglia: Istituto "Giovanni Paolo II." Anno accademico 2001–2002*. Rome: Lateran University Press, 2002.

Petrini, Giancarlo. "Appunti sul concetto di nuzialità." In *Dialoghi sul mistero nuziale: Studi offerti al Cardinale Angelo Scola*, edited by Gilfredo Marengo and Bruno Ognibeni, 285–97. Rome: Lateran University Press, 2003.

Place, Michael D. "*Familiaris Consortio:* A Review of Its Theology." In *The Changing Family: Views from Theology and the Social Sciences in the Light of the Apostolic Exhoration*, Familiaris Consortio, edited by Stanley L. Saxton, Patricia Voydanoff and Angela Ann Zukowski, 23–46. Chicago: Loyola University, 1984.

Póltawski, Andrzej. "Person and Family in the Thought of Karol Wojtyła." In *The Family in the Modern World*, edited by Carl Anderson and William Gribbin, 53–64. Washington, DC: American Family Institute, 1988.

Porter, Lawrence Bruce. "Gender in Theology: The Example of John Paul II's *Mulieris Dignitatem*." *Gregorianum* 77 (1996): 97–131.

Proietti, Pamela Werrbach. "The Future of Family Values: Moral Truths and the Future of the American Republic." *Journal of Interdisciplinary Studies* 12 (2000): 21–44.

Prokes, Mary Timothy. "The Nuptial Meaning of the Body in Light of Mary's Assumption." *Communio* 11 (1984): 157.

———. *Toward a Theology of the Body*. Edinburgh: T&T Clark, 1996.

———. "The Body: Precious Sacramental or Processed Artifact." *National Catholic Bioethics Quarterly* 3 (2003): 139–62.

Radford Ruether, Rosemary. "John Paul II and the Growing Alienation of Women from the Church." In *The Church in Anguish: Has the Vatican Betrayed Vatican II?*, edited by Hans Küng and Leonard J. Swidler, 279–83. San Francisco: Harper & Row, 1987.

Reig Pla, Juan Antonio. "Presupuestos antropologicos para educar la sexualidad." In *Dialoghi sul mistero nuziale: Studi offerti al Cardinale Angelo Scola*, edited by Gilfredo Marengo and Bruno Ognibeni, 299–314. Rome: Pontificia Università Lateranense, 2003.

Reimers, Adrian. "Human Suffering and John Paul II's *Theology of the Body*." *Nova et Vetera (English)* 2 (2004): 445–60.

———. "The Significance of Suffering." *National Catholic Bioethics Quarterly* 3 (2003): 53–58.

Rice, Joseph P. "Destined for Liberty." *Review of Metaphysics* 56 (2002): 183–5. Genova: Marietti, 2003.

Riches, Denis, ed. *The Civilization of Love: Proceedings of a Symposium for the International Year of the Family, Oxford, 29 October 1994*. Oxford: Family Publications, 1995.

Rousseau, Mary F. "Deriving Bioethical Norms from the *Theology of the Body*." *National Catholic Bioethics Quarterly* 3 (2003): 59–67.

Rubio, Julie Hanlon. *A Christian Theology of Marriage and Family*. New York: Paulist Press, 2003.

Saward, John. *Christ Is the Answer: the Christ-Centered Teaching of Pope John Paul II*. New York: Alba House, 1995.

Saxton, Stanley L., Patricia Voydanoff, and Angela Ann Zukowski, eds. *The Changing Family: Views from Theology and the Social Sciences in the Light of the Apostolic Exhoration*, Familiaris Consortio. Chicago: Loyola University Press, 1984.

Schindler, David L. "Catholic Theology, Gender and the Future of Western Civilization." *Communio* 20 (1993): 200–239

———. "The Pontificate of John Paul II." *Communio* 24 (1997): 713–842.

———. "Reorienting the Church on the Eve of the Millennium: John Paul II's New Evangelization." In *The Legacy of Pope John Paul II: His Contribution to Catholic Thought*, edited by Geoffrey Gneuhs, 94–127. New York: Crossroad, 2000.

Schmitt, Thomas. "John Paul II and Therese Lisieux." *Communio* 24 (1997): 541–49.

Schmitz, Kenneth L. *The Gift: Creation, Aquinas Lecture, 1982*. Milwaukee: Marquette University Press, 1982.

———. "The Passage of Love: Wojtyła's Radiation of Fatherhood." *Communio* 22 (1995): 99–106.

———. "Jacques Maritain and Karol Wojtyła: Approaches to Modernity." In *The Bases of Ethics*, edited by William Sweet. Milwaukee: Marquette University Press, 2000.

Schneider, Birgit. *Wer Gott dient, wird nicht krumm: Feministische Ethik im Dialog mit Karol Wojtyła und Dietmar Mieth*. Mainz: M.-Grünewald, 1997.

Schu, Walter. *The Splendor of Love: John Paul II's Vision for Marriage and Family*. New Hope, KY: New Hope Publications, 2003.

Schumacher, Michele, ed. *Women in Christ: Toward a New Feminism*. Grand Rapids, MI: Eerdmans, 2004.

————. "A Speyrian Theology of the Body." In *The Virgin Mary and Theology of the Body*, 243–78, edited by Donald H. Calloway. Stockbridge, MA: Marian Press, 2005.

Scola, Angelo. "'Claim' of Christ, 'Claim' of the World: On the Trinitarian Encyclicals of John Paul II." *Communio* 18 (1991): 322–31.

————. "L'imago Dei e la sessulalità umana: A proposito di una tesi originale della '*Mulieris Dignitatem*.'" *Anthropotes* 8 (1992): 61–73.

————. "Following Christ: On John Paul II's Encyclical *Veritatis Splendor*." *Communio* 20 (1993): 724–27.

————. "The Formation of Priests in the Pastoral Care of the Family." *Communio* 24 (1997): 57–83.

————. "The Dignity and Mission of Women: The Anthropological and Theological Foundations." *Communio* 25 (1998): 42–56.

————. "The Nuptial Mystery at the Heart of the Church." *Communio* 25 (1998): 630–62.

————. "*Familiaris Consortio* e mistero nuziale." *Anthropotes* 17 (2001): 203–05.

Séguin, Michel. "The Biblical Foundations of the Thought of John Paul II on Human Sexuality." *Communio* 20 (1993): 266–89.

Seifert, Josef. "Truth, Freedom, and Love in Wojtyła's Philosophical Anthropology and Ethics." In *Philosophy and Culture*, edited by Venant Cauchy, 536–41. Montreal: Montmorency, 1988.

Semen, Yves. *La Sexualité selon Jean-Paul II*. Paris: Presses de la Renaissance, 2003.

Shivanandan, Mary. "The Anthropological Background of *Fides et Ratio*." *Anthropotes* 17 (2001): 129–48.

————. "Body Narratives: Language of Truth?" *Logos* 1 (2000): 166–93.

————. "Body-Soul Unity in Light of the Nuptial Relation." In *Dialoghi sul mistero nuziale: Studi offerti al Cardinale Angelo Scola*, edited by Gilfredo Marengo and Bruno Ognibeni, 369–81. Rome: Pontificia Università Lateranense, 2003.

————. "The Ecumenism of *Redemptoris Mater* and *Mulieris Dignitatem*." *Diakonia* (2000), 251–64.

————. "Natural Family Planning and the Theology of the Body: A New Discourse for Married Couples." *National Catholic Bioethics Quarterly* 3 (2003): 23–32.

————. "The New Evangelization of John Paul II." *Hear O Islands: Theology and Catechesis in the New Millennium*, pp. 195–208 (London, UK: Veritas, 2002).

————. "The Pope, Man, and Woman." In *The Achievements of John Paul II, Occasional Papers*: vol. 3, pp. 19–26 (Oxford University Chaplaincy) 2001.

————. "Subjectivity and the Order of Love," *Fides Quaerens Intellectum* 1, no. 2 (Winter 2002): 251–74.

Shivanandan, Mary and Joseph C. Atkinson. "Person as Sustantive Relation and Reproductive Technologies: Biblical and Philosophical Foundations." *Logos* 7 (2004): 124–56.

Simpson, Peter. *On Karol Wojtyła*. Belmont, CA: Wadsworth/Thomson Learning, 2001.

————. "What It's Like to Be a Christian." *First Things* 144 (2004): 23–28.

Slipko, Tadeusz. "Le développement de la pensée éthique du Cardinal Karol Wojtyła." *Collectanea Theologica* 50 (1980): special fascicle: 61–87.

Smith, Janet E. *Humanae Vitae, a Generation Later*. Washington, DC: Catholic University of America Press, 1991.

————. ed. *Why* Humanae Vitae *Was Right: A Reader*. San Francisco: Ignatius, 1993.

————. "John Paul II and the Family: The Family: A Communion of Persons." In *A Celebration of the Thought of John Paul II*, edited by Gregory R. Beabout, 85–103. St. Louis: St. Louis University, 1998.

Smith, Russell E., ed. *Trust the Truth: A Symposium on the Twentieth Anniversary of the Encyclical* Humanae Vitae. Braintree, MA: The Pope John Center, 1991.

Smolenski, Stanislaw, Tadeusz Slipko, Jules Turowicz, Georges Bajda, and Charles Meissner. "Les fondements de la doctrine de l'Eglise concernant les principes de la vie conjugale: Un mémoire rédigé par un groupe de théologiens-moralistes de Cracovie." *Analecta Cracoviensie* 1 (1969): 194–230.

Snyder, Patrick. *La femme selon Jean-Paul II: Lectures des fondements anthropologiques et théologiques et des applications pratiques de son enseignement*. Montréal: Fides, 1999.

————. "Le féminisme selon Jean Paul II: L'impasse du déterminisme." *Studies in Religion/Sciences religieuses*, (2000): 313–24.

Sorgia, Raimondo. "Approcio con l''opera prima' di K. Wojtlyla." *Angelicum* 57 (1980): 401–23.

Styczen, Tadeusz. "Der Mensch als Subjekt der Hingabe seines Selbst. Zur Anthropologie der Enzyklika '*Familiaris Consortio*.'" In *Die Würde des Menschen: Die theologisch-anthropologischen Grundlagen der Lehre Papst Johannes Pauls II*, edited by Gerhard Höver, Rainer Öhlschläger, Heinz Theo Risse, and Heinz Tiefenbacher, 123–49. Mainz: Grünewald, 1986.

Sutton, Agneta. "Facing the Sexual Revolution: John Paul II's Language of the Body." In *John Paul the Great: Maker of the Post-Conciliar Church*, edited by William Oddie, 131–50. London: Catholic Truth Society & The Catholic Herald, 2003.

Swierzawski, Waclaw. "Die Würde des Menschen: Über die theologisch-anthropologischen Grundlagen der Lehre Papst Johannes Pauls II." In *Die Würde des Menschen: Die theologisch-anthropologischen Grundlagen der Lehre Papst Johannes Pauls II*, edited by Gerhard Höver, Rainer Öhlschläger, Heinz Theo Risse, and Heinz Tiefenbacher, 77–91. Mainz: Grünewald, 1986.

Tettamanzi, Dionigi. *Alle sorgenti della vita: Humanae vitae attualità di un'enciclica*. Casale Monferrato: Piemme, 1993.

————. *L'esortazione sulla famiglia: Familiaris consortio: Introduzione alla lettura*. Milan: Massimo, 1982.

Vásquez, Manuel A., and Marie F. Marquardt. "Premodern, Modern, or Postmodern? John Paul II's Civilization of Love." In *Globalizing the Sacred: Religion across the Americas*, viii, 255. New Brunswick, NJ: Rutgers University, 2003.

Villarejo Garaizar, Antonio. *El matrimonio y la familia en la "Familiaris Consortio."* Madrid: Ediciones Paulinas, 1984.

Walch, Roland. *Die körpersprachliche Botschaft der Sexualität als Ausgangspunkt für eine Theologie der Geschlechtlichkeit.* Vienna: Institut für Ehe und Familie, 1989.

Waldstein, Michael. "The Common Good in St. Thomas and John Paul II." *Nova et Vetera,* English edition, 3 (2005), 569–78.

Walsh, J.C.D., Msgr. Vincent M. *The Theology of the Body: A Simplified Version.* Merion, PA: Key of David Publications.

Weigel, George. "The Soul of John Paul II." In *Occasional Papers,* vol. 3: *The Achievements of John Paul II,* edited by Oxford University Catholic Chaplaincy, 36–45, 2001.

———. *Witness to Hope: The Biography of Pope John Paul II.* New York: Harper Collins, 1999.

Wierzbicki, Alfred. "La barca interiore: Affinità spirituale del pensiero di Karol Wojtyła con il pensiero di San Giovanni della Croce." In *Karol Wojtyła: Metafisica della persona: Tutte le opere filosofiche e saggi integrativi,* edited by Giovanni Reale and Tadeusz Styczen, 3–20. Milan: Bompiani, 2003.

Wilder, Alfred. "Community of Persons in the Thought of Karol Wojtyła." *Angelicum* 56 (1979): 211–44.

Williams, George Huntston. *The Mind of John Paul II: Origins of His Thought and Action.* New York: Seabury Press, 1981.

Woznicki, Andrew N. *The Dignity of Man as a Person: Essays on the Christian Humanism of His Holiness John Paul II.* San Francisco: Society of Christ, 1987.

Wrenn, Michael J. *Pope John Paul II and the Family: The Text with a Theological and Catechetical Commentary with Discussion Questions on the Apostolic Exhortation of Pope John Paul II on the Role of the Christian Family in the Modern World (Familiaris Consortio).* Chicago: Franciscan Herald Press, 1983.

Zoffoli, Enrico. *Ecumenismo ed umanesimo di Giovanni Paolo II: Assoluta ortodossia del Papa alla luce del tomismo.* Rome: Libreria Editrice Vaticana, 1995.

Index of Words and Phrases

The index is based on the Italian text and is thus independent of the English translation. English translations often differ or overlap according to context. For words marked with an asterisk (*) only a selection of references is presented.

A

A posteriori, see Historical *a posteriori*

Ability, Capability, Capacity, Power (*capacità*) 46 times: 14:6; 15:1, 4; 16:4. The original power of mutual self-communication, 29:2–3; 32:3; 49:6; 54:2–4; 56:1, 5; 57:3; 71:3–4; 107:3; 115:2; 123:6; 125:6; 127:1–2; 128:1, 3; 129:5–6; 130:1–2, 4; 132:4

Ability (*abilità*): 54:2; 56:5

Abortion (*aborto*): 122:1

Abstinence (*astensione*) 20 times: 20:2; 44:5; 54:3–4; 56:1, 5; 57:3; 84:2, 6, 8; 85:1–2, 4, 7; 86:5, 8. *See also* Continence, Celibacy, Virginity

Abstinence (*astinenza*): 44:5

Adam 43 times: 4:3; 8:3; 15:4; 16:1; 20:2; 21:2, 5–6; 22:1, 5–6; 27:2, 4; 31:6; 36:1; 44:5; 70:4, 6–7; 71:2–4; 72:2; 96:5; 97:5; 101:6; 110:7; 114:1; 116:1

Adultery* (*adulterio*) 220 times

The commandment, "You shall not commit adultery," 24:1–2; 26:3; 34:5; 35:1–5; 36:1, 5–6; 37:1, 6; 38:1; 40:1; 41:1; 42:1, 4, 7; 43:2, 5–6; 44:1, 3; 45:1; 46:1; 47:1; 48:1; 49:1, 4; 50:1, 4; 57:6; 58:1, 4; 59:1; 63:1; 100:5–6; 107:1

Adultery in the heart: Consists in an act of concupiscence (*see* 43), 24:1, 4; 25:1, 3–4; 26:3; 28:4; 34:1, 5; 35:1, 4; 38:1, 6; 39:1, 5; 40:1; 41:1; 42:1, 3–4, 6–7; 43:1–3, 5; 44:1, 3, 6; 45:1, 5; 46:1; 47:1; 48:1; 49:1;

50:1, 5; 58:1, 3–4; 59:1; 60:5; 62:5; 63:1; 77:4; 100:5; 107:1; 133:1

Affection (*affetto*) 17 times: 94:8; 95:1, 4; 104:2; 109:1; 111:2; 115:3; 128:6; 129:1, 6; 132:2. *See also* Arousal, Emotion, Attraction, Passion, Sentiment

Manifestations of affection (*manifestazioni di affetto*) 5 times. Phrase derived from *Humanae Vitae* 21: 128:6; 128:6; 129:1; 129:6; 132:2

Affective manifestations of spousal unity (*manifestazioni affettive*) 13 times. Phrase quoted from *Humanae Vitae* 21: 59:6–7; 124:2; 128:3, 5–6; 131:1–2, 4–5. *See also* Emotional

Affective (*affettivo*) other use: 54:3

Affectivity (*affettività*): 18:2

Affectionate (*affettuoso*): 37:3; 104:5; 112:2

Analogy (*analogia*) 139 times. In most cases "analogy" refers to the analogy between the love of husband and wife and the love of God and his people, 8:3; 12:2; 14:6; 27:2; 33:3–4; 36:5; 37:3–5; 38:1; 50:4; 52:3; 54:6; 63:5, 7; 80:4; 87:4; 89:8; 90:1–4, 6; 91:1–4, 8; 92:1–3, 5; 93:1–3; 94:6–7; 95:2, 4–6. The analogy of marriage applies to the historical dimension of the mystery (Christ and the Church), and not to its eternal dimension (the Trinity), 95:7; 95b:1–6; 97:2, 4; 98:2; 99:1; 102:1, 7; 104:1–2, 4, 8; 106:1; 107:1; 108:1, 3, 8; 114:4; 117:6; 117b:1. *See also* Metaphor

Appease, *see* Satisfy

Appropriate* (verb, *appropriare*) 3 of 17 times: Concupiscence appropriates the other person as an object of use, frequently for pleasure, 32:6; 33:1. It is in the end impossible to appropriate a person, 113:3

> Appropriation (*appropriazione*) 9 times: Appropriation is the opposite of the gift of self and of receiving another person as a gift. It is the key defining mark of concupiscence, 17:3; 32:6; 33:1, 3; 62:3; 113:3

Aristotle (*Aristotele*) 6 times: 5:6; 53:5. Meditation on the resurrection led Thomas Aquinas to adopt Aristotle's as opposed to Plato's account of the relation between body and soul, 66:6

> Aristotelian (*aristotelico*): The Aristotelian definition of man as rational animal is confirmed by man's original experience as revealed in Gen, 5:5–6; 72:5

Arousal (*eccitazione*) in the sense of sexual arousal, 14 times: 48:4. The role of sexual arousal in relation to erotic emotion, 128:1; 129:4–6; 130:1–2. *See also* Emotion, Pleasure

Artificial (*artificiale, artificioso*): 42:1; 80:7; 122:3; 123:1, 6–7; 125:4; 133:4

Ascesis (*ascesi*) 9 times: From the Greek *askeō*, practice, exercise, train. Used by *Humanae Vitae* 21 to describe the discipline of abstinence from sexual intercourse in the natural regulation of fertility, 44:5; 59:6; 82:5; 124:2; 125:2; 128:3–4; 131:2

Aspire (*aspirare*): 58:4; 84:4

> Aspiration (*aspirazione*) 20 times: 30:5. Desire is an aspiration to an end, 40:5; 47:1; 48:5; 49:2, 7; 51:2; 71:3–4; 79:7; 84:1; 101:5; 112:3; 113:2

Attitude (*atteggiamento*) 25 times: 14:1. The meaning of the body is what shapes the person's attitude or ethos, 31:5–6; 37:1; 43:3; 45:3; 50:3; 55:3; 57:2; 60:2; 63:4; 78:4; 79:5; 83:3, 9; 84:2; 89:1; 124:4, 6; 125:7; 132:4. *See also* Mentality, Ethos, Spirituality, Virtue

> Attitude (*attitudine*): 25:2; 54:2, 4

Attraction (*attrazione*) 19 times: 32:1–2; 40:2–3, 5; 41:1–2, 4–5; 47:2–3; 48:1; 108:6. *See also* Affection, Arousal, Emotion, Heart, Passion, Sentiment

Attractiveness, Attraction (*attrattiva*) 10 times: 10:2; 21:5; 43:3; 46:5; 47:2; 48:2, 4; 49:5; 54:3; 109:1

Audience (*udienza*): The regular Wednesday general audience, 1:5; 60:7; 70:1. *See also* Analysis, Catechesis, Consideration, Conversation, Meditation, Reflection, Study

Authentic (*autentico*) 82 times: 6:1; 9:4; 10:3; 17:6; 19:2; 23:3; 26:2; 27:1; 31:2–3; 32:3, 6; 33:2; 35:1; 37:1; 38:1; 40:1; 41:4; 45:3, 5; 48:1, 3; 51:4; 53:3–4; 57:3; 58:1, 6; 59:2, 4; 61:2; 62:4; 63:7; 64:3; 65:6; 68:2–3; 69:6; 72:4; 75:1; 77:1–2, 6; 78:4; 79:3; 81:2–4; 82:1; 86:4; 95:3; 102:3–4; 110:4, 7–9; 112:1; 117:6; 120:1–2; 121:2–3; 123:4; 124:6; 125:5; 126:3, 4; 127:1, 4; 128:2; 129:1–2; 131:6; 133:3

Authority (*autorità*) 8 times: 1:4; 35:2; 65:6; 104:3; 105:2; 106:1–2

Aware, conscious (*consapevole*) 19 times: 6:3; 14:6; 56:4; 60:5; 62:3; 76:4; 77:3; 81:2–3; 85:4–5; 98:5; 100:7; 102:3; 106:2; 115:5; 116:4; 121:2

> With awareness, Consciously (*consapevolmente*) 9 times: 6:2; 22:4; 61:3; 76:3; 78:5; 85:7; 101:3

> Awareness (*consapevolezza*) 26 times. Awareness of the body and of its sense, 6:3; 7:1; 9:2. Awareness of the meaning of the body in the mutual self-gift of persons, 10:4. Primordial awareness of the spousal meaning of the body, 19:1, 3. Awareness of participation in God's creative gift through procreation, 21:6; 27:4; 34:2; 42:7; 43:7; 44:3. Awareness of the redemption of the body, 56:5; 69:3; 77:2. Awareness of the freedom of the gift, 80:5; 96:1. Awareness of the holiness of life when it is passed on through procreation, 101:5–6; 132:5. *See also* Analysis, Catechesis, Consideration, Conversation, Meditation, Reflection, Study

Axiological (*assiologico*) 5 times, from the Greek *axios* (worthy). Highlights the aspect of good, value, moral obligation, etc., in contrast to "ontological," which highlights the aspect of being, 9:1; 40:3–5; 49:7

B

Beatific vision (*visione beatifica*), 67:4; 68:2

Beatifying (*beatificante*) 21 times: 14:1, 3–5; 15:2–3, 5; 16:1–2, 5; 17:2; 30:4; 67:5; 68:2–4. *See also* Blessed, Happiness

Beatitudes (*beatitudini*) 5 times: 50:1, 3–4; 57:5

Beauty (*bellezza*) 34 times. Beauty is a key aspect of the overall argument in TOB. John Paul II attempts to let love show its own beauty and thus its own persuasive power. The original beauty of the relationship between man and woman, 15:4; 32:6; 37:2; 38:4–5; 57:3; 63:5. An important purpose of the discussion of the "beginning" is to discover the original beauty of the vocation to marriage, 76:5. The call to celibacy shows the spousal meaning of the body in all its beauty, 81:3; 91:8; 92:3–4; 104:6; 109:1; 110:6; 111:4; 112:3; 117b:5–6; 132:4

> Beautiful (*bello*) 40 times: 22:4; 37:2; 38:4; 46:5; 47:2, 5; 48:1; 91:8; 92:2. Physical beauty, 92:4; 108:6–8; 109:3; 110:4; 111:3; 112:3–4; 113:1

Beginning, Principle (*principio*) 301 times. Most frequently the "beginning" in the sense of God's original intention for human love in the divine plan, and the realization of this intention in the original creation of man, 1:1–5; 2:1; 3:1–2, 4; 4:1, 3–5; 5:1; 7:4; 8:1; 9:2–3; 10:1–2, 5; 11:4, 6; 13:1–4; 14:3–4, 6; 15:1–3, 5; 16:1. The "beginning" is original and beatifying immunity from shame as an effect of love, 16:2–5; 17:1, 6; 18:1, 3–4; 19:6; 20:1; 21:1; 22:1, 3, 5–6; 23:1–6; 24:1–2; 25:1; 26:2, 5; 27:3; 29:1, 4; 30:2; 32:1; 33:2, 5; 34:1–2; 35:4; 36:1; 37:5; 38:1; 39:2, 5; 40:1, 3; 41:5; 44:6; 45:2; 46:5–6; 49:3–4; 51:1, 4; 52:4; 57:3; 58:1–2, 5; 59:2; 60:1; 61:1–2; 63:4; 64:1; 65:5; 66:2–5; 67:5; 68:5–6; 69:1–6, 8; 70:3, 5–6; 71:2–4; 73:1–5; 76:2, 5, 6; 77:1, 3; 78:4; 79:6; 80:2–7; 81:1, 6; 83:2; 85:10; 86:3–4, 6; 87:2, 4, 6; 89:6; 91:6; 92:4; 93:1–2; 95:3; 95b:7; 96:1–2, 4–7; 97:1–5; 98:1, 3; 99:2, 6–7; 100:1–2, 4, 7; 101:11; 102:1–2, 5, 8; 103:2, 4–5; 104:7; 105:2–3; 106:1, 6; 107:1; 108:3; 110:3, 7; 112:3; 115:1; 116:2, 4; 117:1; 117b:3; 119:1, 4; 121:6; 122:1; 123:3; 127:1; 129:2; 131:3; 133:1

From the beginning (*da principio, dal principio*) 98 times, a key phrase in TOB, taken from Jesus' statement, "Have you not read that *from the beginning* the Creator created them male and female?" (Mt 19:3): 1:1–4; 2:1; 3:2; 7:4; 9:2–3; 10:2, 5; 13:2; 15:1, 3, 5; 16:3; 17:6; 18:1, 3–4; 20:1; 21:1; 22:1, 3, 5; 23:1, 3; 29:1, 4; 32:1; 33:2, 5; 34:1; 41:5; 45:2; 46:5; 51:1; 57:3; 58:1; 66:2–4; 67:5; 69:3–6; 70:3; 71:2–4; 73:2, 4; 76:6; 77:1; 78:4; 79:6; 80:2, 3, 6–7; 81:1, 6; 87:6; 93:1–2; 95:3; 96:5–6; 97:3; 98:1, 3; 99:6–7; 100:4, 7; 102:2, 8; 103:2; 104:7; 106:1; 110:7; 115:1; 117b:3; 123:3; 131:3

In the beginning (*in principio*) 8 times: 13:3; 65:5; 69:3, 8; 77:3; 86:3; 95b:7; 103:4

Behavior (*comportamento*) 46 times: 7:1; 23:3, 5; 34:5; 35:3; 36:2; 37:1; 38:1; 42:5; 44:2, 4; 47:3–4; 48:2; 49:5; 50:3; 51:5–6; 52:1, 5; 53:4; 55:7; 56:4; 57:2; 60:2; 62:3–4; 76:3; 84:5; 89:2, 4; 100:7; 105:5; 106:2–3; 107:6; 108:4; 119:2; 121:1; 124:3–4

> Behavior, Conduct (*condotta*) 9 times: 56:3; 57:4; 58:4; 74:3; 91:8; 105:6, 106:2; 121:2

Believe, Have faith (*credere*) 13 times: 8:2; 56:4; 65:3; 69:3; 74:3; 85:3; 87:4; 94:4; 113:4; 119:5; 120:6. *See also* Creed, Faith, Hope, Love

Bible (*bibbia*) 43 times: 2:4; 3:2; 7:4; 8:2–3; 16:1, 3; 20:3–4; 21:1, 5; 22:1–2; 25:1, 3; 26:1; 35:4; 38:3; 43:5; 46:1–2; 59:3; 61:2; 63:3; 66:5; 68:3; 69:8; 74:6; 80:3; 83:9; 91:7; 93:1; 95b:2–3; 108:1; 110:4; 116:2–3; 122:5; 131:3. *See also* Scripture

> Biblical (*biblico*) 168 times: 2:2–3, 6; 3:2–3; 7:1; 8:2–4; 9:1–2, 4; 10:2, 4–5; 11:1–3, 5–6; 12:1, 5; 13:2, 4; 14:6; 15:4; 16:1, 4; 17:5; 20:1–5; 21:1, 3–4, 6; 22:1–2, 4–5, 7; 23:2; 24:4; 25:5; 26:1–4; 27:1; 28:1, 5; 29:1–2, 4–5; 30:5; 31:5–6; 33:3; 39:1–2, 4; 40:1, 5; 44:5; 46:1–2; 47:1–2; 51:6; 57:6; 58:3–4; 60:1; 61:2; 63:3; 64:2; 65:3–4; 67:4; 68:3; 69:3; 70:7; 71:6; 74:2; 80:2, 4; 84:5; 87:3; 88:1; 93:4–5; 95:2, 6; 95b:2, 5; 96:2; 98:7; 104:1; 106:3–4; 108:1, 4; 112:1; 114:2, 7; 117:3, 5; 118:4, 6;

ting instances of rereading texts. A key word in the overall argument, since it (together with Read, Reading) connects the discussion of the spousal meaning of the body in the first two parts of TOB with John Paul II's interpretation of *Humanae Vitae*, which hinges on reading or rereading the language of the body (*see* TOB 118:6). Rereading the language of the body in the truth presupposes that the body has a definite meaning, like an inherited text, which the individual person does not simply determine at will. The spousal meaning of the body in inseparable connection with its procreative meaning is the main criterion for rereading the language of the body in the truth, 104:9; 105:2–3, 5–6; 106:1–3; 107:1, 3–5; 108:3, 8; 110:9; 111:1, 4, 6; 112:1; 113:3; 115:1, 3–4, 6; 116:2, 5; 117:5; 117b:1–2; 118:4

Rereading* the language of the body (noun, *rilettura*) 17 of 19 times: 103:6; 105:2, 5; 108:1; 109:5; 110:6; 111:2, 5; 113:6; 119:1–2. The concept of a morally right regulation of fertility is nothing other than rereading the language of the body in the truth, 125:1

Read the language of the body (verb, *leggere*). Nothing else is at stake here (i.e., in the teaching of *Humanae Vitae*) than reading the "language of the body" in the truth, 118:6

Reading the language of the body (noun, *lettura*) 3 times, 118:4. The moral norm taught by *Humanae Vitae* springs from reading the "language of the body" in the truth, 118:6

BODY 4: *The Drama of the Fall and Redemption of the Body*

Concupiscence of the body (*concupiscenza del corpo*): 23:6; 26:1; 28:3–6; 29:1; 32:1, 4; 36:2; 38:2–3; 77:4

Shame of the body (*vergogna del corpo, pudore del corpo*) 7 times: 16:4; 28:3, 5; 29:3; 31:3

Constraint of the body (*costrizione del corpo*). The constraint of the body

exemplified by the power of sexual instinct over the person when integration is lacking. It is the opposite of the freedom of the gift, 14:6; 15:1, 3; 32:2, 6; 41:3; 43:6; 132:3

Redemption of the body (*redenzione del corpo*). The governing perspective of the whole theology of the body (*see esp.* TOB 86:8), 4:3, 5; 15:5; 23:5; 26:3, 5; 42:7; 43:7; 45:2–3; 46:4; 49:2–4, 6–7; 52:1; 55:3; 56:4–5; 57:1, 5; 58:5; 70:8; 71:1; 75:1; 76:3; 77:4; 79:3; 86:1–8; 87:2; 90:6; 99:4–5, 7; 100:2–7; 101:4, 6–7, 9; 102:3, 6–8; 105:1; 107:2, 5; 117b:6; 119:5; 127:1; 133:1–2, 4

Redemptive meaning of the body (*significato redentore del corpo*): 102:4–5, 8

Ethos of the body (ethos *del corpo*). The ethos appropriate to the body, 18:3; 44:5; 49:1; 59:7; 60:1, 3, 5; 61:1–2, 4

Spirituality of the body (*spiritualità del corpo*): 59:4; 69:8

Pedagogy of the body (*pedagogia del corpo*). A pedagogy of the body based on the theology of the body is particularly necessary in our age, in which people tend to be formed by rationalist natural science and its anthropological dualism, 59:2–5, 7; 122:5. The theology of the body is a pedagogy of the body, 124:3; 125:5; 126:2, 4

Resurrection of the body (*risurrezione del corpo*): 59:7; 65:4; 66:4; 70:8; 72:4, 6; 81:7; 86:4; 101:9

Bodily (*corporeo, corporale*) 27 times: 20:3; 27:1; 29:3; 37:4; 44:5; 50:3; 52:4; 54:2, 4; 58:2; 59:3; 61:3; 63:3; 65:5; 67:1–2; 68:6; 77:3; 78:5; 85:8; 123:7; 129:4, 6; 130:1, 4; 132:5

Somatic (*somatico*) 30 times. From the Greek *sōma* (body) bodily. Somatic differs from bodily (*corporeo*) in two respects: (1) the Greek *sōma* refers only to human and animal bodies, while "body" (*corpo*) and thus "bodily" refers to all extended beings; (2) unlike "bodily," "somatic" is not a common notion of ordinary language, but a technical scientific term used esp. in medicine and psychology, 8:1, 4; 9:5; 20:5; 21:3, 6; 27:4;

28:2; 31:1; 32:2; 36:3; 47:1, 3; 50:3, 5; 55:2–3, 5, 7; 66:5; 71:3; 85:8; 91:1; 123:4; 125:1; 128:1

Somatology (*la somatica*). The science of the body, 55:3

Bodiliness (*corporeità*) 19 times: 7:2; 8:1; 9:4–5; 10:2; 19:3, 5; 21:1. Manifests itself above all through the male and female sex, 44:5; 47:3; 63:3, 7; 66:5; 71:4. The perfection of human bodiliness in the resurrection, 72:2, 4; 96:1

Bond (*vincolo*) 12 times: 2:3; 58:5; 84:2; 91:1; 92:1; 97:5; 103:7; 104:2, 4–5; 105:6; 113:1

Bond, Link (*legame*) 28 times: 4:1; 10:2–3; 11:4; 14:4; 15:5; 16:5; 18:3; 20:1; 36:4; 37:6; 44:2; 49:4; 57:2–3; 85:7; 86:8; 91:2–3; 95:6; 106:3; 114:3; 128:3

Bone (*osso*) 33 times: 3:2; 8:4; 9:4–5; 10:1–2; 14:3–4; 19:1; 21:6; 22:3; 38:4

Bone from my bones (*osso dalle mie ossa*) 9 times. The CEI translation places "flesh from my flesh" first, contrary to the order in the Hebrew original, "bone from my bones and flesh from my flesh," 3:2; 8:4; 10:2; 14:3–4; 19:1

Boundary (*confine*) 12 times: 3:2, 4; 4:1, 3; 9:2; 11:4, 6; 12:2; 23:5; 26:5; 29:5. *See also* Limit

Bride, Spouse, Wife (*sposa*) 124 times: 36:6; 37:1–3; 73:2; 75:3; 78:4; 82:4; 90:2, 5–6; 91:1, 7–8; 92:2–4, 6; 94:5, 7; 95:2–4, 7; 95b:2; 97:5; 99:6; 100:4, 6; 102:4, 6; 103:1–2, 4–5; 104:2, 7, 9; 105:1–2, 5; 108:1, 4–6, 8; 109:1–6; 110:1–2, 4–9; 111:2, 4–6; 112:1, 3, 5; 113:1, 3; 114:2–3, 7; 117:3; 117b:1. *See also* Spouses

Bridegroom, Spouse, Husband (*sposo*) 114 times: 36:5–6; 37:3–4; 75:2–3; 78:4; 79:9; 80:1; 82:5; 90:2, 5–6; 91:1, 7–8; 92:3–4, 6; 94:7–8; 95:1–7; 95b:2; 102:4; 103:1–2, 4–5; 104:2–5, 7; 105:1–2, 5; 108:1, 4–6, 8; 109:1–6; 110:1–2, 5–7, 9; 111:2, 4–6; 112:1–3; 113:3; 114:3; 117:3. *See also* Spouses

Brother (*fratello*) 31 times: 16:3; 18:5; 20:2; 52:4–5; 53:1–2; 64:1–2; 65:1; 83:1, 5, 7; 109:4–5; 110:1, 3; 114:2, 3, 7. *See also* Sister

Fraternal (*fraterno*) 4 times: 110:1, 5–6; 114:3

C

Call (*chiamata*) 65 times: 13:4; 19:6; 21:6; 27:2; 28:1, 4; 31:2; 32:2; 39:5; 40:1–2; 41:2–3; 43:3; 45:4; 46:4–5; 47:2–5; 48:4; 49:7; 61:4; 62:1; 63:2; 73:1; 76:5; 77:1–2, 4; 78:1, 3; 79:1, 3, 8–9; 80:1, 5; 81:2–3, 5, 7; 86:6; 88:1; 93:5; 96:4; 107:2; 110:5; 112:1; 116:4; 117b:1; 128:1; 129:4; 130:3. *See also* Vocation

The call of man and woman to unity, communion, the mutual gift, etc.: 28:4; 31:2; 32:2; 40:1–2; 41:2; 43:3; 47:2; 48:4; 61:4; 62:1; 76:5; 116:4

The sacramental call (to marriage): 39:5

The call to virginity: 73:1; 77:1–2, 4; 78:1, 3; 79:1, 3, 8–9; 80:1, 5; 81:2–3, 5, 7; 86:6

Carnal, *see* Fleshly

Casuistry, Casuistic (*casistica, casistico*) 11 times. From the Latin *casus* (case): an account given of particular cases in moral and legal discussions, not necessarily in a negative sense (for a clearly positive sense of "casuistry," *see Veritatis Splendor* 76), 1:2; 24:4; 35:1–2; 37:6; 38:1; 42:2, 4; 43:5; 64:1

Catechesis (*catechesi*) 9 times. From the Greek *kata* (through, along) and *ēcheō* (to sound): informing or instructing a person. Catechesis is the essential literary genre of TOB (*see* Introduction, pp. 14–18), 129:2; 133:1–2, 4. *See also* Analysis, Audience, Consideration, Conversation, Meditation, Meeting, Reflection, Study

Celibacy (*celibato*), 34 times: 72:7; 73:1, 3–5; 74:1–6; 75:1; 76:1; 77:1; 78:1, 4; 79:7, 9; 80:1; 81:4–5; 82:1; 83:2, 4; 84:5, 7; 102:8. *See also* Abstinence, Continence, Virginity

Celibate (*celibe*): 75:4; 78:3. *See also* Virgin

Certificate of divorce, *see* Divorce

Chapter* (*capitolo*) 3 of 102 times. Only references to parts of TOB as "chapters" are listed here. Uses of "chapter" introduced by UD are set in square brackets, [2:1]; [13:1]; [19:1]; [42:7]; 63:7; [64:1]; 87:1; [94:1]; 114:7

Charismatic (*carismatico*) 10 times. From the Greek *charisma* (gift): having the character of a special and supernatural gift, 56:1; 57:2; 73:4–5; 75:1; 81:5; 84:9; 117b:4

Chastity (*castità*) 32 times: 59:7; 60:5; 61:4; 62:5; 63:6–7; 78:3; 101:4; 104:9; 107:3; 117b:4–5; 121:1; 124:4, 6; 127:5; 128:3, 5–6; 131:1–2; 132:2, 5–6

Church (*chiesa*) 326 times: 9:5; 18:2; 21:1; 23:5; 26:4; 27:2; 51:1, 5; 54:5–6; 55:1; 59:5–7; 73:4–4; 74:5–6; 75:3–4; 77:6; 78:4; 79:3, 7, 9; 80:1; 81:4; 83:7–8; 84:3, 5; 87:1, 3–4; 88:1–3; 89:7–8; 90:1–6; 91:1–8; 92:1–8; 93:1–7; 94:5, 7; 95:1, 6–7; 95b:1, 7, 24; 97:2, 4–5; 98:1–8; 99:1–4, 7; 101:1, 4, 7, 10; 102:1–8; 103:1, 3, 7; 104:1; 105:1–6; 106:1–4; 108:1–2; 112:3; 117:2–3, 5–6; 117b:1; 118:2, 4, 6; 119:1, 3, 5; 120:1, 4; 121:1–3; 122:1, 3; 123:1; 125:3; 126:1; 127:3–4; 128:4; 129:2; 133:2–3

Classical (*classico*) 27 times. Of the first rank or authority; constituting a standard or model, especially in literature, 39:2, 5; 63:5; 65:6; 82:2; 87:3–4, 6; 88:1, 3, 5; 94:6–7; 97:1; 98:2, 4; 99:2, 4, 7; 102:3, 5; 117:1; 117b:1; 127:5; 130:1

Ephesians 5 as the classical text, 20 times: 87:3–4, 6; 88:1, 3, 5; 94:6–7; 96:1; 97:1; 98:2; 99:2, 4, 7; 102:3, 5; 117:1; 117b:1; 127:5

Communicate (*comunicare*) 13 times: 12:4; 13:1; 16:1 (*see also* Give). The original power of communicating oneself, 29:2; 63:4; 67:3, 5; 68:2; 69:6

Communication (*comunicazione*) 17 times: 12:4–5; 60:3; 61:4; 62:1–4; 63:2, 6. *See also* Gift, Giving

Communion (*comunione*) 147 times. Communion arises as a shared life on the basis of the two principles of the life of persons according to *Gaudium et Spes* 24:3: (1) In virtue of their rationality, human beings are capable of the good and can move themselves to the good. This fundamental dignity must be affirmed in all dealings with persons. In this sense persons must be willed for their own sake instead of being used as mere means. (2) Persons can only find themselves in a sincere gift of self, 9:2–3, 5; 10:1–3; 12:1; 13:1. Communion of persons means living in a reciprocal "for," in a relation of reciprocal gift, 14:2, 4, 6; 15:4; 16:5; 17:3, 6; 18:1, 4–5; 23:5; 27:3; 28:1; 29:1. Reciprocal communion; self-communion, 29:2–5; 30:5–6; 31:1–3, 6; 32:1–2, 5–6; 33:1; 37:4–5; 39:5; 40:1, 3; 41:2, 4–5;

43:3; 49:5; 59:2, 4; 61:4; 62:1–3; 63:2, 6; 67:3; 68:1–2, 4; 69:4, 6–7; 73:1; 75:1, 3; 76:5; 77:1–2; 89:6; 95b:4; 100:1; 101:4; 103:5; 104:7; 105:3, 6; 106:2; 107:4, 6; 110:3; 113:5; 115:4; 116:3–5; 117:6; 117b:2; 123:5, 7; 125:1; 127:2, 4; 128:5–6; 129:6; 130:55; 132:5; 132:5. *See also* the Latin term *Communio*

Communion of persons (*comunione delle persone, comunione di persone*) (the phrase echoes *Gaudium et Spes* 12): 9:2–3; 10:2–3; 12:1; 13:1; 14:2, 4; 15:4; 16:5; 17:3, 6; 18:1, 4, 5; 21:7; 27:3; 28:1; 29:1–4; 30:3, 5; 31:2–3, 6; 32:1, 6; 37:4; 39:5; 43:3; 45:2. The deepest substratum of ethics and human culture, 45:3; 47:2; 59:4; 61:4; 62:1, 3; 63:6; 67:3; 69:4; 73:1; 75:3; 76:5; 89:6. Total gift in the trinitarian communion of persons, 95b:4; 100:1; 103:5; 104:7; 105:3; 106:2; 107:6; 110:3; 117:6; 117b:2; 123:5; 130:5

Personal communion (*comunione personale*): 29:3; 32:1–2; 41:5; 123:7; 127:2; 128:5; 130:5; 132:5

Communio (the Latin term *communio*) 18 times, usually in the phrase *Communio personarum* (*see Gaudium et Spes* 12): 9:2–3, 5; 12:5; 33:4; 55:6; 62:3; 68:1, 4. *Communio personarum* is built up by reciprocal self-communication, 69:6; 101:4; 102:2; 103:6; 123:7; 130:5; 131:3

Community (*comunità*) 34 times: 1:1; 3:3; 9:2; 10:3; 13:1; 21:7; 30:3, 5; 51:1; 65:3, 6; 69:6; 70:6; 72:2; 74:3; 77:3; 78:2, 4; 82:1; 88:3; 89:4, 6; 94:4. Reduction of the community to the person, 95b:2; 96:7; 120:4; 121:2; 123:1; 124:3

Communitarian (*comunitario*) 5 times: 69:4; 89:1. Communitarian and personal dimension, 95b:2

Concupiscence (*concupiscenza*) 340 times. *See also* Enjoyment, Lust, Object. Technical term for a corrupt form of desire that unduly appropriates something as a mere object for use, often for the sake of pleasure. This technical theological use of "concupiscence" is based on the Vulgate translation of 1 John 2:16, "All that is in the world—the desire (Greek *epithymia*, Latin *concupiscentia*) of the flesh, the desire of the eyes, the pride of life [or pride in riches]—comes not from the Father but from the world." Neither the Greek "*epithymia*" nor the Latin "*concupiscentia*" has, as such, a negative meaning. Both can be used in a positive or neutral way like the English "desire." Secondarily, however, "*epithymia*" and "concupiscentiae," but especially the English "concupiscence," took on a negative meaning. In present English it is not possible to use "concupiscence" without some negative conntation. The *Osservatore* translation often renders "*concupiscenza*" as sexual "lust." There is a broad consensus in the tradition that sexual lust is only a subspecies of the first of the three forms of concupiscence (*see* Thomas Aquinas, *Summa Theol.*, I–II, 77, 5), 17:3; 23:6; 26:1–3, 5; 27:2; 28:1, 3–6; 29:1, 4–5; 30:4–6; 31:1, 3–6; 32:1, 3–6; 33:1–5; 34:2–3, 5; 35:1, 3; 36:2; 38:2–3, 6; 39:1–2, 4. Sexual concupiscence consists in the detachment of desire from the spousal meaning of the body, 39:5; 40:1–2, 4–5; 41:1–3, 5; 42:4, 6; 43:1–6; 44:1, 45:1–2, 4–5; 46:1–6; 47:1–3, 5–6; 48:1, 4–5; 49:1, 3–6; 50:4–5; 51:1, 5–6; 52:2, 4; 53:3; 55:4; 56:1; 58:3, 5, 7; 59:2, 4–5; 60:2; 61:2–3; 62:5; 63:5; 64:1; 69:6; 70:6; 72:4; 77:4; 84:9; 85:4, 9; 86:4, 6–8; 87:2; 98:4; 100:7; 101:1–5, 7, 9; 106:5; 107:1–6; 117b:5; 123:8; 127:1, 4; 128:1–4; 130:5; 131:5; 132:3; 133:1.

Concupiscence of the Body, *see* Body 4

The threefold concupiscence (*la triplice concupiscenza*) in accord with 1 John: 26:1–3; 27:2; 28:5; 29:4; 30:6; 31:5; 33:4; 34:2, 5; 35:1; 46:1–3, 6; 47:5; 49:3; 50:5; 51:1, 5–6; 53:3; 55:4; 58:3; 61:3; 77:4; 86:7; 98:4; 100:7; 101:1; 107:3; 127:4; 130:5

Concupiscence of the flesh (*concupiscenza della carne*): 26:1–2; 29:4; 30:6; 31:3, 6; 33:4–5; 39:1; 40:1–2, 4; 43:3–6; 44:1; 45:1–2, 5; 46; 47:5; 49:4, 6; 50:5; 51:3; 52:2, 4; 53:3; 55:4; 56:1; 58:4; 59:5; 61:3; 64:1; 84:9; 85:4, 9; 100:7; 101:3, 4, 7, 9; 107:3, 6; 123:8; 127:4; 128:1–2; 130:5; 131:5. *See also* Drive, Lust

Carnal concupiscence (*concupiscenza carnale*): 39:2; 40:5; 45:4; 48:5

Concupiscence of the body, *see* Body 4

Man of concupiscence, *see* Man

Concupiscent (*concupiscente*): 38:6; 41:1; 47:1; 48:1, 5; 62:1; 78:1; 98:5; 100:7

Conjugal* (*coniugale*) 249 times. *See also* Spousal, Matrimonial, Nuptial (at entry for Wedding)

Conjugal act (*atto coniugale*). "Conjugal act" is not a euphemism or antiquated expression for "sex," but sex in its full moral nature and goodness as a personal act in the determinate circumstances of conjugal life. "Sex" is thus related to "conjugal act" somewhat as "eating" is to "dinner," 10:2; 20:2; 25:4; 29:3; 118:2–5; 119:1–2; 120:2; 121:6; 122:1–2; 123:6–8; 127:2, 4; 128:4–6; 129:2, 6; 130:2–3; 131:4–5; 132:2–4, 6. *See also* Conjugal copula, Conjugal knowledge, Conjugal relation, Conjugal union, Know, Knowledge, Marriage act (*Humanae Vitae* 11), Sexual act, Sexual union

Conjugal archetype (*archetipo coniugale*). Applied to the relation between God and his people, 21:1

Conjugal ascesis (*ascesis coniugale*): 131:2

Conjugal betrayal (*tradimento coniugale*): 37:1

Conjugal bond (*vincolo coniugale*): 105:6

Conjugal chastity (*castità coniugale*) 11 times: 107:3; 121:1; 124:4, 6; 128:3, 5–6; 131:1; 132:2

Conjugal copula (*copula coniugale*): 103:2

Conjugal communion (*communione coniugale*): 105:6; 107:4; 123:7

Conjugal community (*comunità coniugale*): 123:1

Conjugal conduct (*condotta coniugale*): 105:6

Conjugal consent (*consenso coniugale*) 16 times: 105:1, 3–6; 106:3–4; 107:2

Conjugal covenant (*alleanza coniugale*): 97:5; 100:3; 107:1

Conjugal covenant, Conjugal contract (*patto coniugale*) 13 times: 10:3; 37:5; 75:3; 80:6; 95:2; 100:5; 103:7; 104:4; 116:4; 117b:2; 127:4. *See also* Covenant

Conjugal "creed" ("*credo*" *coniugale*): 116:2

20:1; 21:1, 5, 7; 22:1–2, 5, 7; 23:1; 25:1; 26:2, 4; 27:2, 4; 28:1; 29:4; 30:5; 32:5; 35:4; 43:6; 45:3; 49:4–5; 50:3; 55:6; 58:1, 3; 59:2; 66:5; 68:3; 69:3; 70:3, 7; 73:5; 76:2; 77:1–3; 79:6; 80:7; 81:1; 86:6; 93:2, 6; 94:8; 95:1, 4–7; 95b:3, 7; 96:3, 6–7; 97:1; 98:1, 3; 99:2, 6; 100:2; 103:2; 104:2; 110:3; 124:4–6; 125:1; 126:1; 127:1; 132:3

Creative (*creativo*) 13 times: 3:1; 14:3, 5; 21:1, 6; 60:2, 4; 63:4, 7; 92:4; 93:5; 117b:3; 126:5

Creative (*creatore, creatrice*) 18 times: 5:4; 8:3; 11:4; 14:4; 18:5; 19:1; 21:1, 3, 5; 39:2; 48:4; 49:4; 50:3; 95b:7; 102:2; 121:6; 124:5

Creature (*creatura*) 24 times: 2:3; 4:1; 5:6; 6:2; 7:4; 11:5; 13:4; 14:3; 15:1, 3, 5; 19:1; 27:2; 32:4; 70:3, 8; 75:3; 95b:4; 114:1; 116:1; 126:1

Creation (*creazione*) 281 times: 1:4; 2:1–6; 3:1–2; 4:3; 5:1–5; 6:1–2, 4; 8:1–4; 9:1, 3, 5; 10:1–2, 4–5; 11:2; 12:1, 3; 13:1–4; 14:1–6; 15:1, 3, 5; 16:1–3, 5; 17:2, 5–6; 18:1, 3–5; 19:1, 3, 5–6; 20:1; 21:1–2, 6–7; 22:3, 5, 7; 23:3; 25:1; 26:2, 4; 27:3–4; 28:1; 29:3–4; 32:1–2; 34:2; 40:1; 46:5–6; 49:2–4; 51:1; 52:1; 55:3; 57:2; 60:7; 63:4, 7; 66:4; 69:3, 8; 70:7; 71:2; 73:3; 76:6; 86:1–3; 90:2; 93:1, 3; 94:1, 5; 95:4; 95b:7; 96:2–7; 97:1–5; 98:1, 3, 8; 99:2, 5, 7; 100:1–2, 5–6; 101:6–7, 9; 102:1, 3–4, 7–8; 103:3, 7; 105:1, 4, 5; 116:1; 117b:2; 123:4; 127:1; 131:4–5

Mystery of creation, *see* Mystery

Creed (*credo*): 116:2. *See also* Faith

Cycle (*ciclo*) 26 times

Cycle as a literary term (instances of Cycle added by UD to the original text of the catecheses are set in square brackets) 1:5; 2:1, 5:1. In 24:1, the first cycle is also called a "chapter." A single cycle that seems to encompass the whole work, 18:1; 22:1; 25:1; 33:1; 34:1; [44:1]; [45:1]; [46:1]; 47:1; 50:1; 58:1–2. Clear transition from the cycle on the Sermon on the Mount to the cycle on the resurrection, 59:7; 63:7; 111:6; 133:2

Other uses of cycle. The cycle of seven days in Gen, 2:1, 3. The cycle of knowledge and generation (Gen 4:1), 22:2, 5, 7

D

Deep, Profound (*profondo*) 144 times. An important concept in TOB since it is closely related to the notion of Expression, and thus to the Spousal meaning of the body, which implies the manifestation of some depth in and through its visible surface, such as the gift of self through the gestures and reactions of sexual union, 1:5; 2:5; 5:5; 6:1; 8:2–3; 9:3, 5; 11:5; 12:4; 13:4; 15:4–5; 16:1, 3; 17:5–6; 19:2; 20:4; 21:3, 7; 23:1; 26:2, 4; 27:1, 4; 29:5; 30:1, 4–6; 31:1, 4; 32:1, 3; 34:5; 35:2, 5; 38:1; 39:2; 40:5; 41:1, 3; 42:3; 43:3, 6–7; 45:1, 3–4; 46:1, 5–6; 47:1, 6; 48:3–5; 49:1, 5–6; 50:3; 57:2–3, 5; 60:7; 61:1–2, 4; 62:1–2; 67:2; 69:2–3; 70:5; 72:3; 76:3–5; 77:1; 80:2, 5; 81:3, 6; 88:2; 89:1, 4, 6; 90:4, 6; 92:5, 8; 100:5, 7; 101:6; 104:2, 7; 110:9; 111:6; 112:5; 113:3; 115:6; 117b:3; 119:4; 120:4; 123:4; 125:3, 5–6; 127:5; 128:2–3, 6; 131:4–5; 132:4–5. *See also* Expression

Deeply, Profoundly (*profondamente*) 61 times: 4:5; 5:4; 8:1; 10:1; 12:1; 14:2; 15:5; 17:3–4; 18:5; 19:5; 22:5; 25:5; 34:2; 36:6; 42:5; 45:2; 49:7; 52:5; 54:4; 55:2; 58:5; 60:2; 61:1, 4; 62:3–4; 69:3; 70:8; 73:1; 74:1; 75:1–2; 81:6; 84:5; 87:6; 90:4; 91:8; 92:2; 94:6; 102:6; 104:2; 107:1; 110:7–8; 113:6; 116:2, 5; 118:3, 5–6; 119:1, 4–5; 128:4; 129:2; 130:3

Depth, Profundity (*profondità*) 68 times: 3:1; 9:1; 10:2, 4; 11:1; 12:1, 5; 13:2–3; 14:3–4; 17:5–6; 18:3–5; 19:3, 5; 20:2, 4–5; 21:2, 6; 24:3; 26:3; 27:2; 31:5; 43:5–6; 44:5; 56:5; 57:3, 6; 61:2; 67:5; 68:3–4; 71:5; 76:6; 79:8; 84:5; 86:3, 5, 8; 95:2; 99:2, 4–5, 7; 100:6–7; 102:3; 104:2, 8; 105:4; 110:6–9; 113:1; 115:3; 116:4; 117b:5

Desire (noun, *desiderio;* verb, *desiderare*), 227 times. *See also* Concupiscence, Enchantment, Enjoyment, Erotic, Fascination, Instinct

Desire (verb), 54 times in a pregnant construction, with a negative sense

and height and, by analogy, other attributes according to which something can be measured in various ways, such as in its level of being, goodness, value, etc.
Dimension of gift. The dimension of gift is decisive for the essential truth and depth of the meaning of original solitude-unity-nakedness, 13:2, 4; 14:4; 19:3; 20:5; 30:1. The dimension of gift is the capacity of expressing love by which, through his or her sex, the person becomes a gift, 32:3, 5; 33:3; 96:1; 110:7; 117b:5; 123:5
Dimension of communion: 10:2; 12:5; 18:4; 30:6; 63:6; 77:1, 3; 91:2; 93:5; 95:7; 97:4; 105:3
Dimension of the person: 33:4; 44:6; 77:2; 95b:2; 103:6; 110:8
Ontological-objective dimension: 2:5; 9:1; 12:3; 20:3; 41:4; 45:2; 60:1–2; 116:5. In the teaching of *Humanae Vitae*, there is a close connection between the ontological-objective and the subjective-psychological dimension, 118:6; 119:2
Interior, subjective, psychological dimension: 8:2–3; 10:1; 11:3; 12:4; 15:4–5; 16:4; 25:2, 5; 28:1; 31:5; 32:5; 40:2; 41:1–2, 5–6; 44:1; 49:7; 50:3; 54:3; 60:1–2; 70:7; 80:4; 100:7; 110:3; 111:2; 112:3; 113:1; 116:5; 118:6; 119:1–2; 121:5; 123:1
Ethical dimension: 9:5; 41:5; 43:4–6; 44:6; 46:6; 48:2; 49:1; 53:1; 56:1, 4; 86:8; 100:5; 122:4; 125:4–5
Cosmic dimension: 52:1; 70:7; 71:2; 86:1–2
Anthropological dimension: 49:1; 86:1–2; 106:5
Dimension of the beginning: 22:5; 68:5; 69:2–3
Dimension of time and history: 24:1; 34:2; 57:5; 65:4–5; 66:4; 68:5; 69:4–5, 8; 79:3; 81:6; 95:7; 95b:7; 96:5; 100:5; 101:7
Eschatological dimension: 24:1; 66:5; 67:5; 68:5–6; 69:2; 99:5; 101:10–11; 117b:1. *See also* Eschatological
Dimension of the totality of life: 77:3; 80:6; 103:5; 106:3; 107:3; 115:5
Spousal and redemptive dimensions of the mystery of Christ: 95:5; 102:4, 6; 104:3

Dimension of covenant and grace of the sacrament of Marriage: 85:6; 87:6; 95:3; 117b:2; 117:1, 5; 133:2
Dimension of sign of the sacrament of Marriage: 87:6; 105:1; 106:1; 107:5; 117:1. The reflections about marriage in the dimension of sign are strictly linked with the teaching of *Humanae Vitae*, 118:3; 133:2
Disinterested (*disinteressato*) 14 times: 15:3; 16:3; 18:5; 22:4; 33:4; 75:4; 92:4; 110:2; 130:1; 132:4. *See also* Sincere, Gift of self
Divinization (*divinizzazione*) 9 times: 51:1; 67:3–5; 69:6; 71:5
Divorce (noun, *ripudio*; verb, *ripudiare*) 30 times: 1:2; 20:1; 23:1–2; 24:1; 34:1; 36:1; 58:1; 73:2; 81:1; 94:8; 95:1, 3; 99:6; 100:4, 6
Divorce (*divorzio*): 59:5
Dominate*, Master, Dominion, Domination, Mastery (*dominare, dominio*)
Master oneself, one's body, one's desire, etc.: 19:3; 28:3; 32:6; 45:2, 5; 48:5; 49:4. The purpose of self-mastery and temperance is the spousal meaning of the body, 49:5–6; 51:5–6; 52:4; 53:5; 54:3; 59:2, 5–6; 67:1, 2; 96:1; 101:1, 4, 9; 121:5; 123:5; 124:2; 127:4; 128:1
Domination of nature: 2:3–4; 5:4; 6:4; 22:2; 27:3–4; 70:7; 123:1
Domination of man over woman: 30:1–3, 5–6; 31:1, 3; 32:2; 33:1–2; 89:3
Drive (*pulsione*) 3 times. Sexual drive in a negative sense related to "concupiscence of the flesh," 128:1. *See also* Desire, Sex
Duet (*duetto*) 10 times. The duet of man and woman in the Song of Songs, 108:5; 109:3, 5; 110:4–5; 114:4; 115:2, 4. *See also* Dialogue
Duty (*dovere*) 18 times. Duty is born from values as the expression of conscience, 24:3, 32:3. The values and scale of values revealed in the Sermon on the Mount point to a duty of the will, 44:2; 56:3, 5; 57:1; 76:4; 85:5–6; 87:1; 91:5; 92:5; 101:2; 117:2, 4; 117b:3; 120:1; 121:2. *See also* Obligation, Virtue
Dynamic, Dynamics, Dynamism (adj., *dinamico*, noun, *dinamica*, noun, *dinamismo*) 14 times. From the Greek *dynamis*

over their impulses, man and woman can reach a higher kind of erotic spontaneity, in which they become aware of the beauty of the body as sign of love, 48:2, 4–5

Eroticism (*erotismo*): 47:3

Eschatology (*escatologia*): From the Greek *eschaton* (last) and *logos* (account): the account of the last things (resurrection, final judgment, etc.) or these last things themselves, 64:2; 65:3; 67:4

Eschatological (*escatologico*) 63 times: 7:4; 24:1; 49:2; 51:4; 57:5; 65:4; 66:2, 6; 67:1, 3–5; 68:1–4; 69:2–3, 5–6, 8; 70:3, 5; 71:4–5; 73:4–5; 75:1; 78:2; 79:2–3; 85:9; 86:3–7; 87:2; 91:8; 94:3; 95:6; 99:5; 101:7–11; 117b:1; 123:3

Eschatological man, *see* Man

Ethics, Ethical (*etica, etico*) 106 times: 2:5; 3:4; 9:5; 24:4; 25:4; 36:4; 38:4–5; 42:5; 44:1; 45:3; 46:2; 47:6; 48:1; 51:1; 53:1–2, 5; 54:2; 56:5; 58:4–5; 61:1; 62:3; 63:4, 7; 72:6; 85:9; 86:4; 100:3–5; 119:4; 122:2; 123:3; 124:4; 125:2, 4–5; 126:3; 128:4; 130:3; 133:3. *See also* Moral

Ethos (ethos) 163 times. *See also* Attitude, Mentality, Spirituality, Virtue. From the Greek *ēthos* (custom, disposition, character) and *ethos* (custom, habit). Ethos differs from virtue in being bound up with actual acts of knowing, as a conscious attitude or position taken up with respect to the good, 12:1; 18:3–5; 19:1–2. Ethos is the interior form, the soul, as it were, of human morality. It is an inner perception of values, 24:3–4; 34:1–2, 5; 35:1–4; 36:6; 38:1–2, 5; 41:6; 42:2, 4, 6–7; 43:4, 6; 44:1–6; 45:3–4; 46:4, 6; 47:1–2, 4–6; 48:1–2, 5; 49:1–7. The nature and structure of evangelical ethos according to Paul, 51:5–6; 52:4; 53:1–2; 57:5; 59:7; 60:1, 3, 5; 61:1–2, 4; 63:1, 6–7; 76:1; 77:4; 81:3, 7; 85:9; 98:5; 100:3, 4, 6–7; 101:2–4, 9; 104:8; 105:6; 107:2–3; 115:1. The ethos and the spirituality of marriage are the same thing, 117b:3, 6; 119:5

Ethos of the Body, *see* Body 4

Ethos of creation (ethos *della creazione*): 49:4

Ethos of redemption (ethos *della redenzione*): 46:4; 47:5. Detailed discussion, 49:2–7. From the perspec-

tive of Paul, 51:5–6; 98:5; 100:3; 107:2

Ethos of the redemption of the body (ethos *della redenzione del corpo*): 46:4. Detailed discussion, 49:2–4, 6–7; 57:5; 100:3; 117b:6; 119:5

Ethos of the Gospel, Evangelical ethos (ethos *del Vangelo*, ethos *evangelico*): 24:2, 4; 38:2; 43:4; 44:1; 47:1; 52:4; 53:1; 100:3

Ethos of the Sermon on the Mount (ethos *del discorso sulla montagna*): 42:4; 44:4; 45:3; 48:5

The new ethos (*il nuovo* ethos): 34:2; 38:1; 42:2, 4, 6–7. Summary overview, 49:2; 53:1; 100:6

Ethos of the Gift (ethos *del dono*): 19:1–2

Ethos of seeing (ethos *del vedere*): 63:6–7

Eunuch (*eunuco*) 25 times. From the Greek *eunē* (bed) and *echō* (have, keep, guard): a bedchamber guard, castrated man, 73:2–3; 74:1, 4, 5; 75:4; 76:4–5; 77:1; 79:1, 4; 80:1; 81:1, 4; 83:4, 6

Evangelical (*evangelico*) 40 times. From the Greek *euangelion* (good news), 24:2, 4; 38:3; 39:4; 42:7; 44:3; 48:5; 52:4–5; 53:1, 4; 55:2; 57:6; 58:5–6; 65:4; 73:1; 75:4; 76:3; 77:6; 78:3, 5; 81:3–4; 83:2–3; 84:1, 6; 85:7, 9; 87:2; 100:3; 107:4; 122:5; 126:4; 133:1. *See also* Gospel

Eve (*Eva*) 16 times: 20:2; 21:1, 5–6; 22:1, 5–6; 31:6; 44:5; 101:6; 110:7; 114:1; 116:1

Evil, Bad (*male*) 62 times: 6:2; 16:4; 35:1, 5; 36:6; 37:5–6; 39:2; 42:3; 44:5–6; 45:2, 4–5; 47:1; 50:4; 51:2, 6; 58:4; 59:1; 62:3; 72:4; 82:6; 86:7; 89:1; 100:7; 104:8; 107:3; 113:4; 115:2, 5–6; 123:7; 124:1; 126:2

Evil in the phrase "tree of the knowledge of good and evil," 37 times: 3:3; 4:1; 6:1; 7:3–4; 11:4–5; 16:3–5; 19:3; 20:2; 21:6; 22:5; 25:1; 26:2, 4; 27:1; 28:2, 4; 59:1; 62:3; 72:3–4; 82:6

Evolutionist, Evolutionistic (*evoluzionista, evoluzionistico*). Connected with a naturalistic understanding of man, 13:2. The evolutionistic mentality, also among theologians, raises objections against a perfect beginning of human life, 15:1

Experience (verb, *sperimentare*), 31 times: 4:5; 7:3; 12:1; 20:4; 22:6; 28:2; 30:4; 32:1,

3; 39:5; 40:1; 44:1; 48:1; 49:6; 55:4, 6; 60:2; 67:1–2, 5; 68:5; 69:1, 5; 70:8; 71:1; 109:4; 112:1; 129:4

Experience (noun, *esperienza*), 215 times. The human experience of love is a legitimate means of interpreting the divine revelation about love, 4:4–5; 6:3; 7:3; 9:1–3; 11:1, 3–6; 12:1–3, 5; 13:2; 14:5; 15:3–4; 16:1, 4–5; 17:1–3; 18:2–3; 19:5–6; 20:2, 4; 21:1, 6; 22:5, 7; 23:3; 25:1; 26:2, 5; 27:2, 4; 28:1, 5; 29:2, 4; 30:1–3; 31:1, 3, 5–6; 32:1–2; 33:5; 34:3; 36:4; 38:2–3, 5; 39:3–5; 40:4; 41:6; 44:5; 47:4; 48:2; 49:6; 55:4, 7. The gift of piety, basis of the experience of the spousal meaning of the body and the freedom of the gift, 57:2–3; 58:7; 59:4; 60:1–3; 67:4–5; 68:2, 5–6; 69:1–3, 5, 7; 70:1, 5–8; 71:1, 3; 74:6; 79:9; 80:1; 82:1–2; 83:3; 87:6; 96:6; 108:6–8; 109:2; 110:3; 111:2, 4, 6; 113:2; 115:2–3; 116:4; 117b:3; 128:6; 129:5

Experience of the Body, *see* Body 3

Express* (*esprimere*) 135 of 225 times, excluding instances of "expression" through words alone. Expression in the sense of a manifestation of the body's interior life in its appearance, e.g., the expression of love by the conjugal act, 7:2; 8:4; 9:3, 5; 10:2; 12:1, 4; 14:4, 6; 15:1, 4; 16:1; 17:3; 19:1, 5; 22:3, 4; 25:3; 27:3–4; 29:3; 32:1–3; 33:3–4; 39:4; 44:5; 45:2; 46:4; 50:5; 51:5; 52:4; 55:2; 57:3; 62:3; 63:4, 6; 67:2; 68:3; 70:3, 7; 75:1; 77:5; 78:4; 79:8; 83:9; 84:1; 85:8; 86:6, 8; 87:5; 90:1; 91:6; 92:6, 7; 97:5; 98:7; 99:7; 101:6; 102:2; 103:3–4, 7–8; 105:4; 107:1, 6; 108:8; 109:1, 4; 110:4, 8; 111:2; 112:5; 113:2; 115:1–3; 116:4; 117:4; 117b:3; 119:3; 122:3; 123:2, 4–6; 124:6; 125:2; 127:1, 4; 128:1, 5–6; 129:1, 4, 6; 131:4; 132:2–4. *See also* Deep, Depth

Expressed* (*espresso*) 26 of 75 times: 12:5; 16:2; 27:4; 29:1; 30:3; 32:4; 40:5; 41:1; 42:6; 43:2; 78:4; 81:2; 95:2; 105:1; 106:1; 109:2; 110:6, 9; 111:4; 123:7; 128:6; 132:2

Expression* (*espressione*) 53 of 178 times: 9:4; 14:4; man appears in the visible world as the highest expression of the divine gift, because he carries the dimension of gift within

himself, 19:3; 21:5; 22:4; 24:4; 27:3; 29:2; 31:2; 32:1–2, 5–6; 44:5; 46:5; 48:4; 52:3; 63:3, 7; 68:3; 69:6; 78:5; 83:3; 89:3; 91:6–7; 92:6; 94:6; 96:1; 101:1; 102:7; 103:5; 104:1, 8; 105:1; 106:1; 107:3; 111:2, 4; 112:5; 113:3; 117:4; 124:6; 125:1, 3

F

Faith (*fede*) 42 times: 4:5; 51:1, 3–4; 52:1, 5; 56:4, 5; 60:7; 64:2; 65:1–3, 6; 67:5; 68:4; 69:3, 7; 70:1–2, 5; 72:7; 76:3, 5; 78:2; 84:1; 93:5; 94:3–5; 97:5; 116:4; 126:4. *See also* Believe, Hope, Love

Faithful (*fedele*) 20 times: 24:4; 27:3; 43:5; 51:1; 53:4; 76:2; 85:4; 93:5; 103:1–2, 5; 107:4; 117:3; 118:4; 119:3; 121:5; 124:6; 125:3; 126:1

Faithfulness (*fedeltà*) 27 times: 16:5; 37:1, 4–5; 51:5–6; 78:3–4; 86:7; 95:3; 104:4, 7–9; 105:1; 106:2; 107:4; 117b:2, 6; 120:3; faithfulness to the divine plan (a plan visible in the two meanings of the conjugal act) is the key principle for responsible parenthood, 121:6; 122:1; 124:6

Unfaithful (*infedele*) 7 times: 37:1–2; 39:1; 57:5; 95:2–3

Unfaithfulness (*infedeltà*) 10 times: 36:6; 94:6–7; 95:3; 104:3–5, 8

Family (*famiglia*) 35 times: 1:1, 5; 18:4; 20:2; 23:2–3; 36:3; 59:5; 64:1; 77:3; 79:3; 81:6; 88:3–5; 89:3; 103:7; 110:1; 121:5–6; 124:2–3; 125:3; 126:2; 129:3; 133:4

Familiar, family, of the family (adj., *familiare*) 21 times: 77:3; 81:3–4; 84:2; 88:5; 105:6; 107:4; 118:1; 120:4; 121:2; 124:3; 125:2, 6; 126:3, 5; 127:3, 5; 129:3; 131:6; 133:2

1980 Synod of bishops *De muneribus familiae christianae*: 1:1; 124:3; 133:2, 4

Post-synodal apostolic exhortation *Familiaris Consortio*: 124:3; 125:1; 133:2, 4

Fascination (*fascino*) 13 times: 38:4; 44:5; 108:5–6, 8; 117b:3–5. *See also* Arousal, Concupiscence, Desire, Enchantment, Enjoyment, Libido, Lust, Object, Passion, Pleasure, Use

Father (*padre*)

The divine Father (*Padre*) 56 times: 9:4; 15:1; 16:2; the fall consists in

45:2; 46:4; 48:3; 49:2, 6; 51:1; 52:5; 53:1–3; 57:2; 58:4, 6; 69:6; 70:7; 72:4; 80:5; 86:1, 3, 8; 99:5; 101:5–6; 110:9; 117b:5; 123:5; 126:1; 128:2–3; 130:4; 132:3, 5

Freedom of the gift (*libertà del dono, libertà di dono*): 15:1–4, 5; 17:2; freedom of the gift is the innermost point of freedom, 18:5; 19:1–2; 32:6; concupiscence brings with itself the loss of the freedom of the gift, 33:1; 39:5; 41:3; 43:6; 46:4; 48:3; 49:6; 57:2; 58:6; 69:6; 80:5; 86:8; 101:5; 110:9; 117b:5; 123:5; 128:2–3; 130:4; 132:3, 5

Freud, Sigmund, Freudian: 8:3; 21:1; 46:1–2, 4, 6; 49:6

Friend occurs only in the feminine (*amica*) 11 times: The bride is called friend in Song 4:7 (CEI translation), 108:6–8; 109:3–4; 111:3; 112:2

Friendship (*amicizia* and Latin *amicitia*) 3 times: 109:4

Fruitful (*fecondo*) 7 times: 2:3–5; 22:3; 74:3; 96:7

Fruitfulness (*fecondità*) 36 times: 2:3; 9:3; 10:2; 14:6; 15:1; 20:1; 30:3; 32:1; 66:4; 69:3; 74:3; 75:2–4; 76:3; 78:5; 97:4; 102:2; 116:1; 123:6; 125:1; 126:3; 129:3, 6; 130:3–4; 131:6. *See also* Birth, Fertility

Fullness (*pienezza*) 72 times: 10:2, 11:4; the fullness of consciousness of the meaning of the body in the original state, 12:2–5; 13:1, 3; 14:3; 16:3; 18:5; 19:1, 6; 24:2; 25:5; 27:2; 28:55; 29:2; 43:7; 46:3; 47:1; 48:1; 49:3–4; 52:5; 53:1, 3–4; 57:3; 65:6; 66:1; 67:3; 71:1; 72:3; 73:1; 75:3; 79:7; 88:1; 90:5; 91:8; 93:3; 94:2, 5; 95b:4; 99:7; 105:4; 115:2; 127:2; 132:3. *See also* Richness

G

Gaudium et Spes. *See also* Council, Vatican II

GS 22:1 By revealing the mystery of the Father and his love, Christ makes man's supreme vocation clear, 86:3, 8; 87:6

GS 24:3, with its three main theses: (1) there is a likeness between the union of divine persons and the union of love between human beings; (2) God wills man for his own sake; (3) man can only find himself in a sincere gift of self: 10:3; 15:1–5; 17:3, 5–6; 19:5; 32:4; 77:2; 80:6; 81:6; 96:6; 100:1; 103:7

Other passages of *Gaudium et Spes*: 59:5; 106:2; 120:1, 3, 6; 121:1–2; 123:1. The traditional teaching on the ends of marriage and their hierarchy is confirmed by *Gaudium et Spes* (*see also* End, Finality, Subordination), 127:3; 129:3

Generative meaning of the body, *see* Body 2

Give* (*dare*) in the context of the gift of self: 10:5; 17:5–6; 18:4; 20:5; 59:1, 4; 73:4; 87:1; 88:1–2; 89:7–8; 90:5–6; 91:3–6; 92:1, 3; 93:1, 3, 6; 94:1, 5; 95:6; 95b:1; 96:4, 7; 97:2, 4; 99:1; 101:10; 102:2–4, 6; 114:5, 7; 126:4

Datum, that which has been given, as distinct from Gift (*donum*): 20:5

Give (*donare*) 47 times: 10:4; 13:4; 14:3–5; 16:1; 17:4–6; 18:5; 31:3; 43:6; 46:6; 47:1; 53:6; 54:1; 58:7; 61:1–2, 4; 62:1, 4; 63:3; 67:5; 79:9; 80:1, 6; 87:5; 90:2, 5–6; 92:4; 97:1, 3; 105:6; 110:7; 111:4; 114:5; 123:5

Gift (*dono*) 338 times. On the belonging of man and woman to each other, expressed by "my" or "mine," *see* 33:3–4. Man and woman become a gift for the other, 13:1–4; 14:1–2. The gift is the fundamental characteristic of personal existence, 14:4–5; 15:1–5; 16:1, 3–5; 17:2–6; 18:1, 3, 5; 19:1. Man appears in the visible world as the highest expression of the divine gift, because he carries within himself the inner dimension of the gift, 19:3, 5; 20:5; 21:1, 3, 6; 22:4; 26:4; 27:2; 30:3; 32:1–6; 33:1–2, 4; 39:5; 40:1; 41:3; 43:6; 46:4; 48:1, 3; 49:5–6; 51:5; 53:3; 56:1, 4; 57:2–4; 58:6–7; 59:2; 60:7; 61:1–2, 4; 62:1–4; 68:2–3; 69:6; 72:6; 73:4; 75:3; 76:4; 77:2–3; 78:4–5; 79:8; 80:5–6; 81:6; 82:2; 83:4; 84:1, 8; 85:4–5, 7–8; 86:8; 88:2; 90:5–6; 91:8; 92:3; 94:1–2, 5; 95:3; 95b:2, 4; 96:1, 3, 5; 97:2; 101:2–3, 5, 10; 103:4–6; 104:4; 110:2, 7, 9; 111:2, 4–5; 113:3; 116:1; 117b:4–5; 123:5, 7; 124:5; 128:1–3; 130:4; 131:1–2, 4–6; 132:1–5. *See also* Gift (*donazione*), Grace

erence to the human subject, the note of appreciation or evaluation of some good by a person. 2:5; 3:3; 4:1; 5:2, 4; 6:1–2; 7:3–4; 8:1, 3; 11:4–5; 13:1, 3; 14:1–2; 16:1, 3–5; 19:3; 20:2; 21:6; 22:5; 25:1; 26:2, 4; 27:1–2; 28:2, 4; 35:1, 5; 37:5–6; 39:2; 44:1, 5; 47:1; 48:2; 50:4; 51:2, 6; 52:4; 53:4; 54:5; 57:5; 58:4; 59:1, 3; 62:3; 72:3–4; 76:5; 77:3–5; 79:7; 82:4–6; 83:1; 84:1, 3; 85:1; 86:7–8; 92:4, 7–8; 96:3; 100:7; 104:8; 110:4; 115:2, 5; 120:6; 121:2; 122:5; 124:6; 125:2–3; 127:2; 133:3. *See also* Value

Good (adj., *buono*) 38 times: 2:5; 9:1; 13:1, 3; 19:3; 21:2; 22:4, 7; 26:2; 27:4; 38:4; 44:3; 46:5; 47:2, 5; 48:1; 53:4; 55:6; 57:2; 83:2; 84:7; 86:2; 92:4; 93:3; 96:3; 111:4; 114:1; 115:1, 5; 116:1; 120:4; 127:1

Gospel (*vangelo*) 81 times: 1:1; 21:5; 23:1; 34:2, 4; 37:5; 38:2; Gen 2:24 ("For this the man will leave his father and his mother and unite himself with his wife and the two will be one flesh") is "the Gospel of the Beginning," 39:5; 42:4; 43:4; 44:1, 6; 45:5; 47:1; 49:3; 51:1; 52:1; 53:2; 57:5; 58:5–6; 59:1, 7; 64:1–3; 65:1; 66:1; 67:2; 68:2; 69:8; 70:1–2, 5; 71:1, 5; 72:1; 73:3–4; 75:3–4; 76:1; 77:1–2; 78:1; 79:8; 80:1; 81:3, 7; 82:1, 3; 83:7–8; 84:3; 85:8; 86:2–3, 7; 93:5; 94:4; 99:4; 100:1–3; 101:1; 104:7; 107:1, 3; 119:5; 121:2; 122:5. *See also* Ethos of the gospel

Grace (*grazia*) 102 times: 4:2; 16:1–2; grace is a participation in the inner life of God, 16:3–4; 18:3; 19:2–3; 27:2; 38:4–5; 46:5; grace is God's self-communication to man, 67:3, 5; 73:4; 75:3; 76:4; 83:9; 84:1, 8–9; 85:4–5; 87:5–6; 88:1; 91:8; 93:3, 5; 94:1–2; 95:3, 6; 95b:4–5; 96:2, 4–5, 7; 97:1–3, 98:1, 7; 99:2; 100:4, 7; 101:2–5, 10; 102:4, 6; 103:3, 6–7; 104:2; 105:1; 106:5; 108:3, 5, 7; 114:7–8; 115:6; 117:1, 5–6; 117b:2; 126:1, 5; 131:3; 133:2

Endow with the gift of grace (*gratificare*) 3 times: 13:4; 96:7; 98:1

Endowment with the gift of grace, Gracing (*gratificazione*) 23 times: 79:7; 96:2, 5; 97:2–3; 98:2–4; 101:5–6; 102:3

Guiding thread (*trama*) 11 times: 18:4; 43:7; 48:1; 55:3; 57:3; 59:1; 110:5; 132:4; other possible translations: woof (the

thread that crosses from side to side in a loom, guided by the shuttle), plot, plan

H

Happiness (*felicità*) 18 times: 2:1; 3:1; 5:4; 14:1, 3; 15:5; happiness is being rooted in Love, 16:1–2, 5; 19:4; 23:5; 66:6; 83:3. *See also* Beatifying

Happy (*felice*) 5 times: 12:3; 30:3; 38:4; 55:6; 88:4. *See also* Beatifying

Heart (*cuore*) 408 times: 1:2; 3:4; 4:1; 12:5; 13:1–2; 16:3–4; 17:1, 3, 6; 18:5; 19:2–3; 20:1; 23:1, 6; 24:4; 25:2, 5; 26:1–5; 27:1; 28:4–6; 29:1; 30:2, 4, 6; 31:5–6; 32:1, 3; 33:1, 5; 34:1–5; 36:3; 37:2; 38:1, 5; 39:2–4; 40:1–4; 41:1–2, 6; 42:7; 43:5–7; 44:1–2, 4; 45:1, 4–5; 46:1–2, 4–6; 47:1, 3–6; 48:2–5; 49:1, 4–7; 50:1–5; 51:1–2, 4–5; 52:1, 3–4; 55:6–7; 56:1; 57:6; 58:4–7; 59:1–2; 60:1; 61:1–3; 62:5; 64:1; 68:5; 69:1; 70:6; 73:2, 4; 78:1; 79:7, 9; 80:1; 82:4; 83:7; 85:10; 86:2–4, 6–7; 87:2; 88:3; 89:2; 95:2; 97:1; 98:5; 99:6; 100:7; 101:1, 3, 5, 7; 103:5; 104:3; 106:6; 107:1; 108:4–6, 8; 109:1, 3; 111:2, 5–6; 112:2–3; 114:4, 6; 115:1, 3–4; 116:2, 5; 126:4–5; 127:4; 128:3; 131:1. *See also* Affective, Arousal, Attraction, Emotion, Passion, Sentiment, Subjectivity

Adultery in the heart, committed in the heart (*adulterio nel cuore, commesso nel cuore*): 24–63

Purity of heart (*purezza di cuore*) 36 times: 16:5; 19:1; 43:5; 48:3, 5; 49:7; 50:1, 3–5; 52:1, 5, 53:4; 55:6; 57:5; 58:4–7; 59:7; 60:1; 62:1; 63:4–5

Help* (*aiuto*) 29 times, Eve as the help given by God to Adam: 5:2, 4; 6:1; 8:3–4; 9:2; 10:3; 12:3; 14:1–2; 76:5; 97:4; 108:4; 114:1; 116:1

Hermeneutics (*ermeneutica*) 25 times. From the Greek *hermeneuō* (to interpret, to translate): the science of interpretation, a systematic interpretation. The subject matter of hermeneutics is meaning, signification. John Paul II's main interest is to unfold "the hermeneutics that has its source in the Bible" (46:1), i.e., the hermeneutics of the gift that brings to light the full spousal meaning of the body, 3:3; 13:2; 16:1; 21:1; 46:1–2, 4, 6; 49:6. Theological hermeneutics, 60:1; 85:10. The linking of the spousal meaning of the body with its redemptive meaning is essential for the hermeneutics of man, which can also be called a hermeneutics of the sacrament, 102:5; 107:1, 5–6. *See also* Interpretation

Hermeneutics of the gift (*ermeneutica del dono*), core of John Paul II's theological method, rooted particularly in St. John of the Cross: 13:2; 16:1

Hermeneutics of the Sacrament (*ermeneutica del sacramento*): 107:5–6

Hermeneutics of suspicion (*ermeneutica del sospetto*): 46:6

Hierarchy (*gerarchia*) 40:3; 48:5; 121:6; Hierarchy of the ends of marriage (*see also* End): *Gaudium et Spes* reaffirms the traditional teaching on the hierarchy of the ends of marriage (primary end procreation, secondary end mutual aid, etc.), but without using that traditional terminology (*see also* Wojtyła, *Love and Responsibility*, 68), 127:3

History (*storia*) 90 times: 4:1, 3; 8:3; 10:1; 15:5; 17:1; 18:4; 19:3–4; 20:1; 22:5–7; 23:5; 25:1–2; 26:2; 30:2, 6; 31:5–6; 34:2, 5; 35:2–3, 5; 36:1; 37:3; 38:2; 43:7; 44:3–6; 46:5; 51:4; 52:4; 55:7; 57:2; 59:1; 60:7; 63:3; 65:3–5; 67:4; 68:2; 69:3–4; 70:3; 72:3; 75:1, 3; 93:2–3, 5; 94:2; 95:2, 7; 95b:7; 96:5; 97:5; 100:1; 106:5; 110:2; 115:6

History of salvation (*storia della salvezza*): 4:3; 8:3; 10:1; 26:2; 31:5; 51:4; 59:1; 75:3; 93:3; 97:5; 106:5

Historical (*storico*) 120 times: 3:1; 4:1–4; 11:1, 4; 15:5; 16:4–5; 17:1–2, 6; 18:2–3; 20:1; 21:6; 23:2; 25:1, 5; 26:1–2; 27:2, 4; 28:2; 29:4–5; 30:2, 6; 31:5–6; 33:2; 34:2–3, 5; 38:5; 43:7; 44:1, 3–5; 45:3; 49:1, 3, 7; 51:1, 4; 55:4, 6–7; 58:3; 61:3; 63:7; 67:1; 68:5–6; 69:1, 4–5; 70:3, 5, 7–8; 72:1; 73:4–5; 74:4; 77:4; 79:3; 85:10; 86:3, 6; 87:2; 93:5; 95:7; 95b:1, 5, 7; 99:5, 7; 100:5–7; 101:4, 7, 11; 106:5; 107:4; 133:4

Historical *a posteriori* (*a posteriori storico*). From the Latin *a* (from) and *posterior* (later): an account "from what is later" rather than from what comes first in time or causality, 16:5; 17:2, 6; 18:3

Historical man, *see* Man

Historicity (*storicità*): 31:5; 40:2

Holy (*santo*) 31 times: 38:4; 68:6; 69:6–7; 74:3; 75:1; 84:4–5; 87:1; 88:1; 89:2; 90:2; 91:5–6, 8; 92:1, 3; 94:1; 95:5; 96:2–4; 97:2–3; 99:1; 102:2–3; 112:3. *See also* Sanctify

Holiness (*santità*) 62 times: 16:1, 3; 19:5; 23:5; 27:2; 53:6; 54:1–4, 6; 55:3, 5, 7; 56:1–2, 4–5; 57:1–3; 58:7; 60:1; 73:4; 75:4; 83:9; 84:5; 88:2; 89:1; 92:3; 93:5; 95:5; 96:4–6; 99:2, 7; 100:6–7; 101:6; 109:2; 116:4; 117b:2; 126:1

Homogeneity (*omogeneità*) 4 times. Together in origin or of the same kind, 8:4; 21:6

Honor, Honorable (*onore, onorare, onorevole*) 19 times: 21:5; 54:5; 55:1, 4–7; 65:3; 75:3; 88:4; 103:1–2, 5; 107:4; 117:3; 118:4. *See also* Reverence, Shame (*vergogna*), as well as Shame (*pudore*)

Honorable, Worthy, Upright (*onesto*) 8 times, morally "honorable" or "upright" method of regulating fertility: 124:1–4; 125:1, 5–7; 126:2; 131:6

Honor, Integrity (*onestà*) 6 times, mainly in the phrase "conjugal honor" or "conjugal integrity": 105:1; 106:2; 107:4; 117b:2, 6

Hope (*speranza*) 48 times: 19:6; 39:2; 49:2; 51:15; 70:7–8; main discussion of "everyday hope," 86:1, 3, 5–7; 99:5; extensive discussion, 101:4, 6–7, 10–11; 102:6; 122:5; 126:4. *See also* Faith and Love

Horizon (*orizzonte*) 24 times: 3:3; 4:3; 7:3; 15:1; 19:6; 20:1; 22:5, 7; 32:4; 40:3–4; 41:2; 51:4; 52:1, 4; 77:4; 99:7; 101:5; 113:5; 114:8; 126:4

Human being (*essere umano*) 53 times: 3:2; 4:1; 5:6; 8:1, 4; 9:1–2; 10:3; 11:1, 3, 6; 12:1, 3; 17:3; 21:1, 3; 23:1, 3; 27:3; 28:4; 29:2–4; 30:6; 31:1, 4–5; 32:6; 33:1; 41:2, 5; 43:6; 44:6; 49:7; 55:4; 56:1; 57:3; 60:1; 66:6; 69:4; 73:4; 86:8; 106:3; 115:3–6; 129:6. *See also* Man

Humanity (*umanità*) 102 times: 2:4; 5:2, 6; 6:2; 7:1, 3–4; 8:2, 4; 9:1, 3–5; 10:2; 12:3; 13:1; 14:6; 15:2; 17:4–5; 18:5; 19:1, 6; 21:1–2, 4, 6–7; 22:1–3; 25:2; 26:4; 27:2, 4; 28:1; 29:2; 30:3, 5; 33:5; 34:2, 4; 43:7; 46:5–6; 49:4; 59:2; 60:4; 62:3, 5; 65:6; 67:3; 69:2, 5, 8; 71:3–4; 72:2–3; 76:6; 77:1, 4; 88:1; 89:7; 90:1; 93:2, 5; 94:3, 5;

I

Intentional (*intenzionale*) 15 times. From the Latin *in* (into) and *tendo* (stretch, aim, tend): a technical term used by Phenomenology to characterize acts that are "about" some object, as seeing red is an act "about" red and in this sense "tends into" red. A toothache is a nonintentional act because it is not in the same way "about" something. The feeling of pain has no object. I can *think about* pain, and this thought has an object; it is intention-

Love (verb, *amare*) 91 times: 33:5; 35:2; 37:1; 47:1; 59:5; 68:3; 72:4; 82:2; 84:1; 87:1; 88:2, 4; 89:7–8; 90:2–3, 5; 91:3–6; 92:1, 3–7; 93:1, 3, 6; 95:3, 6; 95b:1; 97:2, 4; 99:1; 102:2–3, 6; 103:1, 2, 5; 107:4; 109:5; 110:2; 111:4; 112:2; 117:2–4, 6; 117b:3; 118:4; 127:1; 128:3

    Love (noun, *amore*) 465 times: 10:3; 11:3–4; 13:3–4; 14:3–5; 15:1, 4; 16:1–2; 19:1–6; 21:5; 22:2, 4; 26:4; 27:2; 28:6; 29:4; 32:1, 3, 6; 33:3–4; 36:5–6; 37:1–5; 38:5 46:5–6. Love is the supreme value, 46:5–6; 47:1; 49:7; 51:5–6; 53:2; 57:2–3; 59:5–6; 60:7; 63:3; 67:4; 68:1, 3–4; 69:6; 78:4–5; 79:8–9; 80:1, 6; 81:4; 83:3; 84:1; 87:4–5; 89:3–4; 90:1–6; 91:4, 6–8; 92:2–8; 93:1, 6; 94:5–8; 95:1–7; 95b:1–5, 7; 96:1, 6; 97:4; 99:1, 4; 101:1, 7, 10; 102:1–2, 4, 6–8; 104:2–4, 8; 105:1, 6; 106:1–2, 4; 107:4, 6; 108:1, 3–6, 8; 109:1–4, 6; 110:1, 4, 6–7, 9; 111:1–3, 5–6; 112:1, 3–4; 112:4–5; 113:1–6; 114:3–4, 6; 115:1–3; 116:4–5; 117:1–2, 4–6; 117b:1–3, 6; 118:1; 120:1–2, 6; 121:1–2, 4; 123:2–3, 6; 124:2, 5; 125:6; 126:1, 4–5; 127:1–5; 128:2–3; 130:3; 131:1–2, 4; 132:2–3, 6; 133:1

    Love (capitalized) 21 times, in the sense of divine and trinitarian Love: 11:4; 14:4–5; 15:1, 4; 16:1–2; 19:4–6; 26:4; 27:2; 94:5; 96:1; 116:4

    Truth and Love as a conceptual pair to signify trinitarian life (following *Gaudium et Spes* 24:3), in particular the procession of the Son as Word and Truth and of the Holy Spirit as Love: 15:1. Important discussion, 19:4–6; 32:4; 67:4; 69:6; 87:5; 96:1; 100:1; 103:7; 132:6

Love (*carità*) 30 times: 15:1; 32:4; 52:5; 53:1–4; 73:5. The measure of Christian perfection is love, 78:3; 88:1–2; 94:1, 5; 96:2; 100:1; 103:7; 113:4–5; 128:2; 131:3

Lust, Lustful (*lussuria, lussurioso*) 4 times: 39:4; 114:1; 116:3. *Oxf. Engl. Dict.*: "Lust: Sexual appetite or desire. Chiefly and now exclusively implying intense moral reprobation: Libidinous desire, degrading animal passion. (The chief current use.)" Over against four instances of "lust" and "lustful" in the Italian text (to which one can add the few instances

of "*libidinoso*" and "*libido*"), there are more than 170 instances of "lust" in the *OR* translation, often as the equivalent of *desiderio* (desire) and *concupiscenza* (concupiscence). On the problems caused by this proliferation of "lust" see Introduction, p. 13. *See also* Concupiscence, Desire, Enjoyment, Libido, Object, Pleasure

Lustful (*libidinoso*) 6 times: 54:1–4. *See also* Libido

M

Magisterium (*magistero*) 14 times: 18:2; 27:2; 59:5, 7; 118:1–2; 119:3–4; 120:1; 121:1–3

Man*, Human being, Human person (*uomo*) 1,992 times. *See also* Human being (*essere umano*)

    Man of original innocence (*uomo della innocenza originaria*): 28:1; 29:4–5; 55:6; 98:4

    Man of original justice (*uomo della giustizia originaria*): 98:4

    Fallen man (*uomo caduto*): 73:4

    Man of sin (*uomo del peccato*): 92:2

    Historical man (*uomo storico*) 62 times: 4:1–3; 11:4; 16:4; 17:1; 18:2; 20:1; 25:1, 5; 26:1–2; 27:2; 28:2; 29:4–5; 30:2, 6; 34:2–3, 7; 44:1, 3–4; 45:3; 49:1, 7; 51:1, 4; 55:4, 6–7; 58:3; 61:3; 63:7; 67:1; 68:5; 69:1; 70:7–8; 72:1; 86:6; 87:2; 99:5; 106:5; 107:4

    Man of concupiscence (*uomo della concupiscenza*) 33 times: 28:1, 3, 4; 29:4–5; 30:5; 33:1; 34:2–3, 5; 38:2; 45:1; 46:3; 49:1, 4; 51:1; 58:5, 7; 100:7; 106:5; 107; 128:4. *See also* Concupiscence

    Carnal man (*uomo carnale*): 48:5; 69:2

    Sensual man (*uomo sensuale*): 47:1

    Man of earth (*uomo di terra*): 71:3; 72:1

    Man of this world (*uomo di questo mondo*): 71:4

    Old man (*uomo vecchio*) (*see* Rom 6:6): 92:2

    New man (*uomo nuovo, nuovo uomo*) (*see* Eph 2:15 and 4:24): 21:4, 6–7; 22:1, 7; 49:4; 70:7; 88:2; 101:6

    Outer man (*uomo esteriore*) (*see* 2 Cor 4:16): 39:2; 48:3; 51:1

Model, Pattern, Shape (verb, *modellare*) 14 times: 62:3, 5–6; 90:3; 94:3; 99:2–3; 101:4; 102:8; 117:5–6; 122:5; 132:2

Modesty, *see* Shame

Moral, Morality (adj. and noun, *morale*), 142 times: 16:4; 17:3; 20:2; 24:1–3; 25:1; 28:3; 35:2; 36:6; 37:5–6; 38:5; 39:4; 42:3, 7; 43:1. Morality that is alive is always the ethos of human praxis, 44:2–3; 45:4; 46:1–2; 50:2–4; 51:1, 4, 6; 52:3–4; 53:1, 4; 56:1–3; 57:1, 5; 58:4; 59:6–7; 82:2; 83:3; 84:5; 86:8; 88:5; 89:2; 90:3; 92:2–3, 5, 7–8; 94:4; 98:5; 99:7; 100:4; 103:7; 104:2, 8; 107:3; 117:4; 118:1, 3–6; 119:2–5; 120:1–2, 6; 121:1–2, 5–6; 122:1–4; 123:2, 4, 8; 124:1, 3–4; 125:3–7; 126:2; 127:2–3; 128:4; 129:2, 6; 131:2; 133:2

    Morality (*moralità*): 36:4; 86:6; 118:5; 124:4

    Morally (*moralmente*) 24 times: 53:4; 61:1; 107:1; 119:2–3; 122:1–3; 124:6; 125:1–6; 128:6

Mother (*madre*) 45 times

    "The man will leave father and mother" (Gen 2:24) 22 times: 1:2–3; 3:2; 8:1; 9:5; 10:3; 18:5; 19:1, 5; 22:1; 23:1; 58:1; 66:4; 87:1, 3; 91:5; 93:1; 97:2; 99:6; 102:1; 103:2; 133:1

    Mother, in other contexts, 23 times: 10:3–4; 21:1–2, 5–6; 22:5; 31:2; 73:2; 74:1; 75:2; 81:1; 88:4; 92:8; 101:6; 109:5; 110:1, 4; 112:2

    Maternal (*materno*): 21:5–6; 121:5

    Motherhood (*maternità*) 25 times: 10:4; 21:2–6; 22:6; 69:4; 75:2–4; 78:5; 83:3; 97:4; 105:6; 121:3, 5; 127:4; 132:2

    Responsible fatherhood and motherhood, 35 times: 120:6; 121:2–5; 124:1, 4; 125:1–4; 126:2–3; 127:2, 4; 128:5; 129:2, 6; 130:3; 131:5–6; 132:2

Mystery* (*mistero*) 373 times. *See also* Sacrament

    The mystery (*il mistero*). The mystery (see Eph 1:9; 3:3–4, 9, and 5:32) is the communion of divine persons shared by human beings, most fully in the beatific vision, 67:3, 5; 68:1. The mystery is visible in the continuity of God's plan from the spousal union of man and woman in creation to the spousal union of Christ with the Church, 93:3. Extensive historical discussion of "mystery" in footnote, 93:5; 94:1–5. The mystery is revealed in Christ's spousal love, 95:7. Ephesians illumines the sacramentality of marriage by showing how the mystery became visible in a sign, namely, the love between man and woman, 95b:6

    The divine mystery (*il mistero divino*). Ultimately the mystery of the gift of self and communion of persons in the Trinity, 90:4; 94:4; 95b:1, 5–6; 100:7; 107:2; 131:5

    The great mystery, The mystery is great (*il grande mistero, il mistero è grande*) 25 times. The spousal mystery in its continuity from the creation of man and woman to redemption by Christ (*see* Eph 5:32), 9:5; 75:4; 87:1. Important discussion of the continuity of the great mystery, 93:2–4, 6; 95:7; 95b:7; 97:1–2, 5; 98:5; 99:4, 7; 102:1, 4–6, 8; 115:3; 117b:1

    The mystery of the person (*il mistero della persona*). Is visible in the Trinity as a communion of persons, 58:2; 111:1

    The mystery of man (*il mistero dell'uomo*) connected with the inner structure of the person, lies in the meaning of gift inscribed in the body, 62:2

    The mystery of the subject (*il mistero del soggetto*). Is the freedom of the gift of self, 19:2

    The mystery of creation (*il mistero della creazione*) 88 times: is a mystery of divine love and gift, which is an expression and consequence of the eternal reality of gift between the divine persons, 1:4; 3:2; 9:3; 10:1–2, 4–5; 12:1; 13:1–2, 4; 14:3–5; 15:3, 5; 16:1, 3, 5; 17:2, 5–6; 18:3–5; 19:1, 3, 5–6; 20:1; 21:1, 6–7; 22:3, 5; 23:3; 25:1; 26:2; 27:3–4; 28:1; 29:3–4; 32:1–2; 34:2; 40:1; 46:5; 49:3; 55:3; 57:2; 69:3; 70:7; 71:2; 73:3; 76:6; 95b:7; 96:3, 5; 99:7; 100:1–2, 5–6; 101:6, 9; 102:1, 3–4, 8; 103:3, 7; 105:1, 4; 117b:3; 127:1; 131:4

Personal union, unity (*unione personale, unità personale*) 6 times: 31:3; 33:3; 52:1; 55:6; 128:6

Personalistic, Personalist (*personalistico, personalista*) 13 times: 12:5; 81:5; 100:3; 117:3, 5–6; 117b:2; 123:3; 130:3, 5; 133:2–3

Piety (*pietà*, Latin *pietas*) 20 times. Piety is the virtue that regulates one's relation to one's parents, fatherland, ancestors, other family members, and above all one's relation to God, where its proper act is reverence for the holiness of God. Among the gifts of the Holy Spirit, piety is the one most congenial to the virtue of sexual purity, because it is sensitive to the beauty and sacredness of the body as temple of the Holy Spirit. Detailed discussion in 57:2, footnote; 57:2–3; 58:7; 89:1–3, 6; 95:1; 126:4. *Pietas* is the key gift of the Holy Spirit in the spirituality of marriage according to *Humanae Vitae*, 131:2; 132:1, 6

Plan (*disegno*) 24 times. God's plan for human love, 25:1; 34:1; 35:1; 43:6; 45:3; 55:6; 73:5; 88:1; 94:2–3; 96:3; 97:1; 100:2; 101:1, 5; 118:1; 120:6; 123:3; 124:5; 125:1; 126:1

Plan* (*piano*) 35 of 51 times, excluding instances with the meaning "level." God's plan for human love, 51:4; 65:6; 71:3; 78:3; 79:6; 88:1–3; 89:7; 90:2; 93:2, 5; 95b:7; 96:1, 6; 102:1; 118:1; 121:6; 122:1; 123:2; 124:6. "Human love in the divine plan" expresses the theme of the whole work, 133:1

Plato, 14 times: 2:5; 22:4; 47:1–2. Meditation on the resurrection led Thomas Aquinas to abandon Plato's doctrine on the relation between body and soul and adopt Aristotle's, 66:6

Platonic (*platonico*) 9 times: 22:4; 47:1, 4; 66:6; 70:8; 72:4

Pleasure (*compiacimento*) 7 times. *Compiacimento* is used only in the positive sense. A noble [erotic] pleasure, 48:4; 96:3. The mutual [erotic] pleasure of man and woman caused by beauty, 108:6, 8. Mutual fascination and pleasure of man and woman in each other according to the Song of Songs, 117b:3; 132:4. *See also* Arousal, Concupiscence, Desire, Emotional stirring, Enchant-

ment, Enjoyment, Fascination, Libido, Lust, Object, Use

Take pleasure (*compiacere*) 13:3; 113:4; 127:1

Pleasure, Please (verb and noun, *piacere*) 19 times. Mostly in the sense of "pleasing the Lord" and "pleasing one's spouse," 44:5; 51:3; 83:6, 9–10; 84:1, 4; 85:2; 129:6

Potentially procreative meaning, *see* Procreation

Praxis (*praxis*) 6 times. The Greek word *praxis* (act): the sphere of human acts, 44:2–3; 45:3; 48:2, 5

Praxis, Practice (*prassi*) 4 times: 7:1; 20:1; 44:2; 117b:6

Pre-history (*preistoria*) 10 times. Every human being is rooted in his theological pre-history, 4:1–3; 11:1; 15:1; 18:3; 25:1; 31:5–6

Primordial (*primordiale*) 45 times: 1:4; 7:2; 11:1; 19:3–4; 21:1; 28:1; 44:5; 96:1–4, 6; 97:1–2; 98:1–2, 8; 99:2, 7; 100:1, 3–4, 6; 101:7, 9–10; 102:1–2; 104:4; 108:3; 109:2; 110:3; 111:4; 116:4; 117:1. *See also* Original

Procreation (*procreazione*) 44 times: 2:5; 9:3; 10:4–5; 14:6; 15:1; 18:5; 19:1; 21:4; 22:4; 23:3–4; 30:3; 32:1; 35:2; 44:5; 45:3; 66:2; 67:4; 69:3–4; 74:3; 76:5; 96:7; 97:1; 101:6, 11; 121:1; 122:1; 124:1, 6; 125:2–3; 129:6; 132:5; 133:4

Procreative (*procreativo*) 24 times: 4:6; 30:5; 36:2; 39:5; 41:4; 66:4; 69:5; 75:4; 105:6; 106:4; 118:2; 120:2; 123:6; 124:3; 127:3; 128:4–6; 130:3; 132:2. *See also* Unitive

The procreative meaning of the conjugal act is a potentially procreative meaning (*potenzialmente procreativo*) 5 times: 128:5–6; 132:2

Profanation (*profanazione*). Profanation of the body through sexual sin, 56:3

Progress (*progresso*) 8 times: 44:3; 61:2. The essence of the Church's teaching in *Humanae Vitae* consists of raising questions about the stupendous progress made by our age in the domination of the forces of nature, 123:1; 129:2. The issue behind *Humanae Vitae* is that of true as opposed to false progress, a progress measured by persons as opposed to a

Sex (*sesso*) 66 times. Consistently in the sense of the male and the female sex rather than in the sense of the act of sexual intercourse, though some instances are debatable, 2:3; 5:2; 8:1. Theology of sex, of masculinity and femininity, 9:5, 10:1–2; 13:1. The relation between person and sex, 14:3. Sex is the original sign of creative giving, 14:4, 6; 15:1, 3; 17:5–6; 20:3–4. Sex defines the personal identity and concreteness of human beings, 20:5; 21:1–2, 4; 23:5; 25:2; 28:1, 4; 29:2, 4; 30:5; 31:5; 32:5; 36:3; 40:3; 41:4; 44:5; 45:3, 5; 48:3; 62:3; 69:5; 74:4; 77:6; 109:4; 110:7

   Sexual (*sessuale*) 67 times: 8:2–4; 9:4; 12:1–2; 14:6; 16:3; 20:2, 5; 21:1; 22:4; 28:1–2, 4; 29:2–3, 5; 30:5; 32:2; 36:2–4; 40:1, 4; 41:1–2, 4–5; 43:3; 44:5, 47:3; 48:4; 50:2–35; 51:1; 53:5; 54:2, 4; 80:3–5; 123:2, 4; 128:1; 129:4

   Sexual act (*atto sessuale*): 16:3; 20:5; 36:6. *See also* Conjugal act, Conjugal copula, Conjugal knowledge, Conjugal relation, Conjugal union, Know, Knowledge, Marriage act, Sexual union

Sexual union (*unione sessuale*): 44:5

Sexual desire (*desiderio sessuale*): 44:5; 48:4; 53:5; 128:1

Sexual drive (*impulso sessuale*): 128:1

Sexual instinct (*istinto sessuale*). Sexual instinct is sexual desire inasmuch as it arises of its own accord by natural necessity. The term "instinct" can be applied to human beings by likeness to animals, but only in an improper sense (*see* 80:4). "Instinct" is often used in a negative sense, similar to "concupiscence," in the CEI translation of Gen 3:16, "Your desire (*istinto*) shall be for your husband and he will dominate you," 10:2; 14:6; 22:4; 29:3; 30:1–3, 5; 31:1, 3; 32:2; 33:1–2; 43:3; 44:5; 46:4; 59:6; 80:3–5; 121:5; 124:2

   Sexual urge or need (*bisogno sessuale*). Used in a negative sense in the case of "mere satisfaction of sexual urge," 40:4; 41:1–2, 4–5; 43:3; 45:3

Sexology, sexological (*sessuologia, sessuologico*): 36:3; 43:4; 47:3

Shame (*vergogna*) 136 times: 3:2; 11:2–6; 12:1–2, 4–5; 13:1; 14:5–6; 15:1–4; 16:2–4; 17:2–4; 18:1, 5; 19:1–2, 5; 21:2; 22:6; 26:5; 27:1–2, 4; 28:1–4, 6; 29:1–5; 30:1–2, 4, 6; 31:1, 3–4, 6; 40:2; 55:4–7; 61:2–4; 62:1–2; 94:8; 95:1; 96:4; 110:3. *See also* Honor, Reverence

   Shame of the body, *see* Body 4

Shame, Modesty (*pudore*) 33 times. Close in meaning to *vergogna*, but with a more sexual overtone; can also signify the virtue of modesty, 11:3; 12:1–2, 5; 28:4–6; 29:3, 5; 30:5; 36:3; 39:2; 55:7; 56:1; 61:3

Shared life (*convivenza*) 43 times: 12:1; 18:3; 20:4–5; 23:5; 36:1; 37:5; 42:5; 43:6–7; 44:5; 57:3; 60:3; 74:3; 77:3; 83:3; 85:5–7; 101:1, 4; 106:2–3; 117:6; 117b:5; 120:1; 122:5; 125:3; 126:5; 127:5; 128:4–5; 131:1–2, 4, 6; 132:2–4. *See also* Conjugal shared life

Sign (*segno*) 202 times: 8:1, 4; 13:4; 14:4; 15:5; 19:4–5; 20:2; 27:3–4; 28:1–2; 33:4; 37:1, 4–6; 40:4; 44:5; 45:2; 47:3; 48:4–5; 49:5; 51:4; 59:2–4; 62:3; 68:3; 69:6; 73:5; 74:3; 75:1; 76:3; 79:3; 87:5–6; 90:4; 92:2–3; 93:5–6. Ephesians makes a single great sign of marriage as the original sacrament and Christ's redemptive act, 95b:6–7; 96:1, 6; 97:2, 5; 98:3, 7; 99:2; 100:1, 4, 7. Extensive discussion, 103:2–7; 104:1, 9; 105:1–6; 106:1–3, 5–6; 107:1–5; 108:1, 3, 5; 109:2–3; 110:3; 111:4–6; 113:6; 115:1, 3–4, 6; 116:3, 5; 117:1–3, 5; 117b:1–3, 6; 118:3–4; 123:3. The reflections on marriage in the dimension of sign are especially important for understanding *Humanae Vitae*, 123:8; 126:5; 131:4–5; 133:2. *See also* Meaning, Sacrament

   Visible sign (*segno visibile*) 25 times: 19:4–5; 28:1; 87:5; 90:4; 93:5; 95b:7; 96:6; 103:4, 6–7; 105:1–5; 106:2, 5; 108:3; 111:6; 113:6; 117b:3

   Sacramental sign (*segno sacramentale*) 39 times: 87:6; 93:5; 103:2–4; 104:1, 9; 105:1; 106:5; 107:1–5; 108:1, 5; 109:3; 115:1, 3, 6; 116:5; 117:1, 3, 5; 117b:1–2, 6; 118:3–4

Sin (*peccato*) 176 times: 3:2; 4:1–3; 11:4; 15:5; 16:2–4; 18:1–3; 19:2, 6; 20:1–2; 21:2, 6; 22:4, 5; 23:7; 26:2, 4–5; 27:1–2; 28:1; 29:1, 3; 30:1, 6; 31:1, 5; 32:2; 33:1, 5; 34:5; 35:5; 36:1, 5; 37:4–6; 38:1, 4;

41:2–3; 47:2–3; 48:4; 54:4; 60:1–2; 61:1; 67:3; 76:3–4; 79:1; 83:4, 9; 85:8; 104:4; 105:4; 110:4; 111:2; 112:1; 113:1–2; 116:5; 117:2; 118:6; 119:1–2; 126:5; 127:1; 128:5; 129:4; 130:2; 132:2. *See also* Interior, Intimate

Intersubjective (*intersoggettivo*): 73:1; 77:2

Subjectivism (*soggettivismo*): 2:4

Subjectivity (*soggettività*) 64 times. The characteristic feature of the life of persons. It implies both self-awareness and self-determination through which a person is "in" himself or herself, 3:1; 5:4. Subjectivity builds itself through self-knowledge, 5:6; 6:1; 7:2–3; 9:2, 11:3. TOB focuses on the aspect of human subjectivity, 18:1, 5; 19:1; 21:3; 29:4–5; 32:5; 41:1–2; 45:1; 49:6. The category of "heart" is equivalent to "personal subjectivity," 49:7; 54:3; 58:6; 60:1. Human subjectivity is psychosomatic, 67:3. The discovery of the fullness of human subjectivity in the beatific vision, 68:2–4; 71:1; 72:5; 80:4–5; 85:8; 91:4, 6; 92:4–5; 103:4; 109:4; 123:1, 3; 128:1; 129:3; 130:4. *See also* Interiority, Consciousness, Self-determination, Experience, Heart

Intersubjectivity (*intersoggettività*): 23:4; 68:4; 71:5; 75:1

Uni-subjectivity (*uni-soggettività*): 92:5

Bi-subjectivity (*bi-soggettività*): 91:4, 6; 92:4–5

Subordinate, Subordination (*subordinare, subordinazione*) 7 times. The union between man and woman is subordinated to procreation, 30:3. The experience of the spousal meaning of the body is subordinated to the sacramental call, 39:5. Freedom is subordinated to love, 53:2; 67:2; 86:2; 89:3. *See also* End, Finality

Substratum, Substrate (*substrato, sostrato*) 19 times. From the Latin *sub* (under) and *sterno, stratus* (spread), something spread out underneath, a foundation, base, etc. The body is the substratum of the gift of self and of the resulting communion of persons, 26:2; 29:2–3; 32:2. The communion of persons is the deepest substra-

tum of ethics and culture, 45:3; 46:5; 55:6; 62:4; 69:2; 100:5; 101:4; 103:3, 5; 110:4–5

Superabound (*sovrabbondare*) 8 times Of justice according to Mt 5:20: "Unless your justice abounds above that of the Scribes and Pharisees, you will never enter the kingdom of heaven," 24:2–4; 25:5; 35:1

Of revelation: 75:3

Of grace: 97:3

T

Teacher (*il Maestro*) the Teacher, i.e., Christ, 20 times: 1:3–4; 2:5; 18:1; 24:1; 34:3; 38:3; 39:3; 42:4; 43:2, 7; 64:2; 68:5; 69:1; 76:2; 79:5; 82:1–2

Technology, Technique (*tecnica*) 15 times. In the contemporary understanding of man, the person tends to become more an object of technology than a responsible subject, 23:3; 60:3–5; 61:1, 4; 62:1; 63:2, 4. Natural family planning is not primarily a technique, but the exercise of virtue, 124:4; 133:3

Teleology, *see* End, Finality, and Goal

Temple: The body as of the Holy Spirit (*tempio dello Spirito Sancto*) 16 times: 56:1–4; 57:1–3; 58:7; 85:4, 7; 88:1

Temperance (*temperanza*): 49:4. The goal of temperance is the affirmation of the value of the spousal meaning of the body, 49:5–6; 53:5; 54:2–4; 56:1; 58:6–7; 125:4; 128:1. *See also* Purity, Self-Dominion

Theology (*teologia*) 63 times without "theology of the body": 2:5; 3:3–4; 4:4. Theology responds above all to the light of revelation, 4:5; 8:3; 9:5; 16:3; 18:1–2, 4; 23:4; 25:1; 26:1, 3–4; 28:5; 33:5; 34:2; 36:4; 39:4; 44:5; 46:3; 47:1; 51:6; 52:1, 4; 53:5; 54:6; 59:2, 5, 7; 60:1; 64:2; 73:3; 74:5; 79:7; 85:1, 4, 6, 10; 87:2; 95b:4; 98:4; 103:7; 109:3; 124:3; 126:2; 133:2–4

Theology of the body, *see* Body 1

Thomas Aquinas, 8 times: 51:6; 54:2; 66:6; 93:5; 98:7; 130:1

Thread, *see* Guiding thread

Tradition (*tradizione*) not capitalized, 76 times: 2:2; 3:3; 4:3; 5:2, 5–6; 9:5; 15:4; 20:2; 21:1; 35:2–3; 36:5; 37:4–5; 38:4–6; 39:3; 41:4; 50:2–3; 57:6; 58:3; 64:2; 74:2–5; 75:2, 4; 76:1, 5; 78:2–3; 81:3;

6; 67:3; 68:1–2, 4; 72:2; 73:1; 75:1, 3; 77:3; 83:3; 86:7; 87:3; 91:1–3, 8; 92:6–7; 93:3, 5–6; 97:4–5; 98:8; 100:1; 102:1–2, 5, 7–8; 103:7; 105:3; 106:2; 109:4; 110:3, 7–8; 112:5; 115:3–4, 6; 117:4; 117b:1; 123:3, 7; 125:1; 127:2; 128:6; 129:6; 130:2; 131:3, 5; 132:4–5

Conjugal union, *see* Conjugal

Spousal union, *see* Spousal

Unitive (*unitivo*) 8 times: 10:4; 55:6; 118:2; 120:2; 123:6; 127:3; 128:4; 130:3. *See also* Procreative

Unitive meaning of the body, *see* Body 2

Unity* (*unità*) 90 of 122 times in the sense of unity of man and woman, *see also* Original unity: 3:2; 8:1. Double unity, 8:3–4; 9:1–3, 5; 10:1–3, 5; 11:2, 6; 12:3; 13:2; 14:5; 20:1, 4; 21:1; 25:3; 28:2–4; 29:3; 30:2, 5; 31:1, 3; 32:4; 33:3, 5; 37:4, 6; 41:4–5; 43:6; 45:2; 47:2; 52:1; 66:2; 68:1; 69:3–4, 8; 73:5; 76:6; 77:3; 89:4. The unity of man and woman is not ontological, but moral, 92:5–7; 93:1; 100:1–2; 102:1; 115:3, 6; 116:4; 117:3–4

The unity of the two (*unità dei due*) 6 times: 69:4; 76:6; 115:6; 116:4

Unity of the body, *see* Body 2

Unrepeatable (*irripetibile*) 18 times: 4:3; 6:2; 9:1; 10:1; 15:4; 20:5; 34:4; 49:7; 57:3; 60:7; 103:5–6; 106:1; 108:4

Upright, *see* Honorable

Utilitarian, Utilitaristic, Utilitarianism (*utilitario, utilitaristico, utilitarismo*) 7 times. Utilitarianism is the form of ethics congenial to the ambition of power over nature and the consequent mechanistic account of nature, 23:5; 41:5; 43:3; 76:2; 79:5; 125:4

V

Value (*valore*) 142 times. "Value" is the objective goodness of beings inasmuch as that goodness is consciously experienced or "evaluated" by persons. As used in TOB, "value" does not, therefore, have the subjectivist sense of a mere way of valuing (as, for example, in the subjectivist use of "traditional values, modern values"), 2:5; 9:1; 10:2; 12:1; 13:1; 15:4; 22:4; 24:3; 27:4; 28:3, 5–6; 29:3; 31:1; 39:4–5; 40:1, 3, 5; 41:2; 42:2, 4; 44:2; 45:2–5; 46:2, 5–6; 47:1, 3, 6; 48:1–2;

49:5–6; 51:1; 52:4; 54:3; 55:2; 58:3–5; 59:6; 62:3–5; 63:4; 69:6; 73:3; 76:2; 77:2, 6; 78:4; 79:5–6; 81:2–4, 6; 84:5–6; 109:1–2; 110:8; 115:1; 118:4; 119:3; 120:3, 6; 121:2, 6; 124:2–3; 125:3, 6; 127:1–4; 128:1–3; 131:5. *See also* Good

Vatican II, *see* Council

Veneration (*venerazione*) 4 times: 57:2; 131:5; 132:3. *See also* Piety, Reverence

Virgin (*vergine*) 10 times: 20:2; 75:3–4; 81:4; 82:3–4; 109:2. *See also* Celibate

Virginal (*verginale*) 8 times. Virginal value of the person, 10:2. Virginal meaning of being male and female, 67:4. The virginal state of the body in the beatific vision, 68:3. Virginal motherhood of Mary, virginal mystery of Joseph, 75:2. Virginal model of the Church, 84:5

Virginity (*verginità*) 51 times: 68:3; 71:5; 73:1, 4–5; 74:1–2, 4–6; 75:1–2; 76:1; 77:1, 6; 78:1; 79:7, 9; 80:1; 81:4–5; 82:1, 3, 5–6; 83:1, 4; 84:1, 4–5, 7–8; 85:1, 4, 8; 95:3; 101:2; 102:8. *See also* Abstinence, Continence, Celibacy

Virtue (*virtù*) 98 times: 38:5; 44:5; 49:7; 50:4. Extensive discussion with footnote, 51:5–6; 53:4–5; 54:2–4; 55:5; 56:1–3, 5; 57:2–4; 88:2; 107:3; 117b:5; 121:1; 124:4; 125:4; 127:5; 128:1–2, 4; 129:3, 5; 130:1–5; 131:2, 5; 132:2. *See also* Duty, Obligation, Attitude, Ethos, Mentality, Spirituality

Vocation (*vocazione*) 66 times: 5:4; 15:5; 21:6; 23:1, 5; 53:2; 58:2; 73:2–3, 5; 74:1; 76:4–5; 77:1, 5; 78:4–5; 79:6; 81:6; 84:8; 85:2, 4, 9; 86:3, 8; 87:6; 88:2–4; 89:5, 7; 90:2–3; 94:4; 99:3–4; 101:9; 102:5–6; 103:1; 104:7; 106:1–2; 110:3; 116:4; 123:3; 126:1–4; 131:3–4. *See also* Call

W

Wealth, *see* Richness

Wedding, Marriage (*nozze*) 4 times. From the Latin *nuptiae*, wedding: 79:2. Marriage of the lamb, 90:6; 92:4; 103:1. *See also* Spousal

Wedding (*nuziale*) 8 times. In the *Osservatore* translation, the English "nuptial" is used 117 times, mostly as a rendering of "*sponsale* (spousal)" in "nuptial meaning of the body." The Italian text contains only the following instances of *nuziale*, always translated above as "wedding"

Wedding song (*canto nuziale*): 8:4

Wedding garment (*abito nuziale*): 91:8

Wedding night (*notte nuziale*): 114:6, 8; 115:4, 6; 116:4

Wedding (*sposalizio*) 12 times: 91:7–8. The sacrament of redemption, i.e., the wedding between Christ and the Church, corresponds to the sacrament of creation, which has its center in the wedding between the first man and woman, 97:2; 104:1, 5; 114:2, 4; 118:4. *See also* Spousal

Wife (*moglie*) 303 times: 1:2–3; 3:2; 8:1; 10:2–4; 11:2; 17:2; 18:5; 19:1, 5; 20:2, 4–5; 21:1–5; 22:1, 5–6; 23:1; 24:4; 25:1, 3–4; 27:1; 31:2; 34:1; 35:2–4; 36:1–2; 37:1, 4, 6; 38:1, 4–5; 41:5; 42:3–4, 6–7; 43:1–3, 5–6; 50:4; 53:6; 58:1; 64:1–4; 65:1; 66:1–2, 4; 67:1, 4; 68:1–4; 69:1, 3–4, 8; 72:7; 73:1–2, 4–5; 74:5; 75:1; 78:5; 79:4; 81:1, 7; 82:5; 83:1, 3, 5; 84:1, 7; 85:3–5; 87:1–3; 88:4–5; 89:1, 3–5, 7–8; 90:1–3, 5–6; 91:1–6; 92:1, 3–8; 93:6; 94:3, 5; 95:2–3; 95b:1, 6–7; 96:6; 97:2, 4; 98:8; 99:6; 100:4; 101:2, 6, 8, 11; 102:1–2, 5; 103:1–2; 104:2, 5; 105:3; 110:3, 7; 114:1–3, 5, 7; 115:2; 116:1–2; 117:2, 4, 6; 117b:3; 127:3; 133:1. *See also* Husband, Spouses

Wisdom books, Wisdom tradition (*libri sapienziali, tradizione sapienziale*) 15 times: 3:3; 36:1; 38:3–6; 39:1, 3; 45:4; 57:4, 6; 58:3

Who shall she be for him and he for her? Key question, 43:7; 109:3

World* (*mondo*) 297 times

Visible world (*mondo visibile*) 38 times: 2:3; 5:5–6; 6:3–4; 7:1; 8:1; 13:4; 15:1; 19:3–5; 21:7; 27:3–4; 29:3; 69:6; 70:7; 71:4; 86:4; 96:1; 101:9, 11; 108:8; 111:4

Other world (*altro mondo*) 48 times: 64:4; 66:1–5; 67:2–5; 68:2, 4–6; 69:3, 6, 8; 70:1, 6; 71:4; 72:3, 6–7; 73:5; 75:1; 76:3; 79:7–8; 81:6–7; 84:5; 85:1, 10; 86:5; 101:8; 133:1

Worthy, *see* Honorable

Y

Yahweh, 77 times, the divine name according to the revelation of Ex 3:15, in later Jewish tradition, including the Septuagint and the New Testament, read as "Lord": 2:2; 3:1; 5:2, 4, 6; 6:1–2; 7:3–4; 8:2–4; 14:1–2, 4; 15:3; 21:7; 22:5; 26:2, 4; 27:1–2, 4; 30:1, 3–4, 6; 31:1; 33:1–2, 4; 34:1; 35:1; 36:1, 5–6; 37:1, 3–5; 42:2; 94:6–7; 95:2, 6; 95b:2, 5; 104:3–5, 8; 105:1; 116:2

Yahwist, 61 times: 2:2; 3:1, 3–4; 4:1–3; 5:2, 4, 6; 6:1–4; 7:1–2; 8:1–4; 9:2–3; 11:1–5; 12:2–3, 5; 13:2; 14:1, 4–5; 15:3, 5; 18:1; 20:2; 26:4, 5; 27:2; 28:1; 29:2; 30:3; 31:6; 64:2; 70:7; 76:5; 116:1

Scripture Index

Systems of Reference to TOB

THE PRESENT EDITION follows the numbering of the 133 catecheses in the one-volume Italian edition entitled *Uomo e donna lo creò* (UD) produced by the John Paul II Institute in Rome (Rome: Città Nuova and Libreria Editrice Vaticana, 1985, 5th ed. 2001).

Thus TOB 12:3 refers to the twelfth catechesis in UD, third numbered paragraph (paragraph numbers were assigned by John Paul II himself). The reason for following the numbering of the catecheses in UD, despite the (apparently accidental) omission of two catecheses and the consequent shift in numbering, is to allow readers to pass easily back and forth between the English translation and the original Italian. UD is the only easily available Italian text. In the series *Insegnamenti di Giovanni Paolo II*, which contains the authentic Italian text, the catecheses are scattered across ten large volumes.

The new Spanish translation of TOB produced by the John Paul II Institute in Spain contains the UD numbering (as Roman numerals under the title of each catechesis). Readers are thus able to pass quickly back and forth between the English and the Spanish version without the use of a table.

The table below is intended for readers who need to move between this new English edition and one or the other of four other systems of reference that are in use in the English-speaking world.

1. Dates of the 129 catecheses as delivered;
2. Sequential numbering of the 129 catecheses as delivered;
3. Page numbers in the 1997 one-volume edition by Pauline;
4. Page numbers in the four-volume edition by Pauline.[*]

The complex textual situation of TOB, which is the cause of considerable confusion in and between these systems of reference, can be clarified as follows:

John Paul II delivered 129 catecheses.

Preserved in the archives are 135, all of them translated from the Polish into Italian and ready for delivery as catecheses according to John Paul II's

---

[*] 1. *Original Unity of Man and Woman* (1981); 2. *Blessed Are the Pure of Heart* (1983); 3. *The Theology of Marriage and Celibacy* (1986); 4. *Reflections on* Humanae Vitae (1984).

instructions. All 135 catecheses are printed in the 1986 Polish edition of TOB and (with two exceptions) in UD. All of them have been included in this translation.

In its first edition, UD omitted two catecheses that were actually delivered. In later editions, it included one of them in an appendix, but the other is still missing. I have placed these two catecheses in their proper place according to date and numbered them TOB 95b and TOB 117b, in order to preserve the overall numbering of the catecheses in UD.

John Paul II did not deliver TOB 117, perhaps for scheduling reasons. The Polish text is printed in the 1986 Polish edition of TOB and the Italian translation in UD (not in the *Insegnamenti*). The archival materials show that 117 (which has no date of delivery) comes before 117b.

Pope John Paul II had originally prepared six catecheses on the Song of Songs and three on Tobit in both Polish and Italian on the basis of the pre-papal book manuscript. The Italian text of these catecheses is printed in UD. For actual delivery, John Paul II cut the original text to less than half by marking in the Italian typescript (preserved in the archives) which paragraphs were to be read. The reason for cutting the text may have been time pressures. This shorter Italian text is printed in the *Insegnamenti*. In this edition, the two versions are printed synoptically on facing pages.

This edition, following UD	Dates of the catecheses as delivered	Sequential numbering of the 129 catecheses as delivered	One-volume 1997 Pauline edition page numbers	Four-volume Pauline edition page numbers
TOB 1	Sept. 5, 1979	catech. no. 1	p. 25	vol. 1, p. 15
TOB 2	Sept. 12, 1979	catech. no. 2	p. 27	vol. 1, p. 20
TOB 3	Sept. 19, 1979	catech. no. 3	p. 29	vol. 1, p. 27
TOB 4	Sept. 26, 1979	catech. no. 4	p. 32	vol. 1, p. 35
TOB 5	Oct. 10, 1979	catech. no. 5	p. 35	vol. 1, p. 43
TOB 6	Oct. 24, 1979	catech. no. 6	p. 37	vol. 1, p. 50
TOB 7	Oct. 31, 1979	catech. no. 7	p. 40	vol. 1, p. 55
TOB 8	Nov. 7, 1979	catech. no. 8	p. 42	vol. 1, p. 61
TOB 9	Nov. 14, 1979	catech. no. 9	p. 45	vol. 1, p. 70
TOB 10	Nov. 21, 1979	catech. no. 10	p. 48	vol. 1, p. 78
TOB 11	Dec. 12, 1979	catech. no. 11	p. 51	vol. 1, p. 85
TOB 12	Dec. 19, 1979	catech. no. 12	p. 54	vol. 1, p. 92
TOB 13	Jan. 2, 1980	catech. no. 13	p. 57	vol. 1, p. 99
TOB 14	Jan. 9, 1980	catech. no. 14	p. 60	vol. 1, p. 106
TOB 15	Jan. 16, 1980	catech. no. 15	p. 63	vol. 1, p. 113

TOB 16	Jan. 30, 1980	catech. no. 16	p. 66	vol. 1, p. 121
TOB 17	Feb. 6, 1980	catech. no. 17	p. 69	vol. 1, p. 128
TOB 18	Feb. 13, 1980	catech. no. 18	p. 72	vol. 1, p. 135
TOB 19	Feb. 20, 1980	catech. no. 19	p. 75	vol. 1, p. 141
TOB 20	March 5, 1980	catech. no. 20	p. 77	vol. 1, p. 146
TOB 21	March 12, 1980	catech. no. 21	p. 80	vol. 1, p. 153
TOB 22	March 26, 1980	catech. no. 22	p. 83	vol. 1, p. 162
TOB 23	April 2, 1980	catech. no. 23	p. 86	vol. 1, p. 170
TOB 24	April 16, 1980	catech. no. 24	p. 103	vol. 2, p. 19
TOB 25	April 23, 1980	catech. no. 25	p. 106	vol. 2, p. 26
TOB 26	April 30, 1980	catech. no. 26	p. 108	vol. 2, p. 33
TOB 27	May 14, 1980	catech. no. 27	p. 111	vol. 2, p. 40
TOB 28	May 28, 1980	catech. no. 28	p. 114	vol. 2, p. 48
TOB 29	June 4, 1980	catech. no. 29	p. 117	vol. 2, p. 55
TOB 30	June 18, 1980	catech. no. 30	p. 120	vol. 2, p. 61
TOB 31	June 25, 1980	catech. no. 31	p. 122	vol. 2, p. 66
TOB 32	July 23, 1980	catech. no. 32	p. 125	vol. 2, p. 73
TOB 33	July 30, 1980	catech. no. 33	p. 128	vol. 2, p. 79
TOB 34	Aug. 6, 1980	catech. no. 34	p. 130	vol. 2, p. 85
TOB 35	Aug. 13, 1980	catech. no. 35	p. 133	vol. 2, p. 90
TOB 36	Aug. 20, 1980	catech. no. 36	p. 135	vol. 2, p. 96
TOB 37	Aug. 27, 1980	catech. no. 37	p. 138	vol. 2, p. 103
TOB 38	Sept. 3, 1980	catech. no. 38	p. 142	vol. 2, p. 111
TOB 39	Sept. 10, 1980	catech. no. 39	p. 145	vol. 2, p. 118
TOB 40	Sept. 17, 1980	catech. no. 40	p. 147	vol. 2, p. 124
TOB 41	Sept. 24, 1980	catech. no. 41	p. 150	vol. 2, p. 129
TOB 42	Oct. 1, 1980	catech. no. 42	p. 152	vol. 2, p. 134
TOB 43	Oct. 8, 1980	catech. no. 43	p. 156	vol. 2, p. 142
TOB 44	Oct. 15, 1980	catech. no. 44	p. 159	vol. 2, p. 153
TOB 45	Oct. 22, 1980	catech. no. 45	p. 162	vol. 2, p. 161
TOB 46	Oct. 29, 1980	catech. no. 46	p. 165	vol. 2, p. 168
TOB 47	Nov. 5, 1980	catech. no. 47	p. 168	vol. 2, p. 176
TOB 48	Nov. 12, 1980	catech. no. 48	p. 171	vol. 2, p. 184
TOB 49	Dec. 3, 1980	catech. no. 49	p. 174	vol. 2, p. 190
TOB 50	Dec. 10, 1980	catech. no. 50	p. 177	vol. 2, p. 198
TOB 51	Dec. 17, 1980	catech. no. 51	p. 191	vol. 2, p. 205
TOB 52	Jan. 7, 1981	catech. no. 52	p. 194	vol. 2, p. 215
TOB 53	Jan. 14, 1981	catech. no. 53	p. 197	vol. 2, p. 222
TOB 54	Jan. 28, 1981	catech. no. 54	p. 200	vol. 2, p. 228

TOB 55	Feb. 4, 1981	catech. no. 55	p. 202	vol. 2, p. 234
TOB 56	Feb. 11, 1981	catech. no. 56	p. 205	vol. 2, p. 241
TOB 57	March 18, 1981	catech. no. 57	p. 208	vol. 2, p. 247
TOB 58	April 1, 1981	catech. no. 58	p. 210	vol. 2, p. 253
TOB 59	April 8, 1981	catech. no. 59	p. 214	vol. 2, p. 261
TOB 60	April 15, 1981	catech. no. 60	p. 218	vol. 2, p. 269
TOB 61	April 22, 1981	catech. no. 61	p. 220	vol. 2, p. 276
TOB 62	April 29, 1981	catech. no. 62	p. 223	vol. 2, p. 283
TOB 63	May 6, 1981	catech. no. 63	p. 226	vol. 2, p. 290
TOB 64	Nov. 11, 1981	catech. no. 64	p. 233	vol. 3, p. 1
TOB 65	Nov. 18, 1981	catech. no. 65	p. 235	vol. 3, p. 8
TOB 66	Dec. 2, 1981	catech. no. 66	p. 238	vol. 3, p. 17
TOB 67	Dec. 9, 1981	catech. no. 67	p. 240	vol. 3, p. 25
TOB 68	Dec. 16, 1981	catech. no. 68	p. 243	vol. 3, p. 32
TOB 69	Jan. 13, 1982	catech. no. 69	p. 246	vol. 3, p. 39
TOB 70	Jan. 27, 1982	catech. no. 70	p. 249	vol. 3, p. 47
TOB 71	Feb. 3, 1982	catech. no. 71	p. 252	vol. 3, p. 56
TOB 72	Feb. 10, 1982	catech. no. 72	p. 255	vol. 3, p. 62
TOB 73	March 10, 1982	catech. no. 73	p. 262	vol. 3, p. 69
TOB 74	March 17, 1982	catech. no. 74	p. 264	vol. 3, p. 76
TOB 75	March 24, 1982	catech. no. 75	p. 267	vol. 3, p. 83
TOB 76	March 31, 1982	catech. no. 76	p. 270	vol. 3, p. 90
TOB 77	April 7, 1982	catech. no. 77	p. 273	vol. 3, p. 96
TOB 78	April 14, 1982	catech. no. 78	p. 276	vol. 3, p. 104
TOB 79	April 21, 1982	catech. no. 79	p. 278	vol. 3, p. 112
TOB 80	April 28, 1982	catech. no. 80	p. 281	vol. 3, p. 120
TOB 81	May 05, 1982	catech. no. 81	p. 285	vol. 3, p. 128
TOB 82	June 23, 1982	catech. no. 82	p. 287	vol. 3, p. 134
TOB 83	June 30, 1982	catech. no. 83	p. 289	vol. 3, p. 140
TOB 84	July 7, 1982	catech. no. 84	p. 292	vol. 3, p. 148
TOB 85	July 14, 1982	catech. no. 85	p. 296	vol. 3, p. 156
TOB 86	July 21, 1982	catech. no. 86	p. 299	vol. 3, p. 164
TOB 87	July 28, 1982	catech. no. 87	p. 304	vol. 3, p. 171
TOB 88	Aug. 04, 1982	catech. no. 88	p. 306	vol. 3, p. 178
TOB 89	Aug. 11, 1982	catech. no. 89	p. 309	vol. 3, p. 184
TOB 90	Aug. 18, 1982	catech. no. 90	p. 312	vol. 3, p. 191
TOB 91	Aug. 25, 1982	catech. no. 91	p. 314	vol. 3, p. 198
TOB 92	Sept. 1, 1982	catech. no. 92	p. 318	vol. 3, p. 207
TOB 93	Sept. 8, 1982	catech. no. 93	p. 321	vol. 3, p. 215

TOB 94	Sept. 15, 1982	catech. no. 94	p. 324	vol. 3, p. 224
TOB 95	Sept. 22, 1982	catech. no. 95	p. 327	vol. 3, p. 231
TOB 95b	Sept. 29, 1982	catech. no. 96	p. 330	vol. 3, p. 240
TOB 96	Oct. 6, 1982	catech. no. 97	p. 333	vol. 3, p. 247
TOB 97	Oct. 13, 1982	catech. no. 98	p. 336	vol. 3, p. 255
TOB 98	Oct. 20, 1982	catech. no. 99	p. 339	vol. 3, p. 262
TOB 99	Oct. 27, 1982	catech. no. 100	p. 342	vol. 3, p. 269
TOB 100	Nov. 24, 1982	catech. no. 101	p. 344	vol. 3, p. 276
TOB 101	Dec. 1, 1982	catech. no. 102	p. 347	vol. 3, p. 283
TOB 102	Dec. 15, 1982	catech. no. 103	p. 351	vol. 3, p. 293
TOB 103	Jan. 5, 1983	catech. no. 104	p. 354	vol. 3, p. 301
TOB 104	Jan. 12, 1983	catech. no. 105	p. 357	vol. 3, p. 308
TOB 105	Jan. 19, 1983	catech. no. 106	p. 360	vol. 3, p. 316
TOB 106	Jan. 26, 1983	catech. no. 107	p. 363	vol. 3, p. 324
TOB 107	Feb. 9, 1983	catech. no. 108	p. 365	vol. 3, p. 329
TOB 108	May 23, 1984	catech. no. 109	p. 368	vol. 3, p. 335
TOB 109–110	May 30, 1984	catech. no. 110	p. 370	vol. 3, p. 344
TOB 111–113	June 6, 1984	catech. no. 111	p. 373	vol. 3, p. 351
TOB 114–116	June 27, 1984	catech. no. 112	p. 375	vol. 3, p. 358
TOB 117	Not delivered			
TOB 117b	July 4, 1984	catech. no. 113	p. 378	vol. 3, p. 363
TOB 118	July 11, 1984	catech. no. 114	p. 386	vol. 4, p. 1
TOB 119	July 18, 1984	catech. no. 115	p. 388	vol. 4, p. 7
TOB 120	July 25, 1984	catech. no. 116	p. 390	vol. 4, p. 13
TOB 121	Aug. 1, 1984	catech. no. 117	p. 393	vol. 4, p. 19
TOB 122	Aug. 8, 1984	catech. no. 118	p. 395	vol. 4, p. 25
TOB 123	Aug. 22, 1984	catech. no. 119	p. 396	vol. 4, p. 29
TOB 124	Aug. 29, 1984	catech. no. 120	p. 399	vol. 4, p. 35
TOB 125	Sept. 5, 1984	catech. no. 121	p. 401	vol. 4, p. 41
TOB 126	Oct. 3, 1984	catech. no. 122	p. 404	vol. 4, p. 49
TOB 127	Oct. 10, 1984	catech. no. 123	p. 406	vol. 4, p. 55
TOB 128	Oct. 24, 1984	catech. no. 124	p. 408	vol. 4, p. 61
TOB 129	Oct. 31, 1984	catech. no. 125	p. 411	vol. 4, p. 69
TOB 130	Nov. 7, 1984	catech. no. 126	p. 413	vol. 4, p. 77
TOB 131	Nov. 14, 1984	catech. no. 127	p. 415	vol. 4, p. 83
TOB 132	Nov. 21, 1984	catech. no. 128	p. 417	vol. 4, p. 89
TOB 133	Nov. 28, 1984	catech. no. 129	p. 419	vol. 4, p. 95

BOOKS & MEDIA

The Daughters of St. Paul operate book and media centers at the following addresses. Visit, call or write the one nearest you today, or find us on the World Wide Web, www.pauline.org.

CALIFORNIA
3908 Sepulveda Blvd, Culver City, CA 90230	310-397-8676
2640 Broadway Street, Redwood City, CA 94063	650-369-4230
5945 Balboa Avenue, San Diego, CA 92111	858-565-9181

FLORIDA
145 S.W. 107th Avenue, Miami, FL 33174	305-559-6715

HAWAII
1143 Bishop Street, Honolulu, HI 96813	808-521-2731
Neighbor Islands call:	866-521-2731

ILLINOIS
172 North Michigan Avenue, Chicago, IL 60601	312-346-4228

LOUISIANA
4403 Veterans Memorial Blvd, Metairie, LA 70006	504-887-7631

MASSACHUSETTS
885 Providence Hwy, Dedham, MA 02026	781-326-5385

MISSOURI
9804 Watson Road, St. Louis, MO 63126	314-965-3512

NEW JERSEY
561 U.S. Route 1, Wick Plaza, Edison, NJ 08817	732-572-1200

NEW YORK
150 East 52nd Street, New York, NY 10022	212-754-1110

PENNSYLVANIA
9171-A Roosevelt Blvd, Philadelphia, PA 19114	215-676-9494

SOUTH CAROLINA
243 King Street, Charleston, SC 29401	843-577-0175

TENNESSEE
4811 Poplar Avenue, Memphis, TN 38117	901-761-2987

TEXAS
114 Main Plaza, San Antonio, TX 78205	210-224-8101

VIRGINIA
1025 King Street, Alexandria, VA 22314	703-549-3806

CANADA
3022 Dufferin Street, Toronto, ON M6B 3T5	416-781-9131

¡También somos su fuente para libros, videos y música en español!